Lecture Notes in Computer Science 12218

More information about this series at http://www.springer.com/series/7407

Simon K. S. Cheung · Richard Li ·
Kongkiti Phusavat · Naraphorn Paoprasert ·
Lam-For Kwok (Eds.)

Blended Learning

Education in a Smart Learning Environment

13th International Conference, ICBL 2020
Bangkok, Thailand, August 24–27, 2020
Proceedings

Springer

Editors
Simon K. S. Cheung
The Open University of Hong Kong
Hong Kong, China

Richard Li
University of Canterbury
Christchurch, New Zealand

Kongkiti Phusavat
Kasetsart University
Bangkok, Thailand

Naraphorn Paoprasert
Kasetsart University
Bangkok, Thailand

Lam-For Kwok
City University of Hong Kong
Kowloon, Hong Kong

ISSN 0302-9743 ISSN 1611-3349 (electronic)
Lecture Notes in Computer Science
ISBN 978-3-030-51967-4 ISBN 978-3-030-51968-1 (eBook)
https://doi.org/10.1007/978-3-030-51968-1

LNCS Sublibrary: SL1 – Theoretical Computer Science and General Issues

This Springer imprint is published by the registered company Springer Nature Switzerland AG
The registered company address is: Gewerbestrasse 11, 6330 Cham, Switzerland

Preface

Welcome to the proceedings of the 13th International Conference on Blended Learning (ICBL 2020). This year, ICBL 2020 was held at the Kasetsart University in Bangkok, Thailand, during August 24–27, 2020.

Blended learning is one of the promising approaches to teaching and learning. It integrates traditional learning with innovative means to create a new learning environment conducive to effective learning. Like the previous conferences in the series, ICBL 2020 provides a platform for knowledge exchange and experience sharing among researchers and practitioners in this field.

The theme of ICBL 2020 was "Education in a Smart Learning Environment." Our focus was on innovative educational practices of blended learning that creates a new and smart learning environment for effective learning. Such a smart learning environment is able to support a wide range of teaching and learning activities in different subject areas at different levels. ICBL 2020 attracted a total of 70 paper submissions. After a rigorous review process, 33 papers were selected for inclusion in this volume. The selected papers cover various areas in blended learning, including adaptive learning, content and instructional design, smart learning environment, enriched and smart learning experience, and institutional policies and strategies.

We would like to take this opportunity to thank the following parties who made the conference a success: (a) the conference Organizing Committee; (b) the International Program Committee; (c) the conference organizers and co-organizer; (d) the conference sponsors; and (e) all the conference participants.

We trust you will enjoy reading the papers.

August 2020

Simon K. S. Cheung
Richard Li
Kongkiti Phusavat
Naraphorn Paoprasert
Lam-For Kwok

Organization

Organizing Committee

Honorary Chairs

Horace H. S. Ip	City University of Hong Kong, Hong Kong, China
Chongrak Wachrinrat	Kasetsart University, Thailand
Peerayuth Charnsethikul	Kasetsart University, Thailand

Conference Chairs

Lam-For Kwok	City University of Hong Kong, Hong Kong, China
Pornthep Anusornnitisan	Kasetsart University, Thailand

Organizing Chairs

John Hui	The Education University of Hong Kong, Hong Kong, China
Naraphorn Paoprasert	Kasetsart University, Thailand

Programme Chairs

Simon K. S. Cheung	The Open University of Hong Kong, Hong Kong, China
Richard Li	University of Canterbury, New Zealand
Kongkiti Phusavat	Kasetsart University, Thailand

Finance Chairs

Steven Ng	Hong Kong Society for Multimedia and Image Computing, Hong Kong, China
Ramidayu Yousuk	Kasetsart University, Thailand

Local Arrangement Chairs

Suwitchaporn Witchakul	Kasetsart University, Thailand
Praewpran Prayadsab	Kasetsart University, Thailand

Publicity Chairs

Morris Jong	The Chinese University of Hong Kong, Hong Kong, China
Yinghui Shi	Central China Normal University, China
Juta Pichitlamken	Kasetsart University, Thailand

Webmasters

Richard Li	University of Canterbury, New Zealand
Papis Wongchaisuwat	Kasetsart University, Thailand
Sasarose Jaijit	Kasetsart University, Thailand

International Program Committee

Chairs

Simon K. S. Cheung	The Open University of Hong Kong, Hong Kong, China
Richard Li	University of Canterbury, New Zealand
Kongkiti Phusavat	Kasetsart University, Thailand

Members

Oliver Au	The Open University of Hong Kong, Hong Kong, China
Phatcharee Tokaew Thongrattana	Kasetsart University, Thailand
Jan Beseda	Centre for Higher Education Studies in Prague, Czech Republic
Pavel Brebera	University of Pardubice, Czech Republic
Jana Burgerova	University of Presov, Slovakia
Jinnong Cao	The Hong Kong Polytechnic University, Hong Kong, China
C. S. Chai	The Chinese University of Hong Kong, Hong Kong, China
Keith Chan	The Hong Kong Polytechnic University, Hong Kong, China
Peter Chan	Brigham Young University, USA
Chih-Tsan Chang	National Chung Cheng University, Taiwan, China
Wei Chen	Chinese Academy of Agricultural Sciences, China
Guo-Li Chiou	National Taiwan Normal University, Taiwan, China
Thomas Chiu	The University of Hong Kong, Hong Kong, China
Mike Chui	The Education University of Hong Kong, Hong Kong, China
Giuliana Dettori	Istituto di Tecnologie Didattiche del CNR, Italy
Vorasuang Duangchinda	Sripatum University, Thailand
Ludvík Eger	University of West Bohemia, Czech Republic
Supaporn Erjongmanee	Kasetsart University, Thailand
Jittat Fakcharoenphol	Kasetsart University, Thailand
Zbynek Filipi	University of West Bohemia, Czech Republic
Rostislav Fojtík	University of Ostrava, Czech Republic
Yoshiko Goda	Kumamoto University, Japan
Radomira Greganova	Slovak University of Agriculture, Slovakia
Chaiporn Jaikaeo	Kasetsart University, Thailand

Owen Hall Jr.	Pepperdine University, USA
Tianyong Hao	Guangdong University of Foreign Studies, China
Andreas Henrich	University of Bamberg, Germany
Dagmar Hillova	Slovak University of Agriculture, Slovakia
Yoko Hirata	Hokkai-Gakuen University, Japan
Yoshihiro Hirata	Hokkai-Gakuen University, Japan
Wai Shing Ho	Caritas Institute of Higher Education, Hong Kong, China
Norio Hosaki	Waseda University, Japan
Jenq-Muh Hsu	National Chiayi University, Taiwan, China
Ronghuia Huang	Beijing Normal University, China
John Hui	The Education University of Hong Kong, Hong Kong, China
Josef Hynek	University of Hradec Kralove, Czech Republic
Sasarose Jaijit	Kasetsart University, Thailand
Geng Jie	The Chinese University of Hong Kong, Hong Kong, China
Morris Jong	The Chinese University of Hong Kong, Hong Kong, China
Jacky Keung	City University of Hong Kong, Hong Kong, China
Blanka Klimova	University of Hradec Kralove, Czech Republic
Takayuki Konno	Meisei University, Japan
Kenichi Kubota	Kansai University, Thailand
Haruo Kurokami	Kansai University, Thailand
Reggie Kwan	The Open University of Hong Kong, Hong Kong, China
Lam-For Kwok	City University of Hong Kong, Hong Kong, China
Chiu Lin Lai	National Taiwan University of Science and Technology, Taiwan, China
Ivan Lai	City University of Macau, Macau, China
Jeanne Lam	The University of Hong Kong, Hong Kong, China
Jun Le	Guangdong Radio and TV University, China
Keith Lee	The Open University of Hong Kong, Hong Kong, China
Victor Lee	City University of Hong Kong, Hong Kong, China
K. C. Li	The Open University of Hong Kong, Hong Kong, China
Yan Li	Zhejiang University, China
Yi Li	Nanjing University, China
Heng Luo	Central China Normal University, China
Will Ma	Technological and Higher Education Institute of Hong Kong, Hong Kong, China
Jason MacLeod	D'Youville College, China
Martina Manenova	University of Hradec Kralove, Czech Republic
Jaroslava Mikulecka	University of Hradec Kralove, Czech Republic
Kousuke Mouri	Kyushu University, Japan

Anan Mungwattana	Kasetsart University, Thailand
Masayuki Murakami	Kyoto University of Foreign Studies, Japan
Junko Nemoto	Ehime University, Japan
Steven Ng	Hong Kong Society for Multimedia and Image Computing, Hong Kong, China
Jitti Niramitranon	Kasetsart University, Thailand
Somchai Numprasertchai	Kasetsart University, Thailand
Hiroaki Ogata	Kyushu University, Thailand
Makiko Oyama	Osaka University, Japan
Wakio Oyanagi	Nara University of Education, Japan
Naraphorn Paoprasert	Kasetsart University, Thailand
Praewpran Payadsab	Kasetsart University, Thailand
Diana Perez-Marin	Universidad Rey Juan Carlos, Spain
Punpiti Piamsa-nga	Kasetsart University, Thailand
Juta Pichitlamken	Kasetsart University, Thailand
C. K. Poon	Hang Seng University, Hong Kong, China
Linda Pospíšilová	University of Pardubice, Czech Republic
Petra Poulova	University of Hradec Kralove, Czech Republic
Thanawin Rakthanmanon	Kasetsart University, Thailand
Yanghui Rao	Sun Yat-sen University, China
Lucie Rohlikova	University of West Bohemia, Czech Republic
Junjie Shang	Peking University, China
Yinghui Shi	Central China Normal University, China
Ju Ling Shih	National University of Tainan, Taiwan, China
Ivana Simonova	Jan Evangelista Purkyne University, Czech Republic
Chansiri Singhtaun	Kasetsart University, Thailand
Raymond So	The Open University of Hong Kong, Hong Kong, China
Yanjie Song	The Education University of Hong Kong, Hong Kong, China
Niwat Srisawasdi	Khon Kaen University, Thailand
Liana Stanescu	University of Craiova, Romania
Cai Su	Beijing Normal University, China
Prapaisri Sudasna-Na-Ayudthya	Kasetsart University, Thailand
Kobkul Sunphakitjumnong	Kasetsart University, Thailand
Praweenya Suwannatthachote	Chulalongkorn University, Thailand
Hana Svobodova	Masaryk University, Czech Republic
Libuse Svobodova	University of Hradec Kralove, Czech Republic
Jay Tashiro	University of Ontario Institute of Technology, Canada
Shikui Tu	Shanghai Jiao Tong University, China
Olga Vrastilova	University of Hradec Kralove, Czech Republic
Aihua Wang	Peking University, China
Cong Wang	City University of Hong Kong, Hong Kong, China
Shu Ming Wang	Chinese Culture University, Taiwan, China
Shudong Wang	Shimane University, Japan

Worawut Wangwatcharakul	Kasetsart University, Thailand
Suwitchaporn Witchakul	Kasetsart University, Thailand
Billy Wong	The Open University of Hong Kong, Hong Kong, China
Crusher Wong	City University of Hong Kong, Hong Kong, China
Gary Wong	The University of Hong Kong, Hong Kong, China
Raymond Wong	City University of Hong Kong, Hong Kong, China
T. L. Wong	Douglas College, Canada
Papis Wongchaisuwat	Kasetsart University, Thailand
Kris Wongkasem	Kasetsart University, Thailand
Di Wu	Central China Normal University, China
Haoran Xie	The Education University of Hong Kong, Hong Kong, China
You Ru Xie	South China Normal University, China
Philips Wang	The Open University of Hong Kong, Hong Kong, China
Toshiyuki Yamamoto	Kansai University, Japan
Harrison Yang	State University of New York at Oswego, USA
Ramidayu Yousuk	Kasetsart University, Thailand
Y. T. Yu	City University of Hong Kong, Hong Kong, China
Tomáš Zeman	Czech Technical University in Prague, Czech Republic
Zehui Zhan	South China Normal University, China
Liming Zhang	University of Macau, Macau, China
Guodong Zhao	Peking University, China
Jianhua Zhao	Southern University of Science and Technology, China
Yunxiang Zheng	South China Normal University, China
Ying Zhou	Beijing Normal University, China
Sha Zhu	Central China Normal University, China

Organizers

Kasetsart University

City University of Hong Kong

Co-organizer

Hong Kong Society for Multimedia and Image Computing

Sponsors

香港培華教育基金會
Hong Kong Pei Hua Education Foundation

Hong Kong Pei Hua Education Foundation

Springer

Springer Science+Business Media

Keynote Speakers and Panel Chairs

Keynote Speakers

Jiannong Cao	The Hong Kong Polytechnic University, Hong Kong, China
Jiyou Jia	Peking University, China
Karlcharn Kongkatong	Solution One, Thailand
Hugh O'Connell	ICDL Thailand, Thailand
Punpiti Piamsa-nga	Kasetsart University, Thailand

Panel Chairs

Horace H. S. Ip	City University of Hong Kong, Hong Kong, China
Shinichi Sato	Nihon Fukushi University, Japan

Contents

Enriched and Smart Learning Experience

Experience in Blended Learning

Keynotes

A Multimodal Human-Computer Interaction System and Its Application in Smart Learning Environments

Jiyou Jia(✉), Yunfan He, and Huixiao Le

Department of Educational Technology, School of Education, Peking University, Yiheyuanlu 5, Beijing 100871, China
{jjy,heyunfan,lehuixiao}@pku.edu.cn

Abstract. A multimodal human-computer interaction system is composed of the comprehensive usage of various input and output channels. For the information input, apart from the traditional keyboard typing, mouse clicking, screen touching, the latest speech and face recognition technology can be used. For the output, the traditional screen display, the latest speech and facial expression synthesis and gesture generation can be used. After literature review of related works, this paper at first presents such a system, MMISE (Multimodal Interaction System for Education), about its architecture and working mechanism, POOOIIM (Pedagogical Objective Oriented Output, Input and Implementation Mechanism) illustrated with practical examples. Then this paper introduces this system's pilot applications in the epidemic time of novel coronavirus in 2020.

Keywords: Multimodal human-computer interaction · Intelligent tutoring system · Smart learning environment · Mathematics instruction · Learning of English as a foreign language

1 Concept Definition and Research Question

A multimodal human-computer interaction system "seeks to leverage natural human capabilities to communicate via speech, gesture, touch, facial expression, and other modalities, bringing more sophisticated pattern recognition and classification methods to human–computer interaction" (Turk 2014). With the rapid advance in artificial intelligence in the past decade, including natural language processing, machine learning and pattern recognition, the multimodal human-computer interaction research is leveraging keyboard-tipping, mouse clicking, speech, touch, vision and gestures. A multimodal human-computer interaction system should comprehensively use various input and output channels. For the information input, apart from the traditional keyboard typing, mouse clicking, screen touching, the latest speech and face recognition technology can be utilized. For the information output, the traditional screen display, the latest speech synthesis, facial expression synthesis and gesture generation can be utilized.

Two questions arise when a system deals with multiple channels' input and output. The first is how to receive and analyze the multiple input information, and the second is how to generate the appropriate multiple output information.

S. K. S. Cheung et al. (Eds.): ICBL 2020, LNCS 12218, pp. 3–14, 2020.
https://doi.org/10.1007/978-3-030-51968-1_1

2 Related Work

A multimodal human-computer interaction system facilitates the human-like interaction. The human-like interaction between the computer and the user supported by multiple modal technology has been applied in educational technology for a long time, especially in the field of pedagogical agent and intelligent tutoring system (Jia 2015). Johnson and Lester (2018) expected that the anthropomorphic and natural interaction between the pedagogical agent and the student could make the learning easier, more motivating and more participatory. A pedagogical agent is a human-like animation or avatar in a multimedia leaning system, and can support the student's learning by playing part of an expert, a teacher, a tutor, or a friend, which can give a lecture, suggestion, or question (Liew et al. 2017; Schroeder and Adesope 2014). The most played roles by the pedagogical agent include tutors, teachers and trainers, but seldom learning companion, as found by some systematic reviews (Poria et al. 2017; Terzidou et al. 2016).

The effect of a pedagogical agent with human-like interaction has been studied early in the 1990s. Lester et al. (1997) explained the function of a pedagogical agent as persona effect based on the experiment, and believed that the human-like agent, even with a weaker interaction function, could effectively promote the learning. Social presence was first proposed by Short et al. (1976), and defined by Gunawardena (1995) and Lowenthal (2009) as the extent how a virtual agent is regarded as a real human that communicates and connects with the agent. Social clues expressed by a pedagogical agent in a multimedia learning environment like the voice, emotion and facial expression can inspire the learners' social contact schema (Louwerse et al. 2009). This argument was evidenced by the fMRI research conducted by Schilbach et al. (2006). If the social contact schema is stimulated, the learner can process the information coming from the computer deeply and facilitate the more meaningful learning (Mayer and DaPra 2012). Nass and Moon (2000) found more similarity between the computer and the human being can stimulate more social contact of the human users.

The previous studies on pedagogical agent used traditional keyboard text input, natural language and eye or face recognition as input channels. Graesser and his research team applied LSA (Latent Semantic Analysis) and other natural language processing technology in designing intelligent tutoring systems that talk with the student via text or spoken voice in dialogue or trialogue form (Graesser 2016; Graesser et al. 2018).

Lepper and Chabay (1988) found through classroom observations the teachers spent almost as much time on the students to help them with the affective goals as with the knowledge goal. The latest advancement of multimodal emotion recognition and micro emotion recognition improves the performance of affective computing (Wu et al. 2016). Recently the design of pedagogical agents to simulate the human teachers in affective intervention has been a research trend. From the perspective of multimedia learning, the pedagogical agent which can identify learners' emotions can effectively convey more social clues. Positive emotions can help learners focus on current tasks, motivate the learners, and improve the learning effect (Pekrun 2006). Liew et al. (2017) found through the meta-analysis about 30 experiments that the usage of emotional recognition and expression can improve the students' learning motivation, knowledge retention and knowledge transformation.

The output channels of pedagogical agents include text, spoken voice, and animation. Atkinson (2002) found that the pedagogical agents using voices could improve the students' learning performance more effectively than the agents using just the texts. The real human voice used by the pedagogical agents could have better effect than the synthesized voice (Mayer and DaPra 2012). IBM developed the Waston Tutor, which could generate human-like voices with different tones corresponding to the instructional goals and communicate with the students in spoken voices (Afzal et al. 2019). Those findings coincide with the social presence theory arguing that the human voice as a more effective social clue can motivate the learners' social communication schema.

The animating avatar used as a pedagogical agent can behave like a real human being, convey more social clues, and thus improve the learners' performance (Dehn and van Mulken 2000). There are two kinds of animating avatars, the anthropoid or animal-like cartoon (Yilmaz and Kiliç-Çakmak 2012), and the real human avatar (Yung and Paas 2015). Although the real human avatar seems more normal, Schroeder et al. (2013) found in their meta-analysis the anthropoid or animal-like pedagogical agents had significant and positive effect on learning performance, but the real human-like agents did not have significant effect on the learning performance. The reason may be that the learners could be aware of the existence of another human subject and lose their control of the learning (Kim et al. 2016).

The gender of the pedagogical agent is also an important factor in the human-computer interaction. The stereotype of human gender in the reality can be reflected in the relation between the learner and the pedagogical agent. Kim and Baylor (2007) found that the students liked the male agents more than the female agents, and achieved better learning gains by using the male agents. Makransky et al. (2019) found that the students got better learning result by using the same gender agents.

Some researchers have attempted to design the multiple channel output responding to learners' recognized expression. The AutoTutor system (D'mello and Graesser 2013) could recognize the learner's affective status, and then respond with appropriate voice, expression and gesture. Prendinger and Ishizuka (2005) detected the learners' affect by using the skin conductivity sensor and then gave corresponding help and concern, and found the learners felt less pressure.

The above reviewed related studies demonstrate that multimodal input or output technology has been applied in pedagogical agent design. However, the comprehensive consideration of multiple channel inputs and outputs and their application in educational scenarios have not been found in our literature review. This study attempts to fill in this gap. We design a multimodal interaction system for education based on the latest advancement in artificial intelligence, illustrate its workflow and mechanism with practical pedagogical scenarios, and introduce its technical evaluation and pilot application in the epidemic time of novel coronavirus outbreak.

3 The Architecture and Mechanism of the MMISE System

We designed and developed a web-based multimodal human-computer interaction system, MMISE (Multimodal Interaction System for Education). Implemented as a client/server architecture, it is comprised of the client program and the server system, as shown in Fig. 1. The client program deals with the capture, detection and recognition of various input signals on the one side, on the other side generates the synthesized voice and avatar animation. It can be an independent program written in Python or Java, or a webpage written with JavaScript and downloaded from the server. It runs in the client operating system like Windows in personal computers or Android in tablet computers or smartphones. The server system mainly deals with the input-output response mechanism. This client/machine architecture can fully use the computing capability of the user's client machine, and relieve the burden of the server machine.

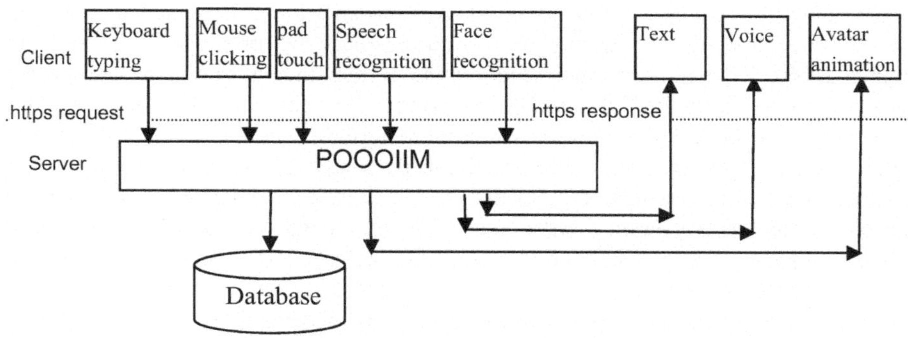

Fig. 1. The architecture of MMISE.

Even if all the inputs in various formats can be detected technologically nowadays, which of them should be captured and recorded into the database for further analysis, depends both on the pedagogical requirement and ethical consideration. Similarly, the output channels should be determined based on the system's pedagogical design objective.

The system can be implemented in three ways: as an independent webpage, as a webpage embedded in other webpages, or as an independent client program running in Windows or other operating system. The user can use the independent webpage or the independent client program, if he or she can concentrate himself or herself on the learning objects. The user should use the webpage format embedded in other webpages, if he or she is easy to lose the concentration or focus on the learning object. Which way to be used is dependent on the pedagogical objective of the system design.

Overall, the input channels, output channels and the implementation approach are all dependent on the pedagogical objectives. This is the mechanism of the MMISE, can be called pedagogical objective oriented output, input, and implementation mechanism, or in abbreviation, POOOIIM or PO^3I^2M. This mechanism can be explained with the following five examples.

The first example is a learning companion system with a MMISE that is hoped to improve the student's concentration on the learning content displayed on the screen, such as a video lecture on demand or a live video lecture. The student's face captured by the video camera is the most important input channel. For this functionality the continuance of facial identification is an important indicator for the student's concentration status of facing the screen. If the MMISE cannot recognize and identify the student's face continuously for a specified period, for example one minute, it should give out some information in the form of spoken voice, because the student does not face the screen and can't read the text message or watch the animation. In this case, the MMISE should be embedded into the lecture display program.

In Fig. 2, the live lecture during the special epidemic time of China was given to the students from Peking University who were located anywhere in the whole country. In the left division, the live video lecture with the lecturer's speech was synchronously displayed to the student, for example, Jack, while in the right division, the learning companion Emina was watching the student' facial expression. Besides, the companion expressed the same emotion with the student. If the student looked happy by watching the lecture, Emina would also looked happy. If the student watched the video in full screen, the companion Emina was hidden, but was still watching the student. If the student left the screen for one minute, Emina would spoke "Where are you now, Jack?".

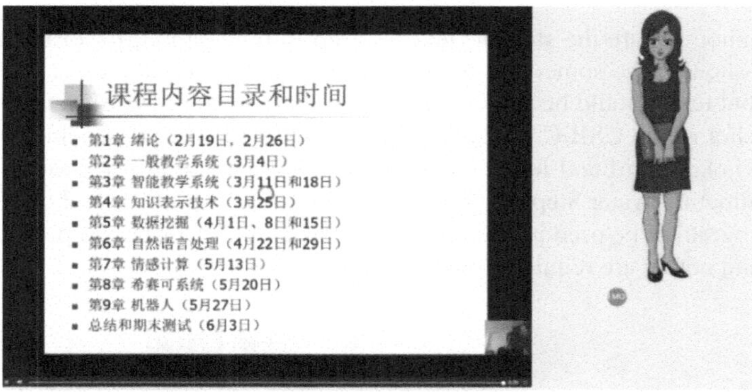

Fig. 2. The screenshot of one live lecture companied by the avatar Emina.

The second example is a tutoring system with the MMISE (Zhang and Jia 2017). The student should input the answers either by clicking the correct one in the multiple choices or fill in the blanks in a given time period, for example in 10 min for the drill, because some students lag behind the required drill duration according to our previous analysis of online learners' drilling behavior (Le and Jia 2018). If the student does not click the mouse or type the keyboard during the given time, the MMISE should alert the student. Furthermore, it should determine the concrete output format, either spoken voice, text or animation. If it detects that the student leaves the screen for a longer time, it should give out spoken text. If the student doesn't leave the screen, the MMISE should keep quiet for a quiz writing system, but function as a tutor with appropriate hints or help in the format text, voice or animation for a tutoring system. Figure 3 shows the screenshot of one online math tutoring system with the learning companion Christoph recognizing the user's face. In this case, the MMISE could be embedded into the dialogue program to enhance the agent effect, and some important issues regarding the voice, the avatar gender and features should be considered, as suggested in the literature review.

The third example is a text dialogue system for language learning with the MMISE. The student's input text is an important indicator of his or her speech behavior. If the

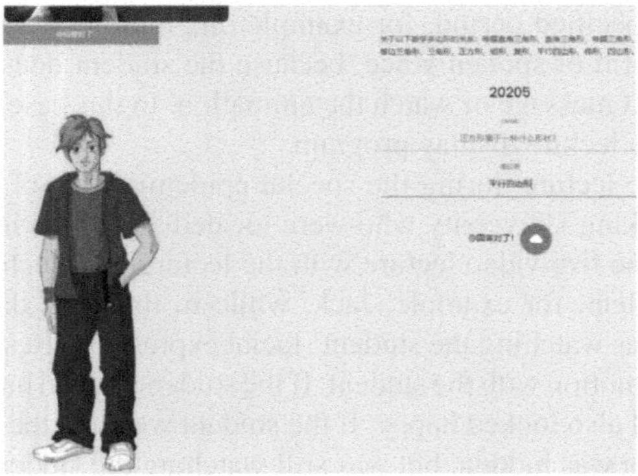

Fig. 3. The screenshot of one online math tutoring system with the user's face recognized.

MMISE cannot capture the student' text for a given time period, for example, for ten minutes, it should give some text messages to the student. On the other hand, all the student' input texts should be responded appropriately by the MMISE. Figure 4 shows one screenshot of the CSIEC system (Jia 2009) where the user is sending message to the avatar via keyboard text input, and receives both text output and spoken utterance from the animation avatar Stephan. In this case, the MMISE could be embedded into the dialogue program or be used just as an independent webpage or program, because only text input and output are required for the dialogue system.

Fig. 4. The screenshot of the CSIEC system

The fourth example is a voice speech dialogue system for language learning with the MMISE. The student's speech is an important indicator for his or her speech behavior. If the MMISE cannot capture the student' speech for a given time period, for example, for ten minutes, it should give some utterances to the student. On the other hand, the student' each input should be responded appropriately by the MMISE. In this case, the MMISE should be embedded into the dialogue program, because the voice speech as the important input channel cannot be separated from the program.

The fifth example is a quiz writing system with the MMISE in online learning. The identification of the examinee and the examination process are critical to the guarantee the fairness of the examination, as cheating often happens in MOOC and other online learning systems (Northcutt et al. 2016). The MMISE should work as the proctors or the examiner in the online examination. With the understanding and the agreement of the examinee, all the input data including keyboard typing, mouse action, speech and face movement should be recorded into the database for future review and analysis. To avoid disturbing the examinee's thinking and question answering process, no output is needed to give out throughout the examination. In this case, the MMISE as the monitor or the proctors should be embedded into the quiz writing system.

For the above examples, the textual output can be continuously presented to the user on the screen. But the voice and animation output should be given in some intervals in order to prevent their overlapping.

4 The Software Systems Used to Implement the MMISE

The advancement of artificial intelligence, including NLP (Natural Language Processing) and machine learning such as deep learning, enables both open source and commercial software systems to be used by implementing the MMISE. We just list some systems.

The continuous speech recognition can be realized by Julius (https://github.com/julius-speech/julius), an "Open-Source Large Vocabulary Continuous Speech Recognition Engine", as a high-performance, small-footprint large vocabulary continuous speech recognition (LVCSR) decoder software for speech-related researchers and developers. Based on word N-gram and context-dependent HMM, it can perform real-time decoding on various computers and devices from micro-computer to cloud server." (Lee et al. 2019). The English model (LM+DNN-HMM) can be downloaded from the Julius Model page (https://sourceforge.net/projects/juliusmodels/files/).

The face, landmark recognition and facial expression recognition can be realized by the FaceAPI.js (https://github.com/justadudewhohacks/face-api.js), a JavaScript API for Face Detection, Face Recognition and Face Landmark Detection of a photo file, a video file, or live webcam capture. It can be embedded in an existing webpage or realized in an independent webpage located in an https webserver server. For face detection, we use the SSD (Single Shot Multibox Detector) model, which computes the locations of each face in an image and returns the bounding boxes together with its probability for each face. The size of the quantized detection model is about 5.4 MB. For face landmark detection, we use the 68 point face landmark detector. The default model file has a size of only 350 kb. For face recognition, a ResNet-34 like architecture is implemented to compute a face descriptor (a feature vector with 128 values) from any given face image, which is used to describe the characteristics of a person's face. We determine the similarity of two arbitrary faces by computing the Euclidean distance. The model achieves a prediction accuracy of 99.38% on the LFW (Labeled Faces in the Wild) benchmark for face recognition. The size of the quantized recognition model is roughly 6.2 MB. For face expression recognition, we use a lightweight and fast model with a file size of roughly 310 kb. It has been trained on a variety of images from publicly available datasets as well as images scraped from the web.

The speech synthesis technology has been matured. It can be realized by commercial providers, such as Chinese iFlyTek (https://www.iflytek.com/), or online Lifelike Text to

Speech ReadSpeaker (https://www.readspeaker.com), whose web version "webReader allows content interaction on a personal level and offers important learning tools that help understanding and improve retention and make it easier to access online content on the go", and whose "speechCloud API is an online text-to-speech API for making desktop/web/mobile applications and Internet-connected devices talk." It can also be realized by open source TTS (Text To Speech) projects, from the old FreeTTS (https://sourceforge.net/projects/freetts/), to Google TTS API, MicrosoftSpeech SDK, and the recent Mozilla TTS (https://github.com/mozilla/TTS), "a part of Mozilla Common Voice. TTS aims a deep learning based Text2Speech engine, low in cost and high in quality." The latest development of TTS is the Real-Time Voice Cloning which claims to "Clone a voice in 5 s to generate arbitrary speech in real-time" (https://github.com/CorentinJ/Real-Time-Voice-Cloning) (Corentin 2020).

The avatar technology can be implemented through 2D or 3D animation software, like live2d (https://www.live2d.com), or game engine Unity (https://unity.com/). We have developed five avatars using the live2d animation software: Christoph, Stephan, Ingrid, Emina, and Christine, and applied them in the above program examples.

5 The Pilot Application of the MMISE

During the epidemic time of the novel coronavirus outbreak in 2020, all Chinese people including students should stay at home. The schools could not run as usually, and the students could not go to the schools. Therefore all the teachers and the students were separated from each other and might be distributed around the whole country. However, in order to maintain the ordinary teaching plan, the educational authorities encouraged and even required the teachers and students to adopt online learning. The teacher used the computer at home or in the school office. Almost all of the students used their computers at home. The access to the Internet was the necessary condition for the online learning. Fortunately, all most all families in China nowadays have the smart phones, and many families have wired Internet connection via optical fiber. The phones can access the Internet via 3G, 4G or even 5G network provided by the ISP (Information Service Provider) and can function as a hot spot to construct a WLAN (wireless local area network), through which the desktop computer, notebook computer or tablet computer can access the Internet. The connection to the Internet could be better and more stable if the family had a wired network through optic fabrics.

Two forms of online instruction approaches are used. The first is instant, synchronous and bidirectional lecture. The second is asynchronous and one-way learning resource browsing and activity participation.

The synchronous lecture was usually implemented in an online conference or meeting system such as Zoom, Classing, Dingding, Tencent, and others. Normally the teacher used the broadcasting function to present the lecture slides like PowerPoint with synchronous aural explanation just as in the traditional classroom or in the lecture hall. The students at home watched the lecture broadcasting as well as the teacher's facial expressions, and listened to the teacher's speech. The teacher could also watch the students' facial expressions through video transmission. However, the teacher's main function was holding the lecture, and could not observer the students' actions for all the time as in the classroom, especially with a large class volume. Because the network bandwidth was limited during the lecture time, the lecture broadcasting together with bidirectional video signals was seldom used. The teacher could not watch the students' facial expression, and could not feel their attitudes and reactions immediately. In such a virtual classroom, the students sitting alone at home could hardly feel the coexistence of other classmates. Only those students with stronger self-regulation could follow the teacher throughout the whole lecture time.

The asynchronous learning resource browsing and activity participation often happened in a course management system such as Moodle or Blackboard. The learning resources include teaching slides file in PowerPoint or other formats, required readings in PDF, Word or other formats, and web pages. The online learning activities include the quiz comprised of multiple choice, blank-filling or other types of questions, the assignment to submit a document or online texts, the feedback or survey, the discussion forum, the Wiki, and online examinations. In the traditional school teaching, similar activities are mostly completed in the paper format. Compared with the traditional paper-format activities, the online learning activities often require the students to have a stronger control over their online learning behavior, because many contents other than the learning content in the Internet, for example, the games, are more attractive to the student, especially the pupils in the schools. If the parents or other adult relatives accompanied the young student or the school pupil, the student could complete the online learning activities on time.

Both forms of pure online learning are different from the traditional classroom learning and the blended learning of traditional classroom learning with computer supported learning including online learning, because the students could not meet the teachers and their classmates on site, and lacked the teachers' face-to-face companion and guidance.

A virtual avatar representing the teacher and accompanying the student's online learning is needed for this special period of virus outbreak. For this practical purpose, we have applied the programs in the examples given in Sect. 3 in the graduate and undergraduate courses in Peking University.

We also applied the program in a web-based intelligent mathematics instruction system for school pupils, "Lexue 100" (https://www.lexue100.com), with the Chinese meaning Happy Learning for 100%. It is a web-based intelligent instruction system for school mathematics, developed by Beijing Lexue 100 Online Education Co., Ltd., and equipped with the OLAI model proposed by the authors' team (Jia and Yu 2017). More than 70,000 quizzes have been designed for the different versions of mathematics textbooks that are used in different provinces and metropolis in China. Writing quizzes is the main learning activity in this system. Each quiz is composed of a series of gap-filling or single-choice questions with predefined standard answers. As soon as one student submits the trial answer to the system, the trial answer can be compared with the standard answer, and the corresponding quiz score and feedback are instantly provided to the student. Users are allowed to pass the quiz only if every answer gets right, meaning that if the first try of one student is wrong, the student will have to try again until the answer hits the point. As we analyzed in previous studies (Jia and Zhang 2019), the school students, especially the students with learning difficulties, are easy to lose their concentration by writing the quiz alone at home, and may copy the answer from other classmates. The learning avatars facilitated with MMISE are embedded in the quiz activity, just like those shown in the above examples, and can improve the student's concentration on the quiz by watching the student's face, and giving appropriate help hints.

6 Limitation and Further Study

This paper just proposes the framework of MMISE (Multiple Modal Interaction System for Education), illustrates its architecture and working mechanism with five pilot examples, and just begins to apply it in education. Its evaluation should be done soon after the user data and evaluation survey result can be collected.

Acknowledgement. The paper is one product of the national educational technology research key project of Central Educational Technology Center China, "Personalized instruction research based on artificial intelligence and big data technology" (Project No.: 176220009). The research is supported by the project "Lexue 100, Smart Education" of Beijing Lexue 100 Online Education Co., Ltd. The authors thank all the teachers and students who have participated in the program.

References

Afzal, S., et al.: The personality of AI systems in education: experiences with the Watson tutor, a one-on-one virtual tutoring system. Childhood Educ. **95**(1), 44–52 (2019)

Atkinson, R.K.: Optimizing learning from examples using animated pedagogical agents. J. Educ. Psychol. **94**(2), 416–427 (2002)

Corentin, J.: Real-time Voice Cloning (2020). https://matheo.uliege.be/handle/2268.2/6801. Accessed 11 Feb 2020

Dehn, D.M., van Mulken, S.: The impact of animated interface agents: a review of empirical research. Int. J. Hum. Comput. Stud. **52**, 1–22 (2000)

D'mello, S., Graesser, A.: AutoTutor and affective AutoTutor: learning by talking with cognitively and emotionally intelligent computers that talk back. ACM Trans. Interact. Intell. Syst. (TiiS) **2**(4), 1–39 (2013)

Graesser, A.C.: Conversations with AutoTutor help students learn. Int. J. Artif. Intell. Educ. **26**(1), 124–132 (2016)

Graesser, A.C., Foltz, P.W., Rosen, Y., Shaffer, D.W., Forsyth, C., Germany, M.-L.: Challenges of assessing collaborative problem solving. In: Care, E., Griffin, P., Wilson, M. (eds.) Assessment and Teaching of 21st Century Skills. EAIA, pp. 75–91. Springer, Cham (2018). https://doi.org/10.1007/978-3-319-65368-6_5

Gunawardena, C.N.: Social presence theory and implications for interaction and collaborative learning in computer conferences. Int. J. Educ. Telecommun. **1**(2), 147–166 (1995)

Jia, J., Yu, Y.: Online learning activity index (OLAI) and its application for adaptive learning. In: Cheung, S.K.S., Kwok, L., Ma, W.W.K., Lee, L.-K., Yang, H. (eds.) ICBL 2017. LNCS, vol. 10309, pp. 213–224. Springer, Cham (2017). https://doi.org/10.1007/978-3-319-59360-9_19

Jia, J.: An AI framework to teach English as a foreign language: CSIEC. AI Mag. **30**(2), 59–71 (2009)

Jia, J.: Intelligent tutoring systems. In: Spector, M. (ed.) Encyclopedia of Educational Technology, pp. 411–413. Sage, Thousand Oaks (2015)

Jia, J., Zhang, J.: The analysis of online learning behavior of the students with poor academic performance in mathematics and individual help strategies. In: Cheung, S.K.S., Lee, L.-K., Simonova, I., Kozel, T., Kwok, L.-F. (eds.) ICBL 2019. LNCS, vol. 11546, pp. 205–215. Springer, Cham (2019). https://doi.org/10.1007/978-3-030-21562-0_17

Johnson, W.L., Lester, J.C.: Pedagogical agents: back to the future. AI Mag. **39**(2) (2018)

Kim, S., Chen, R.P., Zhang, K.: Anthropomorphized helpers undermine autonomy and enjoyment in computer games. J. Consum. Res. **43**(2), 282–302 (2016)

Kim, Y., Baylor, A.L.: Pedagogical agents as social models to influence learner attitudes. Educ. Technol. 23–28 (2007)

Le, H., Jia, J.: Analysis of learner timeout behavior in online tests of a bigdata set based on the OLAI concept. In: Cheung, S.K.S., Lam, J., Li, K.C., Au, O., Ma, W.W.K., Ho, W.S. (eds.) ICTE 2018. CCIS, vol. 843, pp. 285–294. Springer, Singapore (2018). https://doi.org/10.1007/978-981-13-0008-0_27

Lee, A., Kawahara, T.: Julius v4.5 (2019). https://doi.org/10.5281/zenodo.2530395

Lepper, M.R., Chabay, R.W.: Socializing the intelligent tutor: bringing empathy to computer tutors. In: Mandl, H., Lesgold, A. (eds.) Learning Issues for Intelligent Tutoring Systems. COGNITIVE SCIEN, pp. 242–257. Springer, New York (1988). https://doi.org/10.1007/978-1-4684-6350-7_10

Lester, J.C., Converse, S.A., Kahler, S.E., Barlow, S.T., Stone, B.A., Bhogal, R.S.: The persona effect: affective impact of animated pedagogical agents. In: Proceedings of the ACM SIGCHI Conference on Human Factors in Computing Systems, pp. 359–366 (1997)

Liew, T.W., Zin, N.A.M., Sahari, N.: Exploring the affective, motivational and cognitive effects of pedagogical agent enthusiasm in a multimedia learning environment. Hum.-Centric Comput. Inf. Sci. **7**(1), 9 (2017)

Louwerse, M.M., Graesser, A.C., McNamara, D.S., Lu, S.: Embodied conversational agents as conversational partners. Appl. Cogn. Psychol. Off. J. Soc. Appl. Res. Mem. Cogn. **23**(9), 1244–1255 (2009)

Lowenthal, P.R.: The evolution and influence of social presence theory on online learning. In: Kidd, T.T. (ed.) Online Education and Adult Learning: New Frontiers for Teaching Practices, pp. 124–134. IGI Global, Hershey (2009)

Makransky, G., Wismer, P., Mayer, R.E.: A gender matching effect in learning with pedagogical agents in an immersive virtual reality science simulation. J. Comput. Assist. Learn. **35**(3), 349–358 (2019)

Mayer, R.E., DaPra, C.S.: An embodiment effect in computer-based learning with animated pedagogical agents. J. Exp. Psychol. Appl. **18**(3), 239–252 (2012)

Nass, C., Moon, Y.: Machines and mindlessness: social responses to computers. J. Soc. Issues **56**(1), 81–103 (2000)

Northcutt, C.G., Ho, A.D., Chuang, I.L.: Detecting and preventing "multiple-account" cheating in massive open online courses. Comput. Educ. **100**, 71–80 (2016)

Pekrun, R.: The control-value theory of achievement emotions: assumptions, corollaries, and implications for educational research and practice. Educ. Psychol. Rev. **18**(4), 315–341 (2006)

Poria, S., Cambria, E., Bajpai, R., Hussain, A.: A review of affective computing: from unimodal analysis to multimodal fusion. Inf. Fusion **37**, 98–125 (2017)

Prendinger, H., Ishizuka, M.: The empathic companion: a character-based interface that addresses users' affective states. Appl. Artif. Intell. **19**(3–4), 267–285 (2005)

Schilbach, L., et al.: Being with virtual others: neural correlates of social interaction. Neuropsychologia **44**(5), 718–730 (2006)

Schroeder, N.L., Adesope, O.O.: A systematic review of pedagogical agents' persona, motivation, and cognitive load implications for learners. J. Res. Technol. Educ. **46**(3), 229–251 (2014)

Schroeder, N.L., Adesope, O.O., Gilbert, R.B.: How effective are pedagogical agents for learning? A meta-analytic review. J. Educ. Comput. Res. **49**(1), 1–39 (2013)

Short, J., Williams, E., Christie, B.: The Social Psychology of Telecommunication. Wiley, London (1976)

Terzidou, T., Tsiatsos, T., Miliou, C., Sourvinou, A.: Agent supported serious game environment. IEEE Trans. Learn. Technol. **9**(3), 217–230 (2016)

Turk, M.: Multimodal interaction: a review. Pattern Recogn. Lett. **36**, 189–195 (2014)

Wu, C.H., Huang, Y.M., Hwang, J.P.: Review of affective computing in education/learning: trends and challenges. Br. J. Edu. Technol. **47**(6), 1304–1323 (2016)

Yılmaz, R., Kılıç-Çakmak, E.: Educational interface agents as social models to influence learner achievement, attitude and retention of learning. Comput. Educ. **59**(2), 828–838 (2012)

Yung, H.I., Paas, F.: Effects of cueing by a pedagogical agent in an instructional animation: a cognitive load approach. Educ. Technol. Soc. **18**(3), 153–160 (2015)

Zhang, B., Jia, J.: Evaluating an intelligent tutoring system for personalized math teaching. In: Proceedings of International Symposium on Educational Technology 2017, pp. 126–130 (2017)

Learning Analytics Based on Multilayer Behavior Fusion

Yu Yang, Jiannong Cao(✉), Jiaxing Shen, Ruosong Yang, and Zhiyuan Wen

Department of Computing, The Hong Kong Polytechnic University, Kowloon, Hong Kong SAR
{csyyang,csjcao,jiaxshen,csryang,cszwen}@comp.polyu.edu.hk

Abstract. Learning analytics is the measurement, collection, and analysis of data about learners and their contexts for the purposes of understanding and optimizing the process of learning and the underlying environment. Due to the complex nature of the learning process, existing works mostly focus on the modeling and analysis of single learning behavior and thus bears limited capacity in achieving good performance and interpretability of predictive tasks. We propose a research framework for learning analytics based on multilayer behavior fusion which achieves significantly better performance in various tasks including at-risk student prediction. Results of extensive evaluation on thousands of students demonstrate the effectiveness of multilayer behavior fusion. We will report the insights about mining learning behaviors at different layers including physical, social and mental layers from the data collected from multiple sources. We will also describe the quantitative relationships between these behaviors and the students' learning performance.

Keywords: Learning analytics · Multilayer behavior extraction · At-risk student prediction · Automatic text scoring

1 Introduction

Proper education is the foundation of civilization, happiness, and success. Education has thus been an enduring and significant topic at different times. The past decades have witnessed the rapid advancement of wireless sensing, big data, and artificial intelligence. Novel pedagogical improvements have been achieved significantly via community-based learning environments where learners could learn in online communities like discussion forums and various Learning Management Systems (LMS) like Blackboard. These emerging learning paradigms are the foundation of Learning Analytics. The huge amount of data generated through online and offline activities make it possible to trace the learning processes and analyze their relationships with learning outcomes quantitatively. Specifically, learning analytics is defined as "the measurement, collection, and analysis of data about learners and their contexts for the purposes of understanding and optimizing the process of learning and the underlying environment" [1].

Although applications in learning analytics share a similar purpose which is to tailor educational opportunities to the individual learner's need, they are quite diverse ranging

S. K. S. Cheung et al. (Eds.): ICBL 2020, LNCS 12218, pp. 15–24, 2020.
https://doi.org/10.1007/978-3-030-51968-1_2

from performance prediction to course recommendation [2, 3]. For instance, Purdue University exploited data from LMS of a certain course to predict which students may be struggling academically and to provide proactive intervention. The assumption is the students' effort measured by participation in LMS could partially explain academic success. Another example is The University of Alabama improved student retention using a predictive model for at-risk students based on the large data set of their demographics [4].

In various learning analytics applications, different data modalities including text, video, and spatiotemporal data are used to model learners' learning behavior. However, most of them focus on the behavior in a single layer, which bears a limited capacity to model the underlying learning processes that are complex and dynamic in nature. For example, the LMS data reveal the underlying patterns of how students participate in the course. The way students use the LMS like how long (timespan) and how often (frequency) they use certain functionality is closely correlated with their learning performance. The statistical features of timespan and frequency belong to physical behavior. However, learners with the same physical behavior do not necessarily get similar outcomes due to the dynamics in human behavior [21]. Every single human activity takes place within a context. Learning is not an exception. Both relational context and mental context play vital roles in understanding human behavior. The relational context captures social influence and social interaction between learners while the mental context includes individuals' emotion, perception, and motivation.

In this paper, we extract behavior in multiple layers including physical, social, and mental layers which could model the underlying learning process in a more comprehensive way. The vision, however, entails two grand challenges when applied to reality. The first challenge is how to design multilayer behavior features? Most of the related works focus on physical behavior features. How to model the social interaction and mental status of learners remain open challenges. The second challenge is how to fuse the behavior feature from multiple layers? Given features from different behavior, they are usually of different modalities and different granularity which make the fusion task difficult and challenging.

We propose a general research framework indicating how multilayer features are extracted and fused for two learning analytics applications. For the extraction challenge, instead of directly measuring the social interaction in the physical world that is barely possible, we use alternative ways to approximate the social network. For example, both co-occurrences in the physical world and quotation in the cyber world are indicators of social interaction [5]. We also resort to the regularity of different behavior as the measurement of personal characteristics [6]. For the fusion challenge, we propose two types of fusion including feature level fusion and model level fusion as illustrated in two different learning applications. The effectiveness is evaluated in both applications. The results indicate the propose research framework could significantly improve application performance with the help of multilayer behavior fusion.

The remainder of the paper is organized as follows. Section 2 gives an overview of the proposed research framework. Section 3 and Sect. 4 are two case studies of learning applications which illustrate how multilayer behavior features are extracted and fused. The last section concludes the whole paper.

2 Overview

To comprehensively model the learning process, we propose the following research framework as shown in Fig. 1. This framework illustrates how we process typical multi-modal data for significant learning analytics applications of automatic text scoring and at-risk student prediction. Instead of extracting physical behavior only, we extract and fuse social and mental behavior.

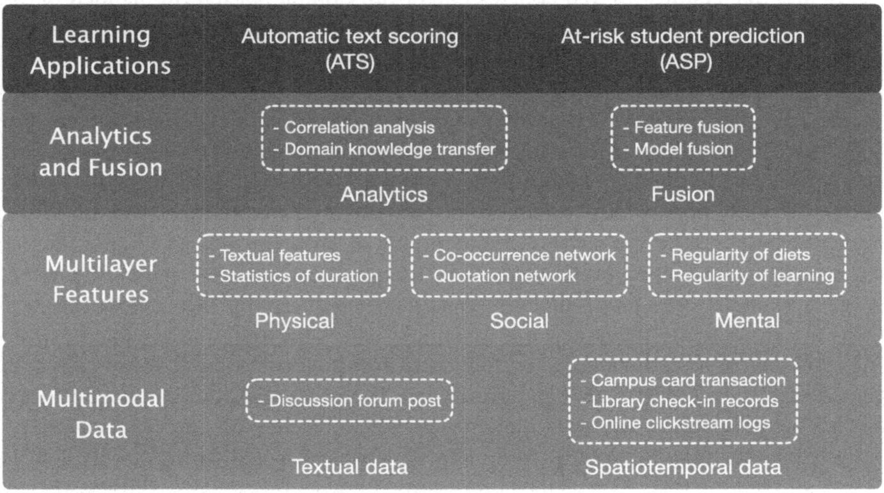

Fig. 1. The proposed research framework.

The Multimodal Data Layer shows the textual data and spatiotemporal data we processed. Specifically, textual data refer to the online discussion forum posts from students and spatiotemporal data include transaction data of daily consumption using campus cards, check-in histories of the library, and operation logs in LMS. In the next layer, we managed to extract multilayer features from physical, social, and mental levels. Physical features are mostly conventional features like statistical features of timespan, frequency of certain activities and textual features from the forum posts. Social features include networks inferred from co-occurrence and quotation. Mental features are the regularity of different behavior. Then in Analytics and Fusion Layer, we transfer domain knowledge and fuse features from different levels for the top layer applications including automatic text scoring (ATS) and at-risk student prediction (ATP).

ATS is to automatically mark the score of given online forum posts. The main focus is textual data where we extract both physical and social features. We consider not only the writing quality but also the quotation relationships between posts using model level fusion. ATP is to predict students that will be academically at-risk. The main inputs are spatiotemporal data from which we extract physical, social, and mental features. The feature-level fusion of all the features is quite effective in predicting at-risk students owing to the capacity of capturing the dynamics of learning processes.

3 Case Study 1: Automated Online Forum Posts Scoring

3.1 Introduction to Automated Online Forum Posts Scoring

With the rapid development of the Internet, online courses ware is spreading worldwide at exponential speed. Numerous colleges and universities have offered fully online or hybrid courses combining online instruction with face-to-face teaching. In 2011, a study from the Pew Research Center reported that, in 2010–11 academic year, 89 percent of four-year colleges and universities offered courses taught fully online, or hybrid/blended online, or other forms of distance instruction. In 2013, 32 percent of all students would enroll in higher education took at least one online course [7]. Meanwhile, instructors start to assign homework online and ask students to submit their homework online. With more and more electrical homework, the requirement of automated grading becomes increasingly urgent. It is a heavy burden for each instructor to mark hundreds of homework within limited time. Besides, unlike objective questions that have explicit answers, the answers of subjective assignments only provide some guidelines so that multiple instructors may give different scores for the same assignment due to different judgments. Last but not least, it is difficult to avoid preferences of instructors' tastes so that some assignments may gain higher scores than other assignments marked by the same instructors. To address the aforementioned issues, it is essential to mark the assignments automatically.

For subjective assignments, textual answers are the most popular way to show the arguments, introduce the method and procedure. Therefore, Natural Language Processing is adopted to analyze those textual answers where researchers largely focus on two types of problems. The first one is Automated Essay Scoring [8] which mainly concentrates on single long text, such as the composition or academic essays. These texts have hundreds of words and were grades by the instructors with a score according to their writing quality. There are usually significantly concrete criteria as guidelines to guide the instructors' marking. The major challenge here is how to represent the writing quality of the long text. The other is Automated Short Answer Grading (ASAG) [9] which pays more attention to the correctness of the student answers. In this task, a question and a correct answer are usually given by the instructors, and the answers are very short, usually one or two sentences. So, the key step to solve this task is to match the consistency between the correct answer and the students' answers.

In online education, online forum is widely used by both educators and students, since asynchronous, threaded discussions can be effective in creating a collaborative learning environment [10]. It benefits online learners via reducing their dropout rates, increasing their performance and course satisfaction, as well as helping and learning from each other [11]. Thus, instructors, especially in the field of social science, usually assign some open topics for students to discuss online as homework. It is inevitable that the instructors are required to grade students' performance by reading all students' posts. However, unlike the aforementioned two tasks, the online discussions show quotation relationships, some posts are more likely to be quoted such that the contents in these posts may carries more significant information. Posts with more quotations could reveal students' innovations since many students are interested in and discuss them. To summarize, this task is to automatically mark all the posts of each student not only considering the writing quality of the posts themselves, but also the quotation relationship among these students.

3.2 Model Fusion of Physical Features and Social Features

We proposed a new model as shown in Fig. 2 to combine the measurement of writing quality and the topology of quotation relationship to grade the students' posts. To evaluating the writing quality, a hierarchical RNN model [12] is used to learn post representations that contain syntactic, semantic and coherence information. Besides, student representation is learned to capture the topology information from the quotation graph. More specifically, to learn the post representation, each post is separated into several sentences, and each sentence is separated into several words. Then, a Long Short-Term Memory (LSTM) network [13] is used to compose a sequence of words to learn sentence representations. Furthermore, another LSTM network is utilized to compose a sequence of sentences to learn post representations. As for student representation, refer to recent network embedding models, a quotation graph is constructed according to the quotation relationship between students. Then, an adjacent matrix is constructed according to the quotation graph. Finally, student representation could be learned via matrix factorization (Singular Value Decomposition) of the constructed adjacent matrix. In total, with learned post representation from text and student representation from the quotation graph, two features are combined to predict the score of the student's post.

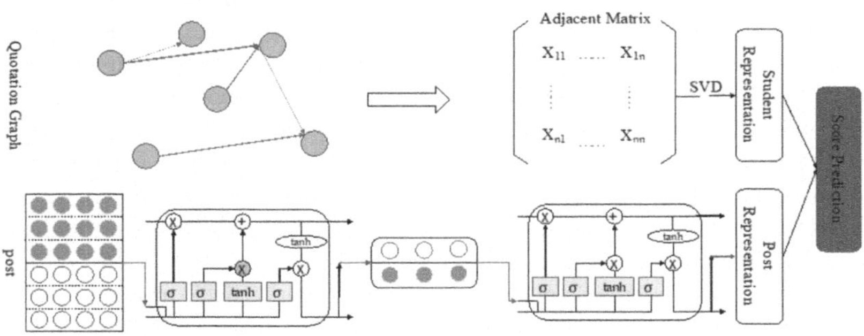

Fig. 2. Methodology framework of automated online forum posts scoring.

3.3 Results of Model Fusion in Automated Online Forum Posts Scoring

We construct a dataset cooperated with Department of Applied Social Science in our university, and two types of evaluation metrics are used, namely correlation measurements including Quadratic Weight Kappa (QWK), Spearman Correlation Coefficient (SCC), and Pearson Correlation Coefficient (PCC), and residuals-based measurements, such as Rooted Mean Square Error (RMSE). As shown in Table 1, we show the experimental results of only using neural network (NN) and using both neural network and matrix factorization (NN + MF). Since the quotation relationship is very sparse and matrix factorization is too simple to learn the quotation relationship topology. The performance of utilizing quotation relationship is lower than only using neural network. However, With the extra quotation relationship, the model gains better QWK values, which shows the effectiveness of quotation relationship.

Table 1. Experiment results.

Model	QWK	SCC	PCC	RMSE
NN	0.405	0.445	0.452	5.60
NN + FM	**0.417**	**0.430**	**0.439**	**5.96**

4 Case Study 2: Early Prediction of At-risk Students

4.1 Introduction to At-risk Student Early Prediction

Early predicting students at risk (STAR) is an effective and significant means of timely prevention of dropout and suicide. STAR are students who require temporary or ongoing intervention for achieving academic success [14]. Universities usually identify STAR by their academic performance which is sometimes too late to intervene. Existing works predict STAR from either online or offline learning behaviors [15–17]. However, neither of them is comprehensive enough to capture the whole learning processes and lead to unsatisfied prediction accuracy. For example, some students may prefer learning online but rarely attend face-to-face lectures. Thus, their offline learning behaviors are inactive which introduces biases in prediction if the whole learning process is not captured.

We aim to identify STAR before the end of a semester using multilayer behavior fusion from both online and offline learning activities. We define STAR as students whose Grade Point Average (GPA) is below 2.0 in a semester. The online learning behaviors are collected from the click-stream logs in the Blackboard, a learning management system (LMS), while the offline one comes from the library check-in records. There three major challenges to be tackled. (1) The number of STAR is far less than that of normal students such that STAR prediction is an extreme label-imbalance classification problem. (2) Comparing to the click-stream traces in LMS, the library check-in records are much sparser causing data density imbalance issues while data fusion. (3) STAR are usually inactive at the beginning of a semester so that their behavior traces are far less than enough for accurate early prediction.

To solve the aforementioned challenges, we propose EPARS for early predicting at-risk students. With the observation that study routines of good students are periodical [18] and STAR usually have more drop-out friends [19], EPARS extracts students' learning regularity patterns by a multi-scale bag-of-regularity approach and embeds their social homophily to accurately predict STAR. The experimental results show that EPARS outperforms baselines and achieves over 61% prediction accuracy in the first week of the semester.

4.2 Feature Fusion of Physical, Social, and Mental Behavior

To encode the regularity as features, we propose multi-scale bag-of-regularity to extract the repeated patterns of learning behaviors in multi-scale manners. First, we represent the learning behaviors as a binary sequence, then we sample subsequences at every nonzero element with length $\ell = 2 + (s - 1) \times z$ where integer s is the scale and z is the step-size between scales. These subsequences actually carry students' behavior patterns. Because regularity is the repeat of the behavior patterns, we filter out those only appearing once and count the number of occurrences of all possible behavior patterns in every scale as features. With this approach, which is robust for sparse data, the regularity features extracted from dense LSM data and sparse library check-ins are in the same scale-space so that it can well solve the challenge of data density imbalance. Figure 3 shows the average occurrence number of each library check-in pattern between STAR and normal students. The horizontal axis represents the library check-in patterns at scale 1 to 4. For example, pattern 110 represents a three-day pattern of students' library check-in behavior in which they continuously go to the library for first 2 days but not go there on the third day. The patterns at scale 1 exactly is the total number of library check-ins. This figure indicates that STAR have less continuous library studies than normal students.

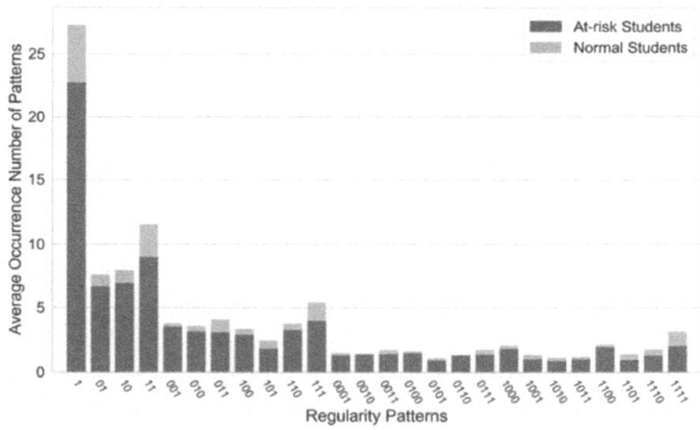

Fig. 3. Regularity patterns of at-risk students and normal students.

To supplement the lack of students' behavior at the early stage of a semester, we construct a co-occurrence network from library check-in records to model students' social relationships. Figure 4 illustrates the constructed co-occurrence network partially. Each red node represents one student, while the edges between nodes indicate the co-occurrences of students when they check-in to the library. The width of the edges shows the number of co-occurrence time between them. Moreover, we use 5 times as the threshold to distinguish the "familiar strangers" and actual friends. The "familiar strangers" are the stranger students check-in to the library together by coincidence; so, the co-occurrence time between those students should be less than actual friends going to the library together. In the figure, solid black edges represent the co-occurrence times between nodes are higher than the threshold, while dashed gray edges represent the co-occurrence times between nodes are lower than the threshold. We model the learning behavior homophily among students by this co-occurrence network, which could further help the at-risk student prediction in the social feature layer. Because of social homophily, the features of students who have similar social connections should be close. We embed the co-occurrence network to encode the social homophily as representation vectors for every student by using Node2Vec [20]. Learning students' social homophily provides extra information for solving the data insufficiency challenges and enables EPARS to early predict STAR.

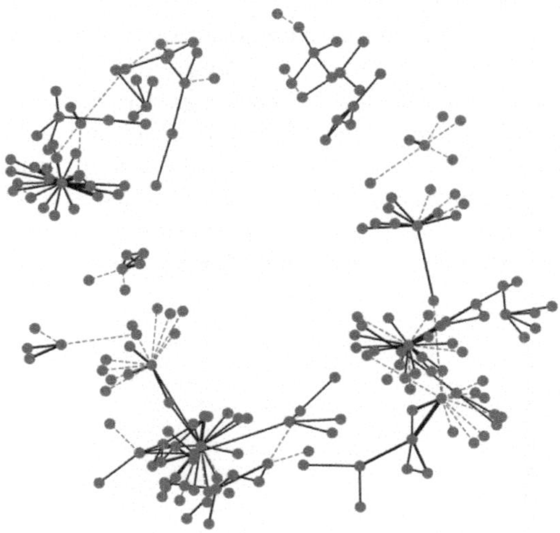

Fig. 4. A constructed co-occurrence network. (Color figure online)

Last but not least, we augment the training samples of STAR by synthesizing new ones using random linear interpolation. After data augmentation, STAR have the same number of samples as that of normal students while training the classifier for prediction. It prevents the classifier from being dominated by the majority of normal students' samples which overcomes the challenge of extreme label imbalance in classification.

4.3 Results of Feature Fusion

We collect the data from 15,503 undergraduate students in an Asian university in 2016 to 2017 academic year for conducting experiments to validate the effectiveness of the EPARS. There are 225 and 319 STAR in two semesters respectively. The experiment task is to predict STAR at the end of every week in the semester. The accuracy of STAR prediction (ACC-STAR) is defined as the amount of true positive predictions divided by the total number of STAR in the test set. The baseline approaches are handcrafted statistically significant behavior features (SF) and its combination with the components of EPARS including data augmentation (DA), regularity features (Reg), and social homophily features (SoH). All experiments are under 5-fold cross-validation and repeat 10 times. The results are reported in Table 2 where the elements represent the average ACC-STAR. The proposed method outperforms all baselines from the first week to the end of the semester which confirms its effectiveness in STAR early prediction. Especially, our EPARS correctly predicts 61.84% STAR from their online and offline learning behaviors in the first week, which outperforms SF, DA, DA-Reg, and DA-SoH 38.22%, 17.50%, 14.62%, and 22.38%, respectively.

Table 2. Results of STAR early prediction.

Weeks	Baseline	DA	DA-SoH	DA-Reg	DA-Reg-SoH
1	0.447	0.526	0.505	0.539	**0.618**
2	0.395	0.421	0.447	0.618	**0.658**
3	0.395	0.408	0.461	0.539	**0.618**
4	0.308	0.368	0.447	0.592	**0.645**
5	0.408	0.421	0.513	0.592	**0.645**
6	0.447	0.447	0.539	0.566	**0.697**
7	0.395	0.500	0.461	0.605	**0.697**
8	0.539	0.421	0.474	0.632	**0.737**
9	0.572	0.408	0.441	0.592	**0.711**
10	0.487	0.444	0.487	0.671	**0.711**
11	0.539	0.582	0.574	0.671	**0.737**
12	0.500	0.582	0.595	0.684	**0.724**
13	0.539	0.608	0.618	0.684	**0.724**

5 Conclusion

In this paper, we propose a general research framework for learning analytics by extracting and fusing multilayer behavior which includes physical, social, and mental behavior. We demonstrate the feasibility and effectiveness of extracting social and mental features from textual data and spatiotemporal data. Also, feature-level fusion and model-level fusion methods reveal the flexibility of multilayer behavior fusion. According to the evaluation of automated online forum posts scoring and at-risk student early prediction, the proposed framework could effectively improve task performance.

Acknowledgements. The work is supported by Human-computer fusion cloud computing architecture and software definition method (project code: 2018YFB1004801). It is also supported by Learning Analytics and Educational Data Mining: Making Sense of Big Data in Education (project code: 1.61.xx.9A5V) and Multi-stage Big Data Analytics for Complex Systems: Methodologies and Applications (RGC No.: C5026-18G).

References

1. Call for Papers of the 1st International Conference on Learning Analytics & Knowledge (LAK 2011). Accessed 12 Feb 2014
2. Sin, K., Muthu, L.: Application of big data in education data mining and learning analytics–a literature review. ICTACT J. Soft Comput. **5**(4) (2015)
3. Avella, J.T., Kebritchi, M., Nunn, S.G., Kanai, T.: Learning analytics methods, benefits, and challenges in higher education: a systematic literature review. Online Learn. **20**(2), 13–29 (2016)

4. Campbell, J.P., DeBlois, P.B., Oblinger, D.G.: Academic analytics: a new tool for a new era. EDUCAUSE Rev. **42**(4), 40 (2007)
5. Crandall, D.J., Backstrom, L., Cosley, D., Suri, S., Huttenlocher, D., Kleinberg, J.: Inferring social ties from geographic coincidences. Proc. Natl. Acad. Sci. **107**(52), 22436–22441 (2010)
6. Silk, J.S., Steinberg, L., Morris, A.S.: Adolescents' emotion regulation in daily life: links to depressive symptoms and problem behavior. Child Dev. **74**(6), 1869–1880 (2003)
7. Allen, I.E., Seaman, J.: Changing course: ten years of tracking online education in the United States. In: Sloan Consortium (2013)
8. Taghipour, K., Ng, H.T.: A neural approach to automated essay scoring. In: Proceedings of the 2016 Conference on Empirical Methods in Natural Language Processing, pp. 1882–1891 (2016)
9. Sultan, M.A., Salazar, C., Sumner, T.: Fast and easy short answer grading with high accuracy. In: Proceedings of the 2016 Conference of the North American Chapter of the Association for Computational Linguistics: Human Language Technologies, pp. 1070–1075 (2016)
10. Cox, B., Cox, B.: Developing interpersonal and group dynamics through asynchronous threaded discussions: the use of discussion board in collaborative learning. Education **128**(4) (2008)
11. Yuan, J., Kim, C.: Guidelines for facilitating the development of learning communitiesin online courses. J. Comput. Assist. Learn. **30**(3), 220–232 (2014)
12. Mikolov, T., Karafiát, M., Burget, L., et al.: Recurrent neural network based language model. In: Eleventh Annual Conference of the International Speech Communication Association (2010)
13. Kalchbrenner, N., Grefenstette, E., Blunsom, P.: A convolutional neural network for modelling sentences. arXiv preprint arXiv:1404.2188 (2014)
14. Richardson, V.: At-risk student intervention implementation guide. The Education and Economic Development Coordinating Council At-Risk Student Committee, p. 18 (2005)
15. He, J., Bailey, J., Rubinstein, B.I., Zhang, R.: Identifying at-risk students in massive open online courses. In: Twenty-Ninth AAAI Conference on Artificial Intelligence (2015)
16. Koprinska, I., Stretton, J., Yacef, K.: Students at risk: detection and remediation. In: Proceedings of the 8th International Conference on Educational Data Mining, pp. 512–515 (2015)
17. Marbouti, F., Diefes-Dux, H.A., Madhavan, K.: Models for early prediction of at risk students in a course using standards-based grading. Comput. Educ. **103**, 1–15 (2016)
18. Yao, H., Lian, D., Cao, Y., Wu, Y., Zhou, T.: Predicting academic performance for college students: a campus behavior perspective. ACM Trans. Intell. Syst. Technol. (TIST) **10**(3), 24 (2019)
19. Ellenbogen, S., Chamberland, C.: The peer relations of dropouts: a comparative study of at-risk and not at-risk youths. J. Adolesc. **20**(4), 355–367 (1997)
20. Grover, A., Leskovec, J.: Node2vec: scalable feature learning for networks. In: Proceedings of the 22nd ACM SIGKDD International Conference on Knowledge Discovery and Data Mining, pp. 855–864. ACM (2016)
21. Yu, Z., Du, H., Yi, F., Wang, Z., Guo, B.: Ten scientific problems in human behavior understanding. CCF Trans. Pervasive Comput. Interact. **1**(1), 3–9 (2019). https://doi.org/10.1007/s42486-018-00003-w

Design a Curriculum with User-Experience Analysis: Case Study Computing Science Curriculum

Punpiti Piamsa-nga[1](✉) and Yuen Poovarawan[2]

[1] Department of Computer Engineering, Kasetsart University, Bangkok, Thailand
pp@ku.ac.th
[2] Kasetsart University, Bangkok, Thailand
yuen@ku.ac.th

Abstract. To improve the education, a new design of curriculum is always a part of the process. However, its development usually relies on the change of body of knowledge and class implementation. As a result, it might not succeed since it is compromised with issues in the deployment. In this paper, we propose to introduce a design concept on user experience (UX), which is extensively studied in the software engineering and computer science research, as a design tool. When the curriculum is improved, not only the body of knowledge is changed, the changes also affect all related resources and activities. If some of them was not well prepared, it would become the obstructions. The UX design/analysis is a process that uses meaningful experiences of all users in all aspects, such as resources, management, usability, and implementation. All related action roles to the system in the past is needed to be analyzed. The new curriculum should be designed based on possibility of implementation and optimized based on the user experience in the future. We introduce the study of computing science curriculum design for basic education. The case study has discussions on the analysis, the objective layout on the curriculum development, and the design of the curriculum.

Keywords: User experience · Computing science

1 Introduction

Thailand is currently facing serious issues and challenges in education. The OECD's Programme for International Student Assessment (PISA) shows that the country's school performance is lower than the OECD averages for all three subject areas: reading, mathematics and science [14]. Despite spending large budget on education [12], the results are unsatisfactory. The Independent Committee for Education Reform (ICER) has a set of mission reports on education reforms [6]. In these reports, identifying underlying problems based on the perspective of many that involved in the system has found the following major issues. First, students lack of critical skills; the traditional schooling is teacher-centered delivery contents to group of students, focusing on rote learning and

S. K. S. Cheung et al. (Eds.): ICBL 2020, LNCS 12218, pp. 25–36, 2020.
https://doi.org/10.1007/978-3-030-51968-1_3

memorization [3]. Second, teachers face many mandatory activities which are exhaustive but unproductive. For example, curriculum and program assessments require long man-hours of paperwork, but do not reflect real statues. Third, curriculum is usually seen as a core element for effective schooling, therefore it is often the object of reforms. However, the contents of each subject cannot be changed drastically. A small change without any new approach or new objective would not make any high impacts. Fourth, resource limitation is a main obstruction for speedy education reform on the large scale. At the national level, there are over 7.7 million of K-12 students, over 200 thousand of educational personnel, and over 10 thousand of schools, major change in curriculum would put pressure on revising teaching materials, teacher training and class management. Fifth, population decline in Thailand means that within 6 years, the number of active students will be reduced to 6.8 million. Seats in many universities will be vacant. In order to survive, universities need to reorganize their business model. The aforementioned problems indicate that a change is necessary but careful consideration should be given to both direct and indirect impacts when drawing new policies/curriculum. Otherwise the new policy may become obstructions to itself.

"Thailand becomes a developed country with security, prosperity and sustainability in accordance with the Sufficiency Economy Philosophy" is the vision as stipulated in the country's current 20-year National Strategy (2017–2036) [16]. The policy of Thailand 4.0 is a new economic model that aims to unlock the country from several economic challenges by moving the country into a new era defined by innovative technology-based manufacturing and services, changing traditional farming to smart farming, traditional SMEs to smart enterprises, traditional services to high-valued services, etc. [19]. To succeed, it requires "smart" citizens. People need to acquire new experiences, skills and knowledge [15]. To this end, the stagnant education system needs to reform to stay coherent with the evolving world.

2 User Interfaces and User Experience

When discussing on the design of software and system, user interface (UI) is a term that is more common and more recognizable. Users access and control the system to reach their objectives by the user interfaces. On the other hand, user experience (UX) is about how each user self-evaluates the system. UX design/analysis is a process to create knowledge models from relevant experiences on design, usability and function from all stakeholders in the system. It can help all users to understand the effects and impacts of the design before the system is implemented [5]. The experience is what users think and judge the system on their own way, not the necessary just on the user interfaces. Many good UI design failed because the users evaluated the system in other aspects. An example of good UI but fail UX is the case of tablet computer. Microsoft failed to deliver Tablet computer in 2000 but iPad succeeded in 2010 [16]. This shows that the success depended on the experience of the users.

Similarly, the curriculum usually is designed on the ideas to achieve goals of the curriculum designer. In this case, curriculum can be compared as the UI. The curriculum, in most case, means its body of knowledge and its contents, not how it is implemented. The case of UX in education is what people have learned on the education not only about the contents but also all related issues to implement the curriculum, such as resource management, personnel, outputs, outcomes, obstructions, risks, and opportunities. Many good curriculums failed by the related issues in the ecosystem of the education, which is not concerned or mentioned in the curriculum [1]. Mainly, the UX analysis are learned on each stakeholder. We believe that using the philosophy of the UX design should make the curriculum more feasibly successful.

3 The Curriculum Design Issues

Some issues of UX for the curriculum are listed as follows. These issues are further discussed in case study in the next section.

Rapid Changes of Technology
Body of knowledge of computing science is not rapidly changed but the technology is. However, the change of information technology affects the learning method. Students become digital native. They can access, manipulate or process the data and knowledge in different ways from the past. Digital contents are in different forms of media. All contents are connected via the Internet. Many of them are visualized multimedia contents, not just a textbook. The learning module becomes more virtualized into the cloud. It is not necessary that learning must be just in the classroom. It is also accessible in parallel. This is an issue that curriculum must fit the new learning method; otherwise, it may not be effective.

Therefore, technologies is not just platforms or tools to delivery knowledge or skills, but become a concept of implementation. Digital learning and active learning are examples of platforms that new curricula must base on.

Focus on the Objectives
Whether using any design tools or not, the philosophy and objectives of the curriculum are still the same. However, curriculum only define characteristics of knowledge of the student, but some important objectives may not be written explicitly [13]. For example, creative thinking is an objective that every student should have. However, there is no subject of "creative thinking" in the curriculum and it can only be taught through some activities in related classes. At the end, there would be no explicit emphasis about creative thinking in the curriculum at all.

To focus on the objectives, the content of curriculum itself must clearly reflect the objectives. In the example of creative thinking, it is a main objective in the curriculum that should be written in the class description. It should be written about how the students can learn to communicate efficiently, think creatively, solve problems systematically, using data and knowledge effectively, and understand new normal of knowledge society. This will make teachers understand the objectives rather than only acknowledge on the body of contents.

The Goals Beyond the Curriculum Design
The success of curriculum is not the success of education system. There are many issues beyond the curriculum design [11]. The extra issues related to the implementation of the

curriculum such as availability and quality of teachers, class materials, class arrangement, and all side effects should be taken into consideration. These will become constraints in the curriculum deployment.

Implementation of the Curriculum
Not only design constraints should be concerned, but the implementation method is also needed to be designed carefully. Usually, implementation is based on availability and cost of current technology. Although the design constraints are obstruction, selecting appropriate implementation methods can make the system more possible. For example, while teaching in an era of Covid-19 virus outbreak is prohibited, the class may be continued using teleconference or broadcasting via the Internet. Most technology has its own cost and benefit. If the designer truly understands choices of implementation method, some obstacles could be avoid.

All-Actors-Centered, Not Just Student-Centered
We must understand clearly, who the students are, who else are in the system, what the specialty of the curriculum is, how all people participate, how much all users are needed to change. By using the UX design, a user is not analyzed as an individual. A user role (actor), which is common behavior and common characteristics of a group of human users, is analyzed instead. User-experience of all actors are needed to be analyzed; then the analysis result is used to design a new UX.

Student is still the most important role in the education system, and it is the centered of the curriculum objective. However, as we know that the system can only continue when everybody from every role can survive in the system. At least, user experiences of student role and teacher role are needed to be analyzed. The UX design of students should make the curriculum succeeded and UX design of teacher should make the curriculum more feasible.

4 Case Study: Computing Science for Basic Education

In this section, we explain the design of the computing science in basic education in Thailand. We demonstrated the backgrounds and explained the design.

4.1 Backgrounds

The basic education curriculum is the national core curriculum which prescribed goals, learning standards and a framework for the development of primary and secondary school curriculum. It is formulated to support the national development plan. Thai government has recognized to important of computer education in today's society and has included Information and Communication Technology (ICT) as one of vocational subjects in basic education curriculum since 1990s [2].

Computer education became distinct subject and one of the mandatory subjects in Thai basic education curriculum in 2017 [7]. It was also given a new name to reflect the new teaching concept, which is about the science of computing applied on any subjects and applications, and it is now called *computing science* [7]. Technology is not the focal point since it changes too fast. The curriculum concentrates instead on the thinking method while programming is deployed as a learning tool. The objective is to develop students to be thinkers, developers, and entrepreneurs, as it has been mentioned in the national development plan. However, although the objective is about computing, the class still has major contents usually found in computer science. Some issues and challenges can be found in [17].

4.2 The ICT Curriculum

The inclusion of ICT in the basic education core curriculum in 1990s was the first time that computer education has been included in Thai curriculum. It was offered as a vocational subject and focused on general uses of computers, such as Office applications, to support subject and topic learning across the curriculum.

During the design process, the user experience analysis was not adopted. The curriculum design team was told to focus on the development of contents. The team consisted of professors from various universities and teachers from some selected schools. The professors knew all about contents of the subject, but they had never had any experiences in the field. On the other hand, the teachers knew the problem in the field, but they lacked understanding on effects of the curriculum changes.

Moreover, there was no available time slot on the students' class schedule. The effect of injecting the new content means some courses in the curriculum must be eliminated. Acquisition of equipment and its required environments, such as computer and internet, is also needed.

The curriculum was not widely successful due to lack of resources, qualified teachers, and interest of students. Computer resources were not widely available. There was no lab for computer exercises in many schools. Lessons were taught by non-specialist teachers since there was shortage of teachers with sufficient knowledge and training new ICT teachers took times. In some schools, the classes were successful at junior high school because the students understood the importance of the subject. However, it was much less interesting to senior high school students since their main focus were university entrance examination and ICT was not part it.

The UX Analysis. To understand the effects of the changes clearly, the UX analysis on all actors are proposed. In this case study, the actors are composed of science teachers, ICT teachers, school administrators, and students. All details are listed during the design process. Examples of UX design/analysis after the ICT course was adopted into the curriculum are shown in Table 1. It shows that user may think in the different way from the design and they always have alternatives. It is very possible that some resource conflicts may occur, and it would become obstruction to the implementation of the curriculum.

Other issues. Some extra lessons learned on the ICT curriculum design and implementation can be listed as follows.

- The design of curriculum was done in form of a committee. Their assignment was to consider only on the body of knowledge, which was usually not too different from any

Table 1. Example of user experience and its effects.

Actor roles	User experience	Effects from the user experience
Student	1. New subject to learn 2. New technology to adopt 3. Another unimportant class since it was not used for the university entrance exam	1. More time to stay in class 2. Possibly extra curriculum needed to be reduced 3. Students not interested to the class
Science teacher	1. Reduced workload because the teaching hour is cut 2. Increased workload because there is no ICT teacher at school	ICT curriculum is a threat to their career
ICT teacher	1. Good opportunity for career 2. No schedule assigned because it was filled by school administrator 3. They are not trained as ICT teacher; need to be developed as well 4. More workload	ICT curriculum is a threat if they do not have backgrounds in computer science
School administrator	1. Need to develop science teacher, or vocational teacher to be ICT teacher 2. Need to acquire computing equipment 3. Re-arranging class schedule and teachers' workload	1. Lots of class and workload management 2. Acquiring and setting up environment needs efforts and time

other curricula in the same subject. Therefore, only the teaching and implementation guidelines, and some exercises were the main control from the conceptual design to the student as a final product.

- Body of knowledges in the curriculum was driven by the situation of the country and trends of available technology.
- The curriculum design was not integrated, and design was separated by subject. Students did not have an opportunity of real-world problems that needs collaborative solution from many subjects to solve it.
- The university entrance exam was a goal of student. The objective of the curriculum was irrelevant to them.
- Besides the class schedules, teachers still had lots of workload, such as class assessments from many organizations. Adding more tasks to teachers seem not to be a good attempt.
- The curriculum is more focus on the content that students should know rather than the life that the students should have. There are many extracurricular activities which students have to learn but are not part of the curriculum and therefore are not scheduled in regular school hours.

– The limit that should be taken into consideration of the curriculum design: action roles of all users, studying hours of students, teaching hours of teachers, teaching resource management, and learning/studying materials.

4.3 The Computing Science Curriculum

The UX design. From the UX analysis of the ICT curriculum, the design issues are listed as follows.

The Philosophy, Objectives and Goals. The curriculum still reflects the philosophy, objectives and goals. In 2010s, the national development plan of Thailand is to promote knowledge economy. Innovative thinking is a key.

UX of the Actors. When the curriculum contents are the main focus without taking the experiences, that the stakeholders will have, into consideration, the outcomes may not be as planned. Everyone always has a choice and it will be the best for him/her. For example, the basic programming is planned to deploy mainly in the junior high level, where it has been initially planned in the senior high level. However, by the UX analysis, students will not be interested in a class that was not a part of national university entrance exam. To avoid that situation, basic skill of computing science, such as Python programming, IoT concept, basic data collection and analysis, was mainly introduced at the junior high level. The class at the senior high level becomes like higher-education class, which has more advanced in software development, data analytics, and project. If some students elect not to continue with the subject at senior high, the curriculum is still successful with slight loss on less important topics.

The Education in the 21st Century. The idea of education in the 21st century brings about the needs of student's characteristics, such as teamwork, leadership, globalization, work/living environment, ethics, design thinking, and engineering senses [8]. However, it was hard to include in the curriculum because the real-world problem requires combination of multiple disciplinaries to solve and the curriculum designer was told to focus only on the computer curriculum.

Focus on a Single Issue, then Expand it. Focus more than one point turns out to be out of focus. Everyone tries to maximize contents into time slots rather than focusing on the ultimate goals first and then extending what to do in details. For example, the focal point of curriculum at level 1 (primary level 1: grades 1–3) is defined as "unplugged". It means that students can solve real-life problems by algorithm without computers or devices. An example to represent outcomes is "student can describe directions from home to school with his/her reasons." It implies how to implement design thinking and critical thinking with the "unplugged" information technology into the curriculum. Focuses of other levels (grades 4–6, 7–9 and 10–12) are "daily life", "primary data", and "secondary data", respectively. Focus on a single issue with further expansion can make the goal of curriculum more understandable and more precise.

Explicitly Emphasis on Goals. A goal must be explicitly written in the curriculum; otherwise, it could not be effective. For example, if the goal is about the integration and problem solving, it is not possible to just talk about IT topics. Therefore, many ICT-related social issues such as fake news and IT laws, are introduced in the computing science class. Previously, these topics were not included in the ICT class. They were more likely be placed in a social science class. However, it is now in the computing science curriculum because it will be more beneficial to build innovative and collaborative thinking to use ICT as parts of solution to the real-world problems than just pure ICT classes.

Design Based on Possible Resources. Resource availability is one of the most important issue to the success of curriculum deployment. The resources in this case includes class hours, teachers, course materials. Moreover, the resource conflict among users in the system should be avoided; otherwise, the curriculum would be rejected.

Curriculum. The curriculum has been deployed since 2007. The curriculum is activity-based, which is responded to the PISA. The activities in the curriculum emphasize on computational thinking and coding. Various platforms of software and IoT can be selected by schools.

The computing science curriculum is separated into 4 grade levels: level 1 primary education grades 1–3 (grades 1–3), level 2 primary education grades 4–6 (grades 4–6), level 3 secondary education grades 1–3 (grades 7–9) and level 4 secondary education grades 4–6 (grades 10–12).

The computing science curriculum has three underlying principles: computational thinking, ICT digital technology and digital, media and information literacy.

Computational Thinking. Acquired analytical, synthetic, constructive, critical and systematic thinking skills, leading to creation of bodies of knowledge or information for everyday life decision-making regarding oneself and society.

ICT Digital Technology. Acquired knowledge of current technologies and have ability to choose and apply them appropriately and ethically.

Digital, Media and Information Literacy. Ability to differentiate fake news and opinions from real news. Aware of cybersecurity and privacy issues.

Some extra design concepts from the above principles are listed as follows.

Technology Class. The computing science was not proposed as a science class, but the new section curriculum called "technology." To avoid name conflict of class with other science class, it is named only "computing." The concept of computing is about design thinking while using computer technology as a major tool.

Knowledge Integration. To use computing science as a thinking method to solve real-world problem is one of ultimate goals. Many tasks and activities in this class is designed from problems in other subjects. STEM concept is also used in the class implementation.

Extensible Design Concept. By the user experiences, the focus points of all four groups are "unplugged", "daily life", "primary data", and "secondary data".

The unplugged was designed from perspective that the student is still very young, and the computing should be the understanding about themselves, thinking and reasoning on their daily life, and presenting or explaining in step by step.

The "daily life" was about how they use computer technology in their daily life, such as searching in the Internet, using online tools, making documents by office software. This group of students becomes familiar with computer technology. A huge number of students have own cell phones even though it is suggested that an under-13 student should not be online. However, dangers of being online has much higher risks. Teaching the risks and how to protect themselves online becomes an important issue in the curriculum.

The third group is the most important to the success of the curriculum. The "primary data" is designed for the junior high students to focus on how they generate primary data rather than what kind of technology they should learn or what programming language skill they should have. The knowledge society will become successful if the society have new knowledge to make new products or new services. Quality data would become quality knowledge. The body of knowledge includes the data processing issues, such as data sensors, data collection, IoT, basic programming, data privacy, copyright and patents, computer and data security, IT laws, etc.

The "secondary data" is designed for senior high student to use their knowledge and programming skills to further build real world application. Students was much less interested in this class since it was not a part of national entrance exam, the class is only appeal to some students who are seriously into computer science and its related technology. Therefore, any very important contents should not be included here. Advanced issues in computing such as AI and data science are also introduced. Datasets are not necessary built by themselves but acquired from others via computing technology. Students are expected to use computing skill and knowledge from other subjects to solve more complex problems from the secondary data sources.

Tools are Selective. Tools are not restricted. Teachers can use any kinds of technologies, programming languages, software packages, operating systems, PC, tablet devices, etc. For example, data collection can be done in paper or online questionnaires. PC is necessary only in a programming skill training class. Python programming language is recommended but not restricted. These are about avoiding problems of resource availability.

Technology Upgrade. Although computer science concept does not change much, the IT technology changes rapidly. New applications such as smart farm, Artificial Intelligence, Internet of Thing, online learning, collaborative tools become the main streams of attentions rather than the office software.

Curriculum Deployment. The curriculum has been deployed throughout the country in 2007. The overview of the curriculum is shown in Table 2. Success of curriculum is still too early to determine since it is still at an early stage of implementation. Obstructions from the resource availabilities, resource conflicts are negligible. The initialization of the deployment was comfortably successful. There were much less resistances. The total teaching hour in the class schedule was not changed. It is still the same as teaching time in the ICT curriculum. The number of teachers is still inadequate due to a graduate with skill in computing is likely to work on other jobs rather than teacher.

Table 2. Example of user experience and its effects.

Level	1	2	3	4
Grades	1–3	4–6	7–9	10–12
Concept keyword	*Unplugged*	*Daily life*	*Primary Data*	*Secondary Data*
Example of skills	Explain the direction from home to school with reasoning	Use computer and the Internet to do daily activities such as searching data and making documents	Collect data from various tools such as basic questionnaire or IoT and write a program to do basic control	Use available data to solve the real-world problem by computer programming
Computer science knowledge	Basic problem solving	Use logic in problem solving	Use programing to solve problems	Apply more advanced computing technology with knowledge from other subjects to solve real-world problems
ICT	Skill to use basic ICT tools	Search data sufficiently and assess its correctness	Collect, analyze, assess, present data and information	
Digital literacy	Protect their private data	Understand rights and responsibilities on data usage	Use ICT with responsibility and understand basic IT laws and ethics	
Example of learning platforms	Unplugged activities	Basic office software tools on available computer platforms	Designed lab with various tools such as KidBright	Programming with provided data sources

Since the technology mentioned in the curriculum was not strictly selected, there are many choices for each technology. The class-material resources such computing equipment and software are also less required. Many learning platforms, such as CodingThailand.org [4] and KidBright [10], have been developed in conjunction with the curriculum deployment. Unplugged programming and Coding are very effective and requires much less resources. Young students pay more attention to the unplugged activities than those in the previous curriculum and teachers also do not need extra training [9]. Coding becomes trendy. It is easy for school to develop IoT or programming class since tools, devices and teaching material are much easier to access or acquire.

5 Conclusions

In this paper, we describe to use of user experience as a part of the curriculum design. User experience design and analysis is a process in computer science to develop software and system based on how the users think of when they use and how they react to the system. It brings about the understanding of projecting obstruction, which can be avoid before the implementation. In the case of curriculum, the users in this case are composed of students, teachers, and administrators. The issues in the analysis that must be taken into consideration are resource availability, resource conflict, and implementation method. The design of new curriculum must learn from the UX analysis of all stakeholders.

The case study demonstrates the development of computing curriculum in the basic education in Thailand. The ICT curriculum has been proposed to include as a science subject of basic education. The proposal was rejected, and it ended up being a vocational class. After analyzing on the user experience, the new curriculum design, namely "computing science", is successfully adopted as a core class in current basic education.

Acknowledgement. We would like to thank Nalina Phisanbut for her English reviews and comments.

References

1. Buasuwan, P.: Rethinking Thai higher education for Thailand 4.0. Asian Educ. Dev. Stud. **7**(2), 157–173 (2018)
2. Bureau of academic affairs and educational standards. Basic Education Core Curriculum B.E. 2008 (Revised B.E. 2017) (2017)
3. Changwong, K., Sukkamart, A., Sisan, B.: Critical thinking skill development: analysis of a new learning management model for Thai high schools. J. Int. Stud. **11**(2), 37–48 (2018)
4. CodingThailand. https://CodingThailand.org. Accessed 13 Apr 2020
5. Deitte, L.A., Omary, R.A.: The power of design thinking in medical education. Acad. Radiol. **26**(10) (2019)
6. Independent Committee for Education Reform: Mission Reports (2019). https://www.thaiedreform.org/knowledge/3127/. Accessed 13 Apr 2020
7. Institute for the promotion of teaching science and technology, Summary of the curriculum and comparison between the ICT curriculum and computing science curriculum (2018)
8. Jedaman, P., Buaraphan, K., Pimdee, P., Yuenyong, C., Sukkamart, A., Suksup, C.: Analysis of sustainable leadership for science learning management in the 21st Century under education THAILAND 4.0 framework. In: AIP Conference Proceedings 1923, Article no. 030062 (2018)
9. Kanyacome, S., Poovarawan, Y.: The relationship between amusement and quality of learning by using gamification approach in creative youth camp. In: 2017 10th International Conference on Ubi-media Computing and Workshops (Ubi-Media), Pattaya, pp. 1–5 (2017)
10. Kid-bright. https://www.kid-bright.org/. Accessed 13 Apr 2020
11. Lee, J., Liu, A., Cheng, Y.C., Ma, S.-P., Lee, S.-J.: Execution plan for software engineering education in Taiwan. In: Proceedings - Asia-Pacific Software Engineering Conference, APSEC (2012)
12. Nitiwong, B.: Cost and pricing towards education industry and business in Thailand. In: The 5th Business, Economics and Communications International Conference (2015)
13. Piamsa-nga, P., Poovarawan, Y.: Engineering education from unlimited vision. In: The 36th Electrical Engineering Conference, Kanchanaburi, Thailand (2013)
14. Thailand Country Note, Programme for international student assessment (PISA) results from PISA (2018). https://www.oecd.org/pisa/publications/PISA2018_CN_THA.pdf. Accessed 13 Apr 2020

15. Sethakul, P., Utakrit, N.: Challenges and future trends for Thai education: conceptual frameworks into action. Int. J. Eng. Pedagogy **9**(2), 8–16 (2019)
16. Royal Thai government. National Strategies (2017–2036) In: Royal Thai Government Gazette, vol. 135, no. 82 (2018)
17. Webb, M., et al.: Computer science in the school curriculum: issues and challenges. In: Tatnall, A., Webb, M. (eds.) WCCE 2017. IAICT, vol. 515, pp. 421–431. Springer, Cham (2017). https://doi.org/10.1007/978-3-319-74310-3_43
18. Wetzlinger, W., Auinger, A., Dörflinger, M.: Comparing effectiveness, efficiency, ease of use, usability and user experience when using tablets and laptops. In: Marcus, A. (ed.) DUXU 2014. LNCS, vol. 8517, pp. 402–412. Springer, Cham (2014). https://doi.org/10.1007/978-3-319-07668-3_39
19. Wongwuttiwat, J., Lawanna, A.: The digital Thailand strategy and the ASEAN community. Electron. J. Inf. Syst. Dev. Countries **84**(3), Article no. e12024 (2018)

Adaptive Learning

Personalising Learning with Learning Analytics: A Review of the Literature

Kam Cheong Li and Billy Tak-Ming Wong(✉)

The Open University of Hong Kong, Ho Man Tin, Hong Kong, China
{kcli,tamiwong}@ouhk.edu.hk

Abstract. Advances have been made in personalised learning by the developments in learning analytics, where useful information can be extracted from educational data and analysed to devise personalised learning solutions. This paper presents a review of the literature in this area, covering a total of 144 relevant empirical articles published between 2012 and 2019 collected from Scopus. It identifies the patterns in the use of learning analytics to personalise learning in terms of the environments (what), stakeholders (who), objectives (why) and methods (how). The results show a clear growth in the number of practices, and diversity in terms of the learning contexts where learning analytics was implemented; the types of data collected; the groups of target stakeholders; the objectives of learning analytics practices; the personalised learning goals; and the analytics methods. The findings also reveal the emergence of practices related to the teacher perspective and some areas which have not been fully addressed, such as personalised intervention for future work.

Keywords: Learning analytics · Personalised learning · Adaptive learning · Personalisation

1 Introduction

Personalisation is a focus in contemporary educational practices. It refers to the tailoring of learning "for each student's strengths, needs and interests—including enabling students' voices and choices in what, how, when and where they learn—to provide flexibility and supports to ensure mastery of the highest standards possible" [1]. In contrast to the conventional "one-size-fits-all" education system, in personalised learning the ways of learning and teaching, as well as assignments and assessments, take into account learners' individual differences and needs.

Learning analytics has been adopted as a major means for implementing personalised learning [2]. It refers to "the measurement, collection, analysis and reporting of data about learners and their contexts, for purposes of understanding and optimising learning and the environments in which it occurs" [3]. With the vast amount of educational data available, new learning analytics approaches have been developed to contextualise the invisible data and improve students' learning experience [4]. The benefits of learning to use analytics have been widely reported in relevant initiatives, such as providing real-time

S. K. S. Cheung et al. (Eds.): ICBL 2020, LNCS 12218, pp. 39–48, 2020.
https://doi.org/10.1007/978-3-030-51968-1_4

feedback based on students' individual progress [5]; recommending the most appropriate materials to fit students' learning proficiency [6]; and dismantling the barriers to lifelong personalised learning [7].

Despite plenty of initiatives on utilising learning analytics for personalising learning, they have yet to be systematically surveyed and reviewed. Related reviews have focused more on the use of other technologies in personalised learning, such as mobile devices and social media [8], or specific aspects of learning analytics, such as interventions [9]. There is therefore a need to review the relevant work in this area.

This paper examines empirical cases of personalised learning through the use of learning analytics. It includes a total of 144 cases published in the period 2012 to 2019. The review covers the data and environment, relevant stakeholders, objectives, and methods of learning analytics, in order to examine the relationship between the use of learning analytics and personalised learning.

2 Literature Review

Personalised learning, as an umbrella term, covers a range of related concepts such as adaptive learning, a flexible learning environment, individualisation, and student-centeredness. The personalisation of learning usually takes into account students' background, learning objectives and preferences. Educational data therefore serve as a vital source of information for personalised learning practices [4]. Santo et al. [10] pointed out that factors, such as effective detection of students' contextual and personal data, are important for a better understating of their individual learning needs. Chatti et al. [11] also stressed that personalised learning solutions which adopt learning analytics can provide students with the learning paths that suit their individual needs or learning resources that reflect their preferences.

There has been a broad range of personalised learning initiatives based on learning analytics for various purposes—such as providing personalised recommendations (e.g. feedback, learning materials and learning paths) [12]; monitoring students' process [13]; providing personal assessment [14]; and predicting students' learning outcomes [15]. These data-driven personalised learning practices have been shown to benefit various stakeholders. For example, students can improve their learning experiences and learning outcomes [15], and teachers can modify their teaching plans to enhance teaching effectiveness [16]. Also, institutions and administrators can review and improve their courses and programme designs [17], and system developers can also develop learning systems which are more suitable for students [18].

However, related reviews have yet to address specifically the adoption of learning analytics to achieve personalised learning. Some of the reviews have covered other types of educational technologies. For example, Berge [19] reviewed the use of mobile devices for enabling learners to choose what, where and how to learn. Also, Scott et al. [20] examined the work on 3D technologies for developing an adaptive virtual learning environment. The literature reviews on learning analytics have focused mainly on its overall practices. For instance, Li et al. [21] analysed the patterns and trends of learning analytics in higher education institutions in Asia, and Wong [22] presented a systematic review of the benefits for higher education. In view of such limitations, there is a need to survey relevant work on personalising learning with the aid of learning analytics.

3 Methodology

This paper aims to identify the patterns in the use of learning analytics for achieving personalisation in educational practices. Related articles published between 2012 and 2019 were collected from Scopus, using the set of keywords [("personalization" OR "personalized" OR "adaptive") AND "learning analytics"]. Initially, 2,682 articles were found. Each of them was further checked to select those which match the inclusion criteria, namely that they (1) were written in English with the full paper accessible, and (2) involved an empirical practice of learning analytics for personalised learning. A total of 144 articles were finally selected for the review. Figure 1 presents the number of articles over the years.

The learning analytics articles were coded according to the Learning Analytics Reference Model proposed by Chatti et al. [11]. The model covers four aspects of the learning analytics practices, viz.

i. What – learning context, learning environment, and data collected
ii. Who – stakeholders
iii. Why – objective of learning analytics, and personalised learning goal
iv. How – learning analytics method.

The patterns of the learning analytics were generalised based on these four aspects.

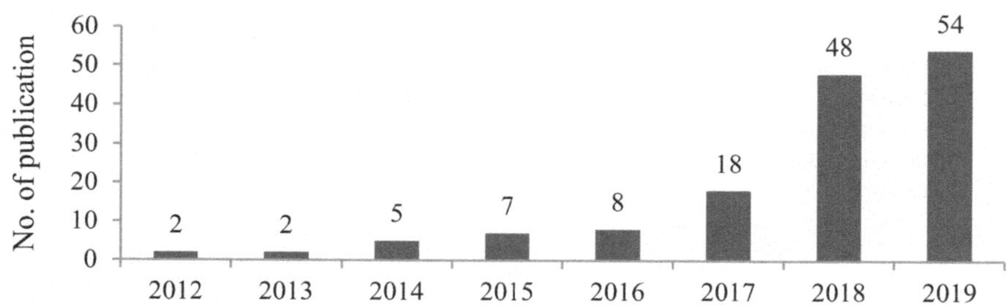

Fig. 1. Number of related articles in various years

4 Results

4.1 What

Learning Context. Figure 2 shows an overview of the learning contexts in the learning analytics practices over the years. In general, a majority of these practices were implemented in formal learning contexts, in particular in tertiary education, followed by informal learning contexts in the form of online learning such as MOOCs. In recent years, primary and secondary education, as well as professional learning (e.g. teacher professional development), have emerged as contexts for learning analytics practices.

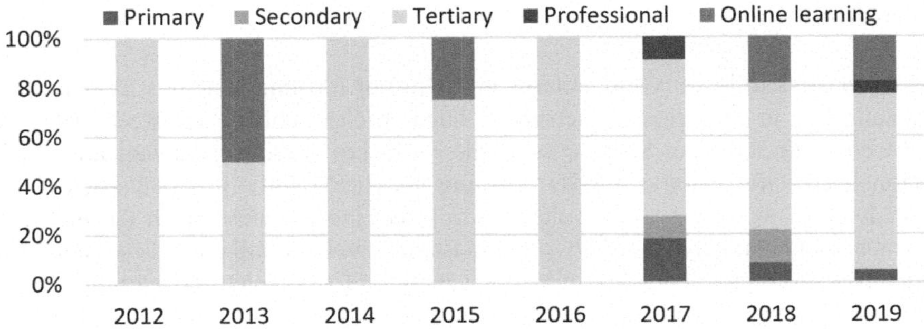

Fig. 2. Learning contexts of the learning analytics practices

Learning Environment. Figure 3 presents the distribution of learning environments for the learning analytics practices. There has been a clear trend for the learning environments to have become more diversified with the increasing number of practices over the years. The online learning systems (developed specially for the learning of specific contents) and learning management systems are the environments most frequently adopted in the practices. This is followed by the classroom environments—online (MOOC) or offline (face-to-face classroom). Other environments—intelligent tutoring systems, learning apps, social media and educational games—have emerged in the practices in recent years.

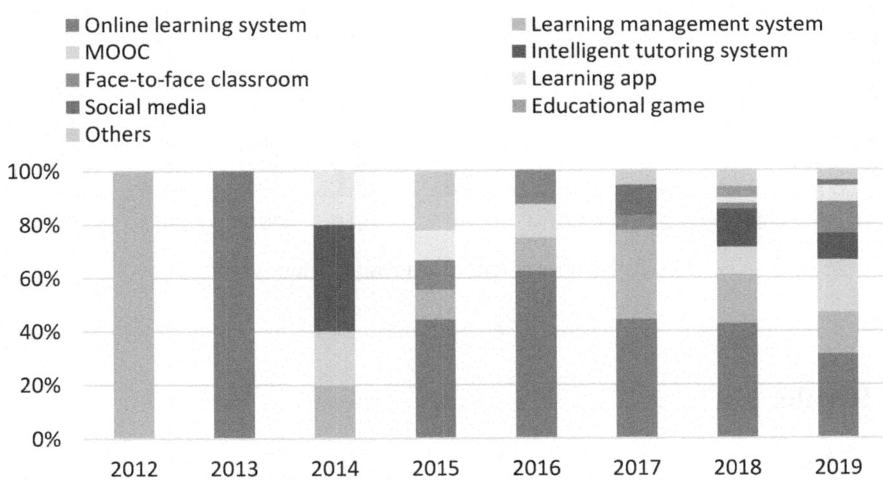

Fig. 3. Learning environments of the learning analytics practices

Data Collected. Figure 4 shows the types of data collected for the learning analytics practices. The largest proportion of data (i.e. 39%) lay in those reflecting the learning process (e.g. log data, times of attempt, and quiz responses in online learning systems). Altogether, nearly half of the types of data used in the practices were contributed by the learners' academic performance (e.g. scores and quiz results); educational backgrounds (e.g. examination scores in prior studies, learning styles and learning preferences); learning outcomes (e.g. completion rates); demographics; and profiles.

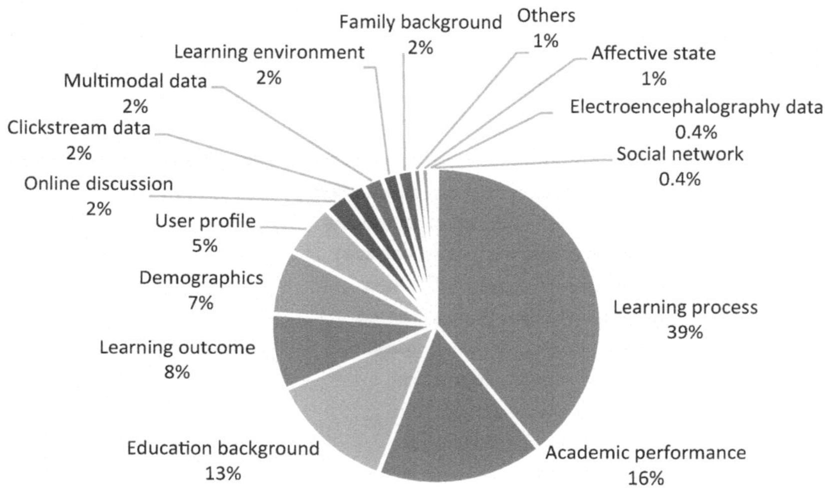

Fig. 4. Types of data collected in the learning analytics practices

4.2 Who

Stakeholder. Figure 5 presents the target stakeholders in the learning analytics practices. Students and teachers have been the stakeholder groups that have dominated the practices throughout the years. Only in some practices have the needs of educational administrators, researchers and system developers been addressed.

4.3 Why

Objective of Learning Analytics. Figure 6 shows the objectives of the learning analytics practices. As expected, personalising the learning experience was the most common objective. Other than that, a number of the practices also targeted monitoring the learning process, predicting students' individual learning outcomes, and providing personalised assessment. There were also practices which addressed the teachers' perspective, with the objectives of assisting the development of teaching plans and examining teaching effectiveness.

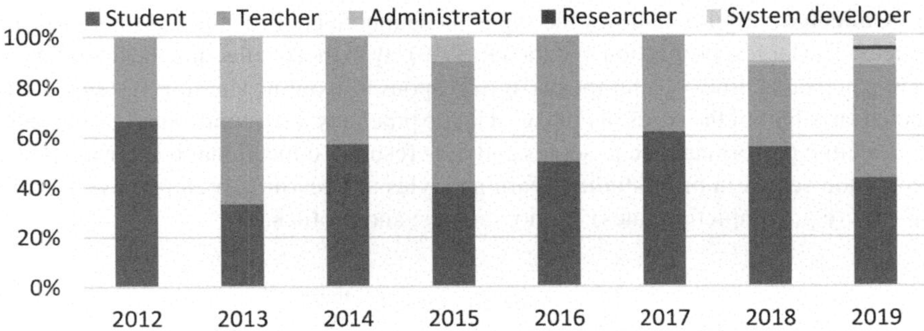

Fig. 5. Stakeholders addressed in the learning analytics practices

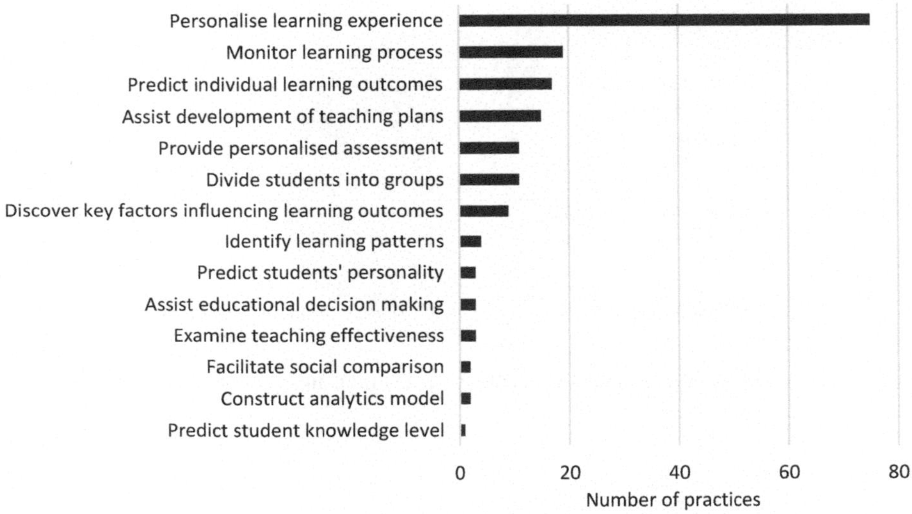

Fig. 6. Objectives of the learning analytics practices

Personalised Learning Goal. Figure 7 summarises the personalised learning goals through the practices of learning analytics. The provision of personal recommendations (e.g. learning paths, resources, feedback and study fields) and the satisfaction of learners' personalised learning needs were the two major goals shown in the practices. There were also other diverse goals, such as coping with learners' learning styles and monitoring their learning outcomes.

4.4 How

Learning Analytics Method. Figure 8 provides an overview of the analytics methods used in the practices. The use of common statistical tests (e.g. ANOVA, correlation, and regression) was the most frequent way, followed by the adoption of classification,

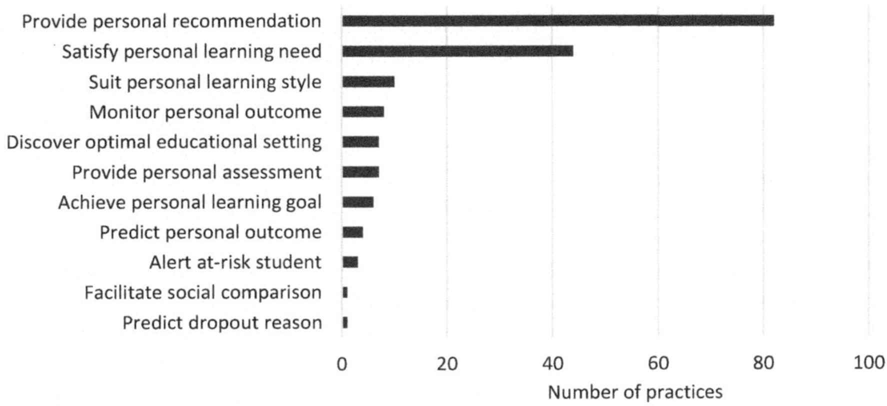

Fig. 7. Personalised learning goals in the learning analytics practices

clustering, and visualisation techniques. Altogether, these four major types of analytics methods were used in about 70% of the practices. There were a number of specific analytics methods used in a small proportion of the practices, such as content analysis, social network analysis, and sparse factor analysis.

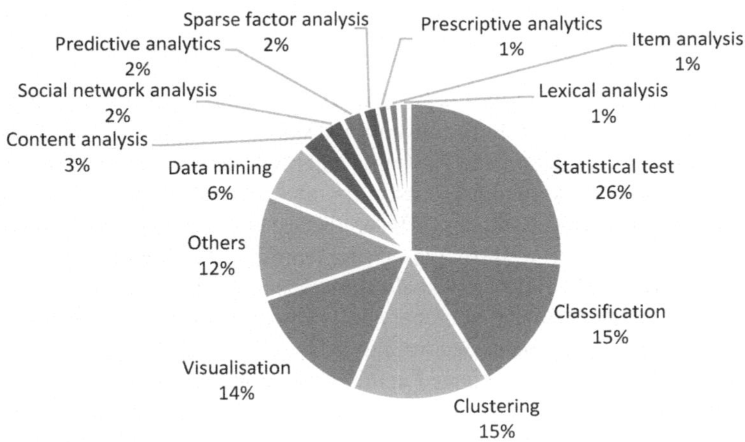

Fig. 8. Types of analytics methods used in the learning analytics practices

5 Discussion

The results of this study indicated that learning analytics has become increasingly prevalent in personalised learning practices. The findings also revealed the patterns of the learning analytics practices in this regard.

There has been a clear trend for a growth in the practice of learning analytics in a broad range of learning contexts. In particular, learning analytics has demonstrated its potential to help in tackling the challenges in informal online learning such as MOOCs, for which the completion rates are known to have been very low in general [23]. The use of learning analytics has benefited from the enormous amount of data available in the online learning environments, particularly the data generated during the learning process which, as shown in this study, was the most frequent type of data collected. In return, the data facilitated the provision of personalised learner support [24].

Students and teachers have been the two major groups of target stakeholders addressed in the learning analytics practices. As shown in the results, students may benefit from personalising learning in terms of having a better understanding of their performance compared with the overall performance of other students [25], and receiving personalised learning resources, learning paths and feedback [26]. From the teachers' perspective, by monitoring students' individual learning processes and outcomes, they are informed about the knowledge gaps of each student and are able to provide suitable interventions [16]. The data-informed practices also help teachers to prepare curricula which are suited better to students' needs [26].

There has been a broad range of objectives for the learning analytics practices. Other than personalising the learning experience, which was mentioned most frequently in the articles, several other objectives have also emerged in recent years. These have included the continuous monitoring of the learning process; prediction of the learning outcomes from unobservable data; and early identification of student needs. They also revealed the recent advances in data tracking and analysis techniques which enabled such objectives to be achieved [17, 27].

Our results also indicated a diversity of analytics methods utilised in the practices. The more frequent ones include both conventional statistical techniques (e.g. descriptive statistics, regression, correlation and ANOVA) and predictive techniques such as classification (e.g. decision trees, random forest, support-vector machines and the Bayesian network) and clustering (e.g. K-means). The predictive techniques were applied for tasks such as predicting dropout rates [16], classifying learning behaviours [28], and estimating learning progress [29]. Besides, visualisation was also a relatively popular learning analytics method, which enabled students and teachers to track learning progress and adjust learning and teaching plans accordingly [13].

The range of relevant work reviewed in this study, however, seldom addressed intervention—the final stage of the learning analytics cycle, following the tracking and analysis of data as well as the generation of insights based on the analysis [30]. This relates to the finding by Wong and Li [9] that intervention has been a great challenge in learning analytics and is yet to be widely implemented. In the context of personalised learning, such a challenge is also revealed by the lack of learning analytics practices which focused on the provision of personalised intervention for at-risk or underachieving learners. This is a potential area to be addressed in future work.

6 Conclusion

This paper presents a comprehensive review of the learning analytics practices which aimed to personalise learning. The results contributed to revealing the patterns of learning analytics practices in this area. They showed a clear trend for a growing number of practices, and diversity in the learning contexts where learning analytics was implemented; the types of data collected; the groups of target stakeholders; the objectives of learning analytics practices; the personalised learning goals; and the analytics methods.

The results also suggest potential areas for future work. There has been an emerging focus of learning analytics practices on the teachers' perspective. Other than the goals, such as developing better teaching plans and assessing teaching effectiveness as shown in the existing practices, the provision of personalised intervention for at-risk or underachieving students is an area which has not been adequately addressed. Besides, the interoperability between learning analytics and other means of achieving personalised learning (such as the flipped classroom and artificial intelligence, as reviewed in Li and Wong [2]) is another area which has yet to be adequately examined. Further efforts devoted to these areas would help to develop more effective and sustainable approaches to personalised learning.

References

1. Patrick, S., Kennedy, K., Powell, A.: Mean What You Say: Defining and Integrating Personalized, Blended and Competency Education. International Association for K-12 Online Learning (iNACOL), Vienna (2013)
2. Li, K.C., Wong, B.T.-M.: How learning has been personalised: a review of literature from 2009 to 2018. In: Cheung, S.K.S., Lee, L.-K., Simonova, I., Kozel, T., Kwok, L.-F. (eds.) ICBL 2019. LNCS, vol. 11546, pp. 72–81. Springer, Cham (2019). https://doi.org/10.1007/978-3-030-21562-0_6
3. Siemens, G., Gašević, D.: Special issue on learning and knowledge analytics. Educ. Technol. Soc. **15**(3), 1–163 (2012)
4. Kravčík, M., Ullrich, C., Igel, C.: The potential of the internet of things for supporting learning and training in the digital age. In: Zlatkin-Troitschanskaia, O., et al. (eds.) Positive Learning in the Age of Information, pp. 399–412. Springer, Wiesbaden (2018). https://doi.org/10.1007/978-3-658-19567-0_24
5. Arnold, K.E., Pistilli, M.D.: Course signals at Purdue: using learning analytics to increase student success. In: Proceedings of the 2nd International Conference on Learning Analytics and Knowledge, pp. 267–270. ACM (2012)
6. Godwin-Jones, R.: Scaling up and zooming in: big data and personalization in language learning. Lang. Learn. Technol. **21**(1), 4–15 (2017)
7. Kalz, M.: Lifelong learning and its support with new technologies. In: Smelser and Baltes (eds.) International Encyclopedia of the Social and Behavioral Sciences, pp. 93–99. Oxford, Pergamon (2014)
8. Gabarre, S., Gabarre, C., Din, R.: Personalizing learning: a critical review of language learning with mobile phones and social networking sites. J. Adv. Res. Dyn. Control Syst. **10**(2), 1782–1786 (2018)
9. Wong, B.T.M., Li, K.C.: A review of learning analytics intervention in higher education (2011–2018). J. Comput. Educ. **7**(1), 7–28 (2020)
10. Santos, O.C., Kravčík, M., Boticario, J.G.: Preface to special issue on user modelling to support personalization in enhanced educational settings. Int. J. Artif. Intell. Educ. **26**(3), 809–820 (2016)
11. Chatti, M.A., Dyckhoff, A.L., Schroeder, U., Thüs, H.: A reference model for learning analytics. Int. J. Technol. Enhanced Learn. **4**(5–6), 318–331 (2013)

12. Yau, J.Y.K., Hristova, Z.: Evaluation of an extendable context-aware "Learning Java" app with personalized user profiling. Technol. Knowl. Learn. **23**, 315–330 (2018)
13. Mejia, C., Florian, B., Vatrapu, R., Bull, S., Gomez, S., Fabregat, R.: A novel web-based approach for visualization and inspection of reading difficulties on university students. IEEE Trans. Learn. Technol. **10**(1), 53–67 (2016)
14. Ma, N., Xin, S., Du, J.Y.: A peer coaching-based professional development approach to improving the learning participation and learning design skills of in-service teachers. J. Educ. Technol. Soc. **21**(2), 291–304 (2018)
15. Lan, A.S., Waters, A.E., Studer, C., Baraniuk, R.G.: Sparse factor analysis for learning and content analytics. J. Mach. Learn. Res. **15**(1), 1959–2008 (2014)
16. Xing, W., Du, D.: Dropout prediction in MOOCs: using deep learning for personalized intervention. J. Educ. Comput. Res. **57**(3), 547–570 (2019)
17. van der Merwe, A., du Toit, T., Kruger, H.: A prescriptive specialized learning management system for academic feedback towards improved learning. J. Comput. Sci. **14**(10), 1329–1340 (2018)
18. Shivanagowda, G.M., Goudar, R.H., Kulkarni, U.P.: CRETAL: a personalized learning environment in conventional setup. In: Proceedings of the 10th Annual ACM India Compute Conference, pp. 143–148. ACM (2017)
19. Berge, Z.L.: If you think socialisation in mLearning is difficult, try personalisation. Int. J. Mob. Learn. Organ. **5**(3/4), 231–238 (2011)
20. Scott, E., Soria, A., Campo, M.: Adaptive 3D virtual learning environments – a review of the literature. IEEE Trans. Learn. Technol. **10**(3), 262–276 (2017)
21. Li, K.C., Wong, B.T.M., Ye, C.J.: Implementing learning analytics in higher education: the case of Asia. Int. J. Serv. Stan. **12**(3/4), 293–308 (2018)
22. Wong, B.T.M.: Learning analytics in higher education: an analysis of case studies. Asian Assoc. Open Univ. J. **12**(1), 21–40 (2017)
23. Tabaa, Y., Medouri, A.: LASyM: a learning analytics system for MOOCs. Int. J. Adv. Comput. Sci. Appl. **4**(5), 113–119 (2013)
24. Clow, D.: MOOCs and the funnel of participation. In: Proceedings of the Third International Conference on Learning Analytics and Knowledge, pp. 185–189. ACM (2013)
25. Chou, C.Y., et al.: Open student models of core competencies at the curriculum level: using learning analytics for student reflection. IEEE Trans. Emerg. Top. Comput. **5**(1), 32–44 (2015)
26. Liu, D.Y.-T., Bartimote-Aufflick, K., Pardo, A., Bridgeman, A.J.: Data-driven personalization of student learning support in higher education. In: Peña-Ayala, A. (ed.) Learning Analytics: Fundaments, Applications, and Trends. SSDC, vol. 94, pp. 143–169. Springer, Cham (2017). https://doi.org/10.1007/978-3-319-52977-6_5
27. Hellas, A., et al.: Predicting academic performance: a systematic literature review. In: Proceedings Companion of the 23rd Annual ACM Conference on Innovation and Technology in Computer Science Education, pp. 175–199. ACM (2018)
28. Papamitsiou, Z., Karapistoli, E., Economides, A.A.: Applying classification techniques on temporal trace data for shaping student behavior models. In: Proceedings of the Sixth International Conference on Learning Analytics & Knowledge, pp. 299–303. ACM (2016)
29. Callies, S., Gravel, M., Beaudry, E., Basque, J.: Logs analysis of adapted pedagogical scenarios generated by a simulation serious game architecture. Int. J. Game-Based Learn. **7**(2), 1–19 (2017)
30. Khalil, M., Ebner, M.: Learning analytics: principles and constraints. In: Proceedings of World Conference on Educational Multimedia, Hypermedia and Telecommunications 2015, Montréal, Canada, pp. 1326–1336 (2015)

Online Gamified Learning Platforms (OGLPs) for Participatory Learning

Kenneth Shiu-Pong Ng[1], Ivan Ka-Wai Lai[1](✉), and Kwan-Keung Ng[2]

[1] Faculty of International Tourism and Management, City University of Macau, Macao, China
{kennethng,ivanlai}@cityu.mo

[2] International Hybrid Learning Society, Hong Kong, China
steven.ng@mail.com

Abstract. Nowadays, students, especially whose majors are practical subjects such as tourism and hospitality in tertiary education, are not interested in ways of learning knowledge through classroom learning. Online Gamified Learning Platforms (OGLPs) are helpful for tertiary education and adult learning, especially for courses involves practical skills. This research aims to identify factors that have significant impacts on tourism and hospitality students to choose OGLPs as their learning tool. This research is based on the Unified Theory of Acceptance and Use of Technology (UTAUT) model. According to the conditions of OGLPs, a new variable 'perceived playfulness' is added and also combined with other theory with variables 'knowledge improvement', 'engagement', and 'immersion'. 272 valid data were collected through questionnaires survey. Data analysis was performed by adopting SmartPLS. The results of the research implied that knowledge improvement, engagement, and immersion influence expectancy of performance and effort. The study has verified the applicability of UTAUT with concepts of fun and learning on studying the tools for gamified learning and participatory learning approaches. It also offers some recommendations for developers of OGLPs to optimize the design of OGLPs as well as a new model for studying the gamified learning and participatory learning approaches.

Keywords: UTAUT · Gamification · Online gamified platform · Perceived playfulness · Knowledge improvement · Engagement · Immersion

1 Introduction

The rapid development and growth of technologies have become popular issues and affect our daily lives. The use of technology benefits a lot of areas for example in education; and varies of mobile apps and computerized platforms are commonly available for educational purposes these days thanks to high-speed internet access. Thence, some educators are probing methods to motivate students using different kinds of mobile technologies with internet access for replenishing traditional classroom learning. Especially in some education fields with practical knowledge in tourism and hospitality education are valuable of bridging the divide between academic knowledge and practical skills as it includes practical knowledge among all education disciplines. However, it's been tough

S. K. S. Cheung et al. (Eds.): ICBL 2020, LNCS 12218, pp. 49–60, 2020.
https://doi.org/10.1007/978-3-030-51968-1_5

to stimulate students' interest as well as motivate them in tourism and hospitality education. Traditional learning approaches are supposed to lack motivation and effectiveness for learning. Though educators devote themselves to enhance the learning approaches, it's known that schools still have troubles increasing student's learning motivation and engagement [1]. Maier and Thomas [2] suggested that online learning platforms bring higher efficiency to most students comparing to traditional classroom design. Filippou, Cheong, and Cheong [3] also recommended gamified learning methods for establishing online learning platforms. They mentioned that gamified learning does better in balance learning and fun than games itself or as entertainment. This kind of online learning platforms is referred to as Online Gamified Learning Platforms (OGLPs), and it is a new concept for education which involves practical learning. To improve OGLPs for related education discipline, the games designed should include more business learning and practical knowledge in real-life. Therefore, it's necessary to identify the factors to implement implementing OGLPs education successfully. Since this study aims to find out the factors those conduce students to accept online gamified learning activities, this study applies UTAUT model which has four variables including performance expectancy, effort expectancy, social influence, and facilitating conditions. It is more suitable to test the acceptance of technology and examining the factors influencing students' behavioural intention (BI) toward using OGLPs. In this research, perceived playfulness will be added as another variable and it represents whether students enjoy the game-like learning activities. Other antecedent variables (knowledge improvement, engagement, and immersion) will also be tested. This study also provides solid recommendations for educators to deliver satisfied game-like learning experiences to students successfully. It offers a new model for understanding the gamified learning for practical knowledge.

2 Literature Review

2.1 Gamification and Education

Kapp, 2012 defined gamification is using game-based mechanics, aesthetics and game thinking to engage people, motivate action, promote learning, and solve problems. Gamification refers to service design aimed at providing game-like experiences to users, commonly with the end-goal of affecting user behaviour [4]. The game has become a common language to bring people together in different aspects with different kinds of game design [5]. A lot of game techniques and elements like points, insignias, leader boards, rewards, rankings, quests, challenges, and virtual loops, were developed by the concept and application of gamification. Dominguez et al. [6] mentioned the positive side of gamification is to facilitate in the process of the selected situation into a gamified experience, by combining the game factors, and letting participation become more interesting and more playfulness. Gamification has become more and more important in business and marketing areas, and has attracted the attention of academics, educators, and practitioners recently from many different areas and also extended into the area of in learning [7].

Gamification education is not a new concept; however, it has been more prominent when combining with technology. Seaborn and Fels suggested that education, the term "gamification" refers to digital game-based learning (DGBL) and serious games in general [7]. In addition, "Gamification" refers to use games as a channel to engage and motivate people to learn and practice how to solve problems in the real world [8]. Maier and Thomas suggested that online learning platforms involved more efficient to learn in practical knowledge for most students over traditional classroom settings [2]. Recently more and more learning platforms, especially online platforms, used gamification as one of the methods to motivate participants' interest and also learn practical skills more easily, even participants with different backgrounds. For example, students are able to utilise the platform of the vocational and professional education and training in Hong Kong (VPET City) to execute flexible learning as well as competency-based and task-oriented instructional strategies [9]. It motivates students to learn practical skills through online gamified methods, for example, Front office operations. In this research, a similar platform is proposed with more gamified elements to raise the participants' interest and learn practical skills in kitchen production. Also, another example is a brand new language learning mobile app DROP launched in 2018. It is a game-based language learning app and became one of the most popular language-learning apps by having more than 10 million downloads all over the world because of their game-based, interesting, and motivated learning approach [10]. Figure 1 shows an example of OGLPs.

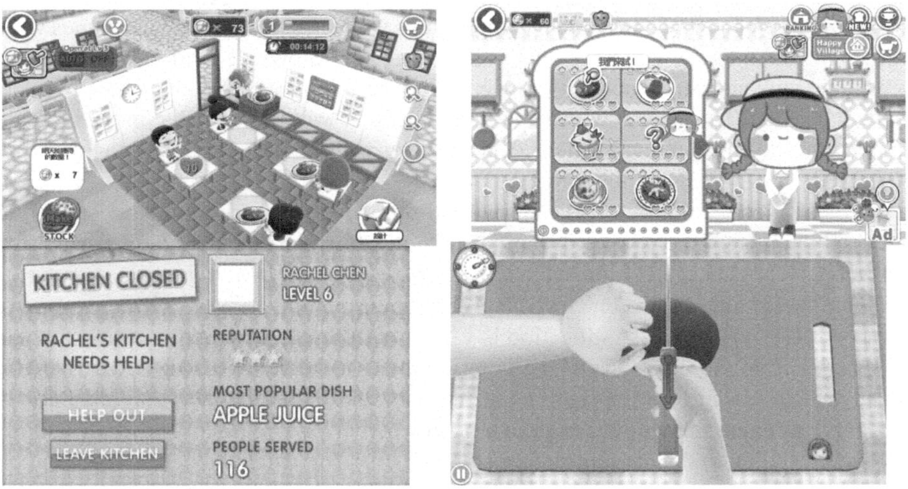

Fig. 1. An example of OGLPs

2.2 The Unified Theory of Acceptance and Use of Technology (UTAUT)

UTAUT was introduced to explain how people adapt to new technology and their further behaviours [11]. In the original UTAUT model, four key factors, including Performance Expectancy (PE), Effort Expectancy (EE), Social Influence (SI), and Facilitating Conditions (FC) were identified and widely used in recent studies. PE refers to the expectancy of people who uses the new system can increase their performance; EE refers to the expectancy of people how much efforts they need to put to use the new system; SI refers to how importance which people use the new technology or not in the social community; FC refers to how well technology organizations and infrastructure support their users when they use the new technology [11]. Using UTAUT to test new technology has been used in online platform already. UTAUT model has been used to test the adoption of mobile tour guide [12] and also the to the acceptance of mobile banking [13]. However, when considering the situation of this research like the interaction and game elements of this new technology, this study proposed to add new factors to modify the original UTAUT model.

In recent studies, additional factors were added to enrich the understandings of UTAUT. For example, Webster & Martocchio defined "Perceived Playful-ness" (PP) as an individual's tendency to interact spontaneously, inventively and imaginatively with computer [14]. In the previous research, researchers tested the relationship between perceived playfulness and usage behaviour on mobile apps [15]. Thus, this study adds PP to the UTAUT to understand whether it significantly impact the BI. In addition, the research in playfulness has been related as a result of fun and cognitive immersion [16]. The results of Filippou, Cheong, & Cheong's study showed that there are relationships among knowledge, engagement, usefulness and immersion [3]. Immersion refers to the degree of which people involved in the game's study and the game's strategies; and engagement refers to the engagement people gains when they are playing the games with enjoyment and interact with the game mechanism [17]. Knowledge improvement refers to whether students perceive their knowledge has been improved or not by adapting the gasified tool [3]. This research tests the relationship between knowledge improvement, immersion, and engagement as antecedent variables with performance expectancy, effort expectancy, and perceived playfulness.

In recent years, a lot of efforts are put on optimising the learning methods by educators while most of them have difficulties in motivating and engaging their students in the schools [1]. User motivation, engagement and enjoyment in non-gaming, computer-mediated environments are enhanced by developing gamification according to previous work. The concept of gamification is valued in different areas in education though the term of it might vary. One of the contributions on the study is to use the UTAUT model which related to acceptance of technology and other elements such as knowledge improvement, immersion, engagement, and perceived playfulness to create a more systematic and up to date approach to test the relationship and behavioural intention of participants for gamification in the education field by using online platforms.

3 Research Hypothesis

This research developed a model to measure students' preference on adapting gamified methods to learn, plus identify factors which affect their perception of using those methods. At a high-level, two different concepts: fun and learning are combined in the model combines. The constructs of Perceived playfulness, Immersion, and Engagement are included in the area of fun while the construct Knowledge improvement is included in the area of learning. The followings explore these constructs further and their connections among each other, which consists of the construction of the conceptual model eventually.

As mentioned previously, this study aims to use the UTAUT model to explain user behavioural intentions towards adopting new technology. As one of the key factors on university students' Behavioural intention (BI) to apply OGLPTs for studying practical knowledge, Perceived playfulness conduce significant impact like the other four constructs (PE, EE, SI, and FC). Knowledge Improvement, Engagement, and Immersion are proposed to be the antecedent factors which affect the students' attitude towards PE, EE, and PP while EE is suggested to be the antecedent factor of PE and PP. Figure 2 shows the research model. Sixteen research hypotheses are listed below:

H1 Performance expectancy of online gamified learning platforms has a positive effect on Behavioural intention.
H2 Effort expectancy of online gamified learning platforms has a positive effect on Behavioural intention.
H3 Social influence of online gamified learning platforms has a positive effect on Behavioural intention.
H4 Facilitating conditions of online gamified learning platforms have a positive effect on Behavioural intention.
H5 Perceived playfulness of online gamified learning platforms has a positive effect on Behavioural intention.
H6-1 Knowledge improvement of online gamified learning platforms has a positive effect on Performance expectancy.
H6-2 Knowledge improvement of online gamified learning platforms has a positive effect on Effort expectancy.
H6-3 Knowledge improvement of online gamified learning platforms has a positive effect on perceived playfulness.
H7-1 Engagement of online gamified learning platforms has a positive effect on Performance expectancy.
H7-2 Engagement of online gamified learning platforms education has a positive effect on Effort expectancy.
H7-3 Engagement of online gamified learning platforms has a positive effect on perceived playfulness.
H8-1 Immersion of online gamified learning platforms has a positive effect on Performance expectancy.
H8-2 Immersion of online gamified learning platforms has a positive effect on Effort expectancy.
H8-3 Immersion of online gamified learning platforms has a positive effect on perceived playfulness.
H9-1 Effort expectancy of online gamified learning platforms has a positive effect on performance expectancy.
H9-2 Effort expectancy of online gamified learning platforms has a positive effect on perceived playfulness.

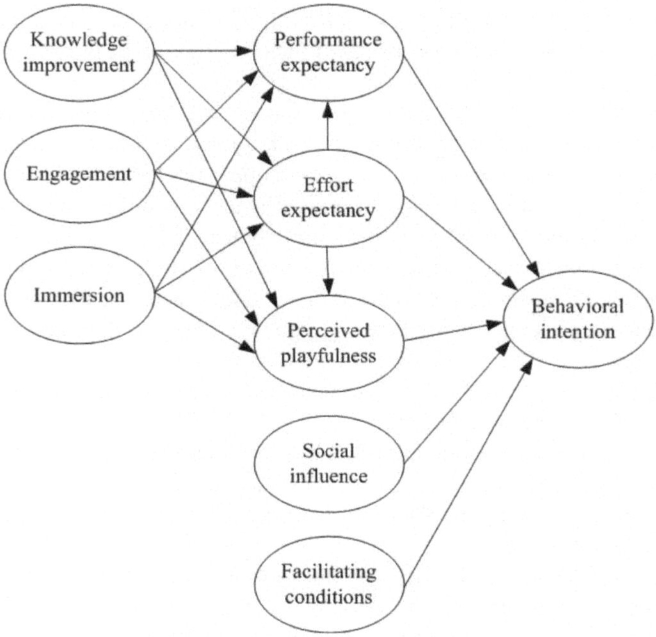

Fig. 2. Research model

4 Methodology

Quantitative methods are research techniques that are used to gather quantitative data or information dealing with numbers and anything that is measurable [18]. This study utilised the UTAUT model as the base theoretical model. This model was evaluated using a series of quantitative data analysis steps that best explain the predominant phenomena of the collected data. This study also aimed to test a set of hypotheses to understand and study the effects among the different constructs. Therefore, a quantitative approach was an appropriate method for this research.

4.1 Survey Design

This study used a questionnaire survey. The measurable items of the questionnaire borrowed from previous studies. The main survey and data analysis were a vital part of the whole study. The first part of the survey consists of 44 questions of the constructs. The second part of the survey consisted of 3 demographic questions to the respondents. The measurable items were the base of the survey and it consists of items from the UTAUT model with Perceived playfulness, Immersion, and Engagement and Knowledge added.

4.2 Date Collection

A pilot test was conducted with twenty questionnaires; the questionnaire has been revised based on the comments from respondents for official research. The researchers delivered the questionnaires to tourism students face to face in Macao University of Science and Technology and the City University of Macao, both Tourism related faculty. There were 300 questionnaires distributed via university students mentioned above in October 2019. 272 data were valid and analysed via SmartPLS software.

5 Findings

5.1 Overview of Survey

Among the 272 respondents, 60% of them are female students. Majority of the students are university's senior-year students (37%). 34.5% of them are 20 years old, while 4% of them are 22 years old.

A 7-point Likert-type scale was applied for the questionnaires. The mean scores of PE, EE, SC, FC, PP, KN, EG, IM, and BI are ranged from 4.89 to 5.84. Comparing to other 8 contracts, IM got the lowest mean; the mean of IM-4 "I changed my feeling for the meaning of time while playing the game" is 4.89, and IM-3 "I temporarily forget worries about everyday life while playing the game" is 4.92. Table 1 illustrates the mean and standard deviation scores of the nine constructs.

Table 1. Mean and Standard Deviation (S.D.) of measurable items

	PE1	*PE2*	*PE3*	*EE1*	*EE2*	*EE3*
MEAN	5.518	5.445	5.426	5.787	5.842	5.809
S.D.	1.011	1.063	1.023	1.108	1.082	1.138
	SC1	*SC2*	*SC3*	*FC1*	*FC2*	*FC3*
MEAN	5.290	5.199	5.044	5.162	5.243	5.566
S.D.	1.095	1.136	1.169	1.139	1.157	1.217
	PP1	*PP2*	*PP3*	*KN1*	*KN2*	*KN3*
MEAN	5.684	5.691	5.669	5.566	5.327	5.551
S.D.	1.186	1.118	1.135	1.083	1.188	1.063
	KN4	*KN5*	*EG1*	*EG2*	*EG3*	*EG4*
MEAN	5.452	5.574	5.57	5.46	5.419	5.235
S.D.	1.149	1.096	1.226	1.153	1.173	1.244
	EG5	*EG6*	*IM1*	*IM2*	*IM3*	*IM4*
MEAN	5.349	5.096	5.136	4.926	4.915	4.893
S.D.	1.286	1.283	1.216	1.270	1.139	1.234
	IM5	*IM6*	*BI1*	*BI2*	*BI3*	
MEAN	5.136	5.004	5.812	5.721	5.768	
S.D.	1.194	1.220	1.017	1.062	1.122	

5.2 Reliability and Validity

As shown in Table 2, reliability is tested by Cronbach Alpha and Composite Reliability, and the convergent validity is evaluated using Average Variance Extracted (AVE).

Table 2. Average Variance Extracted (AVE), Composite Reliability, and Cronbach's Alpha

	AVE	Composite Reliability	Cronbach's Alpha
PE	0.724	0.887	0.809
EE	0.767	0.908	0.849
SC	0.779	0.872	0.695
FC	0.634	0.838	0.711
PP	0.807	0.926	0.880
KN	0.587	0.876	0.824
EG	0.551	0.880	0.838
IM	0.568	0.887	0.847
BI	0.832	0.937	0.899

Furthermore, Table 3 shows the latent variable correlations; 7 out of 9 constructs are having correlation values lower than 0.85 which indicate reasonable and acceptable correlations among them.

Table 3. Latent variable correlations analysis

	BI	EE	EG	FC	IM	KN	PE	PP	SC
BI	*0.912*								
EE	0.439	*0.876*							
EG	0.554	0.483	*0.743*						
FC	0.539	0.388	0.499	*0.796*					
IM	0.480	0.292	0.660	0.496	*0.753*				
KN	0.625	0.585	0.721	0.590	0.539	*0.766*			
PE	0.561	0.499	0.479	0.587	0.456	0.583	*0.851*		
PP	0.626	0.505	0.697	0.555	0.584	0.687	0.494	*0.898*	
SC	0.517	0.388	0.468	0.517	0.413	0.559	0.644	0.447	*0.834*

Remark: AVE - average variance extracted, *Italic* font - square-root of AVE

5.3 The Unified Theory of Acceptance and Use of Technology (UTAUT)

To assess the significance of the path coefficients among these nine constructs, the researchers carried out a bootstrapping analysis in SmartPLS with 272 responses to 5000 samples. According to the SmartPLS results, the p-values of PE, SC, FC, PP and KN are less than 0.05. As a result, H1, H3, H4, H5, H6-1, H6-2, H6-3, are supported. For EG, only H7-2 and H7-3 are supported. While for IM, only H8-1 and H8-3 are supported. H7-1 from EG and H8-2 from IM are neglected because its p-value is over 0.05. For EE, H9-1 and H9-2 are supported but it is neglected on BI due to its p-value is over 0.05. The results of the Partial Least Squares Structural Equation Modeling (SmartPLS) is shown in Table 4 and Fig. 3.

Table 4. Results of SmartPLS analysis

	Beta value	p-value	
H1 Performance expectancy → Behavioural intention	0.179	0.001	Accepted
H2 Effort expectancy → Behavioural intention	0.053	0.314	Rejected
H3 Social influence → Behavioural intention	0.146	0.005	Accepted
H4 Facilitating conditions → Behavioural intention	0.131	0.020	Accepted
H5 Perceived playfulness → Behavioural intention	0.373	0.000	Accepted
H6-1 Knowledge improvement → Performance expectancy	0.343	0.000	Accepted
H6-2 Knowledge improvement → Effort expectancy	0.507	0.000	Accepted
H6-3 Knowledge improvement → Perceived playfulness	0.292	0.000	Accepted
H7-1 Engagement → Performance expectancy	−0.037	0.631	Rejected
H7-2 Engagement → Effort expectancy	0.186	0.029	Accepted
H7-3 Engagement → Perceived playfulness	0.292	0.000	Accepted
H8-1 Immersion → Performance expectancy	0.222	0.000	Accepted
H8-2 Immersion → Effort expectancy	−0.104	0.153	Rejected
H8-3 Immersion → Perceived playfulness	0.194	0.009	Accepted
H9-1 Effort expectancy → Performance expectancy	0.252	0.000	Accepted
H9-2 Effort expectancy → Perceived playfulness	0.137	0.014	Accepted

To sum up, based on the reports and theories above, Perceived Expectancy (PE), Social Influence (SC), Facilitating Conditions (FC), and Perceived playfulness (PP) affect the Behavioural Intention (BI) toward using OGLPs of university students significantly as all hypotheses were supported. Knowledge improvement (KN) showed a most significant influence in PE, EE and PP while some of the hypotheses of Effort Expectancy (EE), Engagement (EG), and Immersion (IM) were not supported.

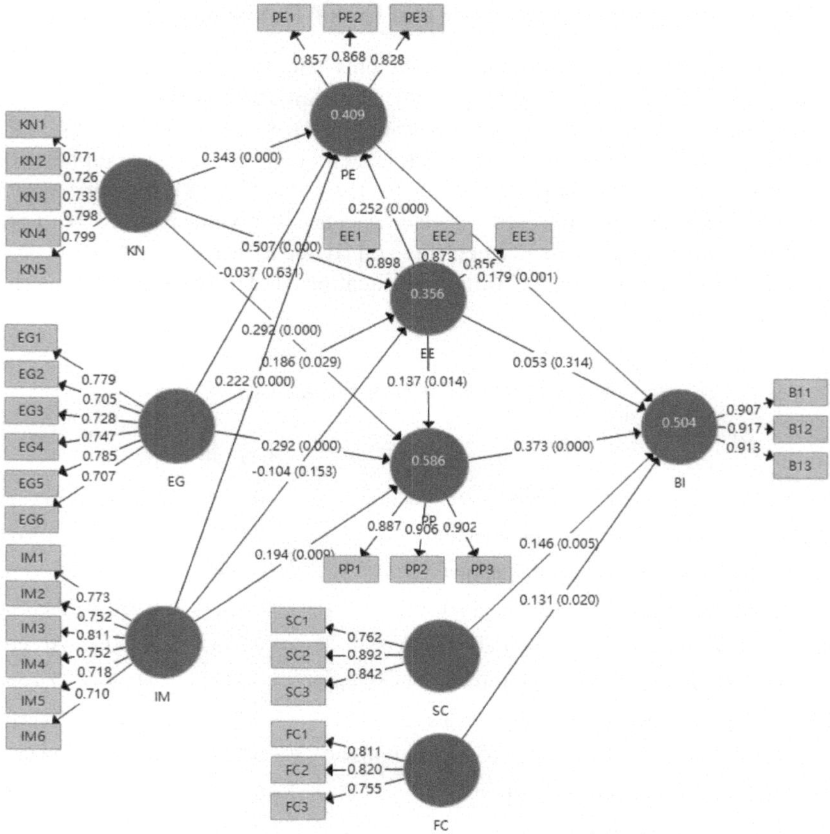

Fig. 3. Results of PLS-SEM analysis

6 Discussion and Conclusion

Nowadays, technology is becoming an important tool in education, particularly in higher education and vocational training that requires much more knowledge out of the textbooks. As visual reflection is a common language around the world, adopting mobiles apps is a way for people of all ages and nationalities to learn practical knowledge more efficiently, especially in industries which relate to service, such as hospitality service training, property management, and so on. It is not only the most popular way in daily communication but also a trend for people to pursue knowledge and skills more manageable and with higher motivation. In addition, online platforms have an advantage of not limited yourselves in a physical environment with nonstop learning when facing special occasion like 2019 Novel coronavirus SARI which affects daily life so much.

For the implications of this research, it uses the UTAUT model by SmartPLS software to analyse university students' BI toward applying OGLPs. It identifies factors which have significant impacts on the BI of university students toward adopting OGLPs; In addition, the results of the research may facilitate industries of service to find out crucial factors to improve staff's flexibility, efficiency, as well service quality by using mobile apps.

As mobile phone apps have been commonly used for many years already, EE is not essential when people choose apps or platforms like OGLPs according to the research results. Also, EG is not essential on PE because when people engaged in one issue, the performance will not be an important consideration as it has a bonding already to the apps.

Last but not least, Immersion is not essential for EE, because when people addicted to one app, the level of effort will not be treated as an important consideration as they will keep using it.

For the limitations of research, as the size of Macao is small, these results might be inappropriate to make generalised conclusions on other countries based on current research settings, and the education phenomenon was different from other areas in the world. Future studies were recommended to perform to test the research model in other regions and countries. In addition, this research added four new factors 'Immersion', 'Knowledge Improvement', 'Engagement' which act as antecedent factors and 'Perceived Playfulness' had positive influences on acceptance of technology towards adopting an ODTSA for the tourists to arrange their travel. Future studies might be considered adding other factors to investigate the relationship between the factors and the behaviour intention toward using ODTSA.

References

1. Lee, J., Hammer, J.: Gamification in education: what, how, why bother? Acad. Exch. Q. **15**(2), 146 (2011)
2. Maier, T.A., Thomas, N.J.: Hospitality leadership course design and delivery: a blended-experiential learning model. J. Hosp. Tourism Educ. **25**(1), 11–21 (2013)
3. Filippou, J., Cheong, C., Cheong, F.: A model to investigate preference for use of gamification in a learning activity. Australas. J. Inf. Syst. **22** (2018)
4. Huotari, K., Hamari, J.: Defining gamification – a service marketing perspective. In: Proceedings of the 16th International Academic MindTrek Conference, Tampere, Finland, 3–5 October (2012)
5. Crawford, C.: The Art of Computer Game Design. Osborne-McGraw-Hill, Berkeley (1984)
6. Domínguez, A., Saenz-De-Navarrete, J., De-Marcos, L., Fernández-Sanz, L., Pagés, C., Martínez-Herráiz, J.: Gamifying learning experiences: practical implications and outcomes. Comput. Educ. **63**, 380–392 (2013)
7. Seaborn, K., Fels, D.I.: Gamification in theory and action: a survey. Int. J. Hum Comput Stud. **74**, 14–31 (2015)
8. Kapp, K.M.: The Gamification of Learning and Instruction: Game-Based Methods and Strategies for Training and Education. Pfeiffer, San Francisco (2012)
9. VPETCITY Programs: VPETCITY Programs (2018). https://sharepoint-auth.vtc.edu.hk/adfs/ls/?wa=wsignin1.0&wfresh=0&wtrealm=urn:sharepoint:2016&wctx=https://sharepoint.vtc.edu.hk/vpetcity?returnUrl=https://sharepoint.vtc.edu.hk/vpetcity/Pages/QESS_TLPs.aspx
10. DROP Language: DROP Language Mobile Apps (2018). https://languagedrops.com/about/
11. Venkatesh, V., Morris, M.G., Davis, G.B., Davis, F.D.: User acceptance of information technology: toward a unified view. MIS Q. **27**(3), 425–478 (2003)

12. Lai, I.K.W.: Traveler acceptance of an app-based mobile tour guide. J. Hosp. Tourism Res. **39**(3), 401–432 (2013)
13. Bhatiasevi, V.: An extended UTAUT model to explain the adoption of mobile banking. Inf. Dev. **32**(4), 799–814 (2016)
14. Webster, J., Martocchio, J.J.: Microcomputer playfulness: development of a measure with workplace implications. MIS Q. **16**(2), 201 (1992)
15. Hur, H.J., Lee, H.K., Choo, H.J.: Understanding usage intention in innovative mobile app service: comparison between millennial and mature consumers. Comput. Hum. Behav. **73**, 353–361 (2017)
16. Ahn, T., Ryu, S., Han, I.: The impact of Web quality and playfulness on user acceptance of online retailing. Inf. Manag. **44**(3), 263–275 (2007)
17. McMahan, A.: Immersion, engagement and presence: a method for analyzing 3-D video games. In: Wolf, M.J.P., Perron, B. (eds.) The Video Game Theory Reader, pp. 67–86. Routledge, London (2003)
18. Easterby-Smith, M., Thorpe, R., Lowe, A.: Management Research, 2nd edn. Sage Publications, Thousand Oaks (2002)

A Sequential Analysis on the Online Learning Behaviors of Chinese Adult Learners: Take the KGC Learning Platform as an Example

Junjie Shang(✉), Rui Xiao, and Yuanyuan Zhang

Lab of Learning Sciences, Graduate School of Education, Peking University, Beijing 100871, China
jjshang@pku.edu.cn

Abstract. The study collected the learning behaviors of 179 adult learners, including video learning, page document learning, assignment submission, and so on. In order to find out the characteristics of online learning behavior of adult learners and provide enlightenment for the improvement of online courses and learning platform design, this paper adopts Lag Sequential Analysis to explore the sequence of learners' behavior transformation. By comparing the behavioral transformation sequence of adult learners with different efficiency, this paper explores the factors influencing learning efficiency. The study found 92 kinds of significant behavioral transformation sequences, reflecting the characteristics of adult learners, such as task-oriented, active exploration and strong self-regulation ability. It is also found that highly efficient learners prefer selective and fast playing pattern, while low efficient learners prefer non-differentiated fast repetition of playing pattern. From this we can get the enlightenment that is helpful to the design of learning platform.

Keywords: Learning analysis · Learning behavior sequence · LSA · The learning efficiency · Learning platform

1 Introduction

With the continuous development of online education, various Internet enterprises have set up platforms to provide learning opportunities for learners of all ages with various learning needs. At present, most researches on online education, whether on the design of online courses or the learning characteristics of online learners, they all focus on open learning platforms such as MOOC (Chen et al. 2017a), Blackboard (Spivey and Mcmillan 2014), LMS (You 2016) or learning management platforms. The current studies of online education, whether it is about the design of the online course, or online learners' learning characteristics, most of them focused on the open learning platforms MOOC or learning management platforms such as Blackboard and LMS. In the learning platforms like MOOCs, although the number of learners is huge, the drop-out rate is high (Yousef et al. 2015) and effective learners are few.

In China, the development of adult online education is in full swing. According to the data of 2019H1 iresearch, higher education and vocational training have always

S. K. S. Cheung et al. (Eds.): ICBL 2020, LNCS 12218, pp. 61–76, 2020.
https://doi.org/10.1007/978-3-030-51968-1_6

been the market subject of online education in China, accounting for about 80% of the total online education market[1]. In China, adult online education, such as vocational training and skill learning, all rely on enterprises' online learning platforms, while the research on online education pays less attention to such learning platforms. Compared with MOOCs and other open learning platforms, there are many unique features of learning in enterprise online learning platforms. For example, due to the profitability of enterprise online learning platforms, there are many unique designs to ensure the learning effect of learners. For example, the KGC learning platform is an enterprise online learning platform, which mainly aims at the skill learning of adults. This platform focuses on the cultivation of practical ability, and does not take test scores as the evaluation standard for learning effect. Instead, it advocates that learners save as much time as possible on the premise of learning skills.

In addition, compared with the main learners of MOOC platform in school, the working adults have strong self-control and clear learning goals. They have a stronger demand for education and training in aspects such as improving their degree, and seeking jobs. These two learning groups have great differences in learning motivation, goal achievement and so on. This study focuses on the online learning platforms in enterprises to explore the different learning characteristics of learners and the characteristics of their behavioral transformation patterns.

2 Literature Review

Along with the learning behavior of learners in the learning platform is recorded, the research of learners' behavior, based on objective data, is becoming possible. In the existing studies on learner behavior characteristics, researchers pay more attention to the relationship between learning engagement, learning behavior pattern and learning effect (Zhao et al. 2019; Le et al. 2019). The key point of these studies lies in the representation of learning engagement, learning behavior patterns and learning effects, and the methods used to analyze their relationship.

2.1 Learning Engagement Behavior

Limited by the data collected by the learning platform, most researchers use some learning behavior as a characteristic variable to represent learners' learning engagement or explore learning behavior patterns, and most of the characteristic variables used are calculated from the perspectives of time and frequency. For example, Lust et al. (2013) used the time spent by students in LMS on network lectures, network link, tests and other contents as variables representing learning behaviors. Hung and Zhang (2008) used the frequency of accessing course materials and the number of reading messages to indicate the level of learners' efforts. In addition, other studies have used the number of times that learners used the login platform (Le et al. 2019; Healy et al. 2005), the number and time of accessing resources (Morris et al. 2005), the total number of times that learners

[1] I Research page, https://www.iresearch.com.cn/Detail/report?id=3452&isfree=0, last accessed 2020/2/19.

visited the course (Asarta and Schmidt 2013) and so on, to reflect learners' learning engagement behaviors. These single behaviors are relatively coarse-grained data, which can hardly reflect learners' cognitive engagement level in detail. These single behaviors reflect learners' learning engagement and learning behavior characteristics rather than learning behavior patterns that should show more about learners' learning behavior path. Previous studies have explored learners' learning path by analyzing learners' behavioral transformation sequence and found learners' backtracking behavior (Hu et al. 2019). In addition, some scholars believe that, compared with the single learning behaviors of learners, the sequence of learning behaviors in the learning process can better reflect the intention and cognitive process of learners' learning behavior trajectory (Yang et al. 2016). Therefore, it can be considered that the behavior transformation sequence can better reflect the learner's learning behavior pattern.

2.2 Behavior Transformation Sequence and LSA (Lag Sequential Analysis)

LSA is used in most studies related to sequences of learning behaviors. This method was proposed by Sackett (1978) to test whether the probability of one behavior occurring after another is statistically significant. In the field of education, LSA takes transitional relationships into consideration to identify temporal differences in learning behavior (Chen et al. 2017b). At present, there are mainly the following types of studies related to learning behavior sequence. The first one is the combination of clustering analysis to define learners with different learning patterns and predict their academic performance by clustering the behavior sequence. For example, Li et al. (2017) explored the online learning behavior sequence and participation pattern of Open University students on Moodle platform through lag sequence analysis. According to the behavior sequence, different online participation patterns of learners are defined, such as low input, shallow level input, performance input, step by step, and random participation. Jiang et al. (2018). used lag sequence analysis to analyze the learning process data on the DEEDS platform, and predicted the learning effect. The second, combined with text analysis, sequence analysis is carried out for the content posted by learners in the forum. For example, Jeong and Allan (2003) conducted sequence analysis of learners' speech content based on text analysis. Similarly, Hou et al. (2009) combined content analysis and sequence analysis to explore learners' learning behavior patterns in the forum. The third is to combine the theoretical framework to explore learners' behavioral transition patterns during knowledge construction (Lan et al. 2012; Lin et al. 2013; Yang et al. 2015). For example, lag sequence analysis is used to analyze the learning patterns of different learners or learners at different stages. Yang et al. (2015) analyzed students' knowledge construction behavior at different activity stages in the collaborative translation process by using lag sequence. Finally, there is a comparative analysis of the differences in learning behavior sequence patterns of learners with high-low achievements (Lai and Hwang 2015). According to the above research, LSA method is an extensive analysis method in the sequence analysis of learning behavior. This study intends to use LSA to explore the learning behavior sequence of Chinese adult learners and analyze the differences of learning behavior sequence of Chinese adult learners with high and low achievement. However, in the above studies, course scores mostly express learners' achievements, which is not suitable for adult learners on the course of KGC learning platform. It is necessary to combine the characteristics of learners, curriculum and learning platform to determine the form of learning effect.

2.3 The Learning Effect of Adult Learners in KGC Learning Platform

Most studies have used test scores (Lin et al. 2013), or self-report through questionnaires (Yang 2016) to reflect learning effect. The score can only reflect the learning effect from the learning result dimension, and the learning efficiency in the learning process is difficult to reflect. In adult learning scenarios such as vocational training, learners not only pay attention to their performance and knowledge, but also pay attention to learning efficiency and time cost. This is the biggest difference between the adult vocational training learning scene and the general online learning scene in the aspect of learning effect. For example, in the KGC learning platform, the design of it is guided by "mastering learning theory", believing that all learners can learn and master relevant knowledge. It's just that the amount of time each person spends is different, and learners should move forward in small steps and strictly monitor the outcome of each step. Only by mastering the current knowledge and skills can learners continue to learn. Under this learning platform, the learning effect is not reflected by test scores, but by the time it takes the learner to reach a certain stage. The shorter the time, the stronger the learner's learning ability, and the higher the learning efficiency. Compared with grades, it is more effective to reflect learning effect from time dimension for vocational skill training. Vocational training courses emphasize a results-oriented approach, unlike many courses in MOOCs. For example, in the MOOC platform of Chinese universities, the scores of most courses are the comprehensive weight of test scores and homework scores, which also contains the input of learning behaviors and other processes at ordinary times. In addition, exams have certain uncertainties, which cannot fully reflect the learning effect of learners. In vocational skills training, the purpose of learners is to master relevant knowledge and skills as soon as possible, so in such learning scenarios, it is more effective to use the time spent in mastering relevant knowledge and skills to reflect the learning effect.

To sum up, we can find that LSA for behavior sequence exploration is a relatively mature analysis technology. Though the behavior sequential analysis, different learning behavior participation patterns can be found. However, most of the above studies were conducted on the courses on open learning platforms, such as MOOCs, and most of them used test scores as learning effects to explore the differences in learning effects of learners with different behavior sequences. For vocational skills training courses in enterprises, learners are mostly adults with clear goals and strong self-control, and the focus of learning effect is not only the mastery of knowledge and skills, but also the cost of time. In such a learning scene, what kind of learning behavior sequence will exist in learners and what kind of learning characteristics will be represented. In addition, studies have also shown that different types of online learning resources can affect learners' learning time and frequency (Yousef et al. 2015). Therefore, it can be seen that different types of learning content may also have a certain impact on learners' learning behavior. Therefore, the purpose of this study is to explore the learning behavior characteristics of adult learners in the context of vocational skills learning, and whether the differences in curriculum content have an impact on them. Further, explore what kind of learning behavior sequence do learners with different learning efficiency have, In order to find ways to improve the learning effectiveness and learning efficiency of learners, and to provide Suggestions and guidance for the design of learning platforms and the learning of online learners.

3 Methodology

3.1 Research Questions

The research collected the data generated by 179 learners in two courses in the KGC learning platform: elementary artificial intelligence: basics of Python introduction(Python introduction) and introduction to data analysis(data analysis). This study explores the behavior sequence of online learners based on this learning platform by using LSA. The questions to be answered in this study are as follows:

1) What are the characteristics of learner's behavior sequence under this learning platform? What learning state can it reflect?
2) In different courses, what are the differences between learners' learning behavior sequences?
3) What are the differences between learners with different efficiency in learning behavior sequence?

3.2 Learning Process of Learners on the KGC Learning Platform

In this case, the learning platform provides online learners with video, documents and other learning resources, as well as calendar module, question and answer module, learning dashboard and so on to assist learners in learning. The main interface of the learning platform is shown in the Fig. 1. This learning platform is characterized by its design of learning baffle based on the mastery learning theory. Learners must master the contents of the previous unit before they can move on to the next unit. In this way, learners can learn the content of each section steadily, so as to achieve a better learning effect. Only by successfully completing the assignments in the previous unit can learners begin to learn the next unit. (Figure 2) In each unit, learners learn mainly by viewing documents, videos and other materials. Besides, the platform also provides learners with several simple test questions to recall the key contents. In addition, learners can also arrange and understand their learning process by adding learning calendar, viewing learning progress, learning duration and other information displayed in the learning dashboard.

3.3 Data Cleaning and Analysis

The learner's learning process is independent, and the learning starts and ends at different times. The study collected 1278,145 log data from 179 learners who successfully completed the two courses from October 2018 to October 2019. After deduplication and cleaning up the invalid data, there are 914938 log data left. According to the learning content types and functions, the study classifies learners' learning behaviors into 7 categories and 26 behaviors in total. The classification and coding are shown in Table 1

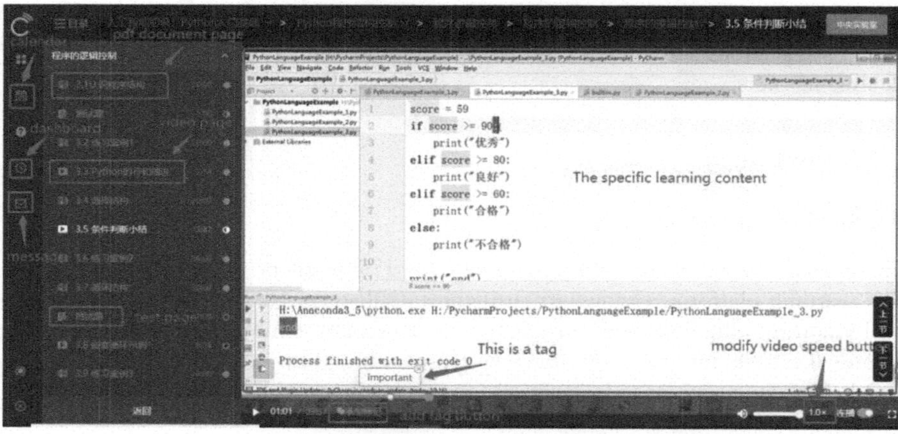

Fig. 1. The main interface of the learning platform

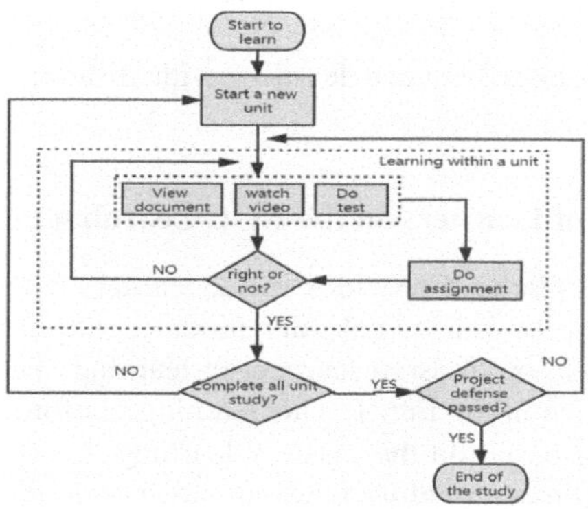

Fig. 2. The course learning process on the KGC learning platform

below. Video is the main learning content of learners. At the same time, according to some summary document pages and test questions provided by the course, learners can conduct a summary review of the content of the video. In each unit, the assignments of the work page are required to be completed by the learner, so that the learner can also know how well he/she has achieved in the unit.

According to the principle of sequence analysis, the transformation from one behavior to another is defined as a sequence of behaviors. The code combination of the two behaviors is used to represent the sequence, and the order of behavior coding in a combination represents the direction of behavior transformation in that sequence. For example, learners enter the document page (ES) first, and then exit the document page (OS), then the behavior sequence is ES → OS. According to the above 26 kinds of behaviors, there are 676 behavioral sequences in theory, but only 443 behavioral sequences are actually produced.

Table 1. Code for 26 learning behaviors

Category	Content type	Learned behavior	Coding
Content learning	Video	Add a tag to the video	AT
		Enter the video learning	EV
		Exit video learning	OV
		Pause video learning	PV
		Continue video learning	CV
		Modify the speed of the video	MS
		Modify the video progress bar to selectively play the content at a certain time	MVP
Summary of learning	Summary document page	Enter the summary document page	ES
		Exit the summary document page	OS
		Download code resource	DR
	Test	Enter the test	ET
		Exit the test	OT
		Submit the test	ST
Effect of learning	The assignments of the work page	Enter the work page	EW
		Do the assignments of the work page	DW
		Submit the work	SW
		Exit the work page	OW
		Apply for reply of the whole course work	AR
		Quit application for reply of the whole course work	QR
		Submit application for reply of the whole course work	SR
Assisted learning	Learning dashboard	View learning progress in the learning dashboard	VP
		View learning duration in the learning dashboard	VT
	Learning calendar	View learning calendar	VC
		Add learning calendar	AC
	Message	View message	VM
		View question and answer module	VQ

4 Result

4.1 Learner Behavioral Sequence Characteristics

According to the LSA method, the GSEQ5.1 software was used to make a frequency table of behavior transformation according 26 learning behaviors, and the standard score conversion was performed to obtain the adjusted residual table (Table 2). When the adjusted residuals value of the behavioral transformation sequence is higher than 1.96, then it was significant at the level of 0.05. It indicates that the occurrence of the behavioral transformation sequence is significant (Bakeman and Quera 1995). The combination of frequency n > 30 was used to screen out the behavioral transformation sequences that reached the significance, and the results showed that only 24 of the 26 behaviors had achieved the significance, and a total of 95 behavioral transformation sequences had achieved the significance. Gephi0.9.2 visualizes these significant behavioral transformation sequences through the Fruchterman Reingold layout, resulting in Fig. 3.

Table 2. The adjusted residual table (Part of the whole table)

	PV	CV	MS	MVP
PV	−151.09	465.1*	−11.03	16.66*
CV	302.95*	−189.35	29.99*	202.8*
MS	47.05*	−14.02	−3.32	33.81*
MVP	180.44*	−16.02	29.33*	−56.63

*P < 0.05

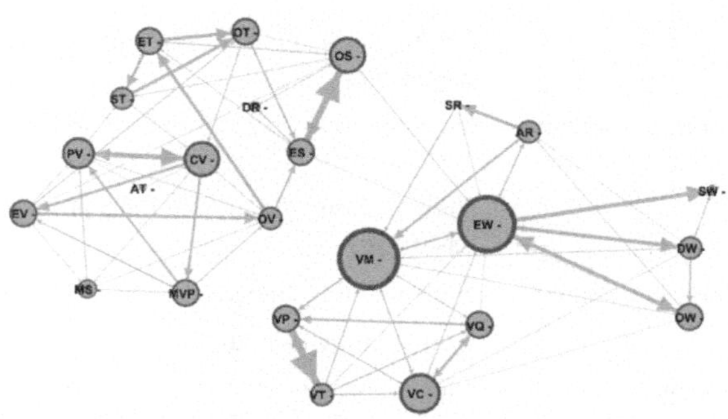

Fig. 3. The sequence diagram of students' overall learning behavior transformation

In Fig. 3, there are 24 nodes, representing 24 learning behaviors, and 95 edges, representing 92 behavioral transformation sequences. The direction of the arrow represents the direction of the behavior transformation, and the thickness of the line represents the probability of the behavior transformation. The size of the node shows the number of degrees of that node. Through the overall sequence diagram of learning behavior transformation of all learners, we can see that viewing message (VM) and entering the work page (EW) are the two largest nodes. It indicates that these two behaviors are the most central behaviors of behavior transformation, and in this platform, learners are driven by homework and good at paying attention to information. According to Fig. 4, it can be seen that there are more wires between the behavior nodes related to Content learning. The behavior nodes related to Summary of learning, Effect of learning and Assisted learning also show similar characteristics, which reflects that learners have more behavioral transformation when learning the same type of content. It may be caused by the setting of the order of learning content on the platform itself. In addition, there are many transformations between Effect of learning and Assisted learning. Moreover, according to Fig. 5, the highlighted nodes connected to the EW or VM nodes are almost "effect of learning" and "assisted learning". it can be found that the transformation between the assisted learning behavior and the work-related behavior is relatively frequent. This indicates that learners' assisted learning behavior is mainly for completing the assignments of the work page, which reflects learners' strong task-oriented learning characteristics under the platform.

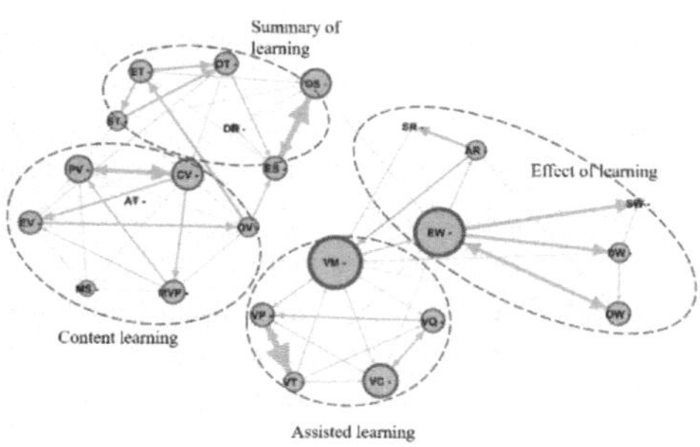

Fig. 4. Sequence diagram of students' behavior transformation to different types of learning content

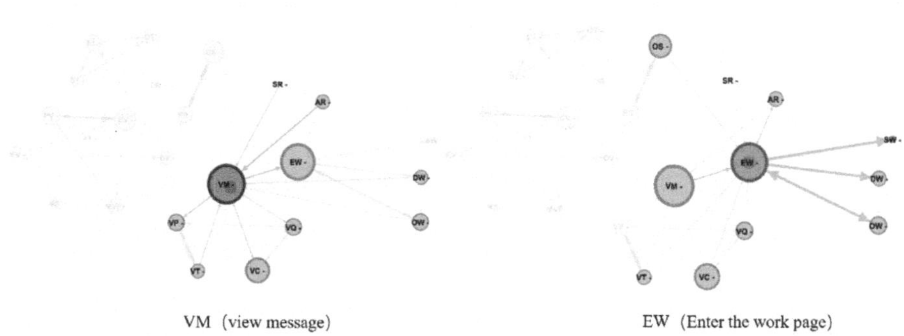

Fig. 5. Behavioral transformation network centered VM and EW respectively

4.2 In Different Courses, the Difference of Learners' Learning Behavior Sequence

The content and instructional goal of the course may influence the sequence of the learner's behavior transition. According to the content and instructional goal of the two courses, it is found that the instructional goal of Python introduction is to let learners learn to write Python code. it requires learners to write more actual code for practice. However, the instructional goal of data analysis is to enable learners to learn the thinking and methods of data analysis. Although the assignments of work page also requires the actual writing of Python code, this course is more inclined to method learning than the course of Python introduction. Therefore, the two courses Python introduction and data analysis are defined as code-drill courses and method learning courses. In order to know the differences of learners' learning behavior sequence in different courses, the study further explored what kind of behavioral transformation sequences these 179 learners had in the two courses.

The same method is used to analyze the behavioral data of learners in these two courses, and Fig. 6 and Fig. 7 are obtained. Through the comparison of the two graphs, it can be found that the behavioral transformation patterns of learners in the two courses are similar in the whole. And the difference is mainly reflected in the transformation between the behaviors related to video learning and assignment completion. Compared with method learning courses, there are more connections between behaviors related to video learning and completing assignment, assisted learning in code-drill course. In combination with the above findings, learners' assisted learning behaviors are mainly for completing assignment, indicating that in code-drill courses, learners frequently switch between assignment completion and video learning, and learners often backtrack the learning video when completing assignment. It reflects that learners in the code-drill course have the characteristics of strong task-oriented and backtrack learning, while in the method learning course, such backtrack learning behavior is less.

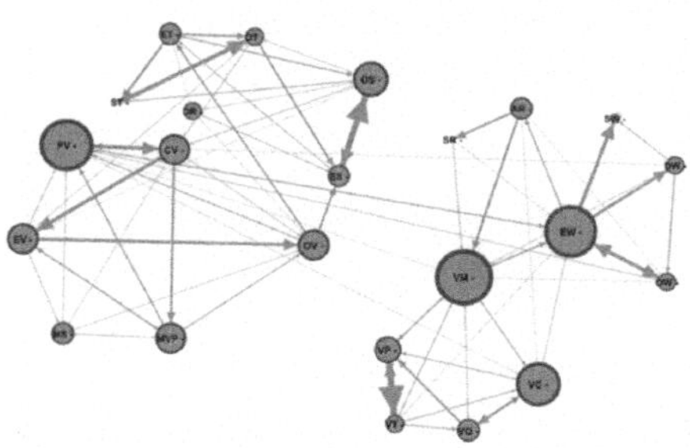

Fig. 6. Sequence diagram of learner behavior transformation in code-drill course

4.3 Differences in Learning Behavior Sequences of Learners with Different Efficiency

In addition to being influenced by the course itself, learners themselves are the most important influencing factor of the behavior sequence. Learners with different efficiency

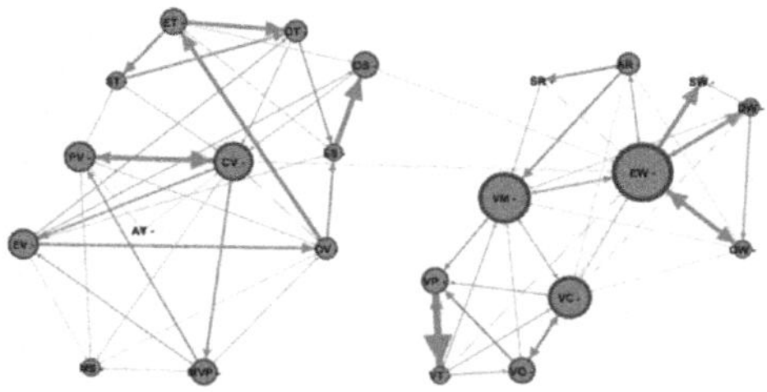

Fig. 7. Sequence diagram of learner behavior transformation in method learning course

may have different learning styles. The study aims to find out the differences in learning styles of learners with different efficiency by exploring the differences in learning behavior sequences of learners with different efficiency, so as to put forward Suggestions conducive to improving learning efficiency.

Distinguish Between Highly and Low Efficient Groups. In order to avoid the influence of different course on learning behavior sequence, this part of the study adopts the learning behavior data of learners in the code-drill course Python introduction. The study differentiates the efficiency of learners according to the time it takes them to complete the course. The average length of time for learners to complete the course is M = 69.15 h, and the standard deviation is 43.49. Learners who completed the course in less than 25.66 h (M-SD) were classified as highly efficient learners, while learners who completed the course in more than 112.64 h (M+SD) were classified as low efficient learners. Finally, there were 30 learners in the highly efficient group and 25 learners in the low efficient group.

Commonality of Behavior Transformation Sequence in Highly and Low Efficient Group. According to the above research results, it can be found that the main learning behaviors of learners are related to document pages, videos and assignments. To further explore the differences of learning behavior transformation between the two groups in the three aspects, a total of 11 behaviors were selected. The result is shown in Fig. 8. As can be seen from the Fig. 8, there was no significant difference in the behavioral transformation patterns of the highly and low efficient groups as a whole. The commonality of these two groups is that in video learning, they not just passively accept knowledge, but also have some behaviors such as pause video learning (PV), modify the video progress bar to selectively play the content at a certain time (MVP). This can reflect that learners have the characteristics of active learning no matter their efficiency is high or low.

In addition, PV → EW and OS → EW, this two significant behavioral transformations, can reflect learners' backtracking behavior towards the previous learning content when doing assignments. The significant behavioral transformation of OS → CV indicates that learners have gone through a series of behaviors including PV → ES → OS → CV, which reflects learners' learning transformation between documents and videos. In this platform, the learning document is the summary of the key content in the video. For this course, the video can explain the operation process more clearly, but it takes time. And the documentation refines the operation code so that learners can quickly access

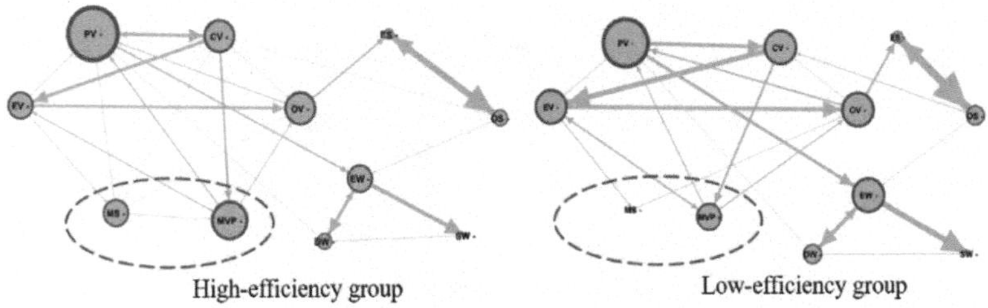

Fig. 8. Learning behavior transformation patterns in different efficiency groups

the method, but there are no detailed steps. Learners switch back and forth between the two types of learning materials, showing learners' active thinking and exploration in the learning process.

Differences of Behavior Transformation Sequence in Highly and Low Efficient Group. Although the highly and low efficient groups are similar in the whole of learning behavior transformation, there are still some differences, mainly reflected in the part shown in circle in Fig. 8. It's about modify the speed of the video (MS) and modify the video progress bar to selectively play the content at a certain time (MVP). The transitions between this two behaviors and the behaviors of pause video learning (PV) and continue video learning (CV) is much more in the highly efficient group. Compared with the low efficient group, the highly efficient group showed the following significant behavioral transformations: CV (Continue video learning) → MS (Modify the speed of the video), MS → PV (Pause video learning), MS → MVP (Modify the video progress bar to selectively play the content at a certain time), MVP → MS. This indicates that during the process of watching the video, there is an intersecting behavior transformation between the four behaviors of pause, continue, modify the video progress bar and modify speed, which reflects that the highly efficient group adopts different learning speeds for different parts of the same video. The significant behavioral transitions associated with the low efficient group were EV (Enter video learning) → MS, MS → OV (Exit video learning). This indicates that in the video learning process, after modifying the playing speed, the low efficient group kept learning at the same speed until the end of the video.

Combined with the investigation on all learners modifying the video playing speed, 83.76% of the video playing speed adjustment is to adjust the speed to higher than the normal playing speed. Among them, the frequency of adjusting the playing speed of the low efficient group was nearly three times that of the highly efficient group, and the average playback frequency of the same video was 2.7 times that of the highly efficient group. Furthermore, according to the accuracy of answering the test for the first time in the highly and low efficient group (see Table 3). It can be concluded that the highly and low efficient group preferred to play the video at a faster speed in video learning. But the highly efficient group played the video quickly and purposefully for some part of the content, and had a higher learning effect. The low efficient group adopted the fast speed without distinction, and returned to repeat learning when the learning effect was low. Therefore, the difference between highly and low efficient groups is mainly reflected in the learning efficiency of videos. The highly efficient group adopted a selective and fast learning method, choosing the main learning content and learning speed more purposefully. The low efficient group adopted the non-differentiated fast repetition learning method, while the content learning method was fast but repeated more times.

Table 3. Highly efficient group versus low efficient group

	Highly efficient group	Low efficient group
The average number of times that a video is played at a speed faster than normal	1.37	3.8
The average number of times a video is played	2.39	6.51
The first correct rate of test	76.45%	61.32%

5 Discussion

Through the study of 179 adult learners, we found that there are many significant learning behavior sequences in the learning process of adult learners in this learning platform. These behavior sequences can significantly reflect that adult learners are driven by task and have strong initiative and self-regulation ability, which is one of the characteristics of excellent learners. Thus, one of the characteristics of online learners is that they are driven by assignments/tasks and have strong goal orientation.

There are differences in the sequence of learners' behaviors in different types of courses. Learners in code-drill courses have strong task-oriented and retrospective learning characteristics, while in method learning courses, such retrospective learning behaviors are rare. This difference may be due to the fact that there are more operational details involved in the code-drill courses, and learners need to constantly recall the relevant details when using what they have learned, while in the method learning courses, after they understand the methods and ideas, they can directly use what they have learned without too much retrospection. According to this difference, in the course design and platform design, learning resources can be arranged in combination with the nature of the course. So as to facilitate learners' learning backtracking behavior, such as providing learners with appropriate summary materials and improving learners' backtracking efficiency.

The study found that there was little difference in the overall behavior transformation pattern of the highly and low efficient group. This indicates that the behavior patterns of learners in this learning platform are similar, but there are some differences in efficiency, and there is no marginal group in learning. This result is different from the disengaged learners (Rodrigues et al. 2016) that appears in MOOC studies. On the one hand, this is because the learner groups are different, and their learning motivation is different. On the other hand, the main reason is the baffle design of the learning platform in this case study, which avoids the "wandering" and "jumping learning" of learners.

In addition, some studies have pointed out that learners in online learning have poor self-monitoring ability and procrastination habit (Hu et al. 2019). In view of this phenomenon, on the one hand, the reward and punishment mechanism should be added in the course design to promote learners' enthusiasm in learning. On the other hand, from the platform design, baffle control can be adopted, which can more mobilize the initiative of learners and reduce their ineffective browsing behavior. In addition, the overall behavior patterns of the highly and low efficient groups were not significantly different, indicating that the most frequent and common behavior transformation patterns were not the main factors affecting the learning effect. As Kinnebrew and Loretz (2013), found, almost all of the most frequent activity patterns in the high and low achievement group were the same or similar. This indicates that the factors influencing learners' learning effect may not be the overall behavioral pattern or the most frequent behavioral transformation pattern, but some key behavioral sequence pattern, such as the video playing behavior patterns found in this study. The highly efficient group prefer to the selective and fast playing pattern, which not only saves time and improves efficiency, but also selectively adjusts itself. And they adopts different learning speeds for different contents to reduce its cognitive load. However, in the low efficient group, non-differentiated fast repetition of playing increased the cognitive load of their learning, resulting in inefficient learning. According to the results, online adult learners can be provided with appropriate learning guidance, so as to prevent them from using indiscriminate and fast playback to save time and learning inefficiency. At the same time, the results provide some inspiration for the developers of video learning materials. In video production, different playing speeds can be presented for different difficult parts of the same video, so that learners can learn video efficiently. At the same time, it also provides inspiration for the feedback design of learning platform. The learning platform can provide feedback to learners about the video learning situation, such as the visual statistical graph of learning times, learning speed, learning time, and learning level in class or group. These can guide students to pay attention to the video learning method, timely find their own learning style problems, and timely adjustment.

6 Conclusion

This study explores the online behavior transformation patterns of adult learners and finds the characteristics of strong task orientation of adult learners. Moreover, this paper explores the differences in learners' behavior sequences from the dimension of course type and learning efficiency, and finds that there are some differences in learners' back-tracking behaviors in the code-drill courses and method learning courses. Learners in code-drill courses have the characteristics of strong task-oriented and retrospective learning, while in method learning courses, such retrospective learning behaviors are rare. Additionally, there are some differences in the video playing patterns among learners in the highly and low efficient group, which may be the main factor affecting the learning efficiency.

Since the conclusion is made by comparing the behavior sequence transformation diagram of the highly and low efficient group, further verification is needed. Besides, there were other limitations, such as the classification of course types. The classification adopted in this study is defined from the perspective of the instructional goals of the course. Later studies can further refine the course types from the knowledge types, so as to further explore which behavioral patterns learners should adopt or which behavioral sequences can have better learning effects for different types of learning contents.

Acknowledgements. This study is funded by Peking University 2020 Novel Coronavirus–infected Pneumonia Prevention and Control (Special) Project "Research on Learning Mechanisms and Key Technologies to Improve the Quality of Online Education (No. 35)".

References

Asarta, C.J., Schmidt, J.R.: Access patterns of online materials in a blended course. Decis. Sci. J. Innovative Educ. **11**(1), 107–123 (2013)

Bakeman, R., Quera, V.: Analyzing Interaction: Sequential Analysis with SDIS and GSEQ. Cambridge University Press, Cambridge (1995)

Chen, B., Fan, Y., Zhang, G., Wang, Q.: Examining motivations and self-regulated learning strategies of returning MOOCs learners. In: International Learning Analytics & Knowledge Conference, pp. 542–543. ACM (2017a)

Chen, B., Resendes, M., Chai, C.S., Hong, H.Y.: Two tales of time: uncovering the significance of sequential patterns among contribution types in knowledge-building discourse. Interactive Learn. Environ. **25**(2), 162–175 (2017b)

Healy, D., et al.: Electronic learning can facilitate student performance in undergraduate surgical education: a prospective observational study. BMC Med. Educ. **5**(23), 1–8 (2005)

Hung, J.L., Zhang, K.: Revealing online learning behaviors and activity patterns and making predictions with data mining techniques in online teaching. MERLOT J. Online Learn. Teach. **4**(4), 426–437 (2008)

Hou, H.T., Sung, Y.T., Chang, K.E.: Exploring the behavioral patterns of an online knowledge-sharing discussion activity among teachers with problem-solving strategy. Teach. Teach. Educ. **25**(1), 108 (2009)

Hu, D., Zhang, M., Zheng, Q.: Visualized analysis of online learners' activity path through lag sequence analysis. e-Educ. Res. **40**(05), 57–65 (2019)

Jeong, Allan, C.: The sequential analysis of group interaction and critical thinking in online. Am. J. Distance Educ. **17**(1), 25–43 (2003)

Kinnebrew, J.S., Loretz, K.M., Biswas, G.: A contextualized, differential sequence mining method to derive students' learning behavior patterns (2013). https://www.researchgate.net/publication/268437308

Jiang, B., Gao, M., Chen, Z., Wang, X.: Learning process analysis and learning achievement prediction with behavioral sequences. Mod. Distance Educ. **31**(02), 103–112 (2018)

Lan, Y.F., Tsai, P.W., Yang, S.H., Hung, C.L.: Comparing the social knowledge construction behavioral patterns of problem-based online asynchronous discussion in e/m-learning environments. Comput. Educ. **59**(4), 1122–1135 (2012)

Lin, T.J., Duh, H.B.L., Li, N., Wang, H.Y., Tsai, C.C.: An investigation of learners' collaborative knowledge construction performances and behavior patterns in an augmented reality simulation system. Comput. Educ. **68**, 314–321 (2013)

Lust, G., Elen, J., Clarebout, G.: Regulation of tool-use within a blended course: student differences and performance effects. Comput. Educ. **60**(1), 385–395 (2013)

Lai, C.L., Hwang, G.J.: A spreadsheet-based visualized Mind tool for improving students' learning performance in identifying relationships between numerical variables. Interactive Learn. Environ. **23**(2), 230–249 (2015)

Li, S., Zhong, Y., Yu, C., Cheng Gang, G., Wei, S.: Exploring the online learning participation behavior pattern based on behavioral sequence analysis. China Educ. Technol. **03**, 88–95 (2017)
Le, H., Fan, Y., Jia, J., Wang, Q.: How do excellent MOOC learners learn——mining learning behavior patterns in MOOC. China Educ. Technol. **385**(02), 77–84 (2019)
Morris, L.V., Finnegan, C.L., Wu, S.: Tracking student behavior, persistence, and achievement in online courses. Internet High. Educ. **8**, 221–231 (2005)
Rodrigues, R.L., et al.: Discovering level of participation in MOOCs through clusters analysis. In: IEEE International Conference on Advanced Learning Technologies. IEEE (2016)
Sackett, G.P.: Observing Behavior: Theory and applications in mental retardation. University Park Press, Baltimore (1978)
Spivey, M.F., Mcmillan, J.J.: Using the blackboard course management system to analyze student effort and performance. J. Financial Educ. **04**, 21–28 (2014)
Yang, X., Li, J., Guo, X., Li, X.: Group interactive network and behavioral patterns in online English-to-Chinese cooperative translation activity. Internet High. Educ. **25**, 28–36 (2015)
Yousef, A.M.F., Chatti, M.A., Wosnitza, M., Schroeder, U.: A cluster analysis of MOOC stakeholder perspectives. Int. J. Educ. Technol. High. Educ. **12**(1), 74–90 (2015)
Yang, X., Guo, X., Yu, S.: Student-generated content in college teaching: content quality, behavioural pattern and learning performance. J. Comput. Assist. Learn. **32**(1), 1–15 (2016)
Yang, X.M., Wang, H., Li, J.: The application of lag sequential analysis method in analyzing learning behavior. China Educ. Technol. **37**(2), 17–23 (2016)
You, J.W.: Identifying significant indicators using LMS data to predict course achievement in online learning. Internet High. Educ. **29**, 23–30 (2016)
Zhao, C., Li, M., Shu, F., Huang, Y.: Research on models of participation in online learning resources and learning effectiveness. Mod. Distance Educ. **41**(4), 20–27 (2019)

School Clusters Concerning Informatization Level and Their Relationship with Students' Information Literacy: A Model-Based Cluster Analysis Approach

Sha Zhu[1], Feixiong Chen[1], Di Wu[1](✉), Jian Xu[1], Xujun Gui[1], and Harrison Hao Yang[1,2]

[1] Central China Normal University, Wuhan 430079, China
dr.wudi@gmail.com
[2] State University of New York at Oswego, Oswego 13126, USA

Abstract. For the concerning about how school utilize information technology to cultivate students adapted to the information age, numerous studies have examined the impacts of schools' informatization on students' information literacy. However, few researches have considered the individual uniqueness of each school. Thus, this study was to investigate the clusters of schools in terms of informatization level and the relationship between the clusters of schools and students' information literacy. Model-based cluster analysis was used to explore the clusters of schools and ANOVA was used to investigate the relation between the clusters of schools and students' information literacy. The results showed that the students of schools with high informatization level tended to perform better in the information literacy test than those of schools with low informatization level. Besides, the clusters of schools were significantly related to the regions of schools. Based on the findings, the authors proposed several suggestions for improving students' information literacy from the perspective of schools.

Keywords: Information literacy · Schools' informatization · Cluster analysis

1 Introduction

In the information society, individuals are increasingly demanded to improve information literacy, which has been described as "the ability of individuals to use information and communications technology (ICT) appropriately to access, manage, integrate and evaluate information, develop new understandings, and communicate with others in order to participate effectively in society" [1]. Especially, information literacy has long been regarded as the basic ability to participate in online activities effectively and efficiently for students [2]. At present, countries around the world attach great importance to the cultivation of students' information literacy [3–5]. It has been widely acknowledged that the cultivation and promotion of students' information literacy is a complex and systematic project, which requires joint efforts from the whole society, including schools, teachers,

S. K. S. Cheung et al. (Eds.): ICBL 2020, LNCS 12218, pp. 77–89, 2020.
https://doi.org/10.1007/978-3-030-51968-1_7

parents, and communities, etc. [6–8]. In particular, schools are extremely important for shaping and cultivating students' information literacy since schools shoulder the main responsibilities of talent cultivation. Studies on the effects of schools on students' information literacy have been well documented. Specifically, numerous studies suggested that schools' informatization level was significantly correlated with students' information literacy [9–11]. The majority of these studies are based on the hypothesis of school homogeneity, where schools were treated as a holistic unit, and their differences were not considered [12]. While one study did attempt to categorize schools in Europe into different groups [13], however, this study ignored the huge differences among schools within a country. Furthermore, as we know that schools' informatization level varies from country to country, but the existing studies only involved developed countries. Specifically, there is a lack of research that focused on the differential influence of schools' clusters concerning the informatization level on students' information literacy in China, a developing country with huge diversity in terms of schools' informatization level [14].

Therefore, the present study aimed to: (1) examine whether different clusters of schools exist in terms of schools' informatization level, and, if so, (2) investigate the relationship between the identified clusters of schools and students' information literacy. The results of this study could provide new insights into the understanding of the impact of schools' informatization level on students' information literacy and may be beneficial for government and school administrators to make informed strategies to cultivate students' information literacy.

2 Conceptual Framework

2.1 Schools' Informatization

Schools' informatization is an important part of education informatization, which is often understood as the utilization of information technology in schools' education and management process [15]. Many countries, international organizations and researchers have developed assessment frameworks to evaluate education informatization [16, 17], most of which contain school-related content. UK Department of Education and Science published "ICT in Schools: Inspectorate Evaluation Studies", in which schools' management and planning, ICT and the curriculum, staff development, schools' ICT culture, and schools' ICT resources and infrastructures were included as evaluation dimensions [18]. Zhang and Wu [19] proposed that education informatization consisted of four dimensions: ICT application, ICT special expenditure, ICT platform, and ICT terminal.

Based on a thorough review of extant research, the present study is based upon a conceptualization of school informatization with six dimensions: (1) infrastructure, (2) digital resources, (3) management informatization, (4) ICT faculty, (5) ICT operation and maintenance, (6) ICT training. Infrastructure refers to supportive hardware and facilities for teaching and learning in ICT-enhanced environment, such as computer lab, electronic whiteboard, etc. Digital resources refer to electronic resources for teaching and learning, such as e-textbook, instructional video, etc. Management informatization refers to supportive system for school management including administrative management, teaching management, and student management, such as safety monitoring system, electronic financial system, etc. ICT faculty refers to teachers and school administrators familiar with ICT skills. ICT operation and maintenance refer to schools' policy guaranteeing ICT operation and maintenance, such as the mechanism of providing technical support, and the policy of establishing educational informatization funds, etc. ICT training refers to the implementation of ICT training for teacher and administrators in schools, such as training teachers in terms of ICT integration, etc. The concept model of school informatization is shown in Fig. 1.

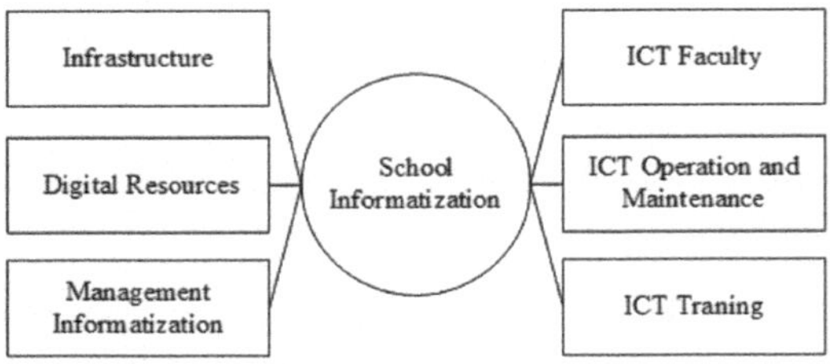

Fig. 1. The concept model of school informatization.

2.2 Information Literacy

Information literacy was firstly proposed by Zurkowski in 1979 to describe the "techniques and skills for utilizing the wide range of information tools as well as primary sources in molding information solutions to their problems" [20]. With the development of information society, the interpretation of information literacy has evolved. Nowadays, the connotation of information literacy includes not only a collection of skills, but also the comprehensive quality required by the information age, such as information ethics, information innovation, information communication, and information awareness [21]. International organizations and researchers have developed different assessment frameworks to evaluate information literacy [22, 23]. In 2018, Our research team also developed the Information Literacy Index System for Primary and Secondary Students [24], which included four dimensions: information awareness and cognition, information scientific knowledge, information application and innovation, and information ethics and law.

Based on a thorough review of extant research, our research team revised the indicator system using the Delphi method and formed a new information literacy index system. As shown in Fig. 2, the current index system contains four dimensions: (1) information awareness and attitude, (2) information knowledge and skills, (3) information thinking and behavior, and (4) information society responsibility. Information awareness and attitude refers to one's sensitivity to information about things or things of interest. Information knowledge and skills refers to one's mastery of information theories, methods, principles of information and information technology, abilities which are used for information acquisition, identification, storage and management, processing, distribution and communication, and innovative applications. Information thinking and behavior refers to one's thinking and behavior of using information technology to solve problems in study and life. Information society responsibility refers to one's moral principles and understanding of the rules governing information activities.

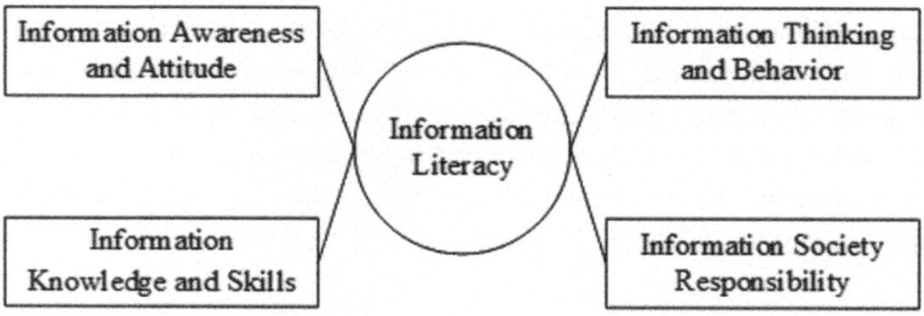

Fig. 2. The concept model of information literacy.

2.3 The Relationship Between Schools' Informatization and Students' Information Literacy

Based on the ICILS 2013 data of four developed countries (Australia, Germany, Norway and the Czech Republic), Gerick et al. [12] found that four aspects regarding with schools' informatization appeared to be crucial for students' computer and informatization literacy score: (1) ICT equipment, (2) professional development of teaching staff, (3) school goals, and (4) views/self-efficacy of teaching staff. In another study, latent class analysis was used to identify clusters of schools based on relevant school-level characteristics, including schools' visions and goals, teachers' professional development and ICT infrastructure [13]. Results showed that 1727 secondary schools in 12 European countries were classified into five clusters of schools, but the school-level factor only have significant relations to students' computer and information literacy in a few countries.

Fraillon et al. [11] analyzed the data of ICILS 2018 and found that the students currently studying ICT subjects got higher scores in computer and information literacy test than those who were not. additionally, in the national contexts survey, many countries agreed the follow six aspects were important for students' cultivation of information literacy: professional development for teachers' pedagogical use of ICT, sufficient ICT infrastructure and resources in schools, development of ICT-related competencies among students, development and provision of digital learning materials, narrowing of the digital divide among students, improvement of administrative and management systems in schools, and communication with parents with ICT.

3 The Present Study

Previous studies have documented how schools' informatization affects adolescents' information literacy. However, to the best of our knowledge, few studies have investigated the uniqueness of each school in terms of the informatization, as well as the impact of distinctive clusters of schools on students' information literacy, especially in a country with huge diversity of schools' informatization level. Against this background, the present study aimed to answer the following two research questions:

RQ1: Do different clusters of schools exist concerning their informatization level? If they do exist, what characterizes them?

RQ2: If RQ1 holds, are the identified clusters of schools related to students' information literacy?

4 Method

4.1 Participants

In December 2018, our research team designed and implemented a National Primary and Secondary School Student Information Literacy Test in China with the support and participation of the National Center for Educational Technology. The participants from secondary schools were selected as the research sample in this study, which consisted of 641 secondary schools and 49546 seventh and eighth grade students. A description of the students' sample is provided in Table 1. The average age range of the students in the seventh and eighth grades was among 12 and 14 years. The schools involved 31 provinces in the east, middle and west regions of China, as shown in Table 2.

Table 1. Demographic composition of the student sample.

Grade	Male	Female	Total
Seventh	12674	12320	24993
Eighth	12325	12228	24553

Table 2. The distribution of schools in each region.

Region	Province	Number of school
East	Beijing, Tianjing, Hebei, Liaoning, Shanghai, Jiangsu, Zhejiang, Fujian, Shandong, Guangdong, Hainan	219
Middle	Shanxi, Jilin, Heilongjiang, Anhui, Jiangxi, Henan, Hubei, Hunan	247
West	Inner Mongolia, Guangxi, Chongqing, Sichuan, Guizhou, Yunnan, Xizang, Shaanxi, Gansu, Qinghai, Ningxia, Xingjiang	175

4.2 Instrumentation

The students' information literacy was measured by 40 multiple-choice questions, which contain four dimensions: information awareness and attitude (12 items), information knowledge and skills (16 items), information thinking and behavior (6 items), information society responsibility (6 items). The sample items of each dimension are shown in Table 3.

The schools' informatization level was measured by the questionnaire developed according to the "China Education Informatization Development Report" [25]. The

Table 3. Sample items of students' information literacy test.

Dimension	Sample item
Information awareness and attitude	Which statement about information is correct? () (A) A newspaper is information (B) A football match published in a newspaper is information (C) Radio is a message (D) A book is an information
Information knowledge and skills	1 KB = () B (A) 256 (B) 1000 (C) 1024 (D) 2048
Information thinking and behavior	Lily wants to understand the world of Harry Potter. If possible, you would suggest her () (A) Read the "Harry Potter" series of books (B) Consult a friend who knows (C) Experience the world of Harry Potter using virtual reality technology (D) Watch Harry Potter movies
Information society and responsibility	Which statement is correct? () (A) When chatting on the Internet, I can say whatever I want to say (B) If I could make computer virus, how great would it be? (C) Since the pirated software is free to use, I can use it (D) We should not browse unhealthy and harmful websites

questionnaire for schools contains 20 items and six dimensions: infrastructure (4 items), digital resources (4 items), management informatization (3 items), ICT faculty (3 items), ICT operation and maintenance (3 items), ICT training (3 items). The questionnaires were filled by school administers who are in charge of schools' development of informatization. The sample items for each dimension are shown in the Table 4.

4.3 Statistical Analyses

The factoextra package, a R package developed by Kassambara and Mundt [26], was used to calculate the Hopkins of the data [27] and to validate the cluster tendency of the data. The best number of the clusters was determined by using BIC. The model-based cluster method in the mclust package, a R package developed by Scrucca et al. [28], was performed on the six dimensions of schools' informatization to explore the classification of the schools. The Chi-square test was applied to analyze the relations of clusters of schools with the regions of schools. ANOVA was conducted to compare the average

Table 4. Sample items of schools' informatization questionnaire.

Dimension	Description	Sample item
Infrastructure	Indicators on supportive hardware and facilities for teaching and learning in ICT-enhanced environment, such as computer lab, electronic whiteboard, etc.	The proportion of multimedia classrooms
Digital resources	Indicators on electronic resources for teaching and learning, such as e-textbook, instructional video, etc.	Teachers' Access to digital teaching resources in schools
Management informatization	Indicators of supportive system for school management including administrative management, teaching management, and student management, such as safety monitoring system, electronic financial system, etc.	Types of management information systems owned by school
ICT faculty	Indicators of teachers and school administrators familiar with ICT skills	The proportion of subject teachers who can use information technology for teaching
ICT operation and maintenance	Indicators of schools' policy guaranteeing ICT operation and maintenance, such as the mechanism of providing technical support, and the policy of establishing educational informatization funds, etc.	Establishment of ICT integration policies
ICT training	Indicators of the implementation of ICT training for teacher and administrators in schools, such as training teachers in terms of ICT integration, etc.	The frequency of providing ICT training sessions per academic year

information literacy test scores of students from the clusters of schools. In addition, post hoc tests were used to examine the differences of all possible pairwise comparisons among the clusters of schools.

5 Result

5.1 Overview of Students' Information Literacy

The results of the students' information literacy test scores are presented in Fig. 3. The overall mean score of the seventh and eighth grade students on the information literacy test was 59.10 (out of a maximum of 100) and SD was 20.94. On the whole, it seemed that the majority of the students got average achievements on information literacy test. Furthermore, according to Table 5, the information literacy test scores of students in the three regions was significantly different from each other in information literacy and the dimensions of information knowledge and skills, and information society responsibility.

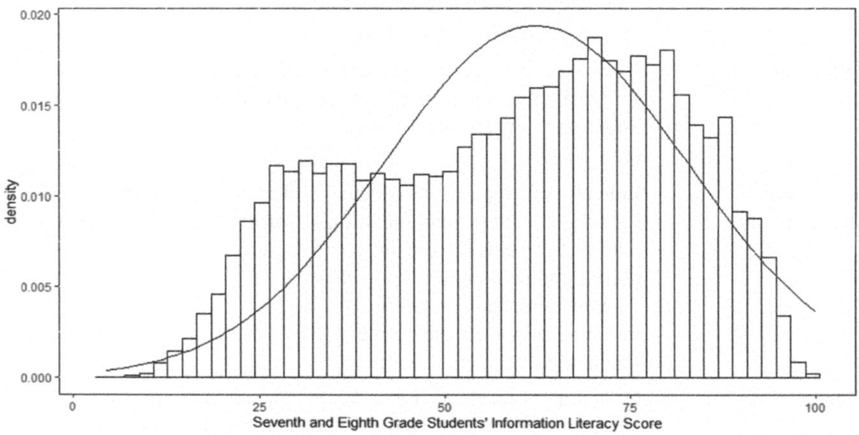

Fig. 3. Information literacy scores distribution of seventh and eighth grade students.

Table 5. Comparison of students' test scores in different regions.

	East	West	Middle	F	Post hoc
Information literacy	64.56	56.89	56.22	797.97*	East > Middle > West
Information awareness and attitude	20.81	18.49	18.48	611.01*	East > Middle, East > West
Information knowledge and skills	10.8	9.38	9.25	674.57*	East > Middle > West
Information thinking and behavior	14.91	13.04	13.02	467.69*	East > Middle, East > West
Information society responsibility	18.05	15.98	15.47	377.08*	East > Middle > West

*p < 0.001

5.2 The Cluster of Schools

The Hopkins of the data is 0.69 over the threshold of 0.5, indicating that the dataset is suitable for cluster analysis. According to the BIC, the best number of clusters is 3. Three clusters of schools resulted from the model-based cluster analysis. The distribution of each cluster on schools' informatization is shown in Fig. 4. The first cluster marked blue was formed by 100 school samples (16.9%) which showed high scores in six dimensions. This cluster was named H. The second cluster marked red was formed by 458 school samples (68.5%) which presented moderate scores in six dimensions. This cluster was named M. The third cluster marked green was formed by 83 school samples (14.5%) which presented low scores in six dimensions. This cluster was named L.

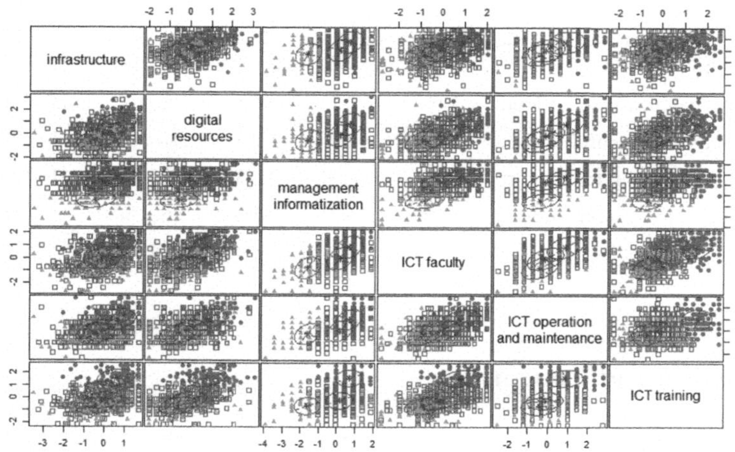

Fig. 4. Description of each cluster on schools' informatization. (Color figure online)

The numbers of schools within each cluster of each region were shown in Table 6. The results of Chi-square test on the clusters and regions of schools was $\chi^2 = 70.27$, df = 4, $p_{value} = 0.000$, which indicated that the clusters of schools and the regions of schools was significantly correlated.

Table 6. The distribution of the schools' clusters.

Cluster	Number of schools in the east region	Number of schools in the middle region	Number of schools in the west region
H	67	19	14
M	143	187	128
L	9	41	33

5.3 The Relationship Between Schools' Informatization Level and Students' Information Literacy

ANOVA was employed to analyze the information literacy scores of students in the three clusters of schools are shown in Table 7. There were significant differences in terms of students' information literacy among the three clusters of schools. The information literacy scores of students from H school cluster were significantly higher than those from M and L cluster. Additionally, the information literacy scores of students from M cluster were significantly higher than those from L cluster.

Table 7. Comparison of students' information literacy test scores among three clusters.

	H	M	L	F	Post hoc
Information literacy	64.39	58.97	53.49	467.78*	H > M > L
Information awareness and attitude	20.64	19.18	17.66	313.04*	H > M > L
Information knowledge and skills	10.64	9.77	8.83	316.81*	H > M > L
Information thinking and behavior	15.00	13.56	12.32	305.81*	H > M > L
Information society responsibility	18.12	16.45	14.68	260.34*	H > M > L

*$p < 0.001$

6 Discussion and Conclusion

This study investigated the clusters of Chinese schools regarding with informatization, and examined the relationship of the clusters of schools and students' information literacy.

For RQ1, the results showed that it is possible to identify three distinct clusters of schools concerning informatization level and the number of schools in the three clusters was normally distributed, with the majority of the schools (62.5%) identified as middle level. Nevertheless, the informatization level of schools in the east region of China was significantly higher than schools in the middle and west regions, indicating that economic development might be an important factor affecting school informatization. For the three clusters, the dimension of ICT training was the most distinguished dimension of school informatization, which indicated that the teacher-related factors might be extremely important for schools informatization and the finding is consistent with previous findings [9, 29].

For RQ2, the results showed that the clusters of schools are significantly related to students' information literacy scores. The cluster with higher schools informatization level showed higher information literacy scores of students. The finding indicated that promoting the development of school informatization could effectively improve students' information literacy. Consequently, the authors suggested that the following strategies could be implemented to improve students' information literacy.

1. Interventions should be made into schools' informatization. It might be useful to increase investment in schools of backward areas on developing informatization to narrow digital divide between urban and rural areas, as well as western and eastern regions. The schools of L cluster should pay more attention to the promotion of management informatization, which is the dimension that distinguish between L

and M cluster. The schools of M cluster should focus on the enhancement of ICT training, which is the dimension that distinguish between M and H cluster.

2. Supporting teachers' professional development with respect to ICT integration. Since teachers are the core of school informatization, teachers' professional development is the key to the promotion of students' information literacy. Researcher [30] claimed that one of the main obstacles for the integration of ICT in schools might be the lack of professional development of teachers with respect to information technology. Petko et al. [29] found that educational technology integration is dependent on teachers' readiness to integrate educational technology, which is based on teachers' perceived skills and beliefs. Therefore, schools should support and encourage teachers to integrate ICT with teaching, such as setting and clarifying ICT integration goal, providing flexible technical support, creating atmosphere of technology integration, establishing platform for communication among teachers in terms of ICT integration, etc.

Acknowledgments. The work was supported by the Fundamental Research Funds for the Central Universities (CCNU19Z02001).

References

1. Dunlea, R.: Ministerial Council on Education, Employment, Training and Youth Affairs (MCEETYA) (2005)
2. McKeever, C., Bates, J., Reilly, J.: School library staff perspectives on teacher information literacy and collaboration. J. Inf. Lit. **11**, 51 (2017). https://doi.org/10.11645/11.2.2187
3. American Library Association: Presidential committee on information literacy. https://libguides.ala.org/InformationEvaluation/Infolit. Accessed 02 July 2020
4. Peacock, J.: Standards, curriculum and learning: implications for professional development. In: Australian and New Zealand Information Literacy Framework: Principles, Standards and Practice, pp. 29–32 (2004)
5. MOE: Notice of the Ministry of Education on printing and distributing the "Education Informatization 2.0 Action Plan". http://www.moe.gov.cn/srcsite/A16/s3342/201804/t20180425_334188.html. Accessed 05 Feb 2020
6. Lanning, S., Mallek, J.: Factors influencing information literacy competency of college students. J. Acad. Librariansh. **43**, 443–450 (2017). https://doi.org/10.1016/j.acalib.2017.07.005
7. Scherer, R., Rohatgi, A., Hatlevik, O.E.: Students' profiles of ICT use: identification, determinants, and relations to achievement in a computer and information literacy test. Comput. Human Behav. **70**, 486–499 (2017). https://doi.org/10.1016/j.chb.2017.01.034
8. Alkan, M., Meinck, S.: The relationship between students' use of ICT for social communication and their computer and information literacy. Large-scale Assessments Educ. **4**, 15 (2016). https://doi.org/10.1186/s40536-016-0029-z
9. Gil-Flores, J., Rodríguez-Santero, J., Torres-Gordillo, J.J.: Factors that explain the use of ICT in secondary-education classrooms: the role of teacher characteristics and school infrastructure. Comput. Human Behav. **68**, 441–449 (2017). https://doi.org/10.1016/j.chb.2016.11.057

10. Wu, D., Li, C.C., Zhou, W.T., Tsai, C.C., Lu, C.: Relationship between ICT supporting conditions and ICT application in Chinese urban and rural basic education. Asia Pacific Educ. Rev. **20**, 147–157 (2019). https://doi.org/10.1007/s12564-018-9568-z
11. Fraillon, J., Ainley, J., Schulz, W., Friedman, T., Duckworth, D.: Preparing for Life in a Digital World: The IEA International Computer and Information Literacy Study 2018 International Report. Springer, Heidelberg (2019). https://doi.org/10.1007/978-3-030-38781-5
12. Gerick, J., Eickelmann, B., Bos, W.: School-level predictors for the use of ICT in schools and students' CIL in international comparison. Large-Scale Assessments Educ. 5 (2017). https://doi.org/10.1186/s40536-017-0037-7
13. Gerick, J.: School level characteristics and students' CIL in Europe – a latent class analysis approach. Comput. Educ. **120**, 160–171 (2018). https://doi.org/10.1016/j.compedu.2018.01.013
14. Wu, D., Li, C.C., Zhou, W.T., Tsai, C.C., Lu, C.: Relationship between ICT supporting conditions and ICT application in Chinese urban and rural basic education. Asia Pacific Educ. Rev. **20**, 147–157 (2019). https://doi.org/10.1007/s12564-018-9568-z
15. Mynbayeva, A., Anarbek, N.: Informatization of education in Kazakhstan: new challenges and further development of scientific schools. Int. Rev. Manag. Mark. **6**, 259–264 (2016)
16. Lonyuduk, N.P., Begi, N.: The application of fuzzy comprehensive evaluations in the college education informationization level. IOSR J. Res. Method Educ. **8**, 8–17 (2018). https://doi.org/10.9790/7388-0803040817
17. Sekulovska, A., Mitrevski, P.: Informatization level assessment framework and educational policy implications. Int. J. Manag. Public Sect. Inf. Commun. Technol. **7**, 11–22 (2016). https://doi.org/10.5121/ijmpict.2016.7402
18. Department of Education and Science: ICT in Schools Inspectorate Evaluation Studies, pp. 1–226 (2008)
19. Zhang, X., Lu, C., Wu, D.: A model based on the factor analysis for assessing the ICT development in basic education and regional comparison. In: Proceedings - 5th International Conference on Educational Innovation through Technology, EITT 2016. pp. 227–231. Institute of Electrical and Electronics Engineers Inc. (2017). https://doi.org/10.1109/eitt.2016.52
20. Zurkowski, P.G.: The information service environment relationships and priorities. Natl. Comm. Libr. Inf. Sci. 1–30 (1974). ERICNumber: ED100391
21. ACRL: Information literacy competency standards for higher education. Community Jr. Coll. Libr. 1–16 (2000). https://doi.org/10.1300/j107v09n04_09
22. Fraillon, J., Schulz, W., Ainley, J.: International computer and information literacy study: assessment framework (2013). https://doi.org/10.15478/uuid:b9cdd888-6665-4e9f-a21e-61569845ed5b
23. Fabbi, J.L.: Fortifying the pipeline: a quantitative exploration of high school factors impacting the information literacy of first-year college students. Coll. Res. Libr. **76**, 31–42 (2015). https://doi.org/10.5860/crl.76.1.31
24. Shi, Y., Peng, C., Wu, Y., Yang, H.: Research on the evaluating indicators system of information literacy for K-12 students. China Educ. Technol. 73–77 + 93 (2018)
25. Ministry of Education Educational Information Strategy Research Base: China Education Informatization Development Report (2017/2018)
26. Kassambara, A., Mundt, F.: factoextra: Extract and Visualize the Results of Multivariate Data Analyses (2019). https://cran.r-project.org/package=factoextra
27. Banerjee, A., Davé, R.N.: Validating clusters using the Hopkins statistic. In: IEEE International Conference on Fuzzy Systems, pp. 149–153 (2004). https://doi.org/10.1109/FUZZY.2004.1375706
28. Scrucca, L., Fop, M., Murphy, T.B., Raftery, A.E.: Mclust 5: clustering, classification and density estimation using Gaussian finite mixture models. R J. **8**, 289–317 (2016). https://doi.org/10.32614/rj-2016-021

29. Petko, D., Prasse, D., Cantieni, A.: The interplay of school readiness and teacher readiness for educational technology integration: a structural equation model (2018). https://doi.org/10.1080/07380569.2018.1428007
30. Pelgrum, W.J.: Obstacles to the integration of ICT in education: results from a worldwide educational assessment. Comput. Educ. **37**, 163–178 (2001). https://doi.org/10.1016/S0360-1315(01)00045-8

Roles of Students' Learning and Motivation: Feedback and External Knowledge

Kongkiti Phusavat(✉), Naraphorn Paoprasert, and Suttharida Suwanphiched

Faculty of Engineering, Kasetsart University, Bangkok, Thailand
{fengkkp,fengnpp}@ku.ac.th, suttharida@gmail.com

Abstract. The study attempts to examine the impacts of feedback and external knowledge on learning and motivation of underprivileged students. This study preliminarily analyzes the type of feedback and external knowledge needed to help students learn and motivate in their study of science experiments and education. It is part of human learning. This study is the extension of the pilot project which began in 2016. This project highlights the use a science experiment to develop a product while tackling waste, and water and soil pollution surrounding schools and students' communities. The initial findings show that feedback in terms of recognition of student's activity through an opportunity to display and purchase of their products from science education, visit by international business committees, and indirect financial support to assist students' activity have reinforced the continuous improvement in learning and development of students. More studies are needed to specifically look at how these feedback and external knowledge have played a role in single- and double-loop learning of students.

1 Introduction

Pedagogical development and effective feedback are essential for students' development (Education Endowment Foundation 2017). Basic education is critical for human capital development of a country. Thailand has several types of schools which are under the jurisdiction and supervision of three ministries. Ministry of Higher Education, Science, Research and Innovation is responsible for all university teacher training schools- representing a very small portion of students and being considered as a top-tier school. Secondly, Ministry of Education is looking after international, Thai public, and Thai private schools which offer the basic education from Grade 1 to Grade 12. More than 85% of the entire student headcounts in the country attend the schools under Ministry of Education.

Lastly, Ministry of Interior also provides basic education services which come under local governmental administrations as well as Bangkok Metropolitan Administration (BMA) and Pattaya City Administration. Approximately 12% of the students' population (of 8 million) for basic education are attending Ministry of Interior schools. The schools in this group are considered to be part of extending education's opportunities to poor or underprivileged students. The reason is that, during the height of Thailand's economic growth, there were large migrations of workers from different regions into urban areas, especially Bangkok.

S. K. S. Cheung et al. (Eds.): ICBL 2020, LNCS 12218, pp. 90–98, 2020.
https://doi.org/10.1007/978-3-030-51968-1_8

Since the available slots for studying at Ministry of Education' schools are allocated to the registered residents, many children who had to accompany their parents could not attend the schools. As a result, the schools were established to help provide the opportunities for these children. However, the schools were not properly prepared and equipped so the reputation and image have not been positive since their inceptions in the late 1970s. Students who attend Ministry of Interior schools are generally considered as underprivileged. At the same time, high teacher turnovers or transfer requests have been high, especially for BMA schools. Thus, the quality of teaching, motivation for learning, and development of students have been problematic.

2 Problem Background

Thailand's education system has been viewed as having shortcomings in developing critical thinking and analytical skills, with too much emphasis on rote learning and reliance on rigid control through extensive inspection and audit as a means of demonstrating high quality teaching and learning (Fry and Bi 2013). Thus, compliance has been a prevailing mindset for teachers which results in long teaching hours and narrow focus only on the subject matter (rather than the skills needed by students).

For those students who attend Ministry of Interior schools, students are faced with even challenges and presumptions, especially at the lower and upper secondary levels during their study on science subjects. The primary reason is that most students in this school group do not plan to continue their education at either vocational or higher education. On the other hand, science education through the curriculum design by Institute for the Promotion of Teaching Science and Technology aims to graduate students who continue in their higher education within the disciplines of basic, engineering, and medical science.

Generally, students who study science at the upper secondary level play to continue their education at a university in the areas of basic, engineering, or medical sciences. So poor behavior and attitude need to be addressed through more exams and classroom time. Therefore, vigorous examinations, long lecturing hours, intensive and specialized experiments in Physics, Chemistry, Biology, and Mathematics are very common. Specially, the examinations are needed to help motivate students. As a result, Ministry of Interior schools' students are unable to catch up with their peers who study at the other two school categories. See Table 1 and the gap of students' development.

Most students perform well in an examination by attending special tutorial sessions. However, students who attend Ministry of Interior' schools generally live in poverty with limited career opportunities. Jobs after-school hours become a necessity to maintain a minimum standard of living. Overwhelming these students with in-depth details on science subjects and payments to a special tutorial session are impractical. A combination of student fatigue from work, poor quality of science laboratory, inability to attend special tutorial sessions, and lack of sense of appreciation to rigid and standardized lessons have contributed to low motivation and poor behavior.

Moving into a digital economy and society implies that students will need to exhibit a stronger sense of civic responsibility while having necessary transferable skills which allow better mobility and adjustment into a changing world (Deep et al. 2019). Science education needs to be extensively reviewed and should be viewed differently from

Table 1. Comparison of international achievement scores from trends in international mathematics and science study or TIMSS (2011)

School category	Mathematics	Science
University Teacher training schools	554	552
Ministry of Education' schools (mainly from public schools)	460	474
BMA schools	425	447
Other Ministry of Interior schools	424	440

Source: Minute of the Meeting prepared by BMA's Department of Education

the past practices. Science skills are critical for future skills on higher cognition (e.g., creativity) through a practice on an enquiring mindset and skills.

Design and improvement on pedagogical practices need to recognize the importance of human learning (e.g., learning process) through empathy and psychology. Specific issues such as student engagement, constructive feedback, team teaching, psychological safety, and creative experiment through product development should be the priority when working with underprivileged students.

To help address the quality of education for underprivileged students, a pilot project was initiated in 2016 to help develop a new pedagogy for science education. Science education should be about science skills. The focus has been on environment and ecology. The highlight from the pilot project is the use a science experiment to develop a product while tackling waste, and water and soil pollution surrounding schools and students' communities.

Since the experiments are conducted outside a laboratory, this provides an opportunity for students to get to know each other better. Extra incomes earned from selling products from science experiments helps strengthen soft skills such as communication, teamwork, planning, entrepreneurship and financial literacy. These skills are essential in students' future employability.

Several tangible impacts on and improvements for both students and teachers can be demonstrated as follows. They have included students' peer-learning community, behavioral improvement described by the parents, and various national awards and recognition relating to students' work on ecology and environment sponsored by Crown Property Bureau Foundation and Utokapat Foundation. Both foundations are under the Royal Patronage of H.M. The King (the late King Rama IX of Thailand).

Two recent recognitions are Outstanding Youth Awards given by National Council on Social Welfare of Thailand under Royal Patronage of H.M. The King, and Thailand's Rotary Clubs during 2018; and Outstanding School Innovativeness Award in 2019 by The Teachers' Council of Thailand. Participating teachers are chosen for the 2018 Outstanding Teacher Award by BMA's Department of Education and the 2019 Princess Maha Charki Award for Outstanding Teachers.

The recent success (e.g., students' behavior, mindset, and attitude as well as teachers' recognition) brings up several critical factors that have contributed to this development. For instance, student's empathy is viewed to be essential, especially for underprivileged students. Understanding their needs and pain points is important to gain students' trust which has been proven with science experiments. Secondly, use of many contemporary approaches and techniques such as Team Teaching have been helpful.

More importantly, when approaching students for their thoughts and reflection, the common reply appears to be the feedback and the importance of external knowledge. The students feel that the typical feedback from an evaluation of exams and paperwork has not been helpful. For some, this feedback would be helpful if they continue their study in a university. As a result, the study focuses on the roles of feedback and external knowledge and the type of feedback that underprivileged students need to help improve learning and motivation. See Fig. 1.

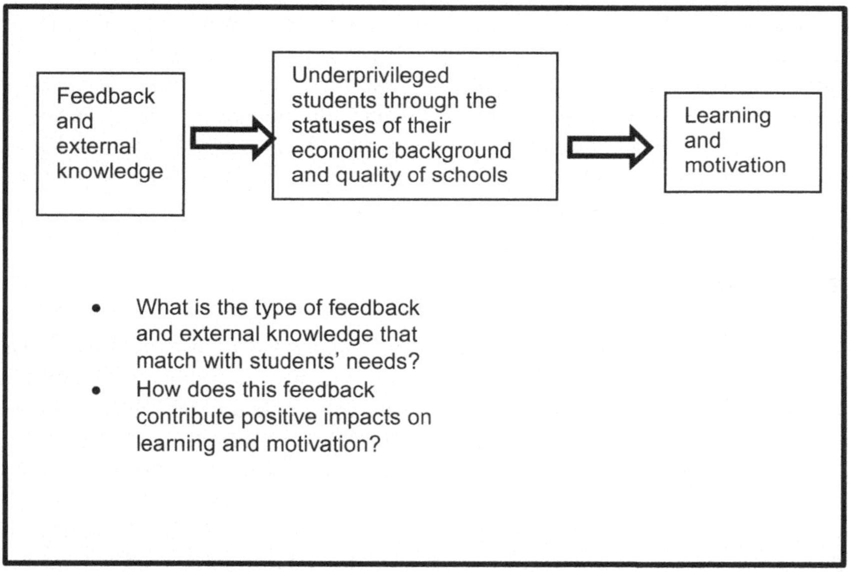

Fig. 1. Scope of the study

3 Objective

The study attempts to gain more insights into the issues relating to motivation and learning for underprivileged students. Since the pilot project has taken place over the past four years with positive impacts on students, it is important to understand the type of and how the feedback and external knowledge have resulted in better learning and motivation. This study takes place at the schools belonging to BMA. Learning and development, especially for science education, by underprivileged students (i.e., students living in poverty and poor quality of a school) has been one of the challenges facing Thailand.

Note that BMA-school students generally live in poverty with a lack of career opportunities after a diploma completion. Often, jobs after-school hours for an evening shift become a necessity for many students to maintain a minimum standard of living. It is important to point out that these schools were created as part of educational opportunity at the primary school level when Thailand experienced a rapid growth in population many decades ago. Ministry of Education could not accommodate the school's needs at that time.

4 Methodology

The study focuses on engaging with students who have already graduated, are graduating, and are studying at two BMA schools which have taken part in the pilot projects since 2016. They are: Matthayom Suwit Serinusorn School and Kaenthong Upatham School. Students from three classes have participated in the discussion on the two previous questions raised in the research's objectives- the type of and how the feedback and external knowledge have resulted in better learning and motivation. Then, the next task is to analyze the students' responses and comments. The concept of human learning, Open-loop Learning, is applied to help with this analysis. This Open-loop Learning concept helps analyze the impacts from feedback and external knowledge.

5 Results and Discussion

Based on the interviews and active engagement with students (from the three classes-those who earlier graduated, who are graduating, and who will move to Grade 12), it appears that the input, comments, and feedback from externa stakeholders has been positive. It reflects the recognition of students' activities and initiatives. By being visible and actively involve students, this has essentially been the type of feedback that students have been lacking for years. A point or a letter grade on the reports and homework (on experimental projects) has not been viewed as helpful to their future. It relates to the fact that most students do not plan to enroll in higher education institutes. In addition, feedback from foreign business communities is rare for underprivileged students. Thus, this has generated a lot of excitement among students. See Fig. 2.

Fig. 2. School visits by international delegates and business communities

According to students, they feel that their work and efforts have been valued by the visits. In addition, these visits indicate that what they have been doing is expected.

In other words, it shows that the students are doing the things in a right way. In fact, the students' interactions with external stakeholders who are willing to share with them unique knowledge/experiences have been repeatedly mentioned as one of the motivating factors for their learning and development. In this pilot project, key external stakeholders involving with these interactions include registered firms in Joint Foreign Chambers of Commerce in Thailand (JFCCT), and foreign Embassies in Thailand.

JFCCT has played a significant role in supporting the innovation project. Small companies in JFCCT have responded to the needs of teachers and students through: a series of workshops on entrepreneurship, product development and costing, financial literacy, and digital literacy from Pure Growth Asia from South African-Thai Chamber of Commerce, and ICDL Thailand from Irish-Thai Chamber of Commerce. Moreover, Thai- Hong Kong Trade Association, a member of JFCCT, purchased many students' products for their members and provided valuable feedback for students, especially in packaging, customer relation, and production planning. Many firms have donated needed instruments to support science experiment such as Felicia Design company which is a member of Thai- Norwegian Chamber of Commerce. See Fig. 3.

Fig. 3. JFCCT's interactions and product development from science education

Excitement and exposure to new and practical ideas, based on the workshops and repeated visits by international delegates from JFCCT, Spouses of Head of Mission or SHOM, and ambassadors, has contributed to higher motivation and commitment. The workshops have focused on product development and entrepreneurship. The delegates have purchased students' products and provided valuable feedback, and have provided needed donations to help science experiments. These donations are based on a request by students after the school visits. Ongoing developments include: (1) active engagement with communities on food waste, (2) experiments on plastic waste, and (3) sharing the experiences with other schools. See Fig. 4 for some of the donations.

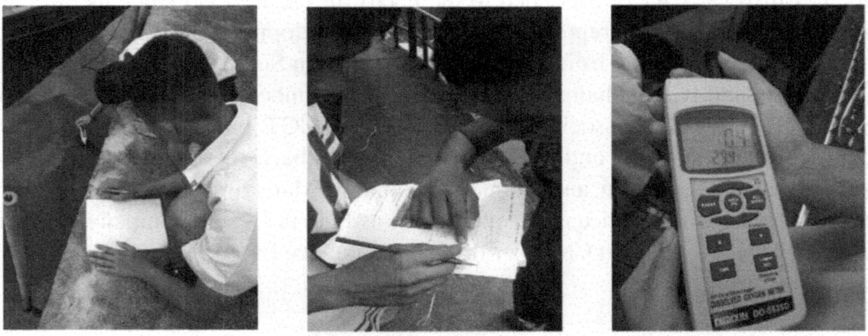

Fig. 4. Example of donations (based on a student's request)

SHOM through the cooperation with JFCCT, has likewise contributed positively to students' motivation and learning. Visiting schools to observe science experiments and to purchase students' products as well as inviting students to display their products at the embassy's events have provided strong acknowledgement to their work and represents a rare opportunity for students to interact with international guests and dignitaries. In addition, financial support from Embassy of Luxembourg helps reinforce students' confidence and pride, and result in extending their initiatives in science experiments. See Fig. 5.

Fig. 5. Display of products (from science education) by SHOM an JFCCT

From the students' viewpoint, general emphasis on uniformity of learners and academic achievement has negatively impacted on the flexibility for teachers to deal with many social problems faced by students (e.g., bullying through physical, verbal, and cyber means; teen pregnancy, dropouts, vaping epidemic and drugs). Poorer performers from the exams likely to be ignored while students who learn at a slower pace than others are likely to be left alone without much engagement from teachers.

To gain better insights into how students learn, motivate, and develop the skills in science education, it is important to apply the Single-loop Learning for this purpose (Smith 2001 and 2013). Based on the preliminary findings, feedback and external knowledge have been essential in their motivation and a change in their behavior. Furthermore, the type of feedback which has positively contributed to students' learning and development is not necessarily academic in nature. Engagement, visits, product display, purchase, references to other entities, donation, and planning together with students and teachers on their future needs represent an opportunity and recognition. For students, this type of feedback has had more impacts than an academic grade as it provides both confirmation and validation that students have done what they are expected to do right or correctly through opportunity and recognition. This can be demonstrated by the Single-loop Concept. See Fig. 6.

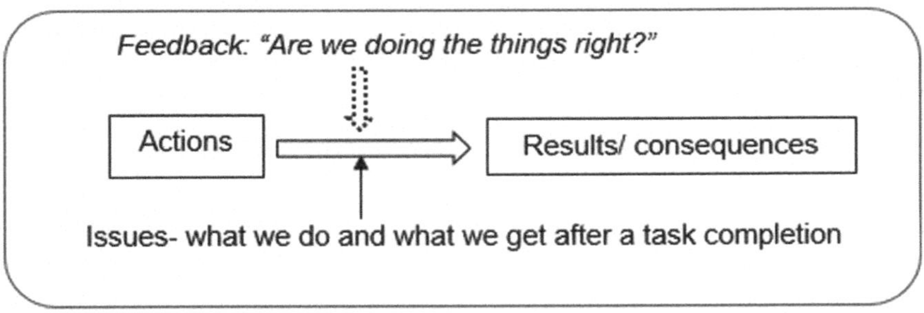

Fig. 6. Roles of feedback in single-loop learning (Adapted from Tosey et al. 2012)

The mindset of feedback (as well as external knowledge) should be further examined. Feedback as part academic assessment and evaluation is critical for learning progress and is required by schools. This pilot project points to another type of feedback (especially for underprivileged students) which can be as (or even) more helpful and effective for learning and development. What and how students learn dealing with pedagogical practices and feedback from assessment and evaluation are critical for human leaning. Identifying the type of feedback (for various spectrums of students) can strengthen learning and development. In addition, the preliminary finding also indicates the applicability of the Open-loop Concept for this purpose.

6 Conclusion

Uniformity in education means more control and compliance which has become a classroom's norm. Production relating to students reinforces that all should uniformly learn the subjects in the same way without recognizing individual development and potential. Participating teaches in the pilot project have witnessed how a thick teaching manual and experimental guidelines with expected answers for science education harmed creativity and critical thinking of students. For underprivileged students, feedback has been very helpful for their learning and development. This study simply points to potential research in the areas of students' learning.

References

Education Endowment Foundation: Measuring teachers' research engagement: findings from a pilot study (2017). https://educationendowmentfoundation.org.uk/public/files/Evaluation/Research_Use/NFER_Research_Use_pilot_report_-_March_2017_for_publication.pdf. Accessed Mar 2018

Deep, S., Salleh, B., Othman, H.: Study on problem-based learning towards improving soft skills of students in effective communication class. Int. J. Innovation Learn. **25**(1), 17–34 (2019)

Fry, G., Bi, H.: The evolution of educational reform in Thailand: the Thai educational paradox. J. Educ. Adm. **51**(3), 290–319 (2013)

Smith, M.: Chris Argyris: theories of action, double-loop learning and organizational learning', the encyclopedia of informal education (2001/2013). http://infed.org/mobi/chris-argyris-theories-of-action-double-loop-learning-and-organizational-learning/. Accessed Jan 2020

Tosey, P.C., Visser, M., Saunders, M.N.K.: The origins and conceptualisations of 'triple-loop' learning: a critical review. Manag. Learn. **43**(3), 289–305 (2012)

Content and Instructional Design

A Comparative Study of Chess Online Educational Products

Qian Dong(✉) and Rong Miao

Department of Educational Technology, Graduate School of Education, Peking University, Beijing, China
st16625m@gse.pku.edu.cn

Abstract. With the development of technology, more and more online educational products emerge in chess, which makes it difficult for different users to choose from. It's important to develop methodologies to assist different levels chess players to learn in varies environment. List method and rubric evaluation has been conducted, and advice has been put forward based on this approach. The results show that chess online educational products were rich in content and full featured, which could be divided into four categories: overall ecology, video tutorial, tactical training, live broadcast product. However, products still need to improve in product positioning and user experience to promote the development of chess online education.

Keywords: Chess · Online education · Products · Comparative study

1 Introduction

The technology of information develops rapidly since the 21 century. Virtual reality, artificial reality, wearable devices are becoming increasingly popular and connected with our daily lives. With the rise of mobile Internet industry, online education has continued to develop. Online educational products changed gradually, from PC to mobile terminals, such as tablets, iPads and mobile phones. Each new version of these products brings innovative features and there is a great potential to change the way how we live, work and study [1]. Information technology changes with each passing day.

The advances of information technology have prompted students, educators and researchers to utilize devices. More and more users begin to choose flexible, convenient and interactive online educational products. According to the report of the Prospective Industry Research Institute, With the promulgation of favorable policies like New Generation AI Development Plan, the number of online education users will continue to grow at a rate of about 15% in the future, and it is expected to exceed 300 million by 2022, owing to the prevalence of Internet, the cultivation of users' habits, the marketing of enterprises [2]. On the one hand, the scale of Chinese netizens has steadily expanded, providing a stable foundation for the rapid growth of the number of online education users. On the other hand, the number of online educational products at home and abroad is growing rapidly. It allows learnings to learn without being restricted by time and place,

S. K. S. Cheung et al. (Eds.): ICBL 2020, LNCS 12218, pp. 101–113, 2020.
https://doi.org/10.1007/978-3-030-51968-1_9

enabling learning wherever they want after class is over. It makes mobile learning, fragmented learning, individual learning occurs naturally through the Internet, giving users a differentiated experience and attracting more people to participate.

There is still a long way to face the challenges in meeting the needs of chess players. There are approximately 700 million chess players in the world, about 50 million of whom are from China. In addition, there are more than 300 features school for chess in China. With the trend of chess online educational products continue upgrading in recent years, more chess players and school teachers begin to use online chess educational products to lean and teach, such as enhance skills, play games, learn courses, practice exercises, watch live, analysis games, etc. Richard Culatta, from the Office of Educational Technology of the United States, pointed out that there would be an increase demand in high-quality educational apps, due to the popularity of mobile devices, the improvement of per capita disposable income and willingness to pay from learners, educators, parents and other stakeholders [3]. But now, owning different design concepts, there are many online chess educational products in the market which focus on different functions in learning chess in different interfaces. For example, chess website like chess.com and Qubang Internet, WeChat applet like Chaoyue chess, applications like Lichess and Chess League. These products have different design concepts, interface presentation, interactive experience, but little research was found on the characters of different chess online educational products.

Based on this area that need further examination, the purpose of this study is to carry out a comparative study of chess educational products, promote the continuous improvement of the interface, content and function, enhance product value, as well as increase the stickiness and activeness of users. This study aims to achieve two goals, which are as follows:

1. Provide more different chess online educational product choices for players to meet their individual needs, and thus help improve the level of individual chess skills and promote the development of chess career.
2. Understand the features of different chess online educational products through comparative research, which helps provide enlightenment for the optimization of product content and function for product development companies and administrative organization.

2 Method

Online education is a method of content dissemination and rapid learning through the application of information and Internet technology [4]. Online educational product refers to the product that spreads content through the application of information and Internet technology around the education goal. In terms of goals, online education products take education as the final goal. From the perspective of usage scenarios, online educational products take the Internet as the media, and use PC, mobile devices (such as smart phones, tablet computers, etc.) to connect online and offline. Users can use it not only in formal education scenarios such as schools or clubs, but also in informal education in other environments such as families. As for the way of learning, it can be blended learning with both online and offline learning, such as under the guidance of offline teachers, students use online education products to complete some training to achieve the established education goals. Besides, it can also be an individual independent personalized learning style, users can use online educational products to complete online learning or expand training. For presentation categories, online educational products mainly include three categories: website, app and WeChat applet.

Edutainment, interactivity and globalization are three big characteristics of chess online educational products. Firstly, the product needs to center on certain educational objectives. Secondly, whether the product is an educational application or a website, it belongs to utility software with certain interactivity. Thirdly, the products are mainly targeted at chess players, who have different cultural backgrounds because chess is a popular intellectual sport in the worldwide. Therefore, the evaluation of chess online educational products is based on instructional design theory, software evaluation theory and cultural psychology theory [5].

There are three methods to evaluate educational products, that is, list evaluation, checklist evaluation and rubric evaluation. The list method is simple and clear, which can help students, teachers and parents to choose proper products. The checklist method is convenient and easy to use. It is more comprehensive and detailed for product evaluation, which is suitable for administrators and teachers to choose specific teaching products. The rubric evaluation is professional and comprehensive, which is appropriate for professional technical developers and administrative personnel.

This study mainly uses the list method and rubric evaluation. It contributes to give access to users with the right products efficiently from the large number of chess online educational products using the list evaluation method. On this basis, continuous use of products can help chess professionals to examine products, make improvements, improve user experience, attract more amateurs, thereby improve the popularity and recognition of international image, continuously enhance players' level of chess skills, enrich the chess culture atmosphere and people's spiritual life.

The list evaluation includes the following three steps: collection and selection, classification and coding, data analysis.

2.1 Collection and Selection

First, we use three ways to search and collect chess online educational products. The first one was keyword searching of websites and application stores (such as chess). The second way was expert interview. The last was snowball searching of the same category (such as chess tiger and chess tiger pro) or publisher (such as chess king).

In this process, products were downloaded and applied. By reviewing and trying, some of the products were narrowed down. A total of 82 products met the criteria to be included in the final study. The filter criteria include three points. Firstly, the product had nothing to do with chess, such as Gobang, Jiuzi chess, Chinese chess, flying chess, go, Japanese chess, checkers and other chess categories. Secondly, the products were not for education, but for games, entertainment, social networking, games, competitions as the main purposes, such as intellectual games, chess multiplayer games, V-Chess, little chess God, Tianli chess, chess mini, open game, etc. Thirdly, the product could not be used normally, such as bilingual chess.

2.2 Classification and Coding

Firstly, according to the presentation, chess online educational products were divided into five categories: app (72), web page (2), APP and web page (4), WeChat applet (3), WeChat subscription and web page (1), as shown in the following Fig. 1.

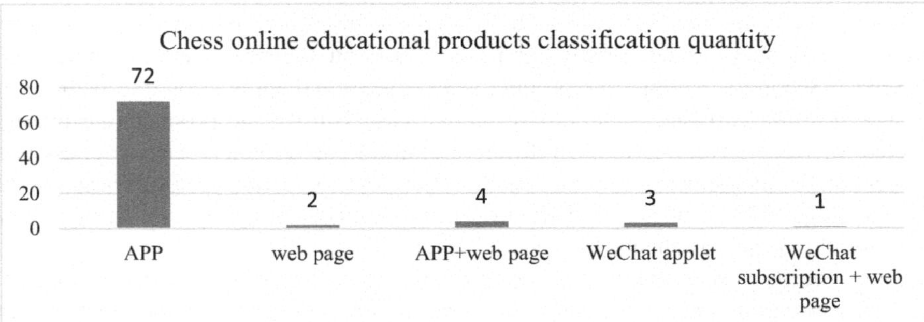

Fig. 1. Classification quantity of chess online educational products

Next, ten types of data were sorted from App Annie, a mobile application data and analysis platform, which comparatively reflected the basic features of a product. Ten items were App's cost, compatibility, category, first tracking time, all version ratings, number of ratings, publisher, language, size, number of version updates. For example, the language was directly related to the region, the cost affected numbers of users. Both would contribute to the globalization of products.

Finally, coding each product through the next process, namely, download, register and log in, deeply use. First, with practical practice, a preliminary coding system were established, and then we coded five apps, two WeChat applets, one website, and one WeChat subscription with a high number of evaluators. In this process, we revised, improved and supplied the coding framework, and established the final coding table. If the coding standard was met, it was marked with "1". If not, it was marked with "0" (Table 1).

2.3 Data Analysis

The apps that met the inclusion criteria were analyzed with a qualitative content analysis method, which was a systematic classification process for analyzing products into categories for the purposes of interpreting meaning [6]. Information from the products relevant to the three research questions was coded and then classified into categories. Then, frequencies for each category were computed and reported in tables. Finally, examples for each category were provided to demonstrate how well the categories represented the data [7].

3 Results

The results of the chess online educational products are described in this section.

Table 1. Chess online educational product code information summary table (part, 82 in total)

No	Name	Basic information: Type	Cost	Compatibility	Classification	First tracking time	Grade	Rating	Requirement	Publisher	Language	Size	Edition	Update times
1	Chess.com	APP Website	99.99USD Diamond Membership 14.99USD Diamond Membership 29.99USD Gold Membership	General	games	before 2008-10-29	4.8	126410	Requires iOS 11.0 or later. Compatible with iPhone, iPad, and iPod touch.	Chess.com	Afrikaans, Albanian, Arabic, Armenian, Azerbaijani, Basque, Belarusian, Bengali, Bosnian, Bulgarian, Catalan, Croatian, [illegible]	93.0MB	1.21—3.8.33	84
2	Chess Tiger	APP	free	General	Games	2010-05-01	4.7	29730	Requires iOS 10.0 or later. Compatible with iPhone, iPad, and iPod touch.	Christophe Théron	English, French, German	42.1MB	2012.05—2019.05	17
3	国际象棋-Learn Chess	APP	free	General	education	before 2009-01-18	3.4	15600	Requires iOS 11.0 or later. Compatible with iPhone, iPad, and iPod touch.	Tom Kerrigan	[illegible], German, Japanese, Korean, Simplified Chinese	4.9MB	1.1.0—1.5.6	14
4	Chess Tiger Pro	APP	9.99USD	General	Games	2011-03-08	4.8	20011	Requires iOS 10.0 or later. Compatible with iPhone, iPad, and iPod touch.	Christophe Théron	English, French, German	41.2MB	2011.01—2019.05	13
5	Play Magnus—Chess	APP	free 8.99 USD Magnomaster Unlimited Use 4.99 USD 77 Extra Levels 2.99 USD Brain Power > 2000	General	games	2014-02-15	4.7	3176	Requires iOS 9.0 or later. Compatible with iPhone, iPad, and iPod touch.	Play Magnus	English, French, German, Italian, Norwegian Bokmål, Russian, Simplified Chinese, Spanish	155.1MB	1.0—3.11.8	64
6	国际象棋. iChess Pro	APP	7.99USD	General	Games	before 2008-11-04	4.2	3089	Requires iOS 11.0 or later. Compatible with iPhone, iPad, and iPod touch.	Tom Kerrigan	[illegible], German, Japanese, Korean, Simplified Chinese	7.2MB	1.0—1.8.1	29
7	Chess Tactics Pro(Puzzles)	APP	free 9.99 USD All-Access Pass 1.99 USD Easy tactics 1.99 USD Intermediate tactics 1.99 USD Hard tactics 1.99 USD Intermediate mates 1.99 USD Easy mates 1.99 USD Hard mates [illegible]	General	Games	2014-09-08	4.7	1417	Requires iOS 9.0 or later. Compatible with iPhone, iPad, and iPod touch.	Emmanuel Mathis	Dutch, English, French, German, Greek, Italian, Japanese, Portuguese, Russian, Spanish, Swedish, Thai, Turkish	26.8MB	1.01—1.19	18
8	Chess for kids	APP Website	free	General	games	2019-04-06	4.2	1071	Requires iOS 9.0 or later. Compatible with iPhone, iPad, and iPod touch.	Chess.com	English	105.2MB	1.0—2.4.14	19
9	[illegible]	APP	free	General	education	2016-04-01	4.1	1196	Requires iOS 10.0 or later. Compatible with iPhone, iPad, and iPod touch.	Beijing Qiyi Technology Co., Ltd	Chinese, English	97.1MB	01.101—4.20	30
10	CT-ART 4.0（国际象棋战术）	APP	free 7.99 USD Full Course	General	games	2016-08-14	4.8	725	Requires iOS 8.0 or later. Compatible with iPhone, iPad, and iPod touch.	Chess King	Dutch, English, French, German, Greek, Italian, Polish, Portuguese	42.6M	0.8.4—1.2	9
11	Chess King	APP	free 7.99 USD Chess From Beginner to Club 10.99 USD Chess King Courses 7.99 USD CT-ART 4.0 (Chess Tactics) 7.99 USD Chess Tactics for Beginners 7.99 USD Chess Opening	General	Games	2017-12-29	4.8	600	Requires iOS 8.0 or later. Compatible with iPhone, iPad, and iPod touch.	Chess King	Dutch, English, French, German, Greek, Italian, Polish, Portuguese, Romanian, Russian, Simplified Chinese, Spanish, Traditional Chinese, Turkish	50.7MB	0.9—1.1.1	10
12	lichess	APP Website	free	General	entertainment	2015-08-05	4.2	474	Requires iOS 10.2 or later. Compatible with iPhone, iPad, and iPod touch.	thibault duplessis	English	19.4MB	1.1.0—6.0.0	47

No	Content and function: Introduction to rules	Tactical training	Chess manual	Explanation to games	Engine analysis	Game practice	Match	Forum	Private data education	Interesting practice	Stage: Opening	Middle game	End game	Level: ABC level	primary level	Intermediate level	Senior level	Master
1	1	1	1	1	1	1	1	1	0	0	1	1	1	1	1	1	1	0
2	1	0	0	0	1	1	0	0	0	0	1	1	1	1	1	1	1	1
3	1	0	0	0	0	0	0	0	0	0	0	0	0	1	0	0	0	1
4	1	1	1	1	1	0	0	0	0		1	1	1	1	1	0	0	0
5	1	1	1	1	0	1	0	0	0	0	1	1	1	1	1	1	1	0
6	0	1	1	0	1	1	0	0	0	0	1	1	1	1	1	1	1	1
7	0	1	0	0	1	0	0	0	1	0	1	1	1	1	1	1	1	1
8	1	1	1	1	1	1	1	1	0	0	1	1	1	1	1	1	1	0
9	0	1	1	0	1	1	0	1	1	1	1	1	1	1	1	1	1	1
10	0	1	1	1	0	0	0	0	1	0	1	1	1	1	1	1	1	1
11	0	1	1	1	0	0	0	0	1	0	1	1	1	1	1	1	1	1
12	1	1	1	1	1	1	1	1	1	1	1	1	1	1	1	1	1	1

3.1 Type

There were 2 websites, 3 WeChat applets, 3 including both app and web pages, 72 apps, and 1 including WeChat subscription and website in 82 online education products (Table 2).

Table 2. Type statistics of chess online educational products

Type	Website	WeChat applet	APP and website	APP	WeChat subscription and website
Number	2	3	3	72	1

3.2 Cost

Seventeen of the 82 online education products were free (such as Lichess, etc.), 15 of them were charged (such as chess tiger pro, etc.), and 50 of them were free for download but charged for their internal products (such as chess king, chess art, etc.). According to this, the total proportion of content payment in chess online educational products was 80% (61% for internal fee, 18% for products). It could be paid not only for the time, like monthly or yearly payments, but also charged by membership level, for example, different level members had different limits of authority. Another way was charged by content or service, such as data private education, video course content, etc. It cost tens to thousands of yuan for different charging ways (Table 3).

Table 3. Cost statistics of chess online educational products

Cost	Free	Internal fees	Charged
Number	17	50	15

3.3 Timeline

Chess online educational product, chess-tchess Pro, developed by publisher Tom Kerrigan first appeared in 2008. Subsequently, the number of products increased year by year in the fluctuation. In 2016, there was a period of rapid growth, with 27 products in a year, of which 19 were launched by the publisher chess king. After 2016, although there were still products launched one after another, it presented the downward trend year by year. With the rapid iteration of products, the early launched products had occupied a certain market. If the follow-up products wanted to make a breakthrough, on the one hand, publishers need to dig out what the users want and deploy new services. On the other hand, publishers need to improve the user experience by optimizing the interface design, enhancing interaction, etc. to attract new users and enhance their viscosity of old users (Figs. 2 and 3).

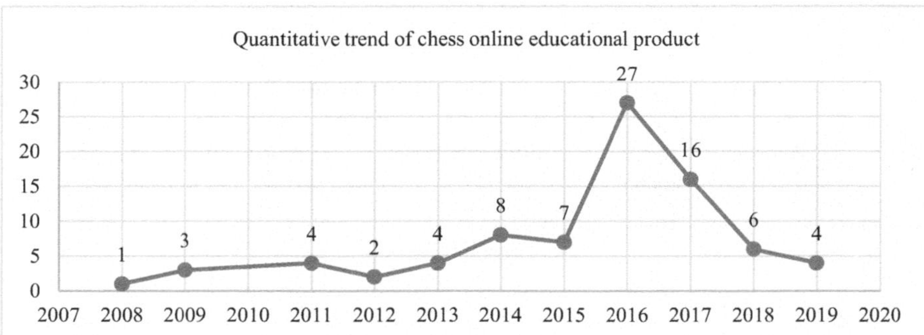

Fig. 2. Quantitative trend of chess online educational products

3.4 Language

There were 31 kinds of languages, including Russian, Turkish, Greek, German, Italian, French, Polish, Chinese, English, Dutch, Portuguese, Spanish, Danish, Hungarian, Norwegian, Czech, Japanese, Korean, Vietnamese, Malay, Indonesian, etc. To some extent, the languages of chess online educational products were rich, which reflected chess was widely distributed. Of all products, Chinese (13 products) and English (69 products) were the most. It was noteworthy that Chinese products usually only supported Chinese, while English products provided multi-national language services.

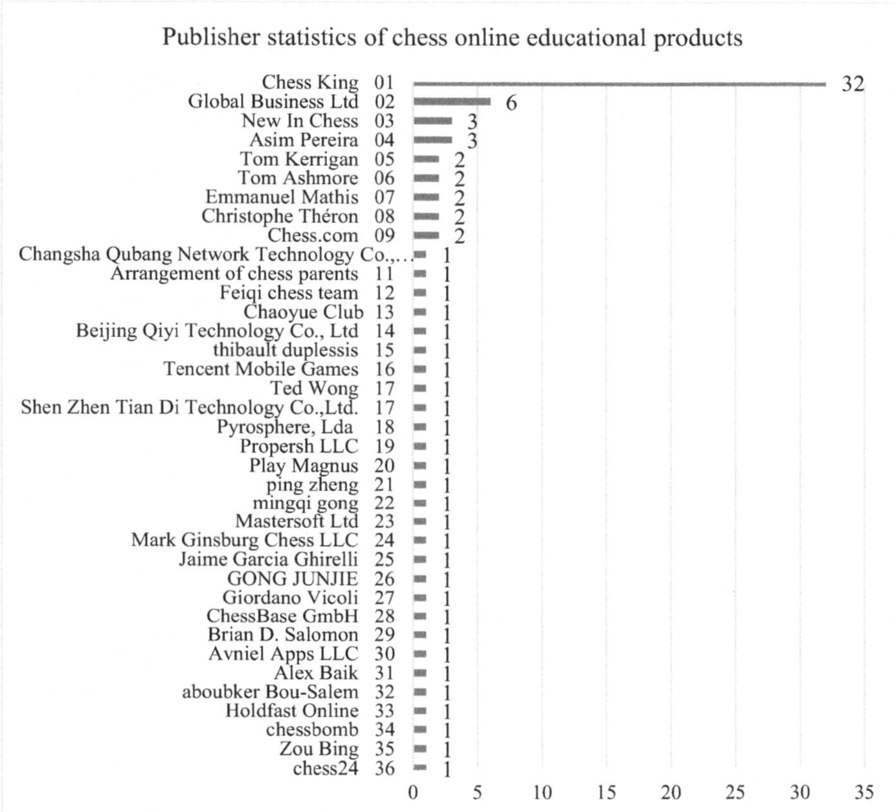

Fig. 3. Publisher statistics of chess online educational products

3.5 APP Category

There were 6 kinds of APP, that is, games (65 products), entertainment (3 products), education (3 products), book (2 products), games board (1), sports (1 products). Although the selected apps had educational function, it was still premier game to enter the market in product positioning and promotion.

3.6 Publisher

There were 36 publishers of 82 products, of which chess king had the largest number (32) of development, followed by Global Business Ltd (6 products). There were 27 publishers developing only one product as their main product.

3.7 Ratings and Participants in Ratings

There were 44 products with rating. However, due to the small number of rating people for some products, the rationality of rating needs to be considered. In this study, 18 products with more than 100 ratings were selected for statistics. Among them, the product with the largest number of ratings was Chess.com, with a population of 126410, which was far higher than other products. The highest rated product was chess tiger pro, chess king and chess tactics for beginners, with a rating score of 4.8. The average rating score of all products with more than 100 users was 4.46 (5 points in total). The rating level could reflect the number of all users and active users. Users' rating of chess online educational products was 4.46 on average, with a high degree of recognition, which also laid a foundation for the product itself and content payment (Table 4).

Table 4. Rating and number of participants in rating statistics of chess online educational product

No.	Name	Rating	Number of participants in rating
1	Chess.com	4.6	126410
2	Chess Tiger	4.7	29738
3	国际象棋-Learn Chess	3.4	25633
4	Chess Tiger Pro	4.8	20011
5	Play Magnus—Chess	4.7	3176
6	国际象棋-tChess Pro	4.2	3059
7	Chess Tactics Pro(Puzzles)	4.7	1417
8	Chess for kids	4.2	1271
9	Chess League - professional chess platform	4.1	1186
10	CT-ART 4.0	4.8	725
11	Chess King	4.8	602
12	Lichess	4.2	474
13	马格努斯·卡尔森（Magnus Carlsen）	4.7	282
14	Chess Openings Pro	4.3	271
15	Chess tactics for beginner	4.8	255
16	Chess Openings Explorer	4.1	247
17	Chess from beginner to expert	4.7	130
18	Small Chess Pro	4.5	125

3.8 Content and Function

Products with tactical training had the largest number, products with chess manual and explanation to games come next, the least were products with interesting practice. Tactical training included one-step kill, two-step kill and other king killing exercises, one-way tactical exercises such as flash attack and containment, and comprehensive exercises such as the most appropriate way of various tactical combinations. The explanation to chess manual included book annotation, video explanation, engine analysis and other forms. Private data education was not only about simple statistics of basic data such as the statistics of accuracy of questions, but also more in-depth analysis of data such as the characteristics of different stages in chess. The forum exchange mainly included the exchange and discussion in the process of playing chess, sending private messages, setting up clubs. Interesting exercises referred to chess breaking, continuous capturing, chess changing or capturing. In the competition, it included not only individual creation Championships, wheel games, etc., but also various challenges organized by the platform, as well as online and offline chess king challenges (Fig. 4).

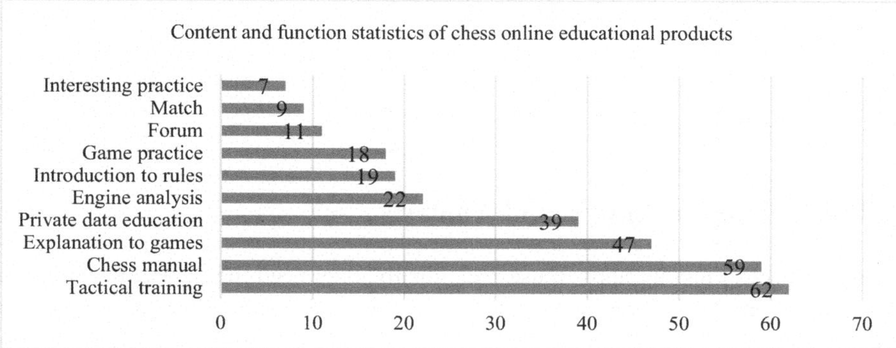

Fig. 4. Content and function statistics of chess online educational products

3.9 Stage

It was relatively similar in the number of chess online educational products in the opening, middle and end games, and many products covered the functions of multiple stages. There were many special products for the opening game, while products which focused on the middle and end games were tactical training, chess manual, explanation to games and engine analysis. Moreover, game practice and match were oriented to the overall stages. It was worth mentioning that the division of the chess game stage was a reference. The transition between the opening and the middle game, and between the middle and the end game were not clear. However, the division of the stages helped players to train more pertinently, and thus improve their chess skills (Table 5).

Table 5. Stage statistics of chess online educational products

Stages	Opening	Middle game	End game
Number	71	75	75

3.10 Level

It showed a decreasing trend for chess online educational products from ABC level to primary level, then to intermediate and senior level, and then to master level, which also basically conformed to the trend of the number of players at all levels as a whole, that is, there were more ABC and primary players, intermediate and senior players were in the middle, and the number of professional players was the least (Table 6).

Although these statistics was not meant to be comprehensive, it provided important findings that could be useful for instructional designers and researchers.

Table 6. Level statistics of chess online educational products

Level	ABC level	Primary level	Intermediate level	Senior level	Master
Number	80	80	74	72	69

4 The Evaluation Rubric and Analysis

For users to select quality apps to use individually, they need the quality resources to do so. This rubric was designed using previously published research while also taking into consideration the changes in chess online education products. This session proposed a chess online educational product evaluation framework, under the guidance of instructional design theory, software evaluation theory, and cultural psychology theory, referring to "A Comprehensive Evaluation Rubric for Assessing Instructional Apps" [8] proposed by Cheng Yuan Lee and Todd Sloan cherner of the coastal University of Carolina and "the evaluation of educational apps domain and dimension design" proposed by Zhao Huichen [9] (Fig. 5).

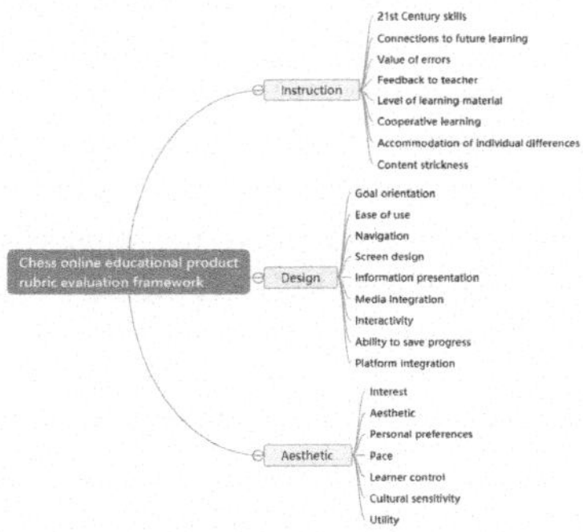

Fig. 5. Chess online educational product evaluation rubric framework

The framework had 3 domains and 24 dimensions, and it aligned to a 5-point Likert scale format so quantitative measures could be established for each dimension. In addition, indicators for the 1-5-point for each dimension were clearly stated to avoid as much ambiguity as possible in the process (Table 7).

The overall framework scores of typical chess online educational products were relatively high. The four kinds of products had a high level of learning materials in instruction, which played an important role in improving user skills and connections to future learning. The differences were mainly reflected in value of errors, feedback to teacher and cooperative learning. In design, it was relatively complete in the dimensions of goal orientation, ease of use, screen design, media integration and interactivity. In aesthetics, although product styles were varied, they were mature in the dimensions of utility, user interest enhancement and learner control. The differences were mainly reflected in cultural sensitivity caused by language. It was worth noting that the above

Table 7. Four categories of chess online educational typical products rubric scores

No	Category	Typical product	Framework scores
1	Overall ecology	Chess.com	120
		Lichess	113
		Chess League	117
		Feiqi Chess	112
2	Video tutorial	Chaoyue Chess	118
		Love Chess	118
		Play Magnus—Chess	107
3	Tactical training	Chess King	112
		Qubang Internet	103
4	Live broadcast	Chess24	111
		Chessbomb	109
		Yizhan	107
		Chisai	107

rubric evaluation results focused on the evaluation of products from the perspective of educational products, and the relevant scores were only referencing within this framework. The purpose was to optimize the content and function of products and improve the quality of online educational products of chess through comparative research.

5 Discussion and Conclusions

In this study, we conducted list method and rubric evaluation to evaluate chess online educational products. By analyzing the collected data, we could draw that chess online educational products began to appear in 2008, and since then the number had increased gradually, reaching the highest in 2016. By 2019, there were 82 chess online educational products from 36 publishers. These products were mainly apps, with rich languages, complete functions and high ratings, covering the opening, middle and end games of chess. Players of different levels can choose according to their needs.

The earliest online chess educational products in China were mainly official websites, personal blogs, etc. mature products started in 2015. In 2016, apps such as Chess League were launched, and then many kinds of chess service management and tactical training functions continued to develop. In 2018, with the development of technology, WeChat small programs such as Feiqi chess and Chaoyue chess were launched. Most of these products are Chinese, few for Chinese and English users. Besides, products can be divided into four categories: overall ecology, video tutorial, tactical training, live broadcast product. With the development of educational informatization, there are two important aspects to improve for chess online educational products.

5.1 Product Positioning

The positioning of chess online educational products needs to excavate the personalized needs of users. Product development is closely related to product positioning. In the process of product upgrading and iteration, publishers need to consider who needs the product to meet, what needs these people have, whether the product meets the needs of the target users, how to achieve the needs, and how to combine the user needs with the features provided. Through the rubric evaluation, it can be found that many products have low scores in the two dimensions of teacher feedback and cooperative learning in education. The product can further consider whether the user is an online autonomous learner, or to seek integration of online and offline, through the construction of the teacher side and other ways to connect the offline traditional teaching and online training, to help teachers timely grasp the progress of students' learning, and promote the communication and feedback between teachers and students. For cooperative learning, whether the product is to activate internal users through the development of new activities or functions, or to attract more other users through the development of multilingual environment and expand communication, is also directly related to the subsequent technical design. In addition, with the increasing number of chess events, it is worth thinking whether to add a standardized unified event release and registration service platform to the overall ecological platform. After clear target positioning, we can further consider whether the components meet the positioning needs, product ease of use, interaction, information presentation, media integration and other issues in technical design. In aesthetics, with the growing maturity of products, according to Maslow's hierarchy needs theory [10], on the basis of meeting the needs of users for product content and function, it will become more and more important for how to excavate product features, constantly excavate and meet the personalized needs of users in the future.

5.2 User Experience

Chess online education products need to improve user experience. User experience is a pure subjective feeling established by users in the process of using products. User status, system performance and environment are three factors that affect user experience. In the future, in the process of product design and development, developers need to further investigate users to understand the use status, system performance and product application environment of target users. For example, whether the user adopts the fragmented mobile learning mode such as subway and public transportation, or prefers the traditional learning in classroom or club environment, whether the user carries out independent learning according to interests, or under the guidance of teachers or parents, according to a certain plan, whether the user can adjust the interface, chessman state, content learning progress, etc. in a personalized way. These users' usage status and application environment information affect the system performance and product promotion of product content settings, content presentation, network environment, payment mode, etc. Therefore, chess online educational products need to be further detailed and in-depth research on the premise of clear product positioning. On this basis, it is necessary to continuously improve and optimize products, enhance user experience, product stickiness and use frequency, to promote the participation and activity of more chess players and improve the level of chess skills.

References

1. Zydney, J.M., Warner, Z.: Mobile apps for science learning: review of research. Comput. Educ. **94**, 1–17 (2015)
2. Analysis on the development trend of online education industry, mobile app gradually becomes the mainstream [DB/OL]. http://www.sohu.com/a/230971860_100155997. Accessed 09 May 2018
3. Ed Tech Developer's Guide: A primer for software developers, startup, and entrepreneurs [DB/OL]. http://tech.ed.gov/developersguide. Accessed 21 Apr 2015
4. Baidu Baike: Online education [EB/OL]. https://baike.baidu.com/item/%E5%9C%A8%E7%BA%BF%E6%95%99%E8%82%B2/460304?fr=aladdin
5. Zhao, H., Lu, X., Zhang, Y.: Theoretical analysis and implementation of educational app evaluation. E-educ. Res. **39**(302(06)), 100–108 (2018)
6. Hsieh, H.-F.: Three approaches to qualitative content analysis. Qual. Health Res. **15**(9), 1277–1288 (2005)
7. Graneheim, U.H., Lundman, B.: Qualitative content analysis in nursing research: concepts, procedures and measures to achieve trustworthiness. Nurse Educ. Today **24**(2), 105–112 (2004)
8. Lee, C.Y., Cherner, T.S.: A comprehensive evaluation rubric for assessing instructional apps. J. Inf. Technol. Educ. Res. **14**, 8–15 (2015)
9. Zhao, H., Lu, X., Zhang, Y.: Theoretical analysis and implementation of educational app evaluation. E-educ. Res. **39**(302(06)), 100–108 (2018)
10. Maslow, F.L., (ed.): Human Potential and Value, pp. 162–264. Huaxia Press, Beijing (1987)

A Review of Open Access Textbook Platforms

Simon K. S. Cheung(✉)

The Open University of Hong Kong, Good Shepherd Street, Homantin, Kowloon, Hong Kong
kscheung@ouhk.edu.hk

Abstract. Open educational resources or OER have been gradually evolved as a major source of learning materials. As one form of OER, open access textbooks can be used as official textbooks for classroom-based learning as well as online learning and distance learning. Through a review of six open access textbook platforms, this paper investigates the operation model of open access textbooks, including their set-up, sourcing and updating of contents, open licenses, usages, review and quality assurance. It is revealed that open access textbook platforms were usually initiated by universities and non-profit organizations, partnering with philanthropic foundations and government bodies. The 5Rs (retain, re-use, revise, re-mix and re-distribute) provision via open licenses is the distinguished advantage of open access textbooks, especially in enabling adaptation to cater for specific teaching and learning needs. Peer review is the common practices for ensuring the quality of textbooks. It is evidenced that open access textbooks together with other forms of OER have successfully driven the effective sharing of educational resources to make education well accessible to all.

Keywords: Open educational resources · Open access textbooks · Open licenses · Textbooks · Learning materials

1 Introduction

In the past two decades, the internet penetration has been increasing in different parts of the world, from 8.0% in 2001 to 53.6% in 2019, in percentage of global population using the Internet [1]. Along with the increasing use of digitized online materials, the growing popularity of social media and networking tools, and the evolving open and sharing culture, vast amount of online resources have been developed and provided to the public via the Internet for free access. On average, 1.7 MB of data are created per second by each person and several quintillion bytes of data are created in the Internet every day [2]. Some of them are of educational nature, such as open access textbooks, open online courses and online dictionaries. These open educational resources or OER are free and openly available via the Internet. According to the Organization for Economic Cooperation and Development, OER is defined as the "digitized materials offered freely and openly for educators, students, and self-learners to use and re-use for teaching, learning and research" [3]. It is widely recognized that OER have many advantages and benefits [4–6].

S. K. S. Cheung et al. (Eds.): ICBL 2020, LNCS 12218, pp. 114–125, 2020.
https://doi.org/10.1007/978-3-030-51968-1_10

Similar to other online resources, OER have been expanding at a compound rate. The driving force comes from both students and teachers. Nowadays, students used to retrieve relevant learning materials from the Internet. As reported by the author in some recent studies, OER have been well perceived by most university students as useful resources for learning purposes, despite some concerns on whether the contents are accurate and up-to-dated [7–9]. On the other hand, software tools are well available for teachers to create their own teaching and learning materials in electronic forms. Some of them are open-source software that are free to use. Teachers have become accustomed to create and share their own created teaching materials as OER in the Internet, especially as the copyright issues can be legitimately resolved by open licensing, such as the Creative Commons [10, 11].

It is undeniable that OER have been widely used by teachers and students, not only in higher education but also in primary and secondary education. In general, there are four categories of OER, namely, open courseware and course materials, open online courses and tutorials, open e-books and e-journals, and open-source learning tools [12]. Open courseware are the self-contained course materials for a course of study. Open online courses are online courses delivered via the Internet, including massive open online courses and online tutorials. Open e-books and e-journals are basically e-books and e-journals that are available for open access. These open access e-books cover textbooks and reference books. Open-source learning tools broadly cover online learning platforms, online dictionaries, online plagiarism-checkers and other online software tools that support teaching and learning.

As one form of OER, open access textbooks can be used as official textbooks for classroom-based learning as well as online learning and distance learning. Besides offering open and free usage, open access textbooks allow adaptation. Through the open licensing arrangement which defines different options on revision, re-mixing, and redistribution, open access textbooks effectively cater for diversified learning needs. A number of open access textbook platforms have been developed. College Open Textbooks Collaborative [13], OpenStax CNX [14], OER Commons [15], and Open Textbook Library [16] are some well-known open access textbook platforms. In Hong Kong, the first open access textbook platform, called the Open Textbooks for Hong Kong, was launched in early 2016 [17, 18]. Many open access textbooks have fulfilled the required academic standards and syllabus, which are especially important for primary and secondary education.

This paper reviews a number of representative open access textbook platforms, and then investigates the typical operation model of open access textbooks. Six platforms are selected for review, namely, OpenStax CNX [14], OER Commons [15], Open Textbook Library [16], Open Textbooks for Hong Kong [18], BCcampus [19] and Wikibooks [20]. Based on the review, a typical operation model of open access textbooks, covering the initial set-up, sourcing and updating of textbook contents, licensing options and modes of usage, and review and quality assurance, is derived. Some common practices of these open access textbook platforms are discussed. The rest of this paper is organized as follows. Section 2 is an overview of open access textbooks. Section 3 shows a review of the above-mentioned open access textbook platforms. Section 4 describes the typical operation model of open access textbooks. Section 5 briefly concludes this paper.

2 Open Access Textbooks

Open access textbooks are essentially one specific form of OER, which can be used as official textbooks for teaching and learning. Besides, they are by nature e-books that provide text-based contents as well as media-rich contents such as audio and video clips, animated features and interactive learning objects, which help enrich learning experience. Like the traditional printed textbooks, open access textbooks are coherent in contents, and are aligned to the required academic standards, subject syllabus and curricular guidelines.

Open access textbooks offer many advantages over the printed textbooks [21–23]. Open access textbooks are available for online access. They can be downloaded for offline usage, and or printed as hard copies. The textbook contents can be openly and freely contributed by the general public. This enables knowledge creation and sharing. The textbook contents can be revised, re-used, and re-mixed in order to cater for diversified learning needs. Since the revised and re-mixed textbooks can be re-distributed through the Internet, subsequent revisions and reviews can be deployed in a quick and efficient way. Also, interactive learning objects, multimedia and animated features can be easily incorporated.

In early 2010s, open access textbooks started to evolve. In 2012, Connexions or CNX (renamed as OpenStax CNX in 2014) started to offer peer-reviewed and open-licensed textbooks that are freely available in digital form, while also providing low-cost printed version [14]. Similarly, a number of open access textbook platforms and projects were gradually established. They include Open Textbook Library [16], Open Textbooks for Hong Kong [18], BCcampus [19] and Global Text Project [24]. There are also projects and platforms, originally offering online learning resources, but not purposefully used as official textbooks. These platforms also maintain a repository of open access textbooks. OER Commons was launched as a digital library for open-licensed educational contents in 2007, where open access textbooks were offered some years later [15]. Other examples include Wikibooks [20], Project Gutenberg [25], Saylor Academy [26] and MIT Open Courseware [27]. Flat World Knowledge originally provided open access textbooks that are free for online usage. Owing to financial concerns, in 2012, they changed to offer their textbooks at affordable prices, no longer delivering free open access textbooks. [28].

To enable the operation of open access textbooks, such as openly allowing others to use, re-use, re-mix, and re-distribute the book contents, the copyright issues need to be properly handled, and the provision of open licensing such as Creative Commons is a solution to solve these issues effectively.

The idea of open licensing is to enable one to grant the rights to use, re-use, re-mix and re-distribute their creative works to others. In 2001, Lessig who is a law professor in Harvard University found a non-profit organization, called Creative Commons, dedicated to building a globally-accessible public commons of knowledge and culture [10]. It defines a number of open licensing options for open access contents such as open access textbooks. These open licensing options, called Creative Commons or CC licenses, provide a free, simple and standardized way to grant copyright permissions for creative and academic works, while ensuring proper attribution, and allow others to copy, distribute and make use of those works.

According to Creative Commons, there are four attributes for open licensing. They are attribution, non-commercial, no-derivatives and share-alike, denoted by the codes BY, NC, ND and SA respectively. Attribution (BY) allows others to copy, distribute, display and make derivative work if giving credits to the author. Non-commercial (NC) means that others may copy, distribute, display and make derivative work only for non-commercial purposes. No-derivatives (ND) allows others to copy, distribute and display but not to make derivative work. Share-alike (SA) means that others may distribute work under a license that is identical to the license governing the original creative work. There are six different possible combinations of the four attributes, BY, NC, ND and SA. These combinations become the possible open licensing options [10], as follows.

- CC BY (attribution) : the rights for others to distribute, re-mix, tweak, and build upon the author's work as long as they credit the author.
- CC BY-SA (attribution + share-alike) : the rights for others to re-mix, tweak, and build upon the author's work as long as they credit the author and license new creations under the identical terms.
- CC BY-ND (attribution + no-derivatives) : the rights for others to re-use the author's work for any purpose, but not to be shared in an adapted form, as long as they credit the author.
- BY-NC (attribution + non-commercial) : the rights for others to re-mix, tweak, and build upon the author's work non-commercially as long as they credit the author, while not necessarily to license new creations on the same terms.
- BY-NC-SA (attribution + non-commercial + share-alike) : the rights to re-mix, tweak, and build upon the author's work non-commercially as long as they credit the author and license new creations under the identical terms.
- BY-NC-ND (attribution + non-commercial + no-derivatives) : the rights to use and share the author's work as long as they credit the author, but not to change the author's work in any way or use them commercially.

The CC licenses have been widely adopted in open access textbooks as well as other forms of OER and open licensed materials. At least 1.4 billion works have been licensed under Creative Commons [29].

3 Review of Open Access Textbooks

This section shows a review of six open access textbook platforms or projects, namely, OpenStax CNX [14], OER Commons [15], Open Textbook Library [16], Open Textbooks for Hong Kong [18], BCcampus [19] and Wikibooks [20].

3.1 OpenStax CNX

Based at the Rice University, OpenStax CNX is a non-profit organization, originally found as the Connexions or CNX project in 1999, to provide an online repository of OER for one to contribute and share their educational resources and materials [14]. Connexions started to provide open access textbooks in 2012. Online access to the textbooks is free, while the printed version can be available at low cost. Connexions was subsequently renamed as OpenStax CNX. All their textbooks are peer-reviewed, and open-licensed under the Creative Commons.

Currently, OpenStax CNX provides over 2,000 open access textbooks in six major subject areas, namely, arts, business, humanities, mathematics and statistics, science and technology, and social sciences [14]. They are available for online access or download. Once registered in the system, teachers can have access to all the textbook contents and teaching materials for teachers. Prior verification of the teacher status is required. Adaptation is allowed, where teachers can revise and re-mix the contents, and incorporate them into other teaching materials to cater for specific teaching and learning needs. They can share the adapted, revised and re-mixed contents. According to OpenStax CNX, the textbook contents should be licensed as CC BY, being enabled to be as reusable as possible.

Quality assurance is emphasized by OpenStax CNX. All open access textbooks are developed and reviewed by educational practitioners to ensure that the contents are accurate, readable, understandable, and appropriately organized for a course of study. OpenStax CNX aims to maintain the online version of textbooks always up-to-date. Users (teachers and students) are welcome to help review the textbook contents and submit errata suggestions. Revision of textbook contents would be made, whenever pedagogically required. Small revisions are usually deployed as online updates. New edition of a textbook would be produced, whenever there are significant development and revisions. All revisions need to be reviewed by relevant experts and educational practitioners in the subject area.

OpenStax CNX is a non-profit educational initiative at Rice University, believing that educational resources can be shared, re-used, inter-connected and continually enriched. Not only supported by Rice University, it has been substantially sponsored by philanthropic foundations such as the William and Flora Hewlett Foundation, and Bill and Melinda Gates Foundation.

3.2 OER Commons

OER Commons was established by a non-profit organization, the Institute for the Study of Knowledge Management in Education, in 2007. It was initially launched as a digital library of open-licensed educational resources, which include OER and other instructional materials, by aggregating the educational resources and standardizing metadata from their providers [15]. Several years later, it started to offer open access textbooks. The collected educational resources, including open access textbooks, are licensed under the Creative Commons.

OER Commons offers over 200 open access textbooks in typical subject areas, such as arts and humanities, life sciences, physical sciences and social sciences, from the affiliated resource providers. These resource providers are open access textbook platforms, such as OpenStax CNX [14] and BCcampus [19], and universities and organizations offering open access textbooks. The textbooks are available for online access and download. They are open-licensed under Creative Commons. Teachers are enabled to design their own curriculums and create their own textbook contents and teaching materials, in order to adjust their pedagogies to cater for specific teaching and learning needs. They can openly share their created and modified book contents and teaching materials with others.

OER Commons welcome contributions of open textbook contents. The contributed contents are curated and reviewed for quality assurance and alignment to the required academic standards. Teachers can conduct reviews and provide comments on the textbook contents. Teaching quality can be improved through the sharing of teaching practices. Workshops are provided to help teachers develop curriculums and create textbook contents and teaching materials.

OER Commons was established by the Institute for the Study of Knowledge Management in Education with the support of William and Flora Hewlett Foundation. The Institute establishes alliances between trusted resource providers, and strategic relationships and partnership with other organizations to advance open education and sustain the development of OER Commons.

3.3 Open Textbook Library

The Open Textbook Library was initiated by the University of Minnesota, aiming to provide open access textbooks which can be used, re-used, and re-distributed [16]. The textbooks are freely available for online access or download, while the printed version is available at low cost.

At present, the Open Textbook Library provides about 700 open access textbooks under 14 subject areas, such as engineering, humanities, medicine, sciences and social sciences. These textbooks come from individual authors, open textbook platforms such as OpenStax CNX [14] and BCcampus [19], and universities and organizations offering open access textbooks. The textbooks are open-licensed under the Creative Commons. The Open Textbook Library commits to 5Rs (retain, re-use, revise, re-mix and re-distribute) provision that requires authors to license their contributed contents in CC BY, whilst not accepting CC BY-ND or CC BY-SA-ND. This encourages re-use, re-mix, and re-distribution of textbook contents.

The Open Textbook Library has set out guidelines on the open access textbooks. Besides open-licensed under the Creative Commons, the textbooks must be self-contained and organized as a complete book in portable formats, such as PDF and ePub. They must be in use in some higher education institutions, scholarly societies and professional organizations. They should be original textbooks that are not any derivative of other textbooks, although some exceptions are allowed. Peer review of textbook contents is another quality assurance measure in the Open Textbook Library. About 60% of textbooks have been reviewed.

The Open Textbook Library was established by the University of Minnesota, as a commitment to open education. It is supported by the Open Textbook Network whose members are universities and institutions advocating open education and OER, and philanthropic foundations such as the William and Flora Hewlett Foundation. Some open access textbook platforms, such as OpenStax CNX [14] and BCcampus [19] also offer support by sharing their textbooks.

3.4 Open Textbooks for Hong Kong

The Open Textbooks for Hong Kong project was established by the Open University of Hong Kong in 2012, aiming to provide a platform of open access textbooks for primary, secondary and higher education in Hong Kong [17, 18]. Open-licensed under the Creative Commons and in portable formats such as PDF and ePub, the textbooks are available for online access or download.

The Open Textbooks for Hong Kong provides a complete set of English language textbooks for primary and secondary education in Hong Kong. For post-secondary and higher education, there are 126 open access textbooks, under six subject areas, namely, arts and humanities, business, education, information technology, science and engineering, and social sciences. Some of these textbooks are contributed by the Open University of Hong Kong. Some others are sourced from open textbook platforms such as OpenStax CNX [14] and BCcampus [19], and universities and organizations offering open access textbooks.

The Open Textbooks for Hong Kong has set out guidelines for assuring quality of the open access textbooks. The textbooks for primary and secondary education must follow the curricular guidelines and subject syllabus in Hong Kong. They are required to seek the Education Bureau of Hong Kong for approval. Only approved textbooks are accepted. On the other hand, the open access textbooks for post-secondary and higher education must be peer-reviewed.

The Open Textbooks for Hong Kong was initiated by the Open University of Hong Kong, as a commitment to provide education for all. A significant amount of funding was obtained from the Hong Kong Jockey Club for the initial set-up, also including the recruitment of professional authors and editor to develop the first batch of open access textbooks for primary and secondary education. Ongoing development relies on volunteers who help contribute and review textbook contents.

3.5 BCcampus

Funded by the British Columbia Ministry of Advanced Education, Skills and Training and the Hewlett Foundation, BCcampus was established in 2012 to provide open-licensed textbooks for post-secondary students in British Columbia [19]. It aims to make the post-secondary education in British Columbia more accessible at low cost through the use of open-licensed textbooks and OER. All the textbooks are open-licensed under the Creative Commons.

BCcampus maintains over 300 open access textbooks under typical subject areas, such as business, engineering, law and mathematics. They are contributed by teachers of post-secondary institutions in British Columbia. The contents are newly created, or re-created from other open access textbooks and OER. BCcampus commits to the 5Rs (retain, re-use, revise, re-mix and re-distribute) provision for their textbooks. The textbooks can be adapted to cater for different curriculum and specific teaching and learning needs. They are delivered online or in printed forms.

In BCcampus, all textbooks are created or re-created by professional teachers. The textbook contents must be peer reviewed for quality assurance. BCcampus encourages adaptation and evolution of teaching and learning practices among post-secondary institutions in British Columbia, which would help foster continuous improvement and innovation for post-secondary education.

BCcampus was a key initiative for post-secondary education, made by the British Columbia Ministry of Advanced Education, Skills and Training. Besides funded by the British Columbia government, BCcampus is financially supported by the Hewlett Foundation on specific projects.

3.6 Wikibooks

Wikibooks was established by Wikimedia Foundation as a platform of open access books in 2003. It welcomes open contribution of book contents, and encourages collaborative development of book contents. All contents are open-licensed under the Creative Commons. The books are intended for learning purposes, so the collection mainly covers textbooks and instructional books.

Wikibooks maintains a collection of open access books under seven subject areas, namely, computing, humanities, sciences, mathematics, social sciences, language, and engineering. There is a separate category of books for kids under the age of 12, called Wikijunior. Like Wikipedia, Wikibooks delivers the open access books as webpages, while allowing to download the contents in PDF format. At present, the book contents in Wikibooks amount to over 85,000 pages. According to Wikibooks, the authors maintain the property right to their contributed contents, while welcoming others to re-use, revise, re-mix, and share derivative contents. All books must be open-licensed under the Creative Commons as CC BY-SA to ensure that the contents can always be reproduced or re-distributed.

In principle, there is no restriction for one to contribute book contents, as long as the nature of the contributed book contents are instructional. Fictional books and non-fictional books that are not instructional are not accepted. Verbatim copies of pre-existing works are not permitted whilst annotated texts are allowed. Guidelines are set out in the "deletion policy". Book contents will be deleted if they are too narrowly defined or do not have a decent definition, or they are not meaningful content, or they would no longer be educational resources.

Wikibooks was initiated and hosted by the Wikimedia Foundation which is a non-profit and charitable organization dedicated to the development and distribution of multilingual contents, and to openly provide the contents free of charge. Its operation is sustained by voluntarism and donation.

4 Operation Model of Open Access Textbooks

Based on the review of OpenStax CNX, OER Commons, Open Textbook Library, Open Textbooks for Hong Kong, BCcampus and Wikibooks, this section describes the typical operation model of open access textbooks, which include the initial set-up of an open access textbook platform, sourcing and updating of textbook contents, open-licenses and the 5Rs (retain, re-use, revise, re-mix and re-distribute) provision of textbook contents, and review and quality assurance.

Initial Set-up of an Open Access Textbook Platform. Open access textbook platforms are usually initiated by universities, institutions, governmental and non-government organizations. For example, the OpenStax CNX was initiated by the Rice University, the Open Textbook Library by the University of Minnesota, the Open Textbooks for Hong Kong by the Open University of Hong Kong, the BCcampus by the Ministry of Advanced Education, Skills and Training of British Columbia, the OER Commons by the Institute for the Study of Knowledge Management in Education, and the Wikibooks by the Wikimedia Foundation. They are committed to providing open access textbooks and OER for the general public, and have common belief to promote open contribution and sharing of open access textbooks and other OER through the appropriate open-licensing options. Significant financial supports from foundations and charities are required, for example the William and Flora Hewlett Foundation, and Bill and Melinda Gates Foundation.

Sourcing and Updating of Textbook Contents. There are a number of channels to sourcing open access textbook contents. First, the contents are directly contributed by authors. Second, the contents are adapted and re-used from other open licensed book contents and/or OER. Third, the contents are directly shared from other open access textbook platforms, such as OER Commons, and Open Textbook Library. There are also cases that some textbook publishers would like to contribute some of their textbooks as open access textbooks. It is emphasized in the open access platforms to keep the open access textbooks up-to-dated. Minor revisions on textbook contents are usually made as errata. New releases or editions of the textbooks will be produced whenever major revisions are made. Like typical textbooks, all revisions need to be reviewed or verified before deployment.

Open Licenses and the 5Rs of Textbook Contents. As open access textbooks are by nature OER that are openly available for the general public, the textbook contents must be open licensed to enable open accesses. Almost all open access textbook platforms adopt the open licensing options under the Creative Commons. Besides open-licensed for free usage, many open access textbook platforms encourage their textbook contents to be maximally shared with the 5Rs (retain, re-use, revise, re-mix and re-distribute) provision, for example, OpenStax CNX, OER Commons, Open Textbook Library, Open Textbooks for Hong Kong, and Wikibooks. The OpenStax CNX, Open Textbook Library and Wikibooks even explicitly require the textbook contents to be open-licensed under the Creative Commons as CC BY or CC BY-SA, while not accepting CC BY-ND or CC BY-SA-ND.

Review and Quality Assurance of Textbook Contents. Like other OER, open access textbooks openly welcome contributions from the public. Inevitably, there are valid concerns on how to assure the quality of the textbook contents. In many open access textbook platforms, there are review mechanisms and measures or assuring the quality of the textbook contents. Peer review is adopted by almost all open access textbook platforms. It may not be guaranteed that all the open access textbooks in a platform are fully reviewed. For example, in Open Textbook Library, about 60% of textbooks have been reviewed. Some open access textbook platforms, such as OpenStax CNX, OER

Commons, and BCcampus, require the review to be conducted by professional teachers. The Open Textbooks for Hong Kong even requires that the open access textbooks for primary and secondary education must obtain the prior approval from the Education Bureau of Hong Kong. In Wikibooks, guidelines are set out to remove unqualified textbook contents.

5 Conclusion

For over a decade, open access textbooks have gradually evolved into a major source of textbooks. It is widely accepted that open access textbooks as well as other OER are useful for learning purposes. Initiated by universities, institutions, governmental and non-government organizations, and supported by charities and foundations, many open access textbook platforms have become stabilized to provide reliable textbooks, openly for one to use, re-use, re-mix and re-distribute. The adoption of open access textbooks is essentially a revolutionary change in practices. The success of these open access textbook platforms clearly shows that the open and sharing culture has become mature and earned much support from the general public.

Through a review of six well-established open access textbook platforms, namely, OpenStax CNX, OER Commons, Open Textbook Library, Open Textbooks for Hong Kong, BCcampus and Wikibooks, this paper investigates the typical operation of open access textbooks, including the initial set-up, sourcing of textbook contents, provision of open licenses, and review and quality assurance measures. Among these successful textbook platforms, there are many similarities in operation as well as common belief on the sharing of resources. They commit to advocate the open sharing of educational resources. Open contributions of textbook contents are welcomed. Open licensing is emphasized, and most of them adopt open licensing options that promote maximum sharing, such as CC BY and CC BY-SA. The 5Rs (retain, re-use, revise, re-mix and re-distribute) provision of the textbook contents are their common belief. Quality assurance are emphasized, and peer review is their common practices for ensuring the quality and standards of the open access textbooks.

The sharing of educational resources over the Internet is now a common practice. Open access textbooks, as well as other forms of OER such as massive open online courses and open courseware, have become a driving force for making education well accessible to all. This resembles a paradigm shift for intellectual properties to move towards open access and sharing. Good examples include open-source software such as Linux and Android, and open platforms such as Google. It is favourably believed that open access textbooks would be the order of the day soon.

References

1. Statistics ITU: Global ICT Developments, 2001–2019, International Telecommunication Union (2020). https://www.itu.int/en/ITU-D/Statistics/Pages/default.aspx
2. DOMO, Data Never Sleeps 6.0 (2019). https://www.domo.com/assets/downloads/18_domo_data-never-sleeps-6+verticals.pdf

3. OECD: Giving Knowledge for Free: The Emergence of Open Education Resources, Centre for Educational Research and Innovation. Organization for Economic Cooperation and Development, Paris (2007)
4. Miao, F., Mishra, S., McGreal, R.: Open Educational Resources: Policy, Costs and Transformation. UNESCO, Paris (2016)
5. Krelja Kurelovic, E.: Advantages and limitations of usage of open educational resources in small countries. Int. J. Res. Educ. Sci. **2**(1), 136–142 (2016)
6. Weller, M., de los Arcos, B., Farrow, R., Pitt, R., McAndrew, P.: What can OER do for me? Evaluating the claims for OER. In: Jhangiani, R.S., Biswas-Diener, R. (eds.) Open: The Philosophy and Practices that are Revolutionizing Education and Science, pp. 67–77. Ubiquity Press, London (2017)
7. Cheung, S.K.S.: Distance-learning students' perception on the usefulness of open educational resources. In: Cheung, S.K.S., Kwok, L., Ma, W.W.K., Lee, L., Yang, H. (eds.) ICBL 2017. LNCS, vol. 10309, pp. 389–399. Springer, Cham (2017). https://doi.org/10.1007/978-3-319-59360-9_34
8. Cheung, S.K.S.: Perceived usefulness of open educational resources between full-time and distance-learning students. In: Cheung, S.K.S., Kwok, L., Kubota, K., Lee, L., Tokito, J. (eds.) ICBL 2018. LNCS, vol. 10949, pp. 357–367. Springer, Cham (2018). https://doi.org/10.1007/978-3-319-94505-7_29
9. Cheung, S.K.S.: A study on the university students' use of open educational resources for learning purposes. In: Cheung, S.K.S., Jiao, J., Lee, L.-K., Zhang, X., Li, K.C., Zhan, Z. (eds.) ICTE 2019. CCIS, vol. 1048, pp. 146–155. Springer, Singapore (2019). https://doi.org/10.1007/978-981-13-9895-7_13
10. Creative Commons. Website of Creative Commons (2019). http://creativecommons.org
11. Yuen, K.S., Chow, L., Cheung, S.K.S., Li, K.C., Tsang, E.Y.M.: Overcoming copyright hurdles in the development of learning materials in the digital era. In: Li, K.C., Wang, F.L., Yuen, K.S., Cheung, Simon K.S., Kwan, R. (eds.) ICT 2012. CCIS, vol. 302, pp. 190–200. Springer, Heidelberg (2012). https://doi.org/10.1007/978-3-642-31398-1_17
12. Cheung, S.K.S., Li, K.C., Yuen, K.S.: An overview of open education resources for higher education. In: Lam, J., Li, K.C., Cheung, S.K.S., Wang, F.L. (eds.) ICT 2013. CCIS, vol. 407, pp. 26–34. Springer, Heidelberg (2013). https://doi.org/10.1007/978-3-642-45272-7_3
13. Website of College Open Textbooks Collaborative (2020). http://www.collegeopentextbooks.org
14. Website of OpenStax CNX (2020). https://openstax.org
15. Website of OER Commons (2020). https://www.oercommons.org
16. Website of Open Textbook Library 2020). https://open.umn.edu/opentextbooks
17. Cheung, S.K.S.: The open textbooks for Hong Kong: from conceptualization to implementation. In: Cheung, S.K.S., Kwok, L., Shang, J., Wang, A., Kwan, R. (eds.) ICBL 2016. LNCS, vol. 9757, pp. 150–160. Springer, Cham (2016). https://doi.org/10.1007/978-3-319-41165-1_14
18. Website of Open Textbooks for Hong Kong (2020). http://www.opentextbooks.org.hk
19. Website of BCcampus (2020). https://bccampus.ca
20. Website of Wikibooks (2020). https://en.wikibooks.org/wiki/Main_Page
21. Cheung, S.K.S., Yuen, K.S., Li, K.C., Tsang, E.Y.M., Wong, A.: Open access textbooks: opportunities and challenges. In: Li, K.C., Wang, F.L., Yuen, K.S., Cheung, S.K.S., Kwan, R. (eds.) ICT 2012. CCIS, vol. 302, pp. 201–210. Springer, Heidelberg (2012). https://doi.org/10.1007/978-3-642-31398-1_18
22. Tsang, E.Y.M., Yuen, K.S., Li, K.C., C, S.K.S.: Designing open textbooks for effective teaching and learning. In: Lam, J., Li, K.C., Cheung, S.K.S., Wang, F.L. (eds.) ICT 2013. CCIS, vol. 407, pp. 43–55. Springer, Heidelberg (2013). https://doi.org/10.1007/978-3-642-45272-7_5

23. Cheung, K.S., Yuen, K.S., Li, K.C., Tsang, E., Wong, A.: Open textbooks : engaging education stakeholders to share learning resources. Int. J. Ser. Stand. **10**(4), 225–239 (2015)
24. Website of Global Text Project (2020). http://globaltext.terry.uga.edu/books
25. Website of Project Gutenberg (2020). https://www.gutenberg.org
26. Website of Saylor Academy (2020). https://www.saylor.org
27. Website of MIT Open Courseware (2020). https://ocw.mit.edu/index.htm
28. Website of Flat World Knowledge (2020). https://catalog.flatworldknowledge.com
29. Website of the State of Creative Commons (2020). https://stateof.creativecommons.org
30. Website of Wikipedia (2020). https://www.wikipedia.org

Students' Assessment of a Communication-Oriented E-Learning Platform

Yoko Hirata(✉) and Yoshihiro Hirata

Hokkai-Gakuen University, 1-40, Asahimachi 4 chome, Toyohiraku, Sapporo, Japan
hira@eli.hokkai-s-u.ac.jp, hirata@hgu.jp

Abstract. E-learning packaged platforms have become highly popular in Japanese tertiary English education as tools to assist students with completing standardized English certifications such as TOEIC and IELTS. However, little research has been conducted into the experiences of students with newer communication-oriented e-learning platforms. This paper assesses a class of Japanese undergraduate students who completed a year-long course of English study which made extensive use of one such e-learning platform. Students were surveyed regarding the benefits and drawbacks of their e-learning experiences, including the impacts on their overall English abilities and their opinions about the platform. The findings show that students primarily expressed appreciation for the increased opportunity to expand their learning with well-organized and more contextually diverse content. The primary drawbacks included some students finding the difficulty level to be inappropriately high. The results also give instructors valuable insights into how to incorporate communication-oriented e-learning platforms into their classrooms.

Keywords: E-learning · Japanese students · Blended language learning

1 Introduction

As a result of numerous improvements in efficiently and convenience made possible by computer technology, online learning options have become vital additions to universities and other educational institutions the world over. With respect to language learning in particular, e-learning is believed to give students a deeper wealth of language learning opportunities beyond the usual the classroom schedule [1, 2]. Japan is no exception when it comes to experimenting with e-learning, with some research claiming that "[E]-learning is being carried out in all levels of schooling, especially in higher education" [3]. Japan remains very much behind when it comes to overall adoption of these new methods [4]. However, when it comes to English language learning, *blended learning* has become fairly normalised in higher education settings. This includes online activities included simultaneously during regular face-to-face classes, as well as assigned for homework [5]. In addition to open or free online learning resources, web and mobile based commercial e-learning platforms have also come into widespread use. These systems make it possible for educational organizations to provide students with distance learning, online

S. K. S. Cheung et al. (Eds.): ICBL 2020, LNCS 12218, pp. 126–135, 2020.
https://doi.org/10.1007/978-3-030-51968-1_11

collaboration with students at different campuses, and autonomous self-study [6]. The obvious benefits for students include easy and convenient access to learning resources anytime from anywhere. For teachers, it enables managing and grading students' progress with relative ease, owing to many processes being automated. Varying from platform to platform, some of drawbacks might include the inability for instructors to customise the content, and students being unable to self-motivate, either due to the monotony of the content or other criticisms. Customisable platforms are vital for different students with different educational background and abilities. Where these platforms are specifically language learning oriented, they are most commonly used as practical training for the preparation of taking standardised tests, often necessary when applying for certain careers or graduate programmes [7].

In Japan, packaged e-learning platforms have become highly popular among students taking English courses in tertiary organisations as tools to assist students with completing standardised English certifications, such as TOIEC, IELTS, and other supplementary materials. These materials expand students' English learning opportunities and help familiarise them with the expectations of their future employers. However, it remains common to have students work on these programmes in lockstep without having the flexibility to choose what lessons or topics to focus on. This drawback is among others that are well understood by researchers, but the benefits remain much more numerous and pronounced [3, 8] . When conducting this research Wang et al. [3] consider the following to be the most important consideration:

> "It is clear that when e-learning is employed, learners' learning devices, learners' learning styles, their preferred learning time and other learning habits should be taken into consideration. Fully understanding students' e-learning habits should help e-learning teachers design an appropriate and effective e-learning program" (p. 222).

Studies have shown that investigation of students' preferences, backgrounds, and different opinions on the use of computers in language learning is crucial knowledge for teachers to be able to provide online education successfully [9, 10]. Nonetheless, investigations of Japanese students' own evaluations of packaged e-learning platforms remain sparse. A previous study on Japanese students' perceptions of a similar e-learning platform as the one used in the Fpresent study suggests that different students success with e-learning varies according to their individual needs and preferences [7], a result which is in accordance with similar findings by Smart and Cappel [8]. In addition, students' perceptions were strongly influenced by their previous language learning experiences [7] and their own proficiency levels [9]. Furthermore, Japanese students lack a great deal of verbal communication training since throughout their school years there is a persistent emphasis on standardised entrance examinations focused on grammar, vocabulary, and reading ability [11]. Therefore, those students who remain passionate about learning English tend to be eager to develop these skills above all else [12]. As yet, little research has been conducted into the experiences of students with newer communication-oriented e-learning platforms in Japan. There is a need for research concerning how these platforms might need to be developed and presented differently, for these students and others who have a strong desire to improve their communication skills.

2 The Study

2.1 Purpose

The primary aim of this study was to investigate how a class of Japanese students, who otherwise lacked substantial prior English speaking and online language learning experience, perceived a specific communication-oriented e-learning platform. Based on similar blended learning research conducted by Kobayashi and Little [9], students in this study were surveyed in order to provide answers to the following research questions:

1. What do students consider to be the benefits and drawbacks of the communication-oriented e-learning platform with respect to their own learning experiences and progress?
2. How do the students perceive the benefits and drawbacks of the platform in terms of its design, functionality, ease of use, etc.?

Answering these questions may help instructors develop their own frameworks for assessing whether a given e-learning platform is appropriate for their communication-oriented blended learning classrooms, and how to introduce them to students.

3 Procedure and Settings

3.1 Participants and Settings

The participants were fifteen full-time second year male students at a Japanese university, majoring in electronics and information engineering, and life science and technology. Through their studies, the students are all sufficiently computer savvy. In addition, all the students are experienced with smartphones. They are also accustomed to the almost exclusively pen-and-paper lecture-style language classrooms typical to Japanese secondary schools. In these classrooms, the focus is on training for examinations and speaking opportunities are very limited [13]. All the students had learned English for seven years and had attained a beginners' or a lower-intermediate level of proficiency. While students did have various amounts of experiencing using digital resources and e-learning systems, none of the students had prior experience working with online language learning in their classrooms or beyond. As a result, only a small number of students were particularly enthusiastic about the online component of the course – an experience mirrored by Kobayashi & Little [9] in their research.

3.2 Course Description

The class, in which the present research was conducted, was scheduled for one and a half hours each week in a computer room during a 15-week, two semester-long elective English courses, as a part of students' general education requirement. These courses are based on a blended learning structure combining face-to-face conventional teacher-directed instruction with an accompanying textbook, and an e-learning module. These courses are designed to encourage students to improve their speaking ability and expand their lexical and grammatical skills based on communicative learning methods. These courses are among the choices students have for their last compulsory English course that they will take as part of their regular university programmes. Therefore, they play an important role in determining how students will perform in pursuit of their engineering careers. Students were required to work on the e-learning platform both inside and outside the classroom.

3.3 Platform Description

The e-learning platform used in this study is called 'Business Speaking' [14] which provides a wide variety of English language learning exercises and practical activities. In this platform, students engage in various realistic business situations such as attending formal meetings and negotiations, making business phone calls, and conducting interviews. In order to extend students' vocabulary and expand their comprehensive knowledge of business English, these exercises cover more than 600 English expressions typically used in business situations. This platform contains 30 lessons in total, with each lesson estimated to take approximately 45 to 60 min to work through. The lessons include a variety of fundamental communicative functions which are vital for university students to acquire before they graduate from university. Examples of these functions include, agreeing and disagreeing, showing interest in other people, exchanging information euphemistically, as well as understanding intercultural communication. Another notable characteristic of this platform is that six different English dialects (American, Canadian, British, Australian, Singaporean and Indian) were used to familiarise students with different accents. Each lesson is divided into roughly five sections: listening comprehension exercises, description of lexical and grammatical phrases in the listening, grammar exercises and listening drills, pronunciation exercises requiring students to record themselves, listening skills practice, and a review test to see what students have learned throughout the lesson. These units, which include multiple choice questions, help students go over what they have learned according to a regular routine. The platform also enables students to look at audio scripts and explanations of the target grammar. This platform has been created to help students achieve a B1 level [15], commensurate to a TOEIC (Test of English for International Communication) L & R score of 550–780. This platform also enables instructors to monitor how far students have progressed with their lessons. This is a computer-based platform and is compatible with smartphones.

An additional component of this platform, which was not available to students in this course, is an interactive conversation exercise conducted with a real person using internet video chat. Later speculation is offered in the discussion section regarding how this might have affected students' responses if it was included.

3.4 Student Feedback

After the courses had been completed data was collected from a 30-item anonymous questionnaire, which was distributed to the students. The aim of collecting the data was to seek opinions on the 'Business Speaking' e-learning platform. Then from their feedback, evaluate how effectively individual students were able to utilize the platform for improving their verbal communication skills, and what they thought of the platform in terms of its design, presentation, and content suitability. The rating scale used in the questionnaire was a 10-point Likert Scale with 1 representing "strongly disagree" and 10 representing "strongly agree". The responses were totalled and averaged to attain a mean response for each question. A standard deviation was also obtained, and the findings are presented as mean ± SD. Due to the small sample size, the data was carefully checked for outliers and none of responses needed to be eliminated. Students were also given space to provide their written responses to general questions about the quality of the platform. These written responses were used to verify the numerical scores and add insight to the overall findings.

4 Results

4.1 Survey Scores

Overall students' responses appeared lukewarm throughout the questionnaire, with an overall average score of 6.2. However, students were especially satisfied with the quantity and quality of the exercises (Q3, Q4) along with the variety of words and phrases (Q1), while being most critical of the still limited opportunities to practice speaking (Q10). Students also expressed difficulty understanding their own progress (Q9), and often struggled with the pre-recording listening content (Q2). On the whole, students tended to be quite divided, giving consistently low or consistently high scores for each question. The descriptive evaluations of these scores are made holistically with considerations for students' written feedback and classroom observations (Table 1).

Table 1. Results of the questionnaire: students' satisfaction with the platform 1

	Questions	Average (±SD)
1.	I was able to learn the various words, phrases, and sentences	6.8 (1.2)
2.	The listening content was easy to follow as a non-native speaker	5.5 (1.6)
3.	The number of exercises was appropriate	6.7 (2.0)
4.	The quality of exercises was appropriate	7.0 (1.8)
5.	The course provided me with the skills and knowledge necessary for business situations	5.5 (1.6)

Students were divided on whether the skills and knowledge taught in the course was necessary for them in future business situations (Q5). However, they were somewhat more positive about being able to picture themselves in these scenarios (Q7). Although most students were satisfied with the quality of the explanations given for the answers to questions in the course (Q6), students were very divided about the appropriateness of the course's difficulty (Q8) (Table 2).

Students were divided on whether the course provided a valuable English learning experience (Q11). Those whose scores for this question were low expressed that they struggled with the difficulty of the exercises and, therefore, could not fully appreciate the

Table 2. Results of the questionnaire: students' satisfaction with the platform 2

	Questions	Average (±SD)
6.	The quality of the explanations for the solutions was appropriate	6.6 (1.8)
7.	I was able to picture myself in these business situations	6.5 (2.1)
8.	The lessons were appropriate to my English level	5.4 (2.3)
9.	The platform enabled me to recognize my own learning progress	5.3 (1.8)
10.	The platform provided me with opportunities to practice speaking	5.1 (2.3)

course (Q15). These same students did not experience any increase in their motivation to Study English as a result of completing the course (Q12). On the other hand, half of them still appeared to believe that the e-learning style of English study was right for them (Q13). There was also some controversy among students with regards to how well each of the four skills was catered to (reading, listening, writing and speaking) (Q14) (Table 3).

Table 3. Results of the questionnaire: students' satisfaction with the platform 3

	Questions	Average (±SD)
11.	The platform helped me to have valuable English learning experiences	6.5 (2.0)
12.	The platform helped me enhance my motivation to study English more	6.1 (2.3)
13.	The platform was compatible with how I like to learn English	6.1 (2.3)
14.	The four skills were provided in a well-balanced way	5.7 (2.3)
15.	Completing the course gave me a sense of accomplishment	5.7 (1.9)

Unfortunately, just over half of the students reported feeling a low sense of accomplishment (Q15) and found the course content difficult to navigate (Q18). However, overall students were satisfied with the design and functionality of the course (Q16, Q17, Q19) (Tables 4 and 5).

Table 4. Results of the questionnaire: students' satisfaction with the functions 4

	Questions	Average (±SD)
16.	The platform had a simple and clear screen layout	7.1 (2.0)
17.	The platform had an easy-to-use interface	7.1 (1.6)
18.	The platform was easy to navigate	5.6 (1.5)
19.	The platform had an easy-to-use audio playback system	6.7 (2.0)
20.	The lessons were well-laid-out and easy to follow	6.7 (2.0)

Table 5. Results of the questionnaire: students' satisfaction with the overall assessment 5

	Questions	Average (±SD)
21.	Were you satisfied with the "explanation of the exercises" section?	6.5 (1.9)
22.	Were you satisfied with the "listening exercises" section?	6.3 (1.8)
23.	Were you satisfied with the "Review of the words and phrases" section?	6.3 (1.9)
24.	Were you satisfied with the "basic grammar" section?	6.9 (1.8)
25.	Were you satisfied with the "pronunciation" section?	6.0 (2.2)
26.	Were you satisfied with the "review" section?	6.4 (1.8)
27.	Were you satisfied with the "Test" section?	6.3 (2.2)
28.	Were you satisfied with the "Score with explanation" section?	6.5 (2.1)

4.2 Written Responses

Students' written feedback provides significant insights into how they view their e-learning experiences. When asked about the benefits of the course, students provided various encouraging responses. Students thought the lessons "well-organized" and "well-written" and expressed satisfaction with being able to monitor their own learning through being "able to see [their] own progress and scores." Students also appreciated how the course would provide them with "repeated exposure" to the "large number" and "wide variety" of exercises. Students pointed out the effectiveness of being able to learn through having to do "grammar and listening exercises at the same time." More than half of the students pointed out the ease of "doing exercises with software" as opposed to having to "open up paper-based textbooks [or] exercise books." Students also expressed surprise at being "able to use [their] smartphones," something that was new to their language learning experiences. In addition, some students also stated that "the explanations and instructions were easy and straightforward to understand." There were two students who expressed that they found the exposure to the different English dialects useful. The majority of students commented favourably on the "opportunity to listen to conversations" whose "contexts were clear" or presented in "easily imagined real-life situations," which is in contrast to the exclusively exam-oriented materials from their previous English education.

It was clear from many of the students' comments that they recognised some contradiction in the goal of learning spoken English using a mostly listening-based system. Some students expressed difficulty "imaging what real conversations are like" in many of these business situations. Other students found the speakers in the listening exercises "talked too fast" for them to be able to follow. Students also expressed "disappointment with [having] limited verbal exercises" throughout the course. There were three students who lamented the fact that the course was mostly multiple-choice questions and answers. One of those students recommended improving the platform with support for voice recognition. Another student expressed that he was "unable to improve [his] pronunciation," with another noting "irrelevance between illustrations and the conversations." There was also a student who requested videos, instead of illustrations.

There were some other minor usability issues students expressed having with the platform. For example, students expressed frustration with the repeated need to provide their passwords to log in and get started. Another student wished to be able to control the speed of the listening sections. There were also various complaints about the difficulty of navigating through the system.

There was nothing in the written results that contrasted significantly with the questionnaire responses given previously.

5 Discussion and Conclusions

This small-scale study of Japanese university students' views on the benefits and drawbacks of the communication-oriented e-learning platform was too small to provide reliably generalisable results or robust data. However, given that these courses are taught by the researcher (as *active research*), the accompanying wealth of qualitative observation may serve as valuable information for instructors who intend to implement e-learning into their own blended language classes, or for researchers intending to pursue larger studies. In terms of the unique contributions of using an e-learning system, in general students reported that the platform provided them with ample opportunity to self-improve their English ability with well-arranged and presented lesson and exercises. They enjoyed the familiar multiple-choice question-answer assessment style coupled with the less familiar immediate instructional feedback made possible by a software solution. Many students also highly rated the ability to monitor their own progress and scores, recognising the course's value as a self-learning tool. For Japanese who are often believed to prize conformity and controlled variation, this e-learning platform is likely to be well received by both instructors and students alike. However, given one of the ideals of online learning is the opportunity for flexibility and autonomy in the pursuit of learning goals [5], the e-learning platform does fail in this regard, making it somewhat less than ideal as a pioneering system. With regards to language learning more generally, students reported that the course helped them to improve their listening comprehension skills. This is an experience common to students participating in e-language learning courses, since improvements to listening skills are a principle benefit of blended learning [9]. The course also helped students appreciate how the business-oriented scenarios presented were true to real-life conversations which they could easily imagine. Due to the ease of doing lessons made possible by the software solution, they thought the course was effective in preparing them well for success in their future workplace, expressing confidence that the various expressions they had learned would serve them well.

However, it is clear that the primary key to success for students in this course was whether or not the content was appropriate to their language level. For those whom the lessons were appropriate, they had little difficulty acquiring the new unfamiliar functions and language characteristics. In contrast, students who reported low scores for the appropriateness of the content did not engage with exercises in productive ways throughout the course. This is of course true of any course of language learning, whether electronic or pen-and-paper based. Therefore, it remains unclear from these findings, whether or not the students performed better using this e-learning platform than they would have if they had learned the same content from a traditional Japanese English language classroom. This is an area where more research is needed, because if students do not diversify away from the learning approaches that they are used to, they may remain unable to motivate themselves to further improve and practice their speaking and other language skills [16].

The major drawback of this particular learning platform, which presents itself as a speaking course, is that many students quickly realised they would not need to rely upon their speaking skills to complete the course. Students who were enthusiastic about making improvements in this area heavily criticized the use of multiple-choice assessment and some were specifically sceptical about the legitimacy of such an assessment method in a communication-based course. This lack of speaking practice is very likely to have resulted in the majority of students failing to achieve a strong sense of accomplishment. It is hypothesized that the large amount of in-class speaking practice students were given may have emphasised the passivity and monotony generated by the aforementioned inflexibility of this particular e-learning platform. A study conducted by Lee and Im [17] agrees that as students become accustomed to online learning, their expectations and imaginations about what may be possible tend to grow. Since technologies such as voice recognition are now widely available, it makes sense that some students would wonder why this kind of feature isn't already available. This suggests that the majority of students saw the need for a close relationship between what they might do face-to-face with real interlocutors and what they learn to do using an e-learning platform. It is important to mention here that the platform can be packaged with a speaking component utilising live internet video chat with English teachers. If students had had a chance to use this component, they could have improved their speaking skills.

Overall, the e-learning course reviewed in this study proved effective in providing students with a large selection of English language content featuring many of the beneficial features intrinsic to computerised learning, including an ability to learn at one's own pace, in one's own time, with real-time feedback and progress reporting. However, in terms of the course's specific objective to improve speaking skills, this course did not provide any uniquely encouraging features. With that being said, students were largely satisfied with the included content, which focused on business English. Despite the lack of speaking practice, students who completed the course still expressed a keenness to improve their overall language skills, especially their speaking skills in the future.

In order to maximize the effectiveness of communication-oriented e-learning itself though, it appears clear that a means to increase students' opportunities to engage in conversation is essential, just as it is essential in offline learning environments as well. Whether or not e-language-learning can substitute for these more resource intensive learning environments, especially in countries where conversation with native speakers of English are difficult to achieve, remains an important avenue for future research.

References

1. Hinkelman, D.: Blending Technologies in Second Language Classrooms. Palgrave Macmillan UK, London (2018). https://doi.org/10.1057/978-1-137-53686-0

2. Wichadee, S.: Significant predictors for effectiveness of blended learning in a language course. JALT CALL J. **14**, 25–42 (2018)
3. Wang, S., Iwata, J., Jarrell, D.: Exploring Japanese students' e-learning habits. JALTCALL J. **14**, 211–223 (2018)
4. Obe, M., Okutsu, A.: Coronavirus forces Japan schools to grapple with online education. Nikkei Asian Review (2020)
5. MacKenzie, D., Promnitz-Hayashi, L., Jenks, D., Geluso, J., Delgado, R., Castellano, J.: Blended learning spaces: synchronous blending. JALT CALL J. **7**, 43–60 (2011)
6. Mindog, E.: Apps and EFL: a case study on the use of smartphone apps to learn English by four Japanese university students. JALT CALL J. **12**, 3–22 (2016)
7. Hirata, Y.: E-learning courseware for language education in Japan: its application and student perceptions. Open Learn. J. Open Distance e-Learn. **33**(2), 83–98 (2018)
8. Smart, K.L., Cappel, J.J.: Students' perceptions of online learning: a comparative study. J. Inf. Technol. Educ. **5**, 201–219 (2006)
9. Kobayashi, K., Little, A.: Learner perceptions on the usefulness of a blended learning EFL program. JALT CALL J. **7**, 103–117 (2011)
10. Hinkelman, D.: Blended learning: issues driving an end to laboratory-based CALL. JALT Hokkaido J. **9**, 17–31 (2005)
11. Aspinall, R.W.: International Education Policy in Japan in an Age of Globalisation and Risk. Global Oriental, London (2015)
12. Bao, D.: Understanding Silence and Reticence: Ways of Participating in Second Language Acquisition. Bloomsbury, London (2014)
13. Humphries, S., Burns, A.: In reality it's almost impossible: CLT-oriented curriculum change. ELT J. **69**, 239–248 (2015)
14. Business Speaking. Reallyenglish, Tokyo
15. Common European Framework of Reference for Languages (CEFR). https://www.coe.int/en/web/common-european-framework-reference-languages/table-1-cefr-3.3-common-reference-levels-global-scale
16. Shea, D.P.: Oriented to English: motivations and attitudes of advanced students in the university classroom. JALT J. **39**, 139–164 (2017)
17. Lee, O., Im, Y.: The emergence of the cyber-university and blended learning in Korea. In: Bonk, C., Graham, C. (eds.) The Handbook of Blended Learning: Global Perspectives, Local Designs, pp. 281–295. Pfeiffer, San Francisco (2006)

Research on the Development of STEM Courses in Junior Middle School–Take "the Making of Aromatherapy Wax Product" as a Case

Xingnan Wang, Jing Qiu, Yunxiang Zheng(✉), and Yun Liu

School of Educational Information Technology, South China Normal University, Guangzhou 510631, China
zyx@scnu.edu.cn

Abstract. The nature of STEM education is to cultivate interdisciplinary talents with scientific spirit and innovative ability. To this end, it is advisable and fundamental to build effective STEM courses systematically, so that both teachers and students can follow. This study refined and proposed the development process of STEM courses in junior middle school via literature review. Based on it, a two-round action research was conducted in practice to showcase, test and optimize the course development process, taking "the Making of Aromatherapy Wax Product" as a case. The results showed that the course developed on the basis of this process helped to effectively reach the course objectives and promote students' scientific inquiry spirit, engineering thinking, mathematical literacy, and technical ability. In addition, it also had a positive impact on students' communication and collaborative ability, which provides a reference for the practice and application of STEM education in middle schools in China.

Keywords: STEM education · Course development · STEM course

1 Introduction

STEM is the abbreviation of science, technology, engineering, and mathematics. In the 21st century, the demand for talents has been changing from professional to diversified and innovative talents. Traditional discipline-based teaching lays a good foundation for students, but it cuts off the links among disciplines and hinders students from developing the ability to solve problems using comprehensive knowledge and skills. The advent and widespread of STEM education help to solve this problem gradually. STEM education is characterized by interdisciplinary learning, emphasizing the use of multidisciplinary knowledge to solve problems in real situation. Through STEM education, students' scientific spirit and innovative practical ability can be improved, which meets the need of cultivating new-era talents.

The fundamental way to develop STEM education is to design and implement STEM courses. Driven by national policies, both domestic and foreign scholars have attached great attention to it. However, how to build an effective STEM course systematically is

S. K. S. Cheung et al. (Eds.): ICBL 2020, LNCS 12218, pp. 136–147, 2020.
https://doi.org/10.1007/978-3-030-51968-1_12

still a challenge in this field. Literature reviews show that studies on STEM courses in recent years mainly focus on integration methods, teaching models and course development. (1) Integration methods. Numerous interpretations of integrating the STEM disciplines have appeared in the literature. Ranging from a single discipline to multidisciplinary and transdisciplinary perspectives [1], the notions of STEM integration remain vague and often contentious [2]. Herschbach proposed two integration models of STEM courses [3]: the correlated curriculum and the broad-fields curriculum. Lyn D. English argues for a greater focus on STEM integration, with a more equitable representation of the four disciplines in studies purporting to advance STEM learning [4]. (2) Teaching models. In the need of guiding the practice of STEM course, scholars gradually turn to the exploration of teaching models. Nowadays, typical STEM teaching models used outside China are the 5E-teaching model [5] based on constructivism and the 6E-teaching model [6] based on engineering design theory. Specifically, the basic steps of the 5E-teaching model include Engage, Explore, Explain, Elaborate, and Evaluate. By referring to the 5E model, the 6E-teaching model integrates engineering design to promote students' cognition of engineering process. (3) Course development. Local schools and water companies in Melbourne built a STEM course called Melbourne's Water Story [7] to promote students' awareness of water conservation. The Mars education program [8] developed by Arizona state university (ASU) and NASA's jet propulsion laboratory (JPL) served as a classic case of STEM practice.

Taking CNKI as the source, 851 articles were retrieved with "STEM course" and "STEM curriculum" as keywords, of which only 35 were related to curriculum or course development. Moreover, as most of the articles talked about the development and implementation of teaching cases, little attention was paid to the course development process comprehensively. Therefore, we proposed a development process of STEM courses in junior middle school as a solution to solve this problem and used action research method to verify its feasibility, enriching the theory and practice of STEM course design.

2 The Development Process of STEM Courses

According to the theories of Taylor [9], Schwab [10], Bobbitt [11] and other scholars, the elements of a course development mainly include goals, content, evaluation, and activities. While STEM emphasizes real problem situation, project-based learning and collaborative interaction in groups, the development process of STEM courses can be captured by seven steps: preliminary analysis, defining theme, setting learning goals, choosing learning content, designing learning activities, designing learning evaluation and designing learning support, as shown in Fig. 1.

1. Preliminary analysis: (1) Analyze school condition, including school features, financial support, teaching facilities and resources; (2) Analyze teachers' qualification, such as the number of teachers in each subject, and whether they have STEM teaching experience; (3) Analyze learners' characteristics, including the initial level and learning attitude.
2. Defining theme: (1) Collect learning topics from different ways, including real life problems, subject knowledge, frontiers of science and technology, special culture,

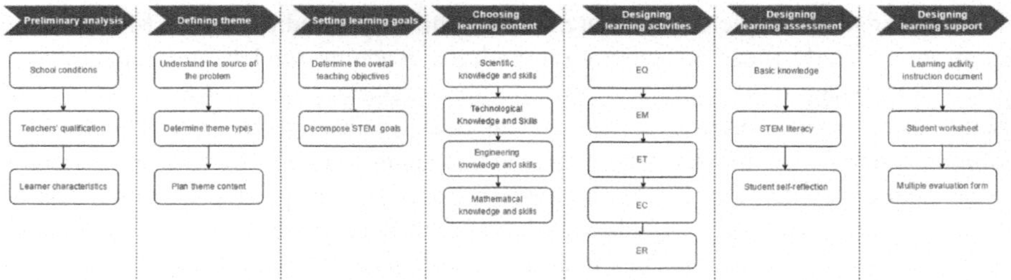

Fig. 1. Flow chart of the development process of STEM courses in junior middle school.

etc.; (2) Determine the type of the theme, including but not limited to verification type, inquiry type, design type and creative type; (3) Finalize the theme content according to the following factors: school education concept, facilities and resources, teachers' background, students' interests and so on.

3. Setting learning goals: (1) Determine the overall teaching goals, which can be divided into three parts: knowledge and skills, process and methods, emotional attitude and value; (2) Decompose the goals from STEM perspective, i.e. science, technology, engineering and mathematics respectively.
4. Choosing learning content: Not only pay attention to the integration of interdisciplinary knowledge (chemical, biological, physical, etc.), but also distinguish the content of different knowledge and skills (scientific, technical, engineering and mathematical) related to the theme of the course.
5. Designing learning activities: According to the 5EX interdisciplinary learning activity design model proposed by Kedong Li [12], the teaching procedure can be divided into five stages: Enter and Questions (EQ), Exploration and Mathematics (EM), Engineering and Technology (ET), Expansion and Creativity (EC), and Evaluation and Reflection (ER). Specifically,

   – EQ means that teachers provide students with videos, reading materials, surveys, etc., enabling students to get involved in real situations, arouse their interest, and then post questions to trigger students' preliminary thinking during the introduction phase.
   – EM focuses on arranging activities targeting to questions or tasks that previously proposed, which requires students to find solutions through scientific inquiry methods (experiments, on-site observations, investigations, etc.) and mathematical methods (measuring, calculating, etc.).
   – ET aims to improve students' hands-on ability by encouraging them to undertake tasks, take part in engineering design process, complete tasks collaboratively with technology and tools. That is exactly what "learning by doing" implies.
   – EC is to empower students to connect theory to practice, and propose creative ideas to make the existing solution more polished or extensive.
   – ER concentrates on multi-dimensional evaluation for comprehensive mastery of knowledge and skills, including teacher evaluation, student self-evaluation and peer assessment. In general, basic knowledge, STEM literacy, and student self-reflection should all be included in the evaluation index system.

6. Designing learning evaluation: (1) Basic knowledge, including basic concepts which are closely related to the associated subjects. They can be tested by means of questionnaires, paper-and-pencil standardized tests, study notes, etc.; (2) STEM literacy, including science literacy, technology literacy, engineering literacy and mathematical literacy. They can be tested by paper-and-pencil tests, in-class observations, study notes, presentations, product displays, etc.; (3) Students' self-reflection, which can be collected by PMIQ form (P stands for Plus, which represents what I have learned; M stands for Minus, which represents what I have missed; I stands for Interest, which represents what I'm interested in; Q stands for question, which represents questions I still have).
7. Designing learning support: Prepare resources and materials students may use during the learning process, including the guidance of learning activities (e.g. popular science materials, operating instructions, evaluation criteria of works), student worksheets, multi-dimensional forms (student self-evaluation form, teacher evaluation form, PMIQ form), etc.

3 Implementation and Improvement of the Development Process

In this section, a two-round action research was conducted to showcase, test and optimize the above course development process, taking "the Making of Aromatherapy Wax Product" as a case.

3.1 Course Introduction

The realistic problem of this course is that about 27% of the people in the world are suffering from sleep disorders. This may not only cause emotional problems but also increase the risk of diabetes and heart disease. Therefore, it is necessary to find an easy way to effectively improve the sleep quality. For this purpose, the theme of this course is set to encourage students to use a certain kind of essential oil and wax to design and make an aromatic product with total cost less than 50 RMB (in order to save resources and costs). The Chinese name of this course is "Cui Xiang Mian", where "Cui" means the extraction of essential oils, "Xiang" means aromatic, and "Mian" means improving the sleep quality. The teaching content includes several parts, such as candle-making, scientific inquiring experiments, as well as the classification, extraction, and the history of aromatherapy.

3.2 Methodology

Participants. The participants involved in this study were the students of class 1 and class 2 in the second grade of Dongguan Songshanhu Experimental Middle School. There were 30 students in each class, with 22 males and 38 females. Some of them had the experience of engaging in STEM competitions and had a strong desire to participate.

Instrumentation. This study used two-round action research method, survey method and qualitative analysis method to test the feasibility of the development process and optimize it. Specifically, action research was utilized in this study to seek transformative change in the process of the course development. Conforming to the development process we proposed, the preliminary process of this course is illustrated in Fig. 2.

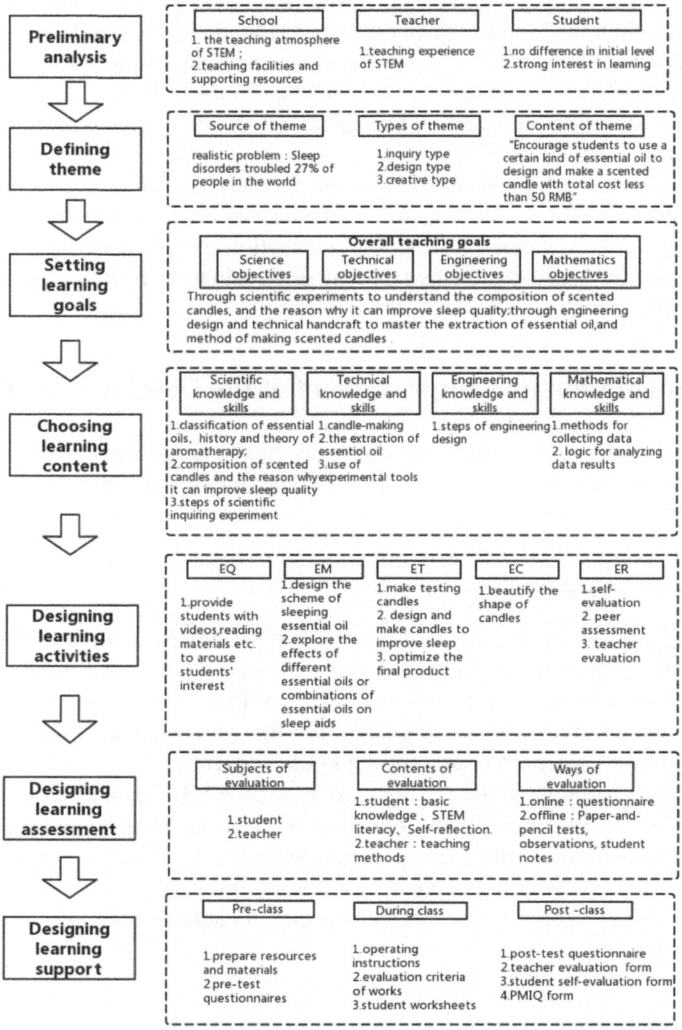

Fig. 2. Preliminary development process of this course.

Survey method was used to collect data in pre-test and post-test. The questionnaire was adopted from an assessment scale developed by the Connecticut Science Center [13], science curriculum standards of junior high school of Chinese compulsory education (2011 edition) [14], and integrated with the characteristics of this course. There were 17 questions in pre-test and post-test respectively to investigate students' learning attitudes, teachers' teaching methods, students' learning effects, and students' STEM literacy. The result from SPSS showed that the questionnaire had high reliability and validity, with the reliability coefficient value 0.662 and validity value 0.704.

Qualitative analysis method was used to collect teachers' and students' opinion on the course and their experience, acquisition and suggestions, including student worksheet, teacher evaluation form, student self-evaluation form, and PMIQ form. Specifically, student worksheet was used in class to record student's learning process and take notes during the experiments, which typically consisted of fill-in blanks of basic knowledge points, inquiry plans, engineering design drafts, etc. Teacher evaluation form was a subjective evaluation scale to assess students' performance by teachers. It contained lists of teachers' opinions on students' in-class performance in 9 activities, which was ranked by level A (exemplary) to level D (beginning). Student self-evaluation form was similar to teacher evaluation form, which was ranked by the students themselves instead of the teachers about their learning satisfaction and gains. PMIQ form was for student summary and reflection, including what students have learned, what they have missed, what they're interested in and the questions they still have.

Data Collection and Analysis Procedures. In the first round of action research, we formulated an experimental plan and designed the STEM course by implementing the development process, then optimized it by analyzing the survey result and data collected through in-class observation. After the optimization, we made the second-round practice. Data collected from the survey and in-class observation were analyzed again. Note that before and after each round, students were required to fill in the questionnaire (pre-test and post-test) so that teachers could know students' learning situation to optimize the process. Finally, we summarized the experience in combination with the results of qualitative analysis (teacher evaluation form, student self-evaluation form, and student worksheets) so as to propose suggestions for future improvement.

As usual, before the survey was administered, permission was granted to conduct the research. All student participation was both anonymous and voluntary. The survey was administered in paper format during the participants' mid-class break. All responses were entered into Microsoft Excel and then imported into SPSS for statistical analysis. In addition, the responses to teacher evaluation form, student self-evaluation form, and student worksheets were all examined carefully by teachers after the course.

3.3 Teaching Implementation and Results

Effect and Improvement of the First-Round Teaching. This STEM course started in September 2018, and contained 9 lessons. The first-round teaching started from September to mid-November. Before the first round of action research, the students in the two classes were surveyed through a pre-test questionnaire and the results were tested through SPSS independent-samples T test. The results showed that there was no significant difference in the initial level of the students in these two classes.

Due to space limitation, the first-round teaching process was omitted. We only listed the in-class observation and improvement suggestions.

Observation

- Observation of teachers. Through the observation of teachers, we found that the teacher gave too much guidance to the students during experimental class while they were supposed to explore independently. In addition, due to the teacher's ignorance of emphasizing the standard of filling out the worksheets and the evaluation form, the quality of these documents was generally low.
- Observation of students. Through the observation of students, we found that the students were interested in this STEM course. However, due to the lack of basic knowledge of aromatic candles, hand-made experience, and scientific and engineering thinking ability, students failed to complete the experimental design and self-exploration within the given time. Besides, the students were good at information searching and sorting but had difficulty in scientific exploration and sketching.

Improvement Suggestions

- Choosing learning content: try to make students familiar with the types of raw wax, and introduce experimental tools to them beforehand, so as to save time and materials that may cause by improper use.
- Designing learning activities: add "Experiments of essential oil extraction" to the scientific inquiry section to stimulate students' interest and improve the skills of using experimental tools.
- Designing learning assessment: check students' worksheet on completion and standardization before evaluation.
- Designing learning support: provide students with additional reading material in the introduction period; provide students with handouts for instruction; redesign the worksheet to make it clear and concise.

Effect and Improvement of the Second-Round Teaching. The process described in Fig. 2 was then updated according to the above suggestions. Based on it, the second-round teaching started from mid-November to the end of January. Again, the in-class observation and improvement suggestions are shown below.

Observation

- Observation of teachers. Compared to the first round, the teacher succeeded in raising heuristic questions to inspire students' active thinking. However, without previous experience in the experiment of essential oil extraction, the teacher overran, leading to class delay.
- Observation of students. The students showed great interest in the content of the course. Meanwhile, their learning ability and self-confidence were improved a lot. Especially in the EC section, students undertook experimental tasks initiatively and their hand-making capability was improved.

Improvement Suggestions

- Designing learning activities: In the EC section, encourage students to make candle molds with materials close at hand, so as to stimulate students' love for life and cultivate their practical ability. What's more, an additional interview activity seems meaningful for students to collect first-hand data from people around them (teachers and parents) about their feelings after using their aromatic products, which in return gives feedback to make the course better.

- Designing learning support: In the EC section, teachers should prepare experimental materials in advance and make accurate estimated time.

After two rounds of action research, the development process of this course was optimized and finalized, as shown in Fig. 3.

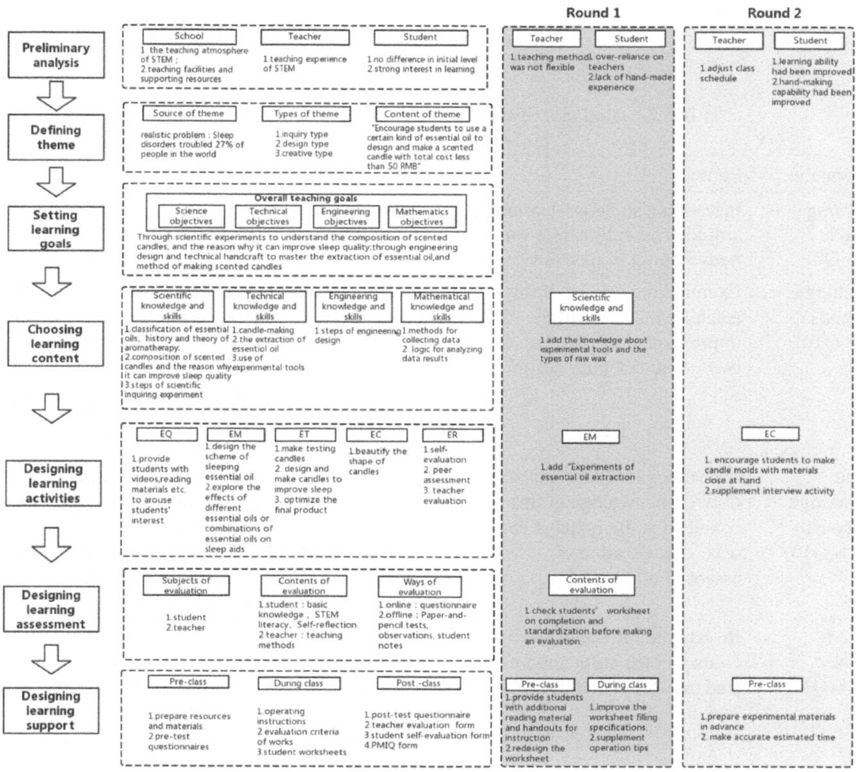

Fig. 3. Finalized development process of the course after two rounds of action research

Effect Analysis of the Two-Round Teaching Implementation. As stated above, the effect of the teaching implementation was measured by both quantitative and qualitative analysis, i.e. pre-test and post-test questionnaires, teacher evaluation form, student self-evaluation form, student worksheet, and PMIQ form. For space limitation, some important details are listed below.

Analysis of Pre-test and Post-test Questionnaire. The result of paired sample test of the post-tests of the two-round teaching effect is shown in Table 1 and analyzed in Table 2.

Table 1. Paired sample test of the post-tests of the two-round teaching effect.

	Paired differences					t	df	Sig. (2-tailed)
	Mean	Std deviation	Std. error difference	95% confidence interval of the difference				
				Lower	Upper			
post-test1 - post-test2	−.40341	.32519	.08130	−.57669	−.23013	−4.962	15	.003

Table 2. Analysis of the results of the pre-test and post-test.

Dimension	Purpose	Result
Learning attitude (Q1–Q8)	Investigate students' learning attitude and enthusiasm for participating in the course	As can be seen from Table 1, the effect of the second round was significantly better than that of the first round ($p = 0.003$)
Teaching methods (Q9–Q10)	Examine the impact of this teaching method and the improvement of the two-round teaching design	The students generally preferred to student-oriented teaching methods. After the second round of course implementation, 93.75% of students considered that "centered by student practice and supplemented by teacher guidance" teaching method could improve their learning efficiency, which was 6.25% higher than the first round
Basic knowledge of the course (Q11–Q13)	Investigate students' mastery of basic knowledge of this course, e.g. the types of raw wax, classification of essential oil, etc.	Comparing the data of pre-test and post-test, it can be seen that after two rounds of teaching, the students' mastering level of basic knowledge of the course increased from 30% to 100%, which indicated that the improved course could make the students better understand the required knowledge in this field
STEM literacy (Q14–Q17)	Investigate the impact of this course on the cultivation of student's STEM literacy	For scientific literacy, Q14 showed that the number of students who could master the controlling variable and analyze data went up from 83.33% to 100% and 75% to 93.75% respectively, illustrating that the course could effectively promote the students' science inquiry ability For engineering literacy, Q15 showed that the number of students who were able to choose the correct sequence rose from 87.5% to 100%, indicating that the students were able to recall the engineering design steps correctly For technical and mathematical literacy, Q16–Q17 showed that the students who could complete the design of making aromatic product increased from 87.5% to 93.75%, and the students who could use experimental measurements correctly rose from 87.5% to 100%

Analysis of Teacher Evaluation Form and Student Self-evaluation Form.
For teacher evaluation, results showed that the rate of level A in the first round was 6.25%, while in the second round it rose to 18.75%. For student evaluation, results

showed that the rate of level A increased from 0% to 6.25%, and the rate of level B rose from 56.25% to 75%. It can be seen that after improving the instructional design and process, the teacher was satisfied with the students' performance in the course, and so were the students. Not surprisingly, the students were pleased to attend this kind of course, make things by hand and share their experience with others in class.

Analysis of Student Worksheet. Redesigning the student worksheet and offering handouts helped the students better understand their tasks and paved the way for a more detailed and clear exploration. And the students' writing and sketching skills, experimental ability, and engineering design capability were improved. Samples of student worksheet and product display are show in Fig. 4.

Fig. 4. Samples of student worksheet and product display

4 Conclusion

When carrying out STEM education, it is advisable and fundamental to build an effective STEM course systematically, so that both teachers and students can follow step by step. This study refined and proposed the development process of STEM courses in junior middle school via literature review. Then a two-round action research was conducted in practice to showcase, test and optimize the course development process, taking "the Making of Aromatherapy Wax Product" as a case. The course was taken in Dongguan Songshanhu Experimental Middle School with 60 participants. During our practice, survey method and qualitative analysis method were utilized as measurements. The results demonstrated that the course developed on the basis of this process helped to effectively reach the course objectives and promote students' scientific inquiry spirit, engineering thinking, mathematical literacy, and technical ability. In addition, it also had a positive impact on students' communicative and collaborative ability, which provides a reference for implementing STEM education in middle schools in China. Limitations include teachers' lack of STEM teaching experience, limited resources, and insufficient class preparation. And the scale of the experimental data in this paper is relatively small, therefore a larger scale experiment should be expected. Hope this paper can provide a reference for the application of STEM course in Chinese elementary education.

Acknowledgments. This work was supported by "Entrusted Project by the Policy and Regulation Department of the Ministry of Education of China" under grant Jybzfs2018115.

References

1. Vasquez, J., Sneider, C., Comer, M.: STEM Lesson Essentials, Grades 3–8: Integrating Science, Technology, Engineering, and Mathematics. Heinemann, Portsmouth (2013)
2. Bybee, R.W.: The case for STEM education: Challenges and opportunities. NSTA Press, Arlington (2013)
3. English, L.D.: STEM education K-12: perspectives on integration. Int. J. STEM Educ. **3**(3) (2016)
4. Herschbach, D.R.: The stem initiative: constraints and challenges. J. STEM Teach. Educ. **48**(1), 96–122 (2011)
5. Maryland State Department of Education. 5E Model for Integrated STEM Education. http://mdk12.msde.maryland.gov/instruction/curriculum/stem/pdf/6-8/middleschoolintegratedSemodelforstemeducation.pdf
6. Burke, B.N.: The ITEEA 6E learning by design model: maximizing informed design and inquiry integrative STEM classroom. Technol. Eng. Teach. **73**(6), 14–19 (2014)
7. Melbourne's Water Story. http://www.waterstory.melbournewater.com.au. Accessed 27 Feb 2020
8. Mars Education at Arizona State University. NGSS STEM lesson plans. http://marsed.asu.edu/stem-lesson-plans
9. Ralph, T.: Basic Principles of Curriculum and Instruction. China Light Industry Press, Beijing (2008)
10. Schwab, J.J.: The practical: a language for curriculum. Sch. Rev. **78**, 1–23 (1969)
11. Bobbitt, J.F.: How to Make a Curriculum. Houghton-Mifflin, Boston (1924)

12. Li, K.D., Li, Y.: 5EX design model for interdisciplinary learning activities in STEM education. Electr. Educ. Res. **40**(4), 5–13 (2019)
13. Bai, Y., Ye, Y., Xin, S.T., et al.: Calm analysis of STEM education boom and suggestions for curriculum implementation. Ref. Basic Educ. (5), 3–9 (2018)
14. Ministry of Education. Notice on Printing and Distributing Curriculum Standards for Compulsory Education and Other Subjects (2011 Edition). http://www.moe.gov.cn/srcsite/A26/s8001/201112/t20111228_167340.html

Augmenting the Makerspace: Designing Collaborative Inquiry Through Augmented Reality

Xu Han[1], Yayun Liu[1], Hongzhu Li[2], Zhenying Fan[1], and Heng Luo[1(✉)]

[1] School of Educational Information Technology, Central China Normal University, Wuhan 430079, China
luoheng@mail.ccnu.edu.cn
[2] Baomin Elementary School, Shenzhen 518100, China

Abstract. This study explored the potential of using augmented reality (AR) technology in designing makerspace-based education in the elementary school setting. Employing the design-based research methodology, this study proposed and successively refined a set of instructional design principles for facilitating AR–supported collaborative inquiry through three iterations of design, implementation and revision. The affordances of AR were found to promote student engagement in collaborative exploration and task completion. Moreover, several pedagogical implications based on the empirical data were discussed, highlighting the importance of interdisciplinary integration, general inquiry sequence, proper scaffolding strategies, opportunities for transfer learning, and abundant instruction time for makerspace-based education.

Keywords: Makerspace · Augmented reality · Design-based research · Disciplinary integration · Collaborative inquiry

1 Introduction

The potential of makerspace for education has been acknowledged worldwide, receiving growing attention from both educational researchers and practitioners. The term *makerspace* is a derivative of the maker movement that originated in the 1990s as a technology-supported Do-it-yourself (DIY) culture featured by innovation, creation comma collaboration, and project-completion [1]. Makerspace is defined as a physical space designed to support the maker movement by having makers substantiate their innovative ideas through hands-on design, collective construction, and novel technologies [2]. However, the makerspace conception is also referred to as resources, opportunities, and communities for individuals to engage in creative, higher-order problem solving activities [3].

Valuing the spirit of the maker movement, educators have been advocating to apply makerspace to both K-12 and higher educational contexts for benefits such as increased learner motivation, self-efficacy, learning performance [4], and development of essential skills such as creative thinking, teamwork, and communication [5]. The passion of

S. K. S. Cheung et al. (Eds.): ICBL 2020, LNCS 12218, pp. 148–159, 2020.
https://doi.org/10.1007/978-3-030-51968-1_13

the global community for promoting makerspace in educational practice is shared by Chinese schools and teachers [6]. In 2015, the Ministry of Education of China released official guidelines calling for more effective use of information technology in exploration of novel educational models such as STEAM and maker education for developing digital competencies and innovation among Chinese students. Consequently, an increasing number of makerspaces are being set up in K-12 schools with various forms of maker education being emerged in the past five years [7].

Nevertheless, the implementation of makerspace in K-12 education is also facing several challenges. First, current literature focuses on the pedagogical assumptions of makerspace education, with few empirical studies investigating how such assumptions are being applied to the actual teaching practice. Second, many makerspace interventions simply had students mindlessly using new technologies such as 3D printers or drones to complete routine tasks without proper scaffolding for collaborative inquiry and problem solving. Lastly, many makerspaces lack necessary educational and technical resources to enable hands-on learning experience for every student. For instance, a class of 60 students might share one 3D printer, making it impossible for everyone to benefit from maker education. Those challenges hinder the sustainable development of maker education in China.

Augmented reality (AR) provides a potential solution to those challenges. The technical affordance of VR such as sensory immersion, haptic interaction, and 3D simulation is known to promote both affective and cognitive learning outcomes [8]. AR-based learning environments were found improve students' learning motivation, learning attitude, academic performance [9, 10]. AR is also found to enhance creativity and knowledge construction by engaging students in the inquiry process and supporting integrated disciplinary curriculum such as STEM [11]. Moreover, the visibility of AR makes shared inquiry feasible among students, making it feasible to teach a large class with limited AR resources [12]. Its immense potential for both K-12 and higher education has been recognized in recent years [13]. However, few studies have investigated the design and implementation of AR-supported makerspace in K-12 education, resulting in a lack of empirically validated design principles.

To address such research need, we conducted a design-based research to propose and successively refine a set of instructional design principles for facilitating AR-supported maker education in an elementary school. More specifically, we seek to answer the following research questions:

1. What instructional design principles for AR-supported maker education were valued by the students and the teacher?
2. What are the benefits and limitations of AR-supported maker education in the elementary school setting?

2 Theoretical Framework

The theoretical framework for designing the AR-supported makerspace education is informed by the theories of cross-disciplinary integration, collaborative inquiry, and worked examples.

2.1 Cross-Disciplinary Integration

Cross-disciplinary Integration aims to break down barriers between disciplines and integrate all subject content into new areas of learning. Subject integration is considered as the core concept of "STEM" education, enabling students to develop problem-solving skills and computational thinking through meaning integration of science, technology, engineering and mathematics [14]. Later, the letter A representing "art" was added to STEM to formulate STEAM, highlighting the enriched concept of creative composition during integrated learning [15]. Cross-disciplinary Integration allows students to understand, evaluate and solve complex problems, as well as develop new knowledge [16]. During such process, students can extend their understanding of the theoretical knowledge learned from multiple disciplines and apply it to the practice of problem solving, and thus become a better learners and innovators. Emerging technologies such AR can facilitate cross-disciplinary integration in makerspace as they can be used as a medium to connect inquiry activities in different disciplines.

2.2 Collaborative Inquiry

Informed by both collaborative learning and inquiry-based learning, collaborative inquiry emphasizes on the dialogue and exchange of team members, and joint action to complete mutual tasks. Collaborative inquiry begins with the tasks or problems assigned by the teacher, the learners then work actively in groups of two or more, contributing to the shared group efforts to complete the tasks or solving the problems. As suggested by the theory of zone of proximal development [17], teachers should employ various of scaffolding strategies to provide necessary guidance in collaborative learning and gradually transfer the responsibility of inquiry from teachers to students [18]. Moreover, some researchers argued that, through clear division of labor and role assignment for team members, group cognition can be promoted through collective problem-solving process [19]. While the strategies and effects of collaborative inquiry have been extensively investigated in traditional classroom settings, how can it unfold in technology-rich makerspace settings is still in need of further exploration.

2.3 Worked Examples

The worked example effect is a well-known instructional effect in cognitive load theory [20]. Compared to problem solving without guidance, the effectiveness of worked examples lies in their resource-saving characteristics that enable improved learning performance with reduced cognitive efforts [21]. Worked examples consist of two fundamental elements: a well-formulated task problem and a step-by-step demonstration of a task solution [22]. By guiding learners to complete a given task progressively, a worked example describes an expert's model for completing a specific task problem and provides scaffolding for learning and transfer performance [23]. The literature in general supports the effectiveness of worked examples in inquiry-based learning, reporting benefits such as increased germane cognitive load, higher cognitive arousal, improved test performance, and less acquisition time [24]. Therefore, worked examples have immense potential for maker education as scaffolding tools.

2.4 Theoretical Assumptions for Design

Based on the review of relevant teaching and learning theories above, we proposed four instructional principles for designing AR-supported maker education. The principles, operations, and theoretical origins are listed in Table 1.

Table 1. The principles, operations, and theoretical origins for designing AR-supported maker education.

Instructional principle	Operation in practice	Theories
Integrating subject content from various disciplines for knowledge integration and transfer	Use AR as a medium to connect learning activities such as story writing, artistic creation, information search, science inquiry, 3D construction and 3D printing	Cross-disciplinary Integration, STEAM theory
Assigning different roles to students in a group, with each role specializing in one aspect of the project	Divide the class into groups of 4 and assign specialized roles based on major activities required for the projects. Roles can rotate if needed	Collaborative learning theory, social learning theory
Facilitating student-centered inquiry learning featured by exploration, problem-solving, learner autonomy, and creative project	Assign a creative project of story-based 3D modeling for group completion, allow great learner control in theme selection, art design, and 3D construction	Inquiry learning, problem-based learning, project-based learning
Providing students with adequate scaffolding in various formats to assist their collaborative inquiry	Prepare the following materials for students before class: worksheet for role assignment, step-by-step guidance for project completion, sample product as examples, and a clear rubric for project assessment	Cognitive load theory, scaffolding strategies, worked examples effect

3 Methodology

3.1 Participants and Setting

The research was implemented in an elementary school in Shenzhen, Guangdong Province. As the Future Education Center of Shenzhen, this school takes a leading role in maker education and was elected as one of the best makerspace education centers in the district. Recently, the school had purchased four zSpace STEAM lab stations, which came with AR software named Leopoly for 3D creative modeling and hardware devices such as 3D-tracking glasses, haptic Styluses, and special display screens (see Fig. 1). Unlike other 3D modeling software such as 3Done and 3D Max, Leopoly can provide students with an easy and intuitive way to create, customize and prepare digital objects for 3D printing. As for participants, we chose sixteen fourth-graders randomly to join in the course and they were divided into four groups.

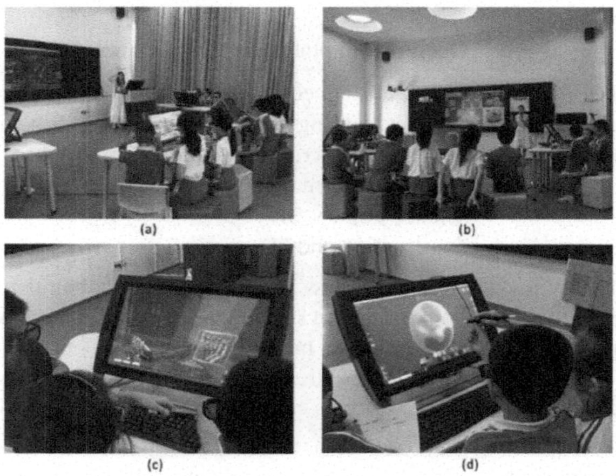

Fig. 1. Teaching environment of this course. (a), (b): four zSpace STEAM lab stations provide hardware support and creates an immersive augmented reality; (c): students wearing 3D glasses are getting familiar with the operation of the device; (d): students are learning the operation of modeling in Leopoly software.

3.2 Instructional Process

Drawing on the affordances of Leopoly, a course named *3D Modeling in Virtual Environment* was conducted among 4th graders in the makerspace of the elementary school. It included three iterations and four classes. The first lesson focused on the AR technology, aiming to prepare students to familiarize with the basic operation of Leopoly and hardware devices for the future classes. The first iteration of class is named *3D model creation-The pig in Chinese zodiac*. This theme came from the twelve Chinese zodiac statues located on campus, closely related to the local and cultural environment of the students. The second iteration allowed students to freely choose from one of twelve Chinese zodiac signs for 3D creation, so as to promote near transfer of learning. The last class (third iteration) required the students to create souvenirs of Chinese culture for international visitors, with the purpose of further advancing the development creativity and innovation and far transfer of learning. The overall process of the designed course is depicted in Fig. 2.

In every iteration, students were divided into groups of 4. In each group, each member assumed a role of storywriter, art designer, 3D modeler, and presenter to complete the

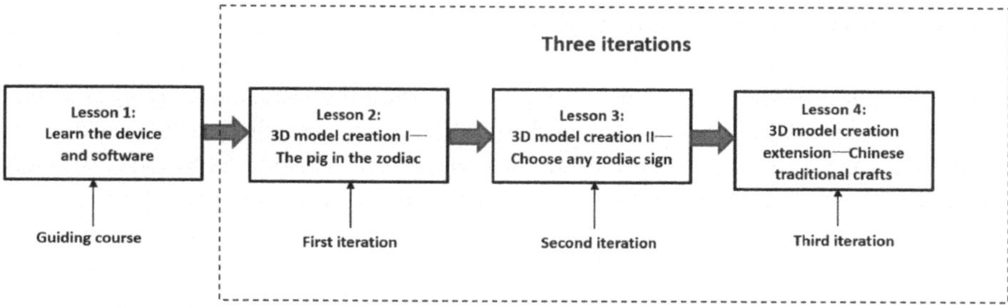

Fig. 2. The overall process of the three iterations.

task in each interaction. The storywriter writes a script with all story elements and include at least two scientific facts in the story content. The art designer designs the image for the leading character/object based on the plot in the story. 3D modeler creates the 3D artifact with key features implied in the story and image. The presenter is also the group leader, coordinating the collaboration process and presenting the final project to the whole class. The key phases in each interaction of class are presented in Fig. 3.

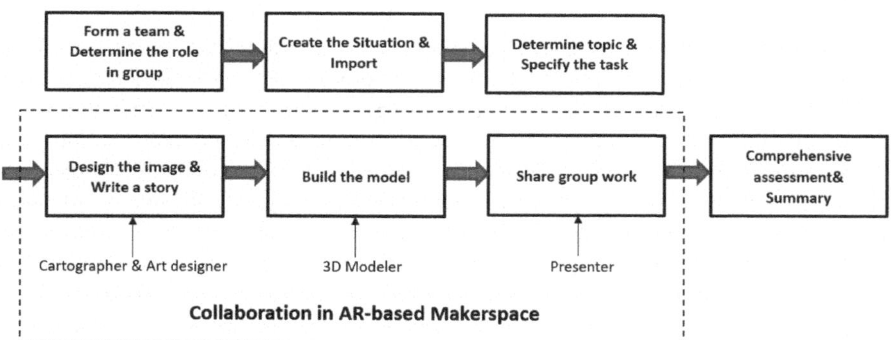

Fig. 3. The key phases and overall sequence of a typical class of maker education.

3.3 Data Collection and Analysis Procedure

Three types of data were collected to evaluate the instructional design. First one is interviews with learners and teachers. According to the performance of learners in the class, 6–8 representative students were selected for semi-structured interviews. The second is the classroom record, including video recording of each class situation, observation of the process of teaching implementation, and critical reflection. The third is student works. We collected three rounds of student works, including story compilation templates, sketch drawing and 3D modeling works.

4 Case Study of Implementation

In every iteration of the maker education, we observed the students' performances in class and conducted interviews with students after class, with the purpose of collecting empirical evidence regarding learning outcomes and learning experience. Critical reflection at the end of each iteration guided our revision for the next iteration.

4.1 First Iteration

Implementation. The first iteration went smoothly as a whole. Firstly, the class topic was introduced by riddles and colorful pictures about animals and students were engaged by the topic. After the introduction, the teacher explained about the pig-zodiac task and assigned tasks to four roles. Priority was given to students' self-exploration and creation, and teacher occasionally helped them to solve difficulties encountered during 3D modeling, such as how to make curly pig tails. In the first half of class, every student played by their roles, but the class started to get a little out of order in the latter phase. Presenters did not perform well in project demonstration, seemed nervous and unconfident. Due to time limit, peer assessment was hastily done, and few students paid attention to it.

Learning Outcomes and Students Experience. Overall, the students were able to complete the assigned task, but the learning outcomes were not satisfactory. Firstly, the quality of group works fell short of the standards and requirements. Students seemed to have difficulty understanding the interdisciplinary nature of the task, and failed to integrate story-writing, design, and scientific facts consistently into the final project. As seen in Fig. 4, the final products from two groups showed high resemblance, indicating students were imitating each other rather than creating innovatively. The ornaments and graphic features on the pig image had little to do with the story plot or scientific facts. Despite increased motivation due to novelty effect, the degree of participation and collaboration within groups was not high, resulting in occasional chaos and misbehaviors in class.

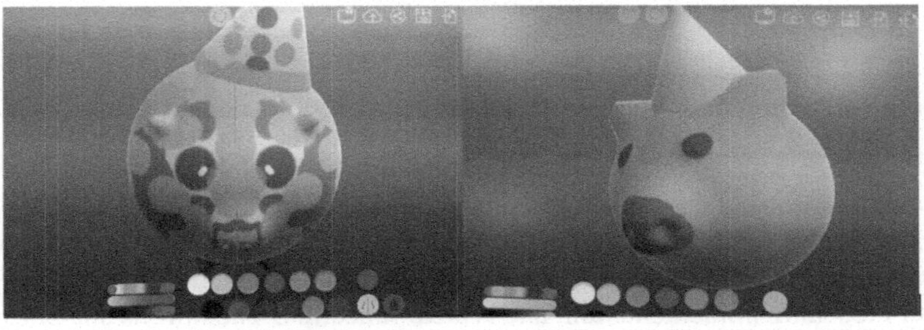

Fig. 4. Comparison of the 3D modeling products of two groups in the first iteration of instruction.

Reflections on Instructional Design. Based on the issues observed in the first iteration, we proposed the following revisions for the second iteration of maker education. We found many students seemed to be distracted by the technology and got a bit overwhelmed by the complexity of the task. As a result, we decided to provide more detailed scaffolding to the students. For example, we created a template worksheet specifying the key elements for story writing (see Fig. 5) so that the activity would offer opportunities for students to practice knowledge and skills of both Chinese and Science. Additionally, the poor execution of project presentation and peer assessment prompted us to create a more detailed assessment rubric, not only for the overall quality of the final product, but also for individual aspects of the product, such as the quality of story, creativity of the image design, and teamwork.

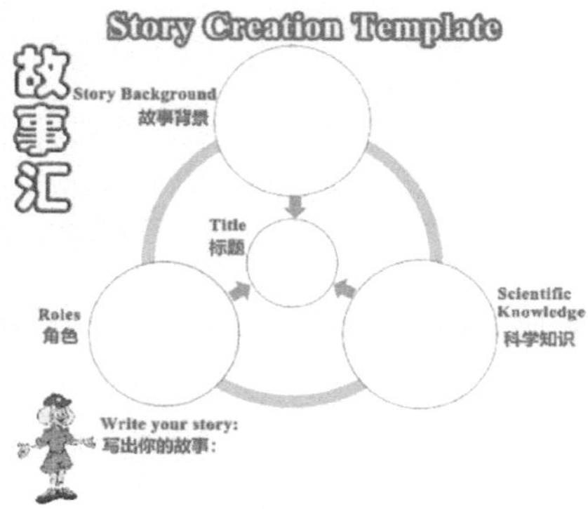

Fig. 5. The template worksheet for story writing used in the second iteration of instruction.

4.2 Second Iteration

Implementation. Compared to the previous class, the second iteration proceeded more smoothly according to the instructional design. The task introduction was about 5 min long, a music videos of the Chinese zodiac and questions about which zodiac animals were mammals were very attractive to students. The template worksheet and project assessment rubric were handed out to the class in advance, which seemed to make students comprehend the requirements of the project task more clearly. In the group collaboration session, students were able to work individually before collaborating with peers and managed to complete the task in shorter period, with improved class discipline and group dynamics. However, the normal length of 45 min per class was still found to be inadequate for the inquiry-based maker education, making everything a bit hasted. For example, the teacher could not elaborate on the requirement of "scientific fact" due to the time constraint, leading to some students confusing common sense with science concepts. The peer assessment was also cut-off by time, making the class ended a bit weak.

Learning Outcomes and Students Experience. The quality of group work improved significantly. Stories were more complete, and the characters were more relevant to the story. For instance, Fig. 6 shows how a storyline about an injured rabbit was reflected in both the image design and 3D model, with the band-aid on an ear as the highlighted feature. Such consistency indicated students comprehended the task requirements and were able to work together to achieve the goal. Moreover, it became clear that AR can be an effective bridge for cross-disciplinary practice. In addition to Chinese and science content, the free shaping and transforming of the virtual clay enabled by Leopoly also allowed for spatial thinking, basic computer operation, and more importantly, the generation and realization of creative ideas.

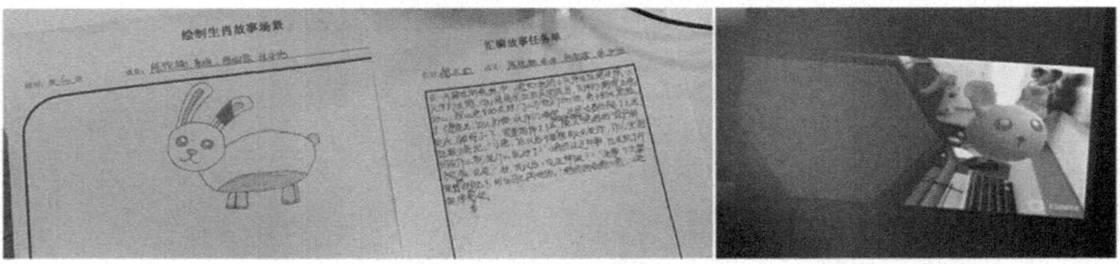

(a) (b)

Fig. 6. One group work display. (a): character design and story; (b): 3D model display.

Reflections on Instructional Design. Despite the apparent improvement, but there were still instructional design decisions in need of revision. Firstly, role-based collaboration was found to cause fragmentation of group work and weak interaction among students in some groups. So, we decided to try the strategy of task-based collaboration, which gave students greater agency regarding the task division and role assignment, with more frequent role rotation during the task completion process. Secondly, class topics of the first two iterations were similar, so we planned to introduce a new topic to examine the far transfer of knowledge and skills in maker education. Thirdly, the perceived benefits of proper scaffolding prompted us to strengthen the use of it by offering a sample product as worked example for the final task. Lastly, upon realizing that insufficient time was a persistent challenge, we decided to double the instructional session by combining two classes together. The first class focused on planning and idea generation whilst the second class focused on technical realization, presentation, and peer assessment.

4.3 Third Iteration

Implementation. This iteration changed the theme into "designing souvenirs for international visitors" and was extended to two periods of planning and development. In collaboration, students were not assigned to specific roles, so they should firstly assign tasks within group and specify individual responsibilities. In terms of disciplinary integration, the teacher emphasized the integration of mathematic concepts and taught about shapes such as cube, sphere and cone. A more detailed template worksheet and assessment rubrics were provided along with a sample souvenir product created by the teacher. With more abundant instructional time, the teacher added a wrap-up and reflection session at the end to guide students to critically reflect on the gains and issues.

Learning Outcomes and Students Experience. Contrary to the common belief, the template worksheet and examples did not restraint the creativity of the students, but rather had them inspire more innovative ideas. For example, some groups decided to add numbers and Chinese characters with symbolic meaning to the souvenir, and managed to decorate not only the side, but also the bottom of the souvenir objects (see Fig. 7). Task-based collaboration worked fine in this session as students no longer complained about the disliked role being assigned to them. But the smooth collaboration might be because students were more familiar with the mode of collaborative inquiry and the responsibility of each role. Meanwhile, enough class time allowed for more practice and trials, making students become more proficient with 3D modeling using AR and have fun in it. Compared to last two iterations, students thought this one was more interesting. One student commented, “this lesson creates a situation for us when foreign friends come to visit. We are more confident to make it better.” It showed that setting up the context and need could stimulate the motivation for students to create innovative artefact in DIY spirit.

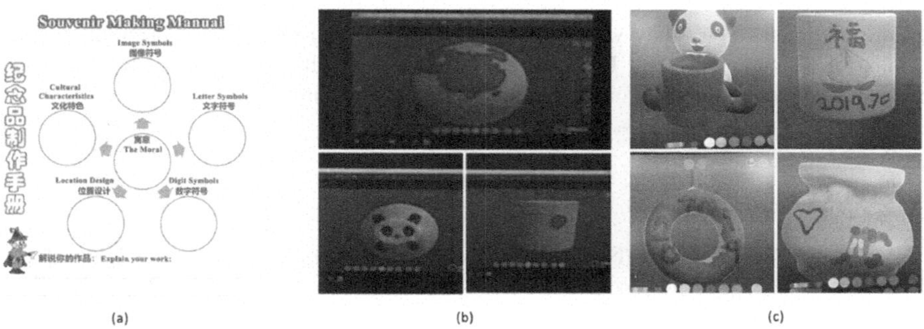

Fig. 7. Scaffoldings and final products in the third iteration of maker education. (a): template worksheet for the souvenir product; (b): Examples of souvenirs created by the teacher; (c) products made by other groups.

5 Conclusion and Implications

This paper explores the design of a makerspace-based instruction in the elementary school setting that promotes collaborative innovation through the technology of AR, presenting a narrative design case in action with empirical evidence and critical reflections on a set of instructional design principles. Technology wise, through three iterations of design, implementation and revision, we found that AR was effective in promoting student engagement in collaborative exploration and task completion, and can be used to integrate inquiry learning from various disciplines such as Chinese, mathematics, science, technology, as well as arts and creativity in particular in this study. Pedagogy wise, despite the young age of students, student-centered collaborative learning turned out to be feasible with proper scaffolding strategies, and necessary due to high student-equipment ratio. Based on the study results, we would like to propose the following six instructional design principles for similar makerspace-based educational contexts:

1. Use makerspace as opportunities to engage learners in higher-order problem-solving activities that focus on cross-disciplinary integration.
2. Follow the general sequence of "engagement-exploration-execution-exhibition-evaluation" to facilitate collaborative inquiry in makerspace.
3. Be flexible about the mode of collaboration, choose role-based or task-based collaboration according to student familiarity and role preferences.
4. Provide students with comprehensive and detailed scaffolding such as template worksheets or examples for complex learning tasks.
5. Manipulate the similarity of the learning task for different classes to promote both near-transfer and far-transfer of learning.
6. Increase class time when needed to allow for more learner exploration, teacher facilitation, project demonstration and reflective evaluation.

Acknowledgment. This study was supported by the National Office for Education Sciences Planning of China under Grant BCA190085. We would also like to thank the Bao'an school district in the city of Shenzhen for their support during the research.

References

1. Anderson, C.: Makers: The New Industrial Revolution. Crown Business, New York (2012)
2. Forest, C.R., et al.: The invention studio: a university maker space and culture. Adv. Eng. Educ. **4**, 1–32 (2014)
3. Smith, A., Hielscher, S., Dickel, S., Soderberg, J., van Oost, E.: Grassroot digital fabrication and makerspaces: reconfiguring, relocating and recalibrating innovation. Sci. Technol. Policy Res. **2**, 1–20 (2013)
4. Blackley, S., Sheffield, R., Maynard, N., Koul, R., Walker, R.: Makerspace and reflective practice: advancing pre-service teachers in STEM education. Aust. J. Teach. Educ. (Online) **42**, 22–37 (2017)
5. Blackley, S., Rahmawati, Y., Fitriani, E., Sheffield, R., Koul, R.: Using a makerspace approach to engage indonesian primary students with STEM. Issues Educ. Res. **28**, 18–42 (2018)
6. Wang, Y.M., Qian, K.L., Hua, J., Guo, J.: Experiencing real learning: towards a new culture of maker education-review of the researches of maker education at home and abroad. E-educ. Res. **2**, 34–43 (2017)
7. Yang, X., Li, J.: The potential value of maker education and its disputes. Mod. Dist. Educ. Res. **2**, 23–34 (2015)
8. Ibáñez, M.B., Delgado-Kloos, C.: Augmented reality for STEM learning: a systematic review. Comput. Educ. **123**, 109–123 (2018)
9. Kerawalla, L., Luckin, R., Seljeflot, S., Woolard, A.: "Making it real": exploring the potential of augmented reality for teaching primary school science. Virtual Reality **10**, 163–174 (2006)

10. Chang, H.-Y., Wu, H.-Y., Hsu, Y.-S.: Integrating a mobile augmented reality activity to contextualize student learning of a socioscientific issue. Br. J. Educ. Technol. **44**, 95–99 (2013)
11. Wang, H.-Y., Duh, H.B.-L., Li, N., Lin, T.-J., Tsai, C.-C.: An investigation of university students' collaborative inquiry learning behaviors in an augmented reality simulation and a traditional simulation. J. Sci. Educ. Technol. **23**(5), 682–691 (2014). https://doi.org/10.1007/s10956-014-9494-8
12. Akçayır, M., Akçayır, G.: Advantages and challenges associated with augmented reality for education: a systematic review of the literature. Educ. Res. Rev. **20**, 1–11 (2017)
13. NMC Horizon Report. https://library.educause.edu/resources/2018/8/2018-nmc-horizon-report
14. Moore, T.J., Guzey, S.S., Brown, A.: Greenhouse design to increase habitable land: an engineering unit. Sci. Scope **37**, 51–57 (2014)
15. Stoneburner, D.: From STEM to STEAM: using brain-compatible strategies to integrate the arts. Roeper Rev. **38**, 129–130 (2013)
16. Lewis, T.: Design and inquiry: bases for an accommodation between science and technology education in the curriculum. J. Res. Sci. Teach. **43**, 255–281 (2006)
17. Vygotsky, L.S.: Mind in Society: The Development of Higher Psychological Processes. Harvard University Press, Cambridge (1978)
18. Belland, B.R.: Handbook of Research on Educational Communications and Technology. Springer, New York (2014). https://doi.org/10.1007/978-1-4614-3185-5
19. Gu, X., Shao, Y., Guo, X., Lim, C.P.: Designing a role structure to engage students in computer-supported collaborative learning. Internet High. Educ. **24**, 13–20 (2015)
20. van Gog, T., Kester, L., Paas, F.: Effects of worked examples, example-problem, and problem-example Pairs on novices' learning. Contemp. Educ. Psychol. **36**, 212–218 (2011)
21. Paas, F., van Gog, T.: Optimising worked example instruction: different ways to increase Germane cognitive load. Learn. Instr. **16**, 87–91 (2006)
22. Clark, R.C., Nguyen, F., Sweller, J., Baddeley, M.: Efficiency in learning: evidence-based guidelines to manage cognitive load. Perform. Improv. **45**, 46–47 (2006)
23. Renkl, A.: Toward an instructionally oriented theory of example-based learning. Cogn. Sci. **38**, 1–37 (2014)
24. Huang, Y.-H., Lin, K.-C., Yu, X., Hung, J.C.: Comparison of different approaches on example-based learning for novice and proficient learners. Hum.-Centric Comput. Inf. Sci. **5**, 5–29 (2015)

Enriched and Smart Learning Experience

Smart Approach to ESP Instruction

Ivana Simonova(✉), Zuzana Prochazkova, Vladimir Lorenc, and Jiri Skoda

Jan Evangelista Purkyne University, Ceske Mladeze 8, 400 96 Ústí nad Labem, Czech Republic
iivana.simonova@gmail.com, {zuzana.prochazkova,vladimir.lorenc,jiri.skoda}@ujep.cz

Abstract. The paper deals with the smart approach to teaching and learning English for Specific Purposes (ESP). First, the theoretical background is introduced providing the definition of the term "smart" and theories examining motivation to learning. Second, in the research part, results of didactic pretests and posttests are compared reflecting learners' types of motivation defined by Plaminek's Inventory, i.e. Coordinators, Explorers, Accurators, Directors. Totally, 119 probands, prospective teachers from the Faculty of Education and experts from the Faculty of Science, participated in this comparative study conducted via quasi-experimental ex-post-facto method for the period of 12 weeks. The smart approach includes the exploitation of smart devices and technologies (applications) in face to face instruction at school and in home preparation for lessons. The findings discovered that the smart approach as applied within this study suited to maximum extent to Coordinators whose increase in knowledge was significantly higher compared to Explorers, Accurators, or Directors.

Keywords: Smart instruction · Higher education · English for Specific Purposes · ESP

1 Introduction

Information and communication technologies (ICT), particularly mobile and smart devices and applications, have been a firm part of the process of instruction at all levels of education. They are reckoned as a strong motivator by numerous authors (e.g. [1–3] and others) supporting both the inner and outer motivation [4]. In English for Specific Purposes (ESP) the smart approach, i.e. exploitation smart devices and tools, has become standard for years. These days, it is even unacceptable to design and conduct the process of instruction without been enhanced by them. As decades ago, when the use of ICT as personal computers and notebooks was under the focus of research, attention is paid to the feature of smartness now. However, a question appears whether all learners are able to acquire the learning content successfully in this way. In other words, do smart devices and applications positively support the process of teaching and learning? Reflecting the above mentioned, in this paper the smart approach to ESP instruction is researched from the view of learners' types of motivation [4]. The main objective of the paper is to compare and analyze their test scores and thus discover whether the smart approach suits to learners of all motivation types.

S. K. S. Cheung et al. (Eds.): ICBL 2020, LNCS 12218, pp. 163–174, 2020.
https://doi.org/10.1007/978-3-030-51968-1_14

2 Theoretical Background

Even though the term "smart" is used rather frequently, not sufficient effort has been devoted to the precise definition. Considering numerous sources, within this paper, the results of review study conducted by Silverio-Fernández et al. [5] are introduced and applied.

2.1 Smart Approach

Silverio-Fernández et al. [5] structured the process towards setting the most appropriate definition into several steps. As the term "smart" is often interchanged and/or confused with "mobile", first, they set a list of key words containing these expressions. Using the online service Google Scholar and Science Direct, the keywords "smart device" and "mobile device" were exploited for search in titles of peer-reviewed journal articles published from 2012 to 2017 in these databases. The results discovered the above mentioned inconsistent use of these words, mostly referring to the same devices. Totally 20 publications were detected having the keyword "smart devices" and 30 ones using the keyword "mobile devices" in the titles. Second, following the White and Marsh [6] design, a systematic content analysis was made which revealed criteria (features) used to define the terms in articles: Autonomy, Connectivity, Context-awareness, Data storage, and User-interaction. The findings show that the occurrence of connectivity was above 50% in both key words (55%; 66.6%), followed by user-interaction (70%; 45%) and autonomy (40%; 16.6%). The occurrence of context awareness is similar (25%; 23.3%), data storage was detected in 20% in both. The feature of "mobility", i.e. the portability, was frequently detected in relation to "mobile device"; however, it rarely appeared with "smart device" key word. Silverio-Fernández et al. [5] agree with Miller [7, p. 9] stating that mobility (of a device) is in contradiction to the user (i.e. a person). Thus they conclude that *autonomy, connectivity and context-awareness* are the key features of "smartness" defined as follows:

Autonomy in smart devices mostly relates to autonomous tasks conducted without direct command of the user having important role in multitasking scenarios [8], or in measuring information through sensors and sending it through autonomously [9]. *Connectivity* refers to establishing a connection to a network of any size for the purpose of gaining sharing information with other devices on the network [10]. *Context-awareness* enables smart devices to perceive information from the environment through sensors such as camera, microphone and Global Positioning System (GPS); thus autonomous decisions can be made, or direct assistance provided to the user. User-interaction, despite been designed for conducting interaction with users via a smart device, was not included in the key features of smartness. The main objection is that devices might never interact directly with users, whereas instead they interact with other devices [7]. Mobility (portability) also was not included in the features of smartness. Been referred as a very characteristic feature of smartphones, tablets and smart watches, it does not apply to every smart device, e.g. on smart board [11], thus proving that the definition of smart devices goes beyond.

To conclude Silverio-Fernández et al. propose following definition of "smartness" [5, no paging]. *"A smart device is a context-aware electronic device capable of performing autonomous computing and connecting to other devices wire or wirelessly for data exchange."* The included features are reflected in the design of ESP instruction described below.

2.2 Motivation to Learning

'To provide joy, to receive results', or 'Do not work. Play. You will produce more'. Could be the motto on how the motivation works in humans (learner's) minds.

Approaches to motivation are based on several motivation theories. However, the main theoretical concepts focus on different matters. Maslow's Hierarchy of Needs [12] states that the individual is willing to produce efforts to at least partially saturate a certain, currently lacking, needs which are structured into five groups of a hierarchic system and have mutual interrelations within the hierarchy. Compared to this, Herzberg's Motivation-Hygiene Theory works with two groups – motivators and hygiene factors. It arises from the precondition that people are/are not able to precisely determine and communicate work conditions which make them satisfied [13]. Those giving them satisfaction are mostly connected with success, recognition, higher responsibility, important tasks etc. On the contrary, feelings not providing satisfaction (in the school environment) are connected with (teacher's) unfair approach, negative relations (to schoolmates), negative (school/class) climate, lack of management and control [2]. Vroom's Expectancy Theory is based on the conviction that people are motivated to conduct any activity if they believe it helps them reach the objective [2]. Thus it can be summarized that the human motivation to doing anything is determined by the importance man sets to the output of efforts multiplied by the trust that it really leads to reaching the objective [14].

Within this research, four types of learners' motivation are considered. Characteristics of single motivation types are defined as follows:

Explorers (dynamics, usefulness). In their behavior, a considerable portion of independence and self-reliance can be found. They are as often impatient and eager for information, and strongly attracted by conquering constraints and challenges. They appreciate freedom and autonomy and cannot stand to be directed. Disagreement is not a means of taking control over others but protecting their own freedom. Their argumentation primarily focuses on the matter, and man is referred only to support the argumentation. They succeed in disciplines in which social skills are not strongly required and maximum rational intelligence and scientific and creative work are needed.

Directors (dynamics, effectiveness). The dynamic part of their motivation does not protect them from running risky activities, the effectiveness determines them for success in social processes and human relations. They are attracted by the possibility to have impact on other people; however, at the same time they strive to achieve maximum freedom for themselves – not within the voluntarily accepted restrictions but the real freedom and unlimited possibilities. They also appreciate to be in the centre of attention and are susceptible to impulses, which is/is not appropriate to the situation. They are able to persuade people about their ideas, being often leaders of social groups (e.g. classmates).

Coordinators (stability, effectiveness). They fully focus on people, their relations, feelings and satisfaction, they like talking to others, asking questions, listening to answers, and they are open to discussions having the ability to understand the others, particularly in the field of feelings and emotions – their empathy is highly developed. They are pillars of social structures so that the environment they work and live in to be warm, human and understanding.

Accurators (stability, usefulness). They are reliable, accurate, hard to themselves and the environment. They appreciate good organization of work, require clear tasks and reach them precisely. Regulations and rules are important for them, they neither like risks, nor negotiating with people. Their communication aims at making the problem clear, collecting and verifying the data etc., thus they seem look calm in social relations. They perform in a rational and emotionally flat way; however, they are open only to those who they closely know and trust. They are loyal to school and teachers they have respect for [2].

3 Research Methodology

3.1 Research Problem, Question, Objective

In this research, the problem relating to smart approach applied in higher education is dealt, when special attention is paid to teaching/learning ESP. Particularly the question appears whether this approach suits to learners of various motivation types. Therefore, a motivation inventory was applied to detect the types within a sample of university students. Analyzing their test scores, *the main objective of the research is to prove whether smart approach as defined below is entitled to be exploited in ESP instruction at higher education level.*

3.2 Research Hypotheses

The main hypothesis was set as follows:

H: When applying the smart approach to ESP instruction, statistically significant difference is detected between learners of various motivation types.

To test the main hypothesis, particular ones were set:

H1: When applying the smart approach to ESP instruction, there exists statistically significant difference in *pretest* scores between groups of Directors, Coordinators, Explorers, and Accurators.
H2: When applying the smart approach to ESP instruction, there exists statistically significant difference in *posttest* scores compared to pretests in groups of Directors, Coordinators, Explorers, and Accurators.
H3: When applying the smart approach to ESP instruction, there exists statistically significant difference in *mean values* of pretest and posttest scores between groups of Directors, Coordinators, Explorers, and Accurators.
H4: When applying the smart approach to ESP instruction, there exists statistically significant *difference* (increase in knowledge) between groups of Directors, Coordinators, Explorers, and Accurators.

3.3 Research Methods and Tools

As smart devices and technologies are widely exploited, it was not acceptable to conduct the pedagogical experiment where the smart approach is exploited in the experimental group, and the control one is taught without. Blended approach as minimum is required by the syllabi of all courses in higher education in the country. Therefore, the comparative study exploiting the quasi-experiment and ex-post-facto method was applied, dealing with differences in acquiring the learning content in learners of different motivation types in the ESP course. Particularly, the increase in test scores between learners' entrance and final knowledge was under the focus. To gather the appropriate data, two tools were used: (1) an inventory detecting learner's type of motivation, (2) didactic tests monitoring learner's test scores. The collected data were processed by appropriate statistic methods (ANOVA, post hoc analysis via Fisher LSD test).

Inventory of Motivation Types

For detecting the motivation type of respondents, the *Inventory of Motivation Types* (IMT) by Plaminek [4] was applied. The tool is structured into two parts. In Part 1, it focuses on the purpose and means of motivation, and differentiates learners on the effectiveness/usefulness scale. This part consists of 14 items. In each of them respondents express their preferences on the five-point scale providing evaluation of pairs of motivators through the intensity of preference in the pair is (possible combinations of points are 5:0, 4:1, 3:2, 2:3, 1:4, 0:5). In Part 2, the inventory concentrates on challenges and safety, and differentiates learners on the stability/dynamics scale using another set of 14 items constructed and evaluated on the identical principle as in Part 1. Then, total score is calculated and the motivation type of each respondent is defined by the combination of scores in both parts of the inventory, i.e. by the effectiveness/usefulness and stability/dynamics scales. Both scales arise from the vitality theory, which belongs to the self-determination theory [15].

Didactic Tests

To measure learners' increase in knowledge after the implementation of smart approach, two didactic tests were applied. The first one, *pretest* detecting learners' knowledge before the process of instruction starts, was exploited at the beginning of the semester; the second one, *posttest* measuring the final knowledge, was used at the end of the semester. The structure of both the didactic tests was identical. Each consisted of 70 tasks reflecting the learning content of ESP, including EAP (English for Academic Purposes). They proportionally covered professional vocabulary from the field of higher education and reflecting probands' study programmes and specializations, professional stylistics and grammar, writing cv and letters, and reading professional texts. All tasks were of open-answer or translation type.

Process of Instruction

Between the pretest and posttest were held, the process of instruction was conducted for the period of 12 weeks. In the process, the smart approach was applied reflecting the key features of this phenomenon defined above – autonomy, connectivity and context-awareness. The smart approach is understood as the exploitation of smart devices and technologies/applications in face-to-face school and after-school learning activities, i.e. using e-sources, particularly parts of MOOCs (Massive Open Online Courses), TED (Technology, Entertainment, and Design) Talks, and various other web pages dealing with professional topics, creating networks which enabled to share information, discuss, or make comments. Probands attended one 90-min lesson per week; the preparation for the next lesson required another 90-min period of after-school (home) work. Face-to-face lessons were mostly devoted to direct (teacher-student, student/s-student/s) conversation, providing feedback on homework and students' questions and problems in learning. This approach met the requirements on individualized teaching in groups (mostly of 15 students, 20 as maximum), when the exploitation of smart technologies/applications available on smart devices satisfied each student's needs towards acquiring the required learning content successfully.

3.4 Research Sample

The research sample consisted of 121 probands detected according to Plaminek's Inventory of Motivation Types as follows: 43 explorers, 33 directors, 23 coordinators, 20 accurators, two probands did not fill-in the questionnaire correctly; final amount was N = 119.

They all were students of Jan Evangelista Purkyne University, Faculty of Education (FE), or Faculty of Natural Sciences (NS), Czech Republic, and they all were involved in the Smart City – Smart Region – Smart Community project within which the research was conducted. The structure of probands was as follows:

- Gender: Male 7%; Female 93%; Age: 19–23 yrs.
- Degree: Bachelor 66% (FE 75%; NS 25%), Master (FE 100%; NS 0%).
- Faculty of Education 82% (M 1%; F 99%) in following study programmes: Teaching at pre-primary schools 39%; Teaching at primary schools 26%; Teaching at primary and SEN (special educational needs) schools 13%; Czech language for media and communication 22%.
- Faculty of Natural Science 18% (M 76%; F 24%) in following study programmes: Information technologies 46%; Toxicology 18%; Biology 12%; Chemistry and Biochemistry 12%; Geography and History 12%.

4 Research Results

The entrance didactic test administered at the beginning of semester (pretest) and final didactic test conducted after 12 weeks of instruction at the end of semester (posttest) provided data for statistic processing which was held in four steps, when comparing: (1) *pretest* scores between groups of Directors, Coordinators, Explorers, and Accurators; (2) *posttest* scores between groups of Directors, Coordinators, Explorers, and Accurators; (3) *mean values of pretests and posttests* between groups of Directors, Coordinators, Explorers, and Accurators; (4) *differences* (increases in knowledge) between *pretest and posttest scores* in groups of Directors, Coordinators, Explorers, and Accurators.

4.1 Results: Comparison of Pretest Scores

In step 1, pretest scores were processed by the method of analysis of variance (ANOVA). Data collected from four groups of learners' motivation types were compared. Results are displayed in Table 1.

Table 1. Comparison of pretest scores between Directors, Coordinators, Explorers, Accurators.

Source	Sum of squares	Df	Mean square	F-ratio	P-value
Between groups	247.211	3	82.4036	**0.51**	**0.6762**
Within groups	25,546.1	158	161.684		
Total (Corr.)	25,793.3	161			

Df: Degree of freedom

The results show that at the significance level $\alpha = 0.05$, the statistically significant differences were not detected between respondents of single motivation types. Groups are equal. **H1 is rejected.**

4.2 Results: Comparison of Posttest Scores

In step 2, posttest scores were processed by the ANOVA method. Data collected from four groups of learners' motivation types were compared. Results are displayed in Table 2.

Table 2. Comparison of posttest scores between Directors, Coordinators, Explorers, Accurators.

Source	Sum of squares	Df	Mean square	F-ratio	P-value
Between groups	1,480.82	3	493.06	**2.86**	**0.0388**
Within groups	27,272.3	158	172.609		
Total (Corr.)	28,753.1	161			

Df: Degree of freedom

The results show that at the significance level $\alpha = 0.05$, the statistically significant differences were detected between respondents of single motivation types. Therefore, the post-hoc analysis exploiting Fisher's Least Significance Difference Test (LSD-test) was applied. Results are displayed in Table 3.

Table 3. Results of Fisher's LSD test.

Contrast	Significance	Difference	± Limits
POST_Director - POST_Coordinator		−4.0682	6.96138
POST_Director - POST_Explorer		4.94996	6.00532
POST_Director - POST_Accurator		2.72678	5.59151
POST_Coordinator - POST_Explorer	*	**9.25678**	6.61177
POST_Coordinator - POST_Accurator	*	**7.0336**	6.23833
POST_Explorer - POST_Accurator		−2.22318	5.14973

*Denotes a statistically significant difference.

The results mean that posttest scores are significantly higher with Coordinators compared to Explorers and Accurators. posttest scores are also higher with Coordinators compared to Directors; however, the difference is not statistically significant. **H2 is accepted.** Differences are displayed in Fig. 1.

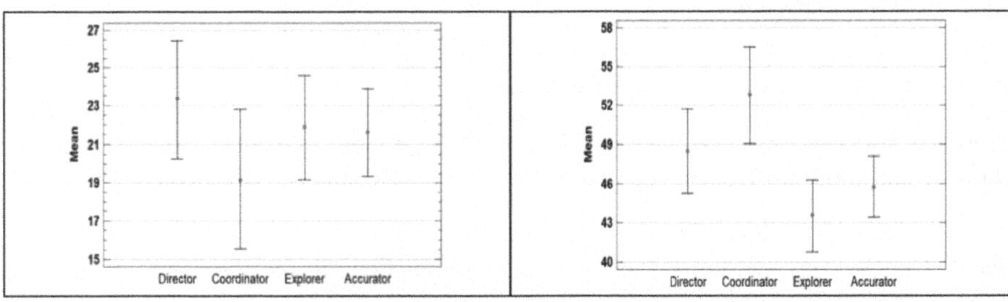

Fig. 1. Results in pretests (left) and posttests (right).

4.3 Results: Comparison of Mean Values of Pretest and Posttest Scores

In step 3, mean pretest and posttest scores were compared in each group of motivation type. Results are displayed in Table 4 for each motivation type.

The null hypothesis is rejected in all motivation types. This result means that at the significance level $\alpha = 0.05$ in all groups mean values of posttest scores are significantly higher compared to pretest scores. Results are displayed in Fig. 2. **H3 is accepted.**

4.4 Results: Comparison of Differences in Knowledge

In step 4, the ANOVA method was applied to compare increases in knowledge between pretest and posttest scores in single groups of motivation types. Results are displayed in Table 5.

The results mean that at the significance level $\alpha = 0.05$, the statistically significant differences were detected in increases in knowledge between respondents of single

Table 4. Comparison of means between Directors, Coordinators, Explorers, Accurators.

95.0% confidence interval for mean of PRE_Director: 23.3636 ± 4.19908 [19.1646; 27.5627] 95.0% confidence interval for mean of POST_Director: 48.4848 ± 4.62248 [43.8624; 53.1073] 95.0% confidence interval for the difference between the means assuming equal variances: −25.1212 ± 6.12477 [−31.246; −18.9964] t test to compare means assuming equal variances: t = −8.19385 P-value = $1.46818.10^{-11}$
95.0% confidence interval for mean of PRE_Coordinator: 19.1667 ± 4.49936 [14.6673; 23.666] 95.0% confidence interval for mean of POST_Coordinator: 52.7917 ± 4.86099 [47.9307; 57.6527] 95.0% confidence interval for the difference between the means assuming equal variances: −33.625 ± 6.44516 [−40.0702; −27.1798] t test to compare means assuming equal variances: t = −10.5015 P-value = 0
95.0% confidence interval for mean of PRE_Explorer: 21.8837 ± 4.03238 [17.8513; 25.9161] 95.0% confidence interval for mean of POST_Explorer: 43.5349 ± 4.25874 [39.2761; 47.7936] 95.0% confidence interval for the difference between the means assuming equal variances: −21.6512 ± 5.77924 [−27.4304; −15.8719] t test to compare means assuming equal variances: t = −7.45008 P-value = $7.55853.10^{-11}$
95.0% confidence interval for mean of PRE_Accurator: 21.6129 ± 3.44674 [18.1662; 25.0596] 95.0% confidence interval for mean of POST_Accurator: 45.7581 ± 3.37022 [42.3878; 49.1283] 95.0% confidence interval for the difference between the means assuming equal variances: −24.1452 ± 4.77235 [−28.9175; −19.3728] t test to compare means assuming equal variances: t = −10.0156 P-value = 0

motivation types. Therefore, the post-hoc analysis exploiting Fisher's LSD-test was applied. Results are displayed in Table 6.

The results show that the increase in knowledge is significantly higher with Coordinators compared to other groups; however, differences between Directors, Explorers, and Accurators are not significant. **H4 is accepted.** Differences are displayed in Fig. 3.

5 Interpretations, Discussions, Conclusions

Referring to the above mentioned motivation concepts, in the school environment it means that the school motivation aims at learners' inner engagement into fulfilling the learning activity in a way which supports their further development. This inner interest forms the basis for development of auto-didactic strategies. Within the school instruction various individual needs of learners' activities should be emphasized, as well as their time and situation variability [2]. On the other side, such situations should be avoided which might induce learners' frustration and dissatisfaction, and thus decrease their motivation.

To sum up, the presented results *prove that the described smart approach is entitled to be applied in ESP instruction of all motivation types at higher education level.* Having the test score of all groups equal at the beginning in pretest (i.e. H1 rejected), statistically

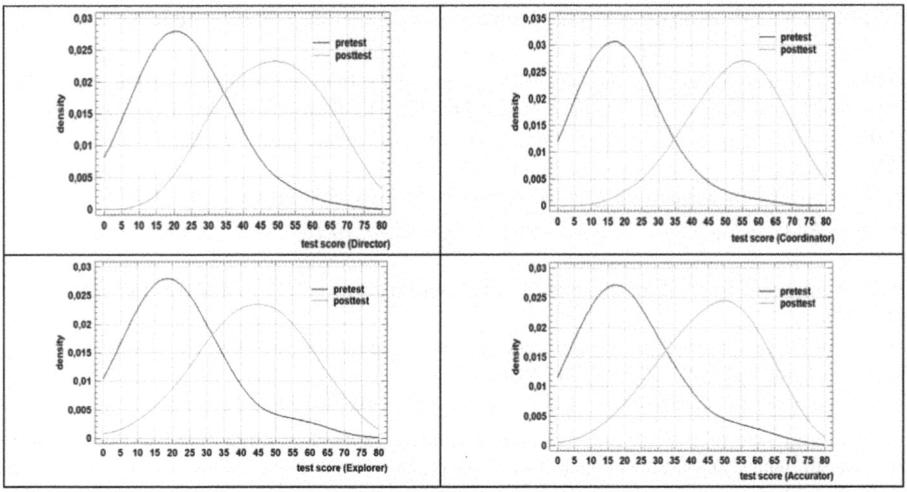

Fig. 2. Comparison of mean values in pretest and posttest scores in single motivation types (Director: upper left, Coordinator: upper right, Explorer: bottom left, Accurator: bottom right)

Table 5. Comparison of increases in knowledge between Directors, Coordinators, Explorers, Accurators.

Source	Sum of squares	Df	Mean square	F-ratio	P-value
Between groups	2,312.19	3	770.73	**3.48**	**0.0174**
Within groups	34,980.6	158	221.396		
Total (Corr.)	37,292.8	161			

Df: Degree of freedom

Table 6. Results of Fisher's LSD test.

Contrast	Significance	Difference	± limits
DIF_Director - DIF_Coordinator	*	**−8.50379**	7.88403
DIF_Director - DIF_Explorer		3.47005	6.80125
DIF_Director - DIF_Accurator		0.976051	6.3326
DIF_Coordinator - DIF_Explorer	*	**11.9738**	7.48809
DIF_Coordinator - DIF_Accurator	*	**9.47984**	7.06514
DIF_Explorer - DIF_Accurator		−2.494	5.83227

*Denotes a statistically significant difference.

significant difference (increase in knowledge) was detected in posttest scores of all groups compared to pretests (H2 accepted), as well as in mean values (i.e. H3 accepted),

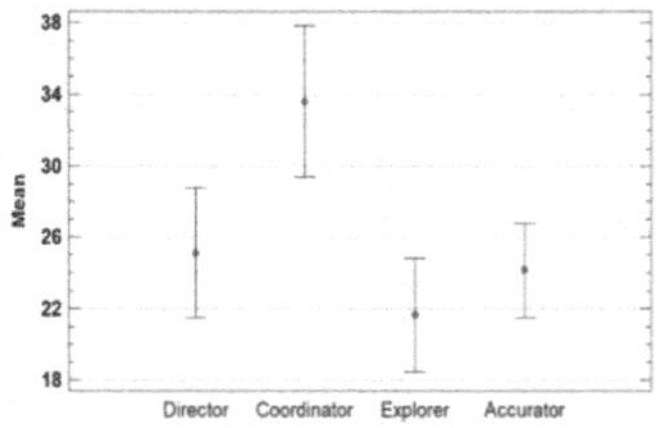

Fig. 3. Differences in knowledge between single motivation types.

and also, statistically significant increase in knowledge was found out in the group of Coordinators compared to Directors, Explorers, and Accurrators (i.e. H4 accepted).

Coordinators, preferring and combining the stability and effectiveness, express emotional intelligence and expect the others to reflect coordinators' empathy in feedback. This feature is strongly required in smart approach where the exploitation of technologies and devices might cause lack of "human" approach. As they prefer relations to results, they make efforts not to fail in meeting the others' expectations; they concentrate on building positive working/learning environment.

However, results of this study are limited, mainly by some characteristics of the research sample. Particularly, there is imbalance in gender (80% of female probands), participating faculties (80% of Faculty of Education), and study programmes (80% of prospective teachers). On the other side, the results entitle the smart approach to be suitable for prospective teachers, and future research activities should be focused on students of other programmes. This finding is very important, as the prospective teachers are those bearing progress in the process of instruction; they have experience in smart approach from both the theoretical and practical view. In agreement with latest works, not to decrease but support to teachers' motivation is a crucial task of the pre-service and in-service teacher training [16, 17]. However, motivation does not only play the vital role but also builds barriers to learning, as emphasized e.g. by Sabah [18], or Ramirez-Arellano [19].

As smart devices and technologies are all around us, the appropriate attention should be devoted to their exploitation in the field of education, with special focus on prospective teachers. In foreign language instruction, the smart approach is rather wide; therefore, further researches monitoring this field are strongly required in the future.

Acknowledgements. The paper is supported by the Smart City – Smart Region – Smart Community project OP VVV, PO1, N. CZ.02.1.01/0.0/0.0/17_048/0007435.

References

1. Cirus, L., Manenova, M., Skoda, J.: Teachers' Attitudes Towards ICT and Their Reflection in the Pupils' Digital Literacy, 1st edn. Educa PF UJEP, Usti nad Labem (2019)
2. Skoda, J., Doulik, P., Bilek, M., Simonova, I.: The effectiveness of inquiry-based science education in relation to the learners' motivation types. J. Baltic Sci. Educ. **14**(6), 791–803 (2015)

3. Ojeda-Guerra, C.N.: Using ICT to motivate students in a heterogeneous programming group. In: Mascio, T.D., Gennari, R., Vittorini, P., De la Prieta, F. (eds.) Methodologies and Intelligent Systems for Technology Enhanced Learning. AISC, vol. 374, pp. 33–40. Springer, Cham (2015). https://doi.org/10.1007/978-3-319-19632-9_5
4. Plaminek, J.: Tajemstvi motivace - jak zařídit, aby pro vás lidé rádi pracovali. [The Secret of Motivation – How to Make People Like Working for You], 2nd edn. Grada, Praha (2010)
5. Silverio-Fernández, M., Renukappa, S., Suresh, S.: What is a smart device? A conceptualisation within the paradigm of the IoT. Vis. Eng. **6**(3), 1–10 (2018). https://doi.org/10.1186/s40327-018-0063-8
6. White, M.D., Marsh, E.E.: Content analysis: a flexible methodology. Libr. Trends **55**(1), 22–45 (2006)
7. Miller, M.: The Internet of Things: How Smart TVs, Smart Cars, Smart Homes, and Smart Cities are Changing the World. Pearson Education, London (2015)
8. Zhang, Y., Mao, M., Rau, P.P., Choe, P., Bela, L., Wang, F.: Exploring factors influencing multitasking interaction with multiple smart devices. Comput. Hum. Behav. **29**(6), 2579 (2013)
9. Schleich, J., Faure, C., Klobasa, M.: Persistence of the effects of providing feedback alongside smart metering devices on household electricity demand. Energy Policy **107**, 225–233 (2017)
10. Cheng, J.W., Mitomo, H.: The underlying factors of the perceived usefulness of using smart wearable devices for disaster applications. Telemat. Inform. **34**(2), 528–539 (2017)
11. Malkawi, N.: The effect of using smart board on the achievement of tenth grade students in English language and on verbal interaction during teaching in public schools. Int. Res. Educ. **5**(1), 197–208 (2017)
12. Maslow, A.H.: A theory of human motivation. Psychol. Rev. **50**(4), 370–396 (1943). http://psycnet.apa.org/record/1943-03751-001. Accessed 29 Jan 2020
13. Miner, J.B.: Organizational Behavior: Essential Theories of Motivation and Leadership. M. E. Sharpe Inc., Armonk (2005)
14. Gagné, M., Deci, E.L.: Self-determination theory and work motivation. J. Organ. Behav. **26**, 331–362 (2005)
15. Deci, E.L., Ryan, R.M.: Self-determination theory: a macrotheory of human motivation, development, and health. Can. Psychol. **49**(3), 182–185 (2008)
16. Min, Q.S., Wang, Z.F., Liu, N.: Integrating a cloud learning into English-medium instruction to enhance non-native English-speaking students' learning. Innov. Educ. Teach. Int. **56**(4), 493–504 (2019)
17. Sanchez-Cortez, I.: Teaching methods, teacher engagement and goals in b-learning. Aula Abierta **48**(3), 311–319 (2019)
18. Sabah, N.M.: Motivation factors and barriers to the continuous use of blended learning approach using Moodle: students' perception and individual differences. Behav. Inf. Technol. Early Access (2019)
19. Ramirez-Arallano, A., Bory-Reyes, J., Hernandez-Simon, L.M.: Emotions, cognitive-metacognitive strategies, and behavior as predictors of learning performance in blended learning. J. Educ. Comput. Res. **57**(2), 491–512 (2019)

A Motivational 3D EdTech in Online Education: Digital Exhibition Space

Hanyuning Lin(✉) and Mathew Pryor

The University of Hong Kong, Pok Fu Lam, Hong Kong SAR, China
lynnlhyn@hku.hk

Abstract. With the outbreak of COVID-19, university classes in Hong Kong have had to transfer into online digital formats. Although no significant difference in learning outcomes between traditional classroom and online learning has been identified, students are still likely to feel distracted or bored. Thoughtful pedagogical strategies and learning design are needed to avoid disengagement which could have negative impact on their academic performance. Regarding the forms of student interactivity or features of online environments, this study examines a motivational EdTech tool - Digital Exhibition Space (DES) - which provides explorative learning experiences for students to foster meaningful peer socialisation. DES creates a 3D visual learning community aimed at enhancing connectivity amongst students, and relatedness between students and their learning artefacts so as to leverage student engagement and learning effectiveness in online education. A quasi-experimental pilot study was undertaken in an entry level class of 106 undergraduates from all faculties of the university. Quantitative results revealed that 1) students in DES learning context reported a higher level of engagement than non-DES context; 2) academic performance in DES groups was better in synoptic assessment than non-DES groups while equivalent in factual knowledge tests.

Keywords: Educational technology · Peer socialisation · Learning motivation

1 Introduction

It is acknowledged that social interactivity plays a key role in learner engagement and knowledge construction in online teaching and learning; online classrooms allow students to learn at anytime and anywhere at their own pace, breaking the distance between the instructor and students [1]. Emerging technologies provide access for those who cannot join face-to-face sessions and participate in collaborative activities. This is especially so in times of emergency, such as the recent COVID-19 pandemic during which campus classes in Mainland China and Hong Kong were suspended and transferred online. Common challenges faced by educators in e-learning, including: student confusion [2]; low motivation [3]; and lack of engagement [4], may become more intense due to emotional anxiety [2], and further limit or deter the expected learning experiences and objectives.

This study examined a 3D Digital Exhibition Space (DES) used as part of the class activities in a common core course at the University of Hong Kong. DES creates a visual

S. K. S. Cheung et al. (Eds.): ICBL 2020, LNCS 12218, pp. 175–186, 2020.
https://doi.org/10.1007/978-3-030-51968-1_15

learning community by allowing students to share a single online space to develop and exhibit their own learning artefacts and review each other's works. The 3D technology allowed students to wander around and explore a central space and adjoining galleries to seek subject-related information. In this process, students feel relaxed and fun, and meaningful peer socialisation and peer learning are promoted. A quasi-experimental pilot study involving 106 undergraduate students in this course was undertaken. The quantitative data revealed that, even in this time of heightened anxiety, students that studied with DES appeared to have 1) a significantly higher level of engagement and 2) better performance in synoptic assessments than the control groups.

In the next session, a brief literature review of several recent socialisation or visualization technologies applied in educational settings is provided. Then, the relevant pedagogical theories and functional interfaces of the Digital Exhibition Space are demonstrated. Followed by a description of the methodology and results of the quasi-experimental pilot study. The final part discusses and concludes the pedagogical practice and research value of this study.

2 Literature Review

2.1 Prior Tech Regarding Socialisation

Past research has identified that the use of Facebook in college education was positively related to student engagement in the perspectives of psychosocial development or cognitive development [5, 6]. Similarly, a wiki including a collection of web pages served as a collective knowledge construction repository to foster effective interaction and reflection amongst students [7–9]. However, a failed experiment was reported on using wiki as an interactive activity in class that none of the students posted anything on wiki possibly out of academic pressure and lack of confidence [10].

Although some studies reported that technology had an affirmative influence on test scores and course grades in primary and secondary schools [11, 12], there was a notable divergence in linkage between technologies and academic achievements in higher education [13, 14].

Recent studies have noted that embracing the use of technology, the alignment of meaningful learning activities/strategies and objectives in online learning environments have yet to be developed [15]. Moreover, online socialisation is still in the stage of being achieved via chat fora or video calls. The use of interactive 3D models to enrich student learning experiences has not been widely explored by researchers due to the limitation of technical efficacy.

2.2 Prior Tech Regarding Visualization

Talking about the concept of socialisation in online learning, naturally leads to virtual learning communities [16, 17]. It was discovered that student perception of community was lower in e-learning environments compared to traditional classes [20]. Many researchers have focused on the process of establishing social networks to support collaborative knowledge construction via virtual classrooms [18, 19]. In recent years, researchers have defined visualization in online learning contexts differently. For example, to visualize student learning trajectories for learning analytics, a circular view diagram (3-level segments) was designed on a serious game-design learning platform in order to identify and solve learning problems [21]; a tool was developed to visualize the data (e.g. used time or scores) collected from student group's participatory behaviours in a game-based assessment with the purpose of refining the activity [22]; and an add-on tool was created and implemented on Open edX [23].

Comparatively, there has been little research that focuses on the learning outcomes, trying to visualize and exhibit student project works or learning artefacts to the public as a group, to motivate and intrigue students to participate more, attempt more and contribute more in their assignments.

2.3 Research Rationale

The research team noted that student engagement was empirically associated with desired learning outcomes referring to their devotion of time and efforts in class activities [24]. Addressing the gaps in educational practices and research studies in higher education context, the team integrated a 3D model technique, designed and developed the Digital Exhibition Space (DES), as a motivational EdTech tool, to enhance both student engagement and academic performances by providing opportunities for explorative learning experiences and emphasizing the visualization of learning outcomes. The hypotheses proposed in this study are, that in online distance learning contexts:

H1: Students using DES will report a higher level of engagement.
H2: Students using DES will have academic performances of better quality.

3 Digital Exhibition Space (DES)

Underpinning the primary stance for the evolution of EdTech are meaningful peer socialisation and relatedness between students and their artefacts. Pedagogical strategies of Technology-facilitated Socialised Learning and Self-determination Theory were the framework of the design of DES.

3.1 Technology-Facilitated Socialised Learning

Technology-facilitated Socialised Learning (SL) is defined as a pedagogy that encourages students with different backgrounds and basic knowledge of their own discipline, to develop social connections and work collaboratively in high-tech environments [25]. Within an SL-designed course, students are tasked to exchange knowledge, regulate their own learning and group members' learning (e.g. goals, progress, quality etc.), offer help or even give some pressures to each other when needed, and critically reflect on themselves continually [25]. In essence, this framework articulates an approach to form a coherent online learning community and assign meaningful collaborative tasks for students to utilise their prior knowledge and learn from each other. By facilitating critical and reflective discourses and regulating socio-emotional interaction [26], higher levels of engagement and better learning outcomes are expected.

3.2 Self-determination Theory (SDT)

Relatedness, competence and autonomy were identified as three essential psychological needs in motivation [27, 28]. Relatedness stands for a sense of attachment and belonging [28]. Competence refers to the need to feel confident and effective [28]. Autonomy is having the freedom to make personal decisions [28, 29]. The former two factors underlie intrinsic motivation; and relatedness facilitates student internalization of extrinsic motivation and promotes positive outcomes in a supportive social environment [30], which are congruent with previous research findings [31]. More specifically, SDT postulates that people tend to internalize the value and regulation driven by extrinsic motivation and turn it into positive behaviours when they experience fulfilment for the needs of relatedness [30].

3.3 Functional Interface

Digital Exhibition Space creates a 3D environment for students to learn collaboratively within their own study groups, and subsequently with the whole class. In DES (see Fig. 1), the whole class is considered as a social learning community while individual student groups are considered as component learning units.

Fig. 1. Overview of 3D digital exhibition space

The format of the DES used in this course was composed of 8 galleries, each of them represents a theme relevant to the course core. Each student learning unit was assigned to a thematic gallery and relevant projects. Several units worked under the same theme but each had their own gallery space (see Fig. 2). The four columns in the central plaza delivered the learning materials and core values of the course provided by instructors.

Within each thematic gallery, the frames on the walls serve as display windows for students to upload and exhibit their project artefacts. Students are required to set the

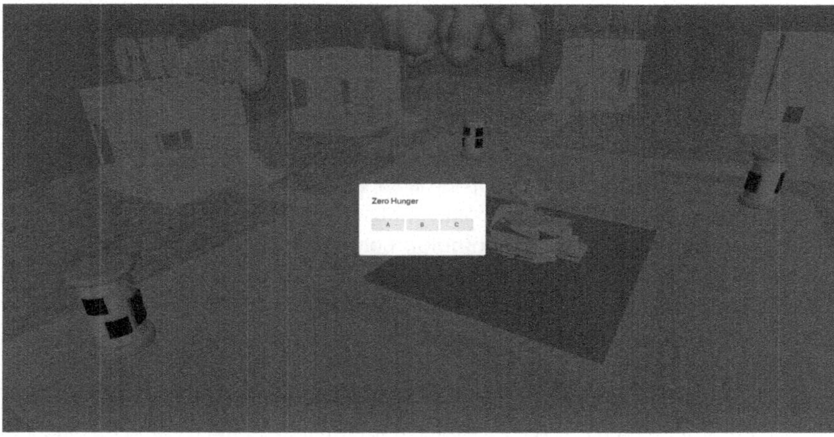

Fig. 2. Student learning units under each theme

cover page for the frames and populate their thematic room with a selection of their works.

Students can visit each other's room to read the title, summative description and author(s) of each frame and click the frame to view detailed contents (see Fig. 3). Access to DES and thematic rooms is open to the whole class via the Internet so that students can share their learning outcomes with anyone as an online exhibition.

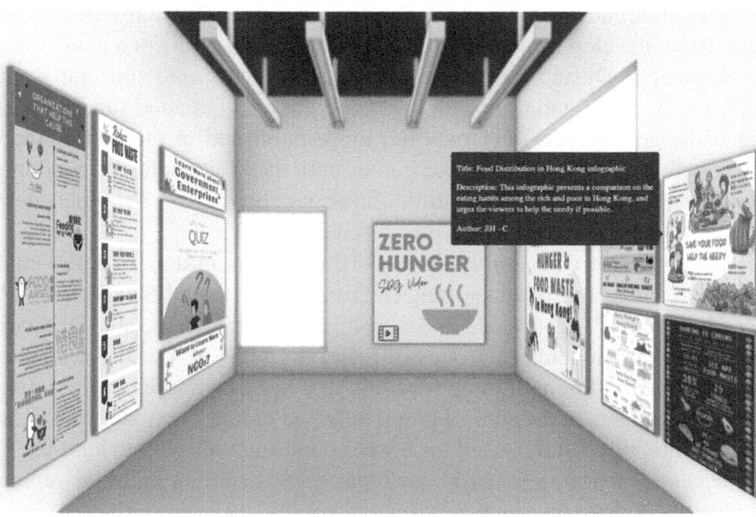

Fig. 3. Individual thematic gallery

4 Quasi-experimental Pilot Study

4.1 Research Context

The University of Hong Kong set a series of common core courses for new undergraduates. The mission is to prepare students to become active and responsible citizens of global and local communities; develop broader and critical perspectives on complex issues; as well as understand the interconnections of these issues and their daily lives.

DES was applied in one of the common core courses which previously ran as a flipped classroom. This CC course investigates the United Nations (UN) sustainable development goals (SDG) and aims to inspire students to think about the way society might construct sustainable cities and communities in future. Students are challenged to use different media and presentational strategies in this course to develop their competence in argumentation and advocacy relating to SDGs in Hong Kong and internationally. However, classes on campus were suspended and transferred into online formats due to the outbreak of coronavirus. This led not only to a shift from a flipped class pedagogy to an online distance teaching, but also had an impact on student emotional engagement and participation.

In DES, the 8 thematic galleries respectively represented 8 different SDGs, such as Zero Hunger, Gender Equality and Quality Education etc. The plaza played the central role of Sustainable Cities and Communities, whose development was constituted and contributed by the surrounding SDGs. Each SDG had three groups of 4 or 5 students (106 students and 24 groups in total, 10 groups of 5 and 14 groups of 4) working on it. There were a set of SDG-relevant assignments that students needed to accomplish individually or with their group mates, for instance preparation of: advocacy videos; infographic diagrams; postcards; and so on. Moreover, students could decide what additional artefacts they would like to develop for their gallery, like developing a quiz or a game for visitors, making a meme, etc. During the learning process, students were constantly uploading and populating the SDG galleries with the works they had created (and were satisfied with). Since the gallery was only required to be published at the end of the course, students were allowed to not publish the frames until they felt confident. Students' work could be updated or amended at any time. Students could also visit other classmate's SDG galleries to learn from their published frames.

In this pilot study, we randomly divided 106 students into an experimental learning environment and a controlled learning environment. In the DES experimental group, there were 55 students (7 groups of 5 and 5 groups of 4) while in the non-DES controlled group, there were 51 students (3 groups of 5 and 9 groups of 4). DES was introduced to students in the experimental group from the first session, and later via online Zoom tutorials. While students in the control group only had online Zoom tutorials. The whole quasi-experimental pilot study lasted for 5 weeks and students in both learning environments had access to learning materials on Open edX. Learning materials uploaded on DES and Open edX were the same.

4.2 Participants and Instruments

89 undergraduates in this course gave their consent and participated in this pilot research study. A quasi-experiment was conducted and amongst participants, 51 of them were

from DES experimental groups, while 38 were from controlled groups; 48 of them were female and 41 of them were male; 74 of them were year 1 students and 15 of them were year 2. The participants were distributed across the university in 9 different faculties which were Faculty of Engineering, Medicine, Arts, Architecture, Law, Business and Economics, Dentistry, Science and Social Science.

Student engagement was measured by a 10-item self-reported questionnaire (Skinner, Kinderman and Furrer 2009), derived from Wellborn (1991), evaluating both behaviour and emotional engagement. Student academic performance was evaluated by the grade of two individual assessments: a reading response and a quiz. The reading response was based on a pre-class given SDG reading, which required a comprehensive understanding and critical mind set on the SDG as it related to personal, territorial (Hong Kong) and global scales. Students were asked to share their ideas and discuss within their groups on Zoom, and individually constructed a short argument after class. Students in the DES experimental group were asked to design a cover page and upload their reading response to their SDG gallery. The quiz was based on two pre-class course videos recorded by the instructor (the second author) testing about the factual knowledge and statistics of a SDG, and conducted in a Zoom tutorial. Marking was an anonymous process in which identifiers like student number and name were removed.

4.3 Data Analysis and Results

Normality test, independent sample t-test and Mann-Whitney U test were undertaken after the data collection to test whether there was a significant difference in engagement and learning performances between experimental groups and control groups.

Engagement. To analyze the collected questionnaire data from both experimental and control groups, the normality of student engagement data distribution was tested in SPSS. Histograms are presented (see Fig. 4 and Fig. 5) and Shapiro-Wilk test suggested a normal distribution in the data of non-DES controlled groups, $W(38) = .959$, $p = .18$; while an insignificant normality was indicated in the data of DES experimental groups, $W(51) = .952$, $p = .038$.

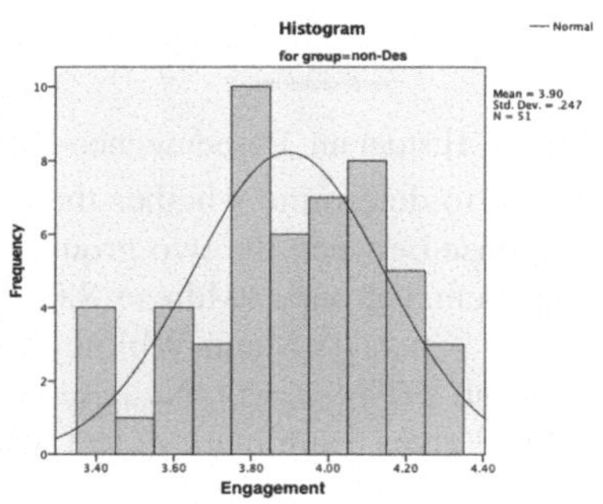

Fig. 4. Histogram_Engagement_non-DES

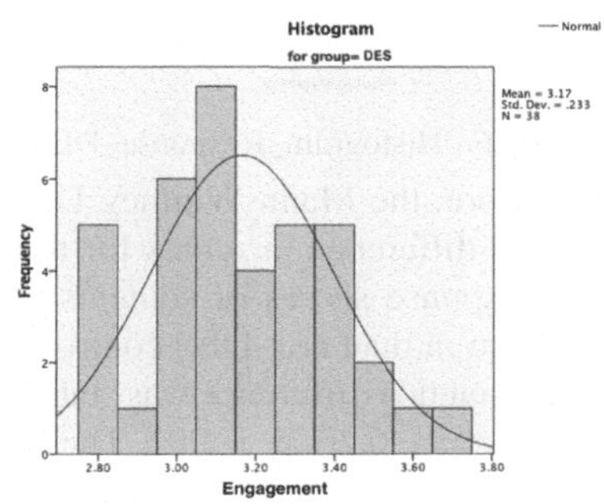

Fig. 5. Histogram_Engagement_DES

Thus, the non-parametric, Mann-Whitney U test, was applied to examine whether significant differences could be found between experimental and controlled groups. The scores of self-reported engagement in DES experimental groups (Mdn = 3.9) were higher than in non-DES controlled groups (Mdn = 3.1). The results of Mann-Whitney U test supported the first hypothesis in this study, postulating that this difference was statistically significant, $U(N_{DES} = 51, N_{non\text{-}DES} = 38) = 36.50$, $z = -7.76$, $p < .001$. Table 1 summarizes the test results.

Table 1. Mann-Whitney U test results_Engagement

Test statistics[a] Engagement			
Mann-Whitney U	36.500	Wilcoxon W	777.500
Z	−7.757	Asymp. Sig. (2-tailed)	.000

[a]Grouping Variable: group

Reading Response. After collecting data from experimental and control groups, the normality of reading response scores in the two independent samples was tested in SPSS. Histograms are presented (see Fig. 6 and Fig. 7) and the Shapiro-Wilk test showed a significant normality in DES experimental groups, $W(51) = .958$, $p = .066$; while a significant departure from normality was observed in non-DES control groups, $W(38) = .647$, $p = .00$.

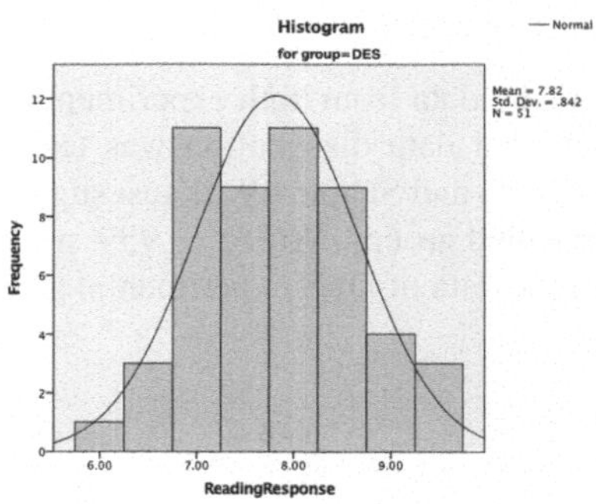

Fig. 6. Histogram_Response_DES

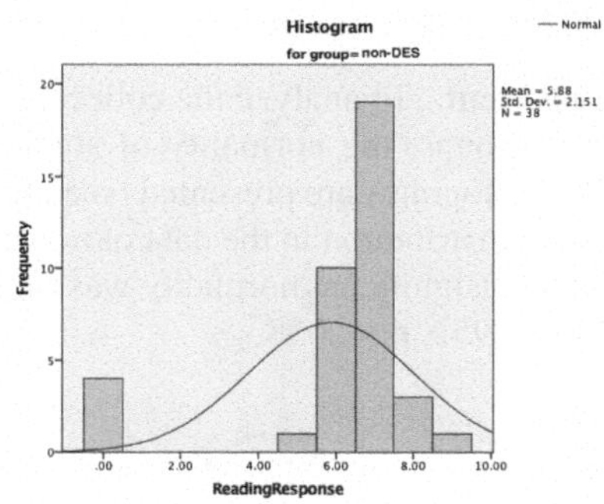

Fig. 7. Histogram_Response_non-DES

Therefore, the Mann-Whitney U test was applied to determine whether there was a profound difference in scores for the reading response between the two groups. The reading response scores of students in DES experimental groups (Mdn = 8.0) were higher those in than non-DES controlled groups (Mdn = 6.5). A Mann-Whitney U test indicated that this difference was statistically significant, $U(N_{DES} = 51, N_{ncn\text{-}DES} = 38) = 222.50$, $z = -6.26$, $p < .001$. The following Table 2 gives a summary of test results.

Quiz. The normality of quiz scores distribution in the two independent samples was also tested in SPSS. Histograms are presented (see Fig. 8 and Fig. 9) and the Shapiro-Wilk test showed a significant normality in both groups, $W(51) = .973$, $p = .30$, and control groups, $W(38) = .949$, $p = .08$.

Table 2. Mann-Whitney U test results_ReadingResponse

Test statistics[a] ReadingResponse			
Mann-Whitney U	222.500	Wilcoxon W	963.500
Z	−6.259	Asymp. Sig. (2-tailed)	.000

[a]Grouping Variable: group

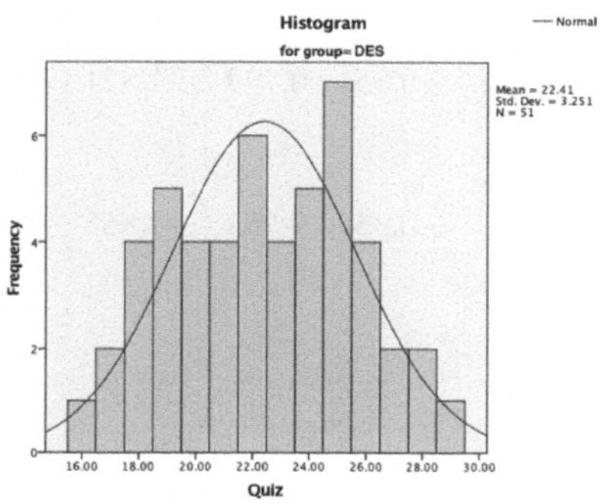

Fig. 8. Histogram_Quiz_DES

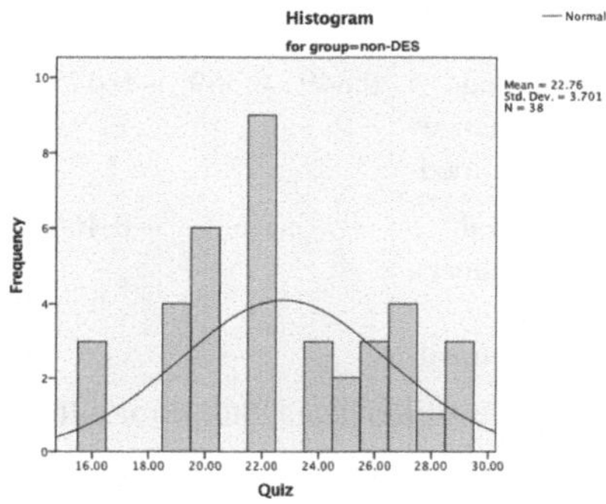

Fig. 9. Histogram_Quiz_non-DES

Therefore, an independent sample t-test was applied. The result indicated that there was no significant difference in quiz scores, $t(87) = -.475$ and $p = .359$, between the 51 students in DES experimental groups ($M = 22.41$, $SD = 3.25$) and the 38 students in non-DES controlled groups ($M = 22.76$, $SD = 3.70$). The following Table 3 and Table 4 give a summary of the test results.

Table 3. Descriptive data of quiz scores in experimental groups and controlled groups

	Group	N	Mean	Std. Deviation	Std. Error Mean
Quiz	DES	51	22.412	3.251	.455
	non-DES	38	22.763	3.701	.600

Hence, the second hypothesis was only partially supported, indicating that the enhancement of learning outcomes with DES is subject to the nature of the knowledge and assessments.

5 Discussion and Conclusion

Researcher has mentioned that online education relies on the creation of learning communities [32]. A sense of community is based upon common goals and needs [26]. DES

Table 4. Independent t-test results on quiz scores in DES groups and non-DES groups

		Levene's test for equality of variances		t-test for equality of means						
		F	Sig.	t	df	Sig. (2-tailed)	MD[a]	SED[b]	95% confidence interval of the difference	
									Lower	Upper
Quiz	Equal variances assumed	0.849	0.359	−0.475	87	0.636	−0.351	0.739	−1.821	1.118
	Equal variances not assumed			−0.466	73.73	0.642	−0.351	0.753	−1.853	1.15

Notes: [a]Mean difference, [b]Std. Error difference

creates an online version of a socialised learning community for the whole class and small learning units for individual student groups. The space structure of connecting the central plaza with SDG galleries shapes the concept that building sustainable cities and communities as a core target in global villages needs to be equally constituted and contributed by different sustainable development goals, which strongly aligns with the learning objectives of the course.

Integrating the 3D model platform, DES provides students with an explorative learning experience via central plaza and SDG galleries as well as transforms students' individual and group artefacts for further peer learning. Through the activity of populating their own SDG gallery and visiting classmate's SDG galleries, students' perspectives towards the sustainability issue have been expanded and diversified; and their way of thinking about the synergy between global issues and themselves has been inspired.

Therefore, even in this challenging time when everybody is anxious, as the pilot study revealed, both student behavioural and emotional engagement in DES learning groups and scores of reading responses were notably higher than the non-DES learning groups. Since knowledge exchange, regulation of learning behaviours and reflections through meaningful peer socialisation were efficient as expected in DES, effective learning behaviours were performed. What is more, visualization and exhibition of selected project works, as well as given autonomy on personalized assignments, foster the students' ownership of their artefacts, which strengthens the sense of relatedness between themselves and their outcomes compared to the usual oblivion after submitting the works. As a result, students feel more ambitious and confident, and more willing to spend time on, and make more contributions to, their projects. Another possible clue could be the novelty of the 3D technology, which raises student curiosity to explore the unknown.

However, the student quiz scores were broadly equivalent between DES and non-DES learning groups. The results indicate that online learning innovation has limited effects on acquisition of factual knowledge, which aligns with the previous research findings that peer socialisation is of less importance if the learning activity is about information acquisition [33]. Synoptic assessment which requires comprehensive understanding and critical mind set on a subject will benefit more from meaningful social interaction.

In conclusion, this study introduces the Digital Exhibition Space (DES) as a new motivational tool to provide students with explorative learning experience through 3D technology and helps to visualize student learning outcomes. Both student socio-cognitive and academic engagement are enhanced due to the increased meaningful socialisation amongst students and intrinsic motivations intrigued by relatedness between students and their artefacts. DES is designed to apply in both blended learning or online learning contexts. The pilot study revealed that, under the circumstances which required all classes to be conducted online, DES managed to help students achieve a higher level of engagement and better academic performance.

References

1. Beldarrain, Y.: Distance education trends: integrating new technologies to foster student interaction and collaboration. Distance Educ. **27**(2), 139–153 (2006)
2. O'regan, K.: Emotion and e-learning. J. Asynchronous Learn. Netw. **7**(3), 78–92 (2003)
3. Keller, J., Suzuki, K.: Learner motivation and e-learning design: a multinationally validated process. J. Educ. Media **29**(3), 229–239 (2004)
4. O'Flaherty, J., Phillips, C.: The use of flipped classrooms in higher education: a scoping review. Internet High. Educ. **25**, 85–95 (2015)
5. Kuh, G.D.: What student affairs professionals need to know about student engagement. J. Coll. Stud. Dev. **50**(6), 683–706 (2009)
6. Gachago, D., Ivala, E.: Social media for enhancing student engagement: the use of Facebook and blogs at a university of technology. S. Afr. J. High. Educ. **26**(1), 152–167 (2012)
7. Godwin-Jones, R.: Emerging technologies, blogs, and wikis: environments for online collaboration. Lang. Learn. Technol. **7**, 12–16 (2003)
8. Parker, K., Chao, J.: Wiki as a teaching tool. Interdisc. J. e-Learn. Learn. Objects **3**(1), 57–72 (2007)
9. Su, F., Beaumont, C.: Evaluating the use of a wiki for collaborative learning. Innov. Educ. Teach. Int. **47**(4), 417–431 (2010)
10. Cole, M.: Using Wiki technology to support student engagement: lessons from the trenches. Comput. Educ. **52**(1), 141–146 (2009)
11. Tienken, C.H., Wilson, M.J.: The impact of computer assisted instruction on seventh-grade students' mathematics achievement. Plan. Chang. **38**(3 and 4), 181–190 (2007)
12. Suhr, K.A., Hernandez, D.A., Grimes, D., Warschauer, M.: Laptops and fourth-grade literacy: assisting the jump over the fourth-grade slump. J. Technol. Learn. Assess. **9**(5), 1–2 (2010)
13. Junco, R.: Too much face and not enough books: the relationship between multiple indices of Facebook use and academic performance. Comput. Hum. Behav. **28**(1), 187–198 (2012)
14. Donlan, L.: Exploring the views of students on the use of Facebook in university teaching and learning. J. Furth. High. Educ. **38**(4), 572–588 (2014)
15. Kabilan, M.K., Ahmad, N., Abidin, M.J.Z.: Facebook: an online environment for learning of English in institutions of higher education? Internet High. Educ. **13**(4), 179–187 (2010)
16. Brown, R.E.: The process of building community in distance learning classes. J. Asynchronous Learn. Netw. **5**(2), 18–35 (2001)

17. Wegerif, R.: The social dimension of asynchronous learning networks. J. Asynchronous Learn. Netw. **2**(1), 34–49 (1998)
18. Haythornthwaite, C.: Building social networks via computer networks: creating and sustaining distributed learning communities. In: Renninger, K.A., Shumar, W. (eds.) Building Virtual Communities: Learning and Change in Cyberspace, pp. 159–190. Cambridge University Press, Cambridge (2002)
19. Hunter, B.: Learning in the virtual community depends upon changes in local communities. In: Renninger, K.A., Shumar, W. (eds.) Building Virtual Communities: Learning and Change in Cyberspace, pp. 96–126. Cambridge University Press, Cambridge (2002)
20. Rovai, A.P.: A preliminary look at structural differences in sense of classroom community between higher education traditional and ALN courses. J. Asynchronous Learn. Netw. **6**(1), 41–56 (2002)
21. Minović, M., Milovanović, M., Šošević, U., González, M.Á.C.: Visualisation of student learning model in serious games. Comput. Hum. Behav. **47**, 98–107 (2015)
22. Melero, J., Hernández-Leo, D., Sun, J., Santos, P., Blat, J.: How was the activity? A visualization support for a case of location-based learning design. Br. J. Edu. Technol. **46**(2), 317–329 (2015)
23. Ruipérez-Valiente, J.A., Muñoz-Merino, P.J., Gascón-Pinedo, J.A., Kloos, C.D.: Scaling to massiveness with analyse: a learning analytics tool for open edX. IEEE Trans. Hum. Mach. Syst. **47**(6), 909–914 (2016)
24. Astin, A.W.: Student involvement: a developmental theory for higher education. J. Coll. Stud. Pers. **25**(4), 297–308 (1984)
25. Lin, H., Pryor, M.: Technology-facilitated socialised learning in a flipped classroom: towards a conceptual framework. In: 2019 18th International Conference on Information Technology Based Higher Education and Training (ITHET), Germany, pp. 1–6. IEEE (2019)
26. Garrison, D.R.: Online community of inquiry review: social, cognitive, and teaching presence issues. J. Asynchronous Learn. Netw. **11**(1), 61–72 (2007)
27. Deci, E.L., Ryan, R.M.: The general causality orientations scale: self-determination in personality. J. Res. Pers. **19**(2), 109–134 (1985)
28. Deci, E.L., Ryan, R.M.: The, "what" and "why" of goal pursuits: human needs and the self-determination of behavior. Psychol. Inq. **11**(4), 227–268 (2000)
29. de Charms, R.: Personal Causation: The Internal Affective Determinants of Behavior. Routledge, New York (2013)
30. Gagné, M., Deci, E.L.: Self-determination theory and work motivation. J. Organ. Behav. **26**(4), 331–362 (2005)
31. Baumeister, R., Leary, M.R.: The need to belong: desire for interpersonal attachments as a fundamental human motivation. Psychol. Bull. **117**, 497–529 (1995)
32. Palloff, R.M., Pratt, K.: Building Learning Communities in Cyberspace: Effective Strategies for the Online Classroom. Jossey-Bass, San Francisco (1999)
33. Picciano, A.G.: Beyond student perceptions: issues of interaction, presence, and performance in an online course. J. Asynchronous Learn. Netw. **6**(1), 21–40 (2002)

The Effects of a Collaborative Learning Approach with Digital Note-Taking on College Students' Learning Achievement and Cognitive Load

Yinghui Shi[1], Huiyun Yang[1], Zongkai Yang[2], Wei Liu[3], and Harrison Hao Yang[1,4](✉)

[1] Central China Normal University, Wuhan 430079, China
harrison.yang@oswego.edu
[2] Xidian University, Xi'an 710071, China
[3] Huazhong University of Science and Technology, Wuhan 430074, China
[4] State University of New York at Oswego, Oswego 13126, USA

Abstract. The purpose of this study was to investigate the effects of a collaborative learning approach with a digital note-taking method on college students' learning achievement and cognitive load in computer network courses. An experiment was conducted using a sample of 42 students from a class of a university in central China. Students were randomly divided into three groups, with each group consists of 14 students. The experimental group A employed a collaborative learning approach with a digital note-taking method and the experimental group B that employed a conventional lecturing approach with a digital note-taking method, while the control group that employed a conventional lecturing approach and traditional note-taking with pen and paper. Students in the classes studied computer network courses for 6 weeks. The pre- and post-tests showed that the students with a collaborative problem-solving approach and employ the digital note-taking method in classroom instruction have a significantly higher learning achievement while significantly lower extraneous load than that of students with the conventional lecturing approach and traditional note-taking with pen and paper.

Keywords: Collaborative problem solving · Digital note-taking · Learning achievement · Cognitive load

1 Introduction

The widespread use of the Internet has made the computer networks course a compulsory one for many universities and colleges [1]. Nowadays, teaching methods in many universities are mainly traditional lecture-based instruction [2], which are led by teachers who use projectors, screens, and blackboards to display teaching materials. This teaching method requires a high level of cognitive ability to integrate the transferred concepts and exert greater pressure [3]. Traditional lecture-based instruction is most often thought of as teacher-centered and content-oriented, which is promoted through practice, with little

S. K. S. Cheung et al. (Eds.): ICBL 2020, LNCS 12218, pp. 187–198, 2020.
https://doi.org/10.1007/978-3-030-51968-1_16

interaction between teachers and students [4], and thus it is of great difficulty to keep students focusing on lectures [3]. Therefore, students may suffer learning problems in gaining acknowledges of the complex concepts and principles of computer networks, and further lose their self-confidence and failed in their learning achievement.

To improve student learning, some researchers have suggested using collaborative learning in the process of teaching [5]. The core elements of collaborative learning are to emphasize the interaction between students, to focus on cooperative incentives, and to work in groups [6]. In collaborative learning, the only role the teacher plays is to help students coordinate activities and offer advice, while students provide and share information with each other in a collaborative problem-solving group [3, 7].

Note-taking is an essential part of classroom activities, it benefits students in learning the materials [8]. The widely use of electronic devices, such as laptops, tablet PCs, takes over the roles of traditional devices in taking notes in the classroom [8]. There is evidence shows that students' learning effect has greatly improved due to the use of digital notes [9]. In comparison with the paper notes, digital notes are more malleable, and one can process the digital notes easily to reflect, recall, synthesize, and collaborate with the learning contents [10]. Moreover, with the support of a cloud-based note-taking system (CNS), students can take notes, share, and review the notes more easily. Collaborative learning combines with digital note-taking in the CNS, opens new possibilities for a conventional course [11].

Cognitive load takes place when the resources of working memory are occupied by the learning activities, resulting in a decrease in the learning potential [12]. According to the cognitive load theory (CLT), there are three types of cognitive load, that is, intrinsic load, extraneous load, and germane load [13, 14]. The CLT can understand the non-surface-level aspects of collaborative learning, making individual learning less effective and efficient than collaborative learning [15]. Meanwhile, the development of technology has made digital notes meet the various needs of students and reduce their cognitive load [16].

Despite that collaborative learning and digital note-taking being the focus of many studies, little research has paid attention to the effectiveness of collaborative learning and digital note-taking. This study examined the influence of collaborative learning and digital note-taking on students' learning achievement and cognitive load.

2 Literature Review

2.1 Digital Note-Taking

Note-taking is a common, complex, and important activity that requires the selection and comprehension of information and written production processes in classroom learning [17]. Several studies confirmed the use of note-taking as a highly effective way of learning. Note-taking can improve the overall recall levels [18] and enhance memory for lecture material [19]. Taking notes can not only ensure the possibility of memorizing information, but also allow us to pay more attention, comprehend and reconsider information more carefully, and organize intentions and plans greater, to improve our learning and retention ability. According to [19], people who take notes do better than those who don't. Therefore, we can conclude that note-taking provide some positive benefit to students' examination performance.

The rapid development of high-quality digital tablets and mobile learning has gradually moved away from traditional notes such as pen and paper to digital note-taking based on personal computers [20]. Digital notes are often used as knowledge management, collaborative learning, and e-laboratory notebooks. Digital notes can help students take more notes. It's believed that students can process more information as they record more notes, which has a stronger influence on their learning [21]. Digital notes are also superior to hand-written notes in many ways: being searchable, editable, easily sharable, more legible, more malleable, and easier to copy, organize, translate and relocate to support reflection, recall, synthesis and collaboration [22]. As a result, it's increasingly common for students to take notes on laptops rather than in longhand.

Note-taking with the laptop has been rapidly spreading in universities (e.g., [23]). Studies have compared digital notes with traditional handwritten notes on students' learning outcomes. On one hand, some studies revealed the positive effects of digital note-taking on students learning achievements. For instance, [21] found that taking notes using a computer led to better overall test performance compared to longhand note-taking. While on the other hand, negative effects were found in several studies. For example, [24] concluded that students who took notes on a laptop performed worse on conceptual questions than students who took notes longhand. Therefore, the mixed results of these studies suggested that the effects of digital note-taking on students' learning achievement remain unclear.

2.2 Collaborative Problem Solving

From the perspective of social constructive theory [25], collaborative problem solving (CPS) is considered as a systematic teaching strategy in a socially constructive teaching context [26], since students can learn various ways of thinking through observations and discussions to improve their knowledge development [27]. In such an environment, the teachers have changed from classroom leaders to observers and guides of student learning, designing classroom teaching, and classroom activities for students. While the students are placed at the focus, and they are the leader of classroom learning, members of the collaborative learning group will be capable of expressing their viewpoints, sharing their experiences, and clarifying their ideas through explaining and debating during the discussions [3].

Mobile or portable devices have been used as major tools in computer-aided collaborative learning projects, with the purpose of tracking and collecting students' learning activities [28]. Studies have suggested that CPS has a positive correlation with student learning achievement [29, 30].

2.3 Cognitive Load

The CLT is related to the way of focusing and using cognitive resources in the learning and problem-solving process [31]. Three types of cognitive load: (1) intrinsic load (IL), which is determined by learner's prior knowledge and the natural complexity of the learning tasks; (2) extraneous load (EL), which is imposed by the instructional features that hinder learners' learning; and (3) germane load (GL), which is caused by the instructional features that are beneficial to learners' learning [32]. The CLT provides a theory-based approach to predict the effectiveness of a learning environment, and it has turned to be one of the basic theories describing the cognitive processes in the learning processes of new technologies, such as web-based instruction or multimedia-based instruction [33].

According to the CLT, one cannot manipulate the IL of learning material, while both the EL and GL of learning material can be manipulated through an instructional design [34]. As pointed out by [32], learners can take part in knowledge elaboration processes that impose GL and further enhance the effect of learning when the IL is at an optimal level and meanwhile the EL is low. Thus, to optimize a particular learner's cognitive load, the design of instructional strategies that induce low EL and optimal GL is needed. Using the cognitive load approach for collaborative learning can better understand why collaborative learning has high effectiveness and efficiency [15]. However, few studies have explored the effects of collaborative learning and digital note-taking on students' cognitive load.

2.4 The Research Questions

To explore the effects of CPS approach and digital note-taking on students' cognitive load and learning achievement, the following research questions were proposed:

1. Do the students who learn with the digital note-taking approach with a CPS approach show better learning achievement than those who learn with either an individual learning or a traditional lecture learning approach?
2. Do the students who learn with the digital note-taking approach with a CPS approach show a more optimized cognitive load than those who learn with either an individual learning or a traditional lecture learning approach?

3 Method

3.1 Participants

The participants of this study were undergraduate students of a university in central China. Forty-two students from a class participated in the experiment. Students were divided randomly into three groups, with two groups designated as the experimental groups A and B respectively, and the third group as the control group. Each group consisted of 14 students. All of the students had a basic knowledge of the computer and able to complete collaborative problem-solving activities. One teacher (Male) with more than ten-year experience in teaching taught all the three groups.

The teaching model of experimental group A was digital note-taking combined with the CPS, where students in this group were divided into small groups, with each group consisted of 4–5 members. The teacher assigned a leader in each small group to maintain the learning status. Students in each small group collaboratively completed the teacher's assignments. Experimental group B was a combination of the digital note-taking and lectures in the teaching mode. Students in this group were asked to complete the teacher's assignments independently; however, they can use the CNS to ask the teacher questions. A conventional pen and paper combined with lectures were employed as the teaching model in the control group. Students in this group completed the teacher's assignments independently, but they can only ask the teacher questions orally or by using conventional pen and paper, instead of using the CNS.

3.2 Cloud-Based Note-Taking System

The Cloud-based Note-taking System (CNS) used in the present study was developed by Tencent Inc., Based on cloud computing technology, the CNS provided superior functions while retaining the same basic functions of note records, providing students with cross-platform and information management functions [35]. The CNS supports both independent [36] and collaborative learning [37]. The CNS can obtain information efficiently and quickly and can be shared and exchanged [38]. Collaborative learning groups will record problem-solving methods on cloud notes after collaborative and completing tasks through discussion, communication, and other methods. Because the CNS is shared in real-time, each group will see what is recorded by other groups on the note in real-time, so while each group is in a collaborative relationship with members of its group, it is also a collaborative relationship with other groups.

In the traditional lecture-based instructional approach, teachers usually use the projector to display multimedia teaching resources for students, such as video and audio files, and various types of documents. As teachers and students cannot operate and write directly on the projector, and thus they have to write contents on the chalkboard, by which the interaction between teachers and students can be achieved. In the traditional lecture-based classroom, the chalkboard is mainly used for the teacher's handwriting and students' answers to exercise questions, while the projector is used only for the presentation of course material.

3.3 Learning Contents

The learning contents in the experiment were four sections of the computer network textbook for college students that majored in electrics and information engineering. The four sections including "Routing", "IPv6", "TCP", and "Application layer". The teacher presented the questions on the screen. The questions were designed according to students' prior knowledge and the teacher would make a brief illustration of the questions to ensure that the students totally understand. Students were asked to present the detailed steps of the solving process to the questions using the CNS.

3.4 Procedure

Before the teaching experiment began, students in all the three groups spent 30 min to complete a pre-test on learning achievement and fill out a pre-questionnaire on cognitive load as well. Each of the learning sessions lasted 90 min and was conducted once a week for six weeks. After the end of the teaching experiment, a post-test on learning achievement and the post-questionnaire on cognitive load were conducted.

Students in experimental groups A and B were asked to bring their laptops or tablet PCs to the classroom to take notes in the CNS during the class. During each session, the teacher divided the session into two parts.

In the first part, the teacher presented the questions on the screen for students to practice. Students' answering processes were divided into two stages. In the first stage, students were asked to answer the questions independently. Students wrote down the answers in the form of digital notes in the CNS. In the second stage, students were asked to answer the questions collaboratively. Members in each group would discuss the questions together, share their viewpoints, and reach a consensus, with the leader of each group plays a leading role.

In the second part, the teacher would view and select one group's answers and show them to other groups and then ask the leader of the group to tell the results of his/her group's discussion. The teacher would give a comment on the answers and conduct a follow-up instruction to the questions according to the answering situation of all the groups. With the help of the CNS, the teacher and the selected group can demonstrate the whole process of problem-solving clearly. Meanwhile, students in other groups could take notes and write down their questions in the CNS. The teacher could give quick feedback to students' questions.

Students in experimental group B have to solve the problems independently. They were not allowed to discuss the questions with their peers during the problem-solving process. In the control group, blank worksheets were distributed to the students at the beginning of the class. The teacher gave lectures and passed on knowledge to the students, and the students took notes and answered questions and involved in discussions with conventional pen and paper. The teacher answered students' questions during the lecturing. Students answered the questions on the worksheet and the teacher would review students' answers after all of them have handed in their worksheets.

3.5 Measuring Tools

The pre- and post-tests of this study were co-designed by the researchers and the teacher. The pre-test was conducted to make sure that all the students in the three groups had the same level of prior computer network knowledge. In the pre-test, there were six fills-up and four multiple-choice questions with only one correct answer. The post-test included 15 multiple-choice questions with only one correct answer and two free-response questions. The full score for both the pre-test and post-test is 100.

The cognitive load scale (CLS) used in this study was modified from the instrument of cognitive load that developed by [33]. We replaced the term "statistics" with "computer networks", to cover the subject and topics of computer networks. There were 10 items in the CLS, and the overall Cronbach's α value of the scale is 0.85, which indicated that the CLS is of high credibility.

4 Results

4.1 Students' Scores on Learning Achievement

A pre-test was conducted to determine the level of students' prior knowledge of computer networks. A one-way analysis of variance (ANOVA) was conducted on student scores of the pre-test. As shown in Table 1, the results revealed no significant difference in the pre-test scores of the three groups ($F = 0.025$, $p > 0.05$). This indicates that no significant difference existed in the three groups' level of prior knowledge before the implementation of the teaching experiment.

Table 1. ANOVA results for the pre-test of the learning achievement.

Variable		Sum of squares	df	Mean square	F
Pre-test	Between groups	14.33	2	7.17	0.025
	Within groups	11,400.07	39	292.31	
	Total	11,414.41	41		

At the end of the teaching experiment, a post-test was conducted to assess students' learning achievement. To eliminate the interference effect of the pre-test scores, a one-way analysis of covariance (ANCOVA) was conducted. Table 2 shows that the ANCOVA results were significant ($F(2, 38) = 3.89$, $p < 0.05$), which indicated that there was a significant difference between the three groups. Therefore, a post hoc comparison was further conducted. The pairwise comparisons show that the post-test score of experimental group A is significantly higher than that of the control group ($p = 0.027 < 0.05$), while no significant difference was found between the two experimental groups or between experimental group B and the control group.

Table 2. ANCOVA results for the post-test of the learning achievement.

Groups	N	Mean	SD	Adjusted mean	SE	F	Post hoc
(1) EG A	14	54.43	13.79	54.51	2.77	3.89^{*}	(1) > (3)
(2) EG B	14	47.71	7.44	47.63	2.77		
(3) CG	14	43.71	8.91	43.72	2.77		

$^{*}p < 0.05$. EG = Experimental group, CG = Control group.

4.2 Students' Scores on Cognitive Load

Students' cognitive load was assessed using the CLS before and after the teaching experiment. A one-way ANOVA was conducted on student pre-test scores of the cognitive load scale before the learning experiment began. As shown in Table 3, there was no significant difference in the three groups' pre-test scores of cognitive load. It's suggested that students in the three groups have a similar level of cognitive load before the teaching experiment.

Table 3. ANOVA results for the pre-test of the cognitive load.

Variables		Sum of squares	df	Mean square	F
IL	Between groups	1.624	2	0.81	1.19
	Within groups	26.64	39	0.68	
	Total	28.27	41		
EL	Between groups	2.23	2	1.11	1.03
	Within groups	42.18	39	1.08	
	Total	44.40	41		
GL	Between groups	0.60	2	0.30	0.54
	Within groups	21.59	39	0.55	
	Total	22.19	41		

After the end of the teaching experiment, a post-test on the cognitive load scale was conducted to assess student cognitive load. A one-way ANCOVA was conducted on student post-test scores of cognitive load, to eliminate the interference effect of the pre-test scores of cognitive load. As shown in Table 4, the ANCOVA results were significant for EL ($F(2, 38) = 3.92$, $p < 0.05$), while no significant effect was found on IL and GL. A post hoc comparison on the post-test of EL was further conducted and the results show that the experimental group A is significantly lower than that of the control group ($p = 0.027 < 0.05$).

5 Discussion and Conclusion

This study examined the effects of a CPS approach in combining with the digital note-taking method on college students' learning achievement and cognitive load in computer network courses. It is found that students with a CPS approach and employ the digital note-taking method in classroom instruction have a significantly higher learning achievement while significantly lower EL than those of students with a conventional learning approach and traditional note-taking with pen and paper.

Students' learning achievement was examined to investigate the different influences of three teaching modes. Students in the experimental group A solved the problems independently at the beginning and after that, they shared their problem-solving processes in the CNS and discussed the problems with their group members. By doing so, students had a better understanding of the concepts of the learning contents, and their

Table 4. ANCOVA results for the post-test of the cognitive load.

Variables	Groups	N	Mean	SD	Adjusted mean	SE	F	Post hoc
IL	(1) EG A	14	2.79	0.80	2.84	0.20	2.01	
	(2) EG B	14	3.48	0.88	3.37	0.21		
	(3) CG	14	3.26	0.75	3.32	0.20		
EL	(1) EG A	14	1.98	0.76	1.90	0.21	3.92*	(1) < (3)
	(2) EG B	14	2.64	1.07	2.55	0.21		
	(3) CG	14	2.50	1.01	2.68	0.21		
GL	(1) EG A	14	3.27	1.00	3.29	0.24	0.20	
	(2) EG B	14	3.59	1.10	3.50	0.25		
	(3) CG	14	3.38	0.89	3.45	0.25		

*$p < 0.05$. EG = Experimental group, CG = Control group.

problem-solving skills were also developed and enhanced during the collaborative processes. As a result, students in experimental group A had a significantly higher learning achievement than those of the control group. This finding is consistent with the results of some previous studies, which stated that the CPS approach could facilitate students' learning and promote their problem-solving abilities and thus improve their learning achievement [29, 39]. Moreover, this finding also confirmed the statements that students have been found to become more actively engaged in the learning process when they learning collaboratively [40], and collaborative learning is more effective and efficient than learning by individuals [15].

The major difference between experimental groups A and B is the instructional approach. Without any CPS process with group members, students in experimental group B completed their learning tasks with the CNS independently. Students can interact with the teachers by asking questions and receiving answers, but not encouraged to actively engage in the learning process. With the help of CNS, the teacher can check students' notes and answers immediately. However, the CNS has little effect in facilitating students' active learning to learn basic concepts of computer networks or improving students' problem-solving abilities. Therefore, it is not difficult to understand why the learning achievement of students in the experimental group B was not as good as that of students in experimental group A.

The major difference between the experimental group B and the control group was the way students take notes. This result was consistent with the findings of [3], which has a similar experimental design. Previous studies pointed out that without an effective learning strategy, the learning achievement wouldn't improve significantly, no matter how advanced the learning tool is [41]. In other words, it's the learning approach or learning strategy rather than the learning tools that do matters to students' learning achievements. Therefore, no significant difference existed in learning achievement between the experimental group B and the control group.

Regarding the effects of three different teaching modes on college students' cognitive load, the results showed that the experimental group A had a significantly lower EL than the control group, while no significant difference was found on IL and GL among the three groups. The post-test showed that the average scores of the three groups' IL were around 3, which indicated that all students have a modest level of IL. As [42] pointed out that when IL is at a modest level and EL is low, students could engage in knowledge elaboration processes that facilitate learning. Therefore, this result can partly explain why students in experimental group A had a significantly higher learning achievement than that of the control group.

It should be noted that this study has limitations. Firstly, this study has a relatively small sample size, because only one subject and one class were included in this initial study. More subjects and larger sample sizes are expecting to involve in future studies. Secondly, this study only examined students' learning achievement and cognitive load, more factors such as motivation, self-efficacy, are suggested to be examined in future studies. Finally, the duration of this experimental study lasts for only six weeks, and it seems that the potential benefits of the collaborative learning approach and CNS are not fully activated. To this end, future studies are suggested to examine the impacts of the collaborative learning approach and digital note-taking method in the long term, in order to make full use of the collaborative learning approach and CNS. In addition, more attention should be devoted to the design and implementation of the collaborative learning approach for classroom instruction, in order to improve college student's learning achievement and optimize students' cognitive load.

Acknowledgment. This work was supported by the Ministry of Education of the Humanities and Social Science project (Project No.: 18YJC880074).

References

1. Aburdene, M.F., Meng, X., Mokodean, G.L.: Analysis of computer networks courses in undergraduate computer science electrical engineering and information science programs. In: 2004 American Society for Engineering Education Annual Conference & Exposition, Salt Lake City, Utah (2004)
2. Samuelson, D.B., Divaris, K., De Kok, I.J.: Benefits of case-based versus traditional lecture-based instruction in a preclinical removable prosthodontics course. J. Dent. Educ. **81**, 387–394 (2017)
3. Huang, C.S.J., Su, A.Y.S., Yang, S.J.H., Liou, H.H.: A collaborative digital pen learning approach to improving students' learning achievement and motivation in mathematics courses. Comput. Educ. **107**, 31–44 (2017)
4. Shi, Y., Peng, C., Wang, S., Yang, H.H.: The effects of smart classroom-based instruction on college students' learning engagement and internet self-efficacy. In: Cheung, S.K.S., Kwok, L.-F., Kubota, K., Lee, L.-K., Tokito, J. (eds.) ICBL 2018. LNCS, vol. 10949, pp. 263–274. Springer, Cham (2018). https://doi.org/10.1007/978-3-319-94505-7_21
5. Efendi, R., Yulastri, A.: Effectiveness of collaborative-problem based learning model of learning computer network courses. In: 5th UPI International Conference on Technical and Vocational Education and Training (ICTVET 2018). Atlantis Press (2019)
6. Prince, M.: Does active learning work? A review of the research. J. Eng. Educ. **93**, 223–231 (2004)

7. Svetsky, S., Moravcik, O.: The practice of CSCL in engineering education within the research on TEL. In: 2015 International Conference on Interactive Collaborative Learning, pp. 283–286. IEEE (2015)
8. Kim, K., Turner, S.A., Pérez-Quiñones, M.A.: Requirements for electronic note taking systems: a field study of note taking in university classrooms. Educ. Inf. Technol. **14**, 255–283 (2009). https://doi.org/10.1007/s10639-009-9086-z
9. Ruan, L., Xiong, Z., Jiang, L., Zhou, X.: Comparison between digital and paper note-taking based on NASA-TLX. In: 2015 IEEE International Conference on Progress in Informatics and Computing, pp. 221–225. IEEE (2015)
10. Willett, W., Goffin, P., Isenberg, P.: Understanding digital note-taking practice for visualization. IEEE Comput. Graphics Appl. **35**, 38–51 (2015)
11. Warwick, P., Mercer, N., Kershner, R., Staarman, J.K.: In the mind and in the technology: the vicarious presence of the teacher in pupil's learning of science in collaborative group activity at the interactive whiteboard. Comput. Educ. **55**, 350–362 (2010)
12. Bujak, K.R., Radu, I., Catrambone, R., Macintyre, B., Zheng, R., Golubski, G.: A psychological perspective on augmented reality in the mathematics classroom. Comput. Educ. **68**, 536–544 (2013)
13. Sweller, J.: Cognitive load theory, learning difficulty, and instructional design. Learn. Instr. **4**, 295–312 (1994)
14. Sweller, J.: Implications of cognitive load theory for multimedia learning. In: The Cambridge Handbook of Multimedia Learning, no. 3, pp. 19–30 (2005)
15. Kirschner, F., Paas, F., Kirschner, P.: A cognitive load approach to collaborative learning: United brains for complex tasks. Educ. Psychol. Rev. **21**, 31–42 (2009). https://doi.org/10.1007/s10648-008-9095-2
16. Belson, S.I., Hartmann, D., Sherman, J.: Digital note taking: the use of electronic pens with students with specific learning disabilities. J. Spec. Educ. Technol. **28**, 13–24 (2013)
17. Piolat, A., Olive, T., Kellogg, R.T.: Cognitive effort during note taking. Appl. Cogn. Psychol. **19**, 291–312 (2005)
18. Di Vesta, F.J.D., Gray, G.S.: Listening and note taking. J. Educ. Psychol. **63**, 8–14 (1972)
19. Peper, R.J., Mayer, R.E.: Note taking as a generative activity. J. Educ. Psychol. **70**, 514–522 (1978)
20. Stacy, E.M., Cain, J.: Note-taking and handouts in the digital age. Am. J. Pharm. Educ. **79** (2015). Article 107
21. Bui, D.C., Myerson, J., Hale, S.: Note-taking with computers: exploring alternative strategies for improved recall. J. Educ. Psychol. **105**, 299 (2013)
22. Grahame, J.A.: Digital note-taking: Discussion of evidence and best practices. J. Phys. Assist. Educ. **27**, 47–50 (2016)
23. Fried, C.B.: In-class laptop use and its effects on student learning. Comput. Educ. **50**, 906–914 (2008)
24. Mueller, P.A., Oppenheimer, D.M.: The pen is mightier than the keyboard: advantages of longhand over laptop note-taking. Psychol. Sci. **25**, 1159–1168 (2014)
25. Vygotsky, L.S.: Mind and Society: The Development of Higher Mental Processes. Harvard University Press, Cambridge (1978)
26. Sung, H.Y., Hwang, G.J.: A collaborative game-based learning approach to improving students' learning performance in science courses. Comput. Educ. **63**, 43–51 (2013)
27. Rogoff, B.: Apprenticeship in Thinking: Cognitive Development in Social Context. Oxford University Press, Oxford (1990)
28. Sugihara, T., Miura, T., Miura, M., Kunifuji, S.: Examining the effects of the simultaneous display of students' responses using a digital pen system on class activity-a case study of an early elementary school in Japan. In: 10th International Conference on Advanced Learning Technologies, pp. 294–296. IEEE (2010)

29. Fakomogbon, M.A., Bolaji, H.O.: Effects of collaborative learning styles on performance of students in a ubiquitous collaborative mobile learning environment. Contemp. Educ. Technol. **8**, 268–279 (2017)
30. Hämäläinen, R., De Wever, B., Malin, A., Cincinnato, S.: Education and working life: VET adults' problem-solving skills in technology-rich environments. Comput. Educ. **88**, 38–47 (2015)
31. Chandler, P., Sweller, J.: Cognitive load theory and the format of instruction. Cogn. Instr. **8**, 293–332 (1991)
32. Leppink, J., Paas, F., Van der Vleuten, C.P.M., Van Gog, T., Van Merriënboer, J.J.G.: Development of an instrument for measuring different types of cognitive load. Behav. Res. Methods **45**, 1058–1072 (2013). https://doi.org/10.3758/s13428-013-0334-1
33. Mayer, R.E.: Multimedia Learning. Cambridge University Press, New York (2001)
34. Brunken, R., Plass, J.L., Leutner, D.: Direct measurement of cognitive load in multimedia learning. Educ. Psychol. **38**, 53–61 (2003)
35. Coursaris, C.K., van Osch, W., Sung, J.: A "cloud lifestyle": the diffusion of cloud computing applications and the effect of demographic and lifestyle clusters. In: 46th Hawaii International Conference on System Sciences, pp. 2803–2812. IEEE (2013)
36. Schepman, A., Rodway, P., Beattie, C., Lambert, J.: An observational study of undergraduate students' adoption of (mobile) note-taking software. Comput. Hum. Behav. **28**, 308–317 (2012)
37. Orndorff III, H.N.: Collaborative note-taking: the impact of cloud computing on classroom performance. Int. J. Teach. Learn. High. Educ. **27**, 340–351 (2015)
38. Numazawa, M., Ai, K., Noto, M.: Education and learning support system using proposed note-taking application. In: 2014 IEEE International Conference on Systems, Man, and Cybernetics, pp. 3617–3622. IEEE (2014)
39. Alvarez, C., Salavati, S., Nussbaum, M., Milrad, M.: Collboard: Fostering new media literacies in the classroom through collaborative problem solving supported by digital pens and interactive whiteboards. Comput. Educ. **63**, 368–379 (2013)
40. Morgan, R.L., Whorton, J.E., Gunsalus, C.: A comparison of short-term and long-term retention: Lecture combined with discussion versus cooperative learning. J. Instr. Psychol. **27**, 53–58 (2000)
41. Hwang, G.J., Chu, H.C., Shih, J.L., Huang, S.H., Tsai, C.C.: A decision-tree-oriented guidance mechanism for conducting nature science observation activities in a context-aware ubiquitous learning environment. Educ. Technol. Soc. **13**, 53–64 (2010)
42. Kalyuga, S.: Knowledge elaboration: a cognitive load perspective. Learn. Instr. **19**, 402–410 (2009)

Developing 21st-Century Competencies for Job Readiness

Yan Keung Hui(✉), Lam for Kwok, and Horace Ho Shing Ip

Department of Computer Science, City University of Hong Kong, 83 Tat Chee Avenue, Kowloon, Hong Kong
yankhui-c@my.cityu.edu.hk, {cslfkwok,cship}@cityu.edu.hk

Abstract. It is a general expectation from the society that new graduates should be job ready with the necessary 21st century competencies more than a good degree. Evidence shows that participation in extracurricular activities can effectively develop students' competencies and enhance their employability. However, information is insufficient for extracurricular activity organizers to plan for the activities and for students to plan for their participation. The City University of Hong Kong has built a central repository called "CRESDA" purposely to provide a smarter way for planning extracurricular activities for different stakeholders such as organizers, students and advisors. This paper reviews the design philosophy of CRESDA and two studies conducted using CRESDA data in the academic year 2016/17 together with employers' feedbacks on placement of computer science students in the following year. It identifies the level of engagement in extracurricular activities, gaps between offering and level of participation, different needs from students of different disciplines, as well as the relationship between the level of engagement and job readiness.

Keywords: 21st-century competencies · Extracurricular activities · Outcome-based learning · Employability · Personal development

1 Introduction

Globalization and rapid technological advancements are changing the ways we live and our expectations of graduates [1]. Employers and the society expect graduates to be equipped with new competencies in order to be job ready when they graduate, and be successful in their career and daily life in the future [2–4]. Students understand that they need new competencies in job searching and career development [5, 6].

Competencies can be developed by participating in extracurricular activities [7]. However, extracurricular activities are not well planned by organizers, students and advisors because of the unstructured nature and difficulty in measurement. Students normally attend extracurricular activities by random based on availability and interest [8, 9]. It reflects that students are not aware of the competencies that they are expected to possess in order to enhance their employability. They also do not have sufficient information to facilitate planning for their learning goals from extracurricular activities.

S. K. S. Cheung et al. (Eds.): ICBL 2020, LNCS 12218, pp. 199–209, 2020.
https://doi.org/10.1007/978-3-030-51968-1_17

In order to solve these issues, the City University of Hong Kong (CityU) developed a system in 2016 called "Central Repository on Student Development Activities (CRESDA)" [10]. It provides information in a structured and systematic manner, to help organizers, advisors and students in planning and reflecting in a smarter way.

2 Literature Review

2.1 21st-Century Competencies

In the 21st century, the society expects graduates to be equipped with new competencies on top of their academic qualifications. These competencies, such as creativity, leadership skills, social skills, communication skills, and global awareness, are generally called the 21st-century competencies (or simply "competencies" or "attributes"). These competencies are the skills and personal attributes that increase graduates' opportunities in gaining employment and succeed in their chosen career [11].

A growing number of educators, politicians, and business leaders believe that students need to develop certain competencies in order to be successful [12]. Institutions are expected to develop students' competencies in order to be job ready [13]. Competencies cannot be learned but can be developed [7], particularly, through participating in extracurricular activities [14, 15]. However, several challenges have been identified. First, competencies cannot be quantified, measured and assessed in a similar way as traditional academic courses because formal examinations are generally not applicable.

Second, the 21st-century competencies may mean different things to different people and different organizations [13]. When preparing employees for a particular career, these competencies are work-related [16]. Therefore, it is expected that students in different colleges/schools may focus on developing different groups of competencies. Students need a smarter way to know "What competencies and to what extend I need to develop them?" and "What and to what extend I have developed on these competencies?".

3 Philosophy of CRESDA

Based on the expected graduate outcomes defined by CityU, we defined a list of 21st-century competencies (called "attributes") in CRESDA and linked them to the extracurricular activities [8]. This provides quantitative data on developing the 21st-century competencies in terms of the duration of an activity leading to each competency developed by students. Graduate outcomes are listed in Table 1.

Each graduate outcome is associated with a set of competencies (or "attributes"). Samples of attributes (9 out of 36) and their corresponding mapping with the graduate outcomes are listed in Table 2 [8].

The learning model associated with CRESDA is shown in Fig. 1. It can capture the attributes that are learned by students in extracurricular activities [8].

Table 1. List of graduate Outcomes of CityU

Graduate Outcome	Description
GO1	Apply effective communication, language, numerical and IT skills to a variety of professional settings
GO2	Apply multi-disciplinary critical thinking skills to solve problems and create new ideas
GO3	Relate cultural awareness to collaborate effectively in a broad range of teamwork situations
GO4	Generate a positive and flexible approach to lifelong learning and employability
GO5	Reflect on the ethical and social responsibilities required for professional citizens in the global society

Table 2. Samples of attributes and their mappings with graduate outcomes

Category	Attribute	Graduate outcome
Internationalization	International perspective	GO3
	Multicultural perspective	GO3
	Understanding global issues	GO5
Social	Interpersonal skills	GO1
	Teamwork	GO3
Psychological/Emotional	Emotional health	GO4
	Self-appreciation	GO4
Professional/Career	Application of professional knowledge	GO2
	Leadership	GO3

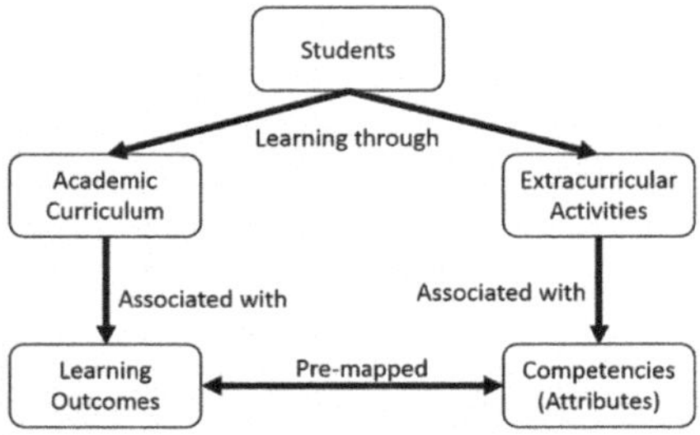

Fig. 1. The learning model associated with CRESDA

4 Results and Discussions

This paper aims at performing an initial study using a qualitative approach to give a high-level understanding of the data being captured in CRESDA in 2016/17. It is followed by the second study which is a quantitative approach on data collected from employers' feedbacks on the placement of computer science students in 2017/18.

4.1 Initial Study

The purpose of the initial study is to identify the gap between extracurricular activities organized and the engagement level, as well as the different needs of students of different disciplines. CRESDA data in the academic year of 2016/17 is used in this initial study. These include students from College of Business (CB), College of Liberal Arts and Social Sciences (CLASS), College of Science and Engineering (CSE), School of Energy and Environment (SEE), School of Law (SLW) and School of Creative Media (SCM). Only completed activities (440 out of 651 extracurricular activities) with attendance records registered in CRESDA (434 out of 440 completed activities), and only full-time undergraduate students (3,428 distinct students who participated in at least one extracurricular activity in the mentioned period) are included in this study.

4.2 Engagement Level

From Fig. 2, it is observed that more than half of the students from SEE (59.88%), about one third of the students from CB (29.95%) and CSE (29.97%) correspondingly, and only 25.16%, 15.47% and 12.5% of the students from CLASS, SLW and SCM respectively have participated in extracurricular activities. Without other information, it is not easy to identify the reasons behind.

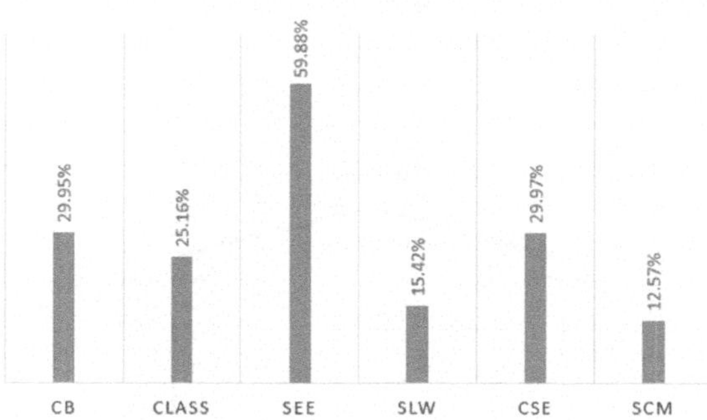

Fig. 2. The participation rate of each college/school

Table 3 shows the participations of students from different cohorts in the academic year 2016/17. It is found that students in their first year at CityU had a higher participation rate in general. In general, the participation rate is not high and it aligns with other findings that students are not engaged in extracurricular activities [5].

Among those who have been participating in at least one extracurricular activity, all the five graduate outcomes have been addressed by at least half of the students with GO4 (82%) and GO1 (79%) being the highest comparing to GO2 (69%), GO3 (62%) and GO5 (49%). It shows students perception and high level of understandings of its importance. It also matches the expectation from the society and employers, and aligns with the trend of globalization and inter-connected cultures.

Table 3. Participation (in hours) across different cohorts and different colleges/schools

College/schools	Cohort					Sub_total (hours)
	2012	2013	2014	2015	2016	
CB	335	256	5,550	13,967	14,363	34,471
CLASS	121	2,026	6,861	12,751	19,916	41,675
SEE	18	296	98	123	594	1,129
SLW	104	477	234	248	222	1,285
CSE	254	3,845	18,410	26,336	72,003	120,848
SCM	–	6,468	1,033	8,885	8,250	24,636
Sub_total (hours)	832	13,368	32,186	62,310	115,348	224,044

4.3 Offered Vs. Participated

Table 4 shows the differences between the activities offered and the activities with highest participation by students. For example, it is obvious that analytical and problem-solving ability ranks high from organizers' perspective (rank #2) but it is ranked at #6 from students' perspective. It is obvious that there is a room for improvement in planning extracurricular activities to match students' needs. It is also found that language proficiency, multicultural perspectives, international perspectives and understanding of global issues are the top four competencies to be gained by students.

4.4 The Diversity of Attributes Learned by Students from Different Colleges/Schools

Different competencies are required in different industries [13, 16]. To understand students' need in a more specific manner, we need to identify the variations of demands of students from different colleges/schools. Table 5 lists the top 5 attributes mostly received by students, in terms of number of hours, from different colleges/schools.

CB students focus more on globalization-related competencies with relatively even distribution, meaning students are trying to participate and gain broader competencies. This matches the vision and value defined by the college that "the College of Business at City University of Hong Kong aims to be a globally-oriented business school, producing

Table 4. Top 10 attributes offered vs. participated

Rank	Offered	Participated
1	Interpersonal skills	Language proficiency
2	Analytical and problem-solving ability	Multicultural perspectives
3	Language proficiency	International perspective
4	Self-learning/Lifetime learning	Understanding global issues
5	Multicultural perspective	Interpersonal skills
6	International perspective	Teamwork
7	Teamwork	Analytical and problem-solving ability
8	Understanding global issues	Integrating international students into the student community
9	Positive attitude	Art appreciation
10	Integrating international students into the student community	Community care and services

innovative and impactful business knowledge, and nurturing leaders for a sustainable future: a key business education hub—in China for the world" [17].

CLASS students focus more on inter-personal-related competencies with a relatively even distribution. This matches the College's mission statement that it "actively cultivates multi-disciplinary and inter-disciplinary collaboration…" [18].

CSE students focus more on language and internationalization-related competencies but clearly with language competencies being significantly higher than all others. This matches findings from other researchers that engineering students, in general, have more rooms for improvement in languages [19].

SEE students focus more on career readiness with almost half of the participants concentrating on career planning. This may be because SEE is a relatively young school which was established in the year 2009 and not many references from previous graduates can guide the new graduates in their careers.

SLW students focus more on inter-person-related skills particularly on teamwork and interpersonal skills. This matches the general understanding that professional services providers such as lawyers rely very much on relationship marketing [20]. At the same time, we can find some competencies such as negotiation, conflict resolution, and communication skills, which may be specific to SLW students.

SCM students focus more on language (37%). But it is worth noting that 16% are participating in community care and services which is not among the top 5 attributes from all other colleges/schools.

4.5 The Second Study

The second study aims at verifying the usefulness of participating in extracurricular activity and the employability. It allows students to know what competencies are critical

Table 5. Top 5 attributes mostly received by students from different colleges/schools. These attributes are arranged in descending order of percentage

College/School	Attributes	Percentage
CB	Multicultural perspectives	14%
	Integrating international students into the student community	14%
	International perspective	9%
	Teamwork	9%
	Traditional cultural heritage	9%
CLASS	Interpersonal skills	11%
	Teamwork	10%
	Emotional health	6%
	Language proficiency	6%
	International perspective	5%
CSE	Language proficiency	30%
	Multicultural perspective	15%
	International perspective	15%
	Understanding global issues	15%
	Interpersonal skills	5%
SEE	Career planning	45%
	Teamwork	16%
	Interpersonal skills	13%
	Art appreciation	11%
	Organization of work	3%
SLW	Teamwork	22%
	Interpersonal skills	18%
	Art appreciation	9%
	Negotiation, conflict resolution, and communication skills	8%
	Integrating international students into the student community	6%
SCM	Language proficiency	37%
	Multicultural perspectives	26%
	Community care and services	16%
	Teamwork	7%
	Analytical and problem-solving ability	4%

to their corresponding disciplines and facilitates them to do planning and learning at an earlier stage. Computer science students of CityU are required, as part of the curriculum, to take a work as placement in a company through their third year of study. At the end of the placement period, employers are required to respond to a standard questionnaire designed by CityU about the work performance of those placement students. The questionnaire contains five sections with a total of nineteen 5-point Likert scale questions. The following three questions are used for analysis purposes:

- Q1: Improvement shown in all aspects since the interim review.
- Q2: Performance compared to newly recruited graduates.
- Q3: Overall performance in the placement year.

We identified that multicultural perspective and interpersonal skills are highly correlated to placement students' work performances. Figure 3 compares the average scores of each of the three questions between the following two groups.

- Group 1: Placement students who never participated in any CRESDA activities related to the corresponding attribute (100 and 89 students for multicultural perspectives and interpersonal skills respectively).
- Group 2: Placement students who have participated in at least one CRESDA activities related to the corresponding attribute (5 and 16 students for multicultural perspectives and interpersonal skills respectively).

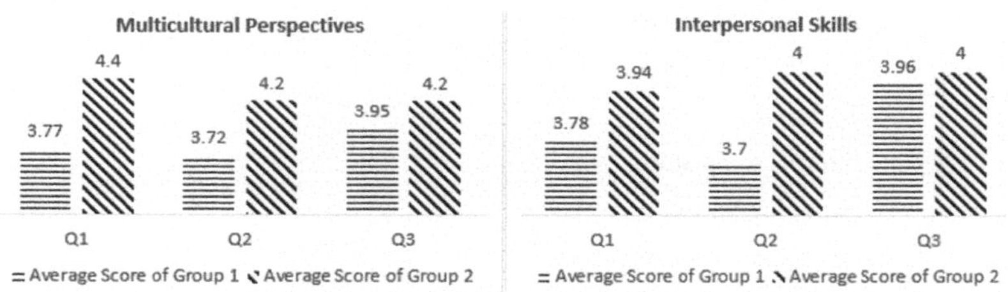

Fig. 3. Participation vs employers' feedback

Despite the relatively small sample size for group 2, the average score of group 2 is significantly higher than that of group 1. This means students participated in extracurricular activities related to multicultural perspective or interpersonal skills could gain higher appreciation and recognition from their employer.

5 Contributions, Limitations and Future Directions

5.1 Practical Contributions

The findings in this paper contribute in practical ways to different stakeholders. First, the organizers of extracurricular activities can identify the gaps between what they are offering and what the students are looking for. This provides valuable references for their smarter planning in organizing extracurricular activities matching the needs of the society, job market and students of different disciplines.

Second, academic advisors can have a consolidated view of students' status on academic and competency development in a holistic way. This can facilitate them in providing smarter and better advising to students.

Third, students can perform reflection on their learning in both academic and non-academic development. This can help them to better understand their strengths and weaknesses on competencies development. This helps students to answer the two questions as mentioned before:

- What competencies and to what extend I need to develop them?
- What and to what extend I have developed on these competencies.

Fourth, institutions benefited from the better use of resources and nurture the right graduates. Ultimately, the society and employers can have a higher chance to have graduates who are more job ready.

5.2 Theoretical Contributions

The findings in this paper contribute in theoretical ways to different research areas. First, it contributes to the research discipline of the 21st-century competencies by providing a more systematic and structured repository with measurement technique.

Second, this study contributes to the way on predicting student success in terms of job readiness and employability based on students' learning behaviors in the non-academic side, which were previously non-structured and difficult to be measured.

5.3 Limitations

Two limitations are observed in this study. First, it is noted that the definition of graduation outcomes of CityU has been refined [21]. It is suggested that CRESDA's coding should be refined accordingly for consistency and better reporting purposes.

Second, with only a year of CRESDA data and a year of employers' feedback on placement students of only one department captured, predictive analysis of students' employability upon graduation is yet to be done. It is suggested that a more in-depth analysis should be conducted to evaluate the predictive power on graduates' job readiness and employability.

5.4 Future Directions

We propose a practical plan for the future development of CRESDA. First, the definition of learning outcomes should align with the latest definition given by the university. Second, promotion and training programmes should be carried out in order to increase the usage and thus enhance the completeness and accuracy of data. Finally, data analysis between CRESDA data and graduate exit survey should be conducted to predict students' employability such as the duration before the first offer is obtained, number of offers, initial salary and company scale.

6 Conclusions

Societies and employers expect new graduates to be job-ready. Therefore, the 21st-century competencies have become more important than academic achievements from employers' and students' perspective in recent years. To make new graduates job-ready with the necessary 21st-century competencies, institutions have the responsibility to develop students according to the market needs. Extracurricular activities have been seen to be the major way to develop students' competencies.

CRESDA was launched by CityU to capture students' participation in extracurricular activities in a more systematic way which associates competencies and intended learning outcomes. This paper reviews the CRESDA design objectives and information model. We conducted analysis the data in the first academic year after CRESDA's launch in July 2016 and the employers' feedback of placement students in the academic year 2017/18. The result shows that students from different colleges/schools have different participation rates and different focuses. The result also shows the gap between what is offered by organizers and what students participated in. Finally, we identified the two competencies that influence placement students' overall performance the most.

The findings are a valuable reference to organizers to better plan and utilize resources when organizing extracurricular activities in the future. Students can also plan their extracurricular activities in order to receive training in the set of 21st-century competencies that his/her future career needs the most.

References

1. Shum, S.B., Crick, R.D.: Learning analytics for 21st century competencies. J. Learn. Anal. **3**(2), 6–21 (2016)
2. Haste, H.: Ambiguity, autonomy and agency. In: Rychen, D., Salganik, L. (eds.) Defining and Selecting Key Competencies, pp. 93–120 (2001)
3. Dede, C.: Transforming Education for the 21st Century: New Pedagogies That Help All Students Attain, Sophisticated Learning Outcomes (2007). http://gseannotopia.blogspot.hk/2010/04/dede-c-2007-transforming-education-for.html
4. Kalantzis, M., Cope, B.: New Learning, Elements of a Science of Education. Cambridge University Press, Cambridge (2008)
5. Greenbank, P.: Still focusing on the "essential 2:1": exploring student attitudes to extra-curricular activities. Educ. Train. **57**(2), 184–203 (2015)
6. Roulin, N., Bangerter, A.: Students' use of extra-curricular activities for positional advantage in competitive job markets. J. Educ. Work **26**(1), 21–47 (2013)
7. Boyatzis, R.E.: Competencies in the 21st century. J. Manag. Dev. **27**(1), 5–12 (2008)
8. Hui, Y.K., Kwok, L.F., Ip, H.H.S.: CRESDA: extending data landscape of learners. Int. J. Innov. Learn. **23**(4), 463–478 (2018)
9. Greenbank, P.: Competing in the graduate labour market: student perspectives on (not) participating in extra-curricular activities. J. Teach. Learn. Grad. Employab. **5**(1), 63–79 (2014)
10. Kwok, L.F., Hui, Y.K.: The role of e-portfolio for smart life long learning. In: Uskov, V.L., Bakken, J.P., Howlett, R.J., Jain, L.C. (eds.) SEEL 2017. SIST, vol. 70, pp. 327–356. Springer, Cham (2018). https://doi.org/10.1007/978-3-319-59454-5_11
11. Stiwne, E.E., Jungert, T.: Engineering students' experiences of transition from study to work. J. Educ. Work **23**(5), 417–437 (2010)

12. Rotherham, A.J., Willingham, D.T.: 21st-century skills: not new, but a worthy challenge. Am. Educ. **34**(1), 17–20 (2010)
13. Soland, J., Hamilton, L.S., Stecher, B.M.: Measuring 21st Century Competencies: Guidance for Educator (2013). https://asiasociety.org/global-cities-education-network/assessing-21st-century-skills-and-competencies-around-world
14. Clark, G.: 'It's everything else you do…': alumni views on extracurricular activities and employability. Act. Learn. High Educ. **16**(2), 133–147 (2015)
15. Fredricks, J.A., Eccles, J.S.: Extracurricular involvement and adolescent adjustment: impact of duration, number of activities, and breadth of participation. Appl. Dev. Sci. **10**(3), 132–146 (2006)
16. Ananiadou, K., Claro, M.: 21st century skills and competencies for new millennium learners in OECD countries. OECD Education Working Papers. 41. OECD Publishing, Paris (2009)
17. CityU: Vision & Values of College of Business. http://www.cb.cityu.edu.hk/aboutus/vision/
18. CityU: Vision & Values of College of Liberal Arts and Social Sciences. http://www.cityu.edu.hk/class/vision_mission.aspx
19. Panyawong-Ngam, L., Tangthong, N., Anunvrapong, P.: A model to develop the english proficiency of engineering students at Rajamangala University of Technology Krungthep, Bangkok, Thailand. Procedia Soc. Behav. Sci. **192**(1), 77–82 (2015)
20. Sarma, N., Patterson, P.G.: The impact of communication effectiveness and service quality on relationship commitment in consumer, professional services. J. Serv. Mark. **13**(2), 151–170 (1999)
21. CityU: City University Graduate Outcomes. http://www.cityu.edu.hk/qac/city_university_graduate_outcomes.htm

Activity Design for Cultivating Students' Critical Thinking Dispositions in a Blended Learning Environment Through a Case Study of Media Literacy Course

Xiaohong Zhang[1(✉)], Kenichi Kubota[2], and Mayumi Kubota[2]

[1] Kumamoto University, Kumamoto City, Kumamoto, Japan
windyzhang0929@gmail.com
[2] Kansai University, Takatsuki, Osaka, Japan

Abstract. A blended learning environment including interactive activities was designed to encourage students to analyze media with multiple views. The purpose of this study was to examine whether the design of interactive activities cultivated students' inquiry-mind and objectiveness of Critical Thinking Dispositions (CTD). This research used a media literacy course in a Japanese university as a case study. The authors developed the questionnaire items which examined interactive activities and the CTD scale for Japanese university students. As a result, the authors found that (1) students highly evaluated activities where they analyzed media with inquiry-mind and objectiveness, (2) the activities positively correlated inquiry-mind and objectiveness, and (3) there were significant differences of inquiry-mind and objectiveness in the low, middle and high groups of participation in LMS activities. The cycle, of thinking activities in the classroom, discussion on LMS and reflection activities, created a critical culture in the blended learning environment in a semester.

Keywords: Activity design · Critical Thinking Dispositions · Media literacy · Critical culture · Blended learning environment · Higher education in Japan

1 Introduction

With the development of the information society, most university students can access and send information freely using mobile phones, the internet and other mass media in Japan. Improving students' media literacy is a big challenge because many students easily accept information without determining if it is true or false and why it is represented in the media.

To avoid accepting information completely, students were asked to think critically about information in the media [1, 2]. However, when asked to analyze media text, some students tended to wait for the teacher to give them the correct answer [3]. Furthermore, in most cases, students avoided disagreeing with opinions stated in the classroom, since Japanese culture, values sameness [4]. Therefore, cultivating students' critical thinking

S. K. S. Cheung et al. (Eds.): ICBL 2020, LNCS 12218, pp. 210–223, 2020.
https://doi.org/10.1007/978-3-030-51968-1_18

dispositions (CTD) to form habits to think and state multiple opinions in university courses is important.

CTD was influenced by the critical culture that encouraged the learners speak or write their ideas and opinions from multiple viewpoints [5]. To create a critical culture, active participation must be designed to foster students' thinking habits and direction [5–7]. Online discussion was used to enhance the effect of active participation in a blended learning environment since there are some limitations in the classroom. This paper focused on the activities designed to cultivate students' CTD in a blended learning, media literacy course.

2 Media Literacy Education and Its Relationship to CTD

2.1 Media Literacy Education in Japanese Universities

Media literacy is the ability to read, understand and use information in media. A goal of media literacy education is for students to critically analyze and judge information in media, before reaching their own conclusions [1, 2]. Students must become active, not passive learners and be critical thinkers in the course. Becoming critical thinkers requires students to be "'rational' and 'skeptical' in their dealing with the media" [2] (P108). To become "rational" and "skeptical" when viewing the media, students must develop critical thinking.

2.2 Critical Thinking and CTD in Media Literacy Education

Critical thinking is reasonable and reflective thinking focused on deciding what to believe or do [8]. Critical thinking includes critical thinking skills (CTS) and CTD. For critical thinking to successfully occur, students should develop their tendencies to think critically [8]. Unfortunately, some students have CTS, but do not use these skills [9, 10]. Tishman, Jay and Perkins call for paying more attention to CTD since CTS cannot occur if students lack tendencies of critical thinking [5].

Morimoto identified critical thinking in media literacy as analyzing media objectively from multiple viewpoints including the perspectives of media production, and social, political and economic backgrounds [9]. The objectiveness of judgement cannot occur unless students inquire and think of new perspectives when exploring information [1, 2]. Thus, analyzing media with inquiry-mind and objectiveness are important CTD in media literacy education.

2.3 Problem Statement

In Japan, universities have large lecture-type classes. One teacher teaches more than 100 students in a lecture hall that seats 300–500 students. Teachers assume the role of the authority who must efficiently teach knowledge. Students listen and take notes. In these classrooms, students assume passive roles in participation and thinking [3]. Therefore, this teaching style does not allow students to analyze media information critically. Furthermore, Japan has a group collective culture, where being in harmony or similar to others is more emphasized than being different. Japanese tend not to express opposition or opinions that differ from their friends and superiors [4]. Therefore, even when asked by the teacher to express their opinions, Japanese students tend not to show their oppositional opinions clearly in the classroom. In this type of learning environment, few Japanese students think about media with multiple perspectives and inquiry mind. Therefore, cultivating Japanese students' inquiry-mind and objectiveness is a great challenge in a media literacy course.

3 Cultivating CTD in Blended Learning Environment

Bukingham indicated that active participation could foster students to analyze media critically [2]. Active participation included group work and dialogue in the classroom. However, there are some limitations of time in a large lecture-type class in Japan. Thus, a blended learning environment, linked with the learning environment that occurred in the classroom and online [11] was designed to cultivate CTD in the course in a Japanese university. A comparison study between blended learning and traditional learning environments found that students developed their CTD better in a blended learning environment [12].

Online discussions were useful strategies for students to reflect on their learning and formulate new ideas [13, 14]. Okano and Kubota analyzed the reports submitted on the bulletin board from 30 students in 2006. They identified that students transformed their media perspectives through the process of notion, reflection, and concepts changing [14]. These studies identified how and why students' CTD changed. However, these studies did not identify how students' CTD was foster in a blended learning environment.

Creating a classroom culture was a possible way to foster students' CTD [5, 6]. Classroom culture depended on the features of the lesson or course. In this study, critical culture was defined as a culture where students can freely express their opinions and think critically.

To create critical culture, there are some design principles: **(1) Interaction between students-students and teacher-students.** Tishman, Jay and Pekins identified that the classroom culture where students felt comfortable and easily expressed their opinions was essential. He suggested that encouragement of interaction between students-students and teacher-students was an important principle [5]. This principle was also supported by Bloch and Spataro in 2014[15]. **(2) Students externalizing their thought through language.** Richhart describes externalization through presentation and writing are forces to shape the culture of CTD [6, 7]. Since thinking is a complex and internal occurrence in the head, externalization in language could improve CTS and form CTD. **(3) The teacher's role as a facilitator to provoke students to think.** Teacher should be a facilitator to support students to think rationally and skeptically [1–3]. Michida suggested that an authoritative teacher who has the 'right answer' may inhibit Japanese students from examining different perspectives and judging objectively [3]. **(4) Reflecting on the thinking process.** Reflection could help students to reexamine their previous thoughts in the process of reaching conclusions and rethink their conclusions [11, 16]. Blended learning does not simply combine the learning in classroom and online but trigger students to reflect deeply what and how they think by linking both activities. Thus, designing a blended learning environment that connects LMS and the classroom is crucial.

4 Activity Design in Blended Learning Environment

Based on the theory of cultivating CTD above, activities were designed to foster inquiry-mind and objectiveness in media literacy education. The design included the three components of thinking activities in the classroom, discussion on LMS, a type of bulletin board in Japan, and reflection activities in the next class (Fig. 1). In this course, the lecturer played the role of the facilitator to trigger students to think independently.

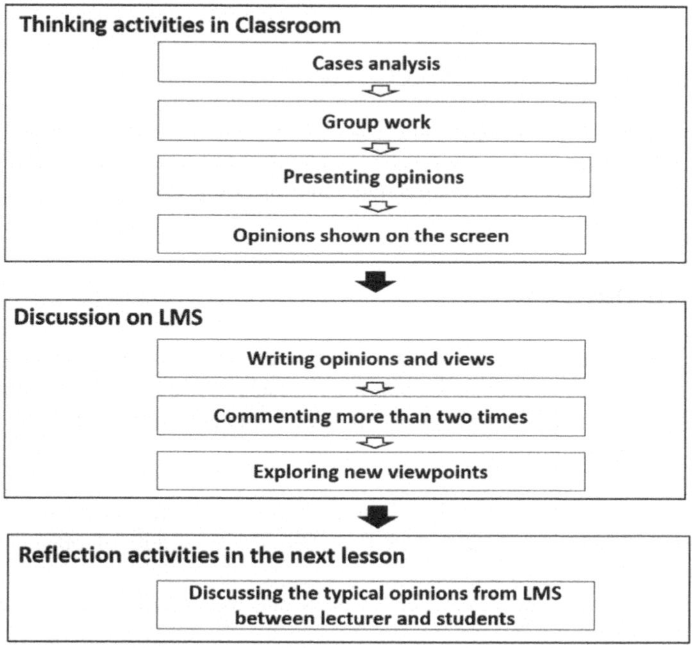

Fig. 1. Activities design to cultivate critical thinking disposition

4.1 Thinking Activities in the Classroom

Some activities in the classroom took about 60 min (one course is 90 min). The activities were as follows: (1) **Cases analysis:** The lecturer showed some cases, such as video, photos or news reporting in media. These cases were unfamiliar to the students and many students felt surprising. (2) **Group work:** Students discussed in groups of 3–4 students, who sat nearby. They exchanged their ideas in the group. (3) **Presenting opinions:** Students were asked to express their answers by raising their hand and asking some thought-provoking questions. If few students stated their answers by raising their hands, they needed to share their opinions quickly into a microphone that was passed around the room. Students were randomly selected to speak into the microphone. (4) **Opinions shown on the screen:** After students shared their opinions, the lecturer posted their answers on a screen in front of the classroom making opinions visible in the classroom.

4.2 Discussion on LMS

After the lesson, students were asked to complete two tasks: post their opinions and views about the discussion topics and classroom lesson, and comment on other students' posts. The design of the active learning on LMS was as follows: (1) **Writing opinions and views:** Every student wrote their opinions and views about the discussion topics. (2) **Commenting on other students' posts:** Students needed to comment on more than two other students' posts. (3) **Exploring new viewpoints:** Students needed to explore new viewpoint based on their judgement.

4.3 Reflection Activities in the Next Lesson

Discussion of a few Typical Opinions from LMS: At the next lesson, some typical opinions on LMS were chosen by the lecturer and introduced. The lecturer discussed the posts with the students, who posted their opinions on LMS.

5 Research Objective

The purpose of this study is to examine the effectiveness of activities designed to combine classroom and LMS interactions. To attain this research objective, the authors used a case study approach in a media literacy course in a Japanese university. Three research questions driving this study are:

1) Do students evaluate whether their inquiry-mind and objectiveness were fostered?
2) What kind of activities were related to their development of objectiveness and inquiry-mind?
3) Are there differences between objectiveness and inquiry-mind in the participation scale of LMS activities?

6 Research Method

6.1 Case of Media Literacy Course

This research examined a media literacy course called "Media Expression" in the spring semester in 2017 as a case study. "Media Expression" was an elective course at K University, Japan. The goals of this course were to foster students' critical thinking and media literacy in a blended learning environment. The students in the class were sophomores, juniors and seniors. This course was designed with 15 lessons in a semester. Two hundred eighty undergraduates participated in this course during the spring semester in 2017.

6.2 Questionnaire and Data Collection

A questionnaire, which included CTD scale and activities in the design, was created. The scale was based on the CTD Scale that Hirayama and Kusumi developed in 2004, which included inquiry-mind, objectiveness, awareness for logical thinking, and evidence based on judgment [17]. Inquiry-mind is the tendency to learn more through communication with different people. Objectiveness is the tendency to make judgments without bias. Awareness for logical thinking is the tendency to think in an orderly sequence when encountering complex problems. Evidence based on judgment is the disposition that leads judgement based on evidence to reach a conclusion. Eleven items of the CTD scales were selected in each factor of inquiry-mind, objectiveness, awareness of logical thinking, and two items from evidence based on judgment were chosen. In addition, eight items about activities based on the design were used (Table 1).

Table 1. Questionnaire Items

Number	Items	Type of items
1	I learned many things through communication with different people in the course	CTD: Inquiry-mind
2	I was interested in the opinions that differ from mine in the course	
3	It was interesting to discuss topics with different people in the course	
4	I tried to think of things not only based on one or two perspectives but as much as possible	CTD: Objectiveness
5	I listened carefully to other people even if I disagreed with them in the course	
6	I reflected on whether I had unconscious bias in the course	
7	I focused on the solution of problems in the course	CTD: Awareness for logical thinking
8	I was confused when I thought about complex problems in the course	
9	I explained my opinions so that everyone can understand me in the course	
10	I checked the evidence to reach conclusions in the course	CTD: Evidence based on judgement
11	I did not firmly believe in all opinions and often doubted them in the course	
12	I said my opinions clearly in the classroom	Thinking activities in classroom
13	I noticed new ideas in group work	
14	I was surprised many times in the classroom	

(continued)

Table 1. (*continued*)

Number	Items	Type of items
15	I compared my opinion with other students' opinions shown on the screen in the classroom	
16	I wrote my opinions clearly on the LMS after the lessons	Discussion on LMS
17	I noticed the difference between myself and other students through the comments on the LMS	
18	I used the ideas of other students in my opinions when I wrote comments	
19	I reflected on my thoughts and behaviors when I read opinions during the feedback time	Reflection activities

The questionnaire used a five-point scale (Strongly agree, agree, neither agree nor disagree, disagree, strongly disagree) for students to answer. The scores were analyzed from five to one with five given to strongly agree and 1 to strongly disagree. Students received questionnaires on July 17, 2017. Of the questionnaires returned, 238 of 246 were valid.

6.3 Analysis Procedure

In this study, data analysis software of Statistical Package for the Social Sciences was used to analyze the data. The analysis procedure is as follows: (1) To ensure the effectiveness of the CTD scale, the authors performed factor analysis based on the data. (2) Descriptive statistics was used to analyze students' course evaluations. (3) Correlation analysis was used to analyze the relation between inquiry-mind objectiveness and activities of CTD. (4) One-Way Analysis of Variance was used to analyze the differences of inquiry-mind and objectiveness in the participation scale of activities relative with LMS.

In One-way Analysis of Variance, three groups were divided as in the following procedure: Firstly, the authors calculated a median score of 4 in LMS activities. Secondly, the authors divided the scores into two groups using median value. The authors divided the class into smaller groups because the class consisted of 238 students. The authors divided students into two additional groups. Few students selected "Disagree" and "Strongly disagree". The numbers of the low group (0–3.99), the middle group (4–4.49) and the high group (4.5–5) were 60, 85, and 93 students respectively.

7 Result and Discussion

7.1 Students' Evaluation for Development in an Inquiry-Mind and Objectiveness

After analysis of the questionnaire that students completed at the end of the course, the authors found that students positively evaluated their development of inquiry-mind and objectiveness (Fig. 2). The results related to inquiry-mind were as follows: (1) 88% of the students agreed that they "learned many things through communication with different people in the course", 9% chose neither agree nor disagree, and 3% selected disagreed. (2) 87% of the students agreed that they were interested in the opinions that differ from theirs, 10% chose neither agree nor disagree, 4% disagreed. (3) 83% of the students agreed that they were "interested in discussing topics with different people in the course", 9% chose neither agree nor disagree, 3% disagreed. This data showed that more than 80% of students agreed that Media Expression fostered their inquiry-mind in the course.

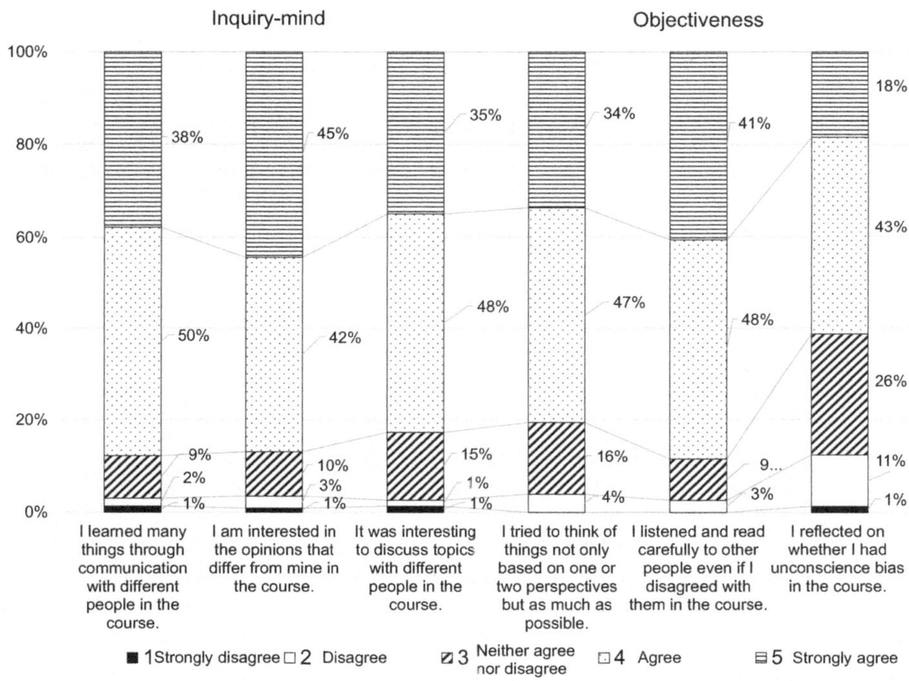

Fig. 2. Students' evaluation after the course

The results related to objectiveness were as follows: (1) Regarding the item "I tried to think of things not only based on one or two perspectives but as much as possible, I thought of many different angles", 81% of the students agreed, 16% chose neither agree nor disagree, 4% answered in disagreement. The data confirms that most students agreed that they tried to think about media from different perspectives. (2) 89% of the students stated that they listened carefully to what others said even if they disagreed with other students' opinions in the course, 9% chose neither agree nor disagree, 3% disagreed. The data showed that students tried to understand and consider opposing opinions in the course. (3) 61% of the students said they reflected on whether they had unconscious bias in the course, 26% chose neither agree nor disagree, 12% disagreed. Thus showing that 61% of students tried to reflect on their unconscious bias. This result was unexpected. The authors predicted that students would reflect on their conscious bias as they did when they wrote their thoughts on LMS and recognized different opinions as a result of participating in the three types of activities. The authors had assumed that some students would reflect on their unconscious bias.

7.2 Correlation Between Activities and Inquiry-Mind and Objectiveness of CTD

Table 2 shows the relationship between the activities and inquiry-mind and objectiveness. Inquiry-mind and objectiveness is based on the average value in three items in questionnaire.

Table 2. Relations between CLD and activities

		Inquiry-mind		Objectiveness	
		Pearson's correlation	Significance	Pearson's correlation	Significance
Thinking activities in classroom	I said my opinions clearly in the classroom	.062	.342	.253***	.000
	I noticed new ideas in group work in the classroom	.493***	.000	.341***	.000
	I was surprised many times in the classroom	.478***	.000	.278***	.000
	I compared my opinion with other students' opinions shown on the screen in the classroom	.416***	.000	.350***	.000
	I wrote my opinions clearly on the LMS after the lessons	.339***	.000	.360***	.000
Discussion on LMS	I noticed the difference between myself and other students through the commemts on the LMS	.510***	.000	.416***	.000
Reflection activities in the next lesson	I used the ideas of other students in my opinions when I wrote comments on LMS	.289**	.000	.221**	.001
	I reflected on my thoughts and behaviors when I read opinions from LMS during the feedback time	.360***	.000	.421***	.000

*p < .05 **p < .01 ***p < .001 (two-tailed)

From the table, inquiry-mind correlates significantly with seven activities. The thinking activities in the classroom, such as "noticing new ideas in group work" (r = 0.493,

$p < 0.001$), "being surprised many times in the classroom" ($r = 0.478$, $p < 0.001$), and "comparing the opinions between my opinions and other students' opinion shown on screen" ($r = 0.416$, $p < 0.001$) had significant correlation.

Furthermore, activities about discussion on LMS also correlated significantly. Particularly, the correlation between inquiry-mind and "noticing the difference between my and other students' comments on LMS" ($r = 0.510$, $p < 0.001$) was strongest among eight items. In addition, reflection activities, in the next lesson, had significant correlation with inquiry-mind ($r = 0.360$, $p < 0.001$). These results of seven items showed that the activities encouraged the cultivation of an inquiry-mind.

Students needed to acquire new information before they could make conclusions [1–3]. Students obtained new information about how and why information was transmitted in the media, in the classroom, through group work and by observing student opinions displayed on a screen at the front of the room. According to Piaget [18], surprising experiences triggered students to avoid a quick judgement before they found new information to inspect. Students with surprising experiences also think of what the media reports in the news and how media intentionally represents images in society.

The interactive comments posted on LMS continued to allow students to find new perspectives based on feedback from other students. These interactive comments motivated them to reconsider whether their opinions were correct or suitable, and whether there were alternative perspectives. Since students could browse freely through many opinions and comments on LMS, the authors conjectured that different and opposite opinions increased depending on the students' access to LMS. Since students couldn't read all online comments, the typical opinions, chosen by the lecturer and shown at the next lesson, assisted students in gaining new perspectives.

Expressing opinions clearly in the classroom had no significant relationship with inquiry-mind ($r = 0.062$, ns). This may indicate the limitations of promoting student from inquiring about new ideas in a lecture hall. Culturally Japanese students prefer not to oppose or state differing ideas [3, 4]. Therefore, they may feel pressured when asked to state their opinions clearly.

All activities related positively with students' objectiveness. Particularly, the items "I reflected my thoughts and behaviors when I read the opinions picked from LMS during the feedback time" related to objectiveness was the highest among eight items ($r = 0.421$, $p < 0.001$). The items, "I noticed the difference between my opinion and other students' opinions through the comments on LMS", was also the second highest item related to objectiveness ($r = 0.416$, $p < 0.001$).

Communication with people who think about things from different perspectives could improve objectiveness [1–3]. In this case, more than 200 students stated their opinions about media issues and exchanged comments with each other on LMS. Thus, many different opinions were presented on LMS. Students, who read other students' opinions and wrote comments, realized multiple perspectives on the same issues. Thus, their objectiveness could be cultivated in an online environment. As Bankingham and Kolb indicated, students reflecting on their process of analysis was important in allowing them to judge their conclusions objectively [2, 16]. The reflecting activities, when the lecturer posted typical opinions during the feedback portion in the next lesson, helped students reflect deeply and with greater perspective.

7.3 Difference of Inquiry-Mind and Objectiveness in the Participation of Activities

Table 3 and 4 contains the results of differences of inquiry-mind and objectiveness in the low, middle and high groups of LMS activities. The average value of participation scale of discussion on LMS and reflection activities in the next lesson was 3.99. By the analysis of variance, there were significant differences of inquiry-mind and objectiveness in low, middle and high groups of LMS activities (Table 3, 4). Inquiry-mind was F (2, 235) = 28.05, $p < 0.001$. Objectiveness was F (2, 235) = 31.26, $p < 0.001$.

Table 3. ANOVA for Inquiry-mind

	Sum of squares	df	Mean square	F	Sig.
Between Groups	17.68	2	8.84	28.05	0.000
Within Groups	74.07	235	0.32		
Total	91.75	237			

Table 4. ANOVA for Objectiveness

	Sum of squares	df	Mean square	F	Sig.
Between Groups	17.62	2	8.81	31.26	0.000
Within Groups	66.23	235	0.28		
Total	83.85	237			

A Tukey Multiple Comparison Test was necessary to determine group differences after significant differences in scores were revealed. Table 5 illustrates the data between group comparisons at low, middle and high groups of LMS activities. The average of inquiry-mind in the low group was 3.91(SD = 0.71), middle group was 4.25 (SD = 0.45) and high group was 4.60 (SD = 0.42). Inquiry-mind between the low and middle groups (I-J = −0.34, p < 0.001), middle and high groups (I-J = −0.35, p < 0.01), low and high groups ((I-J = -0.69, p < 0.001) had significant differences.

The average of objectiveness in low group was 3.72(SD = 0.55), middle group was 4.04 (SD = 0.56) and high group was 4.40 (SD = 0.45). Objectiveness between the low and middle groups (I-J = −0.31, p < 0.001), middle and high groups (I-J = −0.37, p < 0.001), low and high groups ((I-J = −0.69, p < 0.001) has significant differences.

These results above showed that inquiry-mind and objectiveness had significant differences between the low and middle groups, middle and high groups, and low and high groups. These results indicated that the participation scale of LMS activities affected the strength of inquiry-mind and objectiveness. The more student engaged in activities, the

Table 5. Tukey HSD - CTD between groups

	Low group	Middle group	High group	Low–Middle	Middle–High	Low–High
Inquiry-mind	3.91(0.71)	4.25(0.45)	4.60(0.42)	* * *	* *	* * *
Objectiveness	3.72(0.55)	4.04(0.56)	4.40(0.45)	* * *	* * *	* * * * * *

*p<.05 **p<.01 ***p<.001

greater their CTD increased. The engagement of discussion online often depended on the individual and it was easy to have different participation levels [19]. In this course, the engagement time and the levels of effort to make inquiries about new information and make objective conclusions depended on the individual student. Furthermore, student participation varied when the lecture introduced typical opinions from LMS in the reflection activities in the next lesson. The data indicated that students participated better in the activities related to LMS, and their inquiry-mind and objectiveness were higher.

8 Discussion

Analysis of the data found (1) students positively evaluated that Media Expression course fostered their inquiry-mind and objectiveness; (2) participating in seven activities significantly affected students' inquiry-mind and objectiveness, but stating opinions in the big hall only affected students' objectiveness; (3) there were differences in inquiry-mind and objectiveness in the participation scale of LMS activities.

Kusumi et al. found that objectiveness improved but inquiry-mind did not when activities were designed in the classroom [20]. In contrast, this study showed that activity design cultivated Japanese students' inquiry-mind and objectiveness. The authors considered that there was a cycle of thinking activities in classroom, discussion on LMS, and reflection activities in the next lesson in Media Expression course (Fig. 3).

The activities, including writing their opinions about media, commenting on other students' posts, noticing new opinions then discussing, occurred on LMS. Students could express their opinions freely without worry, anxiety or embarrassment. Thus, a culture developed that promoted free expression of opinions online. Next, reflection activities at the next lesson linked their online discussions with the traditional classroom. During this activity the lecturer facilitate the introduction and discussion of typical opinions. These designs were helpful to form a culture that questioned information. Next, the process involved group work, analyzing activities in the lecture hall. Classroom culture was created through different activities during various periods in the semester [5–7]. Thus, a critical culture formed in the course.

As Ogihara and Mochizuki indicated, Japanese students were embarrassed to present their difference or state opposite opinions in the classroom [4]. In a critical culture,

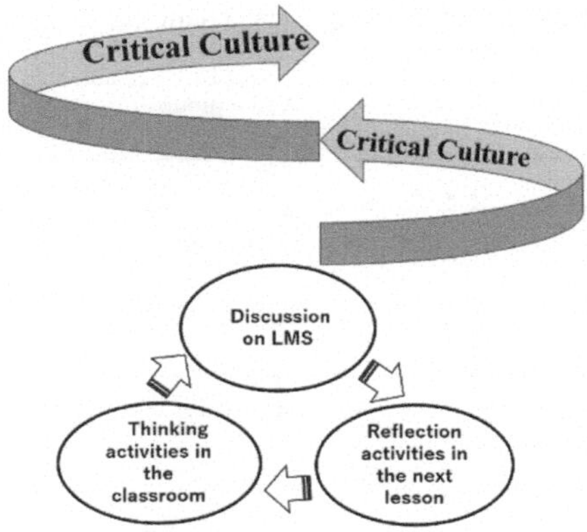

Fig. 3. The cycle of forming critical culture

students could more easily read about, listen to and accept different viewpoints since expressing differences became the norm and sameness was uncommon. This critical culture countered Japanese culture that values being the same. Students felt safe and comfortable to externalize their thoughts in this environment.

9 Conclusions, Implication and Future Perspective

This study examined the design of activities in a blended learning environment that cultivated inquiry-mind and objectiveness in the disposition of students. Results showed that students highly rated their analyzing media with their development of inquiry-mind and objectiveness. There were significant differences of inquiry-mind and objectiveness in the low, middle and high groups of participation scale of LMS activities. The cycle of thinking activities in classroom, discussion on LMS, and reflection activities in the next lesson promoted the critical culture forming in the course.

As Ogihara and Mochizuki indicated, as in Japan, other Asian countries have a collective culture where it is difficult to state differing or opposing opinions to teachers [4]. This study identified that the inquiry-mind and objectiveness of Japanese university students could be fostered through forming a critical culture in the course. This activity design may also bring classroom cultural change that will cultivate students' CTD in media literacy courses in other Asian countries.

This study only focused on students' evaluation after they completed the course. Therefore, this study did not examine students' inquiry-mind and objectiveness of CTD through a comparison of pretest and posttest. Future studies can examine whether inquiry-mind and objectiveness improved through a pretest and posttest in a semester.

Acknowledgements. We greatly thank for the support from the teaching assistants in this field.

References

1. Masterman, L.: Teaching the Media. Comedia, London (1985)
2. Buckingham, D.: Media Education: Literacy, Learning and Contemporary Culture. Polity Press, Cambridge (2003)
3. Michita, Y.: Some suggestions from critical thinking study to media literacy. Comput. Commun. **9**, 54–59 (2000)
4. Ogihara, S., Mochizuki, T.: In search of an Asian model of teaching critical thinking: educational practice in the universities in Southeast Asian countries. Osaka Univ. Knowl. Arch. **4**, 43–52 (2007)
5. Tishman, S., Jay, E., Perkins, D.: Teaching thinking dispositions from transmission to enculturation. Theory Pract. **32**, 147–153 (1993)
6. Ritchhart, R.: Cultivating a culture of thinking in museums. J. Museum Educ. **32**(2), 137–154 (2007)
7. Ritchhart, R., Turner, T., Hadar, L.: Uncovering students' thinking about thinking using concept maps. Metacogn. Learn. **4**, 145–159 (2009). https://doi.org/10.1007/s11409-009-9040-x
8. Ennis, R.H.: A taxonomy of critical thinking dispositions and abilities. In: Baron, J.B., Sternberg, R.J. (eds.) Teaching Thinking Skills: Theory and Practice. Psychology Series, pp. 9–26. W. H. Freeman and Company, New York (1987)
9. Facione, P.A.: Critical thinking what it is and why it counts, pp. 1–30. Insight Assessment (2015)
10. Morimoto, Y.: How students can acquire "Critical" Thinking through Media Literacy Education? Toshindo, Tokyo (2014)
11. Thorne, K.: Blended Learning: How to Integrate Online and Traditional Learning. Kogan Page, London (2003)
12. Yu, W.W., Lin, C.C., Ho, M., Wang, J.: Technology facilitated PBL pedagogy and its impact on nursing student's academic achievement and critical thinking dispositions. Turk. Online J. Educ. Technol. **14**(1), 97–107 (2015)
13. Iwasaki, C., Kubota, K.: Analysis of learning process on media literacy: qualitative research on Bulletin Board System. Jpn. Assoc. Educ. Media Study **11**(2), 57–65 (2005)
14. Okano, T., Kubota, K.: Analysis of transformation process and factors of students' Media perspectives. Jpn. Assoc. Educ. Media Study **12**(2), 1–16 (2006)
15. Bloch, J., Spataro, E.S.: Cultivating critical thinking disposition through business curriculum. Bus. Prof. Commun. Q. **77**(3), 249–265 (2014)
16. Kolb, D.A., Rubin, I.M., McIntyre, J.M.: Organizational Psychology: An Experiential Approach to Organizational Behavior. Prentice Hall, London (1994)
17. Hirayama, R., Kusumi, T.: Effect of critical thinking disposition on interpretation of controversial issues: evaluating evidences and drawing conclusions. Jpn. J. Educ. Psychol. **52**, 186–198 (2004)
18. Piaget, J.: The Equilibration of Cognitive Structures: The Central Problem of Intellectual Development. University of Chicago Press, Chicago (1985)
19. Yang, V.Y., Chou, H.: Beyond critical thinking skills: investigating the relationship between critical thinking skills and dispositions through different online instructional strategies. Br. J. Educ. Technol. **39**(4), 666–684 (2008)
20. Kusumi, T., Tanaka, Y., Hirayama, R.: Teaching critical thinking in the first-year experience of higher education. Cogn. Stud. **19**(1), 69–82 (2012)

Experience in Blended Learning

Effectiveness of the Blended Learning Approach in Teaching and Learning Selected EFL Grammar Structures at a University Level – A Case Study

Blanka Klímová(✉) and Josef Toman

Department of Applied Linguistics, Faculty of Informatics and Management, University of Hradec Kralove, Hradec Kralove, Czech Republic
{blanka.klimova,josef.toman}@uhk.cz

Abstract. Grammar seems to be the backbone of any foreign language learning, including English as a foreign language (EFL). Currently, the most common approach to teaching EFL, especially at a university level, appears to be a blended learning approach, which is a combination of traditional, face-to-face teaching and online learning. The purpose of this study is to evaluate the effectiveness of the use of the blended learning approach to teaching and learning selected grammar structures in a university Course of Practical English Language. The blended learning approach in this study reflects the use of traditional, face-to-face teaching and mobile learning, more specifically, the use of a mobile application, outside the classroom settings. The research methods of this article include a literature review of available studies on the research topic and statistical methods of the analysis and evaluation of the results of students' pre- and post-tests, which focused on the selected grammar structures. The findings of both literature review and the statistical analysis indicate that the blended learning approach contributes to the effectiveness of student's learning of the selected grammar structures since the results confirm that the success of teaching and learning depends on a variety of methods used.

Keywords: Blended learning · Mobile application · English · Grammar · Learning · Effectiveness

1 Introduction

Together with vocabulary, grammar represents a significant foundation of learning English as a foreign language (EFL). Grammar as part of linguistic competence, inevitably connected with language accuracy, is one of the pillars of communicative competence [1, 2]. In fact, grammar is the structural foundation of person's ability to express herself/himself [3]. Knowing the grammar structures helps a person with the form, meaning, and the use of language [4]. As Chomsky [5] states, grammar is a set of finite rules which, if learnt and mastered, can generate an infinite set of sentences. The

S. K. S. Cheung et al. (Eds.): ICBL 2020, LNCS 12218, pp. 227–236, 2020.
https://doi.org/10.1007/978-3-030-51968-1_19

knowledge of grammar is a prerequisite of effective communication. If one makes grammar mistakes in a conversation, it may lead to misunderstanding and disagreement [6]. Thus, grammar seems to be the backbone of learning any foreign language, including EFL. At present, teaching grammar is a bit underestimated since the emphasis is put on a communicative approach, whose objective is to make people communicate successfully in the target language, regardless of grammar mistakes. However, as it has been stated above, without a good command of grammar structures, meaning cannot be properly conveyed [7]. Therefore, teachers have to focus on teaching grammar structures and stimulate their learners to study them. There are different approaches to teaching grammar. The most typical is a traditional translation method to teaching grammar, which most of the students find boring. However, with the emergence of modern technologies, there are other opportunities how to make learners motivated to study the grammar structures.

Currently, the most common approach to teaching EFL, especially at a university level, appears to be the blended learning approach [8–13]. Frydrychova Klimova [14] sees blended learning as a combination of traditional, face-to-face teaching and online learning. In this mode, the online component is practiced outside the face-to-face classes, which enables the integration of traditional learning with innovative methods of learning in order to create an effective learning environment aiming to enrich learning experience [15]. As the findings of several research studies [16, 17] indicate, the blended learning approach has a positive impact when learning EFL grammar. The results of these research studies show that the experimental groups, using the blended learning approach, achieved better results in the grammar post-test in comparison with the control groups, taught by conventional methods. In addition, students in the experimental groups were more satisfied and motivated to learn the EFL grammar.

More recently, thanks to the rapid development of mobile assisted language learning (MALL) [18], mobile applications (apps) have become an integral part of the blended learning approach [19]. After the mobile apps used for assessing and learning vocabulary, grammar learning mobile apps seem to be the second most exploited mobile apps used in EFL learning [20].

The purpose of this study is to evaluate the effectiveness of the use of the blended learning approach to teaching and learning selected grammar structures in a university Course of Practical English Language.

2 Materials and Methods

2.1 Participants

Altogether 29 students attended the Course of Practical English Language in their third year of study of Management of Travel and Tourism at the Faculty of Informatics and Management of the University of Hradec Kralove, Czech Republic. They were all full-time students. Their level of English according to the Common Reference Framework for Languages (CERF) was B2-C1 [21]. The course lasted for 13 weeks, from the last week in September till the third week in December 2019. The face-to-face classes were held regularly for 90 min every Tuesday.

Although the course is aimed at developing and practicing all four language skills (i.e. speaking, writing, listening, and reading), some lessons focus on the selected grammar structures, which still seem to be slightly difficult even for the advanced students of English. These grammar structures include the use of tenses, modal verbs, conditional sentences, and wish clauses.

2.2 Study Design and Hypothesis

The blended learning approach consisted of the face-to-face classes, as it has been described above, and the use of mobile application Anglictina TODAY, which is used both for learning and practicing new EFL vocabulary, as well as practicing grammar structures. The app is available both for the Android operating system and iOS and was developed on the basis of students' needs analysis, as far as EFL grammar learning is concerned. Students were notified at least twice a week to study the relevant section of grammar structures. Figure 1 below demonstrates the mobile app screen with the menu.

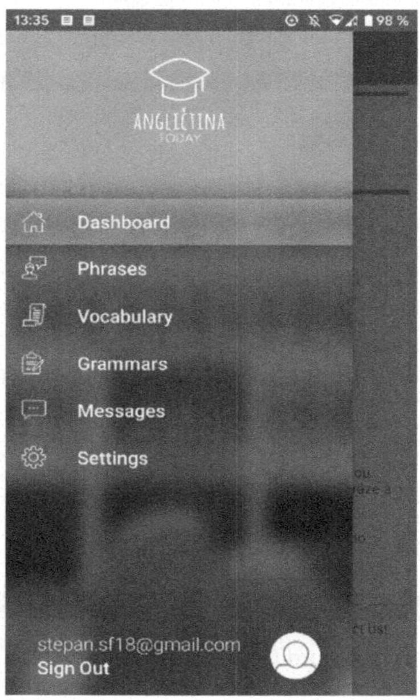

Fig. 1. Student's menu on the mobile app screen.

Figure 2 then illustrates one of the grammar structures on practicing modal verbs, which students have to fill in. As one can see, the practicing of grammar is not based on the traditional translation grammar method, but on the contrary, students have to deduce and understand the meaning of the sentence, which is provided in a short context. On the basis of their knowledge of grammar rules and their understanding of the sentence meaning, they have to fill in the right modal verb together with the given semantic verb.

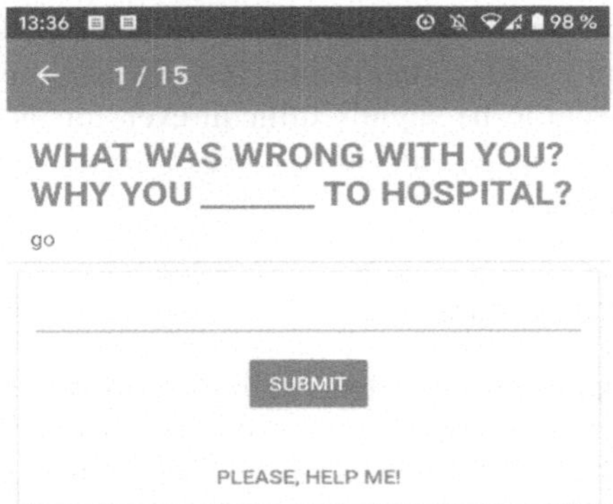

Fig. 2. Example of a grammar structure on modal verbs in the mobile app.

In addition, to the mobile app, students have access to the learning materials used at school in an online Blackboard course (Fig. 3) [22].

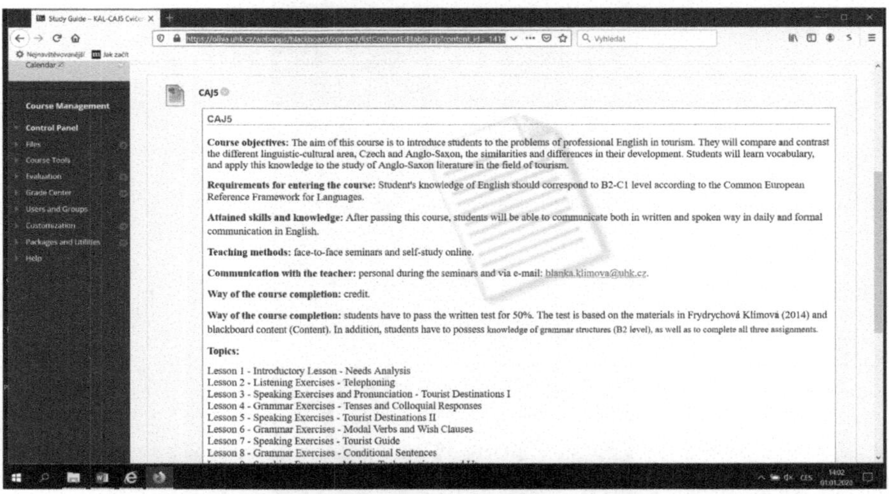

Fig. 3. Online Blackboard Course on Practical English Language.

The methods also included statistical methods of the analysis and evaluation of the results of students' pre- and post-tests focused on the selected grammar structures. The pass mark for the fulfillment of both tests was 50%, i.e., 40 points. The authors set the following hypothesis:

H: The blended learning approach contributes to the effectiveness of student's learning of the selected grammar structures.

3 Results

In the statistical analysis of the impact of the use of the blended learning approach on students' learning of the selected grammar structures, a sample of 25 students participated in the pre grammar test at the beginning of the semester and a sample of 28 students took the post grammar test at the end of the semester 2019. The reason for the uneven number of students was that at the beginning of the semester four students still were abroad on their study stays and the same was true for one student at the end of the semester. The following calculations were made using the IBM SPSS Statistics 25 software.

Important is the difference between pre- and post-education knowledge for one and the same group of students. The cumulative data obtained from both tests obtained before and after the training block are summarized in Table 1 in the second and third columns (test_before/pre-test, test_after/post-test). The fourth column of the same table shows the data calculated (difference A-B) from the second and third columns. The missing data is indicated by the value "99".

Table 1. Number of students and results from the pre-test and post-test and their difference.

No_student	pre_test	post_test	post_minus_pre
	[B]	*[A]*	*[A-B]*
1	6	17	11
2	7	20	13
3	7	23	16
4	7	24	17
5	10	25	15
6	11	28	17
7	11	29	18
8	13	32	19
9	16	35	19
10	17	38	21
11	19	38	19
12	19	39	20
13	20	41	21
14	20	41	21
15	20	41	21
16	21	42	21
17	22	42	20

(*continued*)

Table 1. (*continued*)

No_student	pre_test	post_test	post_minus_pre
	[B]	*[A]*	*[A-B]*
18	22	43	21
19	23	44	21
20	23	44	21
21	24	45	21
22	25	45	20
23	28	46	18
24	31	46	15
25	35	47	12
26	99	47	99
27	99	48	99
28	99	49	99

Assuming the normality of the difference data (A-B), a paired t-test can be used for this situation. Based on the normality test performed, according to the recommendations for small groups, the Shapiro-Wilk test is used (Table 2 below).

Table 2. Test of normality.

	Kolmogorov-Smirnov[a]			Shapiro-Wilk		
	Statistic	df	Sig.	Statistic	df	Sig.
post_minus_pre	0,192	25	0,018	83,40%	25	0,001

a. Lilliefors Significance Correction

According to the Saphiro-Wilk test (Sig < 0.05), i.e. the distribution of the "pre- and post" test difference differs significantly from the normal distribution and therefore the presumption of normality is not met. For this reason, the non-parametric Wilcoxon Signed Rank Test method is used (Table 3). As the findings in Table 3 reveal, the mean score in the pre-test was 18 points, while in the post test, it was two times higher.

Table 3. Descriptive statistics of the results from the pre-test and post-test.

	N	Mean	Std. deviation	Minimum	Maximum	Percentiles
						25th
post_test	28	37,82	9,322	17	49	29,75
pre_test	25	18,28	7,76	6	35	11

Table 4 below shows that 25 students had a higher level of knowledge in the post-test than in the pre-test.

Table 4. Wilcoxon Signed Ranks Test.

		N	Mean rank	Sum of ranks
pre_test-post_test	Negative ranks	25[a]	13	325
	Positive ranks	0[b]	0	0
	Ties	0[c]		
	Total	25		

a) B < A b) B > A c) B = A

This result is statistically significant with respect to the results shown in Table 5, see p-value. Asymp. Sig. (2-tailed) 0.000 < 0.05, i.e. it is a statistically significant difference in score in the "post" test and "pre" test at a significance level of 0.05), i.e. it is not a random result.

Table 5. Wilcoxon Signed Rank Test – test statistics.

	pre_test-post_test
Z	−4,399[b]
Asymp. Sig. (2-tailed)	0,000

b. Based on positive ranks.

4 Discussion

The results described above show that the set hypothesis was confirmed. The blended learning approach contributes to the effectiveness of student's learning of the selected grammar structures. Although there was no control group, the variety of the used methods: traditional teaching, the mobile app, as well as the use of the materials in the online blackboard course prove a significant improvement of students' achievement results. The effectiveness of the blended learning approach was thus manifested in the fact that students succeeded in passing the final post-test significantly better. In addition, they felt that they had improved their language skills. Therefore, the blended learning approach was effective because students not only performed well and thus were able to construct new knowledge, but they were also motivated to study on their own. As Kintu et al. [23] point out, the effectiveness of blended learning is influenced by design features of blended learning, e.g. technology quality, interactions, LMS tools and resources and face-to-face support, as well as by learner characteristics, such as self-regulation, attitude, computer competence, age, or social support.

The findings of this study also reveal that there are certain benefits, which enrich student's learning environment thanks to the use of additional, supporting component of the blended learning approach, i.e. the mobile app. These are as follows:

- accessibility of learning materials at anytime, anywhere, and on one's own pace;
- easiness of the use of mobile app;
- further deepening and retention of student's knowledge of a particular language aspect thanks to the interactivity of the mobile app;
- almost instant corrective feedback on the mobile app tasks;
- use of formative assessment;
- development of student's autonomous study; or
- stimulation for student's study.

The findings of this study are in line with the findings of other research studies [16, 17, 19], which consider blended learning as an effective approach to the enhancement of student's grammar. In addition, mobile learning itself seems to have a positive impact on learning EFL grammar. For instance, Laban [24] reports that students in his experimental group using mobile apps achieved statistically better results than those in the control group being exposed to the traditional teaching methods. Similarly, Wang and Smith [25] claim that mobile learning is effective in improving students' grammar ability.

Furthermore, research shows that the implementation of formative assessment, i.e. continuous assessment, in a blended learning environment may improve the learning quality [26], as well as it may have a significant effect on higher academic achievement levels [27, 28]. This was evidenced by the results from the post-tests in this study since students achieved twice as higher scores than in the pre-tests.

The limitations of this article consist in a small sample of the respondents and a lack of the control group. However, the results comply with the findings of the research studies stated above.

5 Conclusion

The results of this study confirm that the success of teaching and learning depends on a variety of methods used. According to Khan [29], a valuable learning process is created by employing various learning methods, tools and techniques. In this sense, the blended learning approach appears to be a relevant solution since it combines a traditional, classroom way of teaching and an additional component, such as mobile learning.

Nevertheless, it is the teacher who is responsible for the implementation of the most relevant teaching and learning approaches/methods in order to generate higher learning outcomes.

Acknowledgments. This study is supported by the SPEV project 2020, run at the Faculty of Informatics and Management, University of Hradec Kralove, Czech Republic.

References

1. Celce-Murcia, M.: Teaching English as a Second or Foreign Language, 2nd edn. Newbury House, New York (1991)
2. Usó-Juan, E., Martínez-Flor, A.: Current Trends in the Development and Teaching of the four Language Skills. Mouton de Gruyter, Berlin (2006)
3. Crystal, D.: A twenty-first century grammar bridge. Second. Engl. Mag. **7**(5), 24–26 (2004)
4. Richards, J., Theodore, S.R.: Approaches and Methods in Language Teaching: A Description and Analysis. CUP, Cambridge (2001)
5. Chomsky, N.: Knowledge of Language: Its Nature, Origin and Use. Praeger, New York (1986)
6. Dalil, Z.: The Importance of Grammar in Second Language Teaching (2013). https://www.academia.edu/12284393/The_importance_of_grammar_in_second_language_teaching_and_learning
7. Vernon, S.: Is Grammar Really Important for Second Language Learners? (2019). https://www.teachingenglishgames.com/grammar-really-important-second-language-learners
8. Klimova, B.: evaluation of the blended learning approach in the course of business english – a case study. In: Huang, T.-C., Lau, R., Huang, Y.-M., Spaniol, M., Yuen, C.-H. (eds.) SETE 2017. LNCS, vol. 10676, pp. 326–335. Springer, Cham (2017). https://doi.org/10.1007/978-3-319-71084-6_37
9. Frydrychova Klimova, B., Poulova, P.: Forms of instruction and students' preferences - a comparative study. In: Cheung, S.K.S., Fong, J., Zhang, J., Kwan, R., Kwok, L.F. (eds.) ICHL 2014. LNCS, vol. 8595, pp. 220–231. Springer, Cham (2014). https://doi.org/10.1007/978-3-319-08961-4_21
10. Buran, A., Evseeva, A.: Prospects of blended learning implementation at technical university. Procedia Soc. Behav. Sci. **206**, 177–182 (2015)
11. Simonova, I., Kostolanyova, K.: The blended learning concept: comparative study of two universities. In: Cheung, S.K.S., Kwok, L.-f., Shang, J., Wang, A., Kwan, R. (eds.) ICBL 2016. LNCS, vol. 9757, pp. 302–311. Springer, Cham (2016). https://doi.org/10.1007/978-3-319-41165-1_27
12. Černá, M.: User evaluation of language websites as a way of students' engagement into blended learning process case study. In: Cheung, S.K.S., Kwok, L.-f., Shang, J., Wang, A., Kwan, R. (eds.) ICBL 2016. LNCS, vol. 9757, pp. 269–280. Springer, Cham (2016). https://doi.org/10.1007/978-3-319-41165-1_24
13. Garrison, D., Kanuka, H.: Blended learning: uncovering its transformative potential in higher education. Internet High. Educ. **7**(2), 95–105 (2004)
14. Frydrychova Klimova, B.: Blended learning. In Mendez Vilas, A. et al. (Eds.) Research, Reflections and Innovations in Integrating ICT in Education, pp. 705–708. FORMATEX, Spain (2009)
15. Mikulecky, P.: Blended learning in smart learning environments. In: Moura Oliveira, P., Novais, P., Reis, L.P. (eds.) EPIA 2019. LNCS (LNAI), vol. 11805, pp. 62–67. Springer, Cham (2019). https://doi.org/10.1007/978-3-030-30244-3_6
16. Qindah, S.: The effects of blended learning on EFL students' usage of grammar in context. Eurasia Proc. Educ. Soc. Sci. **10**, 11–22 (2018)
17. Al Bataineh, K.B., Banikalef, A.E.A.A., Albashtawi, A.H.: The effect of blended learning on EFL students' grammar performance and attitudes: an investigation of Moodle. Arab World Engl. J. **10**(1), 324–334 (2019)
18. Kukulska-Hulme, A., Shield, L.: An overview of mobile assisted language learning: from content delivery to supported collaboration and interaction. ReCALL **20**(3), 271–289 (2008)

19. Klímová, B., Pražák, P.: Mobile blended learning and evaluation of its effectiveness on students' learning achievement. In: Cheung, S.K.S., Lee, L.-K., Simonova, I., Kozel, T., Kwok, L.-F. (eds.) ICBL 2019. LNCS, vol. 11546, pp. 216–224. Springer, Cham (2019). https://doi.org/10.1007/978-3-030-21562-0_18
20. Heil, C.R., Wu, J.S., Lee, J.J., Schmidt, T.: A review of mobile language learning applications: trends, challenges and opportunities. EUROCALL Rev. **24**(2), 32–50 (2016)
21. Common European Reference Framework for Languages (2019). https://en.wikipedia.org/wiki/Common_European_Framework_of_Reference_for_Languages
22. Online Blackboard Course on Practical English Language (2020). https://oliva.uhk.cz/webapps/blackboard/content/listContentEditable.jsp?content_id=_141902_1&course_id=_1107_1&mode=reset
23. Kintu, M.J., Zhu, C., Kagambe, E.: Blended learning effectiveness: the relationship between student characteristics, design features and outcomes. Int. J. Educ. Technol. High. Educ. **14**, 7 (2017). https://doi.org/10.1186/s41239-017-0043-4
24. Laban, M.M.A.: The Effectiveness of Using Mobile Learning in Developing Eleventh Graders' English Grammar Learning and Motivation for English (2017). https://www.mobt3ath.com/uplode/book/book-10432.pdf
25. Wang, S., Smith, S.: Reading and grammar learning through mobile phones. Lang. Learn. Technol. **17**(3), 117–134 (2013)
26. Febriani, I., Abdullah, M.I.: A systematic review of formative assessment tools in the blended learning environment. Int. J. Eng. Technol. **7**, 33–39 (2018)
27. Ozan, C., Remzi, Y.: The effects of formative assessment on academic achievement, attitudes toward the lesson, and self-regulation skills. Educ. Sci.: Theory Pract. **18**(1), 85–118 (2018)
28. Carrillo-de-la-Pena, M.T., Bailles, E., Caseras, X., Martinez, A., Ortet-Fabregat, G., Perez, J.: Formative assessment and academic achievement in pre-graduate students of health sciences. Adv. Health Sci. Educ. **14**(1), 61–67 (2009). https://doi.org/10.1007/s10459-007-9086-y
29. Khan, B.: Learning features in an open, flexible and distributed environment. AACE J. **13**(2), 137–153 (2005)

What Drives Rural Students' Behavioral Engagement in Synchronous Online Classrooms? Examining the Effects of Discourse Interaction and Seating Location

Mingzhang Zuo[1], Yujie Yan[2(✉)], Kunyu Wang[1], and Heng Luo[1]

[1] School of Educational Information Technology, Central China Normal University, Wuhan 430079, China
[2] National Engineering Research Center for E-Learning, Central China Normal University, Wuhan 430079, China
yanyujie@mails.ccnu.edu.cn

Abstract. Classroom discourse can affect various aspects of student learning. To provide better learning experience in distance learning, the present study examines interactions between classroom discourse based on IRF-discourse and related behavioral engagement of students in front, middle and rear seating locations in synchronous online classrooms. We observed 24 third-grade music classrooms using the behavioral engagement scale. Results from these observations indicate that classroom with more discourse interactions, specifically teacher's elicitation for student responses may result in increased students' behavioral engagement. The study also revealed significant differences in behavioral engagement of students from different seating location. Moreover, the results showed that positive behaviors dominated students' classroom activities, but students demonstrated more teacher-prompted behaviors rather than self-initiated behaviors.

Keywords: Classroom discourse · Behavioral engagement · Interaction · Seating location · Synchronous online learning

1 Introduction

Educators have responsibilities to take active and effective measures to ensure educational equity for rural children to offer them an opportunity to change the current life and achieve upward mobility. The integration of technology into all walks of life has also brought profound changes to the field of education, with information and communication technologies (ICTs) being one of the most feasible driving forces to achieve education equality. Distance learning has enabled more advanced schools in city district to extend learning opportunities to students who are otherwise unable to benefit from them due to time and location constraints [1]. Under the concept of technology-assisted education, we explored the synchronous online classrooms to promote rural revitalization. In the synchronous online classrooms, teachers in urban schools are selected as main instructors, while teachers in rural small schools play the role of assistant to help organize the

S. K. S. Cheung et al. (Eds.): ICBL 2020, LNCS 12218, pp. 237–248, 2020.
https://doi.org/10.1007/978-3-030-51968-1_20

process of learning. The synchronous online classrooms emphasize that online teachers and students can interact in real time via ICTs such as online streaming service and is considered promising to revitalize rural education.

Student engagement is an important indicator to measure the time and effort of students' learning and has been widely investigated. Researchers have reported a positive association between student engagement and academic achievement [2–4]. As suggested by the literature, student engagement at school is influenced by various factors concerning individual, family and school environment. The current literature largely focused on the effect of the school environment, because school is where student engagement actual occurs. Behavioral engagement, as a key dimension of engagement, is an intuitive external manifestation of emotional and cognitive engagement more or less [5], and thus is a key construct of the present study. Supportive teacher-student relationship is a critical aspect of the interpersonal dynamic in schools [6]. Research has indeed shown that Supportive teacher-student relationships play an important role in shaping behavioral engagement [7]. Prior research has argued that teacher goal-oriented instructional practices and public performance feedback affect behavioral engagement [8]. Academic staff explored factors that affect behavioral engagement focused on teacher-student interaction. Due to the specificity of classroom environment, technical conditions, and the teacher-student relationship, interaction in synchronous online classrooms varies from that in traditional classrooms, featured by different types of discourse interaction. However, previous research has seldom investigated the effectiveness of different discourse interaction pattern in supporting students' behavioral engagement in the online settings [9]. Mehan suggested that instructional discourse in the classroom focusing on initiation-response-feedback (IRF) exchanges [10], which is identified the most common sequence in classroom speech events [11, 12]. Therefore, it is feasible to explore the effect of teacher-student discourse interaction based on IRF-discourse. Additionally, we also examined the impact of the seating location on students' behavioral engagement, as it is known to have an impact on classroom discourse and behavioral engagement.

In sum, informed by the IRF-discourse analysis framework, this study examined the effect of classroom discourse on the behavioral engagement of students in front, middle and rear seating in synchronous online classrooms. Specifically, we seek to answer the following questions:

1. What types of discourse interaction and students' behavioral engagement mainly occur in synchronous online classrooms?
2. What is the relationship among students' behavioral engagement, discourse interaction pattern, and seating location?

2 Literature Review of Key Concepts

Fredricks summarized behavioral engagement into three categories: initiation, no violations or destructive behaviors, and performance in learning or academic tasks such as hard work, persistence, concentration, questioning [13]. Specifically, researchers argued that behavioral engagement includes seven behaviors: involvement, persistence, helplessness, participation in discussion, and concentration [14]. The learning engagement subscales compiled by Lan assessed active participation, concentration, and persistence as key elements of behavioral engagement [15]. As a result, behavioral engagement investigated in this study included five aspects: *involvement, persistence, concentration, interaction, initiation*, as synthesized from previous works in the literature. Since behavioral engagement is believed to predict student achievement and success in school, the role of interaction in facilitating engagement continues to be a primary focus. Compared with other forms of interaction, teachers' use of classroom discourse is more likely to attract attention by students in synchronous online classrooms.

Discourse has been defined as an interplay between "word, acts, values, beliefs, attitudes, and social identities" [9], which contribute jointly to sense-making and construction of meaning within a group of individuals in a specific setting. Researchers have noted the potential of teacher-student dialogue to scaffold student cognition and lessen the cognitive load created within the inquiry environment. Teachers' initial questioning and follow-up strategies can serve as scaffolding to support students' construction of conceptual understandings of science concepts [16]. As the study of classroom discourse progressed, Mehan showed that instructional discourse in the classroom was featured by initiation-response-feedback exchanges, which consisted of three moves: initiation move (I) – traditionally in the form of a teacher question, a response move (R) – during which a student answers the question, and a follow-up move (F) – referring to the feedback usually given by the teacher to the student's response [10–12]. Previous research has clearly showed that instances of substantive student participation are often driven by the nature of teacher questions during question and answer sessions [17]. Early research investigated the relationship between dialogic instruction and student engagement within classrooms, and concluded that evaluative discourse may affect the distribution of student engagement [18]. According to self-determination theory, students who receive motivational support such as teacher discourse that respond to students' progress and accomplishments may facilitate approach behaviors occur. However, much fewer studies investigated how students' behavioral engagement were affected by different discourse pattern. In addition, we include indicators of teacher guidance move after observation and analysis of the synchronous online classroom. The language of teacher guidance is an essential part of classroom discourse, and plays an irreplaceable role in imparting knowledge and guiding students' learning especially for elementary school. Hence, the discourse interaction between teachers and students based on IRF-discourse can be observed by the following constructs: *teacher guidance move, teacher initiation move, teacher follow-up move, student follow-up move, and student response move.*

In addition to investigating behavioral engagement in face-to-face classrooms, it is important to understand how classroom discourse pattern that, through discourse interaction between teachers and students, contribute to students' active behavioral engagement in distance education environments. Simultaneously, showing students' behaviors in five aspects concretely is dispensable in this study. These issues have been studied and are relatively well understood in face-to-face learning environments. However, opinions on the role of discourse interaction on learners' engagement in web-casting classrooms vary greatly. Synchronous online classrooms emphasize timely pedagogical practice of knowledge transmission and feedback between different regions. It is necessary to pay more attention the acceleration of classroom discourse form urban teachers for left-behind children growing up in poor-education rural areas abandoned by the rapidly developing economy. Regarding effects of seating location on student participation, previous studies have found that students in front rows showed greater participation than students sitting in the rear rows [19]. However, such finding was found in the traditional classroom setting, it is worthwhile to determine if the finding is transferrable to much smaller classrooms in distance learning environment, as commonly seen in the rural small schools in China.

3 Method

3.1 Participants

324 students led by two male third-grade music teachers participated in the study, including 150 female and 174 male students. Student socioeconomic status, as determined by parents' level of education and occupation, is in general at the lower end of China's social hierarchies, and nearly a third of them were left-behind children whose parents were not around for most of the year. "Study changes destiny" is a firmly held belief for youth growing up in high-poverty rural areas.

3.2 Procedures

Hubei Collaborative Innovation Center is an organization aiming for meeting the shortage of Music and Art courses in rural small schools featured by their incomplete grade setup (usually from grade 1 to grade 3) through synchronous online classrooms. Weekly, collaborative lesson preparation is organized, which ensures that learning activities can be carried out around the same topics and objectives. Considering senior students present more stable performance and have more learning experience with synchronous online classrooms that adapting to the changes that technology brought to the classroom, the research took more attention on the grade 3. After observing the classroom, we focused on the music class. Because music class showed more discourse interaction, compared to art class that required longer time for students to paint independently. To enhance the internal validity of the research design, two male third-grade music teachers were purposefully selected for investigation. The teachers were roughly equivalent in teaching experience, teaching style, professional credentials. Accordingly, 24 classrooms be selected.

We conducted a week-long video-recorded the selected classrooms' music class. Recorded video of synchronous online classrooms' learning context can be seen in Fig. 1. According to videos, we clustered classrooms based on five discourse moves identified in this study to get a classification of discourse interaction pattern. Considered the impact of seating location on behavioral engagement, this study divided the classroom space into three areas based on students' seat: front, middle, and rear due to the arrangement of chairs in straight rows. Each area contains 5 to 10 students. Hence, in addition to distinguishing student's behaviors in different discourse interaction patterns, it is more critical that we recorded students' behavior by area. Before coding the behaviors of the target students in 24 classes, two observers read related observation protocol carefully to ensure the accuracy and reliability of the observation.

Fig. 1. Context of synchronous online classrooms

3.3 Instrumentation

We used an observation protocol developed by use to capture the types and time sequence of teacher-student discourse. The observation protocol focused on five discourse moves: initiation move, including teacher's promoting replies, repeating elicitations, and simplifying elicitations; response move, such as student voluntarily answer questions or is answered by name; teacher follow-up move, including attention, support, iteration, and evaluation for student [20]; guidance move, such as the languages of imparting knowledge and guiding students to open the book, look up, thinking; and student follow-up move, such as feedback on teacher guidance in language, action, and emotion. As for students' behavioral engagement, in the present inquiry, we examined its quality by using observational techniques. Behavior categories that were used to observe were depicted in Table 1. Students' behavioral engagement in synchronous online classrooms is further classified into two aspects, that is, positive behavioral engagement and negative behavioral engagement. It is important to note that this observation protocol does not attempt to capture all indicators of behavioral engagement, only that the features it includes core indicators of behavioral engagement in the synchronous online classrooms and meet the definitional criteria specified in recent authoritative reviews of the concept.

Table 1. Behavior categories and corresponding description

	Category	Description
Positive	Involvement	Following teachers' instructions, answering a question, communicating with others
	Initiation	Raising hand, volunteer to sing or show
	Effort	Listening to teacher persistently, attempting to solve problems
Negative	Inattentive	Exhibiting trivial actions not related to learning
	Disengaged	Dreaming or working on contribution not related to learning
	Giving up	Disrupting a classmate or teacher with nonacademic issues, walking around idle in class

3.4 Data Collection

According to our observation, teacher-student discourse interaction between teacher and student usually occurred during the middle session of an asynchronous class, since teacher typically gave lectures in the beginning and at the end for preview and summary, without talking to the students. So, during the period from the 6 to 30 min of videos, each dialogue between teacher and student was recorded and analyzed according to the principle of classification. Updated records when a new move of classroom discourse occurs. For both moves of classroom discourse, data was reported as the percentage of occurrences of the records out of the total number of records. Cluster analysis was conducted to make 24 observed classrooms into similar sets, using the percentage of each discourse move as the unit of analysis, to determine what types of discourse interaction classrooms. Within the same time sampling, the behavioral engagement was measured using a form of time-sampling technique, in which an observer recorded whether a student exhibited a predetermined category of behavior during a 20 s interval. So, observation of each area consisted of 75 20-s intervals. Within each observation interval, the consistent behavior exhibited by majority of students in the area was recorded as students' behavioral engagement during the 20 s in this area. Each aspect of behavioral engagement was reported as the percentage of occurrences of the records out of the total number of records.

4 Result

Below is the statistical analysis report in response to research questions. The following calculations were made using the IBM SPSS Statistics version 23.

4.1 Classroom Discourse Classification Based on IRF

Through clustering, 2 groups became obvious, and we chose to stop at two clusters instead, which were represented by Type 1 Classroom and Type 2 Classroom. Each Classroom correspond specific phenotype: two classrooms' discourse interaction mainly include guidance-follow up interaction, but the frequency of initiation-response interaction in Type 1 Classroom was much higher than the frequency in Type 2 Classroom. Therefore, we defined the Type 1 Classroom' discourse interaction pattern as mainly guidance-follow-up and initiation-response interactions, and Type 2 Classroom' discourse interaction pattern was largely dominated by guidance-follow-up interactions. Dendrograms for cluster analysis was shown as Fig. 2.

4.2 Discourse Interaction Effects

Table 2 summarized the descriptive statistics for the behavioral engagement in two types of classrooms. The n in the table represented the number of classrooms of each type of classroom contains. Students exhibited behaviors in specific category were presents as M and SD. Values of M and SD indicated that behavioral engagement was more frequently recorded as effort such as listening to the instructor and attempting to solve problems

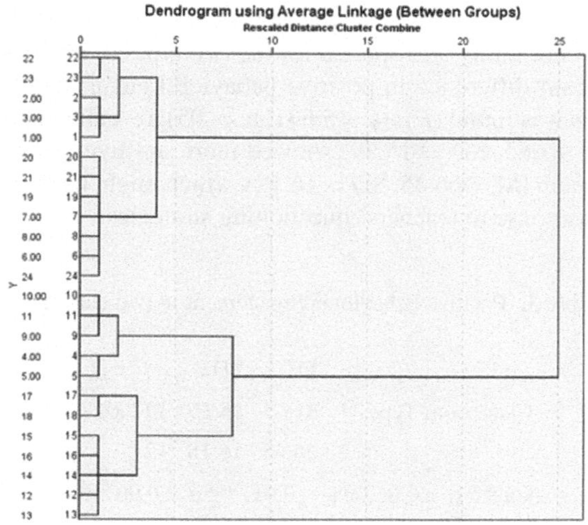

Fig. 2. Dendrogram for cluster analysis

raised by the instructor. Inevitably, inattentive and involvement behaviors were also commonly seen in the students. However, students were found to exhibit few initiation behaviors during the synchronous online learning process. Overall, positive behaviors (i.e., involvement, initiation, and effort) dominated students' behavioral engagement in the two types of classrooms. However, students' behavioral engagement in terms of effort was more frequently seen in Type 1 Classroom when comparing with Type 2 Classroom. It's worth noting that students in Type 2 Classroom showed more initiation behaviors than students in Type 1 Classroom, which can be attributed to learning autonomy was stimulated under the fewer guidance of teachers.

Table 2. Means and standard deviations for different aspects of behavioral engagement in two types of classrooms

Behavioral engagement	Type 1 classroom			Type 2 classroom			Total		
	M	SD	n	M	SD	n	M	SD	n
Involvement	17.00	9.24	12	10.33	9.50	12	13.67	9.78	24
Initiation	7.55	7.44	12	12.43	6.84	12	9.99	7.42	24
Effort	53.62	14.25	12	44.49	13.95	12	49.05	14.55	24
Inattentive	15.56	13.66	12	19.57	14.00	12	17.57	13.69	24
Disengaged	2.34	3.25	12	11.00	10.45	12	6.67	8.76	24
Giving up	0.74	.88	12	2.95	5.26	12	1.84	3.86	24

One-way ANOVAs were conducted to examine the difference in positive behavioral engagement between Type 1 and Type 2 of synchronous online classrooms. Assumption about normality and homogeneity of variance was examined prior to the analysis. No serious violation of normality was spotted for the two types of classrooms. As showing in Table 3, significant difference in positive behavioral engagement between the two types of classrooms was found ($F_{1,23} = 5.631, p < .05$), revealing that students in Type 1 Classroom (M = 81.65, SD = 15.29) showed more positive behavioral engagement than Type 2 Classroom (M = 66.45, SD = 16.18), which might be the result of increased student efforts in response to teachers' questioning strategies.

Table 3. Positive behavioral engagement in two classrooms

		M	SD	n	*p*
Classroom Type	1	81.65	15.29	12	.027*
	2	66.45	16.18	12	

Note: * p < 0.05, **p < 0.01, ***p < 0.001, the same below.

4.3 Seating Location Effects

Table 4 summarized the descriptive statistics for the behavioral engagement in each aspect by seating location of front, middle, and rear area. The n in the table means the number of areas, each of which consisted of 5 to 10 students. The result revealed that, for all aspects of behavioral engagement, students in the front seats performed better than those in the rear seats: Front-seating students exhibited more behavioral engagement in terms of involvement, initiation, and effort, and exhibited less inattentive, disengaged, and giving-up behaviors, when compared with rear-seating students. Interestingly, rear-seating students also demonstrated greater variance in negative behavioral engagement, suggesting seating in the back tend to have different influence on students attending synchronous online classrooms.

Table 4. Means and standard deviations for the behavioral engagement in each aspect by seating location

Behavioral engagement	Front seating			Middle seating			Rear seating		
	M	SD	n	M	SD	n	M	SD	n
Involvement	13.94	9.83	24	13.50	9.12	24	10.31	7.70	15
Initiation	10.95	7.88	24	10.00	7.84	24	8.40	6.86	15
Effort	57.14	16.02	24	50.47	14.53	24	40.31	16.82	15
Inattentive	13.83	13.50	24	20.28	15.11	24	19.82	19.70	15
Disengaged	3.28	6.22	24	4.64	8.27	24	16.44	15.30	15
Giving up	.95	2.82	24	1.36	2.83	24	4.71	8.87	15

ANOVA results revealed significant difference in students' positive behavioral engagement among different seating locations in synchronous online classrooms ($F_{2,60} = 7.278, p = 0.001$). Average level of positive behavioral engagement of student seat in the front, middle, and rear gradually decreased, corresponding to M = 82.14, M = 73.79, and M = 59.02. The result was consistent with findings regarding traditional classroom that students in front rows were usually more active and engaged in learning activities than students sitting in rear rows. The behavioral engagement seemed to be negatively correlated with the distance between student and projection screen, the further students were away from the screen, the less likely they would demonstrate positive behavioral engagement. Results are illustrated in Table 5.

Table 5. Positive behavioral engagement in different seating location

		M	SD	n	*p*
Seating location	Front	82.14	17.21	24	.001***
	Middle	73.97	16.62	24	
	Rear	59.02	22.69	15	

To further explore the impact of seating location and classroom type on positive behavioral engagement, we also examine the interaction effects of location by type and included it in the ANOVA model. However, the result did not show significant interaction effect of the two variables ($F_{2,22} = 2.452, p = 0.727 \geq 0.05$). The lack of interaction effect can be clearly seen in the profile plot in Fig. 3.

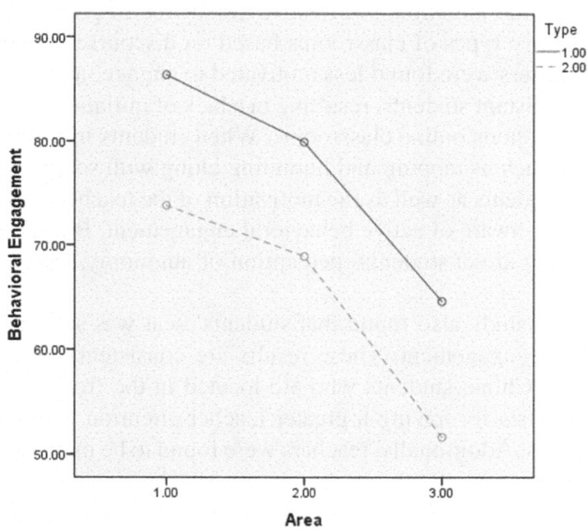

Fig. 3. Interaction effect of discourse interaction and seating location on behavioral engagement

5 Discussion

The present study compared 324 students' performance of behavioral engagement in two types of classrooms based on discourse interaction classification: guidance-follow-up plus initiation-response interactions and mainly guidance-follow-up interactions. Additionally, the impact of seating location on student behavioral engagement was also investigated. Three major findings emerged in our analysis and are discussed in below.

First, significant difference was found in behavioral engagement between the two types of classrooms based on discourse interaction classification. In terms of providing guidance, teachers who asked more questions prompted students to elaborate more on learned concepts in their responses, which is consistent with the literature showing the importance of prompting questions [21, 22]. Questions could serve as cues to direct student attention to important information otherwise might be neglected. Furthermore, when classroom discourse is relatively sparse and the students' enthusiasm is obviously reduced, teachers can help improve the problem by increasing their questioning frequency and changing the way of discourse guidance [15]. In this study, teachers' questions are mostly for all students, but rarely for individual students, which makes the results of students' behavioral engagement improved at the overall rather than individual level of the class.

Second, most students followed instructor's instructions in synchronous online classrooms, but few showed initiative behaviors inspired by intrinsic motivation. Teacher as the main initiator of classroom discourse could influence the richness and liveliness of dialogue to greater extent. One possible reason behind such phenomenon is the disincentive of teachers. Teachers who deliver knowledge through network are expected to be proficient in their computer and internet skills and have high computer self-efficacy [23]. However, workload, burnout, and emotional loss due to lack of face-to-face dialogue have received little attention. We believe this is one of potential reasons for the clustering results of two types of classrooms based on discourse interaction classification. More often teachers were found less motivated to engage in deeper-level of social interactions with the distant students, resulting in a lack of initiation-response dialogical interactions in synchronous online classrooms. When students in a class showed fewer initiative behaviors, such as tapping and humming along with songs, it may be implicitly influence other students as well as the motivation of the teacher. Over time, students gradually become less aware of active behavioral engagement. But too many questions asked by teachers may affect students' perception of autonomy, which in turn reduces their initiation.

Third, the present study also found that students' seat was significantly correlated with their behavioral engagement. These results are consistent with our experiences in K-12 education in China: students who are located in the front rows usually attain better learning outcomes for having a greater teacher attention, compared to students seating in the rear rows. Additionally, teachers were found to be more inclined to arrange outstanding students in front seating, leading to increased gap in behavioral engagement between high-performing and low-performing students. Moreover, the impact of peer influence was highlighted in many studies, suggesting that young students are susceptible to the environmental influence [24]. Therefore, a less-engaged student sitting in the front rows might be motivated by other highly engaged students around them, and vice versa.

6 Conclusion

In conclusion, the results of this study shed light on whether discourse interaction and seating location can affect the behavioral engagement of students in asynchronous online classrooms. The specific pattern of discourse interaction was found to be a significant predictor for behavioral engagement, with more initiation-response interaction leading to more positive behavioral engagement. Also, seating location is one of reasons affecting behavioral engagement, yielding a negative correlation between the seating distance and observed behavioral engagement in synchronous online classrooms. As a result, two pedagogical implication can be drawn: If necessary, teachers in synchronous online classrooms should use passionate and encouraging words to stimulate students' enthusiasm for initiation engagement, and proper arrangement of seating is necessary to boost the behavioral engagement of the whole class, by placing less-engaged students in the front rows.

There are still some limitations in this study. Firstly, data was collected within a specific context and sample size can be further increased for internal and statistical validity. In future research, we can utilize the findings to extend the scope of instructional contexts to include more content subjects and course settings (e.g., English, Art, and Science), and thus expand understanding and strengthen the generalizability of the research findings. Another limit is that, although behavioral engagement in this study can be objectively measured and reflected internal psychological state of students, it was not meant to reflect students' emotional and cognitive engagement comprehensively. Therefore, additional research should explore the concept of engagement with measurement of emotional and cognitive constructs.

Acknowledgement. This study was funded by the Key Research Project of Education Supported by National Social Science Foundation of China, ACA170010.

References

1. Gunawardena, C., McIsaac, M.: Handbook of Research on Educational Communications and Technology, 2nd edn. Simon and Schuster, New York (1996)
2. Borman, G.D., Overman, L.T.: Academic resilience in mathematics among poor and minority students. Elem. Sch. J. **104**, 177–195 (2004)
3. Connell, J.P., Spencer, M.B., Aber, J.L.: Educational risk and resilience in African-American youth: context, self, action, and outcomes in school. Child Dev. **65**, 493–506 (1994)
4. Sirin, S.R., Rogers-Sirin, L.: Exploring school engagement of middle-class African American adolescents. Youth Soc. **35**, 323–340 (2004)
5. Newmann, F.M.E.: Student Engagement and Achievement in American Secondary Schools. Teachers College Press, New York (1992)
6. Lee, J.-S.: The effects of the teacher–student relationship and academic press on student engagement and academic performance. Int. J. Educ. Res. **53**, 330–340 (2012)
7. Engels, M.C., et al.: Behavioral engagement, peer status, and teacher–student relationships in adolescence: a longitudinal study on reciprocal influences. J. Youth Adolescence **45**(6), 1192–1207 (2016). https://doi.org/10.1007/s10964-016-0414-5

8. Hughes, J.N., Wu, W., West, S.G.: Teacher performance goal practices and elementary students' behavioral engagement: a developmental perspective. J. Sch. Psychol. **49**, 1–23 (2011)
9. Gee, J.P.: Literacy, discourse, and linguistics: introduction. J. Educ. **171**, 5–17 (1989)
10. Mehan, H.: Learning Lessons: Social Organization in the Classroom. Harvard University Press, Cambridge (1979)
11. Kovalainen, M., Kumpulainen, K.: The discursive practice of participation in an elementary classroom community. Instr. Sci. **33**, 213–250 (2005). https://doi.org/10.1007/s11251-005-2810-1
12. Lemke, J.L.: Talking Science: Language, Learning, and Values. Ablex Publishing Corporation, Norwood (1990)
13. Fredricks, J.A., Blumenfeld, P.C., Paris, A.H.: School engagement: potential of the concept, state of the evidence. Rev. Educ. Res. **74**, 59–109 (2004)
14. Miserandino, M.: Children who do well in school: individual differences in perceived competence and autonomy in above-average children. J. Educ. Psychol. **88**, 203–214 (1996)
15. Lam, S., Jimerson, S., Wong, B.P.H., Kikas, E., Shin, H., Veiga, F.H.: Understanding and measuring student engagement in school: the results of an international study from 12 countries. Sch. Psychol. Q. **29**, 213–232 (2014)
16. Smart, J.B., Marshall, J.C.: Interactions between classroom discourse, teacher questioning, and student cognitive engagement in middle school science. J. Sci. Teach. Educ. **24**, 249–267 (2013)
17. Nystrand, M., Wu, L.L., Gamoran, A., Zeiser, S., Long, D.: Questions in time: investigating the structure and dynamics of unfolding classroom discourse. Discourse Process. **35**, 135–196 (2003)
18. Kelly, S.: Classroom discourse and the distribution of student engagement. Soc. Psychol. Educ. **10**, 331–352 (2007). https://doi.org/10.1007/s11218-007-9024-0
19. Sommer, R.: Classroom ecology. J. Appl. Behav. Sci. **3**, 489–503 (1967)
20. Rubio, F.: Second and foreign language learning through classroom interaction (review). Language **78**, 607–608 (2002)
21. Lee, Y., Kinzie, M.: Teacher question and student response with regard to cognition and language use. Instr. Sci. **40**, 857–874 (2012). https://doi.org/10.1007/s11251-011-9193-2
22. Pehmer, A.K., Groschner, A., Seidel, T.: Fostering and scaffolding student engagement in productive classroom discourse: teachers' practice changes and reflections in light of teacher professional development. Learn. Cult. Soc. Interact. **7**, 12–27 (2015)
23. Kale, U., Goh, D.: Teaching style, ICT experience and teachers' attitudes toward teaching with web 2.0. Educ. Inf. Technol. **19**, 1–20 (2012)
24. Jackson, T.A., Evans, D.: Can medical students teach? A near-peer-led teaching program for year 1 students. Adv. Physiol. Educ. **36**, 192–196 (2012)

Sentiment Evolutions in Blended Learning Contexts: Investigating Dynamic Interactions Using Simulation Investigation for Empirical Social Network Analysis

Zhongmei Han[1], Changqin Huang[1,2](✉), Qionghao Huang[1], and Jianhui Yu[2]

[1] South China Normal University, Guangzhou 51000, China
{zmhan,qhhuang}@m.scnu.edu.cn, cqhuang@zju.edu.cn
[2] Zhejiang Normal University, Jinhua 321004, China
Yujh2016@m.scnu.edu.cn

Abstract. Sentiments evolve over time driven by diverse interactions, especially in blended learning contexts. However, there is scarce empirical research to investigate sentiment evolutions with respect to interactions in the longitudinal data of blended learning. Therefore, by gathering the longitudinal data of five time periods from 38 postgraduate students, this study applied simulation investigation for empirical social network analysis (SIENA) and lag sequential analysis (LSA) to analyze sentiment evolutions with respect to interactions in blended learning contexts. As the knowledge constructions progressed in the blended learning context, students tended to deep interactions and sentiments had the tendency of diversity. Additionally, students experienced the confusion and insightful sentiments accompanied by the deep interactions. In the stable stage of interactions, students may express positive and insightful sentiments along with the agreement interactions. Most notably, although joking sentiments and social-emotion interactions occur less than other types of sentiments and interactions, there is correlation between them.

Keywords: Sentiment evolution · Dynamic interaction · Asynchronous discussion-based blended learning · SIENA

1 Introduction

As a combination of face-to-face lectures and online activities, blended learning has made learning more accessible in terms of flexibility and time constrains [1]. Enabled by advanced technology, online supports in blended learning contexts can promote further knowledge construction and learning performance [2], such as supplementary resources, asynchronous discussion. Extensive studies have proven that online discussion could engage students in their learning [2, 3]. In particular, as contended by many researchers [4], asynchronous discussion through online forums is a promising channel to facilitate students' interactions in blended learning environments, e.g., social negotiation, knowledge construction, sentiment engagements. Therefore, a demonstration of move from

S. K. S. Cheung et al. (Eds.): ICBL 2020, LNCS 12218, pp. 249–263, 2020.
https://doi.org/10.1007/978-3-030-51968-1_21

face-to-face to blended learning by adding online discussion shows the synergy between blended learning and online discussion in terms of interactions.

Interaction is defined as the involvement of students' engagement to accomplish a certain learning assignment [5]. Recently, there has been considerable attention on learning interactions to understand the process and outcomes of blended learning. Especially, large scale literature has suggested that online interactions are more effective than face-to-face interactions for knowledge constructions. To deepen the understanding of knowledge, it is important to integrate online interaction into the flow of classroom instructions [6]. Additionally, blended learning serves as a dynamic learning environment for interactions. As such, in interaction process, a great body of studies have demonstrated that sentiments embodied in interactions are viewed as the crucial to learning process and knowledge construction. A dynamic perspective is especially useful for understanding the importance of relations and networks. In this regard, the core issue of blended learning is to identify the dynamics of interactions and sentiment evolutions through the integration of online and offline.

In many studies, a great deal of efforts has been made to employ diverse analysis methods for scrutinizing sentiments and interactions in blended learning contexts. To analyze the interaction changes, social network analysis is a widely used to grasp the network structure [7]. Due to the complicated dependence structures in network data, analyzing social network dynamics is complex and requires sophisticated statistical techniques. Longitudinal network data are typically collected as panel data, where the relations between network actors are observed at two or more discrete time points [8]. However, still very few empirical studies have examined the process and changes of sentiment evolutions by using a longitudinal data. In response to this concern, this study aimed to investigate sentiment evolutions with respect to dynamic interactions from longitudinal interaction statistics in online asynchronous discussion-based blended learning contexts.

2 Literature Review

2.1 Blended Learning

Blended learning combines both online and face-to-face learning to create a cohesive learning experience in shifting time and space. Recently, there is growing interest in investigating the implementations blended learning. Diverse instructional models and best practices of blended learning have been reported from simple use of computer or online mediated technologies to full usages of them for a complete course. Blended learning reduces the number of face-to-face lectures and make learning more accessible [4].

As technology empowered, online supports are viewed as supplementary role of face-to-face learning [3]. As contended by some researchers [9], online resource made a transition from offline to online. Flipped classrooms, as a typical blended learning method, gained attention as a new pedagogical method [9]. It employs asynchronous video lectures and problem-solving practices as students' homework with diverse group-based activities in the classroom. These pedagogical approaches represent a combination of instructional methods online and offline. However, some studies pointed out that online instruments might hinder deep learning due to less interactions. As a remedy, online discussions are essential to high quality knowledge constructions [3]. As a similar approach, online discussion was investigated by designing learning activities [10]. These results highlighted that online discussion might be an available avenue for large-scale students to interact each other. Therefore, as a crucial tool to construct knowledge, online discussions are worthwhile further investigations of interactions among students.

2.2 Interactions and Sentiments in Blended Learning Contexts

A body of studies have paid considerable attention to analyzing interactions in educational settings. Various interaction analysis frameworks were used in the studies. For instance, focusing on the relationships, Kurucay and Inan [11] examined the interactions among instructors, students, and learning contents in online learning contexts. Considering the knowledge constructions, Yang, Li and Xing [12] utilized the interaction analysis model, which has been extensively used. The interaction analysis model included five types of interactions. According to the framework for interactions and cognitive engagement proposed by Wang, Chen and Anderson [13], these five types can be sorted from surface to deep interaction.

Different levels of interactions have relations to sentiments. Sentiments have emerged as a vital indicator of learning performance and cognitive processes in establishing effective interactions [14]. Many studies have explored the effect of student on learning sentiments in blended learning environments. Pham, Vo, Lindsay, Pashna, and Li [15] make a comparison with sentiments between online and face-to-face settings. Their results implied that to a great extent, sentiments reflect the learning attitude of students during learning process while interacting with others. In blended learning contexts, a variety of learning sentiments are embedded in discussions. In particular, some studies have specifically identified the sentiments that occur in online learning environments. Thus, it is worth exploring the sentiments experienced in online learning discussions.

Recent studies have tapped into sentiment classifications. Learning sentiments were categorized into three dimensions: positive (e.g., enjoyment, hope), negative (e.g., anxiety, frustration, boredom) and neutral [16]. Based on the taxonomy [16], Zheng and Huang [17] encompassed six-dimensional sentiments: positive, negative, neutral, insightful, confused, and joking. By following the improved classification proposed by Zheng and Huang [17], this study aimed to provide further insights into learning sentiments.

Similar to the development of learning sentiments mentioned above, investigations of relationships between sentiments and interactions have attracted much attention. For example, the study conducted by Huang et al. [10], found different sentiments could be evoked by different level of interactions. Their results suggested that confusion sentiment related to surface interactions (e.g., disagreement) and deep interactions (e.g., negotiation). Moreover, Kort, Reilly and Picard [18] explored that dynamic sentiments might heavily impact the learning process and experience in blended learning contexts. In this regard, this study intended to uncover how interactions was affected by dynamic learning sentiments.

2.3 Lag Sequential Analysis and Social Networks Analysis

To scrutinize the interaction network and sentiment change, a handful of scholars have employed diverse methods. For instance, Hou, Wang, Lin and Chang [19] employed content analysis and lag sequential analysis (LSA) to investigate interaction patterns in problem-based online asynchronous discussions. Additionally, Lin, Duh, Li, Wang and Tsai [20] used a combination of quantitative content analysis and lag sequential analysis to explore the interaction patterns. LSA not only takes into account the occurrence of each learning interaction, but also demonstrates statistically significant sequence of learning interaction [21]. As pointed out by Cabrera and Reiner [22], qualitative analysis is a way to indirectly observe cognitive process. Quantitative analysis was conducted to obtain the interaction patterns by statistics (e.g., frequencies) [23]. However, the above methods of interaction patterns provided few insights into understanding how the network structure and social relationships among learners might vary with interactions.

Due to the capacity to extract the network structure across the large volumes of interactions among learners, SNA is perceived as a useful method for investigating interaction patterns [24]. Considering the network among students' interactions, most of the studies examined students' interaction patterns using social network analysis. By using social network analysis, Duan, Xie, Hawk, Yu and Wang [7] identified the relational structure of learners in online contexts. Their results indicated that the effects of indirect and direct interactions on knowledge constructions and social communications could be revealed by some network properties (e.g., densities and structures). Although the above SNA can characterize interaction network structure, the network evolution and sentiment dynamics remains to be addressed in terms of longitudinal data.

Simulation investigation for empirical network analysis (SIENA), a relatively new approach accounts for network dynamics. SIENA can gain insights into the changes of the studied network by performing statistical estimation for repeated measures of empirical networks (e.g., role) [25]. Zhang et al. [8] used SIENA to provide the estimates of interaction networks and rates for evolution and sentiment variables. The estimates represent the average number of changes in interaction network. The interaction network function consists of a combination of several parameters representing dynamic interactions, as well as sentiment variables associated with dyadic and individual attributes. However, scholars have not yet fully uncovered the interaction networks in blended learning environments that contribute to sentiment evolutions. In this concern, this study employed SIENA to investigate the sentiment evolutions with longitudinal interaction networks through analyzing a longitudinal data.

3 Hypothesis

To summarize the preceding literature, students' interactions may have a certain role in sentiment evolutions in blended learning contexts. As such, the purpose of the current study sought to probe the interaction network for sentiments evolutions. Additionally, SIENA for blended learning course is conductive to capture the dynamics of sentiments. Consequently, in terms of SIENA longitudinal data of blended learning, the following hypotheses was formulated:

Hypothesis 1 (H1)
Students with surface interactions (i1 "sharing/comparing information", i2 "discovery and exploration of dissonance") tend to experience positive and neutral sentiments.

Hypothesis 2 (H2)
In the process of knowledge constructions, the level of interactions among students would be positively related to the occurrence of negative, confusion, and insightful sentiments.

Hypothesis 3 (H3)
Confusion and insightful sentiments are more likely, with the deeper interactions (i3 "negotiation", i4 "test and modification", and i5 "agreement statement") when students construct knowledge.

Hypothesis 4 (H4)
Among the interaction process, students' sentiments may take a diverse turn, gradually give a rise to negative sentiments.

Hypothesis 5 (H5)
Joking sentiments are more likely if students discuss with i6 "social-emotion interactions".

4 Method

4.1 Participants

The sample included 38 postgraduate students (31 females and 7 males) attending the blended course of "Fundamental Educational Technology Theory Course" in a university in China. Students ranged in age from 22 to 31 years (Mean = 24.40). Due to curricular arrangement, these participants who majored in educational technology had rich online learning experiences during their 4-year undergraduate learning. Therefore, in blended learning contexts, they can adapt to the shift from offline to online.

4.2 Blended Learning Contexts Based on Asynchronous Discussion

Before the blended course, all the participants had been trained to use the online asynchronous discussion platform, namely "Liru Cloud Classroom" (http://moodle.scnu.edu.cn). The platform allowed students to discuss without the constrains of time and space. Comments and replies were posted for knowledge constructions via the asynchronous discussion forum. Considering technical nature of the course, face-to-face learning and online learning were combined. To foster the understanding of educational technology, an instructor and a researcher engaged students in blended learning course by co-designing all learning activities in 15 weeks of learning. Seven learning activities were listed in Fig. 1 marked with gray-dotted lines. Moreover, a chat-oriented topic irrelated to learning was designed because the possibility of obscure sentiments in the discussion messages. Coinciding with festival, this topic encouraged students to share

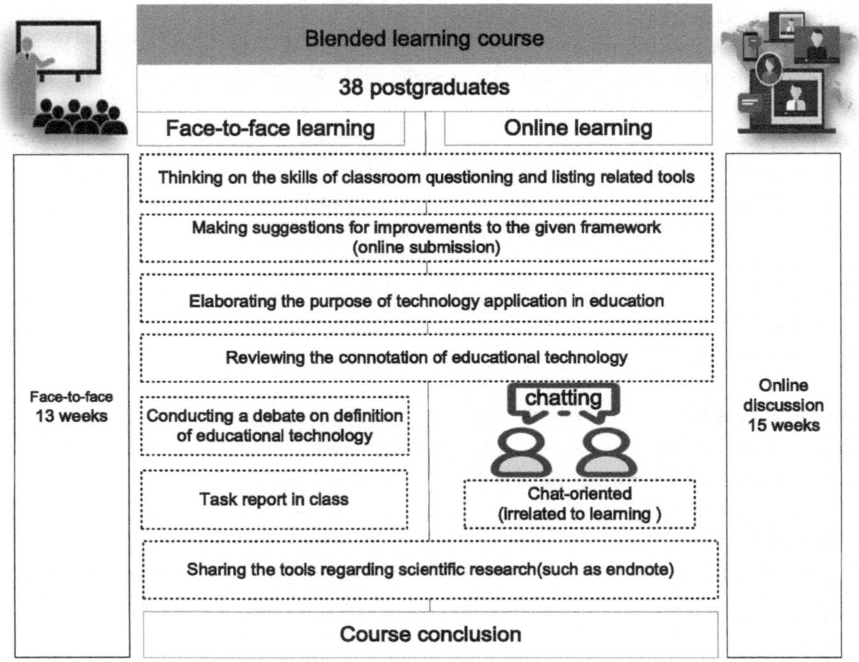

Fig. 1. The procedure of face-to-face and online learning in blended learning contexts

something interesting of the festival. This topic was conductive to adjusting the learning atmosphere and promoting sentiment interactions.

Meanwhile, offline learning (face-to-face) orderly interspersed among the online tasks, shown in Fig. 1. Face-to-face activities consisted of conventional teaching, debate form, and task report in class. In face-to-face learning settings, each student can freely express his opinion and comment/reply others in terms of certain learning theme by asynchronous discussion platform, face-to-face interactions as well. In the course of accomplishing the blended learning, the online discussion posts were recorded automatically in the logs for statistical analysis. Offline interactions can be recorded by videos.

4.3 Coding Schemes

Coding Scheme for Interaction. The coding scheme for interaction analysis was adopted according to the study of Yang et al. [12]. However, some discussions mainly consisted of emotional interactions, such as come on, welcome, and greeting. These messages of discussions were called social-emotional interaction. Accordingly, this study deemed the social-emotional interaction as a new interaction i6. The coding scheme is shown in Table 1.

Table 1. Coding scheme for interaction.

Interaction	Description	Example
Sharing/comparing information (i1)	Sharing/comparing information or proposing similar ideas	I think the definition of educational technology should be discussed at the philosophical level
Discovery and exploration of dissonance (i2)	Discovery and exploration of dissonance or inconsistency among participants	I think electronic scales are not the application of educational technology in your metaphor
Negotiation (i3)	Negotiation of meaning/co-construction of knowledge	I think we should integrate the writing websites and utilize their advantages.
Test and modification (i4)	Test and modification of proposed synthesis or co-construction	With regard to the proposed solution, I personally feel that it is important, so I suggest we should modify the proposal
Agreement statement (i5)	Agreement statement(s)/application of newly constructed meaning	I hereby integrate the views and requests offered, and propose a new approach to solving this problem
Social-emotional interaction (i6)	Expressing feeling about members, such as thanks, sorry etc.	I apologize for my random absences

Coding Scheme for Learning Sentiments. The six-dimension sentiments proposed by Harris, Zheng and Kumar [26], namely, positive, negative, neutral, insightful, confused, and joking, were adopted to identify the sentiments experienced by students in blended learning environments. The coding scheme for learning sentiment analysis is presented in Table 2.

According to the above two coding schemes for interactions and learning sentiments, two coders independently coded 1658 discussion messages by hand. The kappa value of the two coders was 0.89, indicating that the analysis was highly reliable.

4.4 Data Analysis

SIENA are used to examine the evolution of social networks and individual related variables (e.g., interactions, sentiments). In a longitudinal sample of blended course, this study employed SIENA to illustrate the sentiment evolutions with dynamic interactions. The method was implemented in the R package Rsiena (SIENA version 4.0), adopted by Zhang et al. [8].

The prerequisite of SIENA is dynamic networks among students. Therefore, the relationship would be established if two students interact each other. This relationship was characterized by using a binary method: 1 represented a student interact with others

Table 2. Coding scheme for learning sentiments in online learning conversations.

Sentiment	Description	Example
Positive (e1)	Supporting or liking an opinion	This idea is very useful, thanks for your sharing
Negative (e2)	Opposing or disliking the topic	What you said is not true
Neutral (e3)	Ambivalent, or unclear user's sentiment	Some equipment is applied in teaching, such as TV and computers
Insightful (e4)	Conveying some innovative opinions or reflective thoughts	I think problem-solving strategies should include analogy, means-ends analysis, dividing and conquering, and trial and error
Confused (e5)	Transmitting opinions expressing bewilderment or perplexed feelings	I am still confused about these two concepts
Joking (e6)	Meaning a user is only kidding	Yes. My grandmother is more concerned about what I eat and doesn't care what I learn. Enha, biological grandma ☺

in this observation; 0 was denoted as no relation to other students. As such, five networks were obtained (Table 3).

Table 3. Variables and measurement.

Variables	Operationalization	Estimation
Interaction	i1, i2	Surface interactions = 0
	i3, i4, i5	Deep interactions = 1
	i6	Social-emotion interactions = 3
Sentiments	e1, e4	Positive sentiments = 1
	e3	Neutral sentiments = 2
	e2, e5	Negative sentiments = 3
	e6	Joking sentiments = 4

In longitudinal data of blended course, it started with 11 September 2017 and ended with 25 December 2017. During the course, messages related with the chatting-oriented were excluded from data analysis, because these messages had no relevance to knowledge construction. Finally, the evolution network was examined using SIENA with five time periods. As interactions in blended learning course were asynchronous, the network grows with time. As a measure of stability, the Jaccard coefficients for two sequential periods [25], varying from 0.538 to 0.912, indicated that the network dynamics of five time periods were smooth enough, which justified the use of five time periods as appropriate in this study.

First, this study conducted descriptive analysis for interactions and sentiments among five time periods. Subsequently, to draw a sequential transfer diagram, the LSA was conducted to identify and visualize the learners' sentiment change patterns by exploiting the Generalized Sequential Querier 5.1 software. Finally, to further examine the sentiment evolutions with regard to six types of interactions, the SIENA was carried out.

5 Results

In this section, the results are presented in terms of 3 parts, namely descriptive statistics of interactions and sentiments, sequential analysis of sentiments and sentiment evolutions with interaction network results by using SIENA and LSA.

5.1 Descriptive Statistics of Interactions and Sentiments

To explore the interactions contributing to sentiments in the context of blended learning contexts, the interactions and sentiments were coded and analyzed in the five time periods. Descriptive analysis of students' interactions and sentiments was conducted, with the results summarized in Fig. 2.

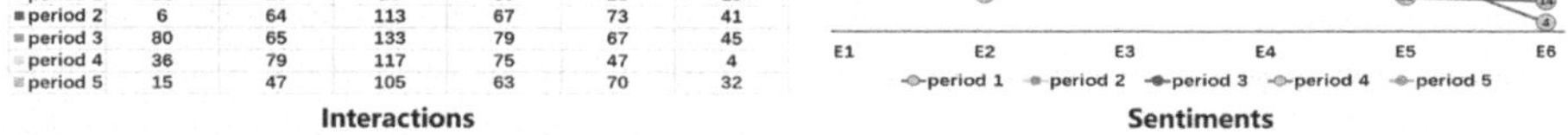

Fig. 2. Descriptive analysis of interactions and sentiments in the five time periods of the blended learning course.

Figure 2 presents some descriptive statistics of interactions. During the five time periods, the frequency of interactions in the period 1 occurs the least than other five observations. Interestingly, students construct knowledge with multiple and increasing interactions in periods 2 to 4. In the last two periods, the frequencies of interactions are similar (period 4 = 358, period 5 = 332), which indicated that interaction network among students tended to stable.

As depicted in Fig. 2, the six types of sentiments varied with five periods. Similar to interactions, periods 3 and 4 seem to have larger fluctuations than other periods. Except for joking sentiments, the frequencies of other five types of sentiments occurred the least in five periods.

5.2 Sequential Analysis of Sentiments by Using LSA

To examine the students' sentiment change exhibited in the online discussion-based blended learning course, a series of sequential analysis was conducted. In terms of the observed five periods, the sequential transition diagram of six types of sentiments was drawn to display the significant sentiment sequences (see Fig. 3). All sequences in the transition diagram were statistically significant.

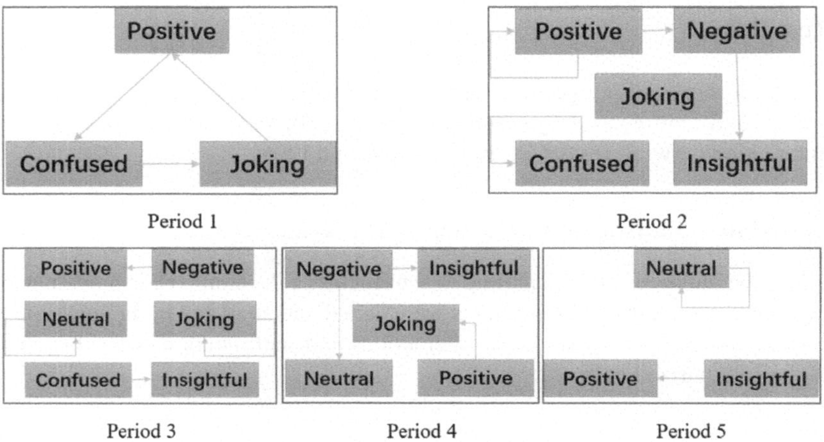

Fig. 3. Significant sentiment sequences of each time period in blended learning contexts.

As presented in Fig. 3, students experienced more and more diverse sentiments among the five periods. At the beginning, the sequence of positive → confused → joking was significant. In the subsequent periods 2–4, negative, confused and insightful sentiments formed transitions to solve the problems in the blended course (negative → insightful, negative → positive, confused → insightful). In the period 5, there were two sequences (neutral → neutral and insightful → positive). The results indicated that learning sentiments are likely stabilized to positive, neutral and insightful sentiments when problems are settled in blended learning course.

5.3 Sentiment Evolutions with Interaction Network via SIENA

To gain insights into sentiment evolution with regard to interaction networks among students, the next step in our analysis was to investigate how much change actually took place during the five periods of longitudinal data. Interactions and sentiments through a series of SIENA were analyzed to evaluate the strength of five observations that affect evolutions in network. Table 4 offered an impression from SIENA analysis of dynamic interaction network (deep and surface interactions) and sentiment change (positive, neutral, negative and joking sentiments). The coefficients were estimated for sentiments with interactions. Taken as a whole, the interaction network established at first time period seems to be scrambled by subsequent periods.

Table 4. Estimation of interaction network and sentiments dynamics of five observations.

Variables	Parameter estimation (λ)	T ratio
Λ (period 1)	0.321***	
Λ (period 2)	1.215**	
Λ (period 3)	1.434***	
Λ (period 4)	0.672*	
Λ (period 5)	0.354*	
Surface interactions		
Positive sentiments	1.315**	0.051
Neutral sentiments	0.246***	−0.013
Negative sentiments	−0.041	0.027
Joking sentiments	0.323*	−0.071
Deep interactions		
Positive sentiments	1.578***	0.023
Neutral sentiments	−0.542	0.009
Negative sentiments	1.324**	−0.034
Joking sentiments	0.759**	0.056
Social-emotion interactions		
Positive sentiments	0.231**	0.003
Neutral sentiments	0.365*	−0.067
Negative sentiments	−0.045	0.092
Joking	0.987***	0.001

*p < 0.1, **p < 0.05, ***p < 0.01

As the simulated network evolved through 1000 iterations, the estimations for the strength of various process were calculated (Table 4). As illustrated in Table 4, there are significant differences among all periods ($p < 0.1$). Additionally, the t ratio values of these variables are less than 0.1 and very close to 0. These results indicated that SIENA had good convergence [25]. In terms of λ, it decreases with the longitudinal data of three time periods (period 3, 4 and 5). The results suggested interactions among students might tend to be stable. The parameter estimates of interactions and sentiments shows the changes in network among the measurement points. Surface interactions are significantly associated with positive and neutral sentiments. This result demonstrated the H1. Regarding the level of interactions, deep interactions have a positive significance with positive, negative and joking sentiments, which revealed that deep interactions would be likely to trigger negative and positive sentiments. Therefore, these findings supported the H2 and H3 about the trigger of sentiments with deep interactions.

In Table 4, the number of deep interactions is even higher than the number of surface interactions in the process of knowledge construction. negative sentiments appear to get a little more settled towards the end of the period, but even then, sentiments of changing periods (2 and 3) are still more abundant and diverse than the stable period (4 and 5). These findings verified H4. Moreover, deep interactions play a role in the evolution of negative and joking sentiments, which further support H4. Additionally, as these are measured at multiple time points, joking sentiment tendency for social-emotion interactions was significant. This further demonstrated the H5.

6 Discussion and Implications

This study was an empirical investigation of the network dynamics of a blended learning course, which contributes to the discussion of how online sentiments can be designed to create and foster a better interaction network. To understanding the sentiment evolutions, SIENA and LSA were used to gain insights into the dynamics of interactions in the context of blended learning.

In blended learning environments, this study is one of the few which investigate the sentiment evolutions and interaction network by using SIENA and LSA. In terms of the sentiments in five time periods, interactions among students may tend to surface interactions (i1 "sharing/comparing information", i2 "discovery and exploration of dissonance") at the beginning. As interactions increase, students may tend to deep interactions (i3 "negotiation", i4 "test and modification", and i5 "agreement statement"), and ultimately to agreement (i6). Despite deep interactions might enhance the progress of knowledge construction, surface interactions are indispensable to drive the deep interactions [13]. Moreover, social-emotion interactions appear occasionally. The possible reason might be that intervention related to sentiment guidance was little, and only one topic was designed to trigger students' sentiment expression. These results are in line with the findings [10]. Although online interactions based on blended learning activities, further study on integrating online into face-to-face interactions would be better to understand the roles of surface and deep interactions.

Pertaining to six types of sentiments, students might tend to start with joking and positive sentiments. As knowledge constructions progress, students' sentiments have a tendency of diversity. Although the joking sentiments occur least than other five types of sentiments, it is significant for them to promote the social relationship and alleviate the climate caused by negative and confusion sentiments [27]. Regarding the evolution of sentiments, six types of sentiments emerging form asynchronous discussion suggested that confusion sentiment might be conductive to problem solving when deep interactions (i3 "negotiation", i4 "test and modification", and i5 "agreement statement") occurs. Deep interaction (i3, i4, and i5) may tend to trigger confusion and insightful sentiments. Notably, it is important for insightful sentiments accompanied by agreement interactions to stimulate the reflection and creative thinking of students. However, surface interactions are also important to start with positive, neutral, and joking sentiments. These sentiments triggered by surface interactions are consistent with dynamic sentiment change proposed by Kort et al. [18], simultaneously are likely to facilitate learning process.

Based on the results from this study, some pedagogical implications were presented for effective interaction when constructing knowledge. In blended learning, instructors should take account of students' sentiments. Instructors should trigger students into employment of online tools for a remedy of offline learning engagement. In this concern, instructors could use online discussions to promote the deep interactions for knowledge constructions. Moreover, it is necessary for instructors and students to evoke joking sentiments when "discovery and exploration of dissonance" occurs. Key components such how to balance the negative sentiments with appropriate interactions (e.g., social-emotion and deep interactions), especially for students and instructors accustoming to online learning contexts. Specially, confusion, as a doubled-edged sentiment, is detrimental to learning if learners fail to resolve confusion [27]. Therefore, to settle the confusion sentiments triggered by cognitive imbalance for instructors, it is crucial to guide the deep interactions (i3 "negotiation", i4 "test and modification", and i5 "agreement statement") for facilitating learning process.

7 Conclusion and Limitation

To conclude, this study adopted SIENA to explore the mechanisms of the sentiment evolutions with interactions in the context of a blended learning course. Investigating how sentiments change over time highlights the unique potential interactions of blended learning. The results emerging from the blended course suggested that there is a need to trigger confusion and insightful sentiments when deep interactions occur among students. Moreover, the joking sentiments and social-emotion interactions are likely to adjust the atmosphere caused by disagreement interactions and negative sentiments.

There are some limitations in this research. First, the samples collected is limited. The generalization of results would be limited due to different population (e.g., learning subject). Therefore, it would be better to have a larger sample for increasing the statistical power. Moreover, although online discussion is beneficial to learning, more online support needs further research, such as intelligent agent, VR/AR resources. Furthermore, although SIENA used the online longitudinal data for the dynamics of interaction networks and sentiment evolutions, face-to-face interactions should be jointly analyzed to gain insights into the evolutions of sentiments and interactions. In particular, multiple methods could be conducted in further work, such as learning analytics and interviews.

Acknowledgments. This work was supported by the Humanities and Social Sciences Planning Fund of the Ministry of Education (No. 18YJA880027), the Key-Area Research and Development Program of Guangdong Province, China (No. 2018B010109002), and the Science and Technology Project of Guangzhou Municipality, China (No. 201904010393).

References

1. Han, F., Ellis, R.A.: Identifying consistent patterns of quality learning discussions in blended learning. Internet High. Educ. **40**, 12–19 (2019)
2. Broadbent, J.: Comparing online and blended learner's self-regulated learning strategies and academic performance. Internet High. Educ. **33**, 24–32 (2017)
3. Delaney, D., Kummer, T.F., Singh, K.: Evaluating the impact of online discussion boards on student engagement with group work. Br. J. Educ. Technol. **50**(2), 902–920 (2019)

4. Martínez, P.J., Aguilar, F.J., Ortiz, M.: Transitioning from face-to-face to blended and full online learning engineering master's program. IEEE Trans. Educ. **63**(1), 2–9 (2020)
5. Çardak, Ç.S., Selvi, K.: Increasing teacher candidates' ways of interaction and levels of learning through action research in a blended course. Comput. Hum. Behav. **61**, 488–506 (2016)
6. Shu, H., Gu, X.: Determining the differences between online and face-to-face student–group interactions in a blended learning course. Internet High. Educ. **39**, 13–21 (2018)
7. Duan, J., Xie, K., Hawk, N.A., Yu, S., Wang, M.: Exploring a personal social knowledge network (PSKN) to aid the observation of connectivist interaction for high-and low-performing learners in connectivist massive open online courses. Br. J. Educ. Technol. **50**(1), 199–217 (2019)
8. Zhang, J., Skryabin, M., Song, X.: Understanding the dynamics of MOOC discussion forums with simulation investigation for empirical network analysis (SIENA). Distance Educ. **37**(3), 270–286 (2016)
9. O'Flaherty, J., Phillips, C.: The use of flipped classrooms in higher education: a scoping review. Internet High. Educ. **25**(25), 85–95 (2015)
10. Huang, C.-Q., Han, Z.-M., Li, M.-X., Jong, M.S.-Y., Tsai, C.-C.: Investigating students' interaction patterns and dynamic learning sentiments in online discussions. Comput. Educ. **140**, 1–18 (2019)
11. Kurucay, M., Inan, F.A.: Examining the effects of learner-learner interactions on satisfaction and learning in an online undergraduate course. Comput. Educ. **115**, 20–37 (2017)
12. Yang, X., Li, J., Xing, B.: Behavioral patterns of knowledge construction in online cooperative translation activities. Internet High. Educ. **36**, 13–21 (2018)
13. Wang, Z., Chen, L., Anderson, T.: A framework for interaction and cognitive engagement in connectivist learning contexts. Int. Rev. Res. Open Distrib. Learn. **15**(2), 121–141 (2014)
14. Wang, Z., Anderson, T., Chen, L., Barbera, E.: Interaction pattern analysis in cMOOCs based on the connectivist interaction and engagement framework. Br. J. Educ. Technol. **48**(2), 683–699 (2017)
15. Pham, T., et al.: Sentiment analysis of student online interaction in a blended postgraduate programme. In: Scholarship of Technology Enhanced Learning Symposium (2019)
16. Pekrun, R.: The control-value theory of achievement emotions: assumptions, corollaries, and implications for educational research and practice. Educ. Psychol. Rev. **18**(4), 315–341 (2006)
17. Zheng, L., Huang, R.: The effects of sentiments and co-regulation on group performance in computer supported collaborative learning. Internet High. Educ. **28**, 59–67 (2016)
18. Kort, B., Reilly, R., Picard, R.W.: An affective model of interplay between emotions and learning: reengineering educational pedagogy-building a learning companion. In: IEEE International Conference on Advanced Learning Technologies, pp. 43–46. IEEE (2001)
19. Hou, H.-T., Wang, S.-M., Lin, P.-C., Chang, K.-E.: Exploring the learner's knowledge construction and cognitive patterns of different asynchronous platforms: comparison of an online discussion forum and Facebook. Innov. Educ. Teach. Int. **52**(6), 610–620 (2015)
20. Lin, T.-J., Duh, H.B.-L., Li, N., Wang, H.-Y., Tsai, C.-C.: An investigation of learners' collaborative knowledge construction performances and behavior patterns in an augmented reality simulation system. Comput. Educ. **68**, 314–321 (2013)
21. Kapur, M.: Temporality matters: advancing a method for analyzing problem-solving processes in a computer-supported collaborative environment. Int. J. Comput.-Support. Collaborative Learn. **6**(1), 39–56 (2011)
22. Cabrera, L.Y., Reiner, P.B.: A novel sequential mixed-method technique for contrastive analysis of unscripted qualitative data: Contrastive quantitized content analysis. Sociol. Methods Res. **47**(3), 532–548 (2018)

23. Maldonado-Mahauad, J., Pérez-Sanagustín, M., Moreno-Marcos, P.M., Alario-Hoyos, C., Muñoz-Merino, P.J., Delgado-Kloos, C.: Predicting learners' success in a self-paced MOOC through sequence patterns of self-regulated learning. In: Pammer-Schindler, V., Pérez-Sanagustín, M., Drachsler, H., Elferink, R., Scheffel, M. (eds.) EC-TEL 2018. LNCS, vol. 11082, pp. 355–369. Springer, Cham (2018). https://doi.org/10.1007/978-3-319-98572-5_27
24. Scott, J.: Social network analysis: developments, advances, and prospects. Soc. Netw. Anal. Min. **1**(1), 21–26 (2011)
25. Snijders, T.A., Van de Bunt, G.G., Steglich, C.E.: Introduction to stochastic actor-based models for network dynamics. Soc. Netw. **32**(1), 44–60 (2010)
26. Harris, S.C., Zheng, L., Kumar, V.: Multi-dimensional Sentiment Classification in Online Learning Environment. In: 6th IEEE International Conference on Technology for Education, pp. 172–175. IEEE (2014)
27. Arguel, A., Lockyer, L., Lipp, O.V., Lodge, J.M., Kennedy, G.: Inside out: detecting learners' confusion to improve interactive digital learning environments. J. Educ. Comput. Res. **55**(4), 526–551 (2017)

Does Flipped Classroom Improve Student Cognitive and Behavioral Outcomes in STEM Subjects? Evidence from a Second-Order Meta-Analysis and Validation Study

Khe Foon Hew(✉), Shurui Bai, Weijiao Huang, Jiahui Du, Guoyuhui Huang, Chengyuan Jia, and Thankrit Khongjan

The University of Hong Kong, Pokfulam Road, Hong Kong SAR, China
kfhew@hku.hk

Abstract. The flipped classroom approach has attracted particular interest from educators in the Science-Technology-Engineering-Mathematics (STEM) subject disciplines. Despite its popularity, the effect of the flipped classroom approach on student outcomes compared with conventional learning has not yet been conconclusively determined. Although previous reviews have reported positive student *perceptions* of flipped courses, this does *not* necessarily imply improved student learning. This study used a *second-order* meta-analysis procedure to summarize more than 10 years of research examining the following question: "*Does the flipped classroom improve student cognitive and behavioral outcomes across STEM subjects as compared with non-flipped classroom?*" A total of 10 primary meta-analyses covering 217 unique STEM studies were analyzed. Results showed that flipped classroom significantly improves student cognitive learning ($g = 0.49$, $p < 0.001$), and student behavioral learning ($g = 1.70, p < 0.001$) as compared to conventional classroom. To validate the results of the second-order meta-analysis, we also conducted a study-level meta-analytic validation. Students' perceptions of using flipped classroom were also analyzed.

Keywords: Flipped classroom · Flipped learning · Meta-analysis · STEM

1 Introduction

1.1 Background

Many education classes now utilize the flipped classroom approach. In flipped classrooms, students are expected to learn the subject content before class usually through watching recorded video lectures [1] and completing some pre-set online exercises. Students then attend classes to complete individual and/or group activities under the instructor's supervision [2]. The whole idea of the flipped classroom approach is to foster more active learning opportunity for students.

The flipped classroom approach has made particular inroads across the science, technology, engineering, and mathematics (STEM) disciplines. Traditionally, the learning of

S. K. S. Cheung et al. (Eds.): ICBL 2020, LNCS 12218, pp. 264–275, 2020.
https://doi.org/10.1007/978-3-030-51968-1_22

STEM disciplines has been characterized by the didactic teacher-lecture approach [3] as these disciplines generally involve the learning of complex concepts before students are able to move on to the practical applications [4]. Instructors have typically spent class time delivering content through lectures and then assigning supplementary homework exercises.

For this reason, increasing numbers of educators have begun experimenting with flipped classrooms. Previous reviews have mainly concentrated on specific subject areas such as nursing or medical education [5–7] and chemistry [8], or have focused on flipped classroom implementation in a particular context, such as Asian universities [9]. In these reviews the researchers generally summarize the characteristics of the primary studies, such as the types of research method used, the types of participants, and the advantages of using flipped classrooms. Some also describe the challenges or disadvantages of flipped classrooms.

To synthesize the findings about learning outcomes, some researchers would merely list the studies that showed an increase in academic performance, e.g. [2], describe the results of each comparison study e.g. [5], or generally report that "flipping the class is a way to improve learning performance" (p. 26) [2]. A few researchers simply used descriptive statistics to summarize the findings of their reviewed studies. For example, Seery [8] counted the flipped classrooms in higher education chemistry that "half of the studies showed no improvement in exam scores" (p. 763). In Bernard's [10] review, 15 out of 24 studies indicated that flipped classroom students outperformed traditional classroom students.

However, what is the overall effect of flipped classroom on STEM student learning achievement? To achieve this aim, several authors have begun to meta-analyze the published individual empirical studies. The main goal of primary meta-analysis, or first-order meta-analysis, is to estimate an overall mean effect from *individual empirical studies*, and to identify possible factors that moderate that effect [11].

Although primary meta-analyses can offer important advantages, it is important to note that they are limited in their scope and focus. Primary meta-analyses usually focus on specific aspects (e.g., subject matter, grade level). Greater generality could be achieved by examining multiple primary meta-analyses and synthesizing their results.

1.2 Purpose of the Present Study

The current study used an approach known as *second-order* meta-analysis to synthesize a number of methodologically comparable primary meta-analyses [12]. A second-order meta-analysis combines the results of multiple primary meta-analyses. This method has two important advantages. First, by summarizing the findings of more than one primary meta-synthesis, a second-order meta-analysis can generate a more robust generalizable result [13]. Second, a second-order meta-analysis can provide a more accurate estimate of the true mean effect sizes in each primary meta-analysis [14].

In this study, we conducted the first-ever second-order meta-analysis to synthesize the results of prior primary meta-analyses on STEM subjects to gain a broader understanding of the effects of flipped classroom use on student learning performance. To validate the results, we also conducted a study-level synthesis of all available effect sizes reported in the primary meta-analyses included in our second-order meta-analysis. Our study is guided by the following questions:

Research question 1: What is the overall effect of flipped classroom used on STEM students' cognitive and behavioral outcomes? Do subject discipline and student grade level moderate the effect of flipped classroom used on students' outcome?
Research question 2: How do participants perceive the use of flipped classroom?

Cognitive Outcomes refer to domain-specific knowledge of a subject. Cognitive outcomes are usually assessed using teacher-developed or standardized tests and exams. *Behavioral outcomes* refer to learners' motor skills or competences in performing a task. Behavioral outcomes are usually assessed through observations such as objective structured clinical examinations (OSCEs).

2 Method

To be as comprehensive as possible, we searched more than ten major academic databases were searched, including ACM Digital Library, all EBSCO host research databases (e.g., Academic Search Premier, British Education Index, ERIC, TOC Premier), Emerald Insight, IEEE Xplore, ProQuest Dissertations & Theses A&I, Science Direct, Scopus, Springer, Web of Science, JSTOR, PubMed, and Google Scholar. To ensure that our search was comprehensive, additional primary meta-analyses identified in Google Scholar were also included. The search string used in this review was: *"meta-analysis" AND ("flip*" OR "invert*") AND ("class*" OR "learn*").* No time restriction was applied to the search, which was completed in November 2019.

For this second-order meta-analysis, a primary meta-analysis was included if it met the following criteria. The primary meta-analysis must: (a) compare the effects of flipped classrooms with those of non-flipped classrooms in STEM specific subjects, including health sciences, general sciences (e.g., chemistry, biology, physics), engineering and/or technology, and mathematics, (b) focus on students' cognitive or behavioral outcome, (c) report an average effect size, (d) provide a list of the primary studies analyzed, and (e) be written in English and publicly available, or available through a library database subscription.

2.1 Data Extraction

For each primary meta-analysis, we extracted the following data: (a) study identification (e.g., author), (b) contextual features (e.g., subject matter), (c) methodological features (e.g., total number of primary studies reviewed, total number of participants), and (d) results (e.g., type of effect size, effect size data). The process of data extraction was conducted by the first author. To test the reliability of the coding, the second author coded five randomly selected meta-analyses independently. There was perfect agreement between the two coders.

2.2 Data Analysis

All of the primary meta-analyses reported the overall effect size using either Hedges' *g* or SMD (standard mean difference, Cohen's *d*). Following Young [15], we assumed that the differences between *g* and *d* would be negligible. Therefore, we used the effect sizes in the original metrics in which they were reported. We retrieved the standard errors (SEs) of effect sizes as directly reported by the authors when available, or computed (SEs) using confidence intervals:

$$SE = (95\%\ CI_{upper\ limt} - 95\%\ CI_{lower\ limit})/3.92 \quad (1)$$

We used the Comprehensive Meta-Analysis software package [16] to conduct effect size synthesis, publication bias and moderator analyses. We conducted a classic fail-safe *N* test, plotted funnel plots [17], and applied the trim-and-fill method [18] to adjust for any possible publication bias.

2.3 Validation of the Second-Order Meta-Analysis

One important issue when conducting a second-order meta-analysis is the issue of study overlap across the various primary meta-analyses [19]. Study overlap occurs when the same empirical studies are included in more than one primary meta-analysis [12]. Although several approaches to addressing study overlap have been proposed, it is not clear which approach is the most appropriate [20].

In this study, we followed the method employed by Young [15] and Tamim et al. [21] in validating the findings of the present second-order meta-analysis. To do this, *individual* effect sizes and sample sizes from available empirical studies reported in the primary meta-analyses were extracted. In this validation sample, all empirical study overlap was eliminated. We then compared the overall mean effect size from the present second-order meta-analysis with the overall mean effect size from the validation sample, where all study overlap had been removed, to determine whether the average effect sizes were similar.

3 Results

As shown in Fig. 1, the initial searches resulted in 42 article abstracts (after duplicates were removed). From these identified 42 documents, 15 were removed after a title and abstract review. Ultimately, 27 full-text primary meta-analyses were assessed for eligibility. Of these 27 full-text primary meta-analyses, 20 were excluded due to a number of reasons, including: no effect size was provided (n = 6); the outcome measure was not student learning performance (n = 6); and non-STEM subjects (n = 8).

The final dataset subsequently used in this study consisted of 10 primary meta-analyses comparing the effects of the flipped classroom and the non-flipped classroom on STEM students' academic performance. Seven primary meta-analyses examined student cognitive learning outcomes [22–28]. These meta-analyses covered a total of 176 unique primary studies with 37,775 participants (19,045 in a flipped class and 19,730 participants in a comparison class). Three primary meta-analyses covering 41

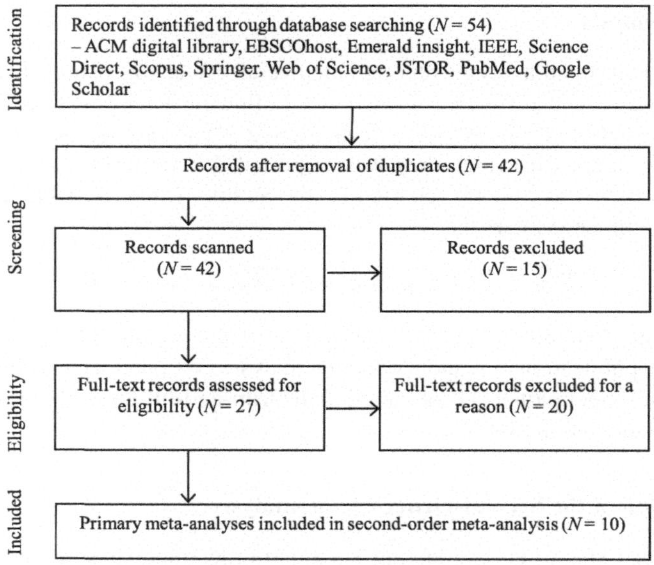

Fig. 1. PRISMA flowchart of article screening process.

unique primary studies with 9,473 examined student behavioral learning outcomes [24, 27, 29].

All 10 primary meta-analyses relied on the effect sizes extracted from primary studies published in peer-reviewed journals. However, four primary meta-analyses included the analysis of *additional* primary studies from conference proceedings and/or dissertations [25, 27–29]. Five meta-analyses focused solely on health sciences education [22–24, 27, 29]. Other meta-analyses focused on science education [28], mathematics education [26], and engineering education [25].

3.1 Effect Size Synthesis: Cognitive and Behavioral Outcomes

We chose the random-effects model to compute the overall effect size of this second-order meta-analysis. The random effects model was considered more appropriate for interpretation because of the wide diversity of settings and subject matter. Under the random-effects model, results revealed a small effect in favor of the flipped classroom approach on student assessed cognitive learning outcomes (Hedges's $g = 0.49$, 95% CI = 0.326 – 0.656, $p < 0.001$), and a large effect on student behavioral outcomes (Hedges's $g = 1.70$, 95% CI = 1.395 – 1.998, $p < 0.001$) (Fig. 2, Fig. 3 respectively). We conducted outlier analysis using the 'one-study-remove' method. Results revealed that all 7 effect sizes for cognitive outcomes fell within the 95% CI of the overall effect size (0.326 – 0.656). Thus, there was no need to remove any meta-analysis.

We conducted sub-group analyses to examine whether the subject discipline and student grade level might moderate the magnitude of the effect sizes (Table 1). The moderator analysis concerning subject discipline suggested no significant effect size

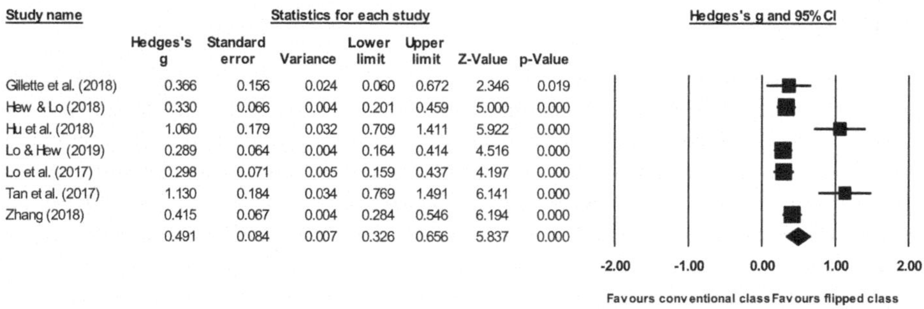

Fig. 2. Forest plot of effect size on student *cognitive* learning outcomes (random-effects)

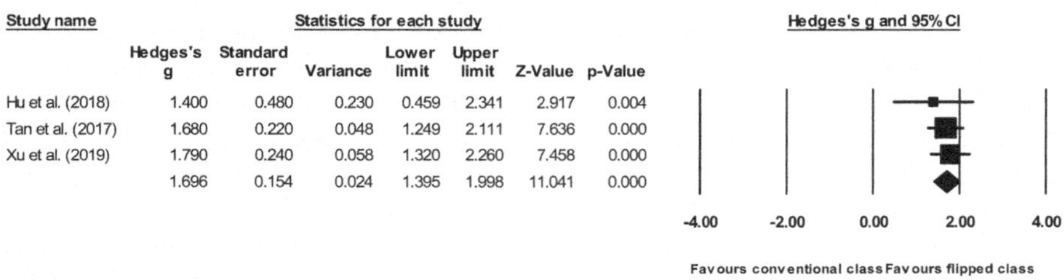

Fig. 3. Forest plot of effect size on student *behavioral* learning outcomes (random-effects)

difference among different disciplines ($Q_B = 1.411$, df $= 3$, $p = 0.703$). The moderator analysis concerning student grade level also suggested no significant effect size difference ($Q_B = 3.374$, df $= 1$, $p = 0.066$).

Table 1. Sub-group analyses.

Sub-group	*N*	*g*	SE	95% CI (LL)	95% CI (LL)	*QB (p)*
Subject discipline						1.411 (0.703)
Engineering	1	0.289	0.404	−0.502	1.080	
Health sciences	4	0.701	0.213	0.284	1.119	
Mathematics	1	0.298	0.405	−0.495	1.091	
Science	1	0.415	0.404	−0.377	1.207	
Student level						3.374 (0.066)
Post-secondary	4	0.662	0.127	0.414	0.910	
K-12 + post-secondary	3	0.334	0.126	0.088	0.580	

We also conducted outlier analysis through the 'one-study-remove' method. Results revealed that all three effect sizes for behavioral outcomes fell within the 95% CI of the overall effect size (1.395 – 1.998). Thus, there is no need to remove any meta-analysis.

3.2 Data Validation

We administered the data validation by extracting the available raw individual effect sizes used in the seven primary meta-analyses and running a regular meta-analysis. A total of 149 independent effect sizes and standard errors were extracted. We computed the overall mean effect size using the random-effects model. The results showed a significant medium effect size in favour of flipped classroom on students' cognitive learning outcome (Hedges's g = 0.51, CI = 0.438-0.599, $p < 0.001$). We also computed the overall mean effect size of student behavioral outcome using the random-effects model among 41 effect sizes. The results showed a significant medium effect size in favour of flipped classroom on students' behavioral learning outcome (Hedges's g = 1.70, CI = 1.387 – 2.010, $p < 0.001$).

In comparing the second-order meta-analysis with the validation study, it is evident that the mean effect sizes for the random-effects model for both student cognitive and behavioral outcomes are closely similar. For example, the mean effect size of the second-order meta-analyses for cognitive outcome was 0.49 (random-effects model), while the mean effect size of the validation study sample was 0.51 (random-effects model). There was only a difference of 0.02, a magnitude which can be deemed trivial [10]. The mean effect size of the second-order meta-analyses for behavioral outcome was 1.70 (random-effects model) which was similar to the mean effect size of the validation study sample (1.70, random-effects model) Thus, the results of the second-order meta-analysis were considered to be a valid representation of the cumulative effects of the primary meta-analyses.

3.3 Publication Bias

Figure 4 shows the funnel plot of the seven primary meta-analyses on student cognitive outcome. The classic fail-safe *N* test result showed that 300 additional studies would be required to invalidate the overall effect.

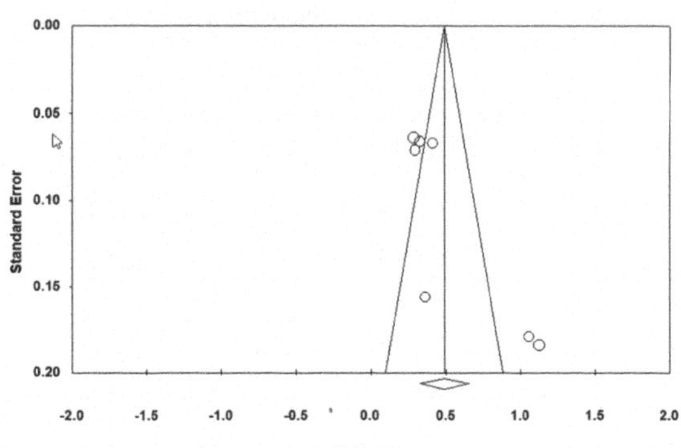

Fig. 4. Funnel plot of seven primary meta-analyses on cognitive learning outcome

We also conducted an examination of publication bias of the cognitive outcomes validation study which consists of 149 independent effect sizes used in the seven primary meta-analyses (see Fig. 5).

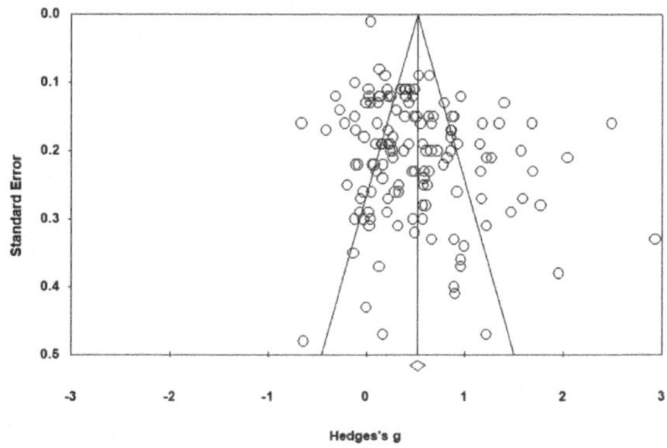

Fig. 5. Funnel plot of the validation study (n = 149 effect sizes) on cognitive learning outcomes

The classic fail-safe *N* was 1,524, indicating that 1,524 null effect studies are needed to invalidate the overall effect for cognitive outcomes. Kendall's Tau was 0.006 (one-tailed $p = 0.456$) which suggested no presence of publication bias. The trim and fill-method, using random-effects model, suggests that 0 studies are missing from the left side of the mean effect.

With regard to student behavioural learning outcome, the classic fail-safe *N* analysis revealed that 82 null effect studies are needed to invalidate the overall effect. Kendall's Tau was 0.000 (one-tailed $p = 0.500$) which suggested no presence of publication bias. The trim and fill-method, using random-effects model, suggests that 0 studies are missing from the left side of the mean effect. We also conducted an examination of publication bias of the behavioral learning outcomes validation study which consists of 41 independent effect sizes used in the three primary meta-analyses (see Fig. 6).

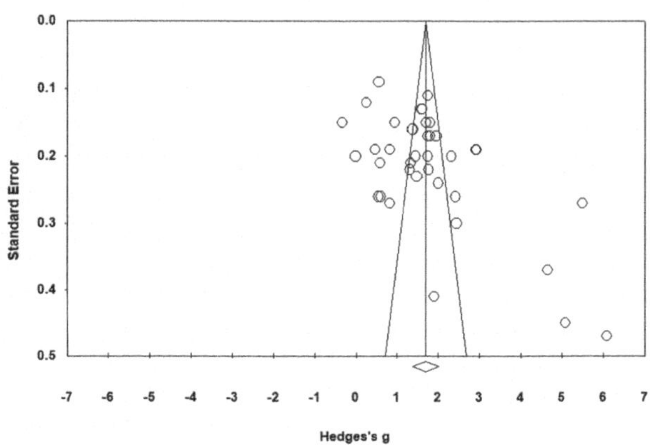

Fig. 6. Funnel plot of the validation study on behavioral outcomes

The classic fail-safe N was 7,940, indicating that 7,940 null effect studies are needed to invalidate the overall effect for behavioral outcomes. Kendall's Tau was 0.215 (one-tailed $p = 0.024$) which suggested a slight presence of publication bias. The trim and fill-method, using random-effects model, however, suggests that 0 studies are missing from the left side of the mean effect. In summary, the results of the classic fail-safe Ns and funnel plots suggest no obvious publication bias for both student cognitive and behavioral outcomes.

3.4 Student Perception of Flipped Classroom

Three primary meta-analyses [25, 26, 28] reported student perception of using flipped classroom. In this section, we briefly synthesize the main findings according to two main categories: benefits of flipped classroom, and challenges of flipped classroom.

Six main benefits of flipped classroom were identified: (a) promote self-paced learning, (b) allow multiple exposures to course materials, (c) help prepare students for class, (d) more opportunity for knowledge application (e.g., problem solving) activities, (e) provide more opportunity for peer-assisted learning, and (f) allow more timely instructor intervention and support. Compared to non-flipped classroom, flipped classroom students have a greater opportunity to do self-paced learning due to the availability of pre-class activity. Students can choose to watch the video or read the course materials at any time and in whatever pace they desire. Flipped classroom also provided students with more than one exposure to the course materials. Students are first exposed to the course materials before class during the pre-class activity. Students engaged with the course materials again later during the in-class session. Multiple exposure to course materials can help improve student understanding of the lesson.

Five main challenges of flipped classroom were also identified. These include: (a) student unfamiliarity with the new approach, (b) student not willing to complete the pre-class activity due to perceived additional workload, (c) student inability to ask questions during the pre-class activity, (d) significant start-up effort on the part of the instructor, and (e) instructor unfamiliarity with the flipped classroom approach.

4 Conclusion

Many individual empirical studies that examined the effects of flipped classroom on student outcomes have been conducted and published in journals, conference proceedings, and dissertations. Along with this growing number of individual empirical studies, there has also been a corresponding increase of meta-analytic studies of the flipped classroom approach in a variety of contexts. The present study used a second-order meta-analysis method to synthesize the findings of ten primary meta-analyses on STEM student cognitive and behavioral outcomes. Overall, we found a significant mean effect size of 0.49, and effect size of 1.70 under the random effects model in favor of the flipped classroom approach in enhancing student cognitive and behavioral outcomes respectively. Findings of our validation study suggest that the results of the second-order meta-analysis can be considered valid representations of the cumulative effects of the primary meta-analyses.

The overall effect size of 0.49 for cognitive outcome may be considered a medium effect [30] and is closely similar to the typical value of 0.40 for student achievement that is reported elsewhere [31]. The overall effect size of 1.70 for behavioral outcome is considered a large effect [30]. An interesting finding is that the effect size of behavioral outcome is much higher than that of the effect size of cognitive outcome. One possible reason why flipped classroom lends itself particularly well to improving behavioral outcome is that it promotes more time for application of knowledge than traditional classroom.

We conclude by highlighting two limitations of previous primary meta-analyses. A majority of the primary meta-analyses did not report whether or how they control for potential student initial equivalence. Student initial differences can result in substantial bias in the outcome measures. If students have different initial knowledge or skill about the subject matter, it becomes unclear whether it is the actual flipped learning pedagogy that caused the effect, or the student's initial knowledge or skill that influenced the outcome. A majority of previous meta-analyses also did not report whether or how they control for instructor equivalence. Since different instructors have different teaching styles (although the content materials remain similar), it becomes unclear whether the actual flipped learning pedagogy caused the effect, or the presence of the instructor confounding variable influenced the outcome. We therefore urge future primary meta-analyses to carefully consider these two issues.

Acknowledgement. The research was supported by a grant from the Research Grants Council of Hong Kong (Project reference no: 17610919).

References

1. Abeysekera, L., Dawson, P.: Motivation and cognitive load in the flipped classroom: definition, rationale and a call for research. High Educ. Res. Dev. **34**, 1–14 (2014)
2. O'Flaherty, J., Phillips, C.: The use of flipped classrooms in higher education: a scoping review. Internet High. Educ. **25**, 85–95 (2015). https://doi.org/10.1016/j.iheduc.2015.02.002
3. Bates, S., Galloway, R.: The inverted classroom in a large enrolment introductory physics course: a case study (2012)
4. Huber, E., Werner, A.: A review of the literature on flipping the STEM classroom: preliminary findings. In: Barker, S., Dawson, S., Pardo, A., Colvin, C. (eds.). Show me the learning. Proceedings ASCILITE 2016, Adelaide, pp. 267–274 (2016)
5. Betihavas, V., Bridgman, H., Kornhaber, R., Cross, M.: The evidence for "flipping out": a systematic review of the flipped classroom in nursing education. Nurse Educ. Today **38**, 15–21 (2016)
6. Chen, K.S., et al.: Academic outcomes of flipped classroom learning: a meta analysis. Med. Educ. **52**, 910–924 (2018)
7. Presti, C.R.: The flipped learning approach in nursing education: a literature review. J. Nurs. Educ. **55**(5), 252–257 (2016)
8. Seery, M.K.: Flipped learning in higher education chemistry: Emerging trends and potential directions. Chem. Educ. Res. Pract. **16**(4), 758–768 (2015)
9. Chua, J., Lateef, F.: The flipped classroom: viewpoints in Asian universities. Educ. Med. J. **6** (2014). https://doi.org/10.5959/eimj.v6i4.316

10. Bernard, J.S.: The flipped classroom: fertile ground for nursing education research. Int. J. Nurs. Educ. Scholarsh. **12**(1), 99–109 (2015)
11. Gurevitch, J., Koricheva, J., Nakagawa, S., Stewart, G.: Meta-analysis and the science of research synthesis. Nature **555**(7695), 175–182 (2018). https://doi.org/10.1038/nature25753
12. Cooper, H., Koenka, A.C.: The overview of reviews: unique challenges and opportunities when research syntheses are the principal elements of new integrative scholarship. Am. Psychol. **67**(6), 446–462 (2012). https://doi.org/10.1037/a0027119
13. Busch, T., Friede, G.: The robustness of the corporate social and financial performance relation: a second-order meta-analysis. Corp. Soc. Responsib. Environ. Manag. **25**(4), 583–608 (2018). https://doi.org/10.1002/csr.1480
14. Schmidt, F., Oh, I.-S.: The crisis of confidence in research findings in psychology: is lack of replication the real problem? or is it something else? Arch. Sci. Psychol. **4**, 32–37 (2016). https://doi.org/10.1037/arc0000029
15. Young, J.: Technology-enhanced mathematics instruction: a second-order meta-analysis of 30 years of research. Educ. Res. Rev. **22**, 19–33 (2017). https://doi.org/10.1016/j.edurev.2017.07.001
16. Borenstein, M., Hedges, L.V., Higgings, J.P.T., Rothstein, H.R.: Introduction to Meta-Analysis. Wiley, Chichester (2009)
17. Egger, M., Smith, G.D., Schneider, M., Minder, C.: Bias in meta-analysis detected by a simple, graphical test. Br. Med. J. **315**(7109), 629–634 (1997)
18. Duval, S., Tweedie, R.: Trim and fill: a simple funnel-plot–based method of testing and adjusting for publication bias in meta-analysis. Biometrics **56**(2), 455–463 (2000). https://doi.org/10.1111/j.0006-341x.2000.00455
19. Polanin, J.R., Tanner-Smith, E.E., Hennessy, E.A.: Estimating the difference between published and unpublished effect sizes: a meta-review. Rev. Educ. Res. **86**(1), 207–236 (2016). https://doi.org/10.3102/0034654315582067
20. Steenbergen-Hu, S., Makel, M.C., Olszewski-Kubilius, P.: What one hundred years of research says about the effects of ability grouping and acceleration on K–12 students' academic achievement: findings of two second-order meta-analyses. Rev. Educ. Res. **86**(4), 849–899 (2016). https://doi.org/10.3102/0034654316675417
21. Tamim, R.M., Bernard, R.M., Borokhovski, E., Abrami, P.C., Schmid, R.F.: What forty years of research says about the impact of technology on learning: a second-order meta-analysis and validation study. Rev. Educ. Res. **81**(1), 4–28 (2011). https://doi.org/10.3102/0034654310393361
22. Gillette, C., Rudolph, M., Kimble, C., Rockich-Winston, N., Smith, L., Broedel-Zaugg, K.: A meta-analysis of outcomes comparing flipped classroom and lecture. Am. J. Pharm. Educ. **82**(5), 433–440 (2018)
23. Hew, K.F., Lo, C.K.: Flipped classroom improves student learning in health professions education: a meta-analysis. BMC Med. Educ. **18**, 38 (2018)
24. Hu, R., Gao, H., Ye, Y., Ni, Z., Jiang, N., Jiang, X.: Effectiveness of flipped classrooms in Chinese baccalaureate nursing education: a meta-analysis of randomized controlled trials. Int. J. Nurs. Stud. **79**, 94–103 (2018)
25. Lo, C.K., Hew, K.F.: The impact of flipped classrooms on student achievement in engineering education: a meta-analysis of 10 years of research. J. Eng. Edu **108**(4), 523–546 (2019)
26. Lo, C.K., Hew, K.F., Chen, G.: Toward a set of design principles for mathematics flipped classrooms: a synthesis of research in mathematics education. Educ. Res. Rev. **22**, 50–73 (2017)
27. Tan, C., Yue, W.G., Fu, Y.: Effectiveness of flipped classrooms in nursing education: systematic review and meta-analysis. Chin. Nurs. Res. **4**(4), 192–200 (2017)
28. Zhang, S.: A systematic review and meta-analysis on flipped learning in science education. Unpublished Master thesis. The University of Hong Kong (2018)

29. Xu, P., et al.: The effectiveness of a flipped classroom on the development of Chinese nursing students' skill competence: a systematic review and meta-analysis. Nurse Educ. Today **80**, 67–77 (2019)
30. Cohen, J.: Statistical Power Analysis for the Behavioral Sciences, 2nd edn. Lawrence Erlbaum Associates, New York (1988)
31. Hattie, J.: Visible Learning: A Synthesis of Over 800 Meta-Analyses Relating to Achievement. Routledge, London (2009)

Blended Versus Traditional Learning: Comparing Students' Outcomes and Preferences

Ludmila Faltýnková(✉)

Faculty of Education, University of Ostrava, F. Šrámka 3, Ostrava, Czech Republic
faltynkova@epol.cz

Abstract. Numerous research studies have already proven that modern approaches such as blended learning can enhance the quality of learning, both in particular subjects and in general. However, quite little is known about how such approaches affect learning outcomes in higher education, and at tertiary schools for medical staff in particular. The submitted paper represents a pilot study with the aim to compare and assess students' perception and preferences concerning blended and traditional format of instruction, as well as their outcomes and learning achievement. In total, twenty-four 1st year students (pharmacy technicians) participated in the pilot research conducted within the English for Specific Purposes course. During one semester, two formats were implemented: the first half of the semester was taught in the traditional face-to-face format while the other one in the blended format. Students reported significantly higher preferences in the blended part of the course in comparison to the traditional one, stating higher motivation, appreciating the possibility of individual pace and independence. They also showed better learning outcomes. Moreover, the students were interested in taking more blended courses, in particular the ones connected with specialized subjects such as anatomy and physiology or pharmacology.

Keywords: Blended learning · Traditional course delivery · Learning outcomes · Tertiary schools for medical staff · Learning preferences · ESP

1 Introduction

Blended learning is a teaching format that has been gaining popularity among higher education institutions for some time as it provides indisputable advantages to both the students and the schools.

Tertiary schools are an inseparable part of higher education in the Czech Republic; however, they are considered a distinction within the educational system. They are established either as part of a secondary technical school or as an independent school, thus forming a cross between secondary and higher education. They maintain education mainly in technical fields, business and health care, and are established by and under the supervision of the Ministry of education. Nevertheless, their study programs follow the university format dividing a study year into two semesters at the end of each there is one-month exam period during which students have to fulfill successfully all the assigned

S. K. S. Cheung et al. (Eds.): ICBL 2020, LNCS 12218, pp. 276–286, 2020.
https://doi.org/10.1007/978-3-030-51968-1_23

exams. At the end of the whole study program, a final exam needs to be accomplished together with a graduation thesis defense.

Tertiary schools for medical staff provide education not only in the specialized fields of medicine, e.g. nursing care, urgent medicine, dental hygiene, but also focus on educating students in English for Specific Purposes, which is part of the final exam. Most of the courses are conveyed in the traditional face-to-face format. However, as Tlučhoř [1] and Hubáček [2] claim, e-learning has become a phenomenon which can broaden the educational methods and be beneficial for both students and teachers. Thus, there have been tendencies to apply blended format into individual courses.

2 Background

Blended learning has gained a great popularity in higher education over the last years and have become widespread. According to Martyn [3], over 90% of higher education institutions use some type of e-learning option. This short summary of the background examines the research across three topics. First, the potential benefits of blended learning in general are examined. Second, the impact on students' learning outcomes is addressed, and third, students' perception of the blended format is explored.

2.1 Blended Learning Benefits

Garrison and Kamuka [4] state that blended learning courses can respond better to the diverse needs and desires of students. They can also adjust to individual students' needs and provide more time to cover increasing curricular demands related to higher education courses (Collopy [5]). Furthermore, Collopy [5] claims that teachers can adjust class time to focus on key questions and vice versa, blended environment can provide the opportunity for the continuation of discussions not completed during limited class time. The blended model can thus utilize the best features of face-to-face and online education. Decreased costs are described as another blended learning advantage as study materials are provided in the digital form (Martyn [3]).

2.2 Impact on Students' Learning Outcomes

Blended learning can overcome various limitations related to face-to-face approach and pure e-learning. An analysis of more than 1,000 studies published between 1996 and 2008 showed that blended learning proved to be more effective than both previously stated learning formats (Means et al. [6]). Clark [7] reports, that e-learning is more efficient than traditional learning formats as learners gain knowledge, skills, and attitudes faster. This efficiency is likely to project into higher student motivation and performance. Furthermore, e-learners demonstrate better utilization of content, resulting in better learning outcomes (Clark [7]).

Numerous researchers have begun to investigate students' experience with the online environment and to examine its potential impact on student learning. According to a study conducted by Dziuban [8], blended courses demonstrate higher percentage of students obtaining an A, B, or C and lower unsuccessful students than comparable face-to-face courses. Singh [9] illustrates demonstration of 10% better learning outcomes than the traditional learning format. Zheng [10] proved continued improvement and sustainable development of student performance mediated by the use of ICT in education, MOOC courses in particular.

2.3 Blended Learning Perception and Preferences

Blended learning can be also described as a mix of delivery methods and study materials that are generally selected and tailored to meet various learning needs. Studies have mostly illustrated students' satisfaction with blended learning increasing with interesting study materials, ease of use, access and interactivity of the environment. (Gibbons and Fairweather [11]) On the other hand, Grandzol [12] found that students' perception of blended learning in terms of enthusiasm, preparation and grading do not differ from the traditional learning. However, Trasler [13] argues that factors as variety, adaptability and flexibility play major role in attracting and motivating students. Moreover, students agree that blended learning is superior to traditional learning method in terms of learning efficiency, accessibility to content and flexible pace of learning, apart from motivation factor and learner autonomy.

3 Research part

For the purpose of this pilot study, the method of comparative analysis was used to compare the test scores and reveal possible differences between the traditional and blended learning format in connection with students' learning outcomes, which are understood a synonym for test scores. Furthermore, a questionnaire was distributed among the research participants in order to obtain data providing evidence about their perception and preferences of the blended learning approach.

3.1 Research Question

Three main research questions were under the focus of research:

Q1: Do students perform better when using the blended format of learning?

Q2: Do students prefer the traditional or blended learning format?

Q3: What is the students' perception of blended learning?

3.2 Research Objective

The main objective of this research was to collect data about students' perception of the blended course delivery and to discover possible differences in their test scores regarding the learning format applied and monitor their learning preferences.

3.3 Research Hypothesis

Based on previous study by Hubáček [2] who presented that blended learning enhances the efficacy of the learning process, the first hypothesis connected with research question 1 was formulated:

H1: In blended format students reach higher test scores compared to the traditional one. Furthermore, it was presumed that: *H2: The frequency of positive evaluation of the blended format will be higher compared to the traditional one;* as Ruiz [14] has revealed in his study on e-learning in medical education.

3.4 Research Sample and Process

The author who designed this pilot research has been teaching at Secondary and tertiary school for medical staff in Olomouc, Czech Republic, since 2014 and started to use blended format in her English for Specific Purposes (ESP) courses in 2018. Similar format has already been used in technical subject courses; however, the e-learning part only in the form of a storage of digital materials used during face-to-face lessons.

The structure of the research sample is displayed in Table 1. All research participants are the 1st year pharmacy technician students attending the compulsory ESP (Medical English) course.

Table 1. Research sample: structure

Measure	Category	Number of students (N)	Percent (%)
Gender	male	4	17
	female	20	83
Age	20–24	24	100
Course	ESP year 1	24	100
Specialization	Pharmacy technician	24	100

This study was conducted during the summer semester 2018/2019. The course lasted from February 01, 2019 to May 31, 2019 (16 weeks).

The ESP course is subsidized with three lessons per week, which are usually organized into one double, and one single lesson a week. A half of the course (8 weeks) was delivered via the traditional face-to-face approach whereas the second half focused on the blended approach providing students with study materials and supplementary exercises in the digital form accessible in LMS Moodle with embedded links to videos, dictionaries and useful web pages.

3.5 Research Method and Tools

Two main research methods were applied: comparative analysis of didactic test scores and questionnaire of students' learning preferences.

Students' performance included two credit tests, one administered after 8 weeks of traditional course delivery and the second one at the end of the 8 week blended format of learning. Test scores were compared in the form of figures presenting results in both study formats. (Figure 1)Test 1 was administered after the first 8-week phase focusing on the traditional approach while Test 2 illustrated students' outcomes after the other 8 week blended approach. Both tests' successful completion was a compulsory part of the subject's fulfillment requiring only information presented in both traditional and blended formats. The tests consisted of questions covering the topics assigned by the syllabus of the course.

Furthermore, a short questionnaire focusing on students learning preferences was administered at the end of the targeted semester in order to find out about students' learning preferences.

Didactic Tests

Both didactic tests were of identical structure. They focused on three parts: professional (i.e. medical) vocabulary, grammar and medical topics. Each took 60-90 min. The cut-off score for passing the tests was 60% altogether out of all the parts. Tables 2 and 3 below show the description of the tests contents.

Table 2. Test 1 content

Test part	Content	Types of tasks	Number of items	Points per item	Points in total
Grammar	Future with will and going to	Filling in	10	1	10
		Translation	5	2	10
		Multiple choice	10	1	10
Vocabulary	Topic related lexical items and phrases	Translation	15	1	15
		Definition	5	2	10
Medical topics	Locomotor's system, Diseases	Open questions	15	2	30

The tables show that the tasks were of identical structure, as well as ratio among single parts. Nevertheless, they focus on different content congruent with the subject syllabus. The total score of test 1 was 85 while test 2 was slightly longer with the total score of 100. The following figures illustrate the tests outcomes connected with both learning formats used. Tests were assessed according to the following criteria: grade **A**: 100% – 90% of max test score, **B:** 89% – 79%, **C:** 78% – 60%, **F:** 59% – 0%.

Questionnaire

This tool consisted of three questions so as to monitor learners' preferences regarding traditional/blended learning and how they perceive the blended process. The questionnaire

Table 3. Test 2 content

Test part	Content	Types of tasks	Number of items	Points per item	Points in total
Grammar	Present perfect and past simple	Filling in	10	1	10
		Translation	10	2	20
		Cloze	10	1	10
Vocabulary	Topic related lexical items and phrases	Translation	20	1	20
		Definition	5	2	10
Medical topics	Central and peripheral nervous system, Hormones	Open questions	15	2	30

consisted of six questions regarding the blended format, all of them either dichotomous or multiple choice. Students' task was to answer the following questions: Q1: *Which approach did you prefer?* Q2: *Would you like to use the blended approach in other subjects as well?* Q3: *Which subjects would you use the blended approach in?* (Max 2 items out of 5), Q4: *Which parts of the online materials were the most useful?* (Max 2 items), Q5: *Which approach was more motivating for your self-study?* Q6: *What did you like about the blended approach?*

4 Results and Interpretation

The ESP course did not require mandatory fulfillment of all e-learning tasks. The course included eight seminars delivered in the traditional way comprising either printed materials or note taking and eight seminars via the blended format offering students digital study materials, supplementary vocabulary, grammar or listening tasks together with recommended complementary sources. However, the students were instructed to use any suitable resources as study materials. The only obligatory in both study formats was 80% attendance and autonomous learning necessary for participation in seminars and successful fulfilling of the credit tests.

4.1 Test scores

Both Figs. 1 and 2 show scores in Test 1 and Test 2. According to these it might be concluded that within the scope of this study there were detected some differences in connection with the two learning formats applied in favour of the blended format, which demonstrated considerably better students' performance within the credit test than the traditional learning format. The most significant difference can be seen in the unsuccessful (F) students whose number decreases from 5 to 2. Number of average students assessed B and C is fairly similar in both groups, nevertheless excellent students (A) represent more numerous group within the blended approach.

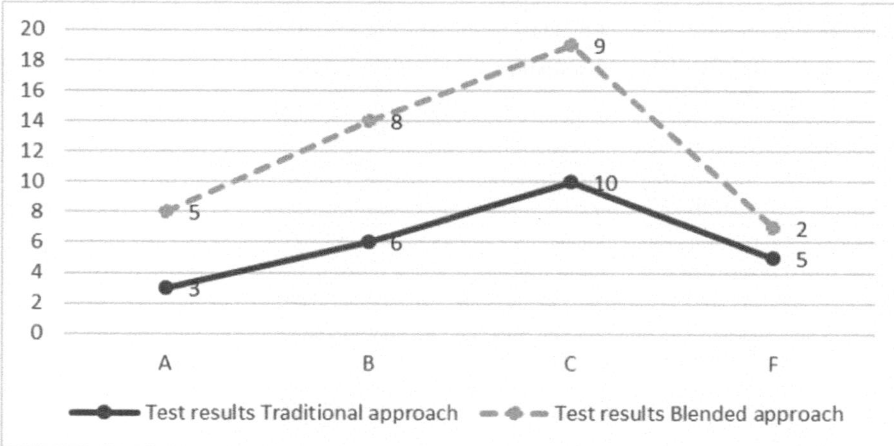

Fig. 1. Test results

For better illustration, Fig. 2 shows the comparison of Test 1 and 2 percentage scores of individual students in both study formats.

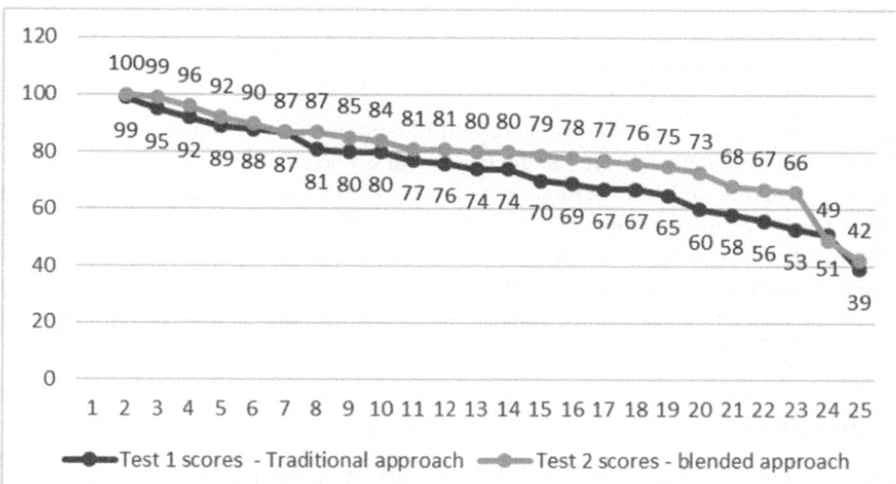

Fig. 2. Test 1 vs test 2 scores

It can be noted, that the students' performances in both learning formats are mostly very close to each other in the interval from 100% to 85%. (N 2 – 7) Then the scores start to diverge with the greatest difference at the point of the cut-off score. (N 8 – 23) The lowest scores again meet at nearly the same point and in both formats do not fall much below 40%. (N 24 – 25)

It may thus be concluded that the use of blended approach in the ESP course of medical English reflected positively at the students test scores.

To sum up, it can be stated that the implementation of blended design into the ESP course increased students' performance in comparison with the traditional way of learning.

4.2 Students' Preferences

Concerning students' course delivery preferences (Q1), only 4% of the respondents were in favour of the traditional course delivery opposed to the vast majority who preferred blended learning. These findings correspond with the prior studies. (Collopy and Arnold [5]). Furthermore, 79% of students would welcome blended approach in other subjects as well. Figure 3 illustrates students' subject preferences in particular.

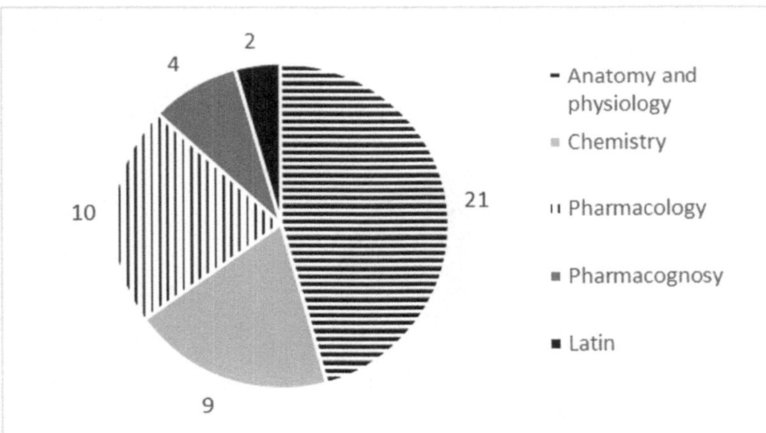

Fig. 3. Q3: Which subjects would you use the blended approach in?

We can clearly see that subjects with the greatest blended learning approach preferences are anatomy and physiology along with pharmacology and chemistry. Surprisingly, even though students expressed strong favour towards blended approach in connection with ESP, they did not share such preferences in case of Latin.

The graph below reflects usefulness of individual implemented study material from the students' point of view.

As can be seen from Fig. 4, 31% of the students marked videos as one of the two possible most useful online materials. Grammar and vocabulary exercises were favoured in about a quarter of instances. The lowest incidence of usefulness was stated in connection with dictionary links and revision of a particular topic in Czech. Extra study materials were appreciated by 10% of respondents.

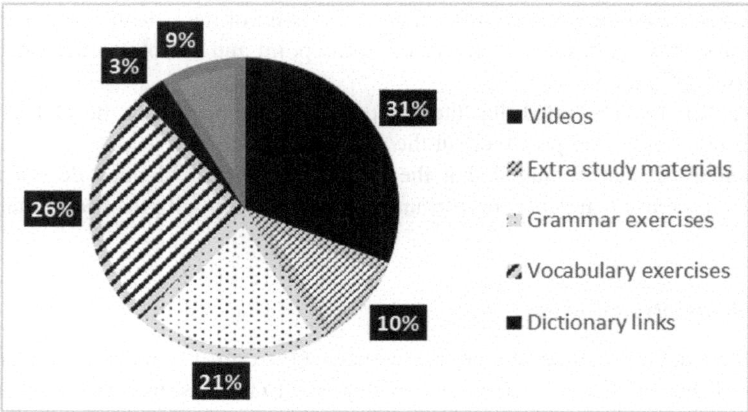

Fig. 4. Q4: Which parts of the online materials were the most useful?

Apparently, Fig. 5 shows students' strong preference of blended approach (62%) in comparison with the traditional one (21%) regarding motivation. Some students (17%) find both approaches equally motivating.

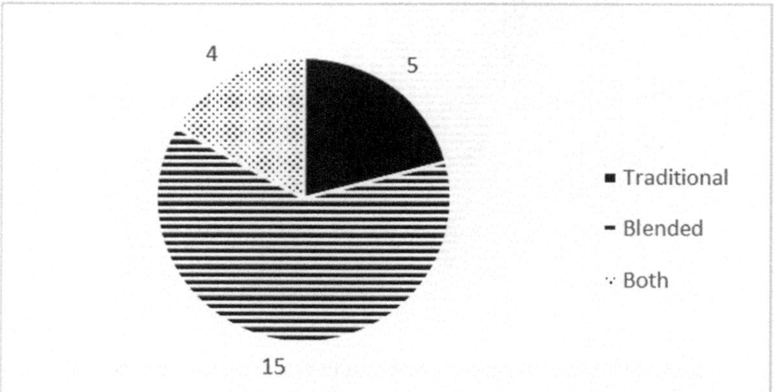

Fig. 5. Q5: Which approach was more motivating for your self-study?

Finally yet importantly, Fig. 6 illustrates aspects of blended approach, which appealed to the students most.

The most valued of blended learning aspects is its ability to meet individual needs (N = 18) along with the possibility to use technologies. Independence and own study pace were appreciated by roughly a third of the respondents. Surprisingly, only 5 students found digital study materials more interesting.

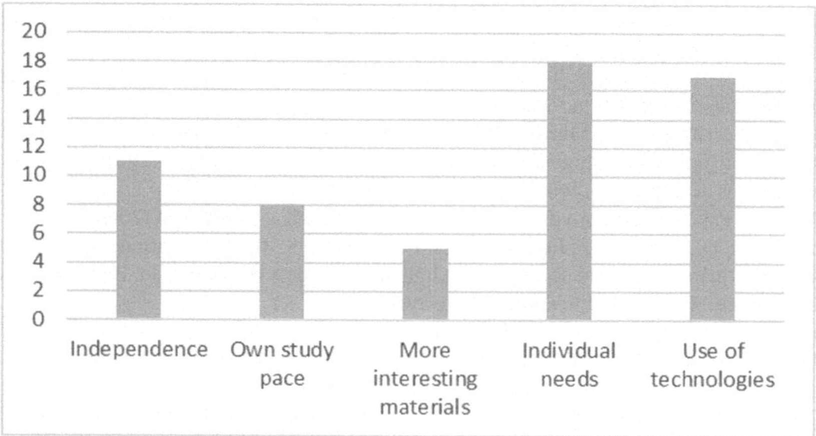

Fig. 6. Q6: What did you like about the blended approach?

5 Conclusion

In accordance to the presented results, it can be concluded that both hypotheses were supported. Blended course delivery contributed to better students' test scores, although the difference compared to the traditional approach was not significant. Moreover, the students expressed strong preference towards blended approach, stating higher motivation, meeting individual needs and supporting their learning independence. Nevertheless, the study was limited by the number of its participants, which might have reflected the outcomes as providing statistically small amount of data. Moreover, all the study participants were members of one study group, which might have influenced their attitudes and study results.

The author suggests conducting a future study of broader range regarding study groups and increasing the number of participants. Furthermore, engaging schools for medical staff in other cities would be worth considering.

Acknowledgements. This paper is supported by the project N. SGS03/PdF/2019-2020; ICT-Enhanced Teaching English.

References

1. Tlučhoř, J.: E-learning a blended learning ve vzdělávacím procesu: [E-learning and blended learning in the educational process]. Západočeská univerzita, Plzeň (2005). ISBN 80-7043-420-1
2. Hubáček, P.: Blended learning na obchodní akademii a VOŠ Valašské Meziříčí – Příprava na distanční vysokoškolské stadium: [Blended learning at secondary business school and tertiary school in Valašské Meziříčí – Getting ready for university distant study]. TVV **4**, 386–388 (2011)
3. Martyn, M.: The hybrid online model: good practice. Educause Q. **26**(1), 18–23 (2003)

4. Garrison, D.R., Kanuka, H.: Blended learning: uncovering its transformative potential in higher education. Internet High. Educ. **7**, 95–105 (2004)
5. Rachel, C., Arnold, J.M.: To blend or not to blend: online-only and blended learning environments. Teacher Educ. Fac. Publ. **15** (2009)
6. Means, B., Toyama, Y., Murphy, R., Bakia, M., Jones, K.: Evaluation of evidence-based practices in online learning: a meta-analysis and review of online learning studies. U.S. Department of Education, Washington, DC (2009)
7. Clark, D.: Psychological myths in e-learning. Med Teach. 24, 598–604 (2002)
8. Dziuban, C.D., Hartman, J., Juge, F., Moskal, P.D., Sorg, S.: Blended learning: online learning enters the mainstream. In: Bonk, C.J., Graham, C. (eds.) Handbook of Blended Learning Environment. Pfeiffer Publications, Hoboken (2005)
9. Singh, H.: Building effective blended learning programs. Educ. Technol. **43**(6), 51–54 (2003)
10. Zheng, Y., Li, H., Zheng, T.: Performance evaluation of ICT-based teaching and learning in higher education. In: Cheung, S.K.S., Kwok, L.-F., Kubota, K., Lee, L.-K., Tokito, J. (eds.) ICBL 2018. LNCS, vol. 10949, pp. 378–390. Springer, Cham (2018). https://doi.org/10.1007/978-3-319-94505-7_31
11. Gibbons, A., Fairweather, P.: Computer-based instruction. In: Tobias, S., Fletcher, J. (eds.) Training & Reraining: A Handbook for Business, Industry, Government, and the Military, pp. 410–442. Macmillan Reference USA, New York (2000)
12. Grandzol, J.: Teaching MBA statistics online: a pedagogically sound process approach. J. Educ. Bus. **79**(4), 237–244 (2004)
13. Trasler, J.: Effective learning depends on the blend. Ind. Commercial Training **34**(4), 191–194 (2002)
14. Ruiz, J.G., Mintzer, M., et al.: The impact of e-learning in medical education. Acad. Med. **81**(3), 207–212 (2006)

Institutional Policies and Strategies

Factors Influencing Students' Willingness to Choose Blended Learning in Higher Education

Youliang Zhang(✉), Tongjie Chen, and Chao Wang

Institute of Higher Education, Beijing University of Technology, Beijing 100124, China
ylzhang@bjut.edu.cn

Abstract. Students' willingness to participate blended leaning has been an interesting topic in the higher education context. This paper aims to examine students' willingness to choose blended learning and identify the influencing factors related to their willingness. A large-scale questionnaire survey was conducted with a collection of 1903 valid responses. Meanwhile, nine students were interviewed. The findings indicated that blended learning have not been widely offered in Chinese universities. Students' participation and understanding of blended learning are relatively limited, but most students have a positive attitude to blended learning and are willing to choose it in the future. Such factors as students' demographic features, curriculum cognition, curriculum design, learning demands will affect their willingness to choose blended learning.

Keywords: Blended learning · Choosing willingness · Curriculum cognition · Students' demands

1 Introduction

Blended learning originated from online education. As a subversive innovation to the traditional education model, online education has gained extraordinary influence due to its features of prestigious schools, famous teachers, excellent courses, openness, free of charge and mobility [1]. However, the low completion rate of online education courses has aroused widespread concern. A large number of students cannot complete their studies without supervision or face-to-face instruction. As a result, the value of traditional school education has been re-examined. In recent years, colleges and universities around the world have explored the integration of online education into various face-to-face instructions and researched the effect of blended learning on students' learning performance [2]. Because blended learning combines the advantages of traditional face-to-face learning and online learning, the education community generally regards blended learning as an ideal model for realizing personalized learning, increasing learning opportunities, and reducing school operating costs [3]. Although faced with plenty of problems in learning and teaching practice, blended learning has become an important components of the higher education in the world.

S. K. S. Cheung et al. (Eds.): ICBL 2020, LNCS 12218, pp. 289–302, 2020.
https://doi.org/10.1007/978-3-030-51968-1_24

In recent years, blended learning has become a hot topic in China's higher education reform. The Chinese government and higher education institutions have been offering increasingly more strategic and policy to encourage the development of blended learning. For example, the Ministry of Education of the People's Republic of China has issued a series of policies to promote the implementation of blended learning in colleges and universities. At present, the blended learning practice in China is thriving, while the research on blended learning obviously lags behind the pace of practice. In order to ensure the effective implementation of blended learning, it is urgent to understand the attitude and capacity of colleges and universities in blended learning [4]. However, in the majority of current research, the voice of students is ignored. There is few research focusing on students' attitude towards the introduction of blended learning in colleges or universities; their willingness to take blended courses offered by the colleges or universities, and what factors may influence their participation in blended learning. Based on these problems, this paper will analyze the cognition of college students on blended learning from their perspective, grasp their willingness to choose blended learning mode and the influencing factors, to provide suggestions for better implementation of blended learning in colleges and universities and promote colleges and universities to construct blended learning model to meet the demands of students.

2 Literature Review

2.1 Definition

Scholars have not reached an agreement on the concept of "blended learning". They have either defined the blended learning too broadly to cover all educational techniques used in classrooms, or regarded it too narrowly as their favorite type mode [5]. Some scholars have also tried to define the concept of blended learning rigorously. Among them, blended learning means that students complete the learning process by combining online learning with learning in entity organizations such as schools. In online learning, students can autonomously control the time, place, path, and pace of learning. In offline learning, students are supervised and instructed by teachers. During the learning process, the online component and offline component form an integrated curriculum system together rather than being separated. Which one meets these conditions is blended learning [3]. However, in the actual practical process, the diversity of blended learning may be far beyond imagination. Most people are confused about the concept and mode of blended learning. The definition of blended learning varies from person to person. However, most researchers believe that blended learning is a mode that organically combines traditional face-to-face learning with online learning [6, 7].

2.2 Effectiveness

With the emergence of blended learning, people urgently need to know which type of learning mode is more effective. In recent years, scholars have carried out comparative studies on the effects of blended learning, online learning and face-to-face learning. Three categories of findings were drawn: (1) some studies support the hypothesis that blended learning is more effective than pure online learning and face-to-face learning. According to a meta-analysis of 47 experimental and quasi-experimental studies on the impact of blended learning and online learning on students' learning performance, the blended learning is more conducive to improving students' learning performance than pure online learning and face-to-face learning [8]. An experiment that applies blended learning to students' foreign language learning shows that blended learning significantly improves students' learning achievement [9]. (2) Only a small amount of experiments have reached the opposite conclusion. An evaluation of the implementation effect of the "Virtual School" project in West Virginia in the United States found that the academic performance of students adopting the blended learning model was significantly lower than that of those students receiving traditional face-to-face instruction [10]. (3) Some experiments also show that there is no significant difference between blended learning and pure online learning, as well as face-to-face learning. For example, some scholars have found that there is no difference in the learning performance of students under the three learning modes, and students have the same satisfaction with their learning experiences [11]. A teaching experiment conducted in a university in Shandong province, China, which compared the effects of traditional learning mode and blended learning model and found that whether blended learning model is adopted or not has no effect on students' performance [12].

2.3 Perception

Although students have different understandings and experience of blended learning, they generally hold a positive attitude towards it, especially those who have participated in blended learning. Students believe that the blended learning model is featured by flexible learning methods and good learning effects, but it encounters problems in time management and technology use [13]. Students are satisfied with blended learning because they generally believe that the learning effect is better than traditional face-to-face learning or online learning [14]. A survey conducted in Malaysia shows that students are satisfied with blended learning regardless of their achievements, and they are willing to continue taking blended courses if given the opportunity. Among the students majoring in accounting and financial management at the University of Winchester in the UK, a study on blended learning cognition was carried out. The results indicate that the students think highly of the courses with good organizational structure and rich resources. These students also hold a positive attitude towards the development of their knowledge and ability in the blended learning environment [15]. According to a survey conducted in Chinese colleges and universities, 72.58% of the students believe that blended learning is helpful to their own development, and most students are highly interested and confident in blended learning [16]. On the whole, students think that blended learning has advantages over traditional education modes and are willing to adopt blended learning mode in the learning process.

3 Methodology

3.1 Research Design

In this paper, "blended learning" refers to a learning model that combines both traditional face-to-face classroom learning and online learning using information technology. This study adopts a progressive research design combined with qualitative interviews and quantitative surveys. At the beginning, nine university students were interviewed to establish a fundamental understanding of the issues. Then, a large-scale quantitative survey questionnaire - Questionnaire on the Present Situation of Blended Learning in Colleges and Universities was well developed to collect quantitative data. After the questionnaire was collected, the data were further cleaned, and the reliability and validity of the questionnaire were tested. Through descriptive statistics of data, this paper analyzes the blended learning's setting in colleges and universities, students' cognition and willingness to participate in blended learning. Logistic regression was used to analyze the influencing factors of students' choice of blended learning. Subsequently, the second cycle interview were conducted after quantitative data collection to provide explanations for the results of quantitative research.

3.2 Research Hypothesis

This study assumes that factors that affect students' choice of blended learning include student's demographic features, students' cognition of blended learning, the design of curriculum structure, and students' learning needs. First of all, there are differences among demographic features of students. Students' acceptability of blended learning may be affected by their learning foundation and learning ability [17]. Due to differences in learning patterns [18], learning strategies [19], subjective initiative and self-discipline [20] among boys and girls, the choice of blended learning may also be different. Second, according to relevant research, students do not enter the classroom without any academic foundation, and cognition of blended learning will affect their behaviour and academic performance [14]. Third, whether the curriculum design is scientific or reasonable directly affects students' feeling of the curriculum. If the curriculum design is well structured and meets students' psychological expectations, they will hold a positive attitude towards it; otherwise students will feel disappointed [21]. At last, traditional face-to-face learning, online learning and blended learning have their own characteristics, which can meet the different learning needs of students. The practice has proved that face-to-face teaching is more effective for students to learn languages. Students decide whether to choose blended learning according to their learning needs in different fields. Based on the above considerations, the following research hypotheses are put forward:

Hypothesis 1: Students' willingness to take blended learning model will be affected by demographic features.
Hypothesis 2: Students' willingness to take blended learning model will be affected by cognition of blended learning.
Hypothesis 3: Students' willingness to take blended learning model will be affected by the curriculum design of blended learning.

Hypothesis 4: Students' willingness to take blended learning model will be affected by their learning demands.

3.3 Date Collection and Analysis

In January 2020, the research group distributed the Questionnaire on the Present Situation of Blended Learning in Colleges and Universities to colleges and universities nationwide online. A total of 1,968 responses were collected, and 1,903 valid responses were obtained after cleaning. Among them, 771 are male, and 1,132 are female, accounting for 40.5% and 59.5% respectively. There were 230 responses from colleges and universities that will be developed into world-class educational institutions, accounting for 12.1%, 805 from universities which focus on building their preponderant disciplines into first-rate ones[1], accounting for 42.3%, and 868 from other colleges or universities, accounting for 45.6%.

The questionnaire consists of three parts: The first part investigates the participants' demographic features, including gender, university, major, grade, academic performance, blended learning experience, and curriculum type preference. The second part investigates students' cognition of blended learning, the design of blended learning and students' learning needs in different fields. Among them, the investigation on students' cognition of blended learning is mainly to analyze the teaching effect, interactive effect and learning gains by comparing different learning modes. The design of blended learning mainly includes nine aspects, which are course resources, learning interest, self-learning ability, learning methods, information technology capability, learning tasks, course difficulty, problem resolution, and course arrangements. In addition, students' learning needs with the choice of blended learning, it mainly includes major course learning, preparing for entrance examination such as postgraduate entrance examination, employment training, language learning, certificate examination guidance, etc. The third part is designed to understand the students' willingness to take a blended course. The question in the questionnaire is "Are you willing to take a blended course in the future?" (Table 1).

In this study, Cronbach Alpha coefficient was used to estimate the internal consistency reliability of the questionnaire, with the overall alpha coefficient of the questionnaire being 0.951, indicating good reliability. After KMO and Bartlett's tests, the KMO value of the scale is 0.985 ($df = 2485$, $Sig = 0.00 < 0.01$), with a good structural validity. The Principal Component Analysis is adopted. The characteristic root is greater than 1, 11 factors appear after the rotation of the maximum variance, and the cumulative contribution rate of the variance reaches 78.418%.

[1] In 2017, Chinese authorities released a selected list of universities and colleges, which will participate in the country's construction plan of world-class universities and first-class disciplines. According to the list jointly released by the Ministry of Education (MOE), the Ministry of Finance (MOF), and the National Development and Reform Commission (NDRC), 42 universities and colleges will be developed into world-class educational institutions, while 95 universities will focus on building their preponderant disciplines into first-rate ones.

Table 1. The description of the variable.

Construct	Variable	Items design
Demographic features	Gender	Male; Female (benchmark)
	Major	Humanities; Science, Agriculture or Medicine; Social science; Engineering (benchmark)
	Class standing	Postgraduate; Senior; Junior; Sophomore; Freshman (benchmark)
	University level	World-class universities; World-class discipline universities; General universities (benchmark)
	GPA ranking	Top 10%; 10%–25%; 25%-50%; The later50%(benchmark)
	Elective experience	Have you participated in blended learning (No as the benchmark)
	Type Preference	Blended learning; Online learning; Face-to-face learning (benchmark)
Cognition	Teaching effects	Blended learning; Online learning; Face-to-face learning (benchmark)
	Interaction effects	Blended learning; Online learning; Face-to-face learning (benchmark)
	Learning gains	Blended learning; Online learning; Face-to-face learning (benchmark)
Design	Course resources	Expanding curriculum resources (No as the benchmark)
	Learning interest	Stimulating learning interest (No as the benchmark)
	Self-learning ability	Cultivating self-learning ability (No as the benchmark)
	Learning methods	Promoting the change of learning methods (No as the benchmark)
	Technology capability	Strengthening information technology capabilities (No as the benchmark)
	Learning tasks	Learning tasks are too heavy (No as the benchmark)
	Course difficulty	Online courses are difficult (No as the benchmark)
	Problem resolution	Learning problems are difficult to solve in time (No as the benchmark)
	Course arrangements	Course arrangements are unreasonable(No as the benchmark)

(*continued*)

Table 1. *(continued)*

Construct	Variable	Items design
Demands	Major course learning	Do you need blended learning in this field? (No as the benchmark)
	Preparing for the entrance examination	Do you need blended learning in this field? (No as the benchmark)
	Employment training	Do you need blended learning in this field? (No as the benchmark)
	Language learning	Do you need blended learning in this field? (No as the benchmark)
	Certificate examination guidance	Do you need blended learning in this field? (No as the benchmark)
Willingness	Choosing willingness	Are you willing to take a blended course in the future? (No as the benchmark)

4 Results

4.1 The Basic Situation of Blended Learning in Chinese Colleges and Universities

The implication of blended learning in Chinese colleges and universities is still in its infancy. According to the data, blended courses are not commonly offered in colleges and universities. Forty-five per cent of the students are not sure whether their universities offer blended courses, seven percent of the students explicitly state that their university does not offer any blended courses. Only 48% of students believe that their universities offer blended courses. Meanwhile, the participation proportion of students in blended learning is relatively low. Fifty-nine point seven percent of the students said that they do not have any experience in participation in blended learning. As to the students who have participated in blended learning, most of them only took 1 to 2 courses, resulting in a limited understanding of blended learning. Among the students investigated, 33.8% for "Never heard about the blended learning", 43.5% for "Know a little about the blended learning", 18.8% for "Know quite a lot about the blended learning", and only 3.9% for "Know much about the blended learning" (Table 2).

4.2 Comparative Analysis of Students' Views on Different Learning Models

It is worth noting that although with the poor proportion of blended courses offered as well as low participation and understanding in blended learning, students still show enthusiasm for this model. Compared with the traditional face-to-face learning model and online learning model, more than half of the students show their preference for the blended learning model. The participants were asked to compare the traditional face-to-face learning, online learning, and blended learning in terms of teaching effect, academic

Table 2. Description of blended learning setting and situation of students' engagement.

Whether your universities offer blended courses?	Don't know	Don't offer	Offer a small portion	Offer a large portion
	856(45%)	133(7%)	773(40.6%)	141(7.4%)
Do you know what blended learning is?	Never heard	Know a little	Know quite a lot	Know much
	644(33.8%)	827(43.5%)	357(18.8%)	75(3.9%)
How many blended courses have you taken?	Zero	One	Two	Three and more
	1137(59.7%)	256(13.5%)	278(14.6%)	232(12.2%)

tasks, teacher-student interaction and learning gains. The survey shows that students gave high response to blended learning. Among them, 47% hold that blended learning is more effective, and 42% believe that they have gained a lot from blended learning. As to the amount of learning tasks, it is believed that the proportion of traditional face-to-face learning and blended learning having a large task burden both exceed 30%, so blended teaching may not be easy. As to the teacher-student interaction, students hold that the traditional learning model is better than the blended learning model, for they generally doubt that whether effective interaction between teachers and students can be realized online (Table 3).

Table 3. Comparative analysis of students' views on different learning models.

	Traditional face-to-face learning	Online learning	Blended learning	Uncertain
Which mode do you like?	644(33.8%)	131(6.9%)	961(50.5%)	167(8.8%)
Which mode has better teaching effect?	721(37.9%)	111(5.8%)	895(47%)	176(9.2%)
Which mode has the largest task burden?	622(32.7%)	354(18.6%)	594(31.2%)	333(17.5%)
Which mode has a better interactive effect?	1114(58.5%)	116(6.1%)	548(28.8%)	125(6.6%)
Which mode did can students achieve more learning gains?	768(40.4%)	127(6.7%)	800(42%)	208(10.9%)

4.3 Analysis of Factors Influencing Students' Willingness to Choose Blended Learning

The binary logistic regression equation is used to analyze the influencing factors of students' choice of blended learning in higher education, with the Cox & Snell R square and Nagelkerke R square of the regression equation is 0.214 and 0.414, respectively, and the results are shown in Table 4.

Table 4. Binary logistic regression analysis of blended course choice willingness.

Independent variable	B	Exp (B)
Gender (Female as the benchmark)	−.537	.585**
World-class discipline universities (General university as the benchmark)	−.298	.742
World-class universities	−.231	.794
Science, Agriculture or Medicine (Engineering as the benchmark)	−.434	.648
Social science	−.133	.875
Humanities	−.456	.634
Postgraduate (Freshman as the benchmark)	.038	1.039
Senior and above	−.112	.894
Junior	−.353	.702
Sophomore	−.476	.621
Top 10%(The later 50% as the benchmark)	.341	1.407
10%–25%	.451	1.570
25%–50%	.102	1.108
Elective experience of blended courses (No experience as the benchmark)	.445	1.561*
Prefer online learning (Traditional face to face learning as the benchmark)	.692	1.998
Prefer blended learning	1.675	5.337***
Online learning effect (Traditional face to face learning as the benchmark)	.286	1.331
Blended learning effect	.610	1.841*
Online learning interaction	.41	1.152
Blended learning interaction	.120	1.128
Online learning gains	−.668	.513
Blended learning gains	.737	2.089**
Expanding curriculum resources(No as the benchmark)	1.414	4.114***
Stimulating learning interest	.882	2.416***
Cultivating self-learning ability	.617	1.853**

(continued)

Table 4. (*continued*)

Independent variable	B	Exp (B)
Promoting the change of learning methods	.595	1.813**
Strengthening information technology capabilities	.368	1.445
Overburdened learning tasks	−.862	.423***
Difficult online courses	−.606	.546**
Untimely problem resolution	−.197	.822
Unreasonable course arrangements	−1.189	.305***
Major course learning (No demand as the benchmark)	1.138	3.119***
Preparing for the entrance examination	.395	1.485*
Employment training	.543	1.721**
Language learning	.068	1.070
Certificate examination guidance	.203	1.225
Constant	−.765	.466

Notes: ***represents $P < 0.01$, **represents $P < 0.05$, *represents $P < 0.1$

In terms of demographic features, a gender difference shows in the choice of blended learning, with male students 41.5% less likely than female students to choose blended learning. The experience of participating in blended learning has an impact on students' choices. The probability that students with participation experience are willing to choose blended learning in the future is 56.1% higher than that of students without experience. The preference for learning mode also influences the choice of students. Compared with the traditional face-to-face learning mode, students who prefer blended learning have a higher probability of choosing this model.

In terms of curriculum cognition, compared with the traditional face-to-face learning model, students who believe that the blended learning model has a better effect are 84.1% more likely to continue to choose such mode in the future; students who believe that they have benefited a lot from blended learning are also more likely to choose such mode.

In terms of curriculum design, according to the data, blended learning has a great attraction to students in terms of enriching curriculum resources, stimulating learning interest, cultivating self-learning ability, and promoting the change of learning methods. The obvious effect of blended learning in these aspects may significantly improve the probability of students to choose this model. While the overburdened learning tasks, difficult online courses, unreasonable curriculum arrangements and other problems in blended learning will affect the probability of students to choose in the future.

In terms of curriculum demands, students with demands on the instruction of specialized courses and entrance examinations, as well as employment training and other fields are more willing to choose blended learning, indicating that students hope to improve their learning effect in these fields through blended learning.

5 Discussions

Chinese students have a high acceptance of blended learning, and colleges or universities have the conditions to offer a wide range of blended courses. According to the data, although students have a low level of understanding and participation in blended learning, nearly half of them hold a positive attitude towards it, with the idea that blended learning can provide them with good learning effect and gains, and tend to choose blended learning in the future. The high acceptance of students towards blended learning lays a foundation for the large-scale popularization of blended learning in colleges and universities [20].

Demographic features influence students' willingness to choose blended learning. On the one hand, compared with male students, female students are more inclined to choose blended learning. Some researchers have found that most female students work harder than male students in online learning and participate positively in online learning activities according to curriculum demands or teachers' suggestions [22], reflecting that female students may be better than male students in time management, learning initiative and participation in the learning process. Therefore, female students are more adaptable to blended learning and show a stronger willingness to choose this model. On the other hand, compared with students who have no experience in participating in blended learning, students with participation experience are more inclined to take blended courses. This research also shows that students' attitudes become more positive after participating in blended learning, and they have formed a clearer understanding of blended learning. Blended learning meets students' learning needs well. Students have experienced the learning effect of blended learning personally and achieved a high degree of satisfaction. This result conforms to the theoretical explanation of the impact of such factors as customer expectations, overall perceived quality and perceived value on customer satisfaction in the customer satisfaction index [23].

Students' cognition influences their willingness to choose blended learning. People who hold a positive attitude towards blended learning are more inclined to attend blended courses. Statistics in this study indicate that students who think that blended learning has a good effect, and have gained a lot from it are more inclined to choose blended learning in their future studies. The technology acceptance model can explain the phenomenon of college students' strong willingness to choose blended learning due to their high recognition of this mode. The model points out that the higher a person's recognition of the use of technology to improve their performance, the more inclined they are to use such technology [24]. Obviously, the cognition of blended learning will affect students' value judgment and future choices, which also confirms Ron Owston's research that students' attitude towards blended learning is closely related to their academic performance and curriculum choices [14].

The design of the curriculum structure will affect students' choice of blended learning. Whether the blended learning mode can achieve better teaching effect depends on the curriculum design. The only well-designed curriculum can attract students to participate in blended learning. The students' willingness to participate in different types of blended learning also depends on the curriculum design. The study finds that scientific and reasonable curriculum design is often favoured by students. In general, the students hold expectations towards blended learning to change the traditional learning mode. Students are fond of learning methods with flexibility, free time arrangement and diversified curriculum resources. However, students do not want blended learning to increase their learning tasks and academic burden, which is a challenge to the reform of education. As Pirkko Jokinen and Irma Mikkonen argued, teachers have to consider the issue in curriculum design. Only the problems in curriculum design are solved can students more actively choose and participate in blended learning [25].

Students' learning needs can also affect their willingness to choose blended learning. The data shows that students tend to choose blended learning in the fields of major course learning, preparing for entrance examination such as postgraduate entrance examination or employment training. Through interviews, it is found that students tend to choose the face-to-face mode in language learning, and online mode in skills training, respectively. When students were choosing a learning mode, they will take the following factors into consideration: which field the knowledge belong to, the degree of mastery required, the time, effort and cost they need to invest, and the learning outcomes. Although students are more inclined to choose blended learning for their compulsory subjects, preparing for an entrance examination or employment training they may have different learning motivation. Student believe that face-to-face learning can effectively solve their puzzles and inspire them to think deeply through interaction with teachers when you study their compulsory subjects. However, Massive Open Online Courses (MOOCs) are rich and varied, and online courses can support repeated learning, which is conducive to mastering professional knowledge. When they need to prepare for the entrance examination and employment, students tend to choose blended learning model as the model seems to be more efficiently, and also hope to obtain practical experience and suggestions through face-to-face communication to help them make scientific and reasonable decisions. In language learning, students generally believe that the greatest difficulty lies in improving listening and speaking ability and practical application of language. Face to face learning method is more convenient for the effective interaction between teachers and students and helps students overcome obstacles in listening and speaking. For the skill training courses, students are more inclined to use the form of online learning because of its flexibility and avoidance of conflicts with daily learning activities and its fast-track to complete the courses within a short time.

6 Conclusion

This paper aims to analyze students' willingness to choose blended learning and its influencing factors. As an important measure to optimize the teaching environment, blended learning not only needs to consider the requirements of the government and the position of teachers but also needs to listen to the voice of students. In the process of education, students are no longer passive subjects and have the right to choose learning model. For colleges and universities, only when they truly understand the demands of students can they provide appropriate education modes. Therefore, it is necessary to analyze the demands for blended learning from the perspective of students.

According to the study, although most students have no experience in participating in blended learning and know a little about it, they generally have a positive attitude to the blended learning model. Compared with the traditional face-to-face learning, students believe that blended learning has a better effect and can benefit more from it, reflecting that the students' expectation to change the traditional learning mode. The students' perceptions of significantly affects their willingness to choose the blended learning model. Students relatively admiring blended learning are more inclined to choose this mode in the future. Compared with online learning and traditional face-to-face classroom learning, blended learning can better meet the demands of students for compulsory courses learning, preparing for postgraduate entrance examination and employment. It should be pointed out that whether blended learning can achieve better effect depends on the design of blended courses. Therefore, the teaching reform of colleges and universities should be guided by the needs of students, scientifically design blended learning to improve the quality of education.

Acknowledgment. This study has been supported by Peking University 2020 novel coronavirus–infected pneumonia prevention and control (special) project "Research on Learning Mechanisms and Key Technologies to Improve the Quality of Online Education "(No. 35), and 2019 Beijing higher education undergraduate teaching reform and innovation project "Relying on High-Quality International Resources to Enhance the Ability of Cultivating Innovative Talents–Taking BDIC as an Example" (No. 162). The authors are grateful to Prof. Junjie Shang from Peking University for his supervision to the current research.

References

1. Johnson, L., Adams, B.S., Cummins, M., et al.: The NMC Horizon Report: 2013 Higher Education Edition. Report. The New Media Consortium, Austin (2013)
2. Jin, H., Shen, N.L., Wang, M.Y.: Key trends and significant challenges in horizon report: development and analysis: based on the 2015–2019 annual report (higher education edition) [《地平线报告》之关键趋势与重大挑战:演进与分析--基于 2015-2019 年高等教育版]. J. Distance Educ. **37**(4), 24–32. (in Chinese)
3. Horn, M.B., Staker, H.: Blended: Using Disruptive Innovation to Improve Schools [混合式学习：用颠覆式创新推动教育革命]. China Machine Press, Beijing (2015). (in Chinese)
4. Feng, X.Y., Wang, R.X., Wu, Y.J.: A literature review on blended learning: based on analytical framework of blended learning [国内外混合式教学研究现状述评--基于混合式教学的分析框架]. J. Distance Educ. **35**(3), 15–26 (2018). (in Chinese)
5. Bliuc, A.M., Casey, G., Bachfischer, A., et al.: Blended learning in vocational education: teachers' conceptions of blended learning and their approaches to teaching and design. Aust. Educ. Res. **39**(2), 237–257 (2012)
6. Garrison, D.R., Kanuka, H.: Blended learning: uncovering its transformative potential in higher education. Int. High. Educ. **7**(2), 95–105 (2004)
7. Graham, C.R.: Blended learning systems: definition, current trends, and future directions. In: Bonk, C.J., Graham, C.R. (eds.) Handbook of Blended Learning: Global Perspectives, Local Designs, pp. 3–21. Pfeiffer Publishing, San Francisco (2006)
8. Chen, C.J., Wang, H.: The effectiveness of blended learning and e-learning on student learning outcomes: a meta-analysis of 47 experimental and quasi-experimental studies [混合学习与网上学习对学生学习效果的影响--47 个实验和准实验的元分析]. Open Educ. Res. **19**(2), 69–78 (2013). (in Chinese)
9. Isti'anah, A.: The effect of blended learning to the students' achievement in grammar class. Indones. J. Eng. Educ. **4**(1), 16–30 (2017)

10. Rockman, et al.: ED PACE Final Report: Submitted to West Virginia Department of Education (2007). https://rockman.com/docs/downloads/edpacefinalreport.pdf. Accessed 10 Jan 2020
11. Yen, S.C., Lo, Y., Lee, A., et al.: Learning online, offline, and in-between: comparing student academic outcomes and course satisfaction in face-to-face, online, and blended teaching modalities. Educ. Inf. Technol. **23**(5), 2141–2153 (2018)
12. Du, S.C., Fu, Z.T.: Blended learning and its empirical research based on MOOC [基于MOOC的混合式学习及其实证研究]. Chi. Educ. Technol. **36**(12), 129–133 + 145 (2016). (in Chinese)
13. Vaughan, N.: Perspectives on blended learning in higher education. Int. J. E-learn. **6**(1), 81–94 (2007)
14. Owston, R., York, D., Murtha, S.: Student perceptions and achievement in a university blended learning strategic initiative. Int. High. Educ. **18**, 38–46 (2013)
15. Osgerby, J.: Students' perceptions of the introduction of a blended learning environment: an exploratory case study. Acc. Educ. **22**(1), 85–99 (2013)
16. Du, S.C.: The Realization Path and Effect Evaluation of Blended Learning in the Context of MOOC [MOOC背景下混合式学习的实现 路径与效果评价研究]. Doctoral Dissertation (2017). http://cdmd.cnki.com.cn/Article/CDMD-10019-1017164583.htm. Accessed 15 Jan 2020
17. Du, S.C., Fu, Z.T.: Research on influencing factors of blended learning acceptance [混合式学习接受度的影响因素研究]. Chi. Educ. Technol. **38**(6), 128–133 (2018). (in Chinese)
18. Emanuel, R.C., Potter, W.J.: Do students' style preferences differ by grade level, orientation toward college, and academic major? Res. High. Educ. **33**(3), 395–414 (1992)
19. Zhou, H.T., Jing A.L., Li, Z.J.: Analysis of undergraduates learning strategies and factors in China [大学生学习策略使用水平及其影响因素分析]. Chi. High. Educ. Res. **29**(4), 25–30 (2014). (in Chinese)
20. Du, S.C.: Research on Blended Learning [混合式学习研究]. China Social Sciences Publishing House, Beijing (2018). (in Chinese)
21. He, W.T., Yang, K.C., Wang, Y.P.: A case study on instructional application of media technology based on IIS map [基于IIS图分析的媒体技术教学应用研究的个案分析]. Chi. Educ. Technol. **37**(4), 48–53 + 66 (2017). (in Chinese)
22. Li, Y., Ma, L., Guan, W.: A Study on the correlation between college students' online learning behavior and personality traits [大学生在线学习行为与人格特征的相关性研究]. Chi. J. ICT Educ. **21**(17), 18-21 (2016). (in Chinese)
23. Knutson, B.J., Singh, A.J., Yen, H.H., et al.: Guest satisfaction in the U.S. lodging industry using the ACSI model as a service quality scoreboard. J. Qual. Assur. Hosp. Tour. **4**(3–4), 97–118 (2004)
24. Davis, F.D.: Perceived usefulness, perceived ease of use, and user acceptance of information technology. MIS Q. **13**(3), 319–340 (1989)
25. Pirkko, J., Irma, M.: Teachers' experiences of teaching in a blended learning environment. Nurs. Educ. Pract. **13**(6), 524–528 (2013)

Identifying Multilevel Factors Influencing ICT Self-efficacy of K-12 Teachers in China

Di Wu, Chi Zhou, Caiyun Meng, and Min Chen(✉)

National Engineering Research Center for E-Learning, Central China Normal University, 152 Luoyu Road, Wuhan, Hubei, China
minchen@mail.ccnu.edu.cn

Abstract. Teacher self-efficacy of information and communication technology (ICT) has an important impact on ICT-based teaching. Teacher ICT self-efficacy is not only influenced by their individual characteristics, but also by various environmental conditions provided by their schools. Studies on teacher ICT self-efficacy have focused on factors at the teacher level, however, have overlooked school environments. To investigate the impact of school environments and teacher characteristics on teacher ICT self-efficacy, this study used a multilevel approach to analyze data from 7629 teachers in 1222 primary and secondary schools in China. The results show that both teacher-level factors and school-level factors contribute to K-12 teacher ICT self-efficacy. Among teacher-level factors, teachers' gender, ICT use, perceived ease of use of ICT and perceived usefulness of ICT make a difference in ICT self-efficacy. Among school-level factors, school type, ICT policy, and internet access are the important factors that impact teacher ICT self-efficacy.

Keywords: ICT self-efficacy · Influencing factor · Multilevel analysis · Large scale survey · Chinese teachers · K-12 education

1 Introduction

The question of how to effectively integrate information and communication technology (ICT) into education has received much attention. Some researchers have explored factors that may influence ICT-based teaching, such as access to technology [1], attitude towards technology [2] and ICT self-efficacy [3]. Among these factors, teacher ICT self-efficacy, which can be understood as their person-al judgment about their capability to adopt ICT to teaching practice [3, 4], plays an important role in improving ICT-based teaching [5, 6]. Teachers with high ICT self-efficacy express greater personal interest in web-based professional development opportunities to improve their ICT teaching [7]. These teachers are often more confident in using ICT for teaching, and more frequently use ICT in teaching activities and often tend to think of how to achieve effective integration of ICT and curriculum in ICT-based lesson designs in class [8]. Improving teacher ICT self-efficacy may enhance the quality of ICT-based teaching [6].

Identifying factors that influence teacher ICT self-efficacy in teaching practice is of great importance. Researchers have explored the influencing factors of teacher self-efficacy in using ICT in the classes [6, 9], however, some findings remain inconsistent.

S. K. S. Cheung et al. (Eds.): ICBL 2020, LNCS 12218, pp. 303–314, 2020.
https://doi.org/10.1007/978-3-030-51968-1_25

For example, López-Vargas et al. surveyed 208 teachers in Colombia and found a significantly negative association between the age and computer self-efficacy of teachers [9]. Anna and Dina, however, surveyed 367 teachers in the Republic of Cyprus and indicated that age is not related to teachers' confidence level in exploiting ICT for teaching [10]. This may be because teachers are in different teaching and ICT contexts (e.g., schools, resources, and policy constraints) [11, 12]. Indeed, some researchers have found that school-level environment may impact the thought, perception, attitude and behavior of teachers, and therefore may influence their ICT self-efficacy [5, 13].

Studies on factors influencing ICT self-efficacy are mostly focused on teacher-level factors, while they overlook the larger educational and social contexts [11, 14]. Therefore, to comprehensively explore the influencing factors of teacher ICT self-efficacy, this study investigates both school-level and teacher-level factors using a multilevel method. The result of this study has positive significance for improving teacher ICT self-efficacy and facilitating teacher ICT-based teaching.

2 Theoretical Background

2.1 ICT Self-efficacy

ICT self-efficacy is rooted in self-efficacy, which was proposed by Bandura [15]. Self-efficacy is defined as a personal judgment about one's capability to adopt certain behaviors and actions to accomplish certain objectives and expected outcomes [14, 15]. It can enhance human accomplishment and well-being, help determine how much effort people will expend on a behavior, how long they will persevere when confronting obstacles and how resilient they will be in face of adverse situations. ICT self-efficacy is based on a formed sense of self-efficacy and represents its fundamental elements applied in the field of use and mastery of ICT. In this case, Aesaert and van Braak defined ICT self-efficacy as personal self-perceived measure of ICT competence [16]. In this study, ICT self-efficacy is considered as the personal judgment about one's competence to adopt ICT to teaching practice.

2.2 Factors Related to ICT Self-efficacy

Teacher ICT self-efficacy develops through the compound effects of factors at school and teacher levels, and school-level factors provide conditions for the operation of teacher-level factors [17]. Following the previous studies, teacher level factors are categorized into background and ICT-related factors, and school level factors are categorized into structural and cultural factors [11, 12]. These four types of factors are discussed in the following.

Teacher Background Factors. Teacher background factors include gender and age. Research has not produced conclusive results about the relationship between gender and ICT self-efficacy [16]. For example, Durndell and Haag found males tend to report greater computer self-efficacy than females [18], while Sang et al. proposed there is no significant difference between male and female preservice teachers' computer self-efficacy [19]. Findings concerning age are also inconsistent. For example, Liang and Tsai found that age negatively affects Internet self-efficacy [20]; on the contrary, Tondeur et al. indicated age is not related to self-perceived ability to use ICT [21].

Teacher ICT-Related Factors. ICT use, perceived ease of ICT use and perceived usefulness of ICT are regarded as important factors that influence ICT self-efficacy. ICT use refers to teachers' use of specific ICT applications in teaching. Perceived ease of ICT use means the extent to which teachers feel comfortable about using computers, while perceived usefulness of ICT means how helpful teachers think of ICT. Mcilroy et al. suggested that people who regularly use ICT have higher self-efficacy than those who do not [22]. Tondeur et al. found that teachers' attitudes towards ICT ease of use has a positive impact on their perceived ICT competence for educational practice [21]. Aesaert and van Braak indicated that ICT attitudes, including computer interest, confidence, and perceived usefulness, have a significant impact on ICT self-efficacy [16].

School Structural Factors. School structural factors, such as school type and ICT infrastructure and access may influence ICT self-efficacy. Hsu investigated the relationship between school type and teacher ICT self-efficacy and indicated that primary school teachers have higher self-efficacy in applying ICT to producing teaching materials and communicating [23]. Furthermore, ICT equipment and access (e.g., computers and Internet) provided by schools is a key factor in ICT integration, which seems to make a difference in ICT self-efficacy [16]. I. K. R. Hatlevik and Hatlevik found that lack of facilitation for using ICT by schools has a negative effect on teacher ICT self-efficacy [6].

School Cultural Factors. School cultural factors refer to school support for integrated ICT into teaching, including ICT policy and ICT related training. While research investigating the relationship between school cultural factors and teacher ICT self-efficacy is scarce, some researchers have investigated the impact of ICT policy on teachers' perceived ICT competence. For example, Tondeur et al. found teachers' perceptions of policy-related factors are significantly associated with ICT integration and teachers' usage of ICT, which may influence teachers' perceived ICT competence [12]. In addition to ICT policy, ICT related training may improve teacher ICT self-efficacy. For instance, Goktas and Demirel suggested the Blog-enhanced version of the ICT training course have a positive influence on teachers' perceived ICT competence [24].

2.3 The Conceptual Framework

Drawing from previous research, we found that various factors at the school level and teacher level have a potential direct impact on teacher ICT self-efficacy. At the teacher level, teacher background factors and teacher ICT-related factors were considered. More specifically, teacher background factors included gender and age, and teacher ICT-related factors consist of ICT use, perceived ease of use of ICT and perceived usefulness of ICT. At the school level, school structural factors and school cultural factors were considered. In terms of school structural factors, school type, ICT infrastructure and access were involved. Concerning school cultural factors, ICT policy and ICT related training were included. In conclusion, to better understand the unique contribution of different factors to teacher ICT self-efficacy, this study has developed a conceptual framework which addresses the impact of a range of teacher-level factors and school-level factors on teacher ICT self-efficacy (see Fig. 1).

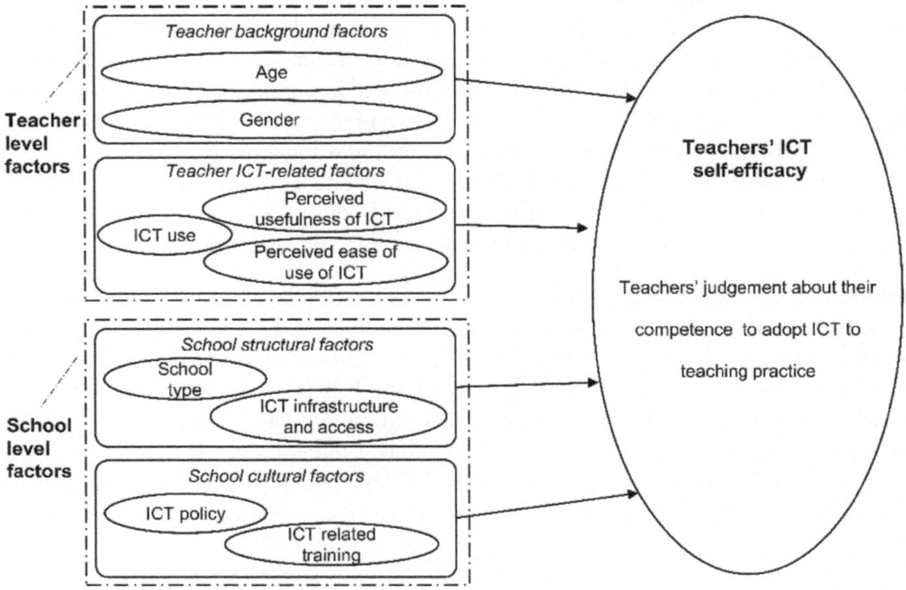

Fig. 1. A conceptual framework of the potential factors influencing teacher ICT self-efficacy.

3 Method

3.1 Participants

A sample of 7629 teachers from 1222 primary and secondary schools in China participated in the study. Of the schools, 54.8% were primary schools and 45.2% were secondary schools. Moreover, 51.6% teachers ($N = 3939$) taught grades 1–6 in 670 primary schools and 48.4% teachers ($N = 3690$) taught grades 7–12 in 552 secondary schools. Of the teachers, 38.7% were male and 61.3% were female. The teachers' age ranged from 21 to 60 years old, with an average age of 37.73 ($M = 37.73$, $SD = 7.95$). On average, teachers had 15.62 ($M = 15.62$, $SD = 8.85$) years of teaching experience, with a minimum of 1 and a maximum of 43 years. The subjects the teachers taught were as follows: Languages accounted for 23.7%, Arts accounted for 27.2%, Human Sciences accounted for 14.7%, and Mathematics and Sciences accounted for 34.4%.

3.2 Instruments

A survey was conducted to explore the impact of teacher-level factors and school-level factors on teacher ICT self-efficacy. The survey included two questionnaires:

one was used to gather information about teacher ICT self-efficacy and teacher-related characteristics, and the other was used to collect information about school-related characteristics.

Teacher ICT Self-efficacy. In the study, teacher ICT self-efficacy was investigated by eight 5-point Linkert items ranging from 1 (strongly disagree) to 5 (strongly agree). The ICT self-efficacy scale was adapted from Aesaert et al. [17]. An example item is "I am convinced that I can master the skills of ICT and curriculum integration." The scale showed a good internal consistency ($\alpha = 0.97$).

Teacher-Related Characteristics. In terms of teacher background characteristics, gender and age were investigated by multiple choice items. In terms of teacher ICT-related characteristics, ICT use was delineated into two categories: supportive ICT use and classroom ICT use [25]. Supportive ICT use, classroom ICT use, ICT ease of use, and ICT usefulness were investigated by 5-point Linkert items, and the more detailed information is shown below.

- The supportive ICT use scale was adapted from van Braak et al. [25], and the scale consisted of six 5-point Likert items (*never, every term, monthly, weekly, daily*). Internal consistency was determined by calculating Cronbach's alpha ($\alpha = 0.71$).
- The classroom ICT use scale was adapted from van Braak et al. [25], and the scale included four 5-point Likert items (*never, every term, monthly, weekly, daily*). The internal consistency of the scale was good ($\alpha = 0.82$).
- The ICT ease of use scale was adapted from Hwang et al. [26]. The scale included six 5-point Likert items (*strongly disagree, disagree, neither agree nor disagree, agree, strongly agree*). The internal consistency was determined by calculating Cronbach's alpha ($\alpha = 0.96$).
- The ICT usefulness scale was adapted from Hwang et al. [26]. The scale consisted of six 5-point Likert items (*strongly disagree, disagree, neither agree nor disagree, agree, strongly agree*). Calculation of Cronbach's alpha reflected a high level of internal consistency ($\alpha = 0.95$).

School-Related Characteristics. At the school level, ICT policy, ICT related training, school type, ICT infrastructure and access were investigated by multiple choice items, and detailed information is shown in Table 1. In detail, ICT policy refers to teachers' ICT competence standard policy; ICT infrastructure and access is about computers and internet.

3.3 Data Analysis

Since the school-level characteristics may influence the teacher-level characteristics [25], the participants of the study were not considered as completely independent. In other words, the 7629 teachers (level 1) of this study were nested in 1222 schools (level 2) and the data has a hierarchical structure. Hierarchical linear modelling (HLM) takes the nested nature of the data into consideration and can avoid statistical and interpretational

Table 1. Description of school-related characteristics.

School-related characteristics	Description
Cultural characteristics	
ICT policy	
- ICT competence standard	The number of policies related to teachers' ICT competence standard
ICT related training	ICT related training hours per teacher in the past year
Structural characteristics	
School type	Primary school or secondary school
ICT infrastructure and access	
- Computers	The ratio of computers to teachers numbers
- Internet	Internet bandwidth

problems [27]. Two-level hierarchical linear modelling was employed to explore both teacher and school-level factors that influence teacher ICT self-efficacy. The effects of teacher ICT-related characteristics, teacher background characteristics, school cultural characteristics, and school structural characteristics on teacher ICT self-efficacy were investigated. Adopting HLM, five models were tested: First, a null model without any explanatory variables was estimated to investigate whether differences in teacher ICT self-efficacy could be found at the teacher level and the school level. In the subsequent models, teacher ICT-related characteristics, teacher background characteristics, school cultural characteristics, and school structural characteristics were added as explanatory variables respectively. During the process, the non-significant factors were deleted from the models before a subset of new variables were added to the models.

4 Results

The analysis of the null model reveals whether it is essential to explore the effects of teacher ICT self-efficacy at multiple levels. In the following steps, teacher-level and school-level factors were added step by step to the model. In this study, only the detail results for the null model and the final model are discussed in the following.

4.1 Null Model

The results of the null model showed that both the within-school variance (teacher level $= 0.228$, $\chi^2 = 86.919$, $p < .001$) and between-school variance (school level $= 0.241$, $\chi^2 = 9327.609$, $p < .001$) differs significantly from zero. This indicated that it is essential to explore the effects of teacher ICT self-efficacy from two levels. Moreover, the results of the intraclass correlation coefficient (ICC) indicated that 51.4% of the variance in K-12 teacher ICT self-efficacy is attributed to differences between schools (ICC $= 0.241/(0.241 + 0.228) = .514$), whereas 48.6% of the variance is due to differences at the teacher level.

4.2 Final Model

After all of the non-significant factors were moved, the final model was presented in the study. As shown in Table 2, in the final model, both teacher-level and school-level factors have an impact on ICT self-efficacy. In detail, the relationship between each factor and ICT self-efficacy will be described in four aspects—teacher ICT-related factors, teacher background factors, school cultural factors, and school structural factors.

Table 2. Model estimates for the two-level analysis of teacher ICT self-efficacy.

	Null model	Final model
Fixed effect		
Intercept (cons)	4.168 (0.015) ***	3.848 (0.077) ***
Teacher ICT-related factors (level 1)		
Supportive ICT use		0.030 (0.013) *
Classroom ICT use		0.029 (0.014) *
ICT ease of use		0.565 (0.018) ***
ICT usefulness		0.301 (0.021) ***
Teacher background factors (level 1)		
Gender (man)		0.025 (0.007) ***
Age		–
School culture factors (level 2)		
ICT policy: ICT competence standard		0.159 (0.030) ***
ICT related training		–
School structure factors (level 2)		
School type		−0.101 (0.029) ***
ICT infrastructure and access: computers		–
ICT infrastructure and access: Internet		0.097 (0.025) ***
Random effect		
School level (between)	0.241 (0.491) ***	0.266 (0.516) ***
Teacher level (within)	0.228 (0.477) ***	0.045 (0.212) ***
Model fit		
Deviance statistics	12682.085	5029.690
χ^2		7652.39533
df		28
P		<.001
Reference		Null model

*p < 0.05, **p < 0.01, ***p < 0.001.

All of the teacher ICT-related factors had a significant impact on teacher ICT self-efficacy. In terms of the relationship between teachers' usage of ICT and teacher ICT self-efficacy, both supportive ICT use (B = 0.030, $t = 2.271$, $p < .05$) and classroom ICT use (B = 0.029, $t = 2.134$, $p < .05$) had positive impacts on teacher ICT self-efficacy. Another two factors were about teachers' beliefs: teachers' perceived ease of use of ICT and perceived usefulness of ICT. Both perceived ease of use of ICT (B = 0.565, $t = 31.007$, $p < .001$) and perceived usefulness of ICT (B = 0.301, $t = 14.639$, $p < .001$) had strong impacts on teacher ICT self-efficacy.

Regarding teacher background factors, teachers' age had no significant influence on ICT self-efficacy. While gender (B = 0.025, $t = 3.660$, $p < .001$) seemed to make a difference in teacher ICT self-efficacy—male teachers had higher ICT self-efficacy than female teachers.

With regard to school cultural factors, ICT related training hours did not seem to be related to teacher ICT self-efficacy. However, ICT competence standard as an ICT policy (B = 0.159, $t = 5.316$, $p < .001$) could significantly influence teacher ICT self-efficacy.

In terms of school structural factors, the relationship between various factors related to ICT infrastructures and self-efficacy is different. Internet access (B = 0.097, $t = 3.844$, $p < .001$) had a significant impact on teacher ICT self-efficacy. On the contrary, the ratio of the numbers of computers to teachers had no significant relationship with teacher ICT self-efficacy. In addition, school type (B = −0.101, $t = -3.473$, $p < .001$) influenced teacher ICT self-efficacy significantly. Primary school teacher ICT self-efficacy was higher than that of secondary school teachers.

5 Discussions

This study explored the impact of school and teacher level factors on the ICT self-efficacy of K-12 teachers. The results revealed a significant amount of variance at the school level explained teacher ICT self-efficacy, indicating that the ICT self-efficacy of teachers is not only influenced by individual factors but also influenced by factors that are related to the school environments. The effects of school and teacher level factors on teacher ICT self-efficacy are discussed below.

5.1 Teacher-Level Factors and Teacher ICT Self-efficacy

Teacher ICT self-efficacy is influenced by their teaching behavior, belief and background characteristics [28]. This study examined the relationship between these factors and teacher ICT self-efficacy. We found that teachers' usage of ICT, perceived ease of ICT use, perceived usefulness of ICT, and gender have significant impacts on their ICT self-efficacy. However, age is not related to teacher ICT self-efficacy.

ICT use is an important factor at the teacher level. This study used the supportive ICT use scale and the classroom ICT use scale to measure teachers' usage of ICT. We found both supportive ICT use and classroom ICT use have positive impacts on teacher ICT self-efficacy. This result suggests that as long as ICT is used for teaching, it could improve teacher ICT self-efficacy. This was consistent with the previous finding [14], which suggested that using software for educational purposes contributes substantially to an increase in computer self-efficacy. Teachers who often use ICT to assist teaching may be more proficient in using ICT and feel that the integration of ICT and teaching is not very difficult.

As for teachers' perceived ease of ICT use and perceived usefulness of ICT, the findings indicated that the easier teachers perceive the usage of ICT, the higher their ICT self-efficacy will be. Similarly, the more useful teachers perceive the usage of ICT, the higher their ICT self-efficacy will be. These positive relationships are consistent with previous studies [12, 21]. When teachers believe that the use of ICT is easier and more useful, they are more willing to use ICT [29], which in turn strengthens their self-efficacy.

In terms of teachers' background characteristics, gender is a strong predictor of teacher ICT self-efficacy. Male teachers have higher ICT self-efficacy than female teachers. This finding supports the previous finding that male's self-reported scores on computer self-efficacy are higher than female's [18]. On the contrary, teachers' age has no significant impact on ICT self-efficacy. Similarly, Gil-Flores et al. found when teacher ICT-related factors are considered, age turn out to be irrelevant in explaining ICT use [13].

5.2 School-Level Factors and Teacher ICT Self-efficacy

The findings indicated school type, ICT competence standard policy, and internet access have significant impacts on teacher ICT self-efficacy, while ICT-related training and the ratio of the number of computers to teachers have no significant impact on teacher ICT self-efficacy.

School type seems to have an impact on teacher ICT self-efficacy. The findings indicated that primary school teachers have higher ICT self-efficacy than secondary school teachers. Hsu and Kuan also found that junior high school teachers do not request students or parents using ICT as often as teachers in elementary school do [11]. A possible reason is that secondary school teachers bear much higher evaluation pressure than primary school teachers do, which makes their usage of ICT is lower than primary school teachers. Then less ICT use leads to weaker ICT self-efficacy.

Findings of the current study showed that the policies of teachers' ICT competence standard have great influences on teacher ICT self-efficacy. Similarly, Tondeur et al. indicated that teachers' perceptions of policy-related factors are significantly associated with teachers' usage of ICT [12]. The reason for the result may be that ICT competence standard policies could help teachers recognize their ICT competence more easily and support teachers' evaluation of their ICT self-efficacy.

ICT related training duration is not significantly associated with teacher ICT self-efficacy in this study. More specifically, it is a noteworthy finding that hours of ICT related training are not a predictor of teacher ICT self-efficacy. Similarly, Paraskeva et al. found that there is no correlation between previous training in computer use and computer self-efficacy [14]. Moreover, they think one of the possible reasons is that the way teachers are trained is not appropriate. As such, future research should use more factors to measure the effectiveness of ICT related training, such as training strategies.

In terms of ICT infrastructure and access, internet access has a significant impact on teacher ICT self-efficacy. The finding is in line with the previous study [11], which found that internet connectivity is essential to teacher's ICT integration. Insufficient bandwidth at school may make teachers feel that ICT teaching is not so easy or useful, which affects their ICT self-efficacy. On the contrary, computers have no significant impact on teacher ICT self-efficacy. Gil-Flores et al. found that computers for instruction do not display a statistically significant relationship with ICT use [13]. One possible reason is that if teachers only have computers and lack other information devices (e.g., software and tablets), they cannot carry out ICT-related teaching activities.

6 Conclusion

Currently, research on teacher ICT self-efficacy has focused almost exclusively on teacher-related characteristics but overlooked the larger educational and social context such as the school-level characteristics. The purpose of this study was to explore the extent to which certain teacher-level and school-level factors were associated with K-12 teacher ICT self-efficacy. To this end, factors were extracted from previous studies and classified into teacher-level factors (e.g., teacher ICT-related factors and teacher background factors) and school-level factors (e.g., school cultural factors and school structural factors). A multilevel analysis method was used to analyze the nest structural data of teachers' and schools' characteristics. The results indicated that K-12 teacher ICT self-efficacy should be considered as a two-level (teacher level and school level) phenomenon. In addition, at the school level, what matters the most is whether the development of teachers' ICT competence is considered in school policies, in other words, whether teachers receive encouragement and drive from the school.

There are some limitations with the current research. Firstly, the multilevel research on teacher ICT self-efficacy is a cross-sectional study, which means all the information is gathered at one single point of time. Future research along these lines could adopt a longitudinal approach to track changes of school-level factors and teacher-level factors related to ICT self-efficacy. Secondly, all information collected from teachers were self-reported data. Such a measurement may weaken the reliability of the results. Further research should try to measure teachers' characteristics more objectively. Finally, why the factors that were found in this study promote or hamper teacher ICT self-efficacy has not been fully analyzed. In other words, in-depth research (e.g., in-depth interview) is needed to unravel the reasons why the factors impact teacher ICT self-efficacy. In spite of these limitations, this study adds to the research on ICT self-efficacy, as it explores factors related to K-12 teacher ICT self-efficacy from a multilevel perspective.

Acknowledgments. This work was supported by the National Natural Science Foundation of China under Grant number 61907018. We would also like to thank all the teachers who participated in this investigation.

References

1. Pelgrum, W.J.: Obstacles to the integration of ICT in education: results from a worldwide educational assessment. Comput. Educ. **37**(1), 163–178 (2001)
2. Aslan, A., Zhu, C.: Investigating variables predicting Turkish pre-service teachers' integration of ICT into teaching practices. Br. J. Educ. Technol. **48**(2), 552–570 (2017)

3. Lemon, N., Garvis, S.: Pre-service teacher self-efficacy in digital technology. Teachers Teach. **22**(3), 387–408 (2015)
4. Han, I., Shin, W.S., Ko, Y.: The effect of student teaching experience and teacher beliefs on pre-service teachers' self-efficacy and intention to use technology in teaching. Teachers Teach. **23**(7), 829–842 (2017)
5. Hatlevik, O.E.: Examining the relationship between teachers' self-efficacy, their digital competence, strategies to evaluate information, and use of ICT at school. Scand. J. Educ. Res. **61**(5), 555–567 (2017)
6. Hatlevik, I.K.R., Hatlevik, O.E.: Examining the relationship between teachers' ICT self-efficacy for educational purposes, collegial collaboration, lack of facilitation and the use of ICT in teaching practice. Front. Psychol. **9**, 935 (2018)
7. Kao, C.P., Wu, Y.T., Tsai, C.C.: Elementary school teachers' motivation toward web-based professional development, and the relationship with Internet self-efficacy and belief about web-based learning. Teach. Teacher Educ. **27**(2), 406–415 (2011)
8. Kreijns, K., Van Acker, F., Vermeulen, M., Van Buuren, H.: What stimulates teachers to integrate ICT in their pedagogical practices? The use of digital learning materials in education. Comput. Hum. Behav. **29**(1), 217–225 (2013)
9. López-Vargas, O., Duarte-Suárez, L., Ibáñez-Ibáñez, J.: Teacher's computer self-efficacy and its relationship with cognitive style and TPACK. Improving Schools **20**(3), 264–277 (2017)
10. Anna, M., Dina, T.: Profiling of English language teachers as trainees in an online course and ensuing implications. Comput. Educ. **126**, 1–12 (2018)
11. Hsu, S., Kuan, P.Y.: The impact of multilevel factors on technology integration: the case of Taiwanese grade 1–9 teachers and schools. Educ. Tech. Res. Dev. **61**(1), 25–50 (2013)
12. Tondeur, J., Valcke, M., van Braak, J.: A multidimensional approach to determinants of computer use in primary education: teacher and school characteristics. J. Comput. Assist. Learn. **24**(6), 494–506 (2008)
13. Gil-Flores, J., Rodríguez-Santero, J., Torres-Gordillo, J.-J.: Factors that explain the use of ICT in secondary-education classrooms: the role of teacher characteristics and school infrastructure. Comput. Hum. Behav. **68**, 441–449 (2017)
14. Paraskeva, F., Bouta, H., Papagianni, A.: Individual characteristics and computer self-efficacy in secondary education teachers to integrate technology in educational practice. Comput. Educ. **50**(3), 1084–1091 (2008)
15. Bandura, A.: Self-efficacy: toward a unifying theory of behavioral change. Psychol. Rev. **84**(2), 191–215 (1977)
16. Aesaert, K., van Braak, J.: Exploring factors related to primary school pupils' ICT self-efficacy: a multilevel approach. Comput. Hum. Behav. **41**, 327–341 (2014)
17. Aesaert, K., van Braak, J., van Nijlen, D., Vanderlinde, R.: Primary school pupils' ICT competences: extensive model and scale development. Comput. Educ. **81**, 326–344 (2015)
18. Durndell, A., Haag, Z.: Computer self efficacy, computer anxiety, attitudes towards the Internet and reported experience with the Internet, by gender, in an East European sample. Comput. Hum. Behav. **18**(5), 521–535 (2002)
19. Sang, G., Valcke, M., van Braak, J., Tondeur, J.: Student teachers' thinking processes and ICT integration: predictors of prospective teaching behaviors with educational technology. Comput. Educ. **54**(1), 103–112 (2010)
20. Liang, J.C., Tsai, C.C.: Internet self-efficacy and preferences toward constructivist Internet-based learning environments: a study of pre-school teachers in Taiwan. Educ. Technol. Soc. **11**(1), 226–237 (2008)
21. Tondeur, J., Aesaert, K., Prestridge, S., Consuegra, E.: A multilevel analysis of what matters in the training of pre-service teacher's ICT competencies. Comput. Educ. **122**, 32–42 (2018)

22. Mcilroy, D., Sadler, C., Boojawon, N.: Computer phobia and computer self-efficacy: their association with undergraduates' use of university computer facilities. Comput. Hum. Behav. **23**(3), 1285–1299 (2007)
23. Hsu, S.: Developing a scale for teacher integration of information and communication technology in grades 1–9. J. Comput. Assist. Learn. **26**(3), 175–189 (2010)
24. Goktas, Y., Demirel, T.: Blog-enhanced ICT courses: examining their effects on prospective teachers' ICT competencies and perceptions. Comput. Educ. **58**(3), 908–917 (2012)
25. van Braak, J., Tondeur, J., Valcke, M.: Explaining different types of computer use among primary school teachers. Eur. J. Psychol. Educ. **19**(4), 407–422 (2004)
26. Hwang, G.J., Yang, L.H., Wang, S.Y.: A concept map-embedded educational computer game for improving students' learning performance in natural science courses. Comput. Educ. **69**, 121–130 (2013)
27. Hu, X., Gong, Y., Lai, C., Leung, F.K.S.: The relationship between ICT and student literacy in mathematics, reading, and science across 44 countries: a multilevel analysis. Comput. Educ. **125**, 1–13 (2018)
28. Krause, M., Pietzner, V., Dori, Y.J., Eilks, I.: Differences and developments in attitudes and self-efficacy of prospective chemistry teachers concerning the use of ICT in education. Eurasia J. Math. Sci. Technol. Educ. **13**(8), 4405–4417 (2017)
29. Terzis, V., Economides, A.A.: The acceptance and use of computer based assessment. Comput. Educ. **56**(4), 1032–1044 (2011)

Extending the COI Framework to K-12 Education: Development and Validation of a Learning Experience Questionnaire

Liyuan Wei, Yue Hu(✉), Mingzhang Zuo, and Heng Luo

School of Educational Information Technology,
Central China Normal University, Wuhan 430079, China
yuehu@mails.ccnu.edu.cn

Abstract. There has been a lack of theoretically framework and research instruments to explain and explore the complexity of learning experience among K-12 students in traditional classrooms. To address this research need, the present study tentatively developed and validated a presence questionnaire for K-12 classroom (PQ-K12) to examine learning experience through the interplay of three perceived presences, as informed by the community of inquiry (CoI) framework. The presence questionnaire was initially designed with 66 items and was administered among 200 primary school students in central China. A three-step validation process comprising item analysis, exploratory factor analysis, and confirmatory factor analysis were conducted sequentially, leading to the removal of 21 items from the overall scale. The revised questionnaire yielded a strong internal reliability and a moderate structural validity. The preliminary results of this study can inform the future revision of the PQ-K12 questionnaire and provide insights on the key characteristics of K-12 education.

Keywords: K-12 education · Learning experience questionnaire · Instrument validity · Community of inquiry · Exploratory factor analysis

1 Introduction

Students' perceived learning experience is an important construct for measuring the meaningfulness of learning outcome from student perspective [1] and can inform the optimal design of instruction in that specific context [2]. As suggested by humanistic educational theories [3], learners are legitimate and important source for evaluating their own learning, and the development of meaningful understanding of the self and perceived changes is an equally important educational goal. As a result, it is argued that to advance our understanding of education, a coherent theoretical framework must be developed to guide investigations into the research and practice of teaching and learning regardless of educational levels, tasks, and contexts.

Our review of recent literature has identified several theoretical frameworks for measuring the learning experience in the context of online higher education, which becomes increasingly popular for its convenience and accessibility for colleges worldwide [4].

S. K. S. Cheung et al. (Eds.): ICBL 2020, LNCS 12218, pp. 315–325, 2020.
https://doi.org/10.1007/978-3-030-51968-1_26

The most recognized framework is the community of inquiry (CoI) framework that employs a social-constructivist perspective to conceptualize online learning experience and suggests it unfolds in the interaction of three types of perceived presences [5]. Since its inception, the CoI framework and the subsequent survey instrument were extensively investigated with the assumptions of validity being empirically validated across disciplines [6].

While the CoI framework is widely acknowledged for its potential for measuring learning experience and diagnosing pedagogical design, it was developed for the unique context of online higher education [5] rather than the context of basic education that is mainly face-to-face. As a result, there has been a lack of theoretically sounding framework and research instruments to explain and explore the complexity of learning experience among K-12 students in traditional classrooms, and thus little is known regarding how higher-order thinking and social discourse are fostered in those classrooms.

With the belief that the key assumptions of CoI on social-constructivism and meaningful learning approaches still apply for basic education in traditional classrooms, this study attempted to extend the CoI framework to K-12 educational settings by designing and validating a learning experience questionnaire with expanded and slightly adjusted items informed by the CoI survey instrument [7]. The study results can cast insights on the applicability of the CoI framework in K-12 settings and can also provide an empirically validated self-assessment instrument that researchers can use to appraise learning process and diagnose pedagogical problems.

2 Theoretical Foundation

The development of the initial questionnaire was guided by the CoI framework proposed by Garrison et al. [8]. The framework guides the examination of the learning experience in terms of three types of perceived presences: teaching presence, social presence, and cognitive presence. The subcategories and content of the three dimensions are listed in Table 1 and are explained in below.

2.1 Dimension I: Teaching Presence

Teaching presence refers to the learners' perception of teaching behaviors to promote the achievement of learning goals and individual meaningful learning or outcomes. In K-12 settings, Due to their younger age, students lack the corresponding self-management skills and need teachers to help manage learning. Management is an important part of teaching. Therefore, this study added a management subcategory to conceptualize teaching presence as having four components based on Anderson, Rourke, Garrison, and Archer's study [9]: (1) Instructional design and organization, refers to the perception of teachers designing, planning, and implementing a course. Its core is everything related to the teaching process, such as teaching goals, teaching activities, teaching content, etc. In K-12 settings, too many or too complex teaching activities may exceed students' cognition, so teaching design and organization should be simple and easy to understand. (2) Facilitating discourse (originally called "building understanding"), it means that the teacher adopts a series of strategies to ensure students' interest, motivation, and

Table 1. The three-dimensions of perceived presence in K-12 education

Dimension	Subcategory and content
Teaching presence	• Design and organization [9] - Instructional content design - Manage teaching activities - Achieve teaching goals • Facilitating discourse [9] - Keep students involved - Stimulate student interest - Focus on discussion activities • Direct instruction [9] - Delivery of instructional content - Provide Feedback • Management - Maintain class discipline - Ensuring effective activities
Social presence	• Affective response [10] - Share something - help others - Play with others • Interactive response [10] - Agree or disagree others - Friendly interaction - Praise others • Cohesive response [10] - Sense of belonging - Tendency of collaboration
Cognitive presence	• Triggering event [11] - Desire for knowledge - Positive thinking • Exploration [11] - Active inquiry - Think about different perspectives • Integration [11] - Ability to analyze, integrate and summarize knowledge - Reflection and discussion • Resolution [11] - Use knowledge to solve problems - Applying knowledge to life

participation in active learning. It emphasizes keeping students focused and engaged. K-12 education is different from online education. It puts more emphasis on face-to-face engagement in discussions, which was not emphasized in the CoI framework. (3) Direct instruction, it means that teachers can use their professional knowledge to deliver instructional content to students. In K-12 settings, it is more about strategies that facilitate face-to-face knowledge transfer. (4) Management, it means that teachers adopt some strategies to maintain classroom order to ensure the implementation of teaching activities. Management is a key part of K-12 education. Teachers use teaching management to help students overcome learning difficulties in the teaching process.

2.2 Dimension II: Social Presence

Social presence is the ability of participants to identify with the community (e.g., course of study), communicate purposefully in a trusting environment, and develop inter-personal relationships by way of protecting their individual personalities [10]. The categories of social presence are affective expression, interactive response, and cohesive response. Affective expression refers to the feeling of intimacy, warmth, and belonging that students experience during social interaction. Interactive response is the ability to support or oppose the opinions and actions of others during the learning process. Cohesive response refers to a kind of emotion generated during the interaction between students and peers, which can shorten the psychological distance between students.

However, social presence in K-12 settings differs from the online higher education in learning environment and student age. In K-12 education, teachers mainly apply face-to-face teaching mode. Compared with online education, students in face-to-face teaching can easily feel the presence of classmates. Therefore, social presence in face-to-face instruction has new implications. Students in face-to-face classroom need to be encouraged to care about their peers and teachers during social collaboration in explicit and implicit forms. In addition, K-12 students are younger than college students, thus their social presence focused more on a sense of collectiveness. They also hope to feel warmth during the learning process and crave for the attention of teachers and peers.

2.3 Dimension III: Cognitive Presence

Cognitive presence refers to the ability of learners to build a cognitive level of meaning through continuous communication during the learning process. Garrison et al. [11] argued that cognitive presence in online learning is developed as the result of a four-phase process. These phases are: (1) a triggering event, where the desire to explore further knowledge; (2) exploration, where students can actively explore learning knowledge; (3) integration, where students can analyze, integrate and summarize knowledge (4) resolution, where students can use knowledge to solve problems. It is argued that participant interactions primarily reside in the first two phases and that moving beyond the exploration phase typically requires enhanced teaching presence to promote higher-level thinking among students [12, 13]. We believe cognitive presences in the K-12 settings and online higher education setting share plenty of similarities. For instance, they all want to stimulate students' interest in learning and be able to actively explore new knowledge. They all agree about the importance of higher-order thinking and knowledge transfer. Therefore, the assumptions of cognitive presence in the CoI framework also apply to the K-12 settings.

However, Shea and Bidjerano [14] suggest that presence included not only teaching, cognition and social presence, but also learning presence. They believe that learning presence represents self-efficacy and other cognitive, behavioral, and motivational structures that support self-regulation in online learning. They also believe that learning the existence may help to gain a more comprehensive understanding of the construction of knowledge in a technology-mediated environment, thereby expanding the descriptive and explanatory power of the CoI framework [15]. From the description of learning presence, we believe that the essence of learning presence is to better measure students' cognition, which is consistent with cognitive existence. Therefore, we decided to keep the original three dimensions of CoI to explore learning experience in K-12 education.

3 Questionnaire Design and Validation

3.1 Initial Questionnaire Design

Based on the aforementioned CoI framework, this study tentatively developed a presence questionnaire for K-12 classroom (PQ-K12) to examine learners' presence in K12 educational contexts. The questionnaire consists of four parts with a total of 66 initial questions. Part one includes 2 items that collect learners' personal data such as grade and school type. Part two includes 23 five-point Likert scale items that have learners rate statements regarding the four components of teaching presence as previously discussed. Part three of the questionnaire consists of 24 five-point Likert scale items, asking learners about the perceived social presence. Part four of the questionnaire includes 17 five-point Likert scale items, having learners rate statements regarding the four components of cognitive presence as previously discussed. The specific items and the measured constructs are shown in Fig. 1.

3.2 Questionnaire Validation

To ensure PQ-K12 with desirable survey reliability and validity, we conducted a pilot validation research and administered the initial questionnaire among 8 different elementary schools located in a city township in central China due to their representativeness of ordinary K-12 schools in China. A total of 189 valid questionnaires were collected, the majority of which were grade 3 and 4 students (63.5%), the rest were grade 5 and 6 students (36.5%). The questionnaire was distributed on site and immediately collected. Three major procedures of data analysis were conducted in this study: item analysis, exploratory factor analysis (EFA) and confirmatory factor analysis (CFA). Data collected were analyzed with SPSS for Windows Version 19.0. Item analysis was conducted first to ensure the reliability and quality of all the items of the PQ-K12, the items failed to meet the standards were deleted and data analysis in latter phases. Then exploratory factor analysis was conducted to further reduce items and verify the structure of the PQ-K12, the expected number of items was around 40 in order to leave space for further research. Finally, confirmatory factor analyses were employed to confirm the fit of the items contributing to its intended factors using AMOS (version 21.0), and the Cronbach's alpha was computed to ensure the internal consistency among the items.

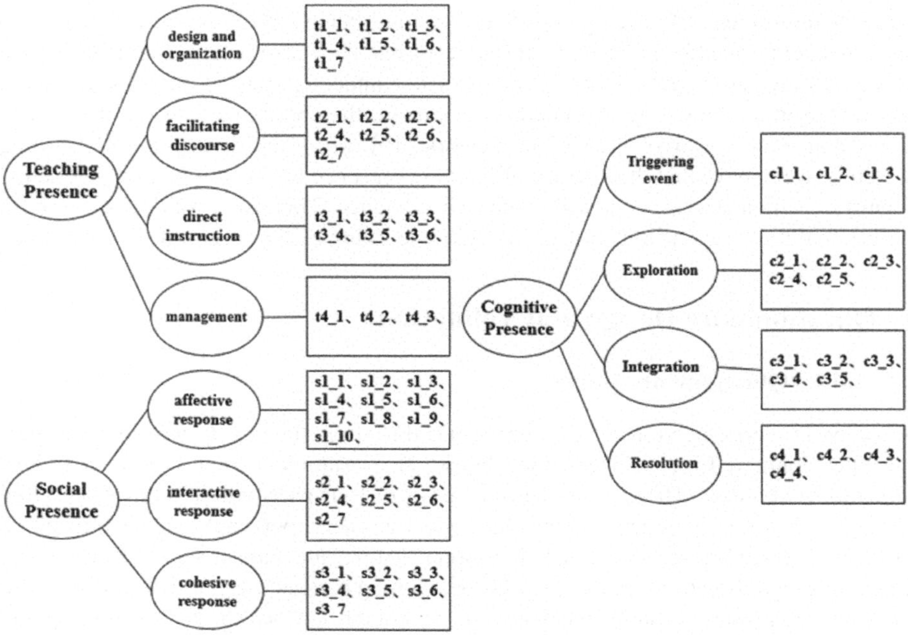

Fig. 1. The relationship between the Initial PQ-K12 items and the three types of presences.

3.3 Item Analysis

To ensure the quality of PQ-K12 questions, it should possess enough discriminating power and each item should be congruent with the overall PQ-K12 testing objectives. First, the critical ration method was used to divide the items into high scoring group and low scoring group: total scores of all items were calculated, and then 27% of the highest and lowest scorers were selected into two groups. The independent sample t-test was used to compute the discrimination between the two groups in each item. According to the significance and t value in this analysis, there were two items with t value below 3.0, if the t value is less than 3.0, it is considered that the discrimination is not up to the standard and should be deleted. Then, the correlation between each item and the total scores of the questionnaire was compared. Pearson correlation coefficients of all items ranged from 0.269 to 0.631, with 14 items yielding Pearson correlation coefficient lower than 0.4, indicating that they had no strong correlation with the total score. Those 14 items also contained the two items with t value less than 3.0, therefore were removed before the exploratory factor analysis.

3.4 Exploratory Factor Analysis

After removing 14 items that did not meet the standard of item analysis, exploratory factor analysis was conducted on the remaining 50 items. The correlation matrix showed that the questionnaire data were suitable for factor analysis with large correlation values mostly higher than 0.45. Bartlett's test of sphericity ($v2 = 5117.65$, $df = 2016$, $p < .001$)

and the Kaiser-Meyer-Olkin (KMO) measure (KMO = 0.848 > 0.8) also indicated that the statistical assumptions of EFA were met in this study. Based on the exploratory factor analysis results, items with small factor loading values and part of items with cross-loading were deleted. In order to further optimize the questionnaire in the later stage, after more than 20 attempts of deleting questions, 7 items (C2_5, s3_5, s3_6, s2_6, t2_5, s3_2, s1_7) were removed successively, and thus 43 items were finally retained. The results of component rotation matrix are shown in Table 1, factor loading value lower than 0.4 are not shown in the component column. As shown in the table, the three extracted components were considered as cognitive, social and teaching presence, as indicated by the guiding theoretical framework. There are some misplaced items between the components of social presence and teaching presence. As a result, the correctly assigned items were marked with "x" in the mark column, whereas the misplaced items were marked with "-", suggesting the presence measured by the items were not what they were initially designed to measure (Table 2).

3.5 Confirmatory Factor Analysis

After EFA, the test consisted of 43 items and its internal reliability was 0.939, as measured by Cronbach's alpha. we extracted three components from EFA results to construct the entire questionnaire model and 3 one-factor models to verify the fit between the questionnaire structure and the guiding theoretical framework. There were 13 items in teaching presence dimension, and 15 items each for social presence and cognitive presence dimension. Then confirmatory factor analyses were employed using AMOS. Based on the confirmatory factor analysis results, the Goodness of Fit Index (GFI), Bentler's Comparative Fit Index (CFI) and Tucker-Lewis Index (TLI) of each one-factor model were greater than 0.9, but the fit measures for the PQ-K12 model were lower than 0.9. Models with GFI, CFI and TLI values greater than 0.9 are considered as an acceptable fit, meaning the one-factor model has obtained acceptable fit index values, however, the PQ-K12 model is not acceptable with this result, we speculate that this result is due to some external factor such as insufficient sample size or, confusing item descriptions, or unclear theoretical construct. The results of Cronbach's alpha and the confirmatory factor analysis results are presented in Table 3.

Table 2. Dimension verification results of the intial PQ-K12 items based on component rotation matrix

Items	Match	Cognitive presence	Social presence	Teaching presence
c3_5. I often analyze, compare and summarize in class	×	.729		
c4_4. I know how to apply what I learned in class to real life	×	.697		
c4_3. I overcame the difficulty well and successfully completed the study task	×	.605		
c2_4. Discussions in and out of class can help me understand the classmates' point of view	×	.583		
c1_3. The content and activities in class often arouse my thinking	×	.543		
c3_4. In order to finish the task better, I adopted different information and perspectives	×	.524		
c4_2. I found a solution to the learning problem given in class and was able to solve it	×	.521		
c1_1. The teacher's questions in class increased my interest in the content	×	.514		
c4_1. I was able to clearly describe how to solve the learning problems given in class	×	.500		
c3_2. Learning activities was able to help me solve problems	×	.465		
c2_3. Search information was able to help me solve problems	×	.446		
s3_7. My classmates and I were able to work together to finish the task	–	.427		
c3_3. The discussion and reflection were able to help me better understand the content of this lesson	×	.425		
c3_1. Combined with the new knowledge, I was able better answer the questions in class	×	.416		
c2_1. I was willing to take the initiative to explore issues in class	×			
s2_2. My ideas were able to get the support of others in study	×		.629	
s2_1. I would supported others' point of view in the study	×		.601	
s1_9. I was willing to take the initiative to share my views with my classmates in study	×		.572	
t3_3. Teacher was able to help us focus our discussion and solve problems in study	–		.566	
t3_6. The teacher was able to summarize and summarize our speech or discussion	–		.557	
t2_6. The teacher was able to guide us through the discussion during the group discussion	–		.544	
s1_10. Students were willing to communicate with me in study	×		.518	
s2_3. I thought about what other people think in study	×		.516	
t2_7. The teacher was able to encourage us to take an active part in the discussion during the group discussion	–		.478	
s1_8. When I argued with my classmates, I could talk with my classmates gently	×		.416	
c2_2. I was willing to find all kinds of materials to solve problems in study	–			
s1_6. The teacher can spoke to me in a gentle voice	×			
t3_1. The teacher could tell me my examination and assignment result in time	–			
s3_1. I know everyone in our class	–			.618
t1_2. The teacher was able to tell us the curriculum goals clearly	×			.573
t2_3. The teacher was able to point out my shortcomings during the group discussion	×			.561

(continued)

Table 2. (*continued*)

Items	Match	Cognitive presence	Social presence	Teaching presence
t3_4. When I had difficulty in my study, the teacher could provide useful help	×		.407	.517
c1_2. Activities in class can arouse my curiosity	–			.493
t1_6. The teacher was able to organize quizzes	×			.476
t2_4. The teacher could help us solve the problem during the group discussion	×			.470
t4_3. When I had a conflict with my partner, the teacher was able to mediate in time	×			.468
s1_4. I was willing to share some things in my life with my classmates	–			.468
t1_1. The teacher could tell us the content of the lecture clearly	×			.455
t3_2. The teacher was able to tell me my strengths and weaknesses	×			.454
t4_1. The teacher could maintain the class order very well during the group discussion	×			.444
s2_5. I was willing to ask my classmates for advice in study	–			.417
t4_2. When my mind wandered, the teacher was able to remind me by word, gesture or eye contact	×			
s1_5. I was very happy when teacher praised me in class	–			

Table 3. The results of Cronbach's alpha and the confirmatory factor analysis

Model	Reliability	GFI	CFI	TLI
PQ-K12	0.939	0.778	0.835	0.826
Teaching presence	0.838	0.915	0.917	0.904
Social presence	0.846	0.931	0.939	0.927
Cognitive presence	0.885	0.918	0.944	0.934

4 Discussion and Conclusion

In this study, we developed a presence questionnaire for K-12 classroom (PQ-K12) that can be used to evaluate teaching and learning process in traditional classroom. Data analysis results prompted us to delete 21 items from original questionnaire, which ensures a strong reliability and structural validity (Cronbach's a = 0.939) for PQ-K12, which consists of a similar three dimensions of teaching presence, social presence, and cognitive presence. The statistical results offer interesting insights on the learning experience in K-12 settings, which are discussed in below.

Firstly, in the process of developing the extended questionnaire from the CoI framework, close attention was paid to the differences between online teaching and traditional classrooms, and the statistical results verify such differences accordingly. The items regarding technical support and self-directed learning in the CoI survey were either removed or revised, since they apply more to online learning and are deemed as inapplicable in PQ-K12. We found that items that emphasize teachers' authority (e.g., t1_2, t2_3) yielded a higher degree of factor loading in teaching presence, indicating that teachers have a more authoritative position in the traditional classroom. In contrast, learning atmosphere of online instruction is featured by more student agency and autonomy, relying less on the authoritative figure of teachers.

Secondly, with a sample size of 200 students, we managed to explore the initial validity of the questionnaire. From EFA results, we can see that several items designed for specific dimensions got mixed in the same dimension based on the factor loading values. In the dimensions of social presence, items such as t3_3, t3_6 and t2_6, originally designed for the dimension of teaching presence, were assigned into the dimension of social presence, possibly because the teaching activities in those items involved class discussion, which is considered as part of social learning. Similarly, cognitive activities (e.g., curiosity arousal) mentioned the item c1_2 got mixed in the dimension of teaching presence, as teachers often started a class with a triggering activity to inspire student interests. Our further analysis of the misplaced items revealed similar issues: the perceived learning experience depicted in those items can be interpreted from more than one dimensions. This finding inspired us to reconsider the design and wording of these items and their dimensions, in which the structure of the presence questionnaire needs to be adjusted to deal with overlapping items.

Lastly, the items with low factor loading values (less than 0.4) indicate that they might be in applicable for the mainstream mode of K-12 education. For example, item c2_1 (I am willing to take the initiative to explore issues in class) suffers from low factor loading in all three dimensions, suggesting that student autonomy might not be emphasized in traditional elementary classrooms. Contrarily, item s1_5 (I was very happy when teacher praised me in class) seems to be too broad with no real implication for the context-specific learning experience. This finding reminds us to pay more attention to the feature of traditional classrooms, to further improve the applicability and validity of PQ-K12. Additionally, low factor loading may also be associated with insufficient sample size, and future study should consider using much larger sample for validation research.

In future research, we need to pay attention to two aspects based on the current research. First, a larger sample size is needed to further support the results of this study. The sample size in the present study was less than 5 times of the total items to obtain stable CFA results. Secondly, the design of specific questionnaire items and the division of the presence structure need to be further optimized according to the data results and the reflection on the feature of the traditional classrooms. These two measures will be conducive to the formation of a better structure and more applicable PQ-K12.

Acknowledgment. This study was funded by the Key Research Project of Education Supported by National Social Science Foundation of China, ACA170010.

References

1. Nehari, M., Bender, H.: Meaningfulness of a learning experience: a measure for educational outcomes in higher education. High. Educ. **7**(1), 1–11 (1978). https://doi.org/10.1007/BF00129786
2. Reigeluth, C.M., Frick, T.W.: Formative research: a methodology for creating and improving design theories. In: Reigeluth, C.M. (ed.) Instructional-Design Theories and Models—A New Paradigm of Instructional Theory, pp. 633–652. Lawrence Erlbaum, New Jersey (1999)

3. DeCarvalho, R.J.: The humanistic paradigm in education. Hum. Psychol. **19**(1), 88–104 (1991)
4. Allen, I.E., Seaman, J.: Grade change: TRACKING online education in the United States. Babson Survey Research Group and Quahog Research Group LLC, Oakland (2014)
5. Garrison, D.R., Arbaugh, J.B.: Researching the community of inquiry framework: review, issues, and future directions. Internet High. Educ. **10**(3), 157–172 (2007)
6. Swan, K., Ice, P.: The community of inquiry framework ten years later: introduction to the special issue. Internet High. Educ. **13**(1–2), 1–4 (2010)
7. Arbaugh, J.B.: Does the community of inquiry framework predict outcomes in online MBA courses? Int. Rev. Res. Open Distance Learn. **9**(2), 1–21 (2008)
8. Garrison, D.R., Anderson, T., Archer, W.: Critical inquiry in a text-based environment: computer conferencing in higher education. Internet High. Educ. **2**(2–3), 87–105 (1999)
9. Anderson, T., Liam, R., Garrison, D.R., Archer, W.: Assessing teaching presence in a computer conferencing context. **5**(2), 1–17 (2001)
10. Akyol, Z., Garrison, D.R., Ozden, M.Y.: Online and blended communities of inquiry: exploring the developmental and perceptional differences. Int. Rev. Res. Open Distrib. Learn. **10**(6), 65–83 (2009)
11. Garrison, D.R., Anderson, T., Archer, W.: Critical thinking, cognitive presence, and computer conferencing in distance education. Am. J. Distance Educ. **15**(1), 7–23 (2001)
12. Pisutova-Gerber, K., Malovicova, J.: Critical and higher order thinking in online threaded discussions in the Slovak context. Int. Rev. Res. Open Distrib. Learn. **10**(1), 1–15 (2009)
13. Schrire, S.: Knowledge building in asynchronous discussion groups: going beyond quantitative analysis. Comput. Educ. **46**(1), 49–70 (2006)
14. Shea, P., Bidjerano, T.: Learning presence as a moderator in the community of inquiry model. Comput. Educ. **59**(2), 316–326 (2012)
15. Shea, P., Bidjerano, T.: Learning presence: towards a theory of self-efficacy, selfregulation, and the development of a communities of inquiry in online and blended learning environments. Comput. Educ. **55**(4), 1721–1731 (2010)

Continuing Professional Development in ICT for Primary School Teachers, Reflections and Issues

Irena Loudova(✉)

University of Hradec Kralove, Hradec Kralove, Czech Republic
irena.loudova@uhk.cz

Abstract. With regard to the main directions of the education policy of the Czech Republic 2030+ , it is clear that the development of information and communication technologies (ICT) in the society brings the necessity to detect the specifics of the teaching profession in the context of current conditions at school. In the future, education should be more integrated with the digital world and respond to technological developments. The upcoming changes will affect virtually all teachers. Computers should be used in the classroom of other subjects, and this may make teachers unwilling to change their practices. Another obstacle to the modernization of teaching is also the lack of school equipment. The Czech School Inspection Authority states that only 9.5% of big primary schools meet the standards for digital education. In small primary schools, it is less than five percent. The aim of our research is to detect, what the real situation is like in the area of professional preparedness in teaching ICT subjects at different types of school with special attention to the perception of the situation by professional teachers. The results of the research confirmed that although teachers have support at school, most of them lack Continuing Professional Development both in the methodology of teaching ICT subjects and in the field of professional ICT subjects. Teachers are rather dissatisfied with the current offer of Continuing Professional Development (CPD) and they would welcome corresponding support.

Keywords: Digital literacy · Continuing Professional Development (CPD) · Didactics of informatics · Competences of ICT teacher

1 Introduction

Continuing professional development programs are meant to provide teachers with opportunities to develop their professional abilities for teaching in particular domains. Current trends in research in CPD view teachers as professionals and CPD programs take the form of providing teachers with learning opportunities to enhance their in-class teaching abilities through processes that engage them in theory-driven pedagogical changes in their teaching practices.

Research in CPD over the past decade has revealed a number of principles that are important in supporting teacher learning during CPD programs and helping teachers

S. K. S. Cheung et al. (Eds.): ICBL 2020, LNCS 12218, pp. 326–337, 2020.
https://doi.org/10.1007/978-3-030-51968-1_27

develop themselves through those programs. Generally speaking, CPD can address a variety of teacher needs, focusing on helping teachers refine their teaching approaches and pedagogy, understanding the need to change their everyday practices in particular areas and helping them implement changes in their daily teaching that will eventually help their students to learn more effectively [1]. Productive CPD programs need to provide teachers with opportunities to identify areas that need to be further developed by teachers themselves, however, the literature suggests that there are issues which are specific to ICT CPD. They are linked to wider approaches to the effective professional development of teachers. These affect the degree to which pedagogy is prioritised in the provision of CPD [2].

Issues which can be identified relating specifically to ICT are:

- An over-emphasis on skills training in itself at the expense of deep understanding and application of skills to developing learning and teaching. This is linked to a perceived need to address a skill 'deficit' in teachers, rather than to develop a focus on pedagogy.
- The challenge of developing an appropriate 'vision' for ICT among school leaders, which is focused on pedagogy and teacher development as a priority.
- 'Policy tensions' which deflect from coherent and consistent development of pedagogy using technologies, and create conflicts over how time and resources are used to embed technologies within schools.

A great deal of skills training has taken place in recent years, and yet there is a persistent lack of integration of technology into teachers' practice. The focus of CPD and the types of CPD activities have not led to the degree of change that was anticipated. This is in contradiction with the new educational policy in the Czech Republic, where with regard to the main directions of the education policy of the Czech Republic 2030+, ICT teachers are placed in a new role: to train teachers of other subjects to use ICT technologies in the instruction.

2 Theoretical Basis

At present, a number of subject didactics talk about the information-communication concept of their field, which underlines the increasing importance of informatics as a science, a teaching subject and a necessary base for efficient use of digital technologies at schools and in practical life [3].

Didactics of informatics is a very young field within the group of subject didactics. An important feature of contemporary informatics is i.e. the processing of text, visual (static and dynamic) and audio information in the form of hypertext. It is desirable for teachers to use a range of methodologies and forms, which they can implement depending on their personality characteristics and vocational focus. The quality teacher acquires several methodologies and teaching strategies and applies them appropriately according to the situation, the particular composition of the pupils in the classroom and other criteria [4].

In the study we focused on the situation in the area of professional preparedness in teaching ICT subjects at primary schools, the emphasis was placed on the perception of the situation by professional teachers. We carried out the detection of didactic resources and overall preparedness of IT teachers for the planned introduction of informatics into non-ICT subjects.

Recently, the rapid development of ICT in education forced teachers to reconsider the lessons' design since ICT have to be incorporated in modern educational scenarios [5]. The integration of technology into curriculum documents in developed countries (most recently in Finland, for example) is through the definition of digital literacy, without which inclusion in educational programs is not possible.

2.1 Digital Literacy

Digital literacy is the ability to use information and communication technologies to find, validate, generate and transmit information that requires both cognitive and technical skills [6]. Digital literacy includes seven elements, see Fig. 1.

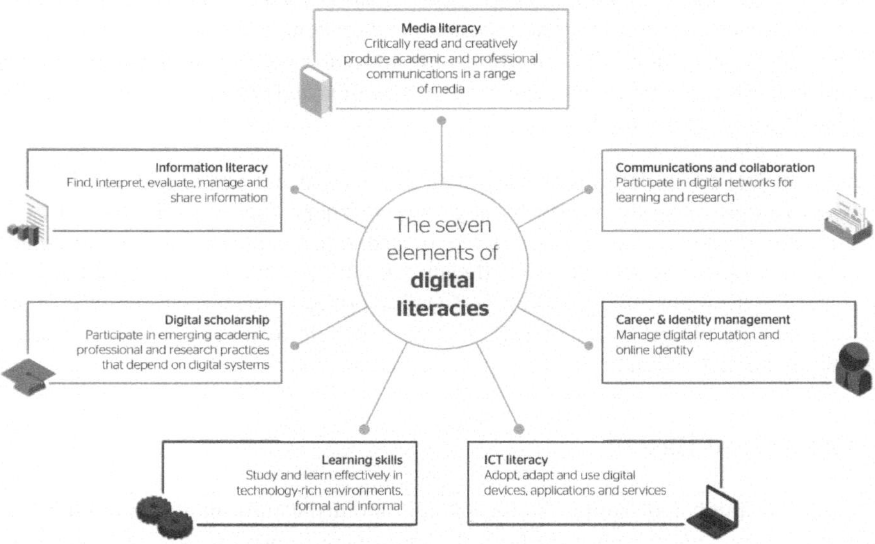

Fig. 1. Seven basic components of digital literacy [6].

In order to develop the concept of information literacy development, it is necessary to know the definitions of concepts and objectives to which information literacy activities should contribute. These goals are often set as standards or as an information literate competence. From a systemic perspective, it is therefore necessary to decompose information literacy into individual skills, abilities and competences. Comparison of approaches used to ICT competences, which is applied in some countries (e.g. USA, UK) or recommended as a model through transnational educational institutions and clusters, seems to be a suitable tool.

2.2 ICT Competences

The European Framework for the Digital Competence of Educators (DigCompEdu) provides a framework describing what it means for educators to be digitally competent. It provides a general reference frame to support the development of educator-specific digital competences, and is directed towards educators at all levels of education, from early childhood to higher and adult education.

DigCompEdu details 22 competences organized in six areas. The focus is not on technical skills. Rather, the framework aims to detail how digital technologies can be used to enhance and innovate education and training [7], see Fig. 2.

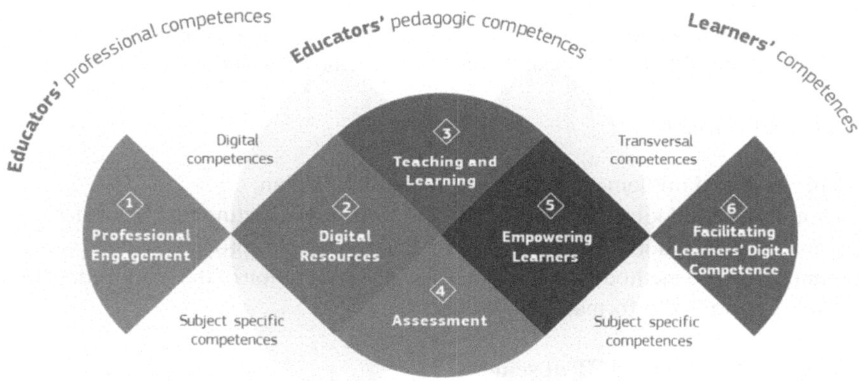

Fig. 2. Seven basic components of digital literacy [7].

Teachers have a large number of different roles in the modern information society, such as facilitators of the educational process, counselors and helpers of pupils and students, co-workers of their colleagues, employees, members of professional associations, professional experts, etc. From this point of view, it is important to realize that when defining teachers' competencies, it is necessary to apply a holistic approach that takes into account the whole spectrum of activities of the teacher.

It would be improper to concentrate on a mere exhaustive list of technological or pedagogical skills accentuated by curricular changes, ignoring the link between the general role of the teacher and the environment and conditions in which teachers operate [8].

The main purpose of ICT teacher training is to equip the graduate with the necessary knowledge, organizational and management skills, and didactic methods, so that the ICT teacher can be qualified in his/her school:

- methodically assist colleagues in integrating ICT into the teaching of most subjects;
- recommend and coordinate further ICT education of teaching staff;
- coordinate the use of ICT in education;

- coordinate software purchases and updates;
- prepare and implement an ICT plan in accordance with the school curriculum;
- coordinate the operation of the school's information system.

The study should fulfill the following **competences** in terms of its content and timing:

Competence for teaching

1. roles, advantages and limits of the use of ICT in the educational process, modern didactic methods;
2. computer use in the educational process;
3. organization of school pupils and student projects;
4. searching and evaluating teaching and information resources on the Internet;
5. using ICT-supported distance and combined learning methods.

Management competence

6. preparation and implementation of the school's ICT plan;
7. elaboration of school security policy (security rules, operating and SW rules);
8. organization of school involvement in regional (national) projects;
9. organization and methodological assistance in the operation of the school educational and organizational information system.

Competences to manage ICT at school

10. basic orientation in new trends in ICT development for education;
11. basic orientation in ICT related legislation;
12. knowledge of principles and possibilities of computer networks;
13. knowledge of principles and possibilities of modern presentation technologies;
14. implementation of new technologies - construction in 3D, 3D printers;
15. sharing materials and using modern communication tools (e-learning, cloud services).

Cheryl Whitfield [9] defines **ICT coordinator** (Technology Facilitator) as a person who should meet the following **characteristics**:

16. experienced teacher;
17. enthusiastic techno-optimist;
18. good lecturer;
19. active mentor;
20. perfect organizer.

We are aware that the list of competencies summarized above is not exhaustive, we intentionally selected only those that are relevant to our research.

3 Research Project

The main goal of the project was twofold, to find out how ICT teachers perceive the current offer of CPD programs focused on information technology, methodology and the subject didactics, and how practicing ICT teachers evaluate their ICT competencies. Based on the above mentioned issues the following research questions were formulated:

1. Does the school management support the ICT teachers' participation of in CPD programs?
2. Are ICT teachers satisfied with the current ICT CPD programs?
3. How do the ICT teachers evaluate the importance of ICT competences based on their teaching practice?

3.1 Methodology

Based on research goals and questions, quantitative research was chosen. An exploratory research method was used and a questionnaire was chosen as the basic research technique. The obtained data were processed by quantitative analysis procedures: tests to verify the psychometric properties of the questionnaire, descriptive statistics, nonparametric test for comparing two or more files - comparison of files to monitored variables: length of practice, overall evaluation of experience, etc. data). The questionnaire had two research parts, the first part was focused on exploration of CPD programs and questions in the form of open items were processed by qualitative analysis (categorical analysis). The second part of the questionnaire was aimed at ICT competencies and Likert scale with five-stage scale items was used. The scale was arranged so that a **value of 1** meant - **very important** and a **value of 5** meant - **unimportant**.

The applied pedagogical research was carried out at 165 primary schools (second level – 11 to 15 years old pupils) in Hradec Kralove Region, and the focus group consisted of 186 ICT teachers with at least 2 years' experience, see Table 1.

Table 1. Characteristics of focus group.

	ICT teachers in focus group
Total number of teachers	186
Male	28
Female	158
Age (AVG)	42.05
Standard deviation	2.4
Minimum	27
Maximum	58
Modus	46
Median	42

4 Research Results

Based on individual scores, we obtained a distribution of respondents in terms of their management support in CPD programs participation. 11% of ICT teachers receives full management support, unlike 42% of ICT teachers who get only limited support from school management to participate in CPD programs. Teachers from the focus group find the main reason in the content offer of provided CPT programs, which according to the school management does not correspond to the current needs in the field of methodology and didactics of ICT subject. see Fig. 3.

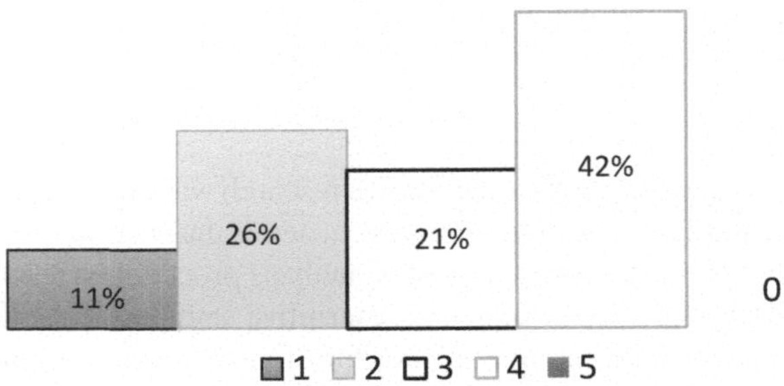

Fig. 3. Does the school management support the ICT teachers' participation of in CPD programs?

Our further objective was to find out if the ICT teachers in the focus group are satisfied with the current content offer of ICT CPD programs. The results of the questionnaire survey show that most ICT teachers (58%) are rather dissatisfied with the content of the CPD programs offer. They miss mainly programs focused on new and current trends (3D printer, robotics, HW…) and of course the methodology of teaching ICT subjects, see Fig. 4.

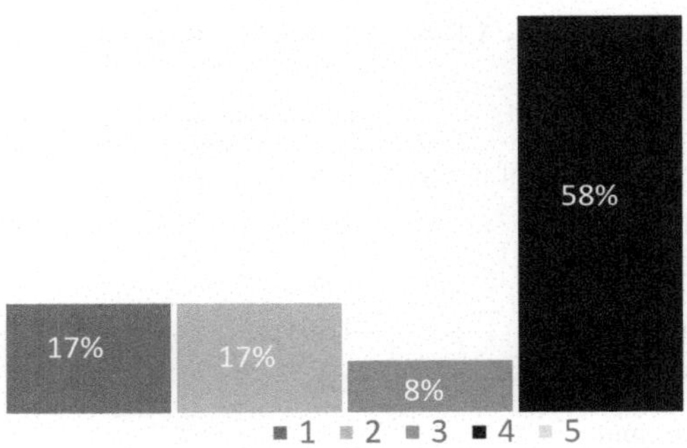

Fig. 4. Are ICT teachers satisfied with the current ICT CPD programs?

In the first part of the research, we found out that even though teachers have the support of school management and can participate in CPD programs, new ICT programs focusing on current trends are not available.

The second part of our research focused on the competences and importance that ICT teachers attach to them. We used the list of competences recorded and numbered in Sect. 2.2. Each number (1–20) represents one competence described in details in Sect. 2.2. The scale values in Table 2 were set as follows: 1- very important, 5 – unimportant, following the Likert scale with five-stage scale items.

Table 2. ICT teachers' evaluation of the importance of ICT competences.

Competence	Mean	SD	Median	Modus
1	1,63	0,07	1	1
2	2,28	1,00	2	2
3	2,03	1,16	2	1
4	3,93	1,22	4	5
5	2,29	1,22	2	1
6	1,98	1,07	2	1
7	2,44	1,11	2	2
8	2,37	1,08	2	2
9	1,37	0,68	1	1
10	1,38	0,63	1	1
11	2,13	1,14	5	5
12*	2,15	1,16	2	–
13	2,26	1,13	2	2
14	2,51	1,30	2	1
15	4.19	1,38	2	1
16	3,08	1,39	3	3
17	1.95	0.99	2	1
18	2,19	0,98	2	2
19	2,5	1,15	2	2
20	1,86	0,98	2	1

*Item 12 has the same frequency of two values, no number is given.

The reliability of the research tool was performed using the Cronbach alpha coefficient: $\alpha = 0.72$.

Descriptive analysis indicated that according to the arithmetic means of individual variables, respondents attach the highest importance in this part of the questionnaire to the following competences: active mentor, use and knowledge of modern didactic methods, knowledge of possibilities of computer network, and good lecturer.

The obtained data were subjected to further investigation; factor analysis was performed. The aim was to analyze the correlations of variables, we worked with the Quartimax rotation. Before the factor analysis itself was used, it was necessary to perform tests that allow its use. We expected that three factors could be used based on the rubble graph, but the extracted factors explained only 30% of the variance, so we used a method of determining the number of factors using the eigenvalue value. Based on eigenvalue >1, 5 factors were extracted for 20 variables, thus explaining 60% of the data variance, see Fig. 5.

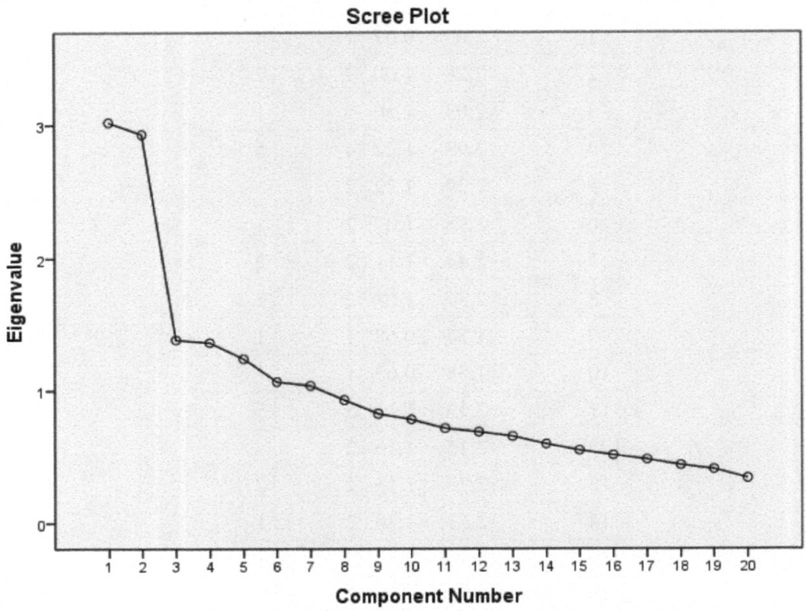

Fig. 5. Rubble chart

A factor is a construct that allows to determine how a group of variables merges into smaller groups (factors). Thus, at first sight, an invisible factor arises that characterizes the common features of the variables. Hendl [10] considers that factors are new variables from which conclusions can be drawn about the context of the original variables. Based on the amount of factor loads, we identified the following five factors (in our case competences):

F1: Competence no. 15 – sharing materials and using modern communication tool (e-learning, Teams, Cloud services);
F2: Competence no. 4 – searching and evaluating teaching and information resources on the Internet;
F3: Competence no. 16 – experienced teacher
F4: Competence 14 – implementation of new technologies – construction in 3D, 3D printers;

F5: Competence no. 7 – elaboration of school security policy (security rules, operating and SW rules).

We used cluster analysis to see if common profiles of respondents and typology of ICT teachers are reflected in the focus group. Numbers 1–5 in Fig. 6 indicate preferred competencies, colored numbers 1 (blue), 2 (red), 3 (green) indicate clusters that determine the types of teacher.

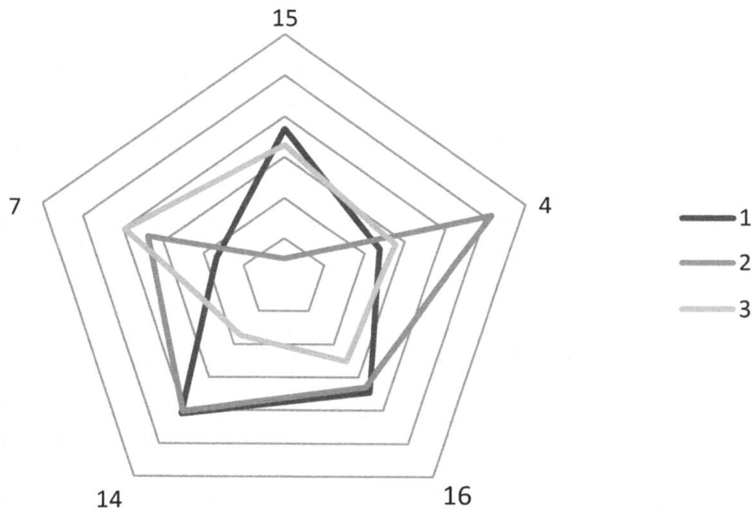

Fig. 6. Cluster analysis: typical respondent in terms of item preferences. (Color figure online)

Based on cluster analysis, the profiles of three types of ICT teachers, which are based on responding item preferences, were defined as follows:

Type 1: in terms of competences, the most important for this type of ICT teacher is to use modern communication tools (e-learning, cloud services) when sharing didactic materials, implements new technologies in the instruction (e.g. 3D printers), and relies on teaching experience;

Type 2: in terms of competences it is necessary for this teacher to evaluate teaching and information resources on the Internet, implement new technologies into the instruction, and elaborate school security policy (security and SW rules);

Type 3: in terms of competences, for this teacher the priorities are school security policy, teaching experience and evaluating teaching and information resources on the Internet.

5 Conclusion

The described research identified the school management support of ICT teachers to participate in CPD programs in Hradec Kralove region. We also investigated whether

ICT teachers are satisfied with the content and offer of CPD programs. The results of the survey showed that even though the teachers are encouraged to further develop and deepen their professional knowledge, there is a lack of courses focused on the implementation of new technologies in ICT instruction, not to mention modern methodological and didactic strategies.

The literature suggests that there are issues which are specific to ICT CPD, which are linked to wider approaches to the effective professional development of teachers. These affect the degree to which pedagogy is prioritised in the provision of CPD. Issues which can be identified relating specifically to ICT are:

- An over-emphasis on skills training in itself at the expense of deep understanding and application of skills to developing learning and teaching. This is linked to a perceived need to address skills 'deficit' in teachers, rather than to develop a focus on pedagogy.
- The challenge of developing an appropriate 'vision' for ICT among school management, which is focused on pedagogy and teacher development as a priority.
- 'Policy tensions' which deflect from coherent and consistent development of pedagogy using technologies, and create conflicts over how time and resources are used to embed technologies within schools [11].

The main feature of successful CPD is that it addresses teachers' individual needs as a priority. Meeting these individual needs takes very different forms, ranging from entirely school-based provision to external programmes. Currently, the National Pedagogical Institute in the Czech Republic is coming up with a number of innovations in CPD ICT programs, which take the form of webinars, workshops and seminars. These courses meet the needs and expectations of ICT subject teachers. In just six months in 2019, over 1,000 teachers participated in ICT webinars that are provided free within the project SYPO (System of the Professional Education Support for Pedagogical Staff and School Management), which is one of the National Pedagogical Institute projects, whose aim is to improve the quality of lifelong education.

Our research also dealt with the issue of ICT competencies and their importance in the teaching process. We found out that the main priorities for practicing ICT subject teachers are the implementation of modern technologies, the use of communication tools such as cloud services, cyber security and the guarantee of quality information obtained from Internet resources. Teaching experience is also very much appreciated.

We are aware that our research is subject to potential limitations, e.g. there is insufficient sample size for statistical measurement and thus we cannot generalize in any way. Despite the limits, we believe that information and communication technology is one of the fastest growing areas and teachers' attitudes to innovations in this area are important for the further development of education. In addition to all the above-mentioned factors that affect CPD programs lifelong education generates professional enthusiasm for teachers' practice of their perceptions, and a call for "hearts and minds" approach is needed [12]. Teachers' CPD participation results in knowledge which shapes teachers' 'minds' but only professional enthusiasm reframes thoughts and put them into action.

Acknowledgement. This research and publication were funded by Deans Office of the Faculty of Education University of Hradec Kralove, Czech Republic.

References

1. Fishman, J.J., Marx, R.W., Best, S., Tal, R.T.: Linking teacher and student learning to improve professional development in systemic reform. Teach. Teach. Educ. **19**, 643–658 (2003)
2. Boylan, M.: Enabling adaptive system leadership: teachers leading professional development. Educ. Manage. Adm. Leadersh. **46**(1), 86–106 (2018)
3. Kopecký, K., Szotkowski, R.: Moderní informační a komunikační technologie ve výuce (průvodce studiem) (2018)
4. Woods, P.: Creative Teachers in Primary Schools. Routledge, Abingdon (2019)
5. Clarke, B., Svanaes, S., Zimmermann, S.: One-to-one tablets in secondary schools: an evaluation study. Tablets for schools (2013)
6. Digital Literacy, Libraries, and Public Policy. (2013). [http://www.districtdispatch.org/wp-content/uploads…]. [cit. 2015-11-26]
7. DigCompEdu. https://ec.europa.eu/jrc/en/digcompedu
8. Cirus, L.: The influence of the teacher on the formation of digital literacy of primary school pupils. Hradec Kralove: Pedagogical faculty of Univerzity of Hradec Kralove, 2017, 195 p. dissertation work (2017)
9. Whitfield, Ch.: The Five Essentials of Technology Facilitators: Successful On-Site Help for Technology Integration. Techlearning (2005). Dostupné na Internetu Accessable from http://www.techlearning.com/story/showArticle.jhtml?articleID=159901663
10. Hendl, J.: Přehled statistických metod zpracování dat: analýza a metaanalýza dat. Portál, sro (2004)
11. Havigerova, J., Haviger, J., Janebova, R., Zikl, P.: Helping professions and normality. Int. J. Psychol. **43**(3–4) (2008)
12. Watson, M.B.: Career Maturity Assessment in an International Context. In: Athanasou, J.A., Perera, H.N. (eds.) International Handbook of Career Guidance, pp. 639–653. Springer, Cham (2019). https://doi.org/10.1007/978-3-030-25153-6_29

Academic Operating Costs Optimisation Using Hybrid MCPSO Based Course Timetabling Tool

Thatchai Thepphakorn[1], Saisumpan Sooncharoen[2], and Pupong Pongcharoen[2(✉)]

[1] Faculty of Industrial Technology, Pibulsongkram Rajabhat University, Phitsanulok, Thailand
[2] Centre of Operations Research and Industrial Applications (CORIA), Department of Industrial Engineering, Faculty of Engineering, Naresuan University, Phitsanulok 65000, Thailand
pupongp@nu.ac.th

Abstract. The course timetabling problem (CTP) is very important for educational institutes. An effective timetable has directly affect to the utilisation of resources and its operating costs. Solving the CTP manually without timetabling tool is extremely difficult, time consuming and may require a group of experts to work for several days. A course timetabling program, named a Hybrid Particle Swarm Optimisation-based Timetabling (HPSOT) tool, has been developed for optimising the academic operating costs. A variant of Particle Swarm Optimisation (PSO) named Maurice Clerc PSO (MCPSO) and its hybridisations with five combinations of insertion operator (IO) and exchange operator (EO) were proposed and embedded in the HPSOT program. The statistical analysis suggested that the results obtained from the hybrid MCPSO were statistically better than those results obtained from the conventional MCPSO for all instances. The average computational times taken by the proposed hybrid methods were quicker than the original MCPSO for all instances.

Keywords: Educational timetabling · Combined ratio · Swarm intelligence · Local search · Metaheuristics

1 Introduction

Smart classroom can be defined as a physical classroom space for showing teaching content, easy for instructional interaction, easy for class management and convenient for accessing educational learning resources [1]. Educational resources can be categorised into living (e.g., students, lecturers) and non-living resources (e.g. teaching rooms, laboratories). During academic semesters, the classrooms in educational institutes is one of the essential supported resources for students' learning as well as teachers' lecturing. There are several types of classroom required by both general study and specific courses [2, 3] such as lecture, laboratories, tutorial, theaters, and smart classrooms. Some classrooms require high initial investments, well maintenance, well-trained staff and operating costs. Thus, the efficient utilisation of academic resources having low operating costs is a common educational institute policy.

S. K. S. Cheung et al. (Eds.): ICBL 2020, LNCS 12218, pp. 338–350, 2020.
https://doi.org/10.1007/978-3-030-51968-1_28

Course timetabling problem (CTP) faced by educational institutions periodically arises every academic semester due to the varying number of students but limited numbers of lecturers and classrooms. For constructing the practical timetables of teachers, students, and classrooms, all hard constraints must be satisfied whereas all users' preferences as well as educational resources' utilisation should be optimised. Therefore, course timetabling is a crucial activity for educational institution [4]. The CTP can be solved either manually by academic staff or automatically using programming tool [5]. Manual solving of large CTP is extremely difficult, time consuming, and requires efforts from a group of experts. CTP is known to be Non-deterministic Polynomial (NP) hard problem, in which the computational time required to find the optimal solutions increases exponentially with problem size [6]. To overcome these difficulties especially for solving very large-size CTP, the preferable design task is to develop an automated timetabling tool embedded with computational intelligence techniques to seek the optimal solutions.

Computational intelligence algorithms, e.g., Particle Swarm Optimisation [7], Frog Leaping Algorithm [8], Artificial Immune System [9], have become very popular for solving large-scale combinatorial optimisation problems [10]. These algorithms have been successfully applied to solve NP-hard problems within acceptable time consuming, but they do not guarantee optimum solutions [11]. PSO has been successfully applied to solve the problems in several domains because of very few parameters to be adjusted, little memory for computations, and easy to understand and implement [12]. Hybridisation strategies for PSO can improve the solution quality through increased exploitation search and can also increase the opportunity to quickly discover the global best solution. However, there is no report on the hybridisation between MCPSO and insertion operator (IO) and exchange operator (EO) to solve the real-world CTP based on minimising academic operating costs.

The objectives of this paper were to: (i) develop a hybrid particle swarm optimisation based timetabling (HPSOT) tool for solving real-world CTP based on academic operating costs; and (ii) compare the performances of the MCPSO and its hybridisations with five combinations of IO:EO ratio in terms of the solution quality (operating costs), convergence speed, and computational time. The next section of this paper briefly explains the CTP. Section 3 describes the PSO and its variants followed by the procedures of the HPSOT program in Sect. 4. Section 5 presents the experimental results and analysis followed by conclusions.

2 Course Timetabling Problem

Course timetabling problem (CTP) is one of the most challenging scheduling problems and also classified into combinatorial optimisation problems due to its complexity and constraints [13]. Constraints found in the CTP can be divided into two categories including hard and soft constraints [11]. Hard constraints (HC) are the most important constraints, in which all candidate timetables must be satisfied to be the feasible timetables [14]. Soft constraints (SC) are more relaxed, in which the total number of SC violations are acceptable but it should be minimised [4]. Both HC and SC constraints considered in this research can be described as follows [15].

HCs considered were: (i) all lectures/laboratories (elements) required for each course must be scheduled and assigned to distinct periods (HC_1); (ii) students and lecturers can only attend one lecture at a time (HC_2); (iii) only one lecture can take place in a room at a given time (HC_3); (iv) lecturers and students must be available for a lecture to be scheduled (HC_4); (v) all courses must be assigned into proper rooms according to their given requirements, including building location, room facilities, and room types (HC_5); and (vi) all lectures within a course requiring consecutive periods must be obeyed (HC_6).

In addition, SC considered were: (i) all courses should be scheduled in the appropriate types of room in order to avoid unnecessary operating or renting costs (currency unit per period) (SC_1); (ii) the courses taught by the given lecturer(s) should be assigned on their available or preferred day and periods in order to save the lecturing or hiring costs (currency unit per period) (SC_2), and (iii) the classrooms should be scheduled in consecutive working periods of a day in order to reduce the number of times to clean or setup after using the rooms (per time) (SC_3).

HC_1-HC_3 are the fundamental constraints, called event-clash constraints, each of which can be found in most of course timetabling problems [11]. HC_4-HC_6 are special requirements for courses, lecturers, and curricula found in many universities in Thailand. SC_1-SC_3 are represented by the objective functions $f(x_i)$ in order to minimise the total university operating costs considered from the candidate timetables following (1);

$$Minimise\ \ f(x_i) = W_1SC_1 + W_2SC_2 + W_3SC_3 \tag{1}$$

$$\text{Subject to} : HC_h = 0, \qquad \forall h, \tag{2}$$

Equation (1) is the objective functions that evaluate the total university operating costs of the SC_1-SC_3. The weightings (W_1-W_3) for each SC are not restricted and depend upon the user preferences for each institution. In this work, W_1–W_3 were specified at 50 (currency units per hour), 300 (currency units per hour), and 2.5 (currency units per times), respectively. Equation (2) checks a timetable to be a feasible timetable, in which all HC must be satisfied. Where h is an index related to the hth hard constraint ($h = 1, 2, 3, \ldots, H$), where H is the number of hard constraints.

3 PSO Variants and Literature Review

Particle Swarm Optimisation (PSO) is population-based metaheuristics and it was introduced by Kennedy and Eberhart in 1995 [16]. PSO was inspired by swarm behaviour in nature such as fish schooling, bird flocking [17]. Due to its simplicity and flexibility, PSO has become one of the most popular swarm intelligent methods and it has been applied to solve many area in optimisation, computational intelligence, and design applications [17]. According to a comprehensive literature review, there are many variants of the PSO including conventional PSO [18], standard PSO (SPSO) [19], and Maurice Clerc PSO (MCPSO) [20], and so on.

The basic concepts of aforementioned PSO variants can be described as follows. The essential parameters of all PSO variants are specified in the initialisation process. Each particle x_i ($i = 1, 2, 3, \ldots, P$) is generated randomly before determining its fitness value via the objective function $f(x_i)$. Where, i is the index of particles whilst P is population size (or number of particles). After that, the iteration best solution $\left(x^t_{best}\right)$ and the global best solution $\left(g^*_{best}\right)$ are identified by the following Eq. (3) [21]. Where, t is the index of iterations whilst I_{now} is the current iteration.

$$x^t_{best} = \min\{f(x^t_i)\}, \quad i \in (1,\ 2,\ 3,\ \ldots, P) \tag{3}$$

$$g^*_{best} = \min\{f(x^t_i)\}, \quad i \in (1,\ 2,\ 3,\ \ldots, P), \quad t \in (1,\ 2,\ 3,\ \ldots, I_{now})$$

In each iteration (generation) of conventional PSO, a new solution (x^{t+1}_i) for particle i is produced by using velocity and position vectors according to Eq. (4) and Eq. (8) [22], respectively. Where v_i is the velocity for particle i; c_1 and c_2 denote the acceleration coefficients, each of which requires a positive constant value; r_1 and r_2 parameters are uniformly random variables distributed within a range from 0 to 1 [21].

$$v^{t+1}_i = v^t_i + c_1 r_1 (x^t_{best} - x^t_i) + c_2 r_2 (g^*_{best} - x^t_i) \tag{4}$$

$$v^{t+1}_i = \omega v^t_i + c_1 r_1 (x^t_{best} - x^t_i) + c_2 r_2 (g^*_{best} - x^t_i) \tag{5}$$

$$v^{t+1}_i = k(v^t_i + c_1 r_1 (x^t_{best} - x^t_i) + c_2 r_2 (g^*_{best} - x^t_i)) \tag{6}$$

$$k = \frac{2}{\left|2 - \varphi - \sqrt{\varphi^2 - 4\varphi}\right|}, \quad \varphi = c_1 + c_2, \quad \varphi > 4 \tag{7}$$

$$x^{t+1}_i = x^t_i + v^{t+1}_i \tag{8}$$

In case of the SPSO, generating a new solution x^{t+1}_i can be achieved by using velocity and position vectors according to Eq. (5) and Eq. (8) [21, 22]. Where ω is the inertia weight used to balance the global exploration and local exploitation [21]. For MCPSO, new velocity and position for a solution x^{t+1}_i can also be updated by using Eq. (6)–(7), and Eq. (8) [22]. Where k is constriction factor for control velocity of particles, φ is a positive parameter depending on the acceleration coefficients [22].

After updating velocity and position, the fitness value for a new solution x^{t+1}_i is evaluated by taking into account the objective function. The x^t_{best} will be replaced by a new solution x^{t+1}_i if the fitness value obtained from the x^{t+1}_i is better than that obtained from the $f\left(x^t_{best}\right)$. Moreover, if the fitness value obtained from the x^{t+1}_i is better than that obtained from the g^*_{best}, the g^*_{best} will be replaced by a new solution x^{t+1}_i. These processes are repeated until getting to the maximum iteration (I) or the given stop criterion.

Generally, constraint optimisation problems are hard to solve only by conventional or standard PSO [23]. Especially in the case of complex multimodal problems, these methods always suffer from premature convergence and low exploration ability [24]. Hybridisation strategy between two or more algorithms has been widely accepted for increasing the algorithm performances to obtain a better solution [25]. Two Local Search (LS) strategies, called insertion operator (IO) and exchange operator (EO), can be embedded for hybridisation with PSO. Both operators are demonstrated for their ability to improve the solution quality according to Eq. (9), Eq. (10) and Eq. (11) [26]. Where w_1 and w_2 are control parameters ranged between 0 and 1 ($w_1 + w_2 = 1$). The parameters can be considered as weight balance for performing two operators (IO:EO ratio) used in the solution improvement process. After conducting LS approaches, measuring the fitness value is applied before updating the x^t_{best} and g^*_{best} again.

$$x_i^{t+1} = x_i^t + IO \quad (9)$$

$$x_i^{t+1} = x_i^t + EO \quad (10)$$

$$x_i^{t+1} = x_i^t + w_1 IO + w_2 EO \quad (11)$$

A focused literature survey on the Scopus database covering the period from the last two decades using "Particle Swarm" and "course timetable*" as keywords for document search in the data records (article title, abstract and keywords) has been conducted and summarised in Table 1.

Table 1. Literature review of PSO variants for solving the UCTP

Authors	Years	UCTP Problems	PSO variants	Hybridisations
Ahandani and Vakil Baghmisheh [19]	2013	Benchmark	SPSO	GA, LS (Hill climbing)
Chen and Shih [18]	2013	Real-world	PSO, SPSO	LS (Interchange Operator)
Irene et al. [27]	2009	Real-world	MCPSO	Constraint-based Reasoning
Irene et al. [20]	2009	Benchmark	MCPSO	Neighbourhood search
Kanoh and Chen [28]	2013	Real-world	SPSO	
Oswald and Anand Deva Durai [23]	2014	Real-world	MCPSO	Local Beam Search
Sheau Fen Ho et al. [29]	2009	Benchmark	MCPSO	
Thepphakorn and Pongcharoen [15]	2019	Real-world	PSO, SPSO, MCPSO	
This research work	2020	Real-world	MCPSO	Local Search (IO, EO)

All PSO variants mentioned above have been applied to solve both benchmark and real-world UCTPs. Heuristics such as Genetic Algorithm, Hill climbing, and Interchange Operator have been adopted for hybridisation with PSO [18] and standard PSO (SPSO) [19] to solve the real-world UCTP. Some approaches, e.g., Constraint-based Reasoning, Local Beam Search, and Neighbourhood Search, have also been hybridised with the MCPSO [20, 23, 27].

4 Hybrid Particle Swarm Optimisation Based Timetabling Tool

The hybrid Particle Swarm Optimisation based timetabling (HPSOT) program has been coded in modular style using the TCL/TK and C programming languages. The HPSOT tool was developed for solving the real world university course timetabling problem (UCTP) by using the Maurice Clerc PSO, in which it received the best performance to solve the real world UCTP from previous research [15]. The main procedures of the HPSOT tool are included in six steps and shown in Fig. 1.

```
Begin                                                                          /*Step 1
   Upload input data and set MCPSO's parameters (including I, P, %IO, %EO)
   Sort a list of courses using heuristic orderings
   Create initial population, x_i (i = 1,2,…,P); initial iteration (t = 0)
   Generate random keys for each x_i
   While t < Max_Iteration(I) do                                               /*Step 2
       For (i=1, i<= Max_Pop(P), i++) do
          Pick random numbers: r1, r2 ~ U(0,1)
          If MCPSO do Update particle's velocity v_i^(t+1) using Eq.(6)-(7)
          Update particle's position x_i^(t+1) using Eq.(8)
          If (x_i^(t+1) = an infeasible timetable) do Repair x_i^(t+1)
          Evaluate objective functions f(x_i^(t+1))                            /*Step 3
          If f(x_i^(t+1))<f(x^t_best) do Replace x^t_best = x_i^(t+1)
          If f(x_i^(t+1))<f(g*_best) do Replace g*_best = x_i^(t+1)
          if MCPSO+EO(100%) do Eq.(10)                 /* 0%:100% ratio        /*Step 4
          Else if MCPSO+IO(25%):EO(75%) do Eq.(11)     /* 25%:75% ratio
          Else if MCPSO+IO(50%):EO(50%) do Eq.(11)     /* 50%:50% ratio
          Else if MCPSO+IO(75%):EO(25%) do Eq.(11)     /* 75%:25% ratio
          Else if MCPSO+IO(100%) do Eq.(9)             /* 100%:0% ratio
          If (x_i^(t+1)' = an infeasible timetable) do Repair x_i^(t+1)'       /*Step 5
          Evaluate objective functions f(x_i^(t+1)')
          If f(x_i^(t+1)')<f(x^t_best) do Replace x^t_best = x_i^(t+1)'
          If f(x_i^(t+1)')<f(g*_best) do Replace g*_best = x_i^(t+1)'
          Update iteration (t = t + 1)
   End Loop while
   Output results and visualisation of g*_best                                 /*Step 6
End
```

Fig. 1. Pseudo code of the HPSOT program

The first step is a solution or timetable initialisation process. All course timetable data were uploaded before assigning the essential parameters for the MCPSO. The total number of events (n) is determined from the number of teaching periods required for all courses. Then, an event list containing a set of n events was generated. The sequence of all events in the list was sorted by using a constructive heuristic, called the largest unpermitted period degree (LUPD) first [30]. This heuristic rule can reduce the probability of getting infeasible timetables or solutions that always occur in the solution initialisation process. Next process is to create an empty timetable, in which the size of that timetable dimension was determined according to the numbers of given rooms, working days per week, and periods per day. After that, all events in the sorted list were assigned into an empty timetable for producing a candidate solution x_i^{t+1} ($i = 1, 2, 3,\ldots, P$), P is the number of given population or particles.

After that, a random key technique [31] was adopted in this work in order to accommodate with a solution evolution process for x_i^{t+1} solutions. A random key list having the same dimension size of the x_i^{t+1} solution was created. Each timeslot of a random key list was then assigned a random number using uniformly distribution ranged between 0 and 1. Both solution initialisation and random key processes for each particle x_i^{t+1} will be repeated until getting to the maximum particles (P).

The second step was the evolution process for MCPSO algorithm. In order to update particle's velocity, each solution/particle x_i^{t+1} was produced by using Eq. (6)–(7). After that, the position of particle x_i^{t+1} for MCPSO was updated by using Eq. (8). The new solution x_i^{t+1} may be either feasible or infeasible timetable; the repair process was therefore applied to rectify infeasible timetables to be feasible timetables.

The third step, the quality of solution x_i^{t+1} was measured by using Eq. (1). If its fitness value is better than $f\left(x_{best}^t\right)$, a particle x_{best}^t is replaced by the x_i^{t+1}. Moreover, a particle g_{gest}^* is replaced by the x_i^{t+1} if the quality of a solution x_i^{t+1} receives the best fitness value. These processes were repeated until all particles were reproduced.

The fourth step was to produce MCPSO's hybridisation with the Local Search (LS) approaches including insertion operator (IO) and exchange operator (EO). In this work, five weight balances of IO:EO ratio, which were MCPSO+IO(100%), MCPSO+EO(100%), MCPSO+IO(75%):EO(25%), MCPSO+IO(50%):EO(50%), and MCPSO+IO(25%):EO(75%), were proposed for MCPSO hybridisation. For examples, MCPSO+EO(100%) means that all particles or solution x_i^{t+1} ($i = 1, 2, 3, \ldots, P$) must be produced by using the EO for each iteration. For an example, the MCPSO+IO(75%):EO(25%) is the 75% of particles in the population will be hybridised using insertion operator whereas the hybridisation of remaining particles (25%) will be conducted using the exchange operator. After this process, a new improvement solution was changed from x_i^{t+1} x_i^{t+1} to $x_i^{t+1\prime}$.

In the fifth step, any infeasible timetables obtained from previous step will be rectified by using the repair process again. Then, the quality of solution $x_i^{t+1\prime}$ will be determined by using Eq. (1) before updating x_{best}^t and g_{gest}^*. Finally, these processes (step 2 to step 5) will be repeated until reaching the maximum iterations (I) followed by the computational report.

5 Experimental Results and Analysis

This research was aimed to solve the university course timetabling problem (UCTP) using the HPSOT program for constructing course timetables with the minimum total university operating costs. The objective of the experiments was to explore and compare the performance of MCPSO hybrid with five combinations of IO:EO ratio, which were 0%:100%; 25%:75%; 50%:50%; 75%:25% and 100%:0%. Eleven real world course timetabling problem instances adopted from the previous research [32] were used in this computational experiment. For the largest instance, there are 323 courses, each of which requires 3 hours per week.

The appropriate parameter setting of MCPSO for this work was adopted from previous research [15]. Personal computer with Core i7 3.20 GHz CPU and 8 GB RAM was used to determine the computational time required to execute experimental runs. The computational run for each instance was repeated ten times by using different random seeds. The computational results were analysed in terms of minimum, maximum, average (currency unit), standard deviation, computational time (minute) and P-value obtained from the analysis of variants (ANOVA) as shown in Table 2.

Table 2. Performance comparisons of the conventional MCPSO and its hybridisations

Problem instance	Analysis	MCPSO	Hybrid MCPSO (IO%:EO% ratio)					ANOVA
			0%:100%	25%:75%	50%:50%	75%:25%	100%:0%	*P-value*
1	Minimum	202,668.50	202,669.00	202,804.00	203,010.50	202,925.00	202,876.00	0.645
	Maximum	203,135.50	203,117.00	203,112.00	203,120.00	203,099.00	203,089.00	
	Average	203,030.80	**202,968.05**	203,009.80	203,041.70	203,042.25	203,002.50	
	Std. Deviation	134.34	186.70	108.36	34.35	49.81	66.50	
	Time (min.)	4.69	1.61	1.87	2.08	2.11	2.08	
2	Minimum	382,239.00	382,481.75	382,245.00	382,281.50	382,232.00	382,239.00	**0.010**
	Maximum	383,409.50	383,723.75	383,415.50	383,423.50	383,415.50	382,980.75	
	Average	382,744.20	383,226.28	382,745.40	382,749.85	**382,734.10**	382,604.20	
	Std. Deviation	391.59	380.10	402.60	388.37	388.29	269.48	
	Time (min.)	19.94	7.84	8.12	8.46	8.98	9.32	
3	Minimum	304,349.25	304,217.75	304,395.25	304,365.25	304,529.25	305,904.25	1.000
	Maximum	306,025.75	306,045.25	306,011.75	305,984.50	305,964.50	306,776.00	
	Average	305,400.33	305,459.90	305,406.53	**305,381.93**	305,396.33	306,352.00	
	Std. Deviation	596.58	630.47	588.61	577.88	471.28	298.85	
	Time (min.)	30.23	12.17	12.37	12.85	13.29	15.45	
4	Minimum	307,855.75	303,713.00	304,018.25	306,349.50	306,648.00	305,857.75	0.415
	Maximum	309,819.75	310,309.00	310,137.00	309,787.25	309,304.25	309,367.50	
	Average	308,821.35	**307,673.00**	307,785.53	308,222.22	307,733.45	308,347.40	
	Std. Deviation	597.81	2,277.09	1,772.47	1,290.22	862.96	973.22	
	Time (min.)	20.47	7.91	8.05	8.33	8.82	9.54	
5	Minimum	492,248.50	492,566.00	492,077.50	492,270.50	491,956.75	492,530.50	0.909
	Maximum	493,737.00	493,921.25	493,734.75	494,061.25	493,675.25	493,370.00	
	Average	493,002.15	493,081.28	492,968.38	493,168.48	493,042.23	**492,949.15**	
	Std. Deviation	500.36	397.97	531.55	501.77	532.04	272.19	
	Time (min.)	36.48	14.87	15.39	15.79	17.09	17.21	
6	Minimum	409,361.50	409,344.75	409,832.25	409,835.00	409,107.75	408,880.25	**0.000**
	Maximum	410,730.00	410,599.25	410,596.75	410,779.00	410,108.75	410,041.75	
	Average	410,328.68	409,958.43	410,187.84	410,167.10	**409,540.36**	409,560.60	
	Std. Deviation	409.93	398.45	263.79	282.43	353.71	389.79	
	Time (min.)	41.47	19.40	20.83	22.63	22.10	23.39	
7	Minimum	418,731.50	413,716.50	414,015.00	414,227.25	415,048.50	417,363.00	**0.036**
	Maximum	420,752.00	421,277.25	420,363.00	420,356.25	419,256.50	419,764.25	
	Average	419,722.18	419,215.90	417,592.33	418,470.98	**417,271.80**	418,966.83	
	Std. Deviation	688.56	2,482.34	2,412.50	2,335.27	1,594.15	832.50	
	Time (min.)	35.03	14.00	14.22	14.75	15.42	17.38	
8	Minimum	587,955.00	586,707.75	588,516.00	587,701.50	587,129.50	588,247.50	**0.022**
	Maximum	589,903.75	589,477.00	589,441.50	589,487.25	588,858.00	589,308.00	
	Average	589,177.85	588,707.28	588,909.53	588,615.75	**588,252.57**	588,762.25	
	Std. Deviation	623.7	878.90	327.79	528.00	620.12	381.66	
	Time (min.)	86.97	30.98	36.44	37.77	40.60	42.71	
9	Minimum	616,349.00	608,436.75	612,932.25	611,974.00	611,149.25	613,422.00	**0.015**

(*continued*)

Table 2. *(continued)*

Problem instance	Analysis	MCPSO	Hybrid MCPSO (IO%:EO% ratio)					ANOVA
			0%:100%	25%:75%	50%:50%	75%:25%	100%:0%	*P-value*
	Maximum	618,259.00	617,638.00	616,545.00	616,096.75	616,663.75	616,290.75	
	Average	617,236.60	614,880.70	615,510.45	**614,465.65**	614,656.13	615,293.73	
	Std. Deviation	612.54	3,474.48	1,151.97	1,428.04	1,623.18	966.60	
	Time (min.)	59.02	21.63	21.71	23.04	23.89	24.65	
10	Minimum	566,033.25	555,947.25	555,038.75	561,096.25	560,539.00	563,620.50	**0.005**
	Maximum	568,658.00	568,574.25	566,740.50	566,867.50	566,242.25	565,769.25	
	Average	567,615.93	565,821.88	**562,962.03**	564,520.63	564,538.45	564,885.23	
	Std. Deviation	1,051.13	3,631.00	4,090.85	1,991.10	1,571.29	718.15	
	Time (min.)	80.95	31.38	32.56	33.86	35.21	36.82	
11	Minimum	956,528.50	943,596.50	952,592.25	950,950.50	950,468.75	952,467.25	**0.000**
	Maximum	961,157.00	959,618.50	957,558.75	957,590.25	956,378.00	955,467.25	
	Average	958,843.10	956,588.75	956,058.43	955,664.61	**953,673.75**	953,942.66	
	Std. Deviation	1,734.03	4,789.36	1,741.44	1,961.10	1,858.93	1,176.38	
	Time (min.)	186.13	72.87	74.36	78.92	82.36	83.14	
Rankings		4th (0:11)	2nd (2:11)	3rd (1:11)	2nd (2:11)	1st (5:11)	3rd (1:11)	

From the statistical analysis in Table 2, it can be seen that the performance of MCPSO+IO(75%):EO(25%) to construct the preference course timetables with the minimum total operating costs was the first ranking. Regarding to the average values of the best so far timetables, five out of eleven problem instances including instance numbers 2, 6, 7, 8, and 11, were better than those values generated by other methods.

MCPSO+EO(100%) and MCPSO+IO(50%):EO(50%) were the second ranking whereas the original MCPSO was the worst. The standard deviations obtained from all proposed methods were marginally different for all problem instances.

The average execution times required by all proposed hybridisations were quicker than MCPSO for all instances (up to 60.85% for the largest instance). Since the number of improved solutions within the population were double after producing the LS improvements (both IO and EO), the number of iterations (I) for the proposed hybrid methods was reduced by half in order to limit the amount of search at the 24,000 candidate solutions. Moreover, the performance differences achieved by all methods were statistically significant with a 95% confidence interval using ANOVA (P-value < 0.05) except some small problem instances.

A comparison of the convergence speed for the proposed hybrid MCPSO using many combinatorial types of IO and EO to investigate the best so far solution is shown in Fig. 2. Problem instance number 11, representing a large problem size, was selected to be an example in this experiment. Although MCPSO+IO(75%):EO(25%) had a lower performance than other hybrid approaches in middle generations, the average of best so far solutions obtained from this hybrid method was the best in the last generation to find the candidate timetables. Therefore, the hybrid strategies with EO and IO improved the performances of MCPSO both in terms of the solution quality and convergence speed.

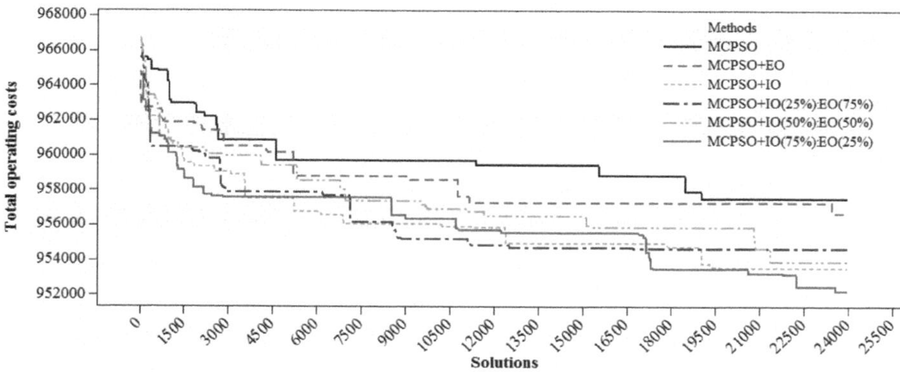

Fig. 2. Convergence plots of hybrid MCPSO with LS for the 11th problem instance

The proposed HPSOT program can be divided into three phases. The first phase was to upload raw timetabling data to the HPSOT tool. Then, all parameters related with MCPSO and problem constraints were assigned via graphic user interface (GUI) as shown in Fig. 3. For the last phase, the best timetables for teachers, students, and classrooms obtained from HPSOT tool will be displayed as shown in Fig. 4

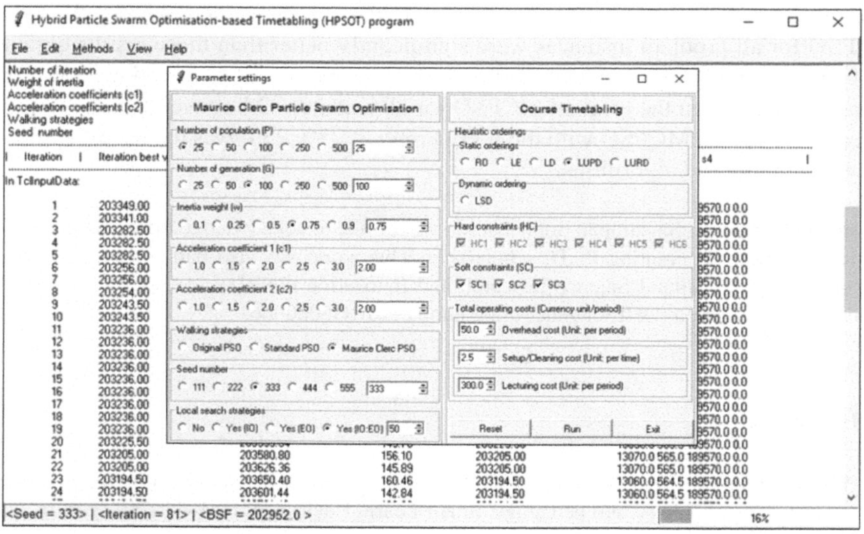

Fig. 3. An example of graphic user interface (GUI) of HPSOT program

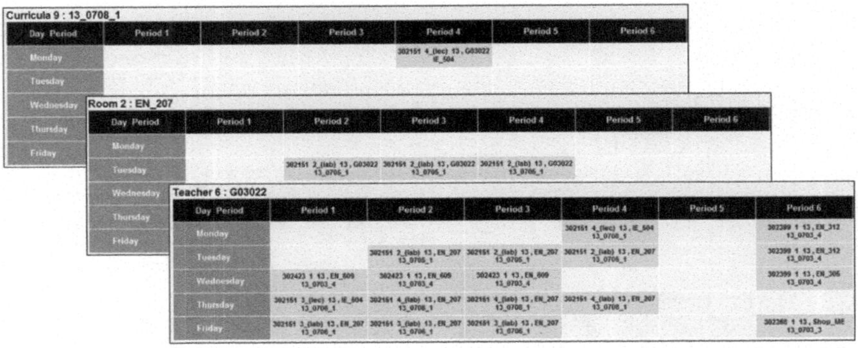

Fig. 4. An example of teacher, student, and classroom timetables obtained from HPSOT tool

6 Conclusions

Hybrid Particle Swarm Optimisation-based timetabling (HPSOT) tool was developed for solving the real-world university course timetabling problem. The MCPSO and its hybridisations with five combinations of the IO and EO ratio were embedded into the HPSOT program for constructing the desirable timetables with minimum academic operating costs. The statistical analysis on the computational results suggested that the averages of the total operating costs associated with the timetables produced by the hybrid MCPSO for all problem instances were significantly better than those results obtained from the original MCPSO. The execution times required by all proposed methods were averagely faster than the original MCPSO for all instances. Moreover, the convergence speed of the hybrid MCPSO with the IO:EO ratio of 75%:25% was the fastest approach among the proposed algorithms.

Acknowledgements. Saisumpan Sooncharoen would like to acknowledge Naresuan University Graduate School for granting Ph.D. scholarship. This work was also part of research project supported by the Thailand Science Research and Innovation (TSRI) and Office of the Higher Education Commission (OHEC) under grant number MRG6080066.

References

1. Yang, J., Pan, H., Zhou, W., Huang, R.: Evaluation of smart classroom from the perspective of infusing technology into pedagogy. Smart Learn. Environ. **5**(1), 1–11 (2018). https://doi.org/10.1186/s40561-018-0070-1
2. Beyrouthy, C., Burke, E.K., McCollum, B., McMullan, P., Parkes, A.J.: University space planning and space-type profiles. J. Sched. **13**, 363–374 (2010)
3. Miranda, J., Rey, P.A., Robles, J.M.: Skeduler: a web architecture based decision support system for course and classroom scheduling. Decis. Support Syst. **52**, 505–513 (2012)
4. Thepphakorn, T., Pongcharoen, P., Hicks, C.: An ant colony based timetabling tool. Int. J. Prod. Econ. **149**, 131–144 (2014)

5. Lutuksin, T., Pongcharoen, P.: Best-worst ant colony system parameter investigation by using experimental design and analysis for course timetabling problem. In: 2nd International Conference on Computer and Network Technology, ICCNT 2010, pp. 467–471 (2010)
6. Pongcharoen, P., Promtet, W., Yenradee, P., Hicks, C.: Stochastic optimisation timetabling tool for university course scheduling. Int. J. Prod. Econ. **112**, 903–918 (2008)
7. Dahmani, I., Hifi, M., Saadi, T., Yousef, L.: A swarm optimization-based search algorithm for the quadratic Knapsack problem with conflict graphs. Exp. Syst. Appl. **148**, 113224 (2020)
8. Dapa, K., Loreungthup, P., Vitayasak, S., Pongcharoen, P.: Bat algorithm, genetic algorithm and shuffled frog leaping algorithm for designing machine layout. In: Ramanna, S., Lingras, P., Sombattheera, C., Krishna, A. (eds.).MIWAI 2013. LNCS (LNAI), vol. 8271, pp. 59–68. Springer, Heidelberg (2013). https://doi.org/10.1007/978-3-642-44949-9_6
9. Pongcharoen, P., Chainate, W., Pongcharoen, S.: Improving artificial immune system performance: inductive bias and alternative mutations. In: Bentley, Peter J., Lee, D., Jung, S. (eds.) ICARIS 2008. LNCS, vol. 5132, pp. 220–231. Springer, Heidelberg (2008). https://doi.org/10.1007/978-3-540-85072-4_20
10. Yang, X.-S.: Swarm intelligence based algorithms: a critical analysis. Evol. Intell. **7**, 17–28 (2014)
11. Lewis, R.: A survey of metaheuristic-based techniques for university timetabling problems. OR Spectr. **30**, 167–190 (2008)
12. Rana, S., Jasola, S., Kumar, R.: A review on particle swarm optimization algorithms and their applications to data clustering. Artif. Intell. Rev. **35**, 211–222 (2011)
13. Jat, S.N., Yang, S.: A guided search non-dominated sorting genetic algorithm for the multi-objective university course timetabling problem. In: Merz, P., Hao, J.-K. (eds.) EvoCOP 2011. LNCS, vol. 6622, pp. 1–13. Springer, Heidelberg (2011). https://doi.org/10.1007/978-3-642-20364-0_1
14. Thepphakorn, T., Pongcharoen, P., Hicks, C.: Modifying regeneration mutation and hybridising clonal selection for evolutionary algorithms based timetabling tool. Math. Probl. Eng. **2015**, 1–16 (2015). Article Number 841748, 16. https://doi.org/10.1155/2015/841748
15. Thepphakorn, T., Pongcharoen, P.: Variants and parameters investigations of particle swarm optimisation for solving course timetabling problems. In: Tan, Y., Shi, Y., Niu, B. (eds.) ICSI 2019. LNCS, vol. 11655, pp. 177–187. Springer, Cham (2019). https://doi.org/10.1007/978-3-030-26369-0_17
16. Kennedy, J., Eberhart, R.: Particle swarm optimization. In: IEEE International Conference on Neural Networks, pp. 1942–1948 (1995)
17. Yang, X.-S.: Nature-Inspired Optimization Algorithms. Elsevier (2014)
18. Chen, R.M., Shih, H.F.: Solving university course timetabling problems using constriction particle swarm optimization with local search. Algorithms **6**, 227–244 (2013)
19. Ahandani, M.A., Vakil Baghmisheh, M.T.: Hybridizing genetic algorithms and particle swarm optimization transplanted into a hyper-heuristic system for solving university course timetabling problem. WSEAS Trans. Comput. **12**, 128–143 (2013)
20. Irene, S.F.H., Deris, S., Mohd Hashim, S.Z.: A combination of PSO and local search in university course timetabling problem. In: Proceedings - 2009 International Conference on Computer Engineering and Technology, ICCET 2009, pp. 492–495 (2009)
21. Zhang, Y., Wang, S., Ji, G.: A comprehensive survey on particle swarm optimization algorithm and its applications. Math. Probl. Eng. **2015** (2015). 38 pages
22. Thangaraj, R., Pant, M., Abraham, A., Bouvry, P.: Particle swarm optimization: hybridization perspectives and experimental illustrations. Appl. Math. Comput. **217**, 5208–5226 (2011)
23. Oswald, C., Anand Deva Durai, C.: Novel hybrid PSO algorithms with search optimization strategies for a university course timetabling problem. In: Proceedings of the 5th International Conference on Advanced Computing, ICoAC 2013, pp. 77–85 (2014)

24. Vafashoar, R., Meybodi, M.R.: Multi swarm bare bones particle swarm optimization with distribution adaption. Appl. Soft Comput. **47**, 534–552 (2016)
25. Fong, C.W., Asmuni, H., McCollum, B.: A hybrid swarm-based approach to university timetabling. IEEE Trans. Evol. Comput. **19**, 870–884 (2015)
26. Talbi, E.-G.: Metaheuristics: From Design to Implementation. John Wiley, Hoboken (2009)
27. Irene, H.S.F., Safaai, D., Mohd, H., Zaiton, S.: University course timetable planning using hybrid particle swarm optimization. In: Proceedings of the 1st ACM/SIGEVO Summit on Genetic and Evolutionary Computation, GEC 2009, pp. 239–245 (2009)
28. Kanoh, H., Chen, S.: Particle swarm optimization with transition probability for timetabling problems. In: Tomassini, M., Antonioni, A., Daolio, F., Buesser, P. (eds.) ICANNGA 2013. LNCS, vol. 7824, pp. 256–265. Springer, Heidelberg (2013). https://doi.org/10.1007/978-3-642-37213-1_27
29. Sheau Fen Ho, I., Safaai, D., Siti Zaiton, M.H.: A study on PSO-based university course timetabling problem, pp. 648–651 (2009)
30. Thepphakorn, T., Pongcharoen, P.: Heuristic ordering for ant colony based timetabling tool. J. Appl. Oper. Res. **5**, 113–123 (2013)
31. Khadwilard, A., Chansombat, S., Thepphakorn, T., Thapatsuwan, P., Chainate, W., Pongcharoen, P.: Application of firefly algorithm and its parameter setting for job shop scheduling. J. Ind. Technol. **8**, 49–58 (2012)
32. Thepphakorn, T., Pongcharoen, P., Vitayasak, S.: A new multiple objective cuckoo search for university course timetabling problem. In: Sombattheera, C., Stolzenburg, F., Lin, F., Nayak, A. (eds.) MIWAI 2016. LNCS (LNAI), vol. 10053, pp. 196–207. Springer, Cham (2016). https://doi.org/10.1007/978-3-319-49397-8_17

Smart Learning Environment

Smart Learning Environments: A Bibliometric Analysis

Xieling Chen[1], Di Zou[2](✉), Haoran Xie[3], and Fu Lee Wang[4]

[1] Department of Mathematics and Information Technology, The Education University of Hong Kong, Tai Po, Hong Kong SAR
s1131872@s.eduhk.hk

[2] Department of English Language Education, The Education University of Hong Kong, Tai Po, Hong Kong SAR
dizoudaisy@gmail.com

[3] Department of Computing and Decision Sciences, Lingnan University, Tuen Mun, Hong Kong SAR
hrxie2@gmail.com

[4] School of Science and Technology, The Open University of Hong Kong, Kowloon, Hong Kong SAR
pwang@ouhk.edu.hk

Abstract. The journal *Smart Learning Environments* (*SLE*) published research work on the issues regarding the reform of learning and teaching methods by advancing existing learning environments. This study presented a systematic review of the 108 *SLE* articles by using bibliometric analysis. This study aimed to 1) examine the trend in the *SLE* articles, 2) identify major contributors to the *SLE*, 3) identify the top influential *SLE* articles, 4) explore the frequently used key phrases within the *SLE* articles, and 5) uncover the major research topics and issues concerned by the *SLE* community. Some interesting results were obtained. First, the annual *SLE* article number had grown from seven to 29. Second, the USA and the *University of North Texas* had contributed the most to the *SLE* community. Also, the "learning environment," "smart learning environment," and "learning process" were the most frequently used key phrases. Additionally, we provided the top ten most-cited *SLE* articles based on the citation counts. This study was helpful in terms of presenting the research status of smart learning environments to researchers and practitioners, as well as raising their awareness of the major issues when considering research topics and project themes.

Keywords: Bibliometric analysis · Highly cited articles · Smart learning environments

1 Introduction

With the advances of novel wireless, ubiquitous, and mobile devices, attempts have been made to investigate the potentials of mobile and ubiquitous learning to facilitate the learning and teaching process and to overcome space and time limitations [1]. Mobile

S. K. S. Cheung et al. (Eds.): ICBL 2020, LNCS 12218, pp. 353–364, 2020.
https://doi.org/10.1007/978-3-030-51968-1_29

learning involves the adoption of mobiles and wireless devices to enable learning while moving [2]. Ubiquitous learning can refer to learning in ubiquitous computing environments, enabling learning anywhere and anytime [3]. Recently, advances in smart devices and online technologies have facilitated the emergence of smart learning environments (SLEs), which involve various connected sensors and devices for delivering services whenever and wherever possible [4]. In this sense, it is understandable that there are some overlaps between mobile learning, ubiquitous learning, and smart learning. According to Lee et al. [5], smart learning refers to learning in interactive, intelligent, and personalized learning environments that are designed with the basis of up-to-date technologies and services, for example, augmented reality, cloud computing, and social networking services.

In recent years, SLEs have increasingly become a research hotspot among researchers worldwide, for example, experts and scholars from computer science and education, most of whom have shown great concern about the development trend and evaluation model of SLEs [6]. In this study, with the use of bibliometric analysis, we conducted a literature review to understand what was going on in SLEs research based on the publications of the journal *Smart Learning Environments* (*SLE*). *SLE* was chosen for the following reasons. First, *SLE* had close relevance to the research target as it aimed to allow different stakeholders of SLEs to receive an in-depth understanding of each other's role in facilitating educational processes as well as how to collaborate to achieve win-win. It sought scientific publications regarding the reform of learning and teaching approaches by advancing the present learning environments towards SLEs. Second, as indicated, it could be insightful to explore the trends, voices, and interpretations of theories and practices within certain areas based on closely relevant journals [7]. Third, *SLE* was open source but did not charge any fee to the authors. Therefore, it was likely to gather wide authorship. In addition, *SLE* offered a fast publication schedule, and articles will be published immediately after acceptance and could be permanently accessed online instantly upon publication. Therefore, the *SLE* articles were undoubtedly in close relation to our research target, and an analysis of the *SLE* publications could provide a better understanding of what was going on in this research field.

Bibliometrics is useful in presenting comprehensive trends of research activities in a particular area. It has been widely adopted in evaluating scientific outputs of a variety of research fields, for example, classroom dialogue [8], social media for healthcare research [9], event detection in social media [10], text mining in medical research [11], artificial intelligence for human brain research [12] and electronic health records processing [13], as well as natural language processing driven medical research [14]. Particularly, bibliometric analysis has also been adopted to evaluate publications of a particular journal, for instance, the *British Journal of Educational Technology* [15] and *Computers and Education* [16].

To that end, this study aimed to identify the trend of the *SLE* article count, major research concerns and issues in the research field of the *SLE*, particularly using a bibliometric analysis method based on articles published by the *SLE*. To be specific, the following five research questions were considered.

RQ1: What was the trend of the *SLE* article count?
RQ2: What were the major contributors to the *SLE* research?

RQ3: What were the top influential *SLE* articles?
RQ4: What were the major issues concerned by the *SLE* community?

2 Materials and Methods

The framework for collecting and analyzing the data is depicted in Fig. 1. As for data collection, since the publications of *SLE* are indexed by Springer, we thus collected all the *SLE* publications published from 2014 to 2019 using the Springer database. In this way, 108 articles were retrieved. We further verified and collected article information used for data analysis by reviewing full-texts of each article, for example, author address information, the article title, the article abstract, and the publication year of the article. As for article citation information, we used the citation information counting up till 11 January 2011, provided by Google Scholar as a measure of article impact.

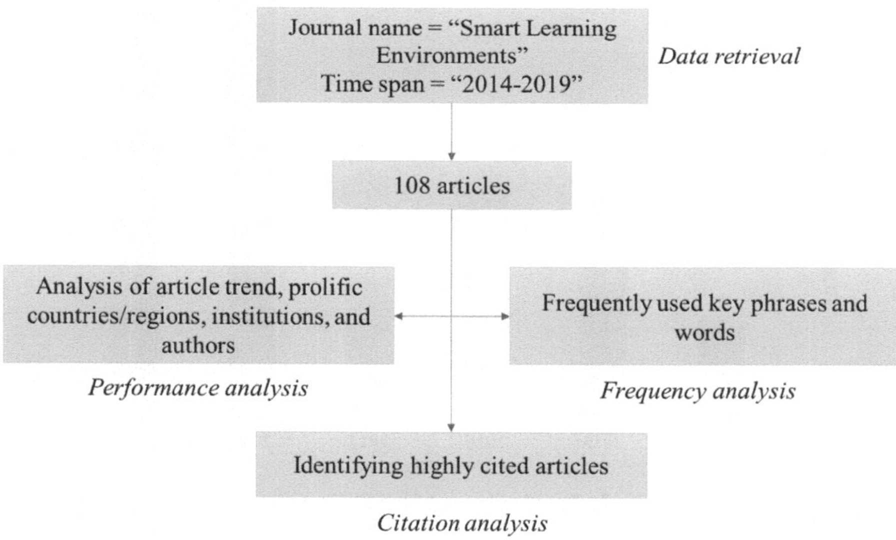

Fig. 1. The framework for data collection and data analysis

With the collected information for all the 108 *SLE* articles, we conducted data analysis mainly in the following four aspects. First, a performance analysis was carried out to analyze the article trend and to identify prolific countries/regions, institutions, and authors. Second, a frequency analysis was adopted to identify the most frequently used key phrases that were extracted from the title and abstract information of each article. Furthermore, we also identified the most frequently used keywords extracted from titles and abstracts of the studied articles. In addition, we identified the top ten highly cited *SLE* articles based on citation analysis.

3 Results

3.1 Analysis of the Article Trend

Figure 2 depicts the timeline of *SLE* articles from 2014 to 2019. On the whole, the total number of *SLE* articles had experienced a significantly increasing trend, from seven articles in 2014 to 30 articles in 2018. In particular, there was a dramatic increase from 2017 to 2018, i.e., from ten articles to 30 articles. However, from 2018 to 2019, there was no much change in the number of articles, with 29 articles in 2019. From the trend analysis of *SLE* articles, we can conclude that since its first appearance, *SLE* had received increasing attention and interest among the authors who were interested in *SLE* research. To a certain degree, this also reflected the growth of research interest in the research field of *SLE*.

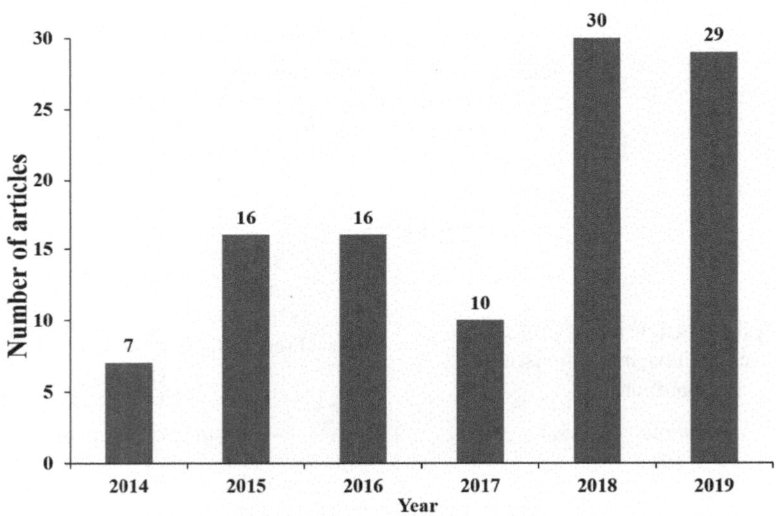

Fig. 2. Trend analysis of the SLE articles

3.2 Analyses of the Countries/Regions, Institutions, and Authors

To analyze countries/regions, institutions, and authors, all participated authors, and all of their affiliated institutions, as depicted in each of the articles, were considered. A total of 40 countries/regions, 130 institutions, and 294 authors made contributions to the publication of the 108 *SLE* articles. However, 42.5% of the countries/regions, 83.85% of the institutions, and 91.16% of the authors contributed to only one article. Table 1 displays 12 most prolific countries/regions with more than three *SLE* articles. From the table, we can see that the USA had contributed the most to the *SLE* research (26 articles), followed by Canada and China, each with 15 articles. From a citation perspective, it is worth noting that although with only eight articles, Taiwan had the most citations as

374, with an index of average citations per article as 46.75, which was the highest within the 12 listed countries/regions. This indicated the wide influence and impact of the *SLE* articles contributed by Taiwan researchers.

Table 1. Top prolific countries/regions

C/R	A	C	ACP	H
USA	26	275	10.58	6
Canada	15	134	8.93	5
China	15	317	21.13	6
Taiwan	8	374	46.75	5
Turkey	6	33	5.50	3
Australia	5	169	33.80	3
Germany	5	33	6.60	3
UK	5	41	8.20	4
Finland	4	15	3.75	2
Greece	4	203	50.75	3
Japan	4	55	13.75	2
Norway	4	55	13.75	4

Abbreviations: C/R: country/region; A: publication count; C: citation count; ACP: Citations per article; H: H-index.

Table 2 displays the top seven prolific institutions with more than two *SLE* articles. From the table, we can see that *the University of North Texas* had contributed the most to *SLE* articles as nine, followed by *Athabasca University* and *Beijing Normal University*, each with seven articles. From a citation perspective, among the listed institutions, the *SLE* articles contributed by *National Sun Yat-Sen University* (with an ACP value as 21.25), *Beijing Normal University* (19.14), and *University of North Texas* (17.44) had significant scientific impact.

Table 3 displays the top nine prolific authors with more than two *SLE* articles. From the table, we can see that *Kinshuk* affiliated with *The University of North Texas* had contributed the most articles (six articles), followed by *Michail Giannakos* affiliated with *Norwegian University of Science and Technology*, and *Nian-Shing Chen* affiliated with *National Sun Yat-Sen University*, each with four articles. From the citation perspective, among the listed authors, it is worth noting that although with only three articles, *Jonathan Michael Spector* affiliated with *University of North Texas* had the most citations as 149, with an index of average citations per article as nine, which was the highest within the nine listed authors. This indicated the wide influence and impact of the *SLE* articles contributed by *Jonathan Michael Spector*.

Table 2. Top prolific institutions

Institutions	C/R	A	C	ACP	H
University of North Texas	USA	9	157	17.44	2
Athabasca University	Canada	7	34	4.86	4
Beijing Normal University	China	7	134	19.14	4
Hacettepe University	Turkey	5	14	2.80	2
National Sun Yat-Sen University	Taiwan	4	85	21.25	2
Norwegian University of Science and Technology	Norway	4	55	13.75	4
University of Eastern Finland	Finland	3	5	1.67	1

Abbreviations are the same as Table 1 except C/R: country/region.

Table 3. Top prolific authors

Authors	Institutions	A	C	ACP	H
Kinshuk	*University of North Texas*	6	24	4.00	3
Michail Giannakos	*Norwegian University of Science and Technology*	4	55	13.75	4
Nian-Shing Chen	*National Sun Yat-Sen University*	4	85	21.25	2
Arif Altun	*Hacettepe University*	3	9	3.00	1
Fathi Essalmi	*Tunis University*	3	24	8.00	3
Hiroaki Ogata	*Kyoto University*	3	54	18.00	2
Jonathan Michael Spector	*University of North Texas*	3	149	49.67	2
Mohamed Jemni	*Tunis University*	3	24	8.00	3
Ronghuai Huang	*Beijing Normal University*	3	18	6.00	2

Abbreviations are the same as Table 1.

3.3 Analysis of the Key Phrases and Key Words

The top 24 most frequently used key phrases are depicted in Table 4, with "learning environment (in 22 SLE articles)" as the most frequently used, followed by "smart learning environment (16)", "learning process (12)," and "learning analytics (11)." Other important key phrases included "smart learning (10)," "case study (7)," "learning experience (7)," "educational context (6)," "learning material (6)," "learning system (6)," and "pedagogical approach (6)." Such key phrase frequency analysis provided insights into what issues had been discussed most within the *SLE* community.

The top 26 frequently used key words are listed in Table 5. There were two learner-related words, including "student (in 52 *SLE* articles)" and "learner (38)," ranking among the top three, indicating that learner was an essential issue concerned by the *SLE* community. Moreover, the application of systems or technologies was also a major concern, with relevant words such as "system (37)," "smart (36)," "application (21)," "online

Table 4. Top 24 key phrases ranked by frequency

Key phrases	A	P	Key phrases	A	P
Learning environment	22	20.37%	Computer science	5	4.63%
Smart learning environment	16	14.81%	Educational resource	5	4.63%
Learning process	12	11.11%	Educational setting	5	4.63%
Learning analytics	11	10.19%	Learning activity	5	4.63%
Smart learning	10	9.26%	Data collection	4	3.70%
Case study	7	6.48%	Educational game	4	3.70%
Learning experience	7	6.48%	Educational system	4	3.70%
Educational context	6	5.56%	Learning approach	4	3.70%
Learning material	6	5.56%	Learning object	4	3.70%
Learning system	6	5.56%	Middle school	4	3.70%
Pedagogical approach	6	5.56%	Significant difference	4	3.70%
Communication technology	5	4.63%	Undergraduate student	4	3.70%

Abbreviations: A: article count; P: percentage.

(19)," and "computer (18)." In addition, issues concerning smart learning environments such as "design (25)," "evaluation (20)," "challenge (19)," and "framework (18)" had also been frequently discussed within the *SLE* community.

Table 5. Top 26 key words ranked by frequency

Key phrases	A	P	Key phrases	A	P
Student	52	48.15%	Evaluation	20	18.52%
Education	40	37.04%	Experience	20	18.52%
Learner	38	35.19%	Method	20	18.52%
System	37	34.26%	Need	20	18.52%
Smart	36	33.33%	Work	20	18.52%
Data	32	29.63%	Challenge	19	17.59%
Model	28	25.93%	Course	19	17.59%
Teaching	27	25.00%	Framework	19	17.59%
Design	25	23.15%	Online	19	17.59%
Content	24	22.22%	Practice	19	17.59%
Tool	24	22.22%	Skill	19	17.59%
Activity	21	19.44%	Teacher	19	17.59%
Application	21	19.44%	Computer	18	16.67%

Abbreviations: A: article count; P: percentage.

3.4 The Top Ten Highly Cited SLE Articles

Based on the Google Scholar citation, the top ten highly cited *SLE* articles were identified. The top ten highly cited *SLE* articles covered particular issues, for example, definitions, characteristics, frameworks, criteria, and challenges conceding SLEs. The top most cited *SLE* article was written by Hwang [17], which presented the definition and criteria of SLEs, proposed a framework of designing and developing SLEs for supporting online and offline learnings, discussed technologies for facilitating SLEs and the characteristics and criteria concerning smart learning, as well as pointing out issues regarding smart learning research. The second most cited *SLE* article was by De Jong et al. [18], which described the Go-Lab philosophy and its initial implementations. The third was by Spector (2014) [19], which presented a framework for various contexts, indicating necessary features specific to typical conditions, and proposed a method to evaluate SLEs. The fourth was by Zhu et al. [20], which discussed the definition of smart education, proposed a four-tier framework of smart instructions, illustrated the major characteristics of SLEs, proposed a technological framework of smart education, and discussed challenges of smart education. The fifth one was by Smeda et al. [21], which proposed a constructivist learning context using digital storytelling, and examined the instructional issues concerning digital storytelling as well as how digital storytelling affected student learning while leaning with digital stories. The sixth one was by Chen et al. [22], which introduced the characteristics and advantages of blockchain technology, investigated several existing blockchain applications for education, and pointed out the benefits and challenges of the adoption of blockchain technologies for educational purposes. The seventh one was by Koper [23], which investigated and defined several key concepts related to SLEs, described the human learning interfaces, presented the definition of SLEs, pointed out a strong challenge for SLEs research, and discussed several research issues concerning human learning interfaces and its adoption. The eighth one was by Gros [24], which discussed key features of smart learning and major challenges for the design of SLEs for supporting personalized learning. Moreover, Scardamalia and Bereiter [25] examined the implications of complexity theory for designing educational technologies. In addition, Mouri and Ogata [26] proposed a novel visualization system by integrating network visualization technologies with a time-map with the basis of ubiquitous learning analytics. They further assessed whether the visualization system was beneficial in terms of discovering relationships between learners and ubiquitous learning analytics, as well as whether the proposed ubiquitous learning graph was easy-to-use.

4 Discussions

This study carried out a bibliometric analysis of *SLE* articles to obtain a thorough review of the status and trends of *SLE* research. The trend analysis of the *SLE* articles indicated a significant growth of the *SLE* publications in academia. This, to a certain degree, reflected an increasing interest in the research concerning smarts learning environments. From the country/region analysis, the USA was the most prolific one that had contributed the most to the *SLE* community. However, from the perspective of the average citations per article, Taiwan was at the first position with an index of average citations per article as 46.75, indicating the wide influence and impact of the *SLE* articles contributed by

Taiwan. From the institution analysis, the *University of North Texas* was the most prolific with nine articles.

Word frequency analysis indicated that the *SLE* articles covered a wide range of interests from multiple research perspectives within the community. This was helpful in terms of enabling a better understanding of the research foci in the *SLE* community. Some important implications concerning research topics and issues are illustrated as follows.

4.1 Important Issues to Be Highlighted

Findings of key phrase analysis offered significant insights into essential concerns among the *SLE* community. The following are worth highlighting.

First, SLEs were frequently discussed within the *SLE* community, with several relevant frequently used phrases, for instance, "learning environment," "smart learning environment," and "smart learning." As indicated by Spector [19], learning environments had changed significantly during the past five decades, particularly due to innovations in information and communication technologies. SLEs are physical contexts created using digital, context-aware, and adaptive devices, aiming at facilitating the learning process [23] and enhancing tailored learning [27] efficiently.

Second, learning analytics was frequently discussed in research about SLEs. As a data-enhanced method aiming to understand better and optimize learning and learning environments, learning analytics can make a great difference to smart learning [28]. Learning analytics involves a variety of tools and methods for collecting and analyzing data gathered in a smart classroom [29]. For example, by using learning analytics, Şahin and Yurdugül [30] proposed an intervention engine with interventions concerning instruction, support, and motivation. Ahad et al. [31] proposed a safeguarded and flexible architecture of an educational model based on the Internet of Everything as well as learning analytics system based on deep learning.

Moreover, there were many authors showing great interest in studying learning processes in SLEs. For example, Martens et al. [32] described an evaluation method proposed in a KOSMOS-2 project for smart support of the process of learning and teaching, while Hartley [33] focused on the conceptualization and support of learning process by using conceptual mapping. In SLEs, learners are required to be conscious of their learning performance in order to realize self-regulated learning [34].

In addition, as indicated, SLEs are learner-centered and aim to achieve effective learning [35]. Therefore, we could see keywords such as "student" and "learner" frequently appearing in the *SLE* articles. In SLEs, systems are able to perceive the scenes of learning activities and identify learners' characteristics and automatically provide them with suitable learning materials [6]. Noh et al. [36] also pointed out that smart leaning usually took place in learner-driven collaborative learning contexts where digital content and services for interaction purposes were involved. SLEs can thus be considered as a learner- and service-driven education approach [5].

4.2 Significance of the Research Findings

The significance of the research findings can be summarized in the following aspects. First, it fills the research gap by presenting generalized insights into the publication trends in *SLE*. Second, it enables scholars and educators to understand the status and trends of *SLE* better. Third, it enables scholars and educators to recognize important contributors to conduct collaborations and share research on smart learning environments. Moreover, it raises the awareness of scholars and educators in terms of predominant research topics concerning SLEs. In addition, the findings can be insightful for companies and governments in terms of resource allocations concerning scientific and technological activities about smart learning.

5 Conclusion Remark and Future Work

This study explored the status and trends of *SLE* research with the utilization of bibliometric analysis. Admittedly, the results and findings were based on only one journal, further studies on more relevant articles collected using keywords search in datasets such as Web of Science and Scopus can be considered. In this way, more comprehensive and solid results can be obtained to enable a more solid understanding of the research field. Moreover, advanced topic modeling methods such as structural topic modeling can be adopted to explore research strength for important contributors. In this way, research strength concerning SLEs of different actors can be identified and appreciated. In addition, manual coding and meta-analysis methods can be further considered to obtain a more in-depth understanding of what has happened as well as what is happening concerning SLEs.

Acknowledgements. This work was supported by the Standing Committee on Language Education and Research (EDB(LE)/P&R/EL/175/2), the Education Bureau of the Hong Kong Special Administrative Region.

References

1. Laru, J., Näykki, P., Järvelä, S.: Four stages of research on the educational use of ubiquitous computing. IEEE Trans. Learn. Technol. **8**(1), 69–82 (2014)
2. Park, Y.: A pedagogical framework for mobile learning: categorizing educational applications of mobile technologies into four types. Int. Rev. Res. Open Distrib. Learn. **12**(2), 78–102 (2011)
3. Shih, S.-C., Kuo, B.-C., Liu, Y.-L.: Adaptively ubiquitous learning in campus math path. Educ. Technol. Soc. **15**(2), 298–308 (2012)
4. Chin, K.-Y., Chen, Y.-L.: A mobile learning support system for ubiquitous learning environments. Proc.-Soc. Behav. Sci. **73**, 14–21 (2013)
5. Lee, J., Zo, H., Lee, H.: Smart learning adoption in employees and HRD managers. Br. J. Educ. Technol. **45**(6), 1082–1096 (2014)
6. Yu, Y., Qi, A.: Teaching system of smart learning environment for aerobics course. Int. J. Emerg. Technol. Learn. **13**(5), 165–176 (2018)

7. Chen, X., Zou, D., Cheng, G., Xie, H.: Detecting latent topics and trends in educational technologies over four decades using structural topic modeling: a retrospective of all volumes of computer & education. Comput. Educ. **151**, 103855 (2020)
8. Song, Y., Chen, X., Hao, T., Liu, Z., Lan, Z.: Exploring two decades of research on classroom dialogue by using bibliometric analysis. Comput. Educ. **137**, 12–31 (2019)
9. Chen, X., Lun, Y., Yan, J., Hao, T., Weng, H.: Discovering thematic change and evolution of utilizing social media for healthcare research. BMC Med. Inform. Decis. Making **19**(2), 50 (2019)
10. Chen, X., Wang, S., Tang, Y., Hao, T.: A bibliometric analysis of event detection in social media. Online Inf. Rev. **43**(1), 29–52 (2019)
11. Hao, T., Chen, X., Li, G., Yan, J.: A bibliometric analysis of text mining in medical research. Soft. Comput. **22**(23), 7875–7892 (2018)
12. Chen, X., Zhang, X., Xie, H., Wang, F.L., Yan, J., Hao, T.: Trends and features of human brain research using artificial intelligence techniques: a bibliometric approach. In: Zeng, A., Pan, D., Hao, T., Zhang, D., Shi, Y., Song, X. (eds.) HBAI 2019. CCIS, vol. 1072, pp. 69–83. Springer, Singapore (2019). https://doi.org/10.1007/978-981-15-1398-5_5
13. Chen, X., Liu, Z., Wei, L., Yan, J., Hao, T., Ding, R.: A comparative quantitative study of utilizing artificial intelligence on electronic health records in the USA and China during 2008–2017. BMC Med. Inf. Decis. Making **18**(5), 117 (2018)
14. Chen, X., Xie, H., Wang, F.L., Liu, Z., Xu, J., Hao, T.: A bibliometric analysis of natural language processing in medical research. BMC Med. Inform. Decis. Making **18**(1), 14 (2018)
15. Chen, X., Zou, D., Xie, H.: Fifty years of British journal of educational technology: a topic modeling based bibliometric perspective. Br. J. Educ. Technol. **51**(3), 692–708 (2020)
16. Chen, X., Yu, G., Cheng, G., Hao, T.: Research topics, author profiles, and collaboration networks in the top-ranked journal on educational technology over the past 40 years: a bibliometric analysis. J. Comput. Educ. **6**, 1–23 (2019). https://doi.org/10.1007/s40692-019-00149-1
17. Hwang, G.-J.: Definition, framework and research issues of smart learning environments-a context-aware ubiquitous learning perspective. Smart Learn. Environ. **1**(1), 4 (2014)
18. De Jong, T., Sotiriou, S., Gillet, D.: Innovations in STEM education: the Go-Lab federation of online labs. Smart Learn. Environ. **1**(1), 3 (2014)
19. Spector, J.M.: Conceptualizing the emerging field of smart learning environments. Smart Learn. Environ/ **1**(1), 2 (2014)
20. Zhu, Z.-T., Yu, M.-H., Riezebos, P.: A research framework of smart education. Smart Learn. Environ. **3**(1), 4 (2016)
21. Smeda, N., Dakich, E., Sharda, N.: The effectiveness of digital storytelling in the classrooms: a comprehensive study. Smart Learn. Environ. **1**(1), 6 (2014)
22. Chen, G., Xu, B., Lu, M., Chen, N.-S.: Exploring blockchain technology and its potential applications for education. Smart Learn. Environ. **5**(1), 1 (2018)
23. Koper, R.: Conditions for effective smart learning environments. Smart Learn. Environ. **1**(1), 5 (2014)
24. Gros, B.: The design of smart educational environments. Smart Learn. Environ. **3**(1), 15 (2016)
25. Scardamalia, M., Bereiter, C.: Smart technology for self-organizing processes. Smart Learn. Environ. **1**(1), 1 (2014)
26. Mouri, K., Ogata, H.: Ubiquitous learning analytics in the real-world language learning. Smart Learn. Environ. **2**(1), 15 (2015)
27. Peng, H., Ma, S., Spector, J.M.: Personalized adaptive learning: an emerging pedagogical approach enabled by a smart learning environment. Smart Learning Environments **6**(1), 1–14 (2019). https://doi.org/10.1186/s40561-019-0089-y

28. Chen, W.: Knowledge-aware learning analytics for smart learning. Proc. Comput. Sci. **159**, 1957–1965 (2019)
29. Aguilar, J., Sánchez, M., Cordero, J., Valdiviezo-Díaz, P., Barba-Guamán, L., Chamba-Eras, L.: Learning analytics tasks as services in smart classrooms. Univ. Access Inf. Soc. **17**(4), 693–709 (2018)
30. Şahin, M., Yurdugül, H.: An intervention engine design and development based on learning analytics: the intelligent intervention system (In 2 S). Smart Learn. Environ. **6**(1), 18 (2019)
31. Ahad, M.A., Tripathi, G., Agarwal, P.: Learning analytics for IoE based educational model using deep learning techniques: architecture, challenges and applications. Smart Learn. Environ. **5**(1), 7 (2018)
32. Martens, A., Sandkuhl, K., Lantow, B., Lehmann, H., Lettau, W.-D., Radisch, F.: An evaluation approach for smart support of teaching and learning processes. Smart Learn. Environ. **6**(1), 2 (2019)
33. Hartley, R.: Conceptualising and supporting the learning process by conceptual mapping. Smart Learn. Environ. **1**(1), 7 (2014)
34. Ferreira, H., de Oliveira, G.P., Araújo, R., Dorça, F., Cattelan, R.: Technology-enhanced assessment visualization for smart learning environments. Smart Learn. Environ. **6**(1), 14 (2019)
35. Widodo, J.: Urban environment and human behaviour: learning from history and local wisdom. Proc.-Soc. Behav. Sci. **42**, 6–11 (2012)
36. Noh, K.-S., Ju, S.-H., Jung, J.-T.: An exploratory study on concept and realization conditions of smart learning. J. Digit. Converg. **9**(2), 79–88 (2011)

The Impact of Cooperative Learning Strategies on Pupils' Learning Engagement in the Smart Classroom Environment

Xue Qin[1(✉)], Yi Zhang[1], Pei Gu[2], and Li Lin[1]

[1] Central China Normal University, Wuhan 430079, China
qinxue@mails.ccnu.edu.cn
[2] Primary School Affiliated to Huazhong University of Science and Technology, Wuhan 430079, China

Abstract. The purpose of this study is to explore the impact of cooperative learning strategies on pupils' learning engagement in a smart classroom environment. This study adopts a one group pre-test and post-test design to study a third-grade music class, "Tiger Molar". This class centers on cooperative learning activities and carries out teaching activities in a smart classroom. The study finds that: (1) In the smart classroom environment, cooperative learning strategies help improve students' learning engagement as a whole. The learning engagement includes positive behavior engagement, negative behavior engagement, positive emotional engagement, and negative emotional engagement. Furthermore, students' negative behavior engagement and negative emotional engagement decreased significantly. (2) When using cooperative learning strategies the smart classroom environment, there is no significant difference in learning engagement between boys and girls.

Keywords: Smart classroom · Cooperative learning strategy · Learning engagement

1 Introduction

The "Smart Classroom" was first proposed by Rescigno in 1988 [1]. The classroom environment should be a kind of new classroom in which teaching content can be optimized to facilitate the acquisition of learning resources to promote classroom interaction [2]. Smart classrooms have evolved from traditional classrooms [3]. Compared with traditional learning environments, smart learning environments facilitate just-in-time learning as they can provide various levels of adaptation and precision of diversified learning conditions for the learners. Some new teaching methods such as cyber synchronous learning, mobile learning, etc. are used in smart classrooms [2, 4]. These learning methods are not available in traditional classrooms.

There is growing evidence that student engagement plays a pivotal role in successful learning and teaching [5]. A higher level of engagement is associated with favorable learning outcomes [6, 7]. However, how to improve students' learning engagement has been plaguing front-line teachers and education researchers. Studies have shown that

S. K. S. Cheung et al. (Eds.): ICBL 2020, LNCS 12218, pp. 365–377, 2020.
https://doi.org/10.1007/978-3-030-51968-1_30

teachers' choice and application of evaluation methods, teaching methods and techniques during learning teaching will have a certain impact on students' learning engagement [8]. Moreover, the learning environment created by smart classrooms can effectively promote students' learning interest, learning motivation, engagement, and effectiveness [9]. For example, Xu Xianlong, Gu Xiaoqing, and other scholars believe that smart classrooms can provide strong technical support for the development of group cooperative learning. Achieve students' transition from lower cognitive goals to higher cognitive goals [10]. Scholars such as Al-Qirim believe that teachers use various learning interaction tools in a smart classroom can stimulate students to actively participate in teaching activities. Therefore, effective and in-depth interaction between teachers and students can be achieved [11].

The literature review shows that articles mainly focus on the positive influence of smart classrooms on students' learning engagement in higher education. However, few scholars have studied the impact of smart classrooms on pupils' learning engagement. In particular, study on the impact of a certain teaching strategy on students' learning engagement in a smart classroom environment. Based on the above study needs, this study uses the following questions guided our study design: (1) What's the impact of cooperative learning strategies on pupils' learning engagement in a smart classroom environment. (2) When using cooperative learning strategies in a smart classroom environment, are there any differences in learning engagement between boys and girls. Finally, from the perspective of improving students' learning engagement, this study puts forward suggestions for teachers on how to implement cooperative teaching strategies in a smart classroom environment.

2 Literature Review

2.1 Research on the Status of Cooperative Learning Strategies

Cooperative learning is a learning model that uses groups as a learning unit to complete learning tasks through mutual learning. Many researchers have shown that cooperative learning strategies have positive effects on students' learning in many ways. Such as improving peer relationships, enhancing class cohesion, increasing learning interest, and improving learning performance on a large scale, especially for the less advanced students [12]. The cooperative research conducted in American universities found that the impact of cooperative learning on students can be divided into the following four aspects: (1) learning success (2) relationship quality (3) psychological adjustment (4) positive attitude towards university experience [13]. In China, Xu Xianlong and other scholars believe that smart classrooms can support for the development of group cooperative learning, effectively improve students' learning engagement and learning interest [10]. However, the impact of applications of cooperative learning strategies on pupils' learning engagement in a smart classroom environment is still lacking in the literature.

2.2 Research on Learning Engagement

Students' learning engagement has been extensively studied since the 1980s [14]. There are many domestic and foreign scales for measuring student learning engagement.

For example, Miserandino revised "the Rochester Assessment Package for Schools" to get a scale that includes two dimensions: behavior and emotion [15]. In China, Wang Yashuang's team designed a five-dimensional scale that includes metacognitive strategies, peer interaction, deep cognitive strategies, teacher-student interaction, and enthusiasm for learning [16]. However, there are relatively few studies on measuring the learning engagement of pupils in smart classrooms. This study hopes to provide a theoretical reference for improving learning engagement in smart classrooms.

3 Course Design and Implementation of Music Class "Tiger Molar"

3.1 Course Introduction

"Tiger Molar" is a music class in the third grade of elementary school. The song used in this class is taken from Chinese classic music. This class creates a story background for the song "Tiger Molar". Students need to create an appropriate soundtrack based on the story. On the one hand, "Tiger Molar" is composed of a variety of folk percussion melody. Students can use the "GarageBand" app on the iPad to simulate different musical instruments for creation. In this way, each student has the opportunity to be exposed to a variety of musical instruments. On the other hand, this song has five sections, which are suitable for group cooperation to reduce the task of students.

The goals of this music are: (1) Students can understand the characteristics of folk percussion instruments in music performance. (2) Students can use their imagination and choose suitable instruments for music creation. (3) Students can use different playing methods of the same instrument to express different images of tigers.

3.2 Environment Analysis of the Smart Classroom

The primary school affiliated to Huazhong University of Science and Technology is a key primary school in Wuhan, China. The smart classroom environment of this study was carried out in the multi-functional hall of this school. The multi-function hall of this school contains basic hardware facilities, teaching recording and broadcasting systems, multimedia teaching systems, iPad and wireless network to assist teaching. Smart classrooms like this have advantages of optimizing the presentation of teaching content and promoting interactive activities in the learning [2]. Compared with traditional classrooms, smart classrooms are more intelligent, which is conducive to stimulating students' learning interest, improving teaching quality, and promoting the integration of information technology and teaching [17]. Teachers can use the AirPlay function on the iPad to project the teaching content onto the LED screen. This not only allows teachers and students to clearly see the learning content but also promotes interactive activities. Teachers can use the learning interactive platform to publish learning tests to understand the students' current learning situation. After the class, teachers can also watch the recorded videos repeatedly to find out problems in the teaching process.

3.3 APT Teaching Model

In the information age, many experts and scholars have proposed models for information technology teaching. These include the "APT model" proposed by Professor Zhang, Bai and Li [18] in Central China Normal University. As an informative teaching model, APT focuses on the integration of assessment, pedagogy, and technology [2]. Studies have shown that teaching based on the APT teaching model has a significant positive impact on pupils' learning interest [18]. The APT model for music class "Tiger Molar" is shown below (Fig. 1). In terms of pedagogy, this class focuses on cooperative learning.

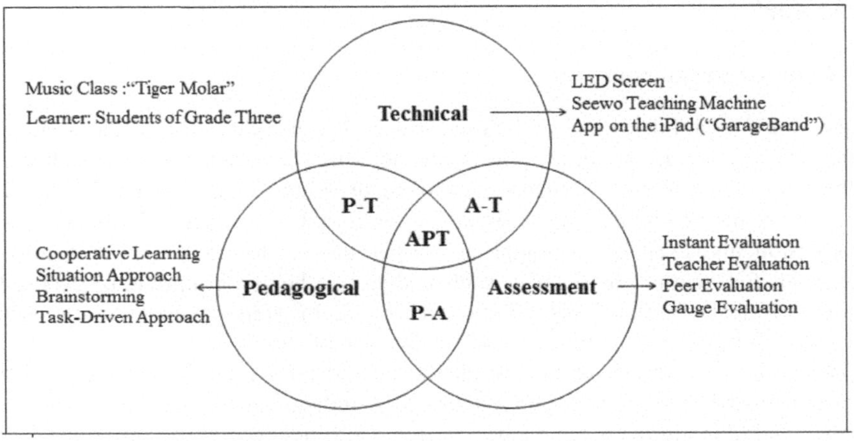

Fig. 1. APT teaching model of "Tiger Molar"

3.4 Tiger Molar Instructional Design and Implementation

"Tiger Molar" is a third-grade music class in elementary school. The course design includes two parts: preview before class and smart classroom teaching. In the first part (preview before class): the teacher divides the whole class into five groups with six people in each group. Students learn to use "GarageBand" on the iPad in groups. In other words, students are already familiar with the use of the iPad before the formal class. In the second part (smart classroom teaching): this part is mainly composed of seven steps: Situational Introduction and Brainstorming, Review Previous Knowledge, First Cooperation, Group Presentation, The Second Cooperation, Class Performance, and Outreach Activity. These teaching activities are shown in Table 1.

The following supplement explains how technology and evaluation support teaching and how cooperative learning activities are carried out. The on-site teaching environment is shown in Fig. 2. The operation interface of the "GarageBand" application is projected on the LED screen.

- Situational Introduction and Brainstorming (0–8 min): The teacher uses the LED screen and the Seewo teaching machine to present courseware and use the situation

Table 1. Teaching activities of "Tiger Molar"

Activities	Description	Assessment/Pedagogical/Technical
Situational Introduction and Brainstorming (0–8 min)	(1) Student A recites the story of "Tiger Molar" without a soundtrack (2) Student A recites the story again with a soundtrack (3) The teacher guides students to think about where the soundtrack has been added to the story and how the soundtrack has influenced the story (4) The teacher guides students to think about which sounds in the story can be simulated with musical instruments? (5) Students use the "GarageBand" application on the iPad to conduct independent exploration	A: Instant Evaluation; P: Situation Approach; Brainstorming T: LED Screen; Seewo Teaching Machine; iPad ("GarageBand")
Review Previous Knowledge (8–13 min)	(1) The teacher leads students to review four rhythm patterns: "x", "xx", "x- "and "x. x" (2) The teacher invites student B to write a four-bar rhythm according to the above rhythm and select a musical instrument to play in "GarageBand" (3) The teacher asks other students to carefully observe whether student B's rhythm is written in norms	A: Peer Evaluation P: Brainstorming T: LED Screen; Seewo Teaching Machine; iPad ("GarageBand")

(*continued*)

Table 1. *(continued)*

Activities	Description	Assessment/Pedagogical/Technical
First Cooperation (13–25)	(1) The teacher distributes task lists and assigns group learning tasks. Each group will write a soundtrack for one of the scenes in the whole story (2) The teacher presents fun evaluation criteria and prompts students to start the five-minute countdown (3) Through teamwork, everyone completes a creative work (4) The teacher allows students to share their work in their own group and each group judges the best work. The team leader uploads the best work to the cloud platform	A: Peer Evaluation Gauge Evaluation P: Task-driven Approach; Cooperative Learning T: LED Screen; Seewo Teaching Machine; iPad ("GarageBand")
Group Presentation (25–34 min)	Each group takes turns to play and other groups give revise opinions	A: Peer Evaluation P: Cooperative Learning T: LED Screen; Seewo Teaching Machine; iPad ("GarageBand")
The second cooperation (34–36 min)	Each group reflects and revises the work based on the revision opinions	P: Cooperative Learning T: iPad ("GarageBand")
Class Performance (36–38)	Each group plays a scene of "Tiger Molar" in turn. Five scenes correspond to five groups	A: Teacher Evaluation P: Cooperative Learning T: LED Screen; Seewo Teaching Machine; iPad ("GarageBand")
Outreach Activity (38-40 min)	The teacher participates in students' presentation. The teacher sings the story while students play together	P: Cooperative Learning T: iPad ("GarageBand")

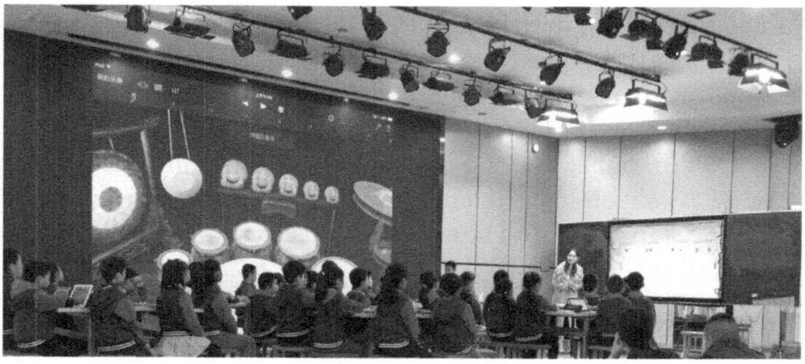

Fig. 2. Smart teaching environment

approach to introduce the course. Then the teacher guides the teaching step by step by continuously asking questions to the students. Students brainstorm to answer questions and the teacher evaluates the students' answers in real time. After brainstorming, students use the iPad to explore.

- Review Previous Knowledge (8–13 min): The teacher presents the content to be reviewed through the LED screen and the Seewo teaching machine. Then the teacher invites student B to write rhythm through the electronic whiteboard function of Seewo teaching machine and perform with "GarageBand". The rest of the students find and point out the problems in the writing and performance of student B through brainstorming.
- First Cooperation (13–25 min): The teacher presents group tasks and evaluation gauges (Fig. 3) through the LED screens and the Seewo teaching machine. Then students use the "GarageBand" app on the iPad to simulate musical instruments for music creation and complete the task list (Fig. 4). When students fill out the task list, the teacher uses "AirPlay" to project the content on the task list onto the LED screen. Students share their work within the group and evaluate others' work according to the gauge. Finally, team leaders uploaded representative works to the cloud platform through the iPad.

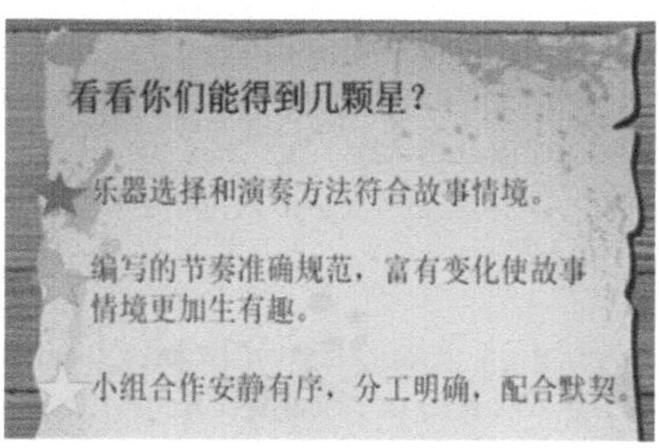

Fig. 3. Evaluation gauge

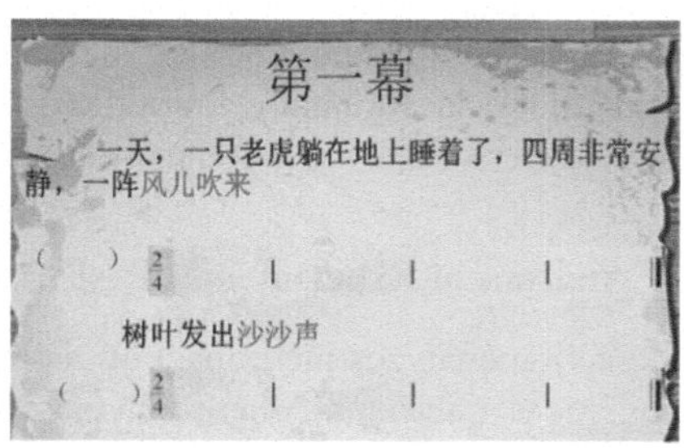

Fig. 4. Task list

- Group Presentation (25–34 min): The teacher downloads group works from the cloud platform. During the group presentation, each student is only responsible for the performance of one instrument. Each group completes the ensemble through cooperation. Through peer evaluation, each group gets revise opinions.
- The Second Cooperation (35–36 min): Discuss and modify the work in groups. Students test on "GarageBand". Team leaders upload the work again via iPad.
- Class Performance (36–38 min): The teacher evaluates the performance of each group.

4 Experiment Design and Data Analysis

4.1 Research Object and Process

This study selects 40 students from the third grade of Primary School Affiliated to Huazhong University of Science and Technology as the research objects, including 22 boys and 18 girls. In this study, researchers conduct a pre-test of students' learning engagement before the experiment course and conduct a post-test of students' learning engagement after the experiment course.

4.2 Measuring Tools

This research mainly uses questionnaires to analyze the impact of cooperative learning strategies on pupils' learning engagement in a smart classroom environment. The measurement tool used by this study is the "Questionnaire on Pupils' Learning Engagement in the Smart Classroom Environment". The questionnaire is adapted from the "Behavioral Engagement and Disaffection Scale" designed by Skinner, Kindermann, and Furrer [19]. The questionnaire used in this experiment is shown in Table 2. It includes two dimensions of positive engagement and negative engagement. The positive engagement level consists of positive behavior engagement and positive emotional engagement; the negative engagement level consists of negative behavior engagement and negative emotional engagement. The questionnaire consisted of 16 questions, of which the second, fourth, sixth, eighth, tenth, twelfth, fourteenth, and fourteenth questions were reverse questions, and the Likert scale was used. The overall Cronbach's Alpha value calculated by SPSS software is 0.851, indicating that the questionnaire has good reliability. To ensure the validity of the questionnaire, the author invited two experts to evaluate the questionnaire, and the experts believed that the questionnaire had good validity.

4.3 Analysis of Experimental Research Data

This section analyzes the impact of cooperative learning strategies on pupils' learning engagement in the smart classroom environment based on data obtained from the questionnaires. A total of 80 questionnaires were distributed in two rounds, and 78 were collected. After excluding the invalid questionnaires, 70 valid questionnaires accounted for 87.5% of the number of questionnaires issued.

Analysis of the Status of Students' Learning Engagement

To explore the impact of cooperative learning strategies on pupils' learning engagement

Table 2. Questionnaire

Components	Item description
Positive behavior engagement	Q1: When I take a music class in a smart classroom, I work as hard as I can
	Q5: When I take a music class in a smart classroom, I participate in class discussions
	Q9: When I take a music class in a smart classroom, I pay attention in class
	Q13: When I take a music class in a smart classroom, I listen very carefully
Negative behavior engagement (-)	Q2: When I take a music class in a smart classroom, I think about other things
	Q6: When I take a music class in a smart classroom, I just act like I'm working
	Q10: When I take a music class in a smart classroom, I don't try very hard.
	Q14: When I take a music class in a smart classroom, I will do things not related to the class
Positive emotional engagement	Q3: When I work on something in a smart classroom, I feel interested
	Q7: The knowledge learned in music class is useful for life
	Q11: When I take a music class in a smart classroom, I enjoy learning new things
	Q15: When I take a music class in a smart classroom, I feel good
Negative emotional engagement (-)	Q4: When I work on something in a smart classroom, I feel bored
	Q8: When the quality of my work is not good, I feel frustrated
	Q12: When I take a music class in a smart classroom, I feel nervous
	Q16: Music classes in a smart classroom are not all fun for me

in the smart classroom environment, the author uses SPSS to conduct paired-sample T-tests based on the data of the questionnaire. The results are shown in Table 3. The scores about negative behavior engagement and negative emotional engagement in the Table 3 have been reversed, because they correspond to the reverse questions in the questionnaire. The scores of post-test in these three dimensions are higher than the scores of pre-test: negative behavioral engagement, positive emotional engagement, and negative emotional engagement. In addition, there are significant differences between the scores before and after the test: negative behavioral engagement ($p = 0.005 < 0.01$) and negative emotional engagement ($p = 0.040 < 0.05$).

Among all the questions, these two questions have the highest scores: "when I take a music class in a smart classroom, I listen very carefully" and "when I work on something in a smart classroom, I feel interested",with scores of 4.800 and 4.771 respectively. This shows that the smart classroom learning environment is very attractive to students. Smart

Table 3. Comparative analysis of learning engagement

Group	Variable	N	Mean	Std. deviation	t	Sig.
Positive behavior engagement	Pre-test	35	4.757	0.390	1.246	0.221
	Post-test	35	4.692	0.518		
Negative behavior engagement	Pre-test	35	3.807	0.905	−3.024	0.005**
	Post-test	35	4.128	0.800		
Positive emotional engagement	Pre-test	35	4.600	0.647	−6.760	0.504
	Post-test	35	4.657	0.535		
Negative emotional engagement	Pre-test	35	4.207	0.993	−2.131	0.040*
	Post-test	35	4.457	0.807		

*$p < 0.05$, **$p < 0.01$, ***$p < 0.001$

Table 4. Comparison of group learning engagement

	Positive behavior engagement	Negative behavior engagement	Positive emotional engagement	Negative emotional engagement	Problems in music works
Pre-test (Group1)	4.857	3.179	4.892	3.678	The sound of playing the musical instruments is too loud
Post-test (Group1)	4.893	3.714	4.892	4.035	
Pre-test (Group2)	4.781	3.812	4.218	4.437	The sound of playing the musical instruments is too loud
Post-test (Group2)	4.812	4.187	4.437	4.625	
Pre-test (Group3)	4.666	4.250	4.625	4.333	The choice of musical instruments is not suitable
Post-test (Group3)	4.500	4.333	4.625	4.375	
Pre-test (Group4)	4.892	3.964	4.785	4.714	Have rhythm problems
Post-test (Group4)	4.642	4.321	4.678	4.821	
Pre-test (Group5)	4.571	3.892	4.537	3.857	Few types of musical instruments
Post-test (Group5)	4.571	4.107	4.678	4.392	

classrooms can support teachers to carry out cooperative learning activities and increase students' interest in the class.

The mean scores of five groups' learning engagement are shown in Table 4. Among them, the problems in the works of Group 1 and Group 2 are relatively light. The data shows that Group 1 and Group 2 have relatively high levels of learning engagement. In other words, a higher degree of learning engagement can make students learn better.

Analysis of Differences in Learning Engagement between Boys and Girls
As can be seen from the Table 5, both boys and girls show a high level of learning engagement in the smart classroom. The scores of girls on the negative behavior level ($4.194 > 4.058$) and negative emotion level ($4.555 > 4.352$) are slightly higher than boys, but there is no significant difference. The scores of boys and girls are roughly the same at the positive behavior level ($4.691 \approx 4.694$) and the positive emotion level ($4.661 \approx 4.652$). Therefore, when using cooperative learning strategies in a smart classroom environment, there is no significant difference in learning engagement between boys and girls.

Table 5. Comparison of learning engagement between boys and girls

	Variable	N	Mean	Exact Sig. [2* (1 − tailed Sig.)]
Positive behavior engagement	Boy	17	4.691	.732[b]
	Girl	18	4.694	
Negative behavior engagement	Boy	17	4.058	.909[b]
	Girl	18	4.194	
Positive emotional engagement	Boy	17	4.661	1.000[b]
	Girl	18	4.652	
Negative emotional engagement	Boy	17	4.352	.832[b]
	Girl	18	4.555	

a. Grouping Variable: Gender
b. Not corrected for ties.

5 Conclusion

This study explores the impact of cooperative learning strategies on pupils' learning engagement in the smart classroom environment. The study finds that: (1) In the smart classroom environment, cooperative learning strategies are conducive to reducing students' negative behavior engagement and negative emotional engagement. However, there are no significant effect on positive behavior and positive emotional engagement. The reason for this phenomenon may be the short implementation time of teaching strategies. Therefore, the research time can be extended in future research so that students can adapt to the relevant environments and teaching strategies. (2) In the smart classroom environment, there is no significant difference in learning engagement between boys and girls. The reason for this phenomenon may be that the sample size is not large enough. Therefore, in future research, the scope of research objects can be expanded, and the number of students in schools, disciplines, and grades can be increased.

Here are some suggestions for developing cooperative learning in smart classrooms: (1) During the research, the author finds that pupils are often attracted by irrelevant content on the iPad when they carry out group cooperation activities in smart classrooms. Therefore, teachers are advised to clarify the rules of group activities and select team leaders to supervise the behavior of team members before class. Teachers should also delete or lock irrelevant apps on iPads before class. In this way, students can work more focused and get better teaching results. (2) In addition, teachers can use a variety of cooperation methods. Cooperation can be within groups, between different groups, and between teachers and students. Technology is like "lubricating oil" that makes the teaching process progress more smoothly. All in all, teachers should make full use of cooperative activities and smart classroom environment to improve student learning engagement and ultimately achieve better teaching results.

References

1. Rescigno, R.C.: Practical implementation of educational technology. The GTE/GTEL smart-classroom. The Hueneme school district experience. Acad. Achi. **27** (1988)
2. Zhang, Y., Li, X., Zhu, L., Dong, X., Hao, Q.: What is a smart classroom? A literature review. In: Yu, S., Niemi, H., Mason, J. (eds.) Shaping Future Schools with Digital Technology. PRRE, pp. 25–40. Springer, Singapore (2019). https://doi.org/10.1007/978-981-13-9439-3_2
3. Huang, R., et al.: The functions of smart classroom in smart classroom age. Open Educ. Res. **18**(2), 22–27 (2012). (in Chinese)
4. Kinshuk, et al.: Evolution is not enough: revolutionizing current learning environments to smart learning environments. Inter. J. Artif. Intel. Educ. **26**(2), 561–581(2016). https://doi.org/10.1007/s40593-016-0108-x
5. Henrie, C.R., Halverson, L.R., Graham, C.R.: Measuring student engagement in technology-mediated learning: a review. Comp. Educ. **90**, 36–53 (2015)
6. Dotterer, A.M., Lowe, K.: Classroom context, school engagement, and academic achievement in early adolescence. J. Youth Adolesc. **40**(12), 1649–1660 (2011)
7. Lee, J.S.: The relationship between student engagement and academic performance: is it a myth or reality? J. Educ. Res. **107**(3), 177–185 (2014)
8. Huang, X.R.: The study on pupils' learning engagement and the influence factors in the smart classroom. Doc. Dis. (2016). (in Chinese)
9. Jena, P.C.: Effect of smart classroom learning environment on learning achievement of rural high achievers and low achievers in science. Int. Lett. Soc. Hum. Sci. **3**(3), 1–9 (2013)
10. Xu, X.L., Wang, X.H., Gu, X.Q.: Design and effectiveness of group collaborative learning in smart classroom. Open Educ. Res. (2017). https://doi.org/10.13966/j.cnki.kfjyyj.2017.04.011. (in Chinese)
11. Al-Qirim, N.: Smart board technology success in tertiary institutions: the case of the UAE university. Educ. Inf. Technol. **21**(2), 265–281 (2014). https://doi.org/10.1007/s10639-014-9319-7
12. Sharan, S.: Cooperative learning in small groups: recent methods and effects on achievement, attitudes, and ethnic relations. Rev. Educ. Res. **50**(2), 241–271 (1980)

13. Johnson, D.W., Johnson, R.T.: Making cooperative learning work. Theory Prac. **38**(2), 67–73 (1999)
14. Appleton, J.J., Christenson, S.L., Furlong, M.J.: Student engagement with school: critical conceptual and methodological issues of the construct. Psychol. Sch. **45**(5), 369–386 (2008)
15. Miserandino, M.: Children who do well in school: individual differences in perceived competence and autonomy in above-average children. J. Educ. Psychol. **88**(88), 203–214 (1996)
16. Wang, Y.S.: An empirical study on undergraduates' learning engagement—based on the data analysis of the 2012 "national college students' learning survey". China High. Educ. Res. **01**, 32–36 (2013)
17. Yang, J.F.: Evaluation and optimization of technology-enhanced learning environment. E-educ. Res. **37**(12), 99–105 (2016). https://doi.org/10.13811/j.cnki.eer.2016.12.014. (in Chinese)
18. Zhang, Y., Bai, Q.Y., et al.: The influence of mobile learning based on the APT teaching model on students' learning interest and performance—a case study of primary school mathematics. China Educ. Tech. **348**(1), 26–33 (2016) https://doi.org:/10.3969/j.issn.1006-9860.2016.01.004. (in Chinese)
19. Skinner, E.A., Kindermann, T.A., Furrer, C.J.: A motivational perspective on engagement and disaffection: conceptualization and assessment of children's behavioral and emotional participation in learning activities in the learning. Educ. Psychol. Meas. **69**(3), 493–525 (2009)

Development and Effect of Primary School Chinese Reading Generative Classroom Model in the Intelligent Environment

Xiaojuan Chen[1], Youru Xie[2(✉)], Jiaying Lin[1], Huiyu Lai[2], Hai Yang[1], Huiwen Zhong[2], and Jiayao Wu[2]

[1] LuDiXi Primary School, Guangzhou, China
[2] School of Educational Information Technology, South China Normal University, Guangzhou, China
764132531@qq.com

Abstract. Classroom revolution is an essential trend in the fundamental education field in China within the education informatization 2.0 era. And it is crucial to deepen talent cultivation model reform and bolster students' creativity and practical ability. Generative teaching, a new teaching model derived from generativist perspectives, emphasizes the traditional classroom reformation and dynamic educational generation. The intelligent environment empowers the development and application of generative classrooms due to its advanced technological characteristics. This study develops a primary school Chinese reading generative classroom model based on theoretical reasoning and practical research. In addition, this study applies the model in teaching practice and produces an evaluation index system to assess its effectiveness. The results indicate that using the generative classroom model can achieve the Chinese reading classroom's teaching objectives, promote students' reading abilities and Chinese literacy.

Keywords: Generative teaching · Chinese reading · Teaching model · Assess effectiveness

1 Introduction

The new round of scientific and technological revolution represented by the fifth-generation mobile communication technology leads to a fundamental change to the society. Under the background of the new era, the calls for "classroom revolution" has gradually become the mainstream. Training people with core qualities has become a new educational task. Among many qualities, reading quality is one of the most basic and critical. Reading is the cornerstone of human acquisition of knowledge and communication. In the digital era with the explosive growth of knowledge, it is particularly

This paper is one of the research results of the national educational information technology research project of "the 13th five-year plan", "the research on the generative teaching mode of intelligent classroom oriented to personality development" (project no.: 174430027).

S. K. S. Cheung et al. (Eds.): ICBL 2020, LNCS 12218, pp. 378–391, 2020.
https://doi.org/10.1007/978-3-030-51968-1_31

important to have the good reading ability. Chinese reading course in basic education is an important way to cultivate students' reading ability. The new curriculum reform puts forward higher requirements for Chinese reading teaching, paying more attention to students' active construction, ability improvement, and personality development in reading courses. Generative teaching is a new teaching model from the perspective of generative philosophy. It pays attention to students' independent inquiry and meaning construction, emphasizes flexible presupposition and dynamic generation of teaching, and becomes an effective way to cultivate students' quality. At the same time, its dynamic generation process is inseparable from the technical support provided by the intelligent classroom teaching environment. The combination of the generated teaching concept and the technical function of the intelligent classroom can effectively change the traditional Chinese reading classroom form, reconstruct the teaching process, and provide more possibilities for the generation and implementation of the Chinese reading class. Based on this, the study applies generative teaching of Chinese reading-related theory as the guide, relying on the Guangzhou LuDiXi primary school as the platform to implement the generative class model within the Chinese reading intelligent environment and advance the research of the model' effect. With the basis of literature research and practice experience, this study intent to construct the Chinese reading generative classroom model from the smart classroom and practice the model in the teaching. Following the model, we also design the corresponding evaluation system to test the model experiments, so as to provide theoretical guidance for Chinese reading teaching reform and practice of reference.

2 Literature Review

2.1 Generative Teaching

Wittrock MC, an American educational psychologist, first proposed the concept of "generative learning". He believed that the generative learning process is the generation process in which the original cognitive structure of the learning subject interacts with the sensory information received from the environment and actively constructs the information meaning [1]. However, professor Ye Lan was the first to put forward the idea of generative teaching in China. She believed that we should "use the concept of dynamic generation to comprehensively understand classroom teaching and construct a new concept of classroom teaching" [2].

At present, the research trending of generative teaching focuses on the theoretical research, action research, model design, teaching application and development strategy of generative teaching. For example, Wang Jian et al. using generative philosophy and other theories as the point of penetration to discussed the main theoretical basis of generative teaching concept, combining with the results of classroom process research, proposed the classroom interaction model of generative teaching [3]; Brinton C G et al. studied user behavior in courses offered by MOOC providers, used linear regression model to analyze forum activity data, and proposed a generative design model [4]; Trespalacios J H compares two learning theories from generative learning and conducts a practical research on how to use virtual teaching AIDS to improve rational number teaching for third-grade students [5]; According to the basic idea of generating curriculum, Yu sheng Quan et al. designed and implemented a teacher-student collaborative curriculum [6]; Taking the electronic schoolbag as an example, Xie You Ru et al. constructed a generative intelligent learning environment and applied it [7]; By analyzing the characteristics and shortcomings of traditional classroom questioning, Zhao Ming Ren et al. studied classroom questioning strategies from the perspective of generative teaching [8].

It can be seen that generative teaching, as a new educational concept, has obtained a certain research basis in theoretical research, model construction and practical application. However, in the field of basic education, there are relatively few teaching models combining the characteristics of specific subjects.

2.2 The Application of Intelligent Technology in Chinese Classroom

Artificial intelligence technology, cloud computing, Internet technology, big data, fusion reality and other intelligent technologies bring new ideas for teaching reform, so in the basic education, more and more attention is paid to the application of these intelligent technologies in the classroom. Under the guidance of the national education informatization construction and development policy, many schools have been equipped with high-speed broadband and related intelligent equipment, and started to carry out educational application experiments of intelligent technology. At present, the research on the application of intelligent technology in Chinese classroom mainly focuses on strategy research, teaching model construction and effect analysis. For example, Huang Tao et al. introduced artificial intelligence technology to assist the teaching of primary school Chinese writing, aiming at the problems of writing obstacles in the teaching of primary school Chinese writing. He also proposed a human-machine collaborative support model of primary school Chinese writing teaching [9]; Huang YongYu made a research on the effective integration of comprehensive Chinese learning in primary school based on intelligent terminal equipment and cultivating students' high-level thinking and its effect [10]; Xue Sheng Lan proposed the "smart phone +Moodle platform" to construct the teaching interactive feedback system, and discussed the implementation method, application mode and practical effect of IRS system based on smart phone applied to Chinese classroom teaching [11].

To sum up, the application of intelligent technology in the Chinese classroom is still in the exploration stage, and some relevant theoretical researches have appeared, but the foundation is weak. In order to form a scientific system, it is necessary to integrate intelligent technology into classroom teaching and summarize the supporting effect of technology on classroom teaching.

3 Model Development

3.1 Rationale

Generative Teaching Theory. The traditional classroom has been difficult to meet the students' personality development and social requirements for talent training, the current teaching reform in China advocates from "pre-learning activities and behaviors" to "generation". Generative teaching is on the foundation of elastic preset, in which teachers and students interact fully and adjust teaching activities and behaviors constantly, jointly construct and form new information and resources of the dynamic process, to achieve the teaching objectives and create supplementary [12]. Besides generative teaching is characterized by nonlinearity, concreteness, diversity, difference, interactivity and creativity [13]. In generative teaching, the interaction between teachers and students can make students actively participate in the teaching process, so as to generate students' reading methods, reading thinking and reading ability. It can let students learn independently, lay a foundation for cultivating students' innovation ability and imagination, and improve students' key competency.

Primary School Chinese Reading Literacy and Teaching Process. We're in an era of information, reading is an important way of human development, and citizens' reading literacy is an important symbol of a country's civilization. Reading literacy refers to the process of individuals' understanding, application, reflection and active participation in reading activities [14]. According to the Chinese curriculum standard for senior high schools issued in 2017 that the key competency of Chinese consists of language understanding and application, thinking development and promotion, aesthetic appreciation and creation, and cultural inheritance and understanding. This provides a reference for the target dimension of Chinese reading teaching in basic education. And it can be seen that reading literacy has become an important part of the key competency of Chinese.

Primary school Chinese reading class is the main way to cultivate reading literacy, is one of the most important classes in the Chinese subject of basic education. In the long-term practice and theoretical research, gradually formed some typical Chinese reading teaching path [15–17]. Combined with literature research and long-term front-line teaching and research experience, this study extracts the general path of Chinese reading teaching, and believes that the teaching model should include primary reading, detailed reading, quality reading, extended reading, writing and other major links.

3.2 Development of Primary School Chinese Reading Generative Classroom Model

Under the guidance of generative teaching theory, we analyze the connotation of Chinese reading teaching and the function of intelligent technology environment. Then we theoretically deduce the primary school Chinese reading generative classroom model in the intelligent environment. This teaching mode is composed of four parts: teaching objectives, generation process, the role of intelligent environment, and teaching evaluation, as shown in Fig. 1.

In this model, the teaching objective is the starting point and end point of teaching activities and teaching evaluation. Teaching activities are the way to implement teaching objectives: The requirements of teaching evaluation on teaching objectives and the adjustment and modification of teaching activities. The technical support of intelligent environment permeates every link of the whole teaching mode, which can provide intelligent tools and platforms for carrying out teaching activities and teaching evaluation, so as to achieve teaching objectives.

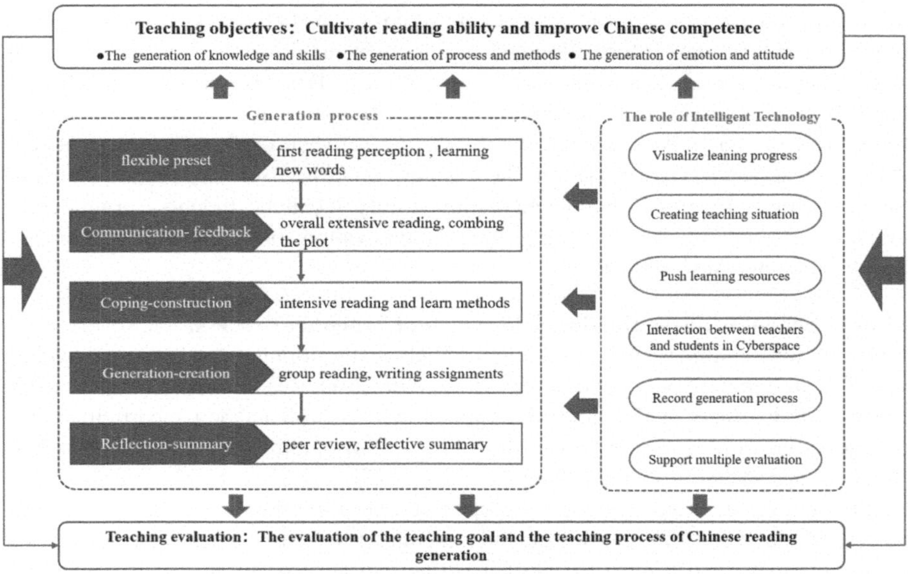

Fig. 1. Classroom model of primary school Chinese reading generation in the intelligent environment

Teaching Objectives. Based on the analysis of Chinese literacy and reading literacy, this study sets the overall teaching goal of Chinese reading generative class as to cultivate students reading ability and improve their Chinese literacy. Combined with the theory of developmental teaching, the new curriculum reform puts forward that the connotation of student development is the three-dimensional integration of knowledge and skills, process and methods, emotion and attitude. Based on this, this study divides the specific objectives of the Chinese reading generative classroom into three dimensions knowledge and skills generation, process and methods generation and emotion and attitude generation.

Generation Process. Guided by the concept of Chinese reading literacy and generative teaching, this study focuses in the classroom teaching of primary school Chinese reading in an intelligent environment. Through an interactive cycle of discussion with subject teachers, trial teaching and modification, the core teaching links were refined, and a classroom teaching process combining generative teaching and reading teaching was formed.

Flexible Preset. This session is conducted before class. The main teaching activities are first reading perception and learning new words. Before class, teachers design and generate teaching objectives based on learning situations, design flexible teaching content and teaching process, and leave free space for students' dynamic generation. Students' activities are mainly to preview the text, understand the main content of the article, from the students' words. This part plays a foreshadowing role in generative learning in class.

Communication-Feedback. This part of the teaching activities is the overall extensive reading, combing the plot. In this part, teacher should pay attention to students' reactions in problem situations, give feedback in time actively, carry out interaction, and use intelligent teaching platform to capture and generate resources. Students grasp the full text by reading quickly and learn new words. This link is the foundation of generating activities in the class and the goal of knowledge and skill generation.

Coping-Construction. The teaching focus of this section is to guide students read intensively and learn methods. Teachers build scaffolding for students learning confusion, help students to carry out exploration, and complete the meaning construction of knowledge learning. Students read independently, explore cooperatively, learn reading methods, and comprehend article emotion. This part is the teaching goal of knowledge generation, methods generation and attitude generation.

Generation-Creation. The content of this link is group reading and writing assignments. Teachers provide students with digital resources for group reading and organize generating activities. Under the guidance of teachers, students can make use of the knowledge and the reading methods they have learned to conduct a personalized reading, practice writing, and express their thoughts. This section guides students to produce visual products to promote the generation of students' emotion.

Reflection-Summary. The teaching activity of this link is peer review and reflective summary. Teachers guide students to appreciate others' works, communicate ideas, summarize classroom teaching content, and sublimate emotion. This link plays the role of deepening the generation.

3.3 Teaching Evaluation

Teaching evaluation aims at assess the achievement of teaching objectives of Chinese generative reading and the teaching process of Chinese generative reading. The teaching objectives of Chinese generative reading class include the generation of knowledge and skills, the generation of process and methods and the generation of emotion and attitude, aiming at improving students reading ability and Chinese literacy. The evaluation of the generative process of Chinese reading teaching should be guided by generative teaching theory and the generative process of reading teaching activities should be evaluated from multiple perspectives. Based on this, this study constructs a Chinese reading generative classroom evaluation scale in an intelligent environment.

3.4 Features of the Intelligent Environment

Based on theoretical research and practical exploration, this study summarizes the six functions of intelligent environment in Chinese reading generative classroom:

Visualize Leaning Progress. The intelligent environment can record and analyze students' answers and works, and visualize the learning progress of each student through learning analysis technology and emotion analysis technology, which is beneficial for teachers to track students' learning progress and adjust teaching timely.

Set Up Teaching Situation. With the help of diversified intelligent multimedia technology, teachers can create a teaching situation and stimulate students' learning enthusiasm by letting students watch videos.

Accurate Push Resources. In an intelligent environment, teachers can use big data analysis technology and artificial intelligence technology to push personalized learning resources and exercises accurately for students before, during, and after class to help students consolidate their learning and broaden the scope and depth of reading.

Interaction Between Teachers and Students in Cyberspace. Rely on the digital teaching space, the intelligent environment provides a platform for the interaction between students and teachers, supports synchronous and asynchronous discussion and writing, supports creation and sharing of works, and provides a platform for teachers and students to communicate, express and create.

Record Generative Process. The intelligent environment can save students' answer records, reading notes, group cooperation process, works and other generative resources, and record the generative process of Chinese reading teaching for teachers and students to see.

Support Multiple Evaluation. Students have different understandings in reading teaching, and the learning process has strong personality characteristics and unique experience. The intelligent environment can store students' electronic file bags and personal logs, provide a variety of evaluation tools, and realize the diversification of evaluation subjects and methods.

4 Model Application and Effectiveness Assessment

4.1 Model Application

We carried out a case study in LuDiXi primary school, Guangzhou, China to apply and assess the effectiveness of the classroom model. 30 fourth-grade students participated in a two-week experimental study to assess the effectiveness of the model in improving reading ability and cultivating Chinese literacy.

Teaching Content Selection. Based on the original teaching progress, this study finally determined the four reading articles in the first volume compiled by the Chinese people's education edition as the teaching materials, which were "Study for the Rise of China" and "Mei Lanfang's beard collection", which both of them are in unit 7, "Xi Menbao's Governance of Ye" and "Story No. 2", which both of them are in unit 8. The teaching theme of unit 7 is "Every man alive has a duty to his country", which aims to cultivate students' patriotism and the reading methods: "pay attention to the main characters and events, and learn to grasp the main content of the article". The teaching theme of the unit 8 is "Time is like a wave washing the sand, and many heroes go down in history", which to cultivate students' capacity of recalling the articles briefly, and paying attention to the order and detail.

Intelligent Environment Analysis. The experimental class of grade 4 selected in this study is the school network experimental class, which is equipped with an intelligent classroom teaching environment. Hardware facilities include Multimedia-one computer, mobile device for teachers and students, recording and broadcasting equipment, interactive whiteboard, exhibition platforms, projectors, etc. Software facilities include a wireless network, V school teaching platform, recording and broadcasting system, and various auxiliary teaching systems and software. The intelligent environment can effectively support accurate push of resources, learning situation creation, teacher-student interaction space, learning process recording, intelligent data analysis, and multiple learning evaluation, providing technical assistance for generative teaching.

Teaching Activities Implementation. This study adopts the primary school Chinese reading generative classroom model to carry out the teaching practice. Take "Study for the rise of China" as an example to show the implementation of specific classroom teaching.

"Study for the Rise of China" tells the story of premier Zhou Enlai who aspired to study for the rise of the China. Combined with the theme of this unit and the national feelings expressed in the article, the classroom teaching takes "foster virtue through education", "generative learning" and "the investigation-oriented study" as the design concept. The teaching objectives are generating students' knowledge and skills, process and methods, emotion and attitude. On the basis of analyzing the learning situation and the text, the teacher determined the main and difficult points of teaching, and designed the teaching strategies of cooperative learning, independent inquiry learning. Along with these, the teaching implementation process is formulated (as shown in Fig. 2).

Before class, prepare the text and collect the information. Students preview the text, learn the new words and phrases, finish the preview list on the tablet, and collect relevant information before class. Teachers carry out flexible teaching design for the text and design generative content in advance.

In class, the first, Sending feedback on learning and familiar with the text. With the help of the data analysis function of the intelligent environment, the teacher analyzes the students' preview situation, explains the situation in a targeted way, and sets up the teaching situation by playing the historical video in multimedia, so as to lead the students to know the text initially. Second, reading the text and prepare to enter the generative process. This link is the "association-feedback" in the generative teaching, students through extensive reading to grasp the whole text. Teachers, through many questions, dialogue, guide students to solve the question, and familiar with the text. Third, exploring methods and construct collaboratively, namely "coping - construction". Teachers organize students to carry out independent and cooperative inquiry activities and learn to read. Fourth, applying methods and create works, namely "generation - creation." With the help of the function of pushing learning resource, teachers can provide extracurricular reading resources such as the story of premier Zhou for students to choose by themselves. Students write their thoughts and upload to the Internet to communicate with each other. Fifth, summarizing and sublimate feelings, namely "reflection - summary." Teachers and students summarize the content of this lesson, reflect on and evaluate it.

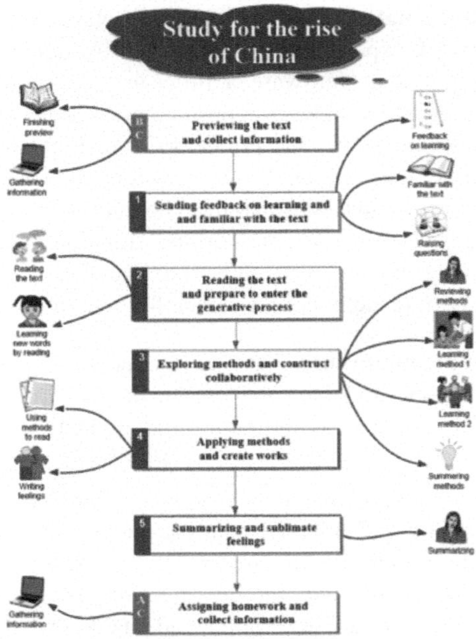

Fig. 2. Teaching implementation process of "Study for the rise of China"

After class, the teacher assigns homework, and the students search relevant historical information with the support of the intelligent environment to further understand the image and spirit of premier Zhou Enlai.

The teaching implementation process of "Study for the Rise of China" basically reaches the teaching objective. From before class to after class, the intelligent environment provides technical support for teaching.

4.2 Effectiveness Analysis

Evaluation System Construction. In order to assess the application effectiveness of the Chinese generative classroom model, we established an evaluation system based on the connotation of generative teaching and the value of primary school's Chinese reading teaching (as shown in Fig. 3). The evaluation system is mainly in two dimensions, which are the evaluation of the language generative teaching goal and the evaluation of the language generative teaching process. The former assesses the students' learning results in accordance with the goal of generative Chinese reading teaching. While the latter assesses the effectiveness of the generative teaching process.

Evaluation of the Achievement of Chinese Reading Generative Teaching Goals. The effectiveness of classroom teaching refers to the development of students through the teaching process. One of the important contents of the evaluation of the teaching effect of Chinese generative reading is the test of the effectiveness of achieving the teaching goals. According to the previous classification of teaching goals in Chinese generative

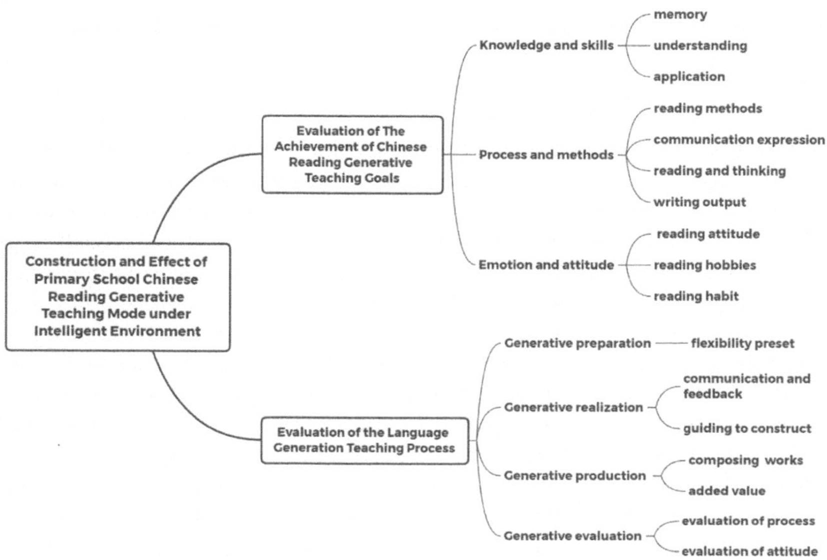

Fig. 3. Evaluation system of the application effect of primary school Chinese reading generative classroom model under intelligent environment

reading, this dimension can be subdivided into evaluations of knowledge and skills, process and methods, emotion and attitude. In terms of knowledge and skills, Chinese scholars use Benjamin Bloom's six levels of educational goals in the cognitive field to propose a three-level classification of "memory, understanding, and use" in primary school teaching. This study combined the specific Chinese reading teaching content to determine that the knowledge and skills in the evaluation system should include the memory, understanding, and application of knowledge and skills. In terms of process and methods, this study is based on the goals and requirements of reading teaching in Chinese curriculum standards, combined with related research, and summarizes them into four dimensions: reading methods, communication and expression, reading and thinking, and writing output. In terms of emotion and attitude, according to D. R. Kraswor's five-level classification of educational goals in the emotion field, combined with the characteristics of reading teaching, we believe that this dimension should include: reading attitude, reading hobbies, and reading habits.

Evaluation of the Language Generation Teaching Process. Another dimension of the effectiveness of the primary school Chinese reading generative teaching mode in the intelligent environment is to evaluate the achievement of the generative teaching process. Based on the connotation and path of generative teaching, we divide the evaluation indicators into four aspects: generative preparation, generative realization, generative production and generative evaluation, to evaluate the normativity and effectiveness of the generative teaching process. Generative preparation refers to the flexible presetting of teaching content before class; generative realization includes communication feedback and guidance construction; generative production includes the creation of works and additional value; generation evaluation includes process evaluation and attitude evaluation.

Application Effectiveness Analysis

Research Design. One class of 30 4th-grade students, from the LuDiXi primary school, Guangzhou, China, was assigned as the experimental group, who received teaching based on the Chinese generative classroom model in the intelligent environment. While another class of 40 4th-grade students from the same school was assigned as the control group, who received traditional classroom teaching. Both experimental and control group were taught the same four articles in two weeks.

According to the above evaluation index system, we designed a Chinese reading test and a Chinese generative reading scale to measure the knowledge and skill acquisition and the rest evaluation indexes respectively. The Chinese reading test aimed at detecting the target dimension of "knowledge and skills" in Chinese reading teaching. The Chinese reading test was jointly developed by the several Chinese teachers from that school. It is prepared for the teaching content of the experiment. It consists of three levels of knowledge, understanding, and application of knowledge and skills learning. It composed of nine objective questions and one subjective question, and the total score is 100 points. On the other hand, Chinese generative reading scale measured the rest indexes of the evaluation index system. The scale was adapted from previous studies and customized by this study. The scale employed the five scales of the Likert scale. There were 28 questions in total, scoring from 1 to 5 to represent "totally disagree" to "totally agree". The standardized Cronbach's α coefficient of the scale reliability test was 0.886, which was greater than 0.7, showing a good consistency and reliability.

Effectiveness Analysis of Achieving Chinese Reading Teaching Goals

a. Knowledge and Skills
   In terms of knowledge and skill generation, 30 test papers were distributed to the experimental class, and 30 valid papers were recovered; 40 test papers were distributed to the control class, and 40 valid papers were recovered. The average score of each level of the experimental class and the control class is as follows (Table 1):

Table 1. Descriptive statistics of knowledge and skills generation in primary school Chinese reading class

Variable		Treatment group			Control group		
First level indicators	Second level indicators (total score)	N	M	SD	N	M	SD
Knowledge and skills	Memorization (32)	30	31.07	2.50	40	23.90	9.69
	Understanding (16)	30	14.40	3.08	40	11.40	5.55
	Application (52)	30	47.60	4.97	40	37.30	10.96
	Total (100)	30	93.07	7.19	40	72.60	31.31

The descriptive analysis results showed that: ① The overall score of the experimental class is better than that of the control class, indicating that the use of the Chinese reading generative mode in an intelligent environment has a significant effect on the generation and acquisition of knowledge and skills. ② There is not much difference between the experimental class and the control class at the level of "Knowledge" and "Understanding". This is related to the nature of learning of "Knowledge" and "Understanding". For students, conventional teaching has been able to meet these two levels of learning. ③ At the "application" level, the experimental class score is significantly higher than the control class, indicating that this model has a significant effect on students' knowledge and skills. "Utilization" is a high-level learning of knowledge and skills in elementary school. The autonomous construction and generation advocated in generative teaching have a positive effect on training students' ability to apply knowledge.

b. Process and Methods and Emotion and Attitude
   In terms of process and method, emotion and attitude generation, 30 questionnaires were distributed to the experimental class and 17 valid questionnaires were recovered; 40 questionnaires were distributed to the control class and 24 valid questionnaires were recovered. An independent sample t test can be obtained from the two sets of data of the experimental class and the control class (Table 2):

Table 2. The analysis results of the process and methods and the generation of emotion and attitude in primary school Chinese reading class

Variable	Treatment group			Control group			*t*
	N	*M*	*SD*	*N*	*M*	*SD*	
Process and method	17	64.53	10.77	24	52.58	12.88	3.13**
Emotion and attitude	17	22.35	2.80	24	19.00	4.56	2.69*

*p < .05. **p < .01.

Two independent t-tests were conducted to compare the "process and methods" and "emotion and attitude" between experimental group and control group. Results showed that the experimental group significantly outperformed the control group in "process and method" ($t = 3.13, p < .01$) and "emotion and attitude" ($t = 2.69, p < .05$).

The performance of the two classes of students in the "process and methods" is quite different, but the difference in "emotion and attitude" is small. This shows that the teaching model constructed by this institute has significant effects in improving students' reading methods, communication, thinking, and writing, but it is less effective in cultivating students' reading attitude, interests, and habits than the former. This is related to students' learning and developmental psychology. The cultivation of emotion and attitude is difficult to form an immediate change effect overnight, so it needs to be explored and realized in long-term teaching practice.

Results of three dimensions of knowledge and skills, process and methods, and emotion and attitude indicated that the Chinese generative classroom model could significantly improve the teaching effect of Chinese reading for primary school students, and promote better achievement of generative goals.

Effectiveness Analysis of Generative Teaching Process of Chinese Reading. In terms of generative teaching process, 30 questionnaires were distributed to the experimental class and 17 valid questionnaires were recovered; 40 questionnaires were distributed to the control class, and 24 valid questionnaires were recovered. An independent sample t-test of the two sets of data from the experimental class and the control class can be obtained (Table 3):

Table 3. The analysis result of the generation process of primary school Chinese reading lesson

Variable	Treatment group			Control group			t
	N	M	SD	N	M	SD	
Generative process	17	35.35	4.90	24	31.63	5.03	2.36*

*p < .05.

An independent t-test was conducted to compare the "generative process" between the experimental and control group. The result showed that the experimental group yielded a significantly better performance in generative process than the control group ($t = 2.36$, $p < .05$). That is, the Chinese generative classroom model was effective in the preparation, realization, generation and evaluation of the generative teaching process, and could meet the requirements of flexible presets, interactive construction and multiple evaluations advocated in the generative teaching. At the same time, it generated additional value and promotes the achievement of generative goals.

5 Conclusion

Based on the generative teaching theory and the Chinese reading pedagogy, we develop a primary school Chinese reading generative classroom model by theoretical reasoning and practical research. Additionally, we apply the model in teaching practice and develop an evaluation index system to assess its effectiveness. The practical results show that this teaching model can effectively achieve the teaching objectives of Chinese reading, promote the generation, and effectively cultivate students' Chinese reading literacy.

This study is targeted at the cultivation standards of reading teaching in primary school Chinese curriculum and students' reading literacy. This study introduces the emerging 'generative teaching' theory of education within the intelligent teaching environment and rebuilds the teaching process, innovates the information technology. This study provides new ideas on the research of Chinese reading teaching and new methods for the technology fusion and innovation of education application in the era of education informatization 2.0.

References

1. Wittrock, M.C.: Generative learning processes of the brain. Educ. Psychol. **27**(4), 531–541 (2010)
2. Ye, L.: Making the classroom full of vitality on the deepening of teaching reform in primary and secondary schools. Educ. Res. **1997**(9), 3–8 (1997)
3. Wang, J., Wang, X.L.: Theoretical basis of generative teaching and classroom interaction model. J. Changchun Normal Univ. (Hum. Soc. Sci. Edn.) **29**(01), 136–140 (2010)
4. Brinton, C.G., Chiang, M., Jain, S., et al.: Learning about social learning in MOOCs: from statistical analysis to generative model. IEEE Trans. Learn. Technol. **7**(4), 346–359 (2014)
5. Trespalacios, J.H.: The effects of two generative activities on learner comprehension of part-whole meaning of rational numbers using virtual manipulatives. J. Comput. Math. Sci. Teach. **29**(3), 327–346 (2010)
6. Yu, S.Q., Wan, H.P., Cui, J.J.: Design and implementation of generative curriculum based on learning element platform. China Educ. Technol. **6**, 7–16 (2015)
7. Xie, Y.R., Yang, Y., Bai, J., et al.: Construction and application of generative intelligent learning environment – a case study of electronic schoolbag. J. South China Normal Univ. (Nat. Sci. Edn.) **48**(01), 126–132 (2016)
8. Zhao, M.R., Pan, C.L.: On the turning of the subject of classroom questions – from the perspective of generative teaching. Educ. Theory Pract. **36**(08), 45–47 (2016)
9. Huang, T., Gong, M.J., Yang, H.L., et al.: Man-machine coordinated support primary school Chinese writing teaching research. Electrochem. Educ. Res. **2020**(02), 1–7 (2020)
10. Huang, Y.Y.: Cultivation of high-level thinking ability in comprehensive Chinese learning in primary schools supported by intelligent terminals. Educ. Inf. Technol. **2016**(12), 26–29 (2016)
11. Xue, S.L.: Design and application research of interactive feedback system for teaching based on smart phone. China Audio-Visual Educ. **2017**(07), 115–120 (2017)
12. Xie, Y.R., Wu, L.H., Li, H.J., et al.: Exploration of generative teaching approach for primary Chinese reading class in the smart learning environment. China Educ. Technol. **6**, 36–42 (2016)
13. Luo, Z.B.: Generative instruction and its rationale. Curric. Teach. Mater. Method **10**, 2–33 (2006)
14. OECD: PISA 2018 Results (Volume I): What Students Know and Can Do, PISA, OECD Publishing, Paris (2019). https://doi.org/10.1787/5f07c754-en
15. Xie, Y.R.: The application of constructivism learning theory in the teaching of "Four Combinations" of Chinese in primary schools. China Educ. Technol. **10**, 9–12 (1997)
16. Wen, R.M.: The concept, characteristics and use suggestions of the Chinese teaching material compiled by ministry of education. Curric. Teach. Mater. Method **36**(11), 3–11 (2016)
17. Qian, M.L.: On Chinese guided reading from historical and present perspective. Curric. Teach. Mater. Method **34**(08), 3–11 (2014)

A Deep Learning Tool Using Teaching Learning-Based Optimization for Supporting Smart Learning Environment

Saisumpan Sooncharoen[1], Thatchai Thepphakorn[2], and Pupong Pongcharoen[1](✉)

[1] Industrial Engineering Department, Centre of Operations Research and Industrial Applications (CORIA), Faculty of Engineering, Naresuan University, Phitsanulok 65000, Thailand
pupongp@nu.ac.th, pupongp@gmail.com

[2] Faculty of Industrial Technology, Pibulsongkram Rajabhat University, Phitsanulok 65000, Thailand

Abstract. Since blended learning has become one of the promising approaches to teaching and learning, the integration of traditional learning with novel innovations should be taken into account. Novel innovations can raise the level of smart learning environments as well as the construction of wisdom classrooms. There are many ways to create these innovations. One of those is to apply the deep learning tool for teaching and learning activities, that can offer the learners to have profound and thorough knowledge experience. This work proposes a novel deep learning tool, which can support teaching and learning activities especially in a topic of scheduling. A computational intelligence algorithm called Teaching Learning-based Optimization (TLBO) was embedded within the tool for solving production scheduling problem. TLBO is a nature-inspired metaheuristic algorithm. It mimics the influential effect of teacher on learners or among learners. The tool was developed and tested upon four case studies.

Keywords: Deep learning · Teaching Learning-based Optimization · Scheduling · Teacher phase · Learner phase

1 Introduction

Smart education is to "improve learners' quality of lifelong learning. It focuses on contextual, personalised and seamless learning to promote learners' emerging intelligence and facilitate their problem-solving ability in smart environments" [1]. The smart education consists of two important components [2]. First is smart pedagogies and second is smart learning environment. Smart learning environment bases its foundations upon smart tools and intelligent innovations [3, 4]. The complexity of some realistic problems like production scheduling may be confusing or difficult to understand. It would be better if the teachers have any tool-based subjects for support the teaching and learning activities to make it more effective and efficient.

This work presents a deep learning tool for supporting the teaching and learning particularly in topic of production scheduling problem. Some important features of this

S. K. S. Cheung et al. (Eds.): ICBL 2020, LNCS 12218, pp. 392–404, 2020.
https://doi.org/10.1007/978-3-030-51968-1_32

tool such as: (i) learners are able to understand about the scheduling parameters, jobs with precedence constraints, related costs, etc. through database's worksheet within the tool, (ii) it also illustrates final production schedule according to the best solution obtained by the algorithm TLBO. From literature review, there has been no report that presents the deep learning tool for scheduling topic and utilizes it for support smart learning environment.

The objectives of this paper were to; (i) present a novel deep learning tool using Teaching Learning-based Optimization (TLBO) to solve complex scheduling problem for support smart learning environment, (ii) explain details of the complex scheduling problem and the procedure of TLBO, (iii) discuss the computational experiments.

The next section of this paper briefly explains related literature review. Section 3 describes the TLBO. Section 4 expresses the production scheduling, Sect. 5 describes the proposed tool using flowchart. Section 6 discusses the computational experiments and Sect. 7 is conclusions.

2 Comprehensive Literature Review

There have been several related comprehensive reviews on the smart education, smart learning, and the application of smart education. Shi, Liu, Gong, Niu, Wang, Jing, Lu, Zhang and Luo [5] presented a comprehensive overview of the research and application of smart education as seven perspectives including Intelligent Tutoring System (ITS), smart campus, Big Data in Education (BDE), knowledge graph, educational robots, virtual teachers, and personalized education. Freigang and Augsten [6] explained how an empirical smart learning environment (SLE) framework is applied inside an established corporation. They also discussed the needs to take into account the tactics, strategies, and practices to adapt frameworks into practice. Agbo, Oyelere, Suhonen and Adewumi [7] illustrated the integration of teach problem-solving skills and programming education with the utilization of computational thinking (CT). Abdel-Basset, Manogaran, Mohamed and Rushdy [8] reviewed the application of Internet of Thing (IoT) for building a smart educational process and also showed the basic concepts, definitions, characteristics, technology, and challenges of the IoT. Vasbieva, Sokolova, Masalimova, Shinkaruk and Kiva-Khamzina [9] explored the uses of education technologies in term of education tools for personalize teaching and learning activities. Huang, Du, Chang, Spector, Zhang and Zhang [10] proposed a smart learning engine in the form of an intelligent personalized learning system. Zhu, Yu and Riezebos [2] focused on four-tier framework of smart pedagogies and ten key features of smart learning environments. Udupi, Malali and Noronha [11] showed the key points of e-learning paradigm and integrated smart technology with big data framework, which leads towards smart learning. Yoo, Lee, Jo and Park [12] used realistic case studies for educational dashboards of smart learning. Shen, Li and Chen [13] expressed a framework of smart education and its application to enhance the activities of teaching and learning.

There are several literatures related to utilized educational tools for support teaching and learning activities. Course timetabling tools have been developed for optimizing the utilization of academic resources using computational intelligence algorithms, such as Genetic Algorithm [14], Ant Colony Optimization [15] and Cuckoo Search [16]. Sharma,

Nand, Naseem, Reddy, Narayan and Reddy [17] took Information Communication Technologies (ICT) driven tools into account for enhancement the ecosystem of smart learning. Mitrofanova, Sherstobitova and Filippova [18] presented Educational Data Mining (EDM) tool for collecting, analyzing, visualizing and presenting students' data in order to make a decision about improving training courses and educational programs. Ribeiro, Moreira, Almeida and Santos-Silva [19] provided mobile seamless learning tool for cancer education. Li, Du and Ma [20] developed smart service tool for collecting students' big data during learning process and providing the individualized service based on the data. Yesalov, Lapiy and Korytnikov [21] presented adaptive learning system tools for increasing the effectiveness of distance learning. Jeong [22] used Effective English Learning Tools to increase university students' perception together with motivation of using digital applications. Hwang, Yun, Park and Moon [23] coded HTML5 to develop a cross-platform tool using the user-oriented environment and e-learning services available for smart phones. Lee and Kim [24] developed an educational evaluation tool for 156 students in middle and high schools. Bae and Lee [25] used smart learning contents authoring tool for development of teaching-learning model with project-based learning. Park, Yun, Kwon, Moon and Kim [26] created a smart-learning platform and content authoring tools that are working on a cloud and web. It is available as a mobile version and a PC version. However, there has been no report that presents the deep learning tool using Teaching Learning-based Optimization for support smart learning environment, which is the contribution of this paper.

3 Teaching Learning-Based Optimization (TLBO)

Teaching Learning-based Optimization [27] was created upon the influence of a teacher on the quality of learners in the class. This class includes a teacher and a population of learners. The quality of each learner is compared with quality of solutions. The TLBO is divided into two phases. First phase is teacher phase. In this phase, the teacher will share his/her knowledge to the learners. As a result, it can lead to better results or higher scores of the learners. TLBO has another one phase. This phase call learner phase. The learner can gain knowledge with interaction among themselves by brainstorming or group discussion activity. The quality of learner in this phase is improved only based on better learner (learner no.1 > learner no.2 > learner no.3). Figure 1 illustrates the deep learning concept in teacher and learner phase of TLBO. The comparison of terminology of the TLBO with one of the most classical metaheuristics (Genetic Algorithm: GA) is shown in Table 1.

4 Problem Description and a Case Study

Nowadays, many industries place importance on the data management system because all activities have been relating to a lot of data, which may be considered in term of big data. Due to the massive volumes of the data, businesses may lose some benefits or opportunities if they are not dealt with the effective and efficient management. Big data involves many sectors such as commercial, construction, financial, service, and manufacturing, etc.

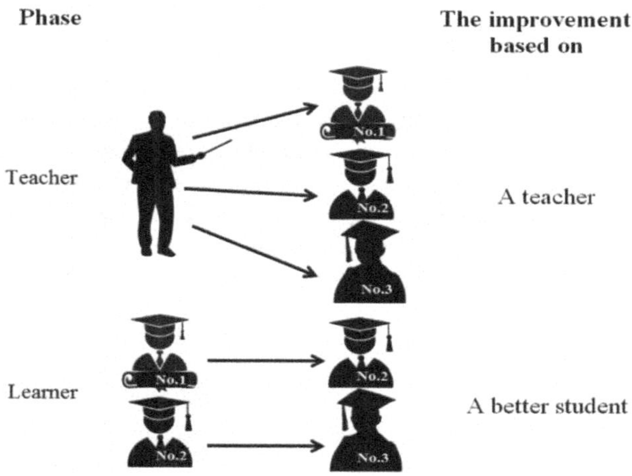

Fig. 1. The deep learning concept in teacher and learner phase of TLBO

Table 1. A comparison of TLBO and GA concept and terminology

Algorithm terminologies	Genetic Algorithm (GA)	Teaching Learning-based Optimization (TLBO)
All of representations	Population	Population
Representation size	Population size	Population size
A representation	A chromosome	A teacher/A student
Representation components	Genes	n/a
Sub-representation components	Allele	n/a
Number of improved rounds	Number of generations	Number of iterations
Selection method	Random	Ordered/Random
Exploitation operator	Crossover	Teacher phase
Exploration operator	Mutation	Learner phase
Evaluation function	Fitness function	Evaluated function
The best so far	The best solution	The best solution

Manufacturing sector, for example, in case of production of multiple assembly stages goods deals with so much related data such as components; subassemblies; main assemblies; processors/machines; inventories; lead times; lot sizes; on hands; suppliers; maximum capacities; etc. It is necessary to have effective and efficient tool for taking charge of production scheduling.

Most of scheduling problems are classified to non-deterministic polynomial time hard (NP-hard) problem [28], which means that the computational time required increases exponentially with problem size. Computational intelligence (CI) algorithms, for instance, TLBO, Artificial Immune System [29], Firefly Algorithm [30], Bat Algorithm [31], Frog Leaping [32] are suitable for solving this type of problem [33]. Deep learning can be appendant to CI procedure to increase ability of searching the optimal solution. For this reason, TLBO was considered in the present work for solving production scheduling in case of multiple assembly stages product.

Figure 2 shows a simplified example of multiple assembly stages product. The final product (the assembly item number A3S2) is operated with four facilities (Fac.1, Fac.2, Fac.3, and Fac.4). Figure 3 demonstrated the production schedule for multiple assembly stages product according to its precedence constraints.

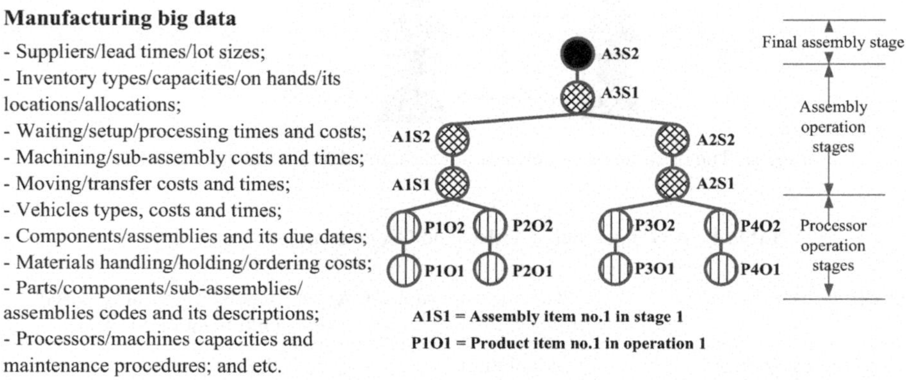

Fig. 2. A simplified example of multiple assembly stages product structure and its related big data

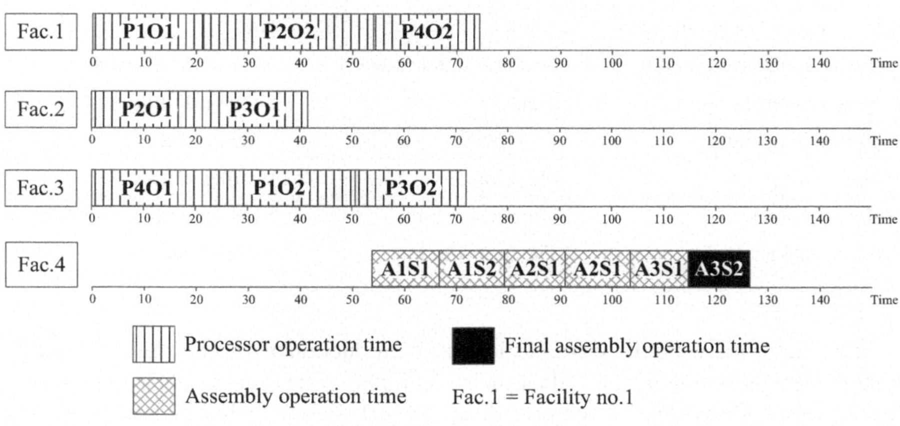

Fig. 3. Production schedule for multiple assembly stages product

5 A Novel Deep Learning Tool Using TLBO for Solving Production Scheduling

In the step of tool development, it is crucial to know step-by-step of the algorithm procedure. This is another way that leads to some benefits to the learners, because this allows understanding about the algorithm used. When the learners clearly understand, they can apply it to other problems easier than ever.

The novel deep learning tool was coded by Visual Basic for Application (VBA) programming language upon modular style. Figure 4 illustrates a flowchart that represents the proposed TLBO used in the tool, which includes the following steps:

1. The tool starts by obtaining input data from database's worksheet;
2. User defined parameters and algorithm used: population size (N), number of iterations (I), number of replications, and selected algorithm TLBO;
3. Problem encoding, and then generate initial population (see Fig. 5) according to N;
4. If any solution in the population is infeasible. Repairing it for all (see Fig. 6);
5. Calculate total cost for all solutions;
6. Rank all solutions from the best (*min.* total cost) to the worst (*max.* total cost);
7. The tool selects teacher phase and set iteration round (i) = 1;
8. Identify a teacher, which is the solution with *min.* total cost;
9. Idenfity a student, which is the solution in population according to n;
10. Randomly select either 1 or 2 to be the value of parameter T_F;
11. Run the swapping procedure (see Fig. 7) according to T_F in step 10 for $X_{old,n\geq 2}$;
12. Generate a random number (r) in the interval [0,1] and calculate number of swap (N_s) following expression [27, 34];

$$N_s = r * \left(X_{best,n=1} - T_F X_{old,n\geq 2}\right) \tag{1}$$

13. Improve $X_{old,n\geq 2}$ based on $X_{best,n=1}$ using the upper-class swapping procedure according to N_s. The $X_{new,n\geq 2}$ was modified as following expression [27, 34];

$$X_{new,n\geq 2} = X_{old,n\geq 2} * N_s \tag{2}$$

    After step 13 are the repair process (see step 4) and calculation total cost (see step 5).

14. Compare new solution ($X_{new,n\geq 2}$) with old solution ($X_{old,n\geq 2}$). If $X_{new,n\geq 2}$ better than $X_{old,n\geq 2}$, replace $X_{old,n\geq 2}$ with $X_{new,n\geq 2}$. Otherwise, reject $X_{new,n\geq 2}$;
15. Repeat at step 8 until $n > N$;
16. If there are remaining iterations go to step 8, otherwise go to step 17;
17. The tool selects learner phase and set iteration round (i) = 1;
18. Select two solutions randomly;
19. Let a better solution be learner $X_{old\text{-}a,n}$;
20. Let a better solution be learner $X_{old\text{-}b,n}$;
21. Improve $X_{old\text{-}b,n}$ based on $X_{old\text{-}a,n}$ using the procedure the same as step 13; and
22. Report the best solution, together with showing the best production schedule. Figure 8 illustrated an example of graphic user interface (GUI) of deep learning tool.

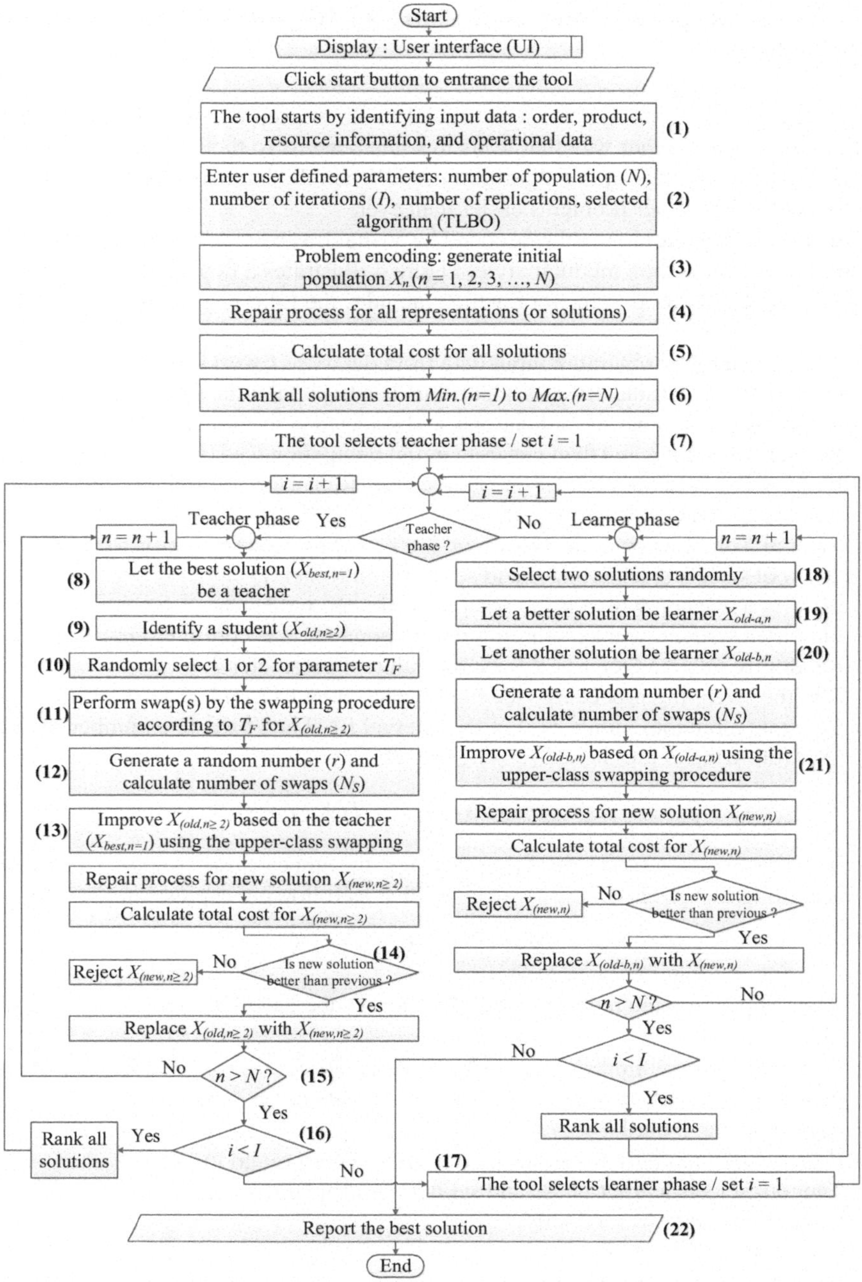

Fig. 4. Teaching Learning-based Optimization deep learning tool flowchart

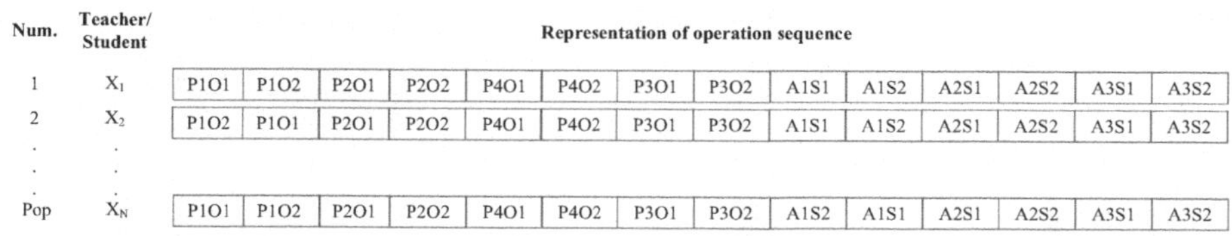

Fig. 5. Representation of a teacher/student of candidate solutions of TLBO

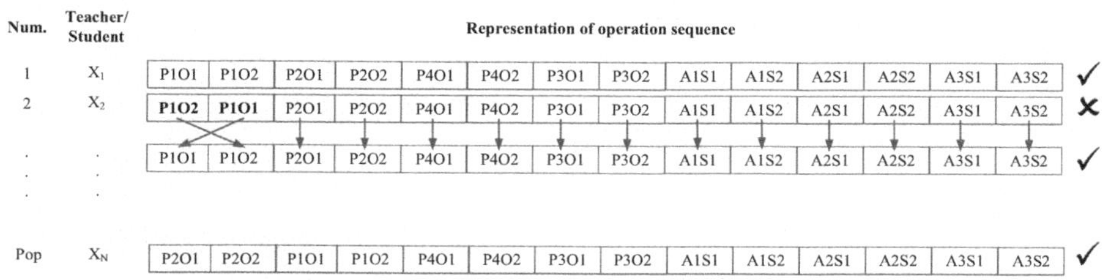

Fig. 6. Repair process for infeasible solutions

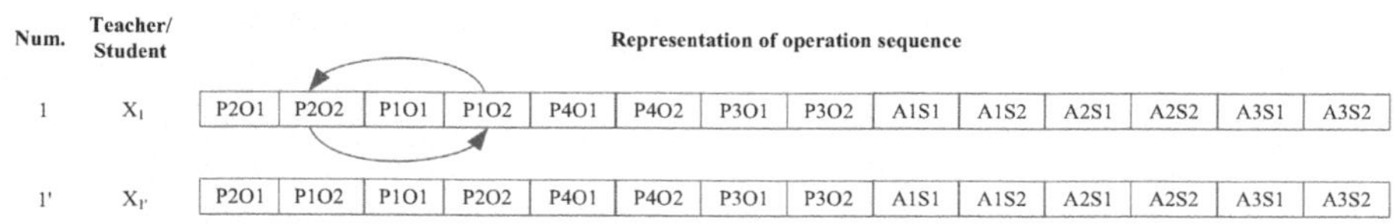

Fig. 7. The swapping procedure

6 Computational Experiments and Discussion

As soon as the tool reported all the results, the statistical analysis was conducted. The research problem used data on four problem instance numbers, which is shown in Table 2. Table 3 presented total cost of schedules obtaining by TLBO using three levels of *N/I* parameters. *N/I* at 100/25 means that the user defines population size with 100 and number of iterations with 25. This determines the amount of search and the computational execution time that was fixed at 2,500. However, the experiment was replicated thirty times, so that the solutions created were $2{,}500 \times 30 = 75{,}000$ in total.

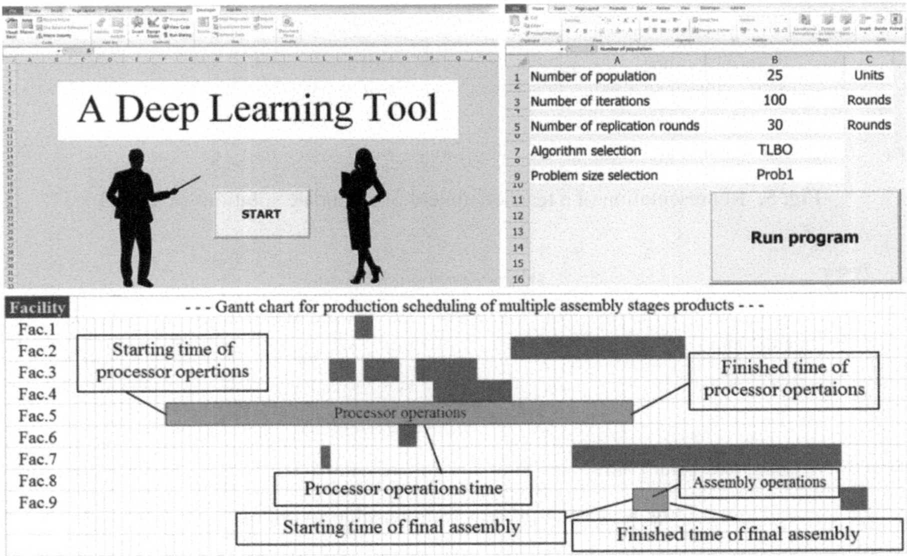

Fig. 8. An example of graphic user interface (GUI) of deep learning tool

Table 2. The characteristics of the four problems

Problem instance number	Number of processors	Number of processor operations	Number of assembly operations	Max. level of operations in product structure	Number of assembly stages
Prob01	8	25	9	11	15
Prob02	7	57	10	17	18
Prob03	17	118	17	19	29
Prob04	25	229	39	20	85

P-value by ANOVA analysis in Table 3 informed that only *N/I* in Prob01 was statistically significant with a 95% of confidence interval, which means that the different level of *N/I* significantly affected the result values. Referring to main effect plots of *N/I* by *Mean* (see Fig. 9), the best parameter setting of TLBO for solving production scheduling problem was 100/25 for prob1, 100/25 for prob2, 50/50 for prob3, and 25/100 for prob4.

Table 3. Total cost of schedules produced by TLBO

Problem instance number	Parameters (*N/I*)	Method: TLBO				*P-value*
		Min	*Max*	*Mean*	*SD*	
Prob01	100/25	13,500.00	13,500.00	13,500.00	0.00	**0.003**
	25/100	13,500.00	15,000.00	14,000.00	719.19	
	50/50	13,500.00	15,000.00	13,800.00	610.26	
Prob02	100/25	34,500.00	34,500.00	34,500.00	0.00	0.372
	25/100	34,500.00	34,500.00	34,500.00	0.00	
	50/50	34,500.00	35,500.00	34,533.33	182.57	
Prob03	100/25	80,000.00	99,000.00	90,683.34	5,230.02	0.881
	25/100	72,500.00	99,500.00	91,166.66	6,363.06	
	50/50	73,500.00	132,000.00	90,183.33	10,170.51	
Prob04	100/25	2,465,000.00	4,338,500.00	3,278,916.25	423,773.97	0.533
	25/100	2,185,500.00	4,603,000.00	3,150,050.25	3,150,050.25	
	50/50	2,423,500.00	3,880,500.00	3,186,967.00	353,679.00	

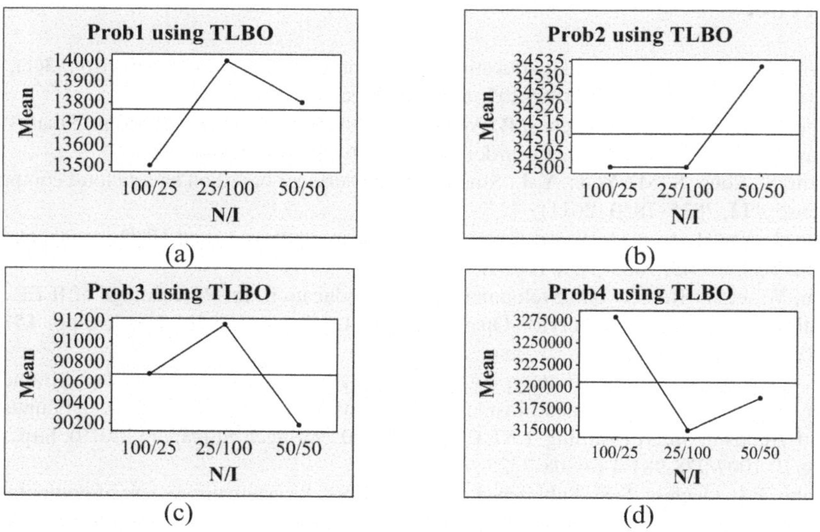

Fig. 9. Main effect plots of *N/I* by *Mean*

7 Conclusions

This work focuses on a deep learning tool using a computational intelligence (CI) called Teaching Learning-based Optimization. This tool was developed to support a wide range of teaching and learning activities especially in topic of scheduling. The tool offers a greater chance of know-how to the learners. It enables the learners understanding the important keys of scheduling problem from database's worksheet within the tool, helps the learners quickly realise the algorithm used for solving the problem, and can be used as an example for other approaches involving the deep learning tool. The result obtained from the tool also gives an opportunity to the learners for statistical analysis of computational experiment. So, the proposed tool is able to answer the concept of blended learning especially in term of the integrated traditional learning with novel innovations. As we know, this work emphasized the process of a deep learning tool development. Our future work is to validate it for the classroom.

Acknowledgements. The first author would like to acknowledge Naresuan University Graduate School for providing his Ph.D. scholarship. This work was also part of research project supported by the Thailand Research Fund (TRF) and Office of the Higher Education Commission (OHEC) under grant number MRG6080066.

References

1. Gros, B.: The design of smart educational environments. Smart Learn. Environ. **3**(1), 1–11 (2016). https://doi.org/10.1186/s40561-016-0039-x
2. Zhu, Z.-T., Yu, M.-H., Riezebos, P.: A research framework of smart education. Smart Learn. Environ. **3**(1), 1–17 (2016). https://doi.org/10.1186/s40561-016-0026-2
3. Kim, S., Song, S.-M., Yoon, Y.-I.: Smart learning services based on smart cloud computing. Sensors **11**, 7835–7850 (2011)
4. Lee, J., Zo, H., Lee, H.: Smart learning adoption in employees and HRD managers. Br. J. Edu. Technol. **45**, 1082–1096 (2014)
5. Shi, W., et al.: Review on development of smart education. In: Proceedings of IEEE International Conference on Service Operations and Logistics, and Informatics, pp. 157–162 (2019)
6. Freigang, S., Augsten, A.: Prototyping theory: applying design thinking to adapt a framework for smart learning environments inside organizations. In: Chang, M., et al. (eds.) Foundations and Trends in Smart Learning. LNET, pp. 177–180. Springer, Singapore (2019). https://doi.org/10.1007/978-981-13-6908-7_25
7. Agbo, F.J., Oyelere, S.S., Suhonen, J., Adewumi, S.: A systematic review of computational thinking approach for programming education in higher education institutions. In: ACM International Conference Proceeding Series (2019)
8. Abdel-Basset, M., Manogaran, G., Mohamed, M., Rushdy, E.: Internet of things in smart education environment: supportive framework in the decision-making process. Concurr. Comput. **31**, 1–12 (2019)
9. Vasbieva, D.G., Sokolova, N.L., Masalimova, A.R., Shinkaruk, V.M., Kiva-Khamzina, Y.L.: Exploring EFL teacher's role in a smart learning environment-review study. XLinguae **11**, 265–274 (2018)

10. Huang, R., Du, J., Chang, T.-W., Spector, M., Zhang, Y., Zhang, A.: A conceptual framework for a smart learning engine. In: Popescu, E., et al. (eds.) Innovations in Smart Learning. LNET, pp. 69–73. Springer, Singapore (2017). https://doi.org/10.1007/978-981-10-2419-1_11
11. Udupi, P.K., Malali, P., Noronha, H.: Big data integration for transition from e-learning to smart learning framework. In: 2016 3rd MEC International Conference on Big Data and Smart City, ICBDSC 2016, pp. 268–271 (2016)
12. Yoo, Y., Lee, H., Jo, I.-H., Park, Y.: Educational dashboards for smart learning: review of case studies. In: Chen, G., Kumar, V., Kinshuk, Huang, R., Kong, S.C. (eds.) Emerging Issues in Smart Learning. LNET, pp. 145–155. Springer, Heidelberg (2015). https://doi.org/10.1007/978-3-662-44188-6_21
13. Shen, B., Li, S.Q., Chen, Y.L.: A framework of smart education and its applications on teaching and learning enhancement. Appl. Mech. Mater. **631–632**, 1353–1356 (2014)
14. Pongcharoen, P., Promtet, W., Yenradee, P., Hicks, C.: Stochastic optimisation timetabling tool for university course scheduling. Int. J. Prod. Econ. **112**, 903–918 (2008)
15. Thepphakorn, T., Pongcharoen, P.: Heuristic ordering for ant colony based timetabling tool. J. Appl. Oper. Res. **5**, 113–123 (2013)
16. Thepphakorn, T., Pongcharoen, P., Vitayasak, S.: A new multiple objective Cuckoo search for university course timetabling problem. In: Sombattheera, C., Stolzenburg, F., Lin, F., Nayak, A. (eds.) MIWAI 2016. LNCS (LNAI), vol. 10053, pp. 196–207. Springer, Cham (2016). https://doi.org/10.1007/978-3-319-49397-8_17
17. Sharma, B.N., Nand, R., Naseem, M., Reddy, E., Narayan, S.S., Reddy, K.: Smart learning in the pacific: design of new pedagogical tools. In: Proceedings of 2018 IEEE International Conference on Teaching, Assessment, and Learning for Engineering, TALE 2018, pp. 573–580 (2019)
18. Mitrofanova, Y.S., Sherstobitova, A.A., Filippova, O.A.: Modeling smart learning processes based on educational data mining tools. In: Uskov, V.L., Howlett, R.J., Jain, L.C. (eds.) Smart Education and e-Learning 2019. SIST, vol. 144, pp. 561–571. Springer, Singapore (2019). https://doi.org/10.1007/978-981-13-8260-4_49
19. Ribeiro, N., Moreira, L., Almeida, A.M.P., Santos-Silva, F.: Mobile seamless learning tool for cancer education. In: Mealha, Ó., Divitini, M., Rehm, M. (eds.) SLERD 2017. SIST, vol. 80, pp. 3–10. Springer, Cham (2018). https://doi.org/10.1007/978-3-319-61322-2_1
20. Li, X., Du, L., Ma, X.: Big data analytics and smart service tool: "smart learning partner" platform. In: Chang, M., et al. (eds.) Challenges and Solutions in Smart Learning. LNET, pp. 141–146. Springer, Singapore (2018). https://doi.org/10.1007/978-981-10-8743-1_20
21. Yesalov, K., Lapiy, A., Korytnikov, O.: Adaptive learning system as a tool for increasing the effectiveness of distance learning. In: 2017 International Conference on Information Science and Communications Technologies, pp. 1–4 (2017)
22. Jeong, K.O.: University students' perception and motivation of using digital applications as effective English learning tools. In: Proceedings of 2017 International Conference on Platform Technology and Service, PlatCon 2017 (2017)
23. Hwang, H.S., Yun, J.S., Park, J.T., Moon, I.Y.: Implementation of smart-learning content authoring tool system utilizing HTML5. Int. J. Multimed. Ubiquit. Eng. **11**, 143–150 (2016)
24. Lee, J.S., Kim, S.W.: Validation of a tool evaluating educational apps for smart education. J Educ. Comput. Res. **52**, 435–450 (2015)
25. Bae, J.H., Lee, H.: Development of teaching-learning model with project-based learning using smart learning contents authoring tool. In: Park, J., Stojmenovic, I., Jeong, H., Yi, G. (eds.) Computer Science and its Applications. LNEE, vol. 330, pp. 1031–1036. Springer, Heidelberg (2015). https://doi.org/10.1007/978-3-662-45402-2_146
26. Park, J.T., Yun, J.S., Kwon, O.Y., Moon, I.Y., Kim, B.J.: Development of a smart-learning platform and content authoring tools that uses a cloud and web. Int. J. Appl. Eng. Res. **9**, 29869–29882 (2014)

27. Rao, R.V., Savsani, V.J., Vakharia, D.P.: Teaching–learning-based optimization: a novel method for constrained mechanical design optimization problems. Comput. Aided Des. **43**, 303–315 (2011)
28. Hajiaghaei-Keshteli, M., Aminnayeri, M., Fatemi Ghomi, S.M.T.: Integrated scheduling of production and rail transportation. Comput. Ind. Eng. **74**, 240–256 (2014)
29. Pongcharoen, P., Chainate, W., Pongcharoen, S.: Improving artificial immune system performance: inductive bias and alternative mutations. In: Bentley, P.J., Lee, D., Jung, S. (eds.) ICARIS 2008. LNCS, vol. 5132, pp. 220–231. Springer, Heidelberg (2008). https://doi.org/10.1007/978-3-540-85072-4_20
30. Khadwilard, A., Chansombat, S., Thepphakorn, T., Chainate, W., Pongcharoen, P.: Application of firefly algorithm and its parameter setting for job shop scheduling. J. Ind. Technol. **8**, 49–58 (2012)
31. Chansombat, S., Musikapun, P., Pongcharoen, P., Hicks, C.: A hybrid discrete bat algorithm with Krill Herd-based advanced planning and scheduling tool for the capital goods industry. Int. J. Prod. Res. **57**, 6705–6726 (2019)
32. Dapa, K., Loreungthup, P., Vitayasak, S., Pongcharoen, P.: Bat algorithm, genetic algorithm and shuffled frog leaping algorithm for designing machine layout. In: Ramanna, S., Lingras, P., Sombattheera, C., Krishna, A. (eds.) MIWAI 2013. LNCS (LNAI), vol. 8271, pp. 59–68. Springer, Heidelberg (2013). https://doi.org/10.1007/978-3-642-44949-9_6
33. Blum, C., Roli, A.: Metaheuristics in combinatorial optimization: overview and conceptual comparison. ACM Comput. Surv. **35**, 268–308 (2003)
34. Vitayasak, S., Pongcharoen, P.: Performance improvement of Teaching-Learning-Based Optimisation for robust machine layout design. Expert Syst. Appl. **98**, 129–152 (2018)

Multiple Device Controlled Design for Implementing Telepresence Robot in Schools

Wichai Puarungroj(✉) and Narong Boonsirisumpun

Computer Science Department, Faculty of Science and Technology, Loei Rajabhat University, Loei 42000, Thailand
{wichai,narong.boo}@lru.ac.th

Abstract. Telepresence robots have shown their capabilities to perform remote teaching. In this research, the telepresence robot was designed and developed specifically for teaching from a remote location. The robot was intended to surpass the limitation of the normal teleconference software regarding the interaction with students. The robot incorporated movement and face display that help create an in-person environment. To use the robot for teaching, the servers were set up to exchange video data between the robot and the software on the remote teacher's side, and to drive the robot's wheels. On the remote teacher's side, the software was designed and developed as a web application to view the classroom environment, control the robot, and control the teaching media within one screen. This enabled the teacher to fully control the equipment while delivering a lecture or talking to students. The robot was tested and evaluated in a real school setting with secondary school students.

Keywords: Telepresence robot · Remote teaching · Interactive video conferencing · IoT · Distance education

1 Introduction

Teaching students in primary and secondary schools is a challenging task due to regularly updated teaching and learning requirements. STEM education, for example, has been recently implemented which educates students in 4 disciplines including science, technology, engineering, and mathematics. These four disciplines could bring troubles to some schools, which lack qualified STEM teachers. A similar problem is also raised in Thailand when new curriculums for primary and secondary schools incorporated computing science subjects following the trend in computer and artificial intelligence education. These subjects combine 3 main parts - computational thinking, digital technology, and media and information literacy. Python language programming is also a part of these subjects. To teach students in these subjects, the schools need to acquire additional special training for their teachers who do not have enough related background. As part of the teaching, additional lessons can be given by scholars outside the schools such as the lecturers in computer science from the universities.

S. K. S. Cheung et al. (Eds.): ICBL 2020, LNCS 12218, pp. 405–415, 2020.
https://doi.org/10.1007/978-3-030-51968-1_33

To facilitate teaching by outside scholars who may not be able to personally present at schools, the research seeks the way to allow teaching from the teachers at the remote sites. This should also provide capabilities of interacting with students in the classroom. One of the solutions to this problem is the use of telepresence robots. The robot can be placed in front of the class while the teacher can connect in from a remote site to deliver a lecture. The teacher can see and talk to students through the robot and vice versa. In this way, the teaching can be common to students than using only one-way communication. From this concept, this research intends to design and develop the telepresence robot that is capable of facilitating teaching from the remote sites. To do so, the robot needs to have the capabilities assimilating a human teacher who stands in front of the class by showing the face of the teacher who delivers the lesson and allowing the teacher to see and interact with his students. The movement abilities of the robot allow the remote teacher to independently turn and move to anyone in the class as if he was there. Therefore, the robot incorporated various features required for representing as a teacher such as face display, movement, and controlling teaching media. On the remote teacher's side, the software was designed to view classroom environment, control the robot movement (move forward, backward, turn left and right), and control teaching media (e.g. slides, video, website). The robot was then tested in a school setting using real class teaching based on a subject taught by a scholar outside the school.

2 Related Work

Telepresence robots provide excellent abilities to overcome the limitation of teleconferencing software. The robots are more flexible in movement, which make them surpass the common use of teleconferencing software. The movement enables interaction between people at the two remote locations [2]. Due to this great performance, telepresence robots have been applied to various fields of applications, for example, remote work [6–8], education [1–3, 5, 9], library [11, 12], and elderly care [4, 10]. Since the robot has been widely used, many studies seek to gain insights into the effect of its use. The study carried out by [6], which focused on the informal communication problem in telework, reported that the telepresence robot was able to be used as a proxy for a remote worker. Meanwhile, the problem of informal communication occurred due to the lack of eye contact, privacy, and disturbance issues. The study suggested various possible solutions for overcoming the problem.

Another experiment carried out by [7] focused on observing the behaviors of teammates when working together with a remote partner. The study reported that there were still obstacles when a remote worker had to collaborate with his teammates, for example, less ease of communication, and feeling less trustworthy. Yang et al. [8] experimented with long distant relationships between two long distant couples. The study found that the robot could improve couples' communication with their distant partners in four aspects: autonomy, unpredictability, movement as body language, and perspectives. These aspects were improved because a robot could replicate a real human in some ways. Thus the couples were satisfied with the quality of in-person interactions of the robot than typical teleconferencing through PCs or smartphones. The robot was also found useful for library services. It could be represented as a librarian who provided several services to patrons [11, 12] or another way round where it represented as a patron who virtually visited the library [12].

In an educational field, the robots have been employed as virtual students for those who are not able to physically present at schools due to serious health problems such as cancer, heart disease, and immune deficiency [1]. Furthermore, the robots have also been deployed by those who are temporarily absent from schools due to some reasons such as mild illness or injury [3]. The research carried out by [3] focused on seeking to understand how robots should be represented students in different conditions: 1) long-term use (due to illness or disabilities), 2) short-term use, and 3) distance learning. The research provided useful suggestions for designing robots such as utilizing microphones and cameras for greater distance, robots' height adjustment capabilities for different ages of students, and using a larger display.

Another study [5] was carried out by observing and interviewing participants who were associated with the use of telepresence robots in schools, for example, home-bound students, parents, teachers, classmates, and school administrators. Each person was associated with the use of the robot in some ways. The study has reported the experience of robot use and opinions towards several perceptions and learning categories such as feeling loneliness, overcoming isolation, social acceptance, negative behaviors, and homebound instruction. In [2], the author had suggested several appropriate properties of a robot for academic use, for example, its interface should be easy to used, and the video should show the user's face close to actual size. Furthermore, the article also reviewed some commercial telepresence robotic devices such as Beam, TeleMe, Double, and vGo as shown in Fig. 1, and provided some information about a tabletop robot called KUBI.

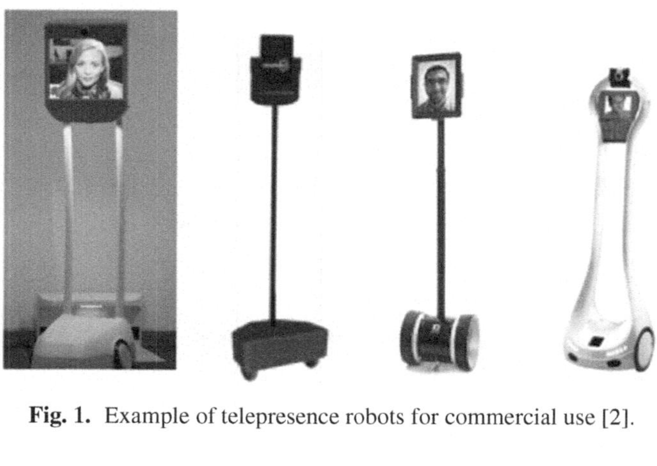

Fig. 1. Example of telepresence robots for commercial use [2].

While most of the prior research reported cases of robot used by homebound students who were unable to show up at schools, not many studies that mentioned about the use of the robot for remote teaching. In some cases, remote teaching may require a specific purpose robot with teaching support functions, which may not be available in general-purpose robots. The research by [9] described the application of telepresence robots for tutoring English. The research developed the robot to be deployed by a remote teacher for delivering English language lesson. The developed robot was tested and evaluated twice by elementary students in interest, confidence, and motivation categories. This shows that the second test yielded a better result in all categories.

3 Research Methodology

3.1 Research Design

The research was intended to design and develop the telepresence robot for facilitating remote teaching in schools. The robot development carried out in 4 steps. Firstly, the robot was designed to incorporate several functions for teaching such as face display, movement, and presentation media control.

Figure 2 illustrates the scenario of the whole system. In this scenario, the robot was brought into the classroom by a teaching assistant. The robot was then set up to connect to the server and the teaching media were stored in a computing device, which was connected to the video projector. When all equipment was ready, the remote teacher used the developed software in his device (e.g. tablet or computer) to connect to the servers through the internet to control both the robot and the teaching media.

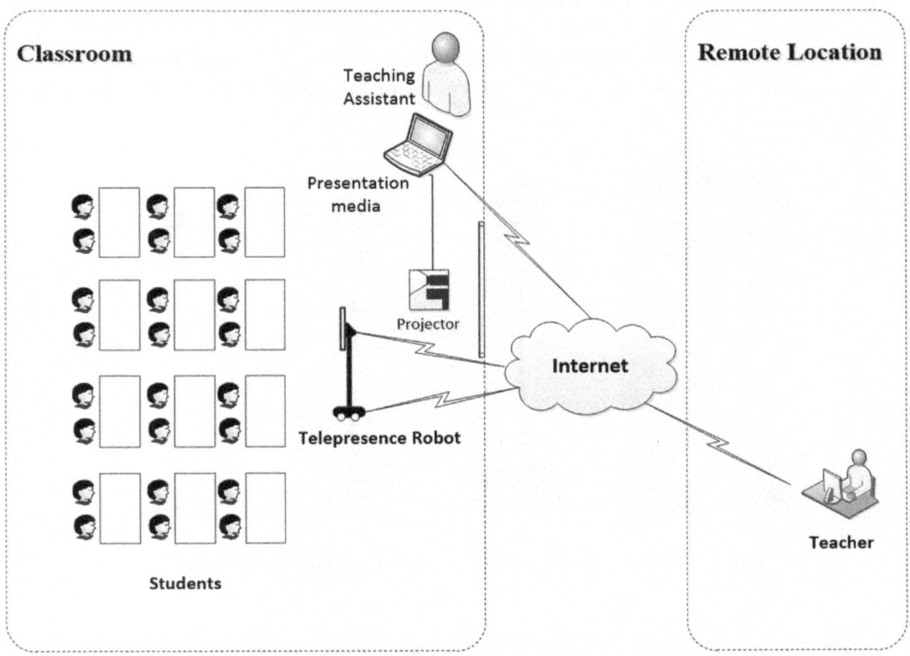

Fig. 2. Robot usage scenario.

The second step was robot development. The robot was constructed based on IoT devices and built with 125 cm tall structure. The structure of the robot was created using an aluminum frame, which was strong enough for holding the robot's head and the wheel equipment and the batteries. Several devices were installed in a base's container placing on the base chassis with four wheels attached. The container stored wireless IOT devices for driving wheels' motors, and the batteries. One 8-in. tablet was attached to the robot's head, which was used for showing the face of the teacher. Another tablet was also prepared as a device for the remote teacher to connect to the robot and teaching media. However, on the teacher's location, a computer or notebook could also be used to control the robot instead of the tablet. In the middle part, a wireless speaker was installed to amplify the volume of the sound. This enabled the robot to increase the voice of the teacher loud enough for hearing in the classroom.

In the third step, two servers were setup. One server was used to manage IoT devices for driving the robot wheels and another server was applied for exchanging the data from cameras from both sides. In the fourth step, the web application for the remote teacher was developed. The application comprised 3 parts for controlling different parts of the robot and teaching media including 1) video display that showed the video of the two sites 2) robot movement control for driving the robot 3) teaching media control for controlling an in-class computing device, which installed the teaching media. After the development, the robot, the servers, and the remote teacher's application were tested together and the errors found were corrected.

3.2 Experiment

The experiment was conducted using one class in a junior high school. The 9th-grade class that needed to study a computing science topic was chosen. The teaching lesson was artificial intelligence. The class of 33 students studied this lesson in a 45 minute-session through the robot while the remote teacher access the system to control the robot, give a lecture, respond to students, and control the teaching slides. The evaluation was carried out after the teaching session end by interviewing with students.

4 Results

The development of the telepresence robot comprised both hardware and software development including server setup, which took 8 months to finish. The robot combined different pieces of robot parts that needed to be designed and printed using 3-D printing machines. During the development, several parts of the robot were adjusted to make it moving smoothly and controlling without difficulty. The developed robot is shown in Fig. 3.

Figure 3 illustrates the developed robot from front and side views. The base installed 4 wheels and the IoT devices were employed to control the motors of the wheels. The wireless speaker was installed in the middle part to make the sound volume loud enough for the whole class, and an 8-in. tablet was installed as the robot head to show the face of the remote teacher.

To control the robot and the teaching media, the software on the remote teacher's side was designed and developed as a web application that integrated the robot control modules, video display, and presentation media control; into one screen to allow

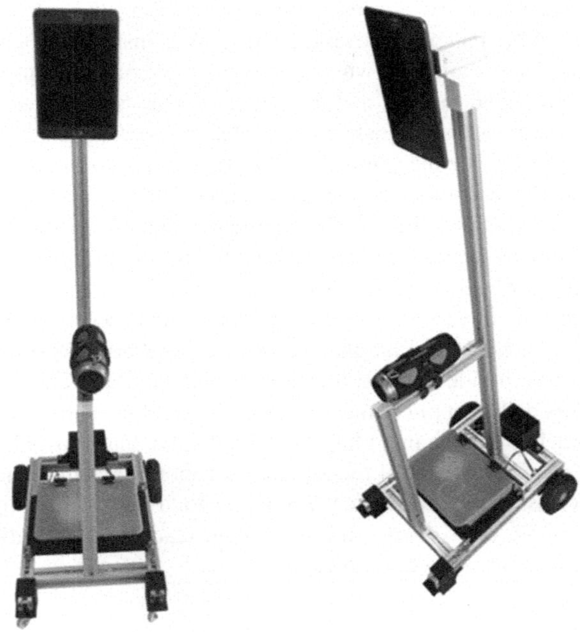

(a) (b)

Fig. 3. The developed telepresence robot: Front view (a) and Side view (b).

operating on a tablet. The remote teacher's screen was divided into two parts: top and bottom. The top screen displayed videos of both teacher and students' sides. Therefore, the screen showed the teacher's face as appeared on the robot's face, and the classroom environment, which helped the teacher visualize his/her students and the path to move the robot. The top screen also provided functions for driving the robot including moving forward and backward and turning left and right. The bottom screen was used for maneuvering the teaching media installed in the classroom's machine. Figure 4 shows the teacher's screen display during class time.

In the experiment, a class of 9th-grade students was informed about the robot usage for teaching while the teacher was in a different location. The robot and teaching slides were set up by the teaching assistant before class. During class time, the teaching was delivered as naturally as possible by combining teacher's communication with students and the robot's movement. The teacher could approach and speak to anyone in the class, ask questions, answer students' questions, give homework, and change presentation slides as in a common classroom. Figure 5 illustrates the classroom atmosphere when teaching with the robot together with presentation media that were fully controlled by the remote teacher.

After class, the authors interviewed students to collect their feedbacks and feelings about robot usage. The answers from students were recorded anonymously. The data were then analyzed and categorized as shown in Table 1.

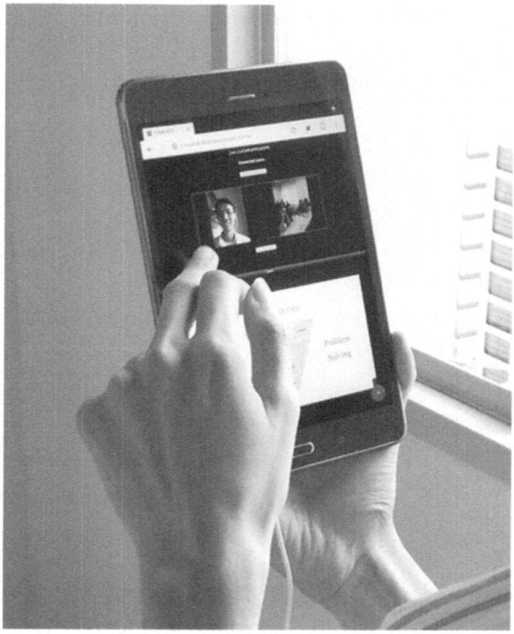

Fig. 4. An application screen on the remote teacher's device can be divided into two parts: the top screen shows real-time videos of the two sides and the robot's movement control when touching; the bottom screen shows the teaching media used in the class.

Fig. 5. Classroom atmosphere: students were surprised when the robot could display the teacher's face, respond, and move towards them.

Table 1. Results from the experiment.

Question	Satisfaction (n = 33)		Opinions
	Yes	No	
1. Do you feel like having a teacher standing in front of the room?	17 (51.5%)	16 (48.5%)	- The robot is too small. It doesn't look like a human
			- The robot interacts with us wonderfully and funny too
2. Do you like the way of communication and interaction with the teacher?	25 (75.8%)	8 (24.2%)	- I like talking to a robot. It's fun
			- The robot seems not as scary as a real teacher
			- Not sure, I cannot see the teacher's face clearly
			- It's like playing a game
3. Is the sound loud enough?	30 (91%)	3 (9%)	- It's loud enough. I can hear it
4. Do you think that the movement of the robot is good for teaching?	30 (91%)	3 (9%)	- If the robot cannot move, it's worthless
			- It's interesting that the robot can move around the room
5. Do you think that it is good if we use the robot as a teacher in some future classes?	26 (78.8%)	7 (21.3%)	- Yes, it can change the classroom atmosphere
			- It seems like fun
			- It looks like we are in the future world
			- I'm not sure whether I can study better with the robot
Average	128 (77.6%)	37 (22.4%)	

In Table 1, there is a mixture of feedback from students. The response to the first question that asked students about their feelings toward the robot whether it could represent as a teacher is interesting. About half of them supported that the robot could serve as a teacher while another half felt the opposite. Some students saw the height of the robot differing from that of their teacher. They said that the robot was too short. The robot was 125 cm tall, which was slightly higher than students' eye levels when sitting. This made students feeling that it could not be compared with the height of the real teachers. In the second question, when asking about the communication with the robot, most students (75.8%) accepted the way they could talk to the robot. However, some students who sit behind the class could hardly see and communicate because their views were blocked by their friends in front. In the third question, the volume level of the robot's sound was mostly accepted (91%). In the fourth question, students were asked to evaluate the robot's movement whether it was good when teaching. The data show that most students (91%) were satisfied with the robot's movement. In the last question, the students were mostly positive (78.8%) when they were asked whether it was good to use the robot in some future classes. At this point, some students believed that the robot could improve the classroom atmosphere, while some other students were still worried about how they could adapt to this new studying environment.

5 Conclusion and Discussion

This research developed a telepresence robot for supporting remote teaching. Remote teaching may be required in some schools especially those with teacher shortage problems in a particular subject. Teaching modern subjects is also a challenging task for schools in recent days, which requires outside support. Many subjects that used to be taught at a university level are nowadays partly provided in primary and secondary schools. These subjects are, for example, programming, computing science, and artificial intelligence. The design of the telepresence robot in this research is to enable remote teaching with interactive, movement, and teaching media control capabilities. In this design, the robot was developed based on IOT devices with 4 wheels for movement and a tablet for displaying the remote teacher's face. A computing device was required in the classroom for storing the teaching media to be displayed while teaching. On the remote teacher's side, the web application was developed for controlling the robot, exchanging sound and video, and controlling the teaching media in one screen. This enabled the teacher to teach their students, move and turn to any students, and control teaching slides or other media. Between the robot and the remote teacher, computer servers were set up for exchanging video and other necessary data. The developed robot was evaluated by a real class teaching with 33 students. The results show that most students satisfied with the robot's movement and sound level. Meanwhile, most of them were also satisfied with the communication and interaction with the robot and agreed to study with it in future classes. The research carried out by [16] also found that students could learn effectively with the telepresence robot, which was called "teacher as robot".

Although the research results suggest positive acceptance of the robot, these results could be affected by the Hawthorne effect [13] where students were motivated or influenced by the experimental set-up during the process of the experiment. The students could be excited by the appearance of the robot when they saw it for the first time. To carry out the research in the future, the long term implementation and observation should be included to explore the actual use of the robot, collect student feedback, and investigate learning outcomes. Another issue of the use of the robot instead of video-based instruction for remote teaching is that the telepresence robot replicates some characteristics of the face-to-face instruction as in a traditional classroom. The remote teachers can make eye contact with their students while the students can ask questions, get immediate feedback, and get additional support from their teachers, which are common practices in the classroom [14]. One interesting point from the experiment is that only half felt like having a teacher standing in front of the class. They mentioned that the robot was shorter than their teachers and may hardly see by students from the back seats. A prior study [2] suggested that the robot height should be approximately human-like sitting or standing. Therefore, the robot design should be considered for further study. To meet the requirement of students who mentioned the robot's height, future research should focus on how to make the robot suitable for students with different groups of ages. Different student groups may require different height design. One solution to this problem is that the robot can be designed by making it height-adjustable. Furthermore, the robot can be improved by applying deep learning methods [15] to help remote teachers recognize students in the class. Moreover, the robot's display screen should be larger to show a clearer view of the teacher's face to students. Lastly, the robot's appearance can be improved by coving the robot structure with materials to increase students' friendly feelings.

Acknowledgments. The authors would like to thank the technical team at The Office of Academic Resources and Information Technology at Loei Rajabhat University for providing support in robot development and also thank the Demonstration School of Loei Rajabhat University for supporting our research.

References

1. Newhart, V.A., Olson, J.S.: My student is a robot: how schools manage telepresence experiences for students. In: Proceedings of the 2017 CHI Conference on Human Factors in Computing Systems, pp. 342–347 (2017)
2. Herring, S.C.: Telepresence robots for academics. Proc. Am. Soc. Inf. Sci. Technol. **50**(1), 1–4 (2013)
3. Cha, E., Chen, S., Mataric, M.J.: Designing telepresence robots for K-12 education. In: 2017 26th IEEE International Symposium on Robot and Human Interactive Communication (RO-MAN), pp. 683–688. IEEE (2017)
4. Koceski, S., Koceska, N.: Evaluation of an assistive telepresence robot for elderly healthcare. J. Med. Syst. **40**(5), 121 (2016)
5. Newhart, V.A., Warschauer, M., Sender, L.: Virtual inclusion via telepresence robots in the classroom: an exploratory case study. Int. J. Technol. Learn. **23**(4), 9–25 (2016)
6. Myodo, E., Xu, J., Tasaka, K., Yanagihara, H., Sakazawa, S.: Issues and solutions to informal communication in working from home using a telepresence robot. ITE Trans. Media Technol. Appl. **6**(1), 30–45 (2018)
7. Stoll, B., Reig, S., He, L., Kaplan, I., Jung, M.F., Fussell, S.R.: Wait, can you move the robot? Examining telepresence robot use in collaborative teams. In: Proceedings of the 2018 ACM/IEEE International Conference on Human-Robot Interaction, pp. 14–22 (2018)
8. Yang, L., Neustaedter, C., Schiphorst, T.: Communicating through a telepresence robot: a study of long distance relationships. In: Proceedings of the 2017 CHI Conference Extended Abstracts on Human Factors in Computing Systems, pp. 3027–3033 (2017)
9. Kwon, O.H., Koo, S.Y., Kim, Y.G., Kwon, D.S.: Telepresence robot system for English tutoring. In: 2010 IEEE Workshop on Advanced Robotics and its Social Impacts, pp. 152–155 (2010)
10. Cesta, A., Cortellessa, G., Orlandini, A., Tiberio, L.: Addressing the long-term evaluation of a telepresence robot for the elderly. In: ICAART (1), pp. 652–663 (2012)
11. Hartsell-Gundy, J., Johnson, E.O., Kromer, J.: Testing telepresence: remote reference service via robotics. Ref. User Serv. Q. **55**(2), 118 (2015)
12. Guth, L., Vander Meer, P.: Telepresence robotics in an academic library. Libr. Hi Tech **35**(3), 408–420 (2017)
13. Wickström, G., Bendix, T.: The "Hawthorne effect"—what did the original Hawthorne studies actually show? Scand. J. Work Environ. Health **26**(4), 363–367 (2000)
14. Boutell, M.: Choosing face-to-face or video-based instruction in a mobile app development course. In: Proceedings of the 2017 ACM SIGCSE Technical Symposium on Computer Science Education, pp. 75–80 (2017)

15. Puarungroj, W., Boonsirisumpun, N.: Recognizing hand-woven fabric pattern designs based on deep learning. In: Bhatia, S.K., Tiwari, S., Mishra, K.K., Trivedi, M.C. (eds.) Advances in Computer Communication and Computational Sciences. AISC, vol. 924, pp. 325–336. Springer, Singapore (2019). https://doi.org/10.1007/978-981-13-6861-5_28
16. Edwards, A., Edwards, C., Spence, P.R., Harris, C., Gambino, A.: Robots in the classroom: differences in students' perceptions of credibility and learning between "teacher as robot" and "robot as teacher". Comput. Hum. Behav. **65**, 627–634 (2016)

Author Index

The manufacturer's authorised representative in the EU is Springer Nature Customer Service Centre GmbH, Europaplatz 3, 69115 Heidelberg, Germany. If you have any concerns regarding our products, please contact ProductSafety@springernature.com

Printed and bound by CPI Group (UK) Ltd, Croydon, CR0 4YY
22/09/2026
02220983-0006